T0076685

A Complete Guide to
PORTALS *AND* **USER EXPERIENCE PLATFORMS**

A Complete Guide to PORTALS *AND* USER EXPERIENCE PLATFORMS

Shailesh Kumar Shivakumar
Senior Technology Architect, Infosys Technologies, India

CRC Press is an imprint of the
Taylor & Francis Group, an **informa** business

CRC Press
Taylor & Francis Group
6000 Broken Sound Parkway NW, Suite 300
Boca Raton, FL 33487-2742

Printed on acid-free paper
Version Date: 20150515

International Standard Book Number-13: 978-1-4987-2549-1 (Hardback)

Library of Congress Cataloging-in-Publication Data

Shivakumar, Shailesh Kumar.
A complete guide to portals and user experience platforms / Shailesh Kumar Shivakumar.
pages cm
Includes bibliographical references and index.
ISBN 978-1-4987-2549-1
1. Web site development. 2. Web portals. 3. User interfaces (Computer systems) I. Title.

TK5105.888.S49155 2016
025.0422--dc23 2015016375

Visit the Taylor & Francis Web site at
http://www.taylorandfrancis.com

and the CRC Press Web site at
http://www.crcpress.com

Printed and bound by CPI Group (UK) Ltd, Croydon, CR0 4YY

I dedicate this book to

my parents, Shivakumara Setty V. and Anasuya T. M., who

are infinite source of love and inspiration,

my wife, Chaitra Prabhudeva, and my son, Shishir, who are eternal sunshine in my life,

my in-laws, Prabhudeva T. M. and Krishnaveni B., who

provided endless support and encouragement,

and

my school teachers who bestowed lots of love and knowledge upon me.

Contents

Preface: A Gateway to Portals and UXPs xxi
Acknowledgments xxxi
Author xxxiii

Section I The Art of Developing Portals

1 Thinking in Portals: Introduction to Portals 3
What Are Portals? 3
Brief History of Portals 3
Portal as a Concept 4
Portal as a Technology 4
Portals as a Business Enabler 5
Core Features of Portals 5
Advantages of Portals 6
Types of Portal 6
Overview of Portals 7
Layer-Wise Portal Components 7
Scenarios for Portals 10
When Do I Need a Portal? 12
Summary 14

2 Make Portal Work for You: Business Transformation through Portals 15
Introduction 15
Business Aspects of Portal 15
Key Business Drivers That Require Portal Technologies 15
Prioritized Portal Value Deliverables 17
Digital Transformation through Portal 17
Enterprise Opportunities for Portal 18
Portal for Building Next-Generation Digital Platform for Business 21
Common Pitfalls While Using Portal 22
Challenges in Portal Adoption 22
Portal Transformation Scenarios and Value Adds 23
Realization of Enterprise Digital Vision through Portal 25
Deriving Portal Program Goals and Principles 27
Sample Portal Usage Scenarios 27
Knowledge Management Portal 27
Enterprise Information Portal 29
Typical Business Domains and Solutions Based on Portal 30
Portal Value Realization Framework 31
Summary 33

3 Choosing Portal Right: Portal Assessment and Evaluation 37
Introduction 37
Do You Really Need a Portal? 37
When Do You Need Portal? 37
Recap of Portal Strengths and Scenarios 38
Portal Fitment Analysis 38
Portal Solution Capability Evaluation 40
Portal Assessment Framework 40
Business Assessment Phase 41
Technology Assessment Phase 44
Product and Technology Evaluation 47
Product Evaluation 47
Technology Evaluation 51
Vendor Evaluation 53
Product Demo Evaluation 54
Proof-of-Concept Evaluation 54
SWOT Analysis 54
Feature Set in Various Portal Products 55
Summary 62

4 Architecting Portals 63
Introduction 63
Portal Capabilities 63
Portal Functional Capability View 63
Capability Solution Mapping 74
Portal Architecture Views 74
Sample Portal Solution Architecture 75
Portal Application Architecture View 77
Portal Component View 77
Portal Data Architecture View 77
Portal Use Case View 81
Portal Information Architecture View 83
Portal Deployment View 84
Portal Security View 86
Portal User Experience Architecture View 87
Portal Content Architecture View 87
Portal Infrastructure Architecture View 88
Portal Architecture Definition 88
Establishing Portal Architecture 88
Portal Strategy Definition Phase 90
Portal Technology Assessment Phase 92
Portal Roadmap Definition Phase 93
Portal Architecture Review 96
Deep Dive into Key Portal Architecture Activities 98
Portal Design Considerations 98
Portal Architecture Best Practices 100
Portal Architecture Principles 103

Portal Road Map Strategy 104
Architecture Concepts for Building Portal Solutions 106
Architecture Concepts of Self-Service Portal 106
Architecting Portal Using Open Source Technologies 106
Summary 110

5 Developing Portals 113
Introduction 113
Portal Terminology 113
Portal Server and Ecosystem 114
Portal Server/Container 114
Portal Ecosystem 115
Servlet versus Portlet 115
Portal Standards, Life Cycle, and Request Processing 116
Portal Standards 116
Portlet Life Cycle 117
Life Cycle of JSR 168 Portlet 117
Portal Request Processing 118
Request Processing for Render Requests 118
Request Processing for Action Requests 118
Request Processing for Resource Requests 119
Portal Elements 120
Portal Objects for Customizing User Experience 120
Portlet Modes 121
Portlet Objects and API 122
Portlet JSP Tags 128
Main Portlet JSP Tags 129
Portlet Window States 130
Portlet Communication 131
Public Render Parameter Interportlet Communication 131
Events 132
Cookies 133
Portlet Packaging and Deployment Descriptor 134
Portlet Deployment Descriptor 134
Portlet Packaging 134
Portal Page Layout and Construction 135
Portal Roles 136
References and Further Reading 137
Summary 137

6 Portal Integrations 139
Introduction 139
Advantages of Integrations 139
Challenges and the Impact of Integrations 140
Business Scenarios for Integrations 140
Technical Scenarios for Integrations 141
Integration Big Picture and Integration Types 142

Portal Integration Techniques ... 144
Link-Based Integration ... 144
iFrame-Based Integration ... 145
Service-Based Integration ... 146
API Gateway–Based Integration ... 149
ESB-Based API Gateway ... 151
Feed-Based Integration ... 152
Clipping and Screen Scraping ... 153
Portlet-Based Integration ... 153
Widget-Based Integration ... 154
Core Portal Integrations ... 155
CMS Integration ... 155
Search Engine Integration ... 156
Social and Collaboration Platform Integration ... 158
Security System Integration ... 160
Business Process Management (BPM), Business Rules, and Workflow Integration ... 161
Knowledge Management Integration ... 162
E-Commerce Integration ... 165
Reports and Business Intelligence System Integration ... 166
Special Forms of Integration: Mashups, Widgets, Plug-Ins, and Extensions ... 167
Mashups ... 168
Widgets ... 168
Plug-Ins and Extensions ... 169
Web Frameworks ... 169
Portal Integration Patterns ... 169
Portal Integration Best Practices to Achieve Optimal Performance, Scalability, and Availability ... 174
Application Integration Design ... 174
Application Development and Testing ... 174
Business Process Integration ... 175
Summary ... 175

7 Portal-Based Content Management ... 177
Portal Content Management Scenarios and Capabilities ... 177
Portal Content Trends ... 178
Portal Content Management Capabilities ... 178
Portal Content Architecture ... 180
Core Content Components ... 180
Content Management System Integration Components ... 182
Portal Service Layer (Content Syndication Services) ... 183
Portal Enterprise Content Services ... 183
External Enterprise Content Sources ... 183
Portal Content Strategy ... 184
Portal Content Design, Authoring, Preview, and Publishing ... 186
User Interface Design Elements ... 187
Content Management Process ... 188
Portal Content Search ... 190
Portal Content Caching ... 191

Web Content Portlet Design 191
Native Web Content Portlet 192
CMS Vendor-Provided Web Content Portlet 192
Custom Web Content Portlet 193
Integration with CMS 193
Portal Content Migration 194
Content Artifacts for Migration 194
Content Migration Methodologies 194
Content Cut-Over Strategy 195
Content Migration Process 195
Portal Content Best Practices 196
Content Authoring 196
Content Workflows 197
Content Testing and Migration 197
Content Publishing 197
Content Presentation 197
Summary 197

8 **Portal Search and Search Engine Optimization (SEO)** 199
Portal Requirements of Search 199
Portal Search Attributes 200
Portal Search Architecture 201
Portal Search Process 203
Indexing Process Using Seed List 203
End-to-End Portal Search Process 205
Search Crawling and Indexing Process 205
Search Engine Crawling of CMS Content 206
Portal Search Execution Process Flow 206
Search Engine Crawling of Feeds 206
Search Engine Crawling of Documents 206
Portal Meta Tags and Personalization 207
Portal Search Best Practices 207
Search Engine Optimization (SEO) 208
Advantages of SEO for Portal Platform 209
Portal SEO Strategy 209
Keyword Optimization 209
Portal Page SEO Optimization 209
Quick Links 211
SEO-Friendly Content Strategy 211
Monitoring and Tracking SEO Effectiveness 211
Summary 211

9 **Securing Portals** 213
Portal Security: An Introduction 213
Portal Security Assessment 213
Portal Security Architecture 214
Portal 214
Identity and Access Management System 216
Security Proxy/Security Manager 216

Web Service Security Proxy ... 216
Web Application Firewall ... 217
External System Integration ... 217
Portal Authentication and Access Control ... 217
Authentication ... 217
Portal Access Control ... 218
Portal Single Sign On ... 218
Web SSO or Internal SSO ... 219
Portal Usage Scenarios ... 220
Federated SSO ... 220
Federated SSO for Web Services–Based Portal Integration ... 222
Federated SSO for APIs-Based Portal Integration ... 222
Portal Usage Scenarios ... 223
Portal User Management ... 223
User Registration and Provisioning ... 223
Portal User Administration ... 226
Security-Related Portal Scenarios ... 226
Secured Integration ... 226
Secure Service Invocation ... 227
Portal Security Vulnerabilities and Prevention Techniques ... 227
Summary ... 229

10 Portal Collaboration, Knowledge Management, and Personalization ... 231
Requirements and Benefits of a Collaborative Portal ... 231
Requirements ... 231
Benefits ... 232
Trends in Portal Collaboration ... 233
Challenges in Achieving Collaboration ... 234
Defining Best Practices–Based Collaboration Strategy ... 234
Knowledge Management in the Portal ... 235
Portal Knowledge Management Architecture ... 235
Portal Services Layer ... 235
Knowledge Management Layer ... 235
Integration Layer ... 237
Enterprise Content Source Layer ... 237
Strategic Goals of a Knowledge Portal ... 237
Challenges to Knowledge Management Portals ... 238
Best Practices and Critical Success Factors in Knowledge Management ... 238
Portal Personalization ... 239
Personalization Concepts ... 241
Personalization Logical Architecture ... 241
Personalization Types ... 243
Rules-Based Personalization ... 243
Demographics-Based Personalization ... 243
Look and Feel Personalization by Show/Hide of Portlets Based on User Group ... 244
Personalized Content and Data Retrieval Using Web Services ... 244
Using User Session Attributes for Personalization ... 244

Anonymous Personalization 244
Recommendation-Based Personalization and Collaborative Filtering 245
Summary 245

11 Portal Testing 247
Challenges in Portal Testing 247
Portal Testing Framework 248
Regular Testing Activities Layer 249
Portal Testing Governance 249
Portal Presentation Components Testing Layer 251
UI Testing 251
Usability Testing 252
Client Side Performance Monitoring and Testing 253
Portlet Testing 253
Localization Testing 253
Multidevice Testing 254
Portal Enterprise Integration Components Testing Layer 254
Service Testing 254
Boundary Scenario Testing 255
Fallback Scenario Testing 256
Interface Testing 256
Special Component Testing Layer 256
Portal Infrastructure Testing 256
Performance Testing 256
Migration Testing 259
Process Testing 259
Multi-Geo Testing 260
End User Testing 260
Security Component Testing Layer 260
Critical Success Factors of Portal Testing 262
Test Automation 262
Test Metrics 262
Agile Approach for Portal Testing 262
Continuous and Iterative Testing 263
Summary 264

Section II User Experience Platforms and Advanced Portal Topics

12 Introduction to User Experience Platforms (UXPs) 267
Introduction 267
Importance of Managing User Experience 267
What Is UXP? 267
Case for UXP 268
UXP Core Capabilities 268
Web Application versus UXP 270
Business Drivers and Motivations for UXP 270
Portals and UXPs 272

Views of UXP ... 273
Business View of UXP ... 273
End User View of UXP ... 276
IT and Operations View of UXP ... 277
UXP Architecture ... 277
Interacting Systems ... 277
Core User Experience Platform ... 278
Web Experience Components ... 278
User Engagement Components ... 279
Prebuilt Accelerators ... 279
Integration Components ... 279
External and Internal Systems ... 280
Security ... 280
Infrastructure ... 280
UXP Capabilities Based on Scenarios ... 281
UXP for Various Customer-Centric Scenario ... 281
Summary ... 281

13 Designing User Experience Platforms ... 283
Introduction ... 283
Design Principles of UXP ... 283
UXP Trends ... 285
User Experience Strategy ... 285
Deep Dive into UXP Design Activities ... 287
User Experience Mapping and Enhancement ... 287
Inventory of Touch Points and Experience Mapping ... 288
Experience Impact Analysis ... 288
Experience Improvement Plan ... 289
User Touch Point Analysis and Improvement ... 289
Identifying Cross-Channel Touch Points ... 290
Analyzing User Expectations across All Channels ... 290
Prioritizing and Planning for Touch Point Experience Enhancement ... 290
Measure, Monitor, and Improve ... 290
UXP Presentation Design ... 290
Banking UXP Design ... 292
Requirements of Banking UXP ... 292
Challenges with Legacy Online Banking System ... 293
Banking UXP Solution ... 293
Features and Capabilities of Next-Generation Banking UXP ... 293
Summary ... 297

14 Portal User Experience and Omni-Channel Enablement ... 299
Portal Responsive UI Architecture ... 299
Portal Omni-Channel Solution Tenets ... 301
Trends in UI and Web Technologies ... 302
Challenges in Portal UX ... 303
Portal UX Strategy ... 303
Portal UX Definition Process ... 303
Implementing Mobile-First Strategy through Portal ... 307

Mobile Portal Design 309
Quality Considerations in Mobile Portal 312
Sample Responsive Design–Based Reference Architecture for Mobile-First Strategy 312
Mobile Portal Based on Responsive Design 312
Portal-Based Hybrid Mobile App 314
Portal UX Best Practices 316
Best Practices in Requirements Elaboration Phase 316
Best Practices in Design Phase 316
Best Practices in Development and Testing Phase 317
Summary 317

15 Portal Best Practices 319
Common Pitfalls and Antipatterns in Portal Programs 319
Portal Best Practices in Project Phases 320
Portal Checklist 324
Best Practices in Portal Security and Performance 324
Portal Security Best Practices 324
Security Best Practices Related to Server and Host Security 327
Portal Performance Best Practices 328
Best Practices in Portal Program Management 329
Tools and Frameworks for Ensuring High Quality 330
Summary 331

16 Portal Analytics, KPIs, and Localization 333
Portal Analytics Introduction 333
Types of Portal Analytics 334
Log File–Based Analytics 334
Page Tagging–Based Analytics 334
Challenges in Establishing Portal Analytics 335
Portal Analytics Architecture 335
One-Time Configuration Setup 337
Setup and Configuration of Google Analytics with Liferay Portal 337
Runtime Web Analytics Flow 338
Tracking Component-Level Events with Google Analytics on Liferay Portal .. 338
Process to Identify Portal Analytics Metrics 338
Portal Key Performance Indicators 339
Portal Localization 341
Portal Localization Design Considerations 342
Summary 344

17 Portal Operations 345
Portal Release Management 345
Portal Release Activities 345
One-Time Setup Configurations and Activities 345
Repeatable Activities 346
Production Smoke Testing and Checkout 346
Portal Production Readiness Checklist 346

Portal Administration 348
Portal Content Administration 348
Other Portal Administration Activities 349
Portal Postproduction Monitoring 350
Internal Monitoring of Portal Infrastructure 350
External Monitoring of Portal Applications 351
Portal Application Monitoring 352
Portal Support and Maintenance 353
Portal Operations Best Practices 355
Portal Maintenance Dashboard 355
Continuous Improvement Process 356
Productivity Improvement Measures 356
Portal Support and Incident Management Process 357
Business Continuity Management in Portal 359
Portal Troubleshooting 360
Sample Portal Issue Categorization 360
Portal Troubleshooting Tips 361
Summary 362

18 Portal Infrastructure and NFR Planning 365
Portal Infrastructure Planning 365
Portal-Sizing Questionnaire 365
Portal Sizing 366
CPU Cores 367
RAM Sizing 367
Portal Virtualization and Cloud 368
Installing Portal on Virtual Machines 368
Cloud Hosting 368
Portal Clustering 370
Vertical Clustering 371
Horizontal Clustering 371
Multitenancy Model and Virtual Portals 372
Portal Disaster Recovery Planning 372
Critical Success Factors for DR Strategy 373
Portal DR Strategy and Setup 373
Portal Infrastructure Testing 374
Challenges in Infrastructure Testing 374
Infrastructure Test Types 378
Portal Nonfunctional Requirements and Planning 378
Summary 378

19 Portal Governance and Program Management 381
Common Portal Project Management Challenges 381
Project Management Stages 382
Program Envision Phase 382
Risks and Mitigation 383
Portal Architecture and Design Phase 384
Risks and Mitigation 385

Portal Solution Development and Testing Phase 385
Risks and Mitigation 386
Portal Maintenance and Evolution 386
Risks and Mitigation 386
Portal Implementation and Roadmap Process 387
Portal Roadmap Definition 387
Portal Governance Model 391
Portal Requirements Prioritization Process 394
Portal Brand Management Process 394
Portal Governance Elements 394
Portal Estimation Model 398
Estimation Risks and Mitigation 400
Portal Release Plan 401
Portal Home Page Release Plan 402
Portal Project Management Best Practices 404
Agile Execution Approach 404
Productivity Improvement 405
Usage of Tools and Accelerators 406
Requirement Traceability Matrix 406
Continuous Integration (CI) 406
Continuous Improvement 407
Risk Management Process 409
Change Management Process 410
Key Performance Indicators of Technical Project Management 411
Summary 412

20 Portal Performance Engineering 413
Introduction 413
Critical Success Factors for Portal Performance 413
Caching 414
Content Types and Portal Caching Scenarios 414
Portal Content Type 414
Portal Caching Scenarios 415
Portal Caching Candidates 416
Portal Caching Layers 416
Browser Cache 418
Edge Caching 418
Web Proxies 418
Reverse Proxy 418
Portlet Caching 418
Portal Caching Methodologies 419
HTTP Cache Headers 419
Object Caching 419
Portal Server Settings 420
Portal Performance Testing Essentials 420
Portal Performance Testing Process 421
Key Steps in Portal Performance Test Execution 421
Performance Load and Stress Testing 422

Portal Performance Testing Types 422
Web Component Testing 422
Portal Performance Testing Checklist 423
Critical Transaction and Process Identification 423
Data-Intensive and Scheduled Jobs 423
Server Monitoring and Reporting 423
Performance Metrics 424
Summary 424

21 Next-Generation Portals and Portal Trends 427
Quick Recap of Portal and Its Utility 427
Traditional Full-Featured Horizontal Portals and Challenges 428
Portal Trends 429
Presentation Technology and User Experience Trends 429
Enterprise Integration Trends 430
Other Technology Trends 431
Business-Specific Trends 431
Operations-Specific Trends 432
Trends in Intranet and External Portals 434
Intranet Portals 434
External Portals 434
Next-Generation Portals 436
Lightweight Web-Oriented Architecture 436
Highly Responsive UX 436
Omnichannel Strategy through Mobile Portal 436
Hyperpersonalized Portal 438
Simple and Robust Platform with Continuous Improvement 438
Accelerators and Prebuilt Components 439
Social and Collaboration Enablement 439
User Experience Platforms (UXP) 440
Vertical Focus 440
Next-Generation Banking Portal 440
Reference Architecture of Next-Generation Portal 441
Portal Architecture 442
Portal Client Layer 442
Portal Server Layer 444
Portal Interface Layer 445
Alternate Scenarios for Next-Generation Lightweight Portals 446
Comparison of Next-Generation Lightweight Portals with Traditional Horizontal Portals 446
Summary 448

22 Why Do Portal Programs Fail? 449
Portal Problems Categories 449
Business-Related Challenges 449
Portal Technology–Related Challenges 451
Operations- and Execution-Related Challenges 454
Summary 455

Section III Case Studies

23 Portal Case Studies ... 459
Intranet Portal Case Study ... 459
Unified Employee Portal Case Study ... 459
Background and Business Scenario ... 459
Internet Portal Case Study ... 461
Retail Portal Case Study ... 461
Background and Business Scenario ... 461
Customer Service Portal Case Study ... 464
Next-Generation Customer Service Portal Case Study ... 464
Background and Business Scenario ... 465
Portal Content Management Case Study ... 467
Scenario before Portal Transformation ... 467
Dynamic Delivery Platform Based on Portal and Enterprise CMS ... 467
Main Benefits of the Portal Solution ... 469

Appendix: Detailed Steps for Development of JSR Portlets ... 471

Further Reading ... 479

Index ... 481

Preface A: Gateway to Portals and UXPs

The Big Picture: Modern Enterprise Digital Platform

A modern digital enterprise needs to engage a wide audience through different channels. Today's digital enterprises need to be agile, adaptable, proactive, and customer-centric, and should constantly adapt to market dynamics. A robust digital platform should provide a 360° view of its customers and business activities and should have an effective feedback loop to continuously improve upon its online strategy. In order to be successful and lead the competition, the enterprise digital platform should differentiate itself through compelling user experiences. The digital platform should constantly adapt to market and technology disruptors such as pervasive mobile technologies, increasing influence of social media platforms, emerging SaaS models, rapid advancements in front-end technologies, and others. In order for this to happen, digital platform strategy depends on various technology enablers, such as the following.

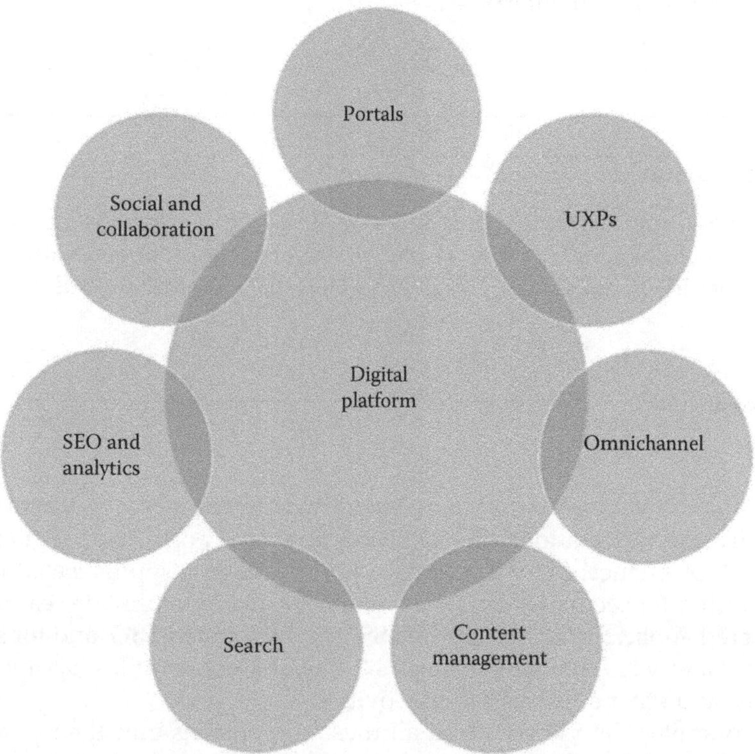

Portals and user experience platforms (UXPs) form the core technology and business enablers for a digital platform. Portal technologies, in fact, weave a lot of other technology components such as content management, search, SEO, analytics, and social and collaboration technologies into an enterprise platform; portals' main strength lies in personalization, content aggregation, and single sign-on, which provide a unified view of all activities.

With prebuilt accelerators, UXPs provide the next-generation customer experience and highly engaging user experience; they cater to a tech savvy and socially active user community. Lean portals and UXPs are now the preferred platform of choice for external-facing digital platforms. Portals and UXPs complement each other to complete the digital platform vision of an enterprise. The technology landscape of the digital platform is vast; it also includes technologies such as digital commerce, Big Data, Internet of Things (IoT), automation technologies, etc. In this book, we focus on the core digital platform capabilities mentioned in the figure. A digital transformation program also reflects the changing trends and disruptions in the industry such as social media becoming mainstream in customer engagement, explosion of data and devices, transaction-based to relationship-based customer engagement, content creation to content aggregation and co-creation, planned marketing campaigns to customer loyalty and advocacy, etc.

In order to build the next-generation forward-looking enterprise digital platform, it is essential to have a good understanding of portal technology and UXPs.

Portal technology is a sweet spot as it is at the intersection of highly interesting and business-critical technologies and is a convergence of various essential functionality. UXPs are essentially user-centric platforms that provide highly engaging and relationship-enhancing experiences to end users. A modern-day enterprise digital strategy naturally involves portals and UXPs at its heart. This book will act as a comprehensive guide in devising a robust digital strategy for an enterprise.

Book Organization

We have organized the book into three sections. The first section discusses the core features of portal technology. The second part elaborates the next-generation digital platforms, UXPs, and advanced topics. The final section discusses case studies.

Portals

The term "portal" is interpreted and understood in different ways by different audiences, resulting in diverse expectations. For business analysts, portal is a digital strategy to provide unified experience; for technologists, portal means a sophisticated personalized aggregation engine; for security teams, it is another platform to provide seamless access to various protected applications through web SSO and federated SSO; and for site administrators, portal is a way to efficiently manage sites, pages, user profiles, permission models, access controls, and other administrative activities.

Portals can definitely be viewed from all these dimensions and their potential utility is much beyond these. Portals can offer value in various business domains such as retail, e-commerce, manufacturing, business intelligence, etc., due to the breadth of technologies it supports. The principal goal of this book is to provide a comprehensive coverage of portal technologies, concepts, and utilities by exploring portals through various dimensions and viewpoints. Since portal technology is of interest to a wide audience that also needs to properly understand how to get the most out of their portal strategy. In the process, they may encounter questions such as the following:

- Should I use portal technology for this scenario or not?
- How do I know for sure that portals are effectively impacting my business and online strategy?
- What are the best practices and rules of thumb during portal development?
- How does a portal fit into emerging UI trends?
- How can I implement mobile-first strategy through portals?
- How can we get real-time insights into customer behavior and action in portals?
- How can I use a portal for managing marketing content and campaigns?
- What are the various business-enabling features in portals?

As we can see, these questions are of concern to varied stakeholders. I have tried to address these questions in various chapters.

In this book, I have tried to explore portals from various viewpoints such as the following:

- Business viewpoints:
  - Business transformation scenarios
  - Critical success factors of portal programs
  - Portal metrics and KPIs
  - Portal value realization framework
- Technology viewpoints:
  - Technology use cases and portal fitment assessment
  - Portal assessment framework
  - Portal capability evaluation
  - Portal development concepts
  - Portal architecture views such as solution view, deployment view, use case view, security view, integration view, data architecture view, user experience view, etc.
  - Portal architecture best practices
  - Portal roadmap strategy
- Project management viewpoints:
  - Portal best practices
  - Portal testing
  - Portal governance and program management
  - Commonly encountered portal challenges
- Portal administrator viewpoints:
  - Portal operations
  - Infrastructure and nonfunctional planning

I have also developed dedicated chapters for the critical portal capabilities such as enterprise integrations, content management, enterprise search, personalization, user experience, localization mobility, analytics, and collaboration. Many of the book chapters are dedicated to the concepts, techniques, and methodologies to realize modern digital platform capabilities such as content management, analytics, SEO, personalization, search, etc.

UXP

Horizontal portals have been in the market since the early 2000s, and they have matured pretty well with various standards governing its development. Having said that, front-end technologies and other ecosystem elements of portals are changing at a very rapid pace. The scenarios for which portals appeared to be an automatic choice now have a variety of options. Horizontal portals are at an interesting turning point: on the one hand, they are slowly evolving into next-generation portals that are lean and lightweight in nature, and, on the other hand, UXPs are leveraging portals in building highly engaging user experiences. Portal products are trying to adapt to the changing trends and accommodate emerging technologies. Lean portal model, mobile portals, web-oriented architecture, widget-based models are gaining popularity. We will have a look at these aspects in chapters related to UXPs and next-generation portals.

We will also discuss some of the advanced features such as performance engineering, portal operations, portal program management, architecting next-generation portals, portal infrastructure planning etc. in the second section. To conclude, we will have a look at some of the portal case studies and portlet code examples in the appendix.

Key Differentiators

The key differentiators and novel aspects of this book are summarized in the following:

- *Reference portal frameworks and models*: The book elaborates many portal frameworks such as portal value realization framework, portal assessment framework, portal testing framework, and portal governance and estimation model. These frameworks are designed based on my rich experience and on real-world portal implementations.
- *UXPs concepts*: Concepts related to UXPs are still evolving and are dependent on the solution vertical. This book explores various UXP concepts such as UXP architecture, various views of UXP, overlapping concerns between portal and UXP, design principles and design activities, etc.
- *Portal evaluation and assessment techniques*: Evaluation and critical assessment of scenarios and use cases are required for optimal portal fitment. The book details evaluation techniques such as strategy mapping to portal metrics, portal scenario assessment, portal fitment matrix, etc. The evaluations and assessment methodologies are based on practical portal consulting engagements.

- *Portal KPI and metrics*: A few chapters provide the main portal tracking metrics, portal KPIs, and analytics metrics that can be used to continuously track and fine-tune the portal platform.
- *Portal best practices*: Guidelines, checklists, and portal best practices are discussed in multiple chapters, with an in-depth discussion in Chapter 15. This includes best practices related to portal architecture, portal integration, portal security, portal content, collaboration, performance, and portal program management.
- *Trends related to portal technologies*: Various technology trends related to user experience, next-generation portals, portal integration, and portal collaboration are detailed in the book.
- *Reference architecture*: Sample reference portal architecture for self-service portals, open source portals, and next-generation portals have also been provided in a few chapters.
- *Applicability in online and digital projects*: Though the book predominantly discusses portal topics, the techniques and methodologies discussed in a few chapters such as program management and testing can be used for any online or digital project.

Motivation for the Book

I was involved in several large-scale digital engagements, playing various roles such as that of a developer, consultant, architect, and business analyst. These varied roles provided me with different perspectives of the digital platform. Though the viewpoints from these perspectives vary, all of them invariably aim toward a quantifiable success of the digital program. I have analyzed these perspectives in the hope that it would help digital technology practitioners, the technical community, and the intended target audience. In the process, I also wanted to highlight the best practices, frameworks, evaluation models, trends, metrics and KPIs, reference architecture, and common pitfalls along with the discussion of core portal elements. As a result, this book has chapters to cover areas catering to various business and technology domains. Though this book is mainly written from a practitioner viewpoint, I have done research into the technology domain to ensure appropriate depth and coverage of all the topics.

Main Themes and Focus Areas

The main themes and focus areas of this book are as follows:

- *Comprehensive coverage of portal technologies*: Portals are viewed from various angles such as business, technology, integration, operations, program management, testing, etc., to provide an adequate coverage.
- *Emergence of UXP*: The role and relevance of UXP in digital architecture is covered from various dimensions. As UXPs are playing a major role in consumer facing application, this book discusses various design concepts, trends, reference architecture related to UXP.

- *Product-agnostic and technology-agnostic view*: All chapters in this book discuss portal concepts and technologies from a generic viewpoint. The methodologies and techniques can be implemented in most of the portal products. The idea is to provide a generic and product-agnostic view of portals. Though we have given sample product features in some chapters, it is only for illustration and information purposes and to make the concepts more clear.
- *Tracking trends in portal technologies*: Emerging trends related to portal technologies such as UX, integration, collaboration, etc., are covered in appropriate chapters.
- *Dedicated focus on core portal technologies*: There are separate chapters dedicated to core portal technologies such as content management, search, analytics, personalization, and security.
- *Challenges and best practices*: While discussing core portal technologies such as integrations, content management, search, etc., the commonly encountered challenges and pitfalls and the best practices have been discussed.
- *Forward-looking technologies*: This book discusses many emerging technologies such as mobility-related technologies, cloud deployment, responsive design, etc. We will look at these topics when we discuss UXP, lean portals, and user experience.

Chapter Organization and Target Audience

This book is organized into three sections. Section I, "The Art of Developing Portals," mainly focuses on the core portal aspects and usage scenarios. Section II, "User Experience Platforms and Advanced Portal Topics," covers the vital elements of UXPs, user experience, and advanced portal topics such as portal governance, program management, operations, best practices, etc. Section III is about portal case studies.

Following are the brief summaries of each of the chapters along with its target audience:

- Chapter 1: Thinking in Portals: An Introduction to Portals—discusses the basic features and utilities of portal technologies
  - Target audience: Students, portal enthusiasts, and portal developers
- Chapter 2: Make Portals Work for You: Business Transformation through Portals—discusses the business aspects of portals such as portal success factors, portal strategy, solution tenets, portal value realization framework, etc.
  - Target audience: Business analysts, business stakeholders, portal program sponsors, project managers, enterprise architects and portal architects
- Chapter 3: Choosing Portal Right: Portal Assessment and Evaluation—provides details about portal evaluation and fitment models
  - Target audience: Business analysts, Enterprise architects, and portal architects
- Chapter 4: Architecting Portals—this is one of the main chapters that elaborates various architecture concepts of portals such as various architecture views, capability solution mapping, portal architecture activities, and portal architecture principles along with sample reference architecture
  - Target audience: Portal architects, enterprise architects, infrastructure architects, and security architects

- Chapter 5: Developing Portals—provides various developmental aspects of portals such as portal standards, life cycle methods, portal elements, portal deployment descriptors, etc.
    - Target audience: Portal developers and portal architects
- Chapter 6: Portal Integrations—elaborates various techniques and methodologies of portal integration along with integration best practices and patterns
    - Target audience: Portal architects, Enterprise Architects, portal developers, and integration architects
- Chapter 7: Portal-Based Content Management—discusses all details about content management such as content strategy, architecture, content workflows, content caching, and content best practices
    - Target audience: Enterprise content architects, portal architects, enterprise architects, portal developers, content authors, and content administrators
- Chapter 8: Portal Search and Search Engine Optimization—mainly focuses on portal search–related aspects such as portal search architecture, search process, and SEO
    - Target audience: Portal architects, enterprise architects, and portal developers
- Chapter 9: Securing Portals—discusses various portal security aspects such as authentication flows, SSO process, user management, etc.
    - Target audience: Portal architects, security architects, portal developers, and enterprise architects
- Chapter 10: Portal Collaboration, Knowledge Management, and Personalization—discusses the main portal utilities such as collaboration, personalization, and knowledge management
    - Target audience: Portal architects, portal developers, content architects, and enterprise architects
- Chapter 11: Portal Testing—provides various insights into portal testing–related aspects such as kinds of portal testing, testing framework, and critical success factors for portal testing
    - Target audience: Quality and validation team, portal architects, portal developers, and project managers
- Chapter 12: Introduction to User Experience Platforms—discusses core capabilities of UXP, different views of UXP, and UXP architecture
    - Target audience: UX designers, UX architects, portal architects, and portal developers
- Chapter 13: Designing User Experience Platforms—the key UXP design principles and design activities such as touch point analysis and experience mapping are discussed in this chapter
    - Target audience: UX designers, UX architects, portal architects, and portal developers
- Chapter 14: Portal User Experience and Omni-Channel Enablement—elaborates user experience aspects of portals such as UX strategy, UX process, mobile-first strategy, etc.
    - Target audience: Portal architects, portal developers, UX designers, and UX architects

- Chapter 15: Portal Best Practices—various portal-related checklists, guidelines, and portal best practices are discussed in this chapter
  - Target audience: Portal architects and portal developers
- Chapter 16: Portal Analytics, KPIs, and Localization—architecture for portal analytics and portal KPIs are discussed in this chapter along with localization-related aspects
  - Target audience: Portal architects, portal developers, business analysts, and project managers
- Chapter 17: Portal Operations—key operational elements of portals such as release management, administration, monitoring, maintaining, and troubleshooting topics are discussed in this chapter
  - Target audience: Portal architects, portal developers, portal administrators, portal support and maintenance personnel, and online operations personnel
- Chapter 18: Portal Infrastructure and NFR Planning—infrastructure components such as sizing, infrastructure planning, and portal nonfunctional requirements are discussed in this chapter
  - Target audience: Portal architects, infrastructure architects, portal developers, and project managers
- Chapter 19: Portal Governance and Program Management—the key aspects of portal program management such as governance model, estimation model, release plan, and project management best practices are discussed in this chapter
  - Target audience: Portal project managers and business analysts
- Chapter 20: Portal Performance Engineering—portal performance optimization techniques, performance testing, caching, and performance metrics are discussed in this chapter
  - Target audience: Portal architects, performance engineering personnel, project managers, portal developers, and quality and validation personnel
- Chapter 21: Next-Generation Portals and Portal Trends—the emerging trends of next-generation portals and a reference architecture of the modern portal are detailed in this chapter
  - Target audience: Portal architects and business analysts
- Chapter 22: Why Do Portal Programs Fail?—some of the commonly encountered pitfalls, ant patterns in portal programs, and the effective means by which these issues can be identified early and addressed are discussed in this chapter
  - Target audience: Portal architects, project managers, and portal developers
- Chapter 23: Portal Case Studies—four portal case studies related to intranet portals, retail portals, customer service portals, and portal content management are discussed along with their business drivers, challenges, portal solutions, and solution benefits
  - Target audience: Portal architects, project managers, and portal developers
- Appendix: Sample codes for JSR 168 and JSR 286 portlets are given in the appendix to complement the portal development chapter

Declaration

- Utmost care has been taken to ensure the accuracy and novelty of the book content. Any inaccuracies found in the book is entirely my own; I sincerely regret that. If you think of any corrections or feedback, please write to shailesh.shivakumar@gmail.com.
- In a few chapters, I have used the features of popular portal products to explain the concepts. The reference is for educational purposes only and is not aimed toward providing an exhaustive coverage of any commercial or open source portal product.
- I have provided feature sets of various popular portal products in Chapter 3 for educational purposes. The feature list provided is indicative and is not intended to be a product or feature evaluation. The concepts of this book are product-agnostic and it provides a product evaluation framework and structured model for evaluation that can be used by readers.
- All open source tools mentioned are in public domain as open source at the time of writing this book.
- Some of the reference architectures discussed in this book depict technologies, tools, and frameworks that can be used for implementing that architecture. Depiction of concrete tools and framework is only for educational purposes and it does not intend to recommend any particular technology or framework. The reference architecture is technology-agnostic and can be implemented by other similar technologies as well.
- I acknowledge the trademarks of all products, technologies, and frameworks being used in this book.
    - Oracle, WebCenter, WebLogic, OHS, ADF, Jdeveloper, Oracle TopLink, OWC Spaces, OracleAS Oracle Access Manager (OAM), Oracle Internet Directory (OID), Oracle Identity Manager (OIM) and Java are registered trademarks of Oracle and/or its affiliates.
    - WebSphere, IBM WCM, IHS, IBM Connections, Rational Application Developer, IBM Tivoli, TAI, and DB2 are registered trademarks of IBM and/or its affiliates.
    - AEM, Omniture and CQ5 are registered trademarks of Adobe and/or its affiliates.
    - SharePoint, Sharepoint Portal, MS Lync, Visual Studio, Microsoft Designer, Sharepoint CMS and SQLServer are registered trademarks of Microsoft and/or its affiliates.
    - Liferay, Liferay CMS and Liferay Developer Studio, is registered trademark of Liferay and/or its affiliates.
    - Intel is trademark or registered trademark of Intel Corporation.
    - All other trademarks or registered trademarks are the legal properties of their respective owners.

Acknowledgments

Many of my colleagues provided great help in the preparation and review of this book. I acknowledge and sincerely thank them for their immense help, support, and cooperation.

I convey my sincere and heartfelt thanks to Elangovan Ramalingam, Arunagiri Kaliappan, Istiaque Hussain, Verma V.S.S.R.K, Jitendra Ranganathan, and Subrat Mishra for their valuable input and review comments. I convey my sincere thanks to managers Shankar Bhat and Rahul Krishnan, who encouraged me in my initiatives. I appreciate the efforts and support given by Verma V.S.S.R.K, Udaykiran Kotla, and Sreenivas Kashyap at Infosys for ensuring a timely review and approval for this book. I recognize and thank Dr. P. V. Suresh, for his constant encouragement and immense support.

My extended family provided the much-needed moral support during the course of this project. I immensely thank Vasanth T. P and Aravind T.C for their care and encouragement.

My special thanks to Aastha Sharma, Marsha Pronin, Alexander Edwards, Richard Tressider and the editors, designers, and the publishing team at Taylor & Francis Group/ CRC Press for providing all the necessary and timely support in terms of review, guidance, and regular follow-ups. I also would like to thank Christine Selvan for timely corrections and content reviews. I owe much of the book's success to them.

Acknowledgments

Author

Shailesh Kumar Shivakumar is a TOGAF 9 certified senior technology architect and practice lead for digital practice at Infosys Technologies Limited, India with over 13 years of industry experience and a research student at PES University. His areas of expertise include enterprise portals, Java enterprise technologies, performance engineering, user interface components, and content management technologies. He is a Guinness World Record holder for successfully developing a mobile application in a coding marathon. He has four patent applications, including two U.S. patent applications in the area of web and social technologies.

He was involved in multiple large-scale and complex digital transformation projects for Fortune 500 clients of his organization. He has also provided on-demand consultancy in performance engineering for critical projects across various units in the organization. He has hands-on experience in a breadth of technologies, including web technologies, portal technologies, and database technologies and has worked on multiple domain areas such as retail, manufacturing, e-commerce, avionics, etc. He was the chief architect of an online platform that won the Best Web Support Site award among global competitors.

He has published a technical book titled *Architecting High Performing, Scalable and Available Enterprise Web Applications* related to enterprise architecture. He is a regular blogger at Infosys "Thought Floor," and many of his technical white papers have been published by Infosys. He has delivered two sessions at the Oracle JavaOne 2013 conference on performance optimization and project management and has presented a paper at an IEEE conference on knowledge management systems. He has also published three white papers related to web performance optimization, social media technologies, and insight driven computing. He has also headed a center of excellence (CoE) for portals and is currently the practice lead for enterprise portal practice. He has led multiple thought leadership and productivity improvement initiatives and was part of special interest groups (SIG) related to emerging web technologies at his organization.

He holds numerous professional certifications, including TOGAF 9 Certification Oracle Certified Master (OCM) Java Enterprise Edition 5, Sun Certified Java Programmer, Sun Certified Business Component Developer, IBM Certified Solution Architect—Cloud computing, IBM Certified Solution Developer—IBM WebSphere Portal 6.1, and many others.

He has won numerous awards, including the prestigious Infosys Award for Excellence 2013–2014, "Multitalented Thought Leader" under Innovation—Thought Leadership category, "Best Employee at Bangalore DC" award, "Brand Ambassador Award" for MFG unit, Delivery Excellency Award, and multiple spot awards, and received honor from the executive vice chairman of his organization. He is featured as "Infy star" in the Infosys Hall of Fame and has recently led a delivery team that won the "Best Project Team" award at his organization.

He holds an engineering degree in computer science and has completed the executive management program from the Indian Institute of Management, Kolkata. He lives in Bangalore, India, and can be reached at shailesh.shivakumar@gmail.com. His LinkedIn profile page can be accessed at in.linkedin.com/in/shaileshkumarshivakumar/.

Section I

The Art of Developing Portals

1

Thinking in Portals: Introduction to Portals

The term "portal" means different things to different people. The legacy definition of portal refers to a portal as a web page with multiple "sections or fragments" whereas modern enterprise architects use formal Java Specification Requests (JSR) such as JSR 168 and JSR 286 to explain portal terminologies. Marketing folks refer to a portal as a tool to provide a holistic user experience and normal web users would perceive a portal as a gateway to all personalized services and functionality. So, obviously, there exist multiple view points for the term "portal".

In this chapter, we will try to understand the key concepts, standards, and motivations for using portal technology. This chapter serves as an introduction to portal concepts such as personalization and content management. We will elaborate on each of the core concepts and scenarios in coming chapters. Portal architects, students, developers, and business analysts would find this chapter useful.

What Are Portals?

Portals are web platforms that provide personalized and secured aggregation platform. Their main strength lies in providing optimal integrations and exceptional user experience to drive business outcomes and cost savings. They enable the business models through various means such as self-service, collaboration, analytics, search, content management, etc. In this section we will look at the various roles of a portal and its features and types.

Brief History of Portals

Portals have a close relationship with the history of web browsers. Early portals emerged in the late 1990s and they provided a link-based gateway for the Internet. Most of the browser vendors were interested in developing a single entry point for the Internet and developed portals for that. First-generation portals mainly were utility based, which contained links to the most popular web sites or functionalities such as stocks, weather sites, search sites, news links, etc. Companies such as AOL and Yahoo! provided early portal-like features. These were mainly static link and functionality aggregation.

Soon, many large software vendors realized the importance of portal functionality and started building fully featured portal products. Those enterprise portal products provided in-built functionality to deploy a full-fledged enterprise portal. Some of the major players in this area built the portal on top of their existing application server infrastructure. These portals mainly provided information aggregation, prebuilt UI components such as themes and skins, personalization, out-of-the-box portlets, site administration features, and user management features. Later, portal standards begin to emerge. JSR 168 standard was created in 2003 and JSR 286 in 2008. Standards helped the developers to develop portable and standards-based portal applications. The portal products leveraged the standards and became the platform-of-choice for delivering personalized content aggregation for enterprises.

Since then, portals have evolved on multiple fronts. The emergence of Web 2.0 technologies such as AJAX and widgets have influenced the front-end technologies in portals; on the integration side, web services and Representational State Transfer (REST) services have gained popularity; cloud hosting is gaining traction on the deployment side of things. We will look at the emerging trends in Chapter 21.

Today, we have mature enterprise portal products that are available in the market such as Liferay Portal, IBM WebSphere Portal, BackBase, Oracle WebCenter portal, Microsoft Sharepoint Portal, etc.

Portals are a unique combination of multiple technologies that have wide potential in multiple business scenarios. Let us try to look at some of the perspectives and viewpoints about portal.

Portal as a Concept

The term "portal" literally means a gateway or an entry point. Historically, portals were used as a unified gateway for other web pages and applications through links. Even today, any reference to portal will include a scenario to provide "unified" or "single-stop shop" or "single point of access" kind of experiences. Portals provide a convergence of various technologies, platforms, and disparate applications and services.

So portal essentially serves as a starting point for any functionality and user journey. In the digital world, portal usually serves as a front-end application that weaves a lot of underlying enterprise applications and functionality.

Portal as a Technology

A portal is a web application that provides a unified and personalized view of applications and functionality through single sign-on (SSO) and content aggregation from multiple sources. Essentially, portal is a "specialized" web application that provides value-added services such as:

- Personalization to provide relevant content, functionality, and user preferences–based experience, content, data, and functionality
- SSO to provide seamless login to all links and applications provided by the portal
- Content management to author, manage, and publish various content formats
- Data aggregation from various sources such as ERP systems, database, web services, legacy systems, third party external applications, etc.
- Secure search facilities to provide a unified and secured search covering all enterprise data source
- Localization of content to provide the content and web pages in various languages
- Multichannel access to provide the functionality on multitude of devices such as PDAs, tables, and smartphones in addition to desktop browsers
- Social and collaboration features such as blogs, wikis, communities, forums, chat, etc.

In addition, a few portals also cater to specialized scenarios such as workflow management, process orchestration, dashboards, analytics, reporting, and business rules management wherever necessary.

Portals as a Business Enabler

Portals are key components of digital journey of an enterprise. Portals are the primary technology enablers for realizing the digital vision for an enterprise. Portals are uniquely positioned to address both business and technical challenges and realize the goals of online strategy.

Portals allow aggregation of heterogeneous applications and data and help in streamlining functionality related to people, process, and technology. Many of the business goals such as providing consistent brand experience, providing consolidated and holistic view of services, productivity enhancements, collaboration, optimizing total cost of ownership (TCO), and self-service can be realized through the effective application of portal technologies.

Core Features of Portals

We have seen the main portal utilities in the earlier section. Following are the main features of the portal technology framework:

- *Single-sign-on (SSO):* Portal will be able to provide SSO with secured applications and services.
- *Enterprise integration*: This is one of the main strengths of portal by which it provides various integration components and plugins to enable easy and extensible integrations with internal and external applications, feeds, and services.
- *Personalization*: The user experience, functionality, and data will be customized based on user preferences and the implicit/explicit attributes. The objective is to enhance the overall user experience and help user find the relevant information in quick time.
- *Multidevice support*: This feature enables portal deliver user experience optimized for all channels.
- *Content management*: This is another main feature of portal that provides built-in web content management features.
- *Enterprise search*: Built-in search and support for external search plugins help portals to crawl and index enterprise content sources.
- *Collaboration*: Portals can be used as collaboration platform to provide features such as chat, wikis, document sharing, web conferencing, communities, etc.
- *Social integration*: One of the main integration scenarios for a portal is to integrate with external and internal social platforms.
- *Process engine*: Portals often provide workflow support for modeling business processes.
- *Rules engine*: Modeling of complex business processes also require configurable rules engine that can be used for handling complex business logic.
- *Plugins and extensions*: To support platform extensibility and accommodate future needs, portals provide plugin architecture through which external systems can be integrated. Extensions help us in customizing the core portal functionality such as security to suit the customer needs.

Advantages of Portals

We have seen that portal is mainly used as an information aggregation platform for providing personalized services. The main advantages of the portal framework from business and technical standpoint are as follows:

- Improved collaboration and knowledge sharing through in-built collaborative features such as chat, communities, wiki, etc.
- Improved productivity through intuitive information architecture and self-service features provided by portal platform
- Reduced integration cost using in-built portal components
- Multidevice support for the portal platform
- Easier content management through portal's web content management features
- Enterprise search for all types of enterprise data that enhances the discovery of relevant information
- Process optimization and process automation to optimize the business process management
- Reduced maintenance and operations cost due to in-built site administration features
- Reduced time to market, which can be achieved through portal accelerators and out-of-the-box portlets and reusable components
- Enables digital marketing and sales channel through business-friendly content publishing and site maintenance features
- Improved customer satisfaction through rich user interface and intuitive features
- Enables self-service features through search and friendlier information architecture
- Provides highly scalable, robust, and extensible platform that can be used for future needs

We will discuss each of the core features in the coming chapters along with their utilities. We have also provided a dedicated chapter about portal features for business enablement.

Types of Portal

Portals are categorized mainly as horizontal and vertical portals. Horizontal portals cater to a variety of industries and organizations. They mainly aggregate the information from various enterprise applications. For instance, a portal application that can be reused for both retail and finance domain will qualify for a horizontal portal. Horizontal portals focus more on the core portal use cases such as information aggregation, personalization, and single sign-on rather than on vertical or domain-specific scenarios. Horizontal portals provide all necessary technology infrastructure to realize the core portal scenarios.

Vertical portals are specialized portals that cater to a specific industry vertical or domain-specific functionality and are designed for fulfilling a specific business function. Business intelligence dashboard portals and health care portals are examples of vertical portals.

This book mainly focuses on horizontal portals though we touch base on vertical portals for a few specific instances.

Sometimes portals are also categorized based on its access: Intranet portals are targeted mainly for internal stakeholders such as employees, sales and marketing team, organization support team, business line managers, etc. The main intranet portals are employee portals, collaboration portals, knowledge portals, process and policy portals, search portals, etc. External portals or Internet portals are external-facing public portals that cater to Internet audience such as dealers, end customers, external partners, resellers, etc. There are a wide variety of external portals such as retail portals, ecommerce portals, enterprise information portals, dealer portals, etc. The topics discussed in this book can be used to build both intranet and external portals.

Overview of Portals

In this section we will look at the key components of portal platform and typical elements of a portal page. We will also look at some of the common usage scenarios for portals. This section serves as an introduction to the world of portals and we will have in-depth discussion on these sections in the coming chapters.

Layer-Wise Portal Components

Let us look at the high-level components in a portal platform. This provides an insight into the capabilities of portal components. Figure 1.1 provides a high level overview of components present at each of the layers in an enterprise portal platform.

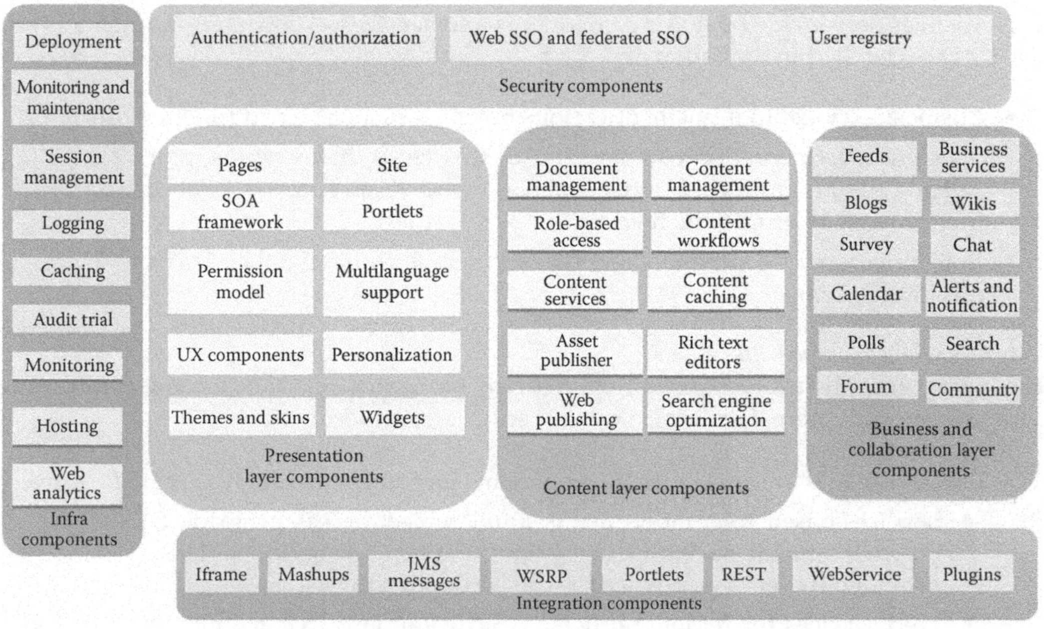

FIGURE 1.1
Layer-wise portal components.

Here is a brief explanation of portal components in each layer.

Presentation layer components
This involves the presentation components like portlets and user experience components:

- *Portlets*: Portlets are main web components that are reusable independent applications.
- *Portal pages*: Portal pages aggregate information through portlets.
- *Themes and skins*: These include standard and consistent header and footer for uniform user experience and branding. Skins provide the branding for individual portlets.
- *Multilanguage support*: Components to internationalize portal pages in various languages.
- *Personalization*: This includes user-specific or group-specific features that can be leveraged to provide customized user experience.
- *Widgets*: Client-side widgets are used to provide Asynchronous JavaScript and XML(AJAX)-based functionalities. This would help enhance overall user experience and improve the page performance. Real-time report data display/refresh, pagination, and search functionality are typical scenarios where this AJAX-based features can be employed.
- *Permission model*: Portal permission model includes coarse-grained access control at page level and fine-grained access control at resource level.
- *UX components*: These include client-side libraries, third-party UI plugins, stylesheets, and static assets that are required for user experience.
- *Site*: This represents the overall site hierarchy and site taxonomy structure.

Business and collaboration layer components
This involves server side business components and services. A few core components and services are detailed in the following:

- Business services to implement various business scenarios and functionality.
- Social and collaboration components such as feeds, blogs, wikis, polls, surveys, calendars, communities, forums, and audio and video chat for collaborating with internal and external stakeholders.
- Enterprise search component to index and search from all data sources with various data formats.

Integration layer components
The layer primarily involves integration components used by portals to connect to various data sources and internal/external systems, services, and feeds.

- Portal provides various in-built components for integration such as the following:
  - Services-based integration using simple object access protocol (SOAP)- and representational state transfer (REST)-based web services. This is usually provided by services proxy and web service portlets.
  - Web services for remote portlets (WSRP) standard to consume external web services through a portlet and to expose the portlet functionality to external systems.

  - Portlet-based integration such as content portlet, feed portlet, iframe portlet, link portlet, web-clipping portlet, etc.
  - Third Party plugins such as widgets or client-side component plugins.
- Message-based integration to support asynchronous message sending and receiving through message queues and topics.
- The integration components can be leveraged to integrate with a variety of systems such as ERP system, reporting systems, third party systems, legacy systems, and content management systems (CMSs).

Security layer components

- Portals provide in-built support for various forms of authentication that can also be extended to suit the custom needs.
- Besides, the portal framework provides coarse-grained authorization at page level and fine-grained authorization at portal resource level.
- Most portals provide in-built support for integration with user registries such as lightweight directory access protocol (LDAP).
- To support web SSO with enterprise-wide internal applications portals provide various plugins and federated SSO with external systems will be achieved through standards such as SAML.

Content layer components

- CMSs will be used to store all the web content and static assets (PDFs, images, media files, and documents). Most portal systems come with bundled CMS, which provide seamless integration. Portals also support pluggable adaptors to connect to various CMS systems.
- Portal-based CMS has built-in features such as asset publishing, search engine optimization (SEO), multilingual content, content workflow, content import and export, role-based content access, rich text editor support, etc.

Infrastructure layer components

- It consists of monitoring components that include internal and external continuous application/system service-level agreement (SLA) monitoring and maintenance that is essential to maintain the availability and performance SLA, system health-check/heartbeat monitoring to ping the availability of portal system, and all interfacing systems to ensure that they are responding within agreed response time. Automatic notification is triggered if any system is down.
- Most of the portal systems provide web analytics plugins to monitor the business-critical process and activities in real time. This could include activities such as page load time, search processing time, user activity, user behavior, etc.
- Other infrastructure components include logging, caching, auditing, and deployment components.

Various portal sections

Let us have a look at the user interface of a typical portal page. A typical portal page is shown with all web components in Figure 1.2.

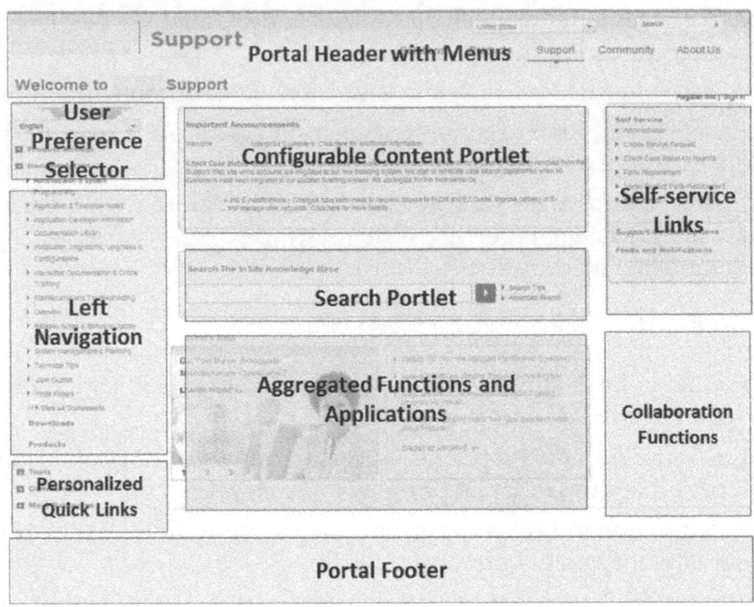

FIGURE 1.2
Portal page elements.

A typical portal page consists of the following components:

- Header and footer that provides a uniform and consistent branding. This is usually implemented by the portal theme component.
- Search functionality that is usually implemented by search portlet.
- Configurable portlets such as content portlet wherein the customer can specify the preferences.
- Custom portlets and widgets for data aggregation from various applications.
- Navigation components such as left navigation, breadcrumbs, etc.
- User preferences selector to select the portlets, user experience, page layout, etc.
- Self-service components such as knowledge base solutions, recommended content, and saved search results.
- Personalized content such as user- and role-specific links; targeted content, promotions, programs, etc.
- Role-based authorization features such as role-based portlet access.
- Client-side widgets and gadgets.
- Collaboration features such as chat, communities, wiki, etc.

Scenarios for Portals

Let us look at various scenarios where portal technologies can be effectively used. This is another crucial factor in deciding the right fit of portals. We have discussed the high-level business and technology scenarios where portals have been proven to be effectively used to realize the intended benefits. This will provide a high level overview of the scenarios and we will discuss them in detail in the coming chapters.

Business scenarios for portals
The list of business scenarios where portal can be used are listed here:

- *Digital marketing*: Portals are the preferred choice for digital marketing scenario, which can leverage the web content management, document management, and workflow features offered by the portal platform. Portals can be widely used for marketing promotions, campaign management, marketing analysis dashboards, etc.
- *Multichannel support*: Portals are also uniquely positioned to implement "mobile-first" strategy to rollout the online platform on mobility devices. One of the important business goals in consumer-facing organizations is to provide unified experience across all channels and a synchronized view of data that can be implemented using in-built features of portal.
- *Self-service model*: Enterprises can use portals to implement self-service model related to their business. Instances of this include self-registration, self-approval, issue avoidance architecture, etc.
- *E-commerce*: Most of the e-commerce sites need unified view of e-commerce features. A dashboard-type view of sales promotions, personalized offers, targeted content, product search, product communities and forums, and chat and support is required for an effective e-commerce program and this can be achieved effectively using portal platform.
- *News portals*: This is one of the traditional use cases of portals wherein the news content is aggregated from multiple sources and displayed to the user according to the user's preferences.
- *Business intelligence dashboards*: Portals are also widely used for analytics and reporting applications wherein a dashboard view of reports and analytical data is presented to business users.
- *Process management systems*: Many process-oriented systems and business domains can also adopt the portals by leveraging the in-built workflow support provided by portals. Process optimization techniques such as reducing process steps, providing quicker process alternatives, and automating processes can be implemented using portals.
- *Unified user experience platform*: Modern UI technologies such as HTML5, CSS3, and responsive web design can be used by portals to provide enhanced user experience. Bringing various applications under a single umbrella with a consistent look and feel and brand identity is another unique value proposition of portal platform.
- *Government portals*: Many governments effectively use portals for providing single-window interface for utilities for its citizens. Government agencies also adopt portal strategy for providing process-related functions.
- *Utility dashboard*: Any business scenario, which requires a single interface or dashboard view of utilities, can leverage on portals. Health care dashboard, sales dashboard, and supply-chain dashboard are all instances of this use case.

Technical scenarios for portals

Following are the main technology-related scenarios where portals can be used.

- *Information aggregation*: When an online or digital strategy involves aggregation of decentralized and separately managed data sources, portal would be a right fit. Portal has all the integration capabilities to satisfy these requirements. It provides various libraries and portlets and supports third party widgets and plugins to aggregate data from multiple data sources.
- *Information gateway scenario*: If a home page or landing page acts as a gateway to all services, applications, and data, then it can be implemented through portal technology. Portal provides an aggregated view of all applications.
- *Security and SSO*: When there are multiple discrete applications hosted internally and externally, it would be natural to have multiple security mechanisms for that. In order to provide seamless navigation and access to those services and applications, underlying platform should support SSO or federated SSO. Portal platform has unique capabilities to satisfy this.
- *Service-oriented architecture*: This is the preferred means for information aggregation. Portal supports wide variety of services such as SOAP, REST, and feed aggregation to aggregate the data in asynchronous fashion. It also provides many pluggable widgets and client-side components for service-based information aggregation

When Do I Need a Portal?

The decision to use portal technologies for implementing an online strategy is the primary step before adopting the portals. In this section, we will discuss about the main scenarios that warrant the use of portal.

- *Consolidated platform*: If the organization has discrete applications and data that needs to be aggregated, then portal would be the technology of choice. Many in-built integration techniques and portlets available within a portal platform will be able to create a unified and consistent branding and user experience in a quick time.
- *Multichannel access*: One of the most recent trends picking up these days is "mobile-first" strategy wherein the web applications are predominantly built for mobile devices. Mobility enablement is another key in-built feature of portal platform, which is provided through various features such as mobile themes (header and footer), automatic device-recognition plugins, mobile rules, etc.
- *To provide personalized experience*: Portals have many features to provide personalized user experience features such as preference-based data aggregation, context-relevant functionality, user-profile-based filtering features, geo- and locale-specific features, etc. Most portal products have in-built tools and rules engine to support personalization.
- *Internal and external collaboration*: Social and collaboration are essential for knowledge sharing and productivity improvements. Some of the core social and collaboration tools such as chat, blogs, wiki, communities, forums, message

boards, and plugins to external social platforms are readily available as portlets in many portal products.

- *SSO and role-based access control*: While accessing information from discrete applications and systems, handling security of all these systems is inevitable. In order to provide seamless access to systems using distinct security mechanisms, it is necessary to establish a SSO for internal systems and federated SSO with external systems. Portals have in-built SSO plugins and provide extensible security and pluggable authentication modules to support these features. Additionally, it is required to provide role-based security at various levels such as coarse-grained security at page and site level as well as fine-grained access control at portlet, data, and content level. Portals provide these features out-of-the-box.
- *Web content management*: For many of the marketing features and web content scenarios, the content is stored in CMS. Most of the portals provide seamless CMS integration and content management features such as content authoring, content tagging, workflow support, content publishing, content translation, content review and approvals, content preview, etc. This feature is mainly used for web marketing and web content management scenarios.
- *Unified enterprise search*: As the main aim of portal is to unify discrete data sources, applications, and systems, search becomes an important tool in aiding information discovery. An enterprise search consists of indexing various forms of structure and unstructured data of various formats from distinct data sources. The indexed data is then ranked based on its relevance and presented to the user. Search is assuming increased prominence in modern portals due to its multidimensional utility. Search can be effectively used as an information discovery tool, as a navigation aid, as a self-service tool, and it can drastically influence the end-user experience. Hence search is being prominently positioned in portal use cases.
- *Self-service*: Portal would unify people, process, and technology in enhancing user experience. The evolution road map of many portal programs include self-service as one of their key end-state objectives. This includes self-service issue resolution, information discovery, approval workflows, collaboration, etc. Most of the process-oriented business scenarios would need self-service as their primary objectives. Portal provides tools and features to enable self-service.
- *Knowledge management*: This is another area where portal is widely used. Managing solution documents, articles, keyword-based search, and controlling user access can be done using portal technologies. Knowledge management portals are used both for internal and external stakeholders.
- *Collaboration*: Portal is an ideal platform where people from various channels can collaborate. Portals provide various types of collaboration features such as chat, message boards, discussion forums, communities, etc., which help people to collaborate and share knowledge. Intranet portal collaboration tools are mainly used for productivity improvement and knowledge sharing whereas extranet portal collaboration tools are aimed at improving the user experience, reducing issue resolution times, and sharing/reusing the knowledge.

We will discuss various scenarios that warrant portal and where portal is an optimal fit in the coming chapters.

Summary

- Portal is a web platform to provide a unified and single-stop shop experience for all enterprise functionalities, applications, and services.
- Portal is a specialized web application that provides personalized experience and other features such as content, data, and functionality aggregation, SSO with enterprise systems, multichannel enablement, collaboration, and content management.
- Portal history dates back to the late 1990s where link-based aggregation was used in initial stages. Later, portal transformed itself into a platform for aggregating content and for providing personalization services.
- Portal can be viewed as a concept, a technology platform, and as a business enabler.
- The main features of the portal include enterprise integration, personalization, multidevice support, content management, enterprise search, collaboration, social integration, process orchestration, rules engine, etc.
- Due to its diverse technology benefits, portals can be of best use in a wide variety of scenarios such as digital marketing scenarios, collaboration scenarios, multidevice support scenarios, for implementation of self-service features, unified experience platforms, utility dashboards, etc.
- Portals are mainly categorized as horizontal and vertical portals based on its utility.
- Portal platform typically implement model–view–controller (MVC) architecture providing components for all layers.
- The main scenarios where portal could be of best fit include information aggregation, personalized experience, SSO use cases, web content management, self-service, knowledge management, etc.

2

Make Portal Work for You: Business Transformation through Portals

Introduction

More often than not, various key program stakeholders have diverse expectations from portal programs and it is important to align all stakeholders in line with program goals and set right expectations about portal possibilities. One of the main reasons for the failure of portal programs is the unrealistic expectations and suboptimal portal fitment for the given scenario. Hence, it is an absolute necessity to ensure that before portal is finalized as the technology solution, we need to thoroughly understand the business scenarios and the applicability of portal technologies in solving business problems. Additionally, there are a few business scenarios where portal can be readily used, leveraging its in-built components to get instant benefits.

This chapter mainly explores various business-related aspects of portal technologies such as portal opportunities, portal adoption challenges, typical business transformation scenarios enabled by portal, portal applicability scenarios for business use cases, and portal value realization framework. Business community, program managers and business analysts would find the techniques and concepts discussed in this chapter useful in understanding the role that portals can play in a digital transformation journey and the methodologies for evaluation and fitment of portal product.

Business Aspects of Portal

We analyzed numerous portal programs and the business scenarios and business drivers in those programs. In this section, we will look at the main business drivers that require portal technologies and the challenges that we normally face during the execution of portal programs and the business capabilities enabled by portal programs. Insights into the ways portals are used in business scenarios and the most effective business applications of portal are provided.

Key Business Drivers That Require Portal Technologies

After analyzing the key business motivations and drivers from various portal engagements, we came up with the list of key business drivers that can be realized by portal technologies. Following are the top 10 categories of business drivers for which portal technologies are most suitable. The categories in Table 2.1 are listed in the order of priority and importance:

TABLE 2.1

Portal Business Scenarios

Business Driver Category	Key Business Drivers
Aggregation and consolidation	• Data, content, and information aggregation • Functionality consolidation • Creation of single source of information • One-stop shop unified experience • Consolidation of data for operational efficiency • Consolidation of technology landscape and better management of the existing infrastructure and IT resources
User experience improvement	• Addressing disjointed user interface and the need to integrate many existing web channels into one • Addressing inconsistent user experience, obsolete content, and inefficient workflow • Creating a uniform, consistent, responsive and engaging brand identity • Driving demand for services through enhanced experience • Friendlier and personalized navigation
Personalized experience	• Personalized content and functionality • Targeted and relevant content • Personalized search • Personalized recommendations, benchmarks, and comparisons to enable users in making informed decisions leading to actions • Customizing the experience so that customers can easily discover the relevant information and can quickly perform tasks
Active user engagement	• Relationship-enhancing and self-service feature enablement • Promotion of common and consistent branding and user experience • Providing ease of use, promoting client-centricity, and driving client satisfaction • Enhancing user engagement • Enhancing user loyalty and aim to become long-term preferred platform for the customer
Business enablement	• Enabling business users and administrators to easily create content and configure pages, providing flexibility and faster time to market • Legacy modernization and replacement of outdated technology through technology consolidation
Integrated platform	• Need for seamless integration with back-end applications • Design for future integration with other systems • Supporting new business strategy of nonlinear growth by acquiring businesses and onboarding all accompanying applications • Reusable, scalable, robust platform based on standards and open architecture, which helps in future integrations and business needs • Building a services-based platform to enable future business growth opportunities
Collaboration and knowledge base	• Improving productivity through solution knowledge base • Creating collaboration platform for internal and external users • Enabling knowledge cocreation and updates
Cost optimization	• Reducing high cost of operations and maintenance due to redundant and duplication of applications • Continuous productivity and quality improvement
Process optimization	• Automating and optimizing business process • Implementing robust business process management platform
Actionable analytics	• Gathering real-time insights based on customer behavior
Omnichannel experience	• Enabling the online access on multiple devices
Self-service experience	• Providing intuitive and easy-to-find self-service features • Efficient completion of tasks and processes with minimal external help

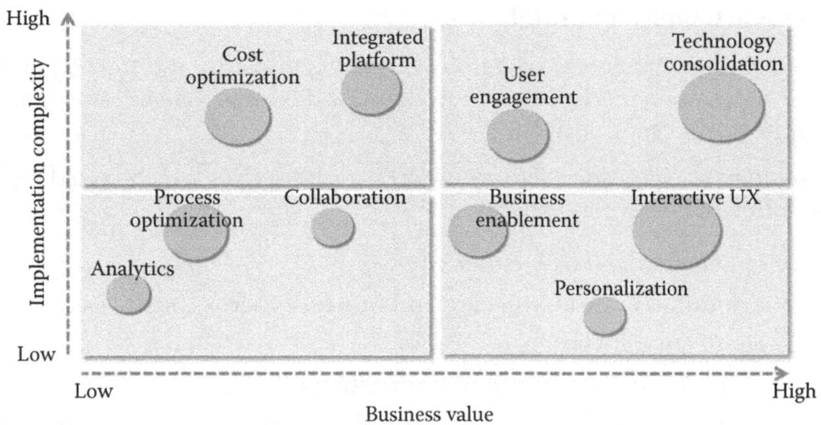

FIGURE 2.1
Business value vs. implementation complexity.

Prioritized Portal Value Deliverables

Normally for most of the portal engagements, we find a common set of business value additions that can be effectively realized through portal platform. It makes perfect business sense to leverage the unique value proposition of portal to fulfil business goals.

A plot of the business value vs. implementation complexity of portal value proposition is shown in Figure 2.1.

Normally during program execution, we will prioritize the "low-hanging fruits" to provide quick wins and achieve faster time to market. With this strategy, we can achieve high business value with relatively lesser effort and enable those capabilities in the initial release. As per Figure 2.1, interactive UX, business enablement functionality, SSO, personalization, and partial technology consolidation will be targeted for the initial releases. Additionally, functionality that can be rolled out leveraging the in-built portal features with little customization will be a part of initial release; this includes features like basic collaboration features leveraging chat portlet; in-built wiki, forum, and community features; enterprise integrations using out-of-the-box portlets, etc.

In subsequent phases, we can prioritize features and functionality based on potential business value. As per Figure 2.1, we can achieve platform consolidation through services, functionality, and application integration and user engagements feature in the next release.

Digital Transformation through Portal

Every organization wants to position portal as the single point of access to all its users and wants to realize their end state objectives. The portal plays a key role in the digital transformation of an organization. In the previous chapter we have already seen the business scenarios that warrant portal technology. Let us now look at the business transformation that can be enabled by portal technology.

Enterprise Opportunities for Portal

We have seen the key business drivers in earlier sections. In addition to those drivers, portal platform can open up further possibilities for business. The following are the main enterprise opportunities for portals:

Portal as a solution to enterprise challenges: Portal technologies can be used to effectively address the following enterprise challenges:

- Absence of personalized user experience
- Expensive, redundant infrastructure and processes across business units
- Absence of effective governance
- Multiple points of access for various applications
- Limited aggregation and integration capabilities and the absence of holistic view
- Nonintuitive information architecture
- Lack of standard user experience design
- Limited ability to support mobile devices
- Absence of integrated experience across various channels with seamless and synchronized user experience
- Business lacking required control (such as business-driven site management and campaign and promotion setup) over sales and marketing initiatives
- Need for improvement in system agility
- Unreliable knowledge, solution, and document management systems
- No easy way to discover relevant and context sensitive information
- High dependency on support team
- Existing systems are not able to scale to meet the increased demand impacting business growth
- Challenges in rolling out new changes at multiple geographies
- Silos of multiple applications leading to inconsistent user experience

Process improvements: There are multiple ways where a portal solution can lead to improved processes.

- Optimizations such as process automation, process optimization, configurable business rules, process customization, and process orchestration
- Identifying and minimizing duplicate or unnecessary process steps
- Leveraging portal for more efficient business process management (BPM)
- Leverage portal as a knowledge management system to improve the employee productivity and for faster response times
- Enabling self-service features through processes such as process automation, self-approvals, etc.

Competitive advantage achieved through portals:

- Portals provide unified interface for multiple roles and personas thereby enabling businesses to rollout new features and functionality in seamless fashion

- Portal helps in achieving efficiency in partnership through seamless collaboration with all channel partners, resellers, suppliers, customers, and employees
- Portals helps in achieving supply chain efficiency leveraging portal technologies such as unified view, seamless secured access to all applications in the chain, etc.
- Personalized and multichannel interface provided by portals enhances user experience and improves site usability
- Portal can implement mobile-first and mobile-ready platform offering personalized services
- Portals provide personalized services based on the user context and past behavior for providing differentiated service thereby achieving increased customer loyalty and retention
- Portals integrated with analytics provide insights into the user activities and uses it to improve the user experience and targeted marketing and promotion
- Portals provide a consistent and synergized multichannel experience
- Portals decreases time to market through faster release cycles and adopting to agile practices

Portal solution as enterprise platform:

- We can standardize and consolidate discrete technologies used at the enterprise using portal.
- Portals can be used to build an extensible platform that can be extended for future initiatives.
- Portal platform can provide a single window to all services, data, and features for enhanced user experience and synchronized access across all channels.
- Portal platform can achieve minimal total cost of ownership in the long term:
    - Simple, configurable, and easy to use administration interfaces such as business rules, workflows, screen flows, etc.
    - Open architecture and standards-based platform to enable future integrations, expansions, and mergers.
    - Ability to support faster time to market initiatives such as campaign management, microsite enablement, etc.
    - Robust platform that can be scalable to increased user demand, multiple geographies, and multiple devices.

User experience and active user engagement:

- Portals can have positive impact on end-user experience through intuitive and responsive UX.
- Portals can provide multidevice access.
- Portal can address the inconsistencies in the user experience and define a common framework for user interface elements.
- Portals can improve the site usability and information discoverability through unified search and intuitive information architecture with clearly defined visual hierarchy.

- Portals enable targeted marketing through user segmentation and personalization.
- Leveraging web analytics along with portal provides vital insights into customer actions and behavior. This can be further used to address the gaps and pain points and enhance user experience.
- Portals enable a wiki-like knowledge repository for users to collaborate and re-use solution artifacts.
- Portal components can be used to develop real, appealing, immersive, interactive, and responsive UI using AJAX toolkits.
- Portals can be used to achieve better and consistent branding and visual appeal through themes and page layout features.
- Portals could be used to engage customers more actively using blogs, feeds, wikis, etc.
- Portals enhance the site usability through
    - Intuitive page layout and responsive user interface
    - Intuitive site taxonomy
- Portals maximize the ease of information access through
    - Intuitive information architecture
    - Intuitive search by positioning search as a primary tool for discovering relevant information
    - Intuitive navigation like breadcrumbs, left navigation, etc.
    - Personalized content and features relevant for the user and the context
- Portals can provide high performing and scalable platform to cater to the increased business demand across geographies.
- Portals can engage end users through collaboration and cocreation.

Cost optimization:

- Enhances productivity improvements through prebuilt portlets and integration components
- Enables easy rollout of new functionality to various geographies
- Minimizes customer service costs through portal self-service features such as
    - Support forums, blogs, wikis, chat and communities
    - Solution knowledge base
- Optimizes customer and employee onboarding cost with a single interface–based functionality
- Minimizes site maintenance cost through in-built site management features

Enhancement of business controls through portals:

- Portal enables business community with easy-to-use and easy-to-manage interfaces to launch sales and marketing campaigns.
- Portals provides configurable and intuitive user interface for business community to easily customize the default behavior to suit business needs.

- Portals can be used to provide dashboard view of reports and program activities for easy and efficient business management.
- Portals provide business-friendly content publishing and content workflows for easier and faster publishing of product content.

Enabling business growth:

- Portal features can be leveraged to expand the digital footprint across multiple geographies, languages, and devices.
- Enables multichannel access to increase reach of customers.

Portal for Building Next-Generation Digital Platform for Business

Due to the breadth and depth of the capabilities of portal technologies, portal is uniquely positioned as the platform of choice for implementing next-generation digital strategy. We will look at these in detail in Chapter 21.

Next-generation digital platform with the following features can be built using portal:

- *Cutting-edge and forward-looking platform*: Competitive advantage can be gained by staying ahead of the curve through industry-leading technologies. Portals help in implementing this future-proof platform through the support of plugins, adaptors, and various frameworks.
- *Mobile-first strategy*: Target the mobile users by enabling multichannel support and provide consistent and synergized cross channel experience. Most of the portal products provide in-built mobile themes and support responsive web design (RWD) for implementing this strategy.
- *Customer-centric platform*: Portals are well-positioned to develop a customer-centric platform that provides personalized and on-demand content and services over multiple channels.
- *Elastic scalability*: The digital platform should be able to meet the growing business demands and increasing data volumes through elastic scalability. Cloud-enabled portals and clustered portals come handy in providing this scalability to the digital platform.
- *Next-generation digital strategy*: The portal has a breadth of technologies to realize the strategic digital transformation for an enterprise by providing presentation, content, and search and integration services. Coupled with real-time analytics, we can also provide targeted content, personalized recommendations, and improve operational efficiencies through portal.
- *Hypercollaborative platform*: The digital platform should keep all its users connected and collaborate through various means such as chat, forum, community, sharing, conferencing, integration with external social sites, etc. Portal platform provides robust in-built social and collaboration features and most portal products provide connectors and adaptors to external social media platforms.
- *Lightweight, nimble platform with quicker time to market*: Portals that are built using web-oriented architecture that use widgets and client-side technologies built using AJAX toolkit provide accelerated development, faster deployment, and quicker time to market.
- *Flexible and robust platform*: The digital platform should be extensible to onboard new applications, functionality, and integrations for future needs. Portals are

very well positioned in this space through various integration components and it can use service-oriented integrations for future integrations and extensions.

- *Social-enabled platform*: Leveraging on portal social connectors we can harness the strength of social media platforms such as social listening, brand management, voice of customer (VOC), crowd sourcing, etc.

Common Pitfalls While Using Portal

We have noticed some recurring problem patterns while using portal for business scenarios. The scenarios are explained in detail in Chapter 22. In this section we will look briefly into some of the common pitfalls while using portal. These pitfalls are focused on business related:

- *Thinking about end user in the final phases of the program*: In some portal programs, portals are built without keeping the end user in mind. This leads to poor customer engagement and reduced user adoption. We need to have a clear customer-centric focus of portal from the beginning. Following are some aspects that need to be thought through:
  - Understand how the portal site will be used including the information, services, pages, functionality, etc.
  - Understand how the page is accessed—the browsers, devices, etc.
  - The expected performance across various geographies
  - Continuous tracking of user's web behavior and updating the portal accordingly
  - The key business process used most frequently by users
- *Lack of monitoring and tracking*: Not having relevant metrics to track the portal usage, effectiveness, and return on investment (ROI) metrics. If we do not have a clear monitoring infrastructure and metrics for comparison, it would not be possible to understand the effectiveness, pain points, usage patterns, etc., of the portal. Tools such as web analytics and real user monitoring tools can be used to continuously monitor the portal performance and provide real-time feedback.
- *Improper positioning of portal*: A portal might be able to do a lot of things, but it should be positioned and expectations should be set appropriately with all stakeholders. Portal may not be a solution to all the problems; even after adopting portal, there could be some amount of manual process steps; all these needs to be clearly communicated to all relevant stakeholders.
- *Lack of proper portal governance*: A portal program is as good as its governance. Without having a clearly defined role–responsibility matrix and standard operating procedure (SOP), portal program would not be successful in the long run.

Challenges in Portal Adoption

For the portal program to be successful, it is important to understand the commonly encountered challenges in the adoption of portal program. The main challenges are given here. A more detailed discussion of reasons that lead to the failure of portal program is discussed in Chapter 22.

Functional and nonfunctional challenges:

- Identifying the comprehensive list of key portal functionality
- Accurately defining the nonfunctional requirements and SLAs
- Minimal or unstructured documentation of business logic
- Implementing portal foundation/platform release as per the specifications
- Aggregating nonstandard technologies and unstructured data from various data sources

Organizational challenges:

- Getting people to change and adopt standardized practices for information access and processing
- Business value management
- Quantatively defining the portal business value and ROI strategy
- Lack of sponsor support and buy-in from all relevant stakeholders in the organization
- Business goals not aligned properly into IT goals
- Challenges in interacting and collaborating with various internal and external groups and subject matter experts (SMEs)
- Requirement of cultural change for effective collaboration

Technology related challenges:

- Nonstandard technologies posing challenges in integration
- Legacy systems without service interfaces
- Logically related information distributed across multiple data sources without any single source of record system
- Not using a proof of concept (PoC) for complex and unknown integrations and complex features
- Inadequate infrastructure

Process related challenges:

- No proper governance for business and technical functionality
- No well-defined process for main business functionality
- Having a lengthy and big-bang release cycle without end-user feedback
- No plan for continuous improvement and productivity improvement
- Absence of business continuity plan

Portal Transformation Scenarios and Value Adds

We now know the main business drivers and enterprise opportunities where a portal can be leveraged. Let us look at the common business scenarios wherein a portal can play a pivotal role in filling the gaps and lead the transformation. The main business scenarios and the portal value additions to those business scenarios is given in Table 2.2.

TABLE 2.2

Business Scenarios and Portal Value Adds

Business Scenario	Portal Value Adds
Challenges in user experience	
• Multiple interface and inconsistent user experience	• Portal themes and skins can be used to provide a consistent and uniform user experience
• No support for mobile devices	• Portal multichannel capability can be leveraged to provide mobile-enabled sites
• Poor customer satisfaction score	• A rich, responsive, and interactive user experience can be developed on portal platform for the active engagement of customers
• Lack of uniform branding	• Self-service features, intuitive navigation, and friendlier information architecture can be used to improve user satisfaction
• Lack of consistent and friendlier navigation	• Template-driven page layouts and content provides a consistent user experience
	• Development of intuitive information architecture using portal navigation features will provide effective navigation and easier information discovery
Nonavailability of robust platform	
• Multiple systems, servers, and technologies used throughout the enterprise	• Portal can aggregate data to provide a single interface for end users
• No consistent or standard way of integrating these systems	• We can standardize the integration technologies as part of portal roadmap implementation. We can service enable interface systems for smoother and extensible integration
• Usage of nonstandard technology and architecture	• Portal technologies can be leveraged to build a platform for future needs and extensions
• High cost incurred due to nonstandard technologies and redundant software components	• Standards-based open architecture can be built using portal technologies
• Usage of proprietary technology leading to vendor lock-in	• Robust portal governance process can minimize technology barriers
	• Portal can be used to build a robust *information aggregation platform*
Launching new features and sites	
• Challenges in launching new website features	• Portal provides lots of in-built features such as site creation, page promotion, multisite management, and virtual portals that can be leveraged for quicker launch of new sites, microsites, brands, etc.
• Challenges in expanding to new geolocations	• Out-of-the-box portlets, integration components, and accelerators can be leveraged for quicker time to market
• Longer time to market	• Process automation, deployment automation, and continuous integration can be done on portal technologies to further reduce development and release cycles
• Configuring new rules to adhere to country/geo-specific rules and regulations	• Portal provides in-built rules engine that can be leveraged for configurable rules definition
• Launching marketing campaigns and microsites	

Realization of Enterprise Digital Vision through Portal

We will look at a sample long-term digital strategy of an enterprise and look at the key portal solution tenets to arrive at the digital end state.

Figure 2.2 shows a typical business transformation that can be done using portal technology.

We can see how the digital strategy can be implemented to achieve business goals that in turn are realized by portal solution tenets.

A typical digital objective for an enterprise is to provide an interactive, personalized, collaborative, and self-service platform that can be used to achieve various business, technology, and operation goals. To achieve this digital vision, a distinct set of business goals need to be achieved. For instance, to build a self-service online platform, the business should provide a robust knowledge platform and a collaborative platform. The main business, technology, and operational goals are depicted in Figure 2.2.

These business goals can be realized through a portal-based solution that possesses these five key solution tenets. In a nutshell, the portal solution architecture should satisfy these high-level solution tenets for a successful transformation.

Let us look closely at each of the solution tenets and its attributes.

Reusability:

- The solution should use services-based architecture for loose coupling during integrations to support future extensions and integrations.
- The solution should try to reuse current investments in technology for solution architecture.
- The solution should be modeled on layered architecture so that individual layers and its components can be reused.

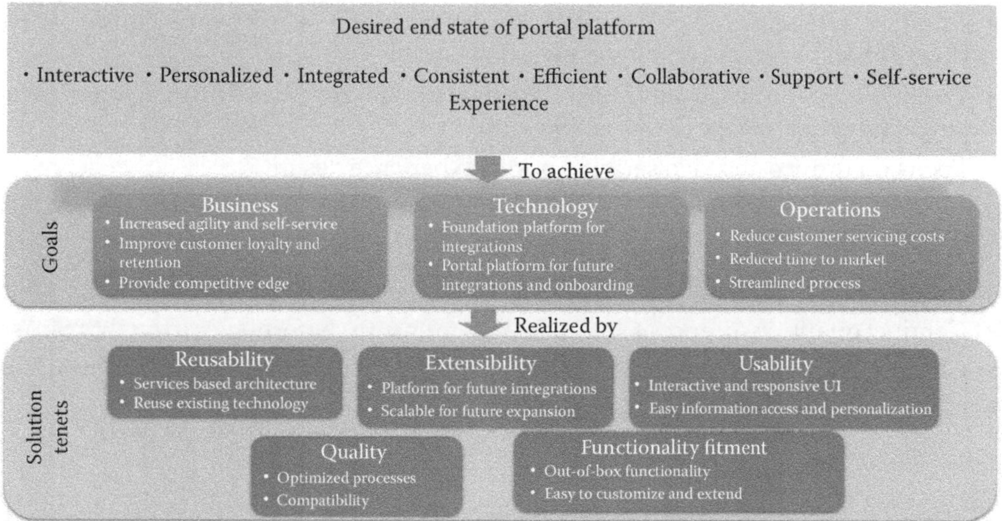

FIGURE 2.2
Business transformation through portals.

- The solution should adopt standards-based implementation (JSR 168/286) to allow porting of functionality to potential alternate portal solutions in the future.
- The solution should have a clear separation of presentation from integration and business services.

Extensibility:

- Create a platform based on portal for all future integrations and enhancements.
- Create progressive technology architecture with forward-looking features to make the solution future proof and align with strategic and long-term goals of the organization.
- Create a platform scalable for future global expansion.
- Adopt performance best practices and proven techniques to optimize the performance by leveraging caching and other techniques at various layers to optimize performance.
- Enable standardized information delivery to support immediate and future business needs.
- Make minimal investments on transient functionality.
- Create a long-term portal roadmap to realize the strategic business goals.

Usability:

- Provide an interactive, personalized, and responsive user interface.
- Improve information discoverability by improving search and by providing intuitive information architecture.
- Position support portal as one-stop shop for all support needs to enhance user's support experience.
- Promote self-service at all possible opportunities like software entitlements, downloads, user registration, password reset, etc.
- Provide unified and intuitive user experience by placing all key functionalities in single interface and easily accessible locations.
- Focus on unified and rich services portal experience design.

Quality:

- Adopt best practices and proven accelerators to provide a quality solution.
- Conduct quality assurance at various stages to ensure conformance to quality SLAs.
- Create a robust continuous monitoring infrastructure to maintain the quality attributes.
- Optimize the business process to improve the overall quality.

Functionality fitment:

- Create a detailed mapping of the solution approach for all specified functional requirements to portal products and ensure the right product and technology fitment.
- Do a product and technology evaluation to ensure the optimal fitment.

- Explore open source alternative before building or procuring the solution components for realizing the functionality.
- The solution platform should be easily extensible and customizable to enable future business and technology needs of the organization.

Deriving Portal Program Goals and Principles

We have seen in the Figure 2.2, how portal solution tenets were derived from business vision and business goals. We will extend this concept and see how we can define portal principles derived from program objectives. This helps the business team to map their vision to specific solution features that enables better tracking of program, defining success metrics, and quantifying the ROI.

We will derive the primary and secondary principles from the overall program objectives. An example is given in the following:

Figure 2.3 shows a steady translation of program-level goals and objectives into portal-specific principles. For instance, a program objective of "continuous process improvement" translates into "process automation and reduced human intervention" as primary principle. This primary principle translates into one or more derived principles such as "workflow automation and KPI monitoring and analysis," and "continuous improvement initiatives." The derived principles can then be mapped to portal product components and features that become the solution components.

Another advantage provided by this mapping is that we can trace each program objective to a solution component that ensures the completeness of the solution and helps in early identification of implementation gaps. As mentioned before, we can also track the end solution components to understand the ROI.

Sample Portal Usage Scenarios

Let us have a focused look at two popular sample portal scenarios from business standpoint. These use cases depict the key business functions enabled by portal functionality.

Knowledge Management Portal

Knowledge management (KM) portal aims to create an organization-wide knowledge repository. The portal fulfils the main business goals such as productivity improvement, self-service, and content sharing. KM portals are mainly used in customer support business and in organizations' intranets. This is one of the natural usage scenarios for a portal. Figure 2.4 is focused mainly on KM portal:

The main feature categories of a KM portal as depicted in Figure 2.4 are intuitive features, social and collaboration, and omnichannel. Almost all the features in these three main categories can be realized by portal technologies (with most of them by in-built components). For example, intuitive features such as chat can be implemented using chat portlet, social and collaboration features can be implemented through in-built portal collaboration features, and document and content management provided by portal web content management. Portals also provide omnichannel access through responsive themes and RWD support.

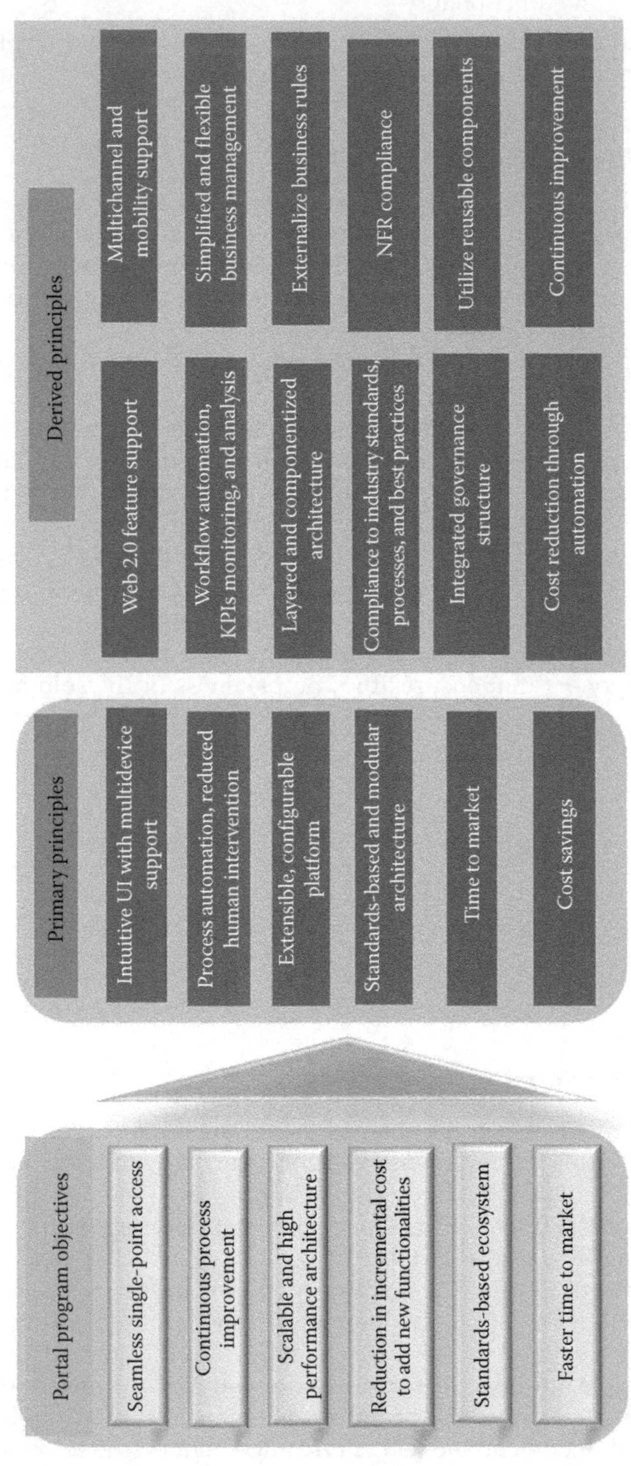

FIGURE 2.3
Portal principles derived from program objectives.

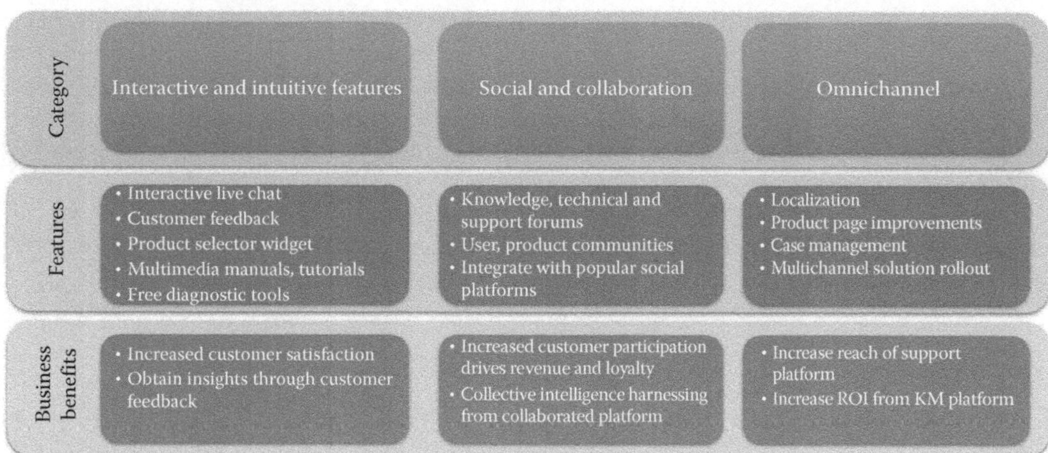

Category
Interactive and intuitive features
Social and collaboration
Omnichannel
Features
• Interactive live chat
• Customer feedback
• Product selector widget
• Multimedia manuals, tutorials
• Free diagnostic tools
• Knowledge, technical and support forums
• User, product communities
• Integrate with popular social platforms
• Localization
• Product page improvements
• Case management
• Multichannel solution rollout
Business benefits
• Increased customer satisfaction
• Obtain insights through customer feedback
• Increased customer participation drives revenue and loyalty
• Collective intelligence harnessing from collaborated platform
• Increase reach of support platform
• Increase ROI from KM platform

FIGURE 2.4
KM portal features.

As we can see, the common technology use cases such as social and collaboration and multichannel enablement are found in this portal scenario as well.

Enterprise Information Portal

In the case of enterprise information portal (EIP), the focus is mainly on the content strategy. The main concern is to provide the information about the organization, brand, and product to the end user. EIPs are mainly used by manufacturing and health care businesses. However, the core features of EIP such as relevant content display are essentially present in almost all portal solutions. Figure 2.5 provides insights into the various aspects of the key features that are expected within the EIP.

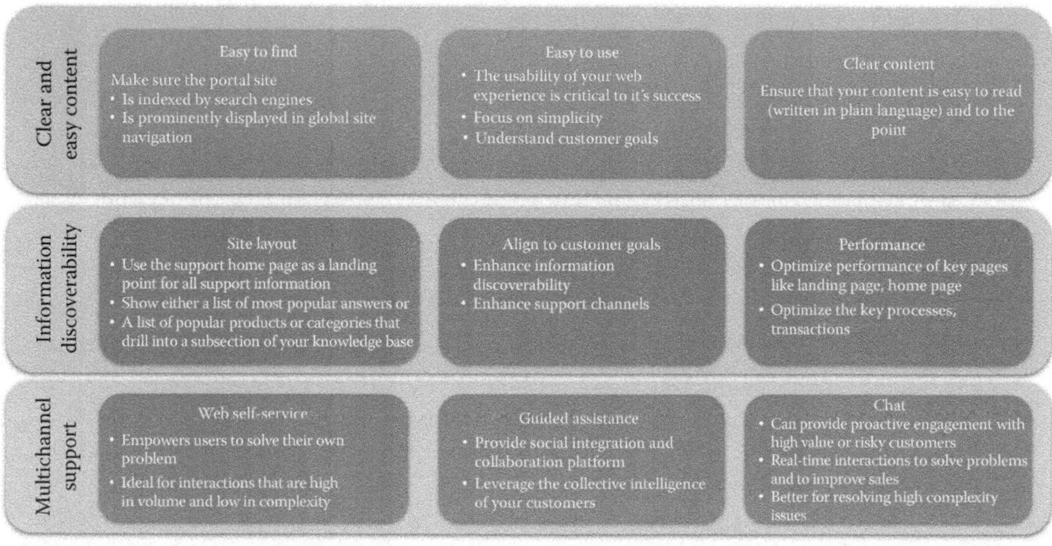

FIGURE 2.5
Enterprise information portal features.

User experience and ability to find the right content at the right time at the right place underscores the principal focus areas in EIP. The feature categories such as "easy to find" can be realized by portal search engine optimization (SEO), clear content objective can be achieved through optimal portal content strategy, site layout through portal site management features, and chat and collaboration through portal collaboration features.

These two examples narrate the business use case scenario of the portal from two different dimensions. We will also look at detailed business scenarios when we look at portal case studies in Chapter 23.

Typical Business Domains and Solutions Based on Portal

The most common business domains where portal would be used most frequently are as follows:

- *Digital marketing*: Portals help digital marketing with robust web content marketing and personalized and targeted marketing.
- *Multichannel support*: A portal site provides omnichannel support through mobility theme and RWD.
- *Self-service model*: Numerous portal features can be leveraged to achieve a self-service model. Portal features such as collaboration, content management, search, and process automation can be used to achieve self-service features.
- *E-commerce*: Portals can not only be front end e-commerce engines, but it can also provide highly personalized recommendations, real-time analytics-based insights, and robust search on top of regular commerce functionality.
- *News portals*: Portals can aggregate news content from various sources and also can distribute it as service or as feeds.
- *Business intelligence dashboards*: Portals are commonly used for constructing dashboard views of various analytical reports.
- *Process management systems*: With inbuilt workflows, rules engine, and business process management features, portals can be used to optimize and manage complex business processes.
- *Unified user experience platform*: Information and data aggregation coupled with widget support positions portal as a unique player in the user experience management space.
- *Government portals*: Portals would cater to multiple government initiatives such as request tracking, policy portal, etc.
- *Utility dashboard*: Portals can be used for various utility functions such as payment functionality, media renting and borrowing, bill payments, etc.
- *Campaign management and microsites*: Sales and marketing team can use portals to launch and manage campaigns and microsites with ease due to its robust content and site administration features.
- *Social and collaboration platform*: Portals provide in-built support for collaboration features such as blogs, wikis, communities, etc., which can be used to build collaboration platforms.

TABLE 2.3
Portals for Various Business Domains

Domain	Portals	Key Portal Features Used
Manufacturing	Information portals, dealer portal, reseller portal	Content aggregation, SSO
Retail	Commerce portals, shopping portals	Personalization, recommendation, SSO, user segmentation, web analytics, SEO
Health care	Health portal, health dashboards	Information aggregation
Education	e-learning portal, research portal, university portal, learning management system	Self-service features
Analytics/BI	Dashboard portal, reporting portal	Service-based integration, widgets
Government	Utility portal, citizen portal, services portal, payment portal	Functionality aggregation, SSO, self-service
Media	News portal	Content aggregation, SSO, personalization, multilingual enablement, federated SSO
Enterprise	Employee portal, search portal, collaboration portal, colleague portal, knowledge portal, document portal, content portal, monitoring portal, dashboard portal, enterprise social portal, legacy modernizer portal, support portal, performance dashboard portal, payment portal, registration portal, idea portal, publishing portal, sales and marketing portal, policy portal	Collaboration, self-service, content management, document management, single sign-on, personalization
Entertainment	Gaming portal, book and movie review portal	Responsive design, widgets, collaboration features
Automobile	Dealer portal, reseller portal	SSO, personalization
Finance	Banking portals, investment portals	Security, fine-grained authorization, personalization

Let us look at some of the most common business domains which can leverage portal technologies in Table 2.3. This will give a broad picture of where a portal would fit in for typical business domains.

Portal Value Realization Framework

One of the main challenges in portal programs is that project sponsors and business community are not able to quantify the benefits realized from portal investment.

Portal value realization framework provides a quantifiable ROI for portal adoption. The framework consists of the following high-level steps in Figure 2.6:

Step-1: *Identification of business value levers*—Business requirements are gathered and prioritized based on its value. During this step we will also identify the organizational and technical capabilities that need to be transformed. This is referred to as "business value levers" in the Figure 2.6.

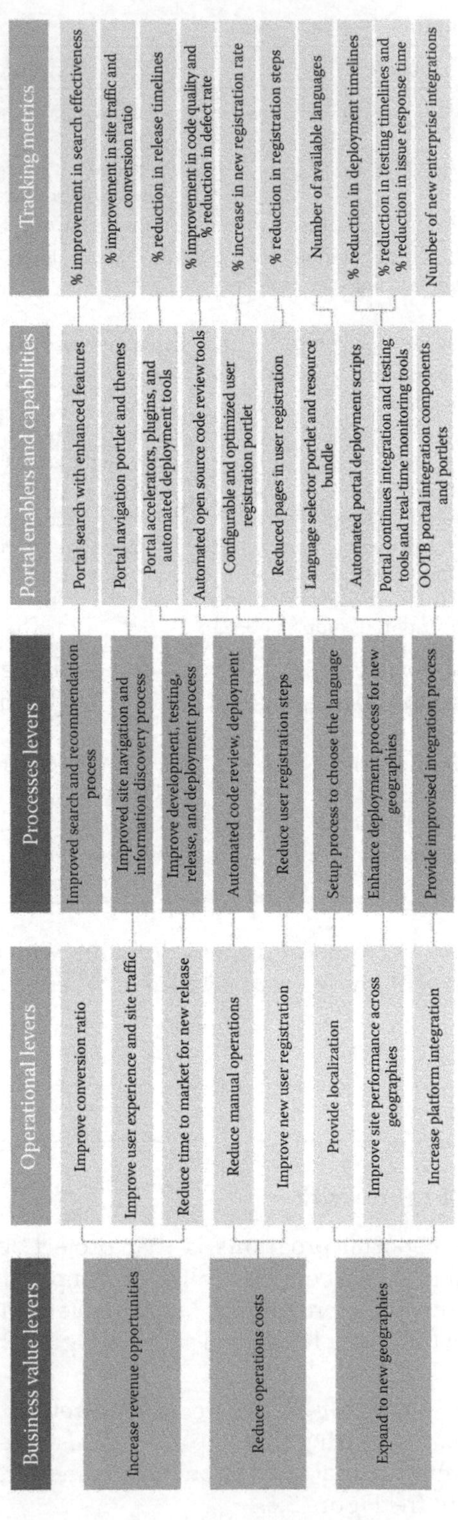
Business value levers
Increase revenue opportunities
Reduce operations costs
Expand to new geographies
Operational levers
Improve conversion ratio
Improve user experience and site traffic
Reduce time to market for new release
Reduce manual operations
Improve new user registration
Provide localization
Improve site performance across geographies
Increase platform integration
Processes levers
Improved search and recommendation process
Improved site navigation and information discovery process
Improve development, testing, release, and deployment process
Automated code review, deployment
Reduce user registration steps
Setup process to choose the language
Enhance deployment process for new geographies
Provide improvised integration process
Portal enablers and capabilities
Portal search with enhanced features
Portal navigation portlet and themes
Portal accelerators, plugins, and automated deployment tools
Automated open source code review tools
Configurable and optimized user registration portlet
Reduced pages in user registration
Language selector portlet and resource bundle
Automated portal deployment scripts
Portal continues integration and testing tools and real-time monitoring tools
OOTB portal integration components and portlets
Tracking metrics
% improvement in search effectiveness
% improvement in site traffic and conversion ratio
% reduction in release timelines
% improvement in code quality and % reduction in defect rate
% increase in new registration rate
% reduction in registration steps
Number of available languages
% reduction in deployment timelines
% reduction in testing timelines and % reduction in issue response time
Number of new enterprise integrations

FIGURE 2.6
Portal value realization framework.

Step-2: *Mapping business value levers to next-level elements*—We will then identify levers that are related to the business value levers. For instance, in Figure 2.5, operational and process levers need to be transformed to achieve the business value levers. Each of the business value levers is mapped to its corresponding operational and process lever elaborating how the business value is realized. This top-down approach provides a 360° view of transformation.

Step-3: *Map-next-level levers to portal capabilities and enablers*—As a next step, we map the next-level levers derived in step 2 to specific portal capabilities, elements, and enablers. Here, we will identify portlets and portal components that will be used to implement the transformation.

Step-4: *Tracking metrics*—Each of the portal components are mapped to metrics that quantify the improvements.

Figure 2.6 shows the sample portal value realization framework steps:

A simple example of the portal value realization framework diagram is shown for an e-commerce portal. As we can see, the main business value levers are revenue increments, reduction in operation cost, and expansion to new geographies. These three key business levers are mapped to corresponding operational and process levers. Further, the portlets and portal components are identified and tracking metrics are mapped to them. For instance, to realize the operation lever "improve user experience and site traffic," the process lever is to provide an optimal navigation and information discovery process and this can be realized by navigation portlets, portal themes, and intuitive information architecture. We can measure this through "percentage increase in site traffic" and from customer satisfaction index scores.

Another example of using portal value realization framework for a support portal is given in Figure 2.7. The main business value levers in this context are the cost reduction and process automation. To realize these business benefits, portal accelerators, self-service features, and collaboration features will be leveraged.

Portal value realization framework can be used to assess the success and effectiveness of portal technologies for the business scenario.

Summary

- The main business drivers that need portal technologies are aggregation and consolidation, user experience improvement, personalized experience, active user engagement, business enablement, integrated platform, collaboration and knowledge base, cost optimization, process optimization, actionable analytics, omnichannel experience, and self-service experience.
- Interactive UX, business enablement functionality, and personalization are some of the quick wins that can be achieved through portals.
- The enterprise opportunities for portals include solution to enterprise challenges, process improvements, achieving competitive advantage, platform approach, user experience and active engagement, cost optimization, enhanced business controls, and enabled business growth.

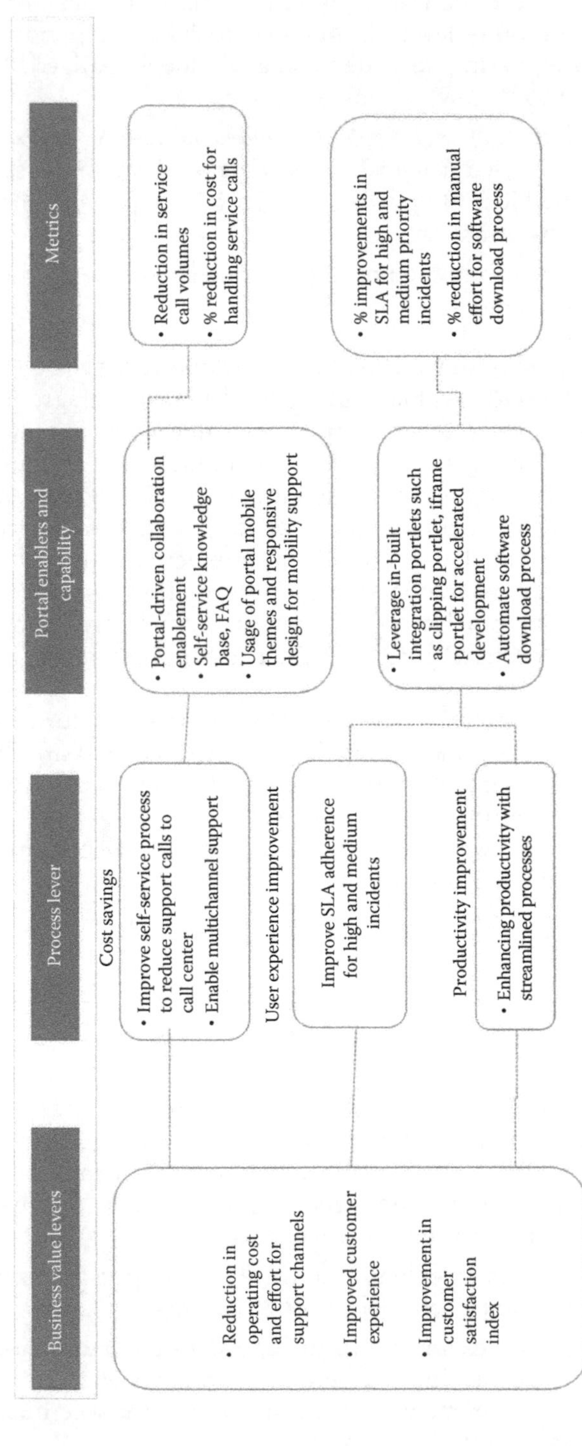

FIGURE 2.7
Portal value realization framework for support portals.

- Portals are well-positioned for building next-generation digital platform for business with features such as mobile-first strategy, customer-centric platform, elastic scalability, and hypercollaborative and social-enabled platform.
- Common pitfalls encountered in portal programs include thinking about end user in the end stages, lack of monitoring and tracking, improper positioning of portal, and lack of proper portal governance.
- Portal challenges would fall into categories such as functional and nonfunctional, organizational, technology related, and process related.
- Portals can be effectively used to address challenges related to user experience, lack of standard, and challenges in launching new features and functionality.
- The main solution tenets for a portal solution are reusability, extensibility, usability, functionality fitment and quality.
- Portal program objectives need to be translated and mapped to primary and secondary principles.
- KM portal and EIP are classical portal fitment scenarios.
- The main business expectations from portals are seamless single point of access, cost, process and productivity optimization, active user engagement, scalable and extensible platform, and competitive advantage through differentiated services.
- Portal value realization framework consist of four steps: Identification of business value levers, mapping business value levers to related process and operational levers, map process and operational levers to portal capabilities, and enablers and tracking metrics.

3

Choosing Portal Right: Portal Assessment and Evaluation

Introduction

In the previous chapter we saw the main business scenarios where a portal can play a vital role. We saw the high level business drivers, use cases and portal value in realizing those business scenarios. Let us say that we have to assess the portal fitment for a new scenario: how do we do the portal fitment assessment? Which scenarios really need a portal? The answers to these questions are important for the ultimate value realization from the portal program. This chapter explores these questions and provides us with a portal assessment framework, portal fitment analysis, and other related aspects.

Portal architects, enterprise architects, and business analysts would find the techniques and concepts discussed in this chapter useful in understanding the role that portal can play in a digital transformation journey and methodologies for evaluation and fitment of portal product.

Do You Really Need a Portal?

The primary step in portal scenario assessment is to thoroughly understand the business scenario and critically analyze the portal fitment for the solution. In this section let us look at portal fitment analysis and portal capability evaluation. These two evaluation methodologies will help in evaluating portal against non-portal technologies and choosing the right fitment of portal.

When Do You Need Portal?

Let us look at the main business requirements and technical scenarios that warrant portal technologies.

The most visible aspect of portal is its presentation layer even though it has robust components in server and integration layers. As we know, we have numerous options for implementing a presentation layer solution, such as custom web applications and open source web frameworks such as Apache Struts, JSF, SEAM framework, and Spring MVC, to name a few. Besides, we also have various package solutions such as reporting web application, CRM application, etc. So it is critical to understand the best fit scenarios for portals and to set the right expectations with all the stakeholders. We have seen a few scenarios wherein portal was recommended where it was not needed; these kinds of suboptimal portal fitment would lead to the following issues:

- Overengineering of the solution even if the solution requires a simple one-off functionality and we use portal to load it with features that may never be used
- If the right expectations are not set, sooner or later it leads to huge expectation mismatch and the collapse of the entire program
- Unnecessary increase in the overall program cost and the total cost of ownership (TCO)

Hence, it is important to find the right technology fitment for the portal and position the portal appropriately. In the coming sections we will look at the various methodologies to understand the technical use cases, business scenarios, and evaluation techniques for portals.

Recap of Portal Strengths and Scenarios

As we have seen in other chapters, the main strengths of portal technologies lie in implementing the following:

- Content, data, and functionality aggregation from multiple discrete sources
- Providing a highly personalized and contextualized information relevant for the user
- Facilitating a seamless access to multiple secured applications through single sign-on
- Providing an engaging user experience through configurable portlets, multichannel delivery, and responsive user interface (UI) elements

On similar lines businesses use cases with requirements as follows:

- A unified, single-window interface to the user providing access to all relevant data, information, and functionality
- A personalized dashboard view of various reports, data, analytics, and charts
- Process-intensive applications such as multistep approvals, user registration, and complex business processes that require automation and that are easy to manage
- An internal or external collaboration platform to communicate, share, and improve the productivity of all the participants
- Creation of simple, yet, robust platform that helps businesses to easily onboard future applications that come during mergers and acquisitions

In the coming sections we will see a few fitment and capability evaluation metric for using portal technologies. A combination of these techniques can be used to assess business and technical scenarios that qualify for using a portal technology.

Portal Fitment Analysis

A sample fitment of portal technology for a given scenario can be done by using the following evaluation guide. Figure 3.1 provides a sample scoring sheet that can be used for high level fitment analysis of portal technology stack for a given business scenario.

Scenario	Scoring	Scoring Guide
Content aggregation (integrate content from multiple data sources such as database, ERP, web service, reports, etc.)		If discrete data source >= 4, score = 5 If discrete data source >3 and <4, score = 4 If discrete data source >2 and <3, score = 3 If discrete data source = 1, score = 2 If discrete data source = 0, score = 1
Personalization (role or user attribute–based customization of user experience)		If the requirement contains page level personalization, section/portlet level personalization, functionality level personalization, data level personalization, role-based access, score = 5 If the requirement contains page level personalization, section/portlet level personalization, functionality level personalization, score = 4 If the requirement contains page level personalization, section/portlet level personalization, score = 3 If the requirement contains page level personalization, score = 2 No personalization requirements, score = 1
Security and SSO requirements		If application has requirements for authentication, authroization, SSO with 2 or more applications, federated SSO with external application, score = 5 If application has requirements for authentication, authroization, SSO with 2 or more applications, score = 4 If application has requirements for authentication, authroization, score = 3 If application has requirements for authentication, score = 2 If application has no authentication, score = 1
Mobility requirements		Fully mobile enabled, score = 5 Partially mobile enabled, score = 4 No mobile enablement, score = 2
User interface requirements		Fully customizable and configurable layout, drag-and-drop page sections, ability to hide page sections based on user profile attributes, in-built branding supporting features, score = 5 Fully customizable and configurable layout, drag-and-drop page sections, ability to hide page sections based on user profile attributes score = 4 Partially customizable and configurable layout, drag-and-drop page sections, score = 3 Partially customizable and configurable layout, score = 2
Collaboration requirements		Requirements for communities, audio/video chat, conferencing, blog, wiki, integration with external social media platforms, score = 5 Any 5 of the above requirements, score = 4 Any 4 of the above requirements, score = 3 Any 3 of the above requirements, score = 2 Any 2 of the above requirements, score = 1 Any 1 of the above requirements, score = 0
If score is between 24 and 30, then it is suitable for portal, else for custom web application		

FIGURE 3.1
Portal fitment scoring sheet.

NOTE:

- The evaluation matrix given is mainly focused on technical scenarios.
- The matrix can be used as a guiding principle and more detailed analysis needs to be carried out on a case-to-case basis.

The aforementioned scoring guide can be used as a rule-of-thumb or as a generic guiding principle for the right fitment of portal product. As we can see from the fitment matrix in Figure 3.1 the solution that depends heavily on personalization, aggregation, SSO, UX, and mobility requirements are ideal candidates for portal fitment. This avoids using portal for simple scenarios that would not need portal technologies.

For instance, if there is a requirement for a web application that just requires a static list of web pages, then that solution can be implemented by using any web technology without the need for portal. Similarly, if the solution has predominantly following characteristics then portal may not be a right fit:

- A solution that requires rendering mainly static informational content
- A solution that does not need authentication, role-based security, or personalization
- A solution that does not need or has minimal content aggregation requirements
- A solution that does not have dynamic content delivery requirements
- A solution that mainly performs single utility function without authentication.

Portal Solution Capability Evaluation

We have now seen where portal fits and where it can be of best use. Let us look at the sample capability evaluation matrix for comparing portal with other alternate web technologies.

Table 3.1 provides a sample capability evaluation matrix for comparing portal technologies with custom web technologies. Similar evaluation needs to be done for all the shortlisted products and technologies before the portal product is finalized.

Portal Assessment Framework

Selection of a most appropriate portal product that can realize the short-term solution and that aligns with the long-term strategic business goals is quintessential for the long-term success of the program. This exercise is easier said than done as there are numerous factors that can influence the evaluation. Constantly changing technologies, build vs. buy decisions, COTS vs. open source framework decisions, non-quantifiable or unstructured success criteria, and nonspecific business goals are some of the challenges that we would face during this process. Hence, we need a robust and all-round portal evaluation and assessment framework that would address these challenges.

Given in Figure 3.2 is an assessment framework that can be used for finalizing the portal product for a given business scenario by factoring in the points and challenges mentioned earlier.

TABLE 3.1

Portal Capability Evaluation Matrix

Category	Capability Parameter	Portal Technology Effort (Low Effort Is Preferred)	Custom Web Application Effort (Low Effort Is Preferred)
Total cost of ownership	Licensing cost of the entire package	Medium (depends on type of portal product)	Medium
	Hardware cost	Medium	Medium
	Training cost	Low (due to open standards)	Low–medium
	Development cost	Medium	High (due to custom development)
	Maintenance and operations cost	Low (due to in-built and supported maintenance tools)	High
	Cost to extend and scale the functionality for future needs	Low	High
Functionality extension and flexibility	New enterprise Integrations	Low–medium (due to the availability of OOTB integration components and portlets)	High
	New feature development to meet future business needs	Medium	High
	Mobility enablement	Medium	High
Security	Effort for implementing coarse-grained and fine-grained access control	Low–medium (due to in-built support for security components)	High
	Availability of web SSO and federated SSO	Low–medium (due to in-built support for SSO components)	High
UX features	Flexible and reusable page layouts	Low (OOTB page layout support)	Medium
	Mobility support	Low–medium	Medium
Time to market	Rollout of new functionality	Low–medium (due to the availability of OOTB portlets and development accelerators)	Medium
Collaboration Support	Chat, blog, wiki, community	Low–medium (due to the availability of OOTB collaboration components)	High
Enterprise integration	Integrate with internal and external application	Low–medium (due to the availability of OOTB integration components)	High

At a high level, it is a three-step process as shown in Figure 3.2.

Each of these phases involves many substeps and internal assessments. The assessment framework can be used when the organization decides to undergo a digital transformation exercise to meet the growing business demands, to remain competitive, or to fill up the existing gaps. Let us look at each of these phases in detail.

Business Assessment Phase

In this phase we basically understand and analyze the following:

- *Key business scenarios assessment*: In this step, the main business use cases that need transformation will be analyzed. It will be documented through various means such as use case documents, functional prototypes, etc.

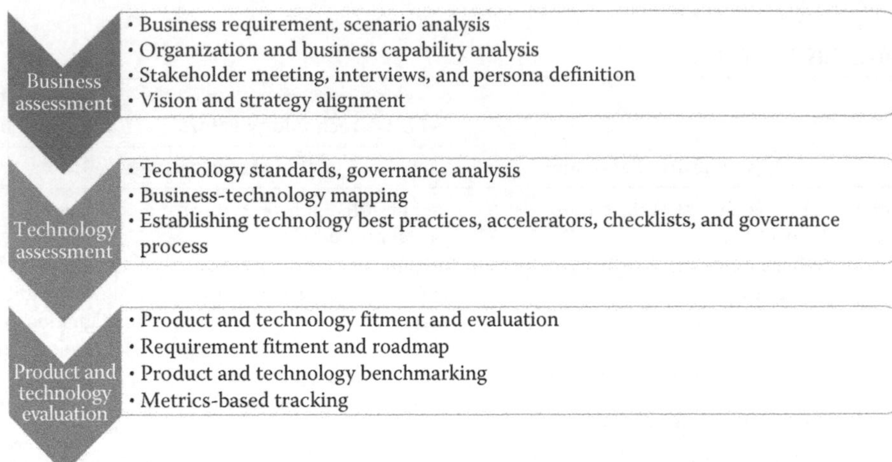

FIGURE 3.2
Portal assessment framework steps.

- *Unique user personas and their user journeys*: The key actors in the business scenarios are identified in this step. The way these personas use the digital channels will also be analyzed.
- *Capability and maturity assessment*: The current maturity levels of the enterprise will be assessed for the transformation. Maturity levels in business processes and governance will be analyzed.
- *Key business drivers and motivation factors assessment*: The main business motivations for the transformation will be compiled. The key performance indicators (KPI) relevant for business will also be identified. We have discussed these key drivers required for a portal transformation in Chapter 2.
- *Analysis of the opportunities and challenges for the transformation*: We also saw the key opportunities and challenges for portal in Chapter 2.
- *AS-IS assessment of key business process and workflows*: All the main business processes will be documented in process flow document.
- *Functional and nonfunctional requirements elaboration and prioritization*: The specific functional and nonfunctional requirements will be gathered and elaborated in functional requirements document. They will also be prioritized based on their business value and alignment with enterprise strategy. This list will be useful for planning releases during transformation. Any opportunities for quick-wins will also be identified here.
- *Understanding of the vision and long-term strategy of the organization*: The main business goals for short-term and long-term are understood.
- Gap analysis to understand the gap between current maturity and the desired end state. Based on the inputs we have gathered from maturity assessment, challenges, and long-term strategy, we will come up with the list of existing gaps and the way those gaps can be addressed during the transformation program.
- *Concerns, pain points, and view points*: The main concerns will be gathered from all the main stakeholders. The key stakeholder communities include business

stakeholders, security team, infrastructure team, and IT team. This provides a holistic view of existing challenges from various dimensions. This also helps us in identifying the business risk in the transformation program.

In order to understand the mentioned points and concepts, we need to have various interaction sessions and workshops. Stakeholder meetings, interviews, all-hands workshops, focused group discussions, and scenario walkthroughs are some of the ways in which we can get various view points from all concerned stakeholders.

At the end of this phase, we will have the business requirements and other topics captured in a structured way in one or more of the following documents:

- *Business requirement document* (*BRD*): This document provides the list of all business scenarios. It also provides main user scenarios, stakeholder concerns, business drivers for the transformation, etc.
- *Functional requirement document*: This provides the detailed functional requirements for the transformation program. It includes the functional specifications, detailed requirements, business rules, and exception flows. Requirements are categorized into various categories such as interface requirements, security requirements, data requirements, and migration requirements. The document also provides various views to effectively communicate the requirements. Some of the diagrams such as data model diagram, context diagram, interface diagram, and security diagram can be leveraged to elaborate the requirements.
- *Use case document*: This standard document details the requirement use cases. Each use case consists of primary flow, exception flow, input/output parameters, validation rules, and other applicable business rules.
- *Process flow diagrams*: Flow diagrams are used to effectively model the complex business processes.
- *Business, technology, and organization maturity assessment reports*: These reports provide insights into the current maturity of the organization to undergo the desired transformation. Standard operating procedures, governance models, maturity of business processes, opportunities for process optimization, and automation will all be analyzed to create these reports.
- *Gap analysis document*: This document details the gaps from business standpoint. Process gaps, maturity gaps, governance gaps, business continuity gaps, and other gaps will be compiled.
- *Business KPI document*: This provides the list of business key performance indicators (KPI) that determine the success criteria for the program.
- *Nonfunctional requirements document*: This includes all nonfunctional or quality-of-service (QoS) requirements such as security requirements, performance requirements, usability requirements, scalability requirement, availability requirement, accessibility requirement, mobility requirement, etc.
- *Governance model assessment*: This document provides the analysis of existing governance model. It provides the list of role–responsibility matrix for existing processes.
- *Business risk document*: The document identifies all the business-related risks.

This will lay the foundation for future stages such as technology mapping, architecture definition, solution development, etc.

Technology Assessment Phase

In this phase, we will assess the technology capabilities and related aspects. Once we finalize all the business requirements from various dimensions we will then define the technology elements for them. The list of key activities is as follows:

- *Define the architecture framework*: This is achieved through identifying key architecture principles and creating the reference and base line architecture. The reference architecture depicts the main building blocks of the overall architecture.
- *Portal fitment*: We will use the portal fitment score sheet and portal solution capability evaluation to evaluate if the portal technology is the right fitment for the given business scenario. The details of these two evaluation methodologies are already discussed in earlier sections.
- *Define the technology best practices and standards that need to be used in the solution*: We will also identify all applicable patterns, standards, and best practices that can be applied for the solution architecture.
- *Map the business requirement to technology capabilities and provide a traceability matrix*: This ensures that all expected business capabilities and transformation objectives are part of the architecture definition.
- *Define the data standards and any applicable application standards*: This includes the encryption standards, data transport policies, data security standards, application compliance levels, accessibility standards, and applicable regulatory standards.
- *Establish architecture compliance framework*: This includes the compliance checklist to ensure that the solution is compliant with guiding architecture principles. Architecture principles define the integration standards, security policies, data access policies, etc., which all the enterprise applications should abide by.
- *Assess current technology capability*: Existing technology and solution stack is analyzed to understand the gaps and to explore the reuse opportunities. This includes detailing strategy for legacy modernization, strategy to replace outdated technology, and migration strategy. At the end of this step, an inventory of current technology components is compiled. As a part of this step, existing data architecture, application architecture, security architecture, and enterprise integration architecture will be analyzed and the capabilities of the technology stack will be assessed.
- *Define technology governance models*: In this step we will define the process for solution design, solution development, testing, deployment, and maintenance. Applicable open-source and COTS products will be leveraged to automate the activities such as code review, deployment, testing, and to accelerate the time to market.
- *Risks and dependencies*: All potential technical risks with the transformation program and dependencies will be compiled in this step. Identified risks are prioritized and they will be accompanied by the mitigation plan.
- *Implementation, roadmap, and migration strategy*: A high level solution implementation plan and technology roadmap will be defined. If the transformation requires a migration effort, the details will be documented. The implementation and roadmap will be designed to address the gap between existing states and the desired state.
- *Enterprise security strategy*: The enterprise security elements such as authentication standards, password policies, data level security, transport level security, and

single sign-on strategy will be documented. This strategy will be compiled in consultation with enterprise security team.

- *Technology gap analysis*: This involves all the steps that need to be taken to fill the technology gap to align with the long-term business strategy and reach the desired end state. Gap analysis can involve filling the technology gaps from various aspects such as security gaps, integration gaps, user experience gaps, functionality gaps, infrastructure gaps, and gaps in all involved technology components. Once a gap is identified, possible solution options to fill the gap will also be designed. A sample gap analysis for portal products based on its capabilities is shown in Figure 3.3.

At the end of this phase we will have following artifacts:

- *Technical traceability matrix*: It maps all the business requirements to technology solution components and architecture elements. This artifact ensures completeness of all business scenarios and requirements.
- *Portal fitment analysis*: The report that provides the fitment analysis for portal technologies. The report provides detailed elaboration of why (or why not) portal technologies would be the best fit for the given scenario.
- *Technical risks and mitigation plan*: A detailed risk and mitigation plan document that prioritizes the risk, categorizes the risk, and provides business impact and the detailed mitigation plan.
- *Reference architecture framework*: Software architecture document or enterprise architecture document details the baseline reference architecture that the solution architecture can use as reference. The solution architecture has to provide the exact solution components for each of the component in the reference architecture. This document also consists of all identified architecture principles, architecture best practices, standards, governance model, various architecture views (deployment view, process view, use case view, data view, security view, etc.), major architecture decisions, architecture diagrams such as flow diagrams, etc.
- *Technology roadmap document*: This document provides the detailed technology roadmap strategy indicating the phases in which technology capabilities will be enabled.
- *Technology assessment document*: This document provides the assessment of current technology capabilities.
- *List of solution accelerators*: We will also compile all solution accelerators, open source frameworks/tools, and productivity improvement measures that can be adopted in the solution.
- *Infrastructure analysis*: This document provides details of the existing infrastructure such as servers, hardware, network, data centers, cloud availability, disaster recovery environment, etc.
- *Finalized list of portal products and technologies*: After finding a fit case for product, we would enlist all potential portal products and related technologies for developing the solution. The list of portal products will be shortlisted based on a number of factors such as their relevance to the transformation program, market share, popularity, and installed base. Other factors such as total cost of ownership, vendor alliance strength, and the presence of related technology stack in the organization will also play a role in some cases.

Capabilities	Portal product 1	Portal product 2	Portal product 3	Portal product 4	Solution gap	Possible options
Content management					Portal product 1: All content cannot be exported to PDF format Portal product 2: No content management feature available Portal product 3: All content cannot be exported to PDF format Portal product 4: No OOTB support for content management	Portal product 1: All office files only can be converted into PDF by using commercial product. Portal product 2: User open source CMS Portal product 3: Integrate with open source CMS Portal product 4: Use open source CMS
Collaborative content					Portal product 1: All requirements met Portal product 2: Simultaneous editing of a page is not supported Portal product 2: All requirements met Portal product 4: Spreadsheets cannot be edited efficiently in the browser.	Portal product 1: Fully compliant Portal product 2: Integrate with enterprise collaboration platform Portal product 3: Fully compliant Portal product 4: Integrate with open source collaboration platform
User experience					Portal product 1: Not complient with requirements (not all browsers supported). Portal product 2: All requirements met Portal product 3: Not complient with requirements Portal product 4: All requirements met	Portal product 1: No alternative Portal product 2: Fully compliant Portal product 3: Custom develop the UI components to fill the gap using RWD Portal product 4: Fully compliant

% of requirements met by the solution	0%	25%	50%	75%	100%

FIGURE 3.3
Sample portal gap analysis matrix.

Product and Technology Evaluation

This is the crucial step of the assessment framework wherein we finalize the portal product and technology that best suits the business requirements and technology framework. As we have shortlisted the portal products and accompanying technologies in the previous phase, it is now time to select the most appropriate portal product and technology.

A comprehensive portal evaluation framework is detailed in Figure 3.4. The figure shows the hierarchical structure and the steps involved in the comprehensive portal evaluation.

As we can see from Figure 3.4, the final product and technology recommendation happens based on five main evaluations: product evaluation, technology evaluation, vendor evaluation, product demo evaluation, and proof-of-concept evaluation. Let us look at each of the evaluations in detail.

Product Evaluation

At a high level, portal products are evaluated based on their functional, technical, and operational capabilities. These three factors are evaluated in the context of the current business scenario.

Scoring in each of these criteria would be directly proportional to the ease of implementation and the degree of alignment. For instance, if a functional or technical requirement is readily available within a portal product then it would be given the highest score. A sample four-point scale scoring is given in the following:

- 3—If the portal product conforms to the requirement out of the box
- 2—If the portal product supports the requirement through configurations or minimal customization
- 1—If the portal product conforms to the requirement through maximum customization or manual coding
- 0—If the portal product does not support the requirement

Let us now look at each of the scorecard criteria in detail:

- A functional scorecard evaluates all the required functional capabilities of the portal product. Each functional capability is assigned a weightage based on its business importance and a score is assigned. The final score will be the weighted sum of individual functional scores.

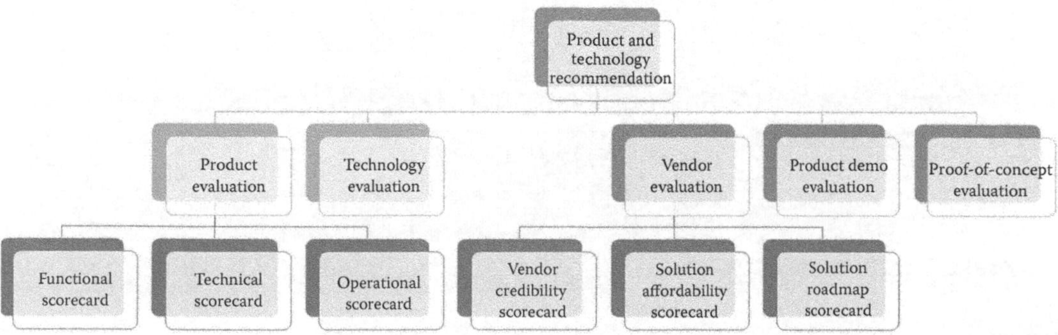

FIGURE 3.4
Portal product and technology evaluation framework.

A sample functional scorecard–based evaluation is shown in Figure 3.5.

A chart representation of the functional capabilities is shown in Figure 3.6:

- Technology scorecard consists of evaluating all the technical capabilities that are required for the solution domain. Compliance and alignment with architecture principles and best practices in the technology assessment phase will also be considered as some of the scoring parameters. The final score would be the weighted sum of individual technical capability scores.

A sample technical scorecard-based evaluation is shown in Figure 3.7.

A chart representation of the technology capabilities is shown in Figure 3.8:

- Operation scorecard consists of evaluating all the operational capabilities that can address the gaps in existing governance and process model. Besides business goals such as time-to-market and release cycle time, productivity improvement expectations will also be considered while evaluating this scorecard. The final score would be the weighted sum of individual operational capability scores.

RFI Ref	Evaluation Parameter	Weights	Portal Product 1			Portal Product 2		
			Rating (1 - 10)	Score	Rationale	Rating (1 - 10)	Score	Rationale
	Functional Capabilities	**40%**		2.82			2.5	
1	**Administration - user, pages**	**15%**		0.96			0.87	
1.1	User Administration	30%	8	2.4	Available OOTB, can be integrated with Directory server	7	2.1	Provides decent capabilities
1.2	Pages and portlets Administration	30%	8	2.4		7	2.1	
1.3	Custom Administration	40%	4	1.6	Need to be Custom Built	4	1.6	Need to be Custom Built
3	**Security and Access management**	**10%**		0.84			0.7	
3.1	SSO Integration	20%	8	1.6	SSO integration can be easily done with all major	8	1.6	Supports SSO with major open source products
3.2	Login and Registration	20%	7	1.4	OOTB Login module is available, and required filters can	5	1	Needs custom development
3.3	User Impersonation	20%	9	1.8	provides OOTB functionality for user impersonation	6	1.2	Provides limited features for user impersonation
3.4	Access Control	40%	9	3.6	Can be easily integrated with the Directory server, and	8	3.2	Provides good access control
4	**Multi Device Support - Responsive**	**12%**		0.66			0.6	
4.1	Multi Device Support	50%	6	3	Product provideds feature where the device type	6	3	Provides multi-device support thorugh device plugins and mobility rules
4.5	Responsive Site Design	50%	5	2.5	Need to include the Responsive UI design	4	2	Suppports responsive design
5	**Customization and Personalization**	**10%**		0.8			0.55	
5.1	User Customization	50%	8	4	Customization an be easily achieved both at Design	5	2.5	
5.2	Personalization	50%	8	4	Provides OOTB support for Configuring Personalization Rules and Scenarios. These can be applied to the CMS	6	3	Provides good personalization features
6	**UI/UX Management**	**8%**		0.6			0.62	
6.1	Themes and Skins	25%	8	2	Themes and skins can be custom built by extending the	8	2	Provides OOTB themes and extensible themes
6.2	Site Design - HTML 5 support	25%	8	2	HTML5 is supported on portal	7	1.75	HTML 5 is supported
6.3	JS Library Support	50%	7	3.5	External JS Libraries can be easily included to create the	8	4	Supports all external JS libraries
7	**Reusable Widget Gallery**	**10%**		0.725			0.55	
7.1	Out of the Box Widgets	50%	8	4	Provided some OOTB Widgets	5	2.5	Provides minimal OOTB widgets
7.2	Custom Widget Development	25%	6	1.5	Does not provide much support for widget	5	1.25	Not much support for widget development
7.3	Support for widget based integration	25%	7	1.75	External widgets can be integrated.	7	1.75	Supports widget integration
8	**Content Management Functionality**	**15%**		1.275			0.87	
8.1	Content Display / Presentation Templates	20%	9	1.8	Provides OOTB support for Presentation templates	6	1.2	Portal CMS supports templates
8.2	Authoring Templates	10%	9	0.9	AvailableOOTB	5	0.5	
8.3	Content Workflows	20%	8	1.6	OOTB Support for Content creation workflows. Custom Actions can be custom built.	6	1.2	Supports Kaleo workflow and content workflow
8.4	Content Aggregation	15%	8	1.2	Supports allmajor integration patterns for content aggregation	7	1.05	Supports content aggregation
8.5	Inline Editing	10%	9	0.9	AvailableOOTB	4	0.4	Needs to be customized
8.6	Content Taxonomy	15%	8	1.2	AvailableOOTB	5	0.75	Needs to be customized
8.7	Content Access Control	10%	9	0.9	AvailableOOTB	7	0.7	Provides support for content access control
12	**Collaboration Features**	**15%**		0.84			1.14	
12.1	Blogs	20%	7	1.4	Available OOTB, with content stored in portal content	8	1.6	OOB
12.2	Fourms	20%	6	1.2	Discussions service are availble which can be utilied to implement the same.	8	1.6	OOB
12.3	Wiki	20%	7	1.4	Available OOTB, with content stored in portal content	7	1.4	OOB
12.4	Micro Blogging	20%	4	0.8	Can be custom Developed using people connections,but	8	1.6	OOB
12.5	Chat, Chat integration	20%	4	0.8	No OOTB Chat, can be integrated with 3rd party Chat	7	1.4	OOB Chat portlet
11	**Multi Lingual Suppport**	**5%**		0.35			0.35	
11.1	Multi Lingual Support	100%	7	7	Can be done using Resource bundles	7	7	Provides multi-lingual support

FIGURE 3.5
Portal functional evaluation scorecard.

(Continued)

	Technology Capabilities	50%		2.5525			2.685	
2	Service Based Integration	60%		2.52			2.67	
2.1	GIS Integration	70%	4	2.8		4	2.8	
2.2	ERP Integration	5%	6	0.3	Provides OOTB Adapters to integrate with major ERP	5	0.25	Provides support for ERP integration
2.3	ESB (Service) Integration	10%	5	0.5	Can be easily integrated with ESB, can also integrate	5	0.5	Provides service oriented integration with ESB
2.4	Payment Service Integration	5%	4	0.2	To be Custom built using Payment service gateway API's	6	0.3	
2.5	Service gateway support	10%	4	0.4	Need to be custom built	6	0.6	Provides suppor for services gateway
9	Search capability	10%		0.52			0.59	
9.1	Search Engine Integration	40%	4	1.6	Need to be Custom built using the Services/API's	5	2	Can use services based integration
9.2	Search Engine Optimization	30%	5	1.5	Meta tags required for SEO can be included both at	6	1.8	Supports SEO
9.3	Inbuild Search Capabilities	30%	7	2.1	Has good Search capabilities	7	2.1	Lucene
10	Cloud Implementation	10%		0.7			0.8	
10.1	Private Cloud Support	50%	7	3.5	Ccan be implemented in Cloud,	8	4	Support through cloud services
10.2	Public Cloud Support	50%	7	3.5		8	4	
13	Non Functional Requirements	10%		0.75			0.8	
13.1	Patches and Upgrades	25%	8	2	Readily available from	7	1.75	Patching tool is OOB
13.2	Compliance to Industry Standards	25%	6	1.5	Has Custom Frameworks which need to be used to	8	2	JSR standard portlet, WSRP etc are supported
13.3	Scalability	25%	8	2	Provides clustered and cloud deployment	8	2	Clustering
13.5	Browser Support	25%	8	2	Supports most of the latest browsers	9	2.25	
14	Portal Requirements	10%		0.615			0.51	
14.1	Designer tool support for page creation	25%	8	2	Pages can built and customized at runtime.	6	1.5	Provides web interface
14.2	configuration driven user registration	20%	6	1.2	Should be Custom Build for integration with Third party	6	1.2	OOB User registration portlet
14.3	Configuration driven user and profile,a ccount	25%	7	1.75	User, profile and Account management can be done	4	1	Needs to be custom built
14.4	Self-service functions such as password	20%	6	1.2	Password management can be done if on-built	7	1.4	Password policies can set
14.5	Workflow Capability	10%	2	0.2	Workflow capability available in CMS, but not in portal	7	0.7	Support through Kaleo
	Monitoring and operational functionalities	10%		0.6			0.425	
15	Monitoring functionalities	50%		3			2	
15.1	System Monitoring	50%	7	3.5	Portal environment can be Comprehensively monitored	4	2	Basic support
15.2	Monitoring Reports	50%	5	2.5	Data can be cheked on the console, but no OOTB	4	2	Basic support
16	Operational	50%		3			2.25	
16.1	Reporting and Analytics	50%	7	3.5	OOTB Analytics provides information about common	4	2	Basic support
16.2	External Analytics Integration Capabilities	50%	5	2.5	Can be integrated by introducing the Analytics script in the pages.	5	2.5	GA can be disabled and other Analytics solution can be implemented

FIGURE 3.5 (*Continued*)
Portal functional evaluation scorecard.

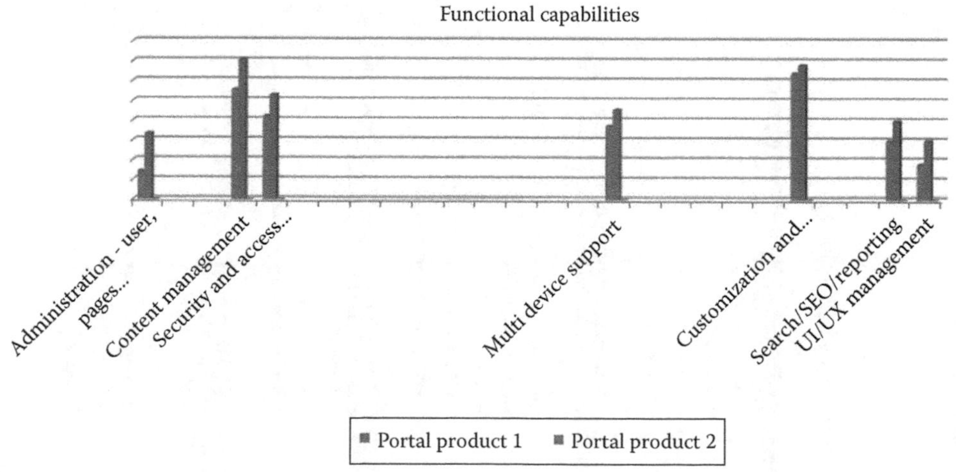

FIGURE 3.6
Portal functional score graph.

No	Evaluation Parameter	Weights	Portal Product 1			Portal Product 2			Portal Product 3		
			Rating (1 - 10)	Score	Rationale	Rating (1 - 10)	Score	Rationale	Rating (1 - 10)	Score	Rationale
	Technology Capabilities	35%		2.3989			2.6684			1.5652	
2	Integration (bi-directional, on-	30%		1.8			1.8			1.44	
2.1	General Integration Scenarios	40%	7	2.8	Separate Liscense required for	9	3.6	Integration with 3rd party	6	2.4	Sharepoint adapter is an add
2.2	Web Services	20%	8	1.6	RPC, SOAP, synchronous, authenti	6	1.2	RESTful webservice, a lea	6	1.2	RESTful WS, SOAP, OAuth 2.0
2.3	Adapters/APIs	20%	9	1.8		9	1.8	Open source integration	6	1.2	
2.4	OOTB Integration with external	20%	8	1.6		6	1.2		6	1.2	
9	Authentication/Access	20%		1.494			1.504			1.152	
9.1	Authentication	15%	8	1.2	Integration of SSO, LDAP. May not	7	1.05	Integration of SSO, LDAP.	5	0.75	SSO integration.
9.2	Access Control	24%	8	1.92	Fine grained authorization. Does c	9	2.16	ACLs can be managed to e	4	0.96	Group level integration with
9.3	Registration and Profile Management	28%	7	1.96		7	1.96	No differentiators	7	1.96	no differentiators
9.4	Security	13%	8	1.04	for encryption of content, integrat	10	1.3	No security loopholes. M	8	1.04	Content itself cannot be enc
9.5	Legal Requirements	5%	6	0.3	Custom code	6	0.3	Custom code	6	0.3	custom code
9.6	Access Management and Identity	15%	7	1.05		5	0.75	Loose integration with 3r	5	0.75	Loose integration with 3rd p
10	System Maintenance/Code	10%		0.56			0.8			0.32	
10.1	CMS Deployment	20%	6	1.2	J2EE skills	8	1.6	J2EE,Packaging of the mo	4	0.8	
10.2	Code Deployment	40%	6	2.4		8	3.2	Content porter for code a	2	0.8	
10.3	Product Upgrades/Maintenance	40%	5	2	Very aggressive product upgrade r	8	3.2	No downtime required fo	4	1.6	Supports ootb performance
13	Product Architecture &	40%		3			3.52			1.56	
13.1	Architecture Concepts	15%	8	1.2	TBD	10	1.5	Integrated Arch,simplisti	2	0.3	
13.2	Architecture Components	15%	8	1.2	Content and metadata can be sep	8	1.2		2	0.3	Content management has to
13.3	Compliance to Industry Standards	15%	7	1.05	No support for JSR170, JSR 168, JSR	9	1.35	Supports all standards as	4	0.6	
13.4	Technology	15%	8	1.2	J2EE Based. Customizations in JSP	10	1.5		4	0.6	
13.5	Templating	10%	7	0.7	JSP	8	0.8		4	0.4	

FIGURE 3.7
Portal technical evaluation scorecard.

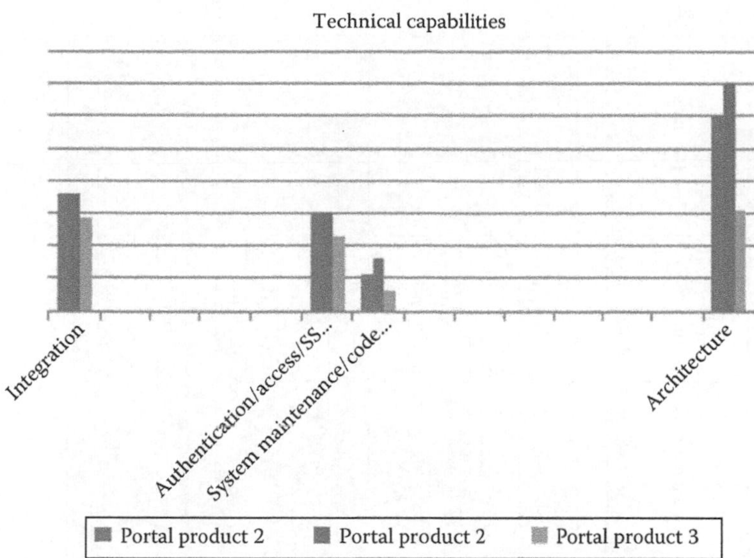

FIGURE 3.8
Portal technology score graph.

A sample operational scorecard-based evaluation is shown in Figure 3.9.

After the scorecard-based evaluation of functional, technical, and operational analysis, a summarized view is shown in Figure 3.10.

Technology Evaluation

Technology evaluation includes the evaluation of constituent technology components such as infrastructure libraries (logging, auditing, encryption, etc.), solution-specific technology components such as web service run time libraries, object-relational mapping (ORM) frameworks, and systems/frameworks in other layers such as database system, ERP system, and systems that are required for end-to-end solution.

At a high level, the technology components for the end-to-end solutions are evaluated based on the following criteria:

- *Conformance to organization standards*: How well the technology components conform and adhere to the specified organization standards and best practices.
- *Alignment to architecture principles and best practices*: How well the technology components and products align with the laid out architecture principles, patterns, and best practices.
- *Affordability*: Total cost of ownership (TCO) of the technology component. We will also evaluate a build vs. buy decision. A most commonly followed practice is to select the components in the following order:
  - Evaluate the reusability of existing technology solution components
  - Explore solution components in open source community
  - Evaluate the cost of suitable COTS (commercial) product
  - Custom develop the component
- *Solution fitment*: How well the solution component satisfies the functional and business specifications.

No	Evaluation parameter	Weights	Portal product 1			Portal product 2			Portal product 3		
			Rating (1–10)	Score	Rationale	Rating (1–10)	Score	Rationale	Rating (1–10)	Score	Rationale
	Operational capabilities	15%		0.41085			0.462825			0.309375	
14	Support and product roadmap	33%		2.739			3.0855			2.0625	
14.1	Support	15%	8	1.2		9	1.35		7	1.05	
14.2	Implementation and training services	10%	8	0.8		8	0.8		7	0.7	
14.3	Documentation	10%	8	0.8		10	1		6	0.6	
14.4	Product vision and roadmap	50%	8	4		10	5		6	3	
14.5	Company profile	15%	10	1.5		8	1.2		6	0.9	
15	Administration	33%		2.739			3.0855			2.0625	
15.1	User administration	15%	8	1.2		9	1.35		7	1.05	
15.2	Process administration	10%	8	0.8		8	0.8		7	0.7	
15.3	Workflow administration	10%	8	0.8		10	1		6	0.6	
15.4	User and account setup	50%	8	4		10	5		6	3	
15.5	Migration capability	15%	10	1.5		8	1.2		6	0.9	
16	Release and deployment	33%		2.64			3.0525			2.145	
16.1	Automated build support	25%	8	2		9	2.25		7	1.75	
16.2	Automated deployment	25%	8	2		8	2		7	1.75	
16.3	Maintenance support	25%	8	2		10	2.5		6	1.5	
16.4	Monitoring support	25%	8	2		10	2.5		6	1.5	

FIGURE 3.9
Portal operational scorecard.

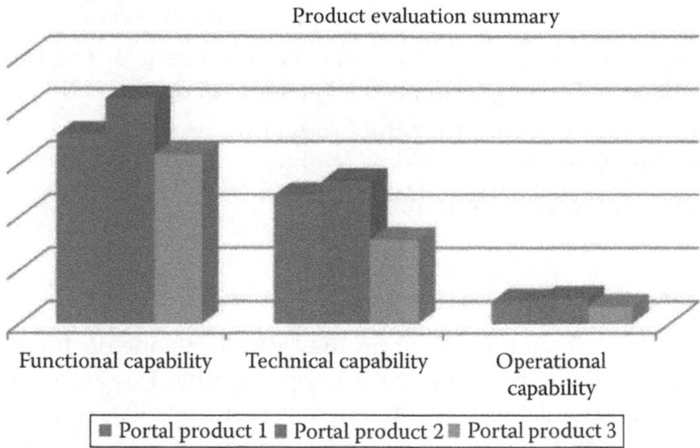

FIGURE 3.10
Evaluation chart for overall portal capabilities.

- *Alignment with solution road map*: How well the technology component is positioned to satisfy the long-term solution road map strategy.
- *Benchmarking*: The technology component is benchmarked against the competitors to understand its strengths and weaknesses.
- Availability of support for the technology.

The evaluation matrix will use the weightage-based scoring similar to the one used in product evaluation framework and at the end of the evaluation phase the list of solution components will be recommended.

Vendor Evaluation

In this evaluation step, we will also assess the capabilities of the portal product vendor using the following criteria:

- *Vendor credibility scorecard*: Here we will take the weighted score of various parameters such as the following:
  - Vendor credentials including the company financials and the alliance relationship
  - Independent analyst ratings of the vendor for the portal product
  - Market share
  - User base
- *Solution affordability scorecard*: This mainly involves finding the optimal choice with respect to
  - License cost
  - Maintenance and deployment cost
  - Support cost
  - Alliance cost
  - TCO over the extended duration of time
  - Learning and training cost for training the employees with the portal technology

- *Solution roadmap*: In this category we will look at how the vendor is aligned to
  - Future trends in the portal space and the alignment of the product to those trends, this includes long-term product vision and road map
  - The commitment of vendor for the product in terms of support and enhancement and bug fixes
  - Vendor thought leadership in portal space

Product Demo Evaluation

A detailed product demo from the portal product vendor is one of the main selection criteria. During this demo, the vendor will get an opportunity to showcase the main features of the product and its applicability to the current scenario. Various stakeholders of the organization participate in the demo to understand the ease of use, flexibility, strength, and other product features. At the end of the demo each of the stakeholders would provide feedback that will be used for the overall evaluation of the product.

Proof-of-Concept Evaluation

Out of numerous shortlisted portal products, a selected few (typically two to three) portal products would be finally shortlisted for the proof of concept (PoC). Important business scenarios and complex technical requirements will be implemented using the final shortlisted portal products in the PoC phase. For instance, organization-specific integrations, a complex business process with multiple business rules, and custom security integration are some of the ideal candidates for a PoC. We will evaluate how easy (or difficult) it is to customize/configure and use the product for organization-specific scenarios during this phase and this will also be factored into the final evaluation. This step sometimes also involves development of quick prototypes that can be later used in the final solution. Focus would be given on *evolving* PoC, which can be reused rather than *throw-away* PoC.

The final portal product would be recommended using the rankings in each of these individual categories. The aforementioned framework may also need to be customized for some cases. For instance, in some organizations, the product vendor alliance will get a heavy weightage due to the relationship with product vendor, in some other cases, the product that closely aligns with existing technology stack or ecosystem may be preferred over other criteria, and in consumer facing external portals, support for user experience and mobility enablement will be of prime importance. So we need to customize the framework by tweaking the weightage and evaluation criteria parameters wherever needed.

SWOT Analysis

In addition to the three-factor product evaluation based on functionality fitment, technology fitment, and operational fitment, a SWOT (strength, weakness, opportunities, threat) analysis is also done in some cases to get various perspectives of the portal product.

SWOT analysis is typically done for the final list of products. This analysis in addition to the PoC evaluation helps in finalizing the portal product that most appropriately addresses the issues.

SWOT analysis helps us in understanding how the portal product can be used beyond the stated functional specifications. It also provides insights into the vulnerabilities and weaknesses that otherwise cannot be obtained through regular means of evaluation.

Strength	Weakness
• Meets around 80% of the requirements • Ranked high in analyst rankings • Supports enterprise integrations through various in-built components • Supports integration through customization and additional scripts • Global customer base and global product support • Fortune 500 clients with large install base • More than 200 resellers and has partnership with more than 50 system integrators • Availability of numerous open source plugins	• Not good in analytics and reporting • Huge learning curve • High release and deployment time • No out-of-the box integration with enterprise ERP system • Some of the core integrations are proprietary
Oppurtunities	**Threats**
• Leverage the services support to build a service-based platform on portal • Leverage the open source plugins to minimize development and testing effort • Focus on content delivery, with plans for personalization functionality, analytics, blog, and wiki support • Provides set of standard APIs to integrate with other applications like CRM • Many of the requirements can be accomplished through customization and additional scripts	• Not able to achieve faster time to market • Difficult to extend the proprietary integration technologies • Competitors can use lower cost disruptive technology

FIGURE 3.11
Portal SWOT analysis.

SWOT analysis has various utilities:

- Leverage the opportunities provided by the product for building the robust platform
- Augment/complement the portal product with other complementary technologies where the product is weak; close any technology gaps through additional tools
- Proactively address the threats listed in the SWOT analysis

Let us look at a SWOT analysis for a portal product in Figure 3.11.

As we can see from the given analysis, we get a clear understanding of opportunities, weaknesses, and threats.

The main takeaway from the aforementioned SWOT analysis is as follows:

- Use the opportunities to build a robust service-oriented platform using portal technologies. Leverage the in-built integrators and APIs to achieve the same.
- Procure additional analytics and reporting components and integrate with portal to fill the gaps.
- Develop an agile execution methodology to achieve faster release and time to market to address one of the key threats.

Feature Set in Various Portal Products

In this section we will look at the main features of popular portal products. This helps us in understanding how portal products implement portal use cases. The list provides a high-level overview of some of the core features of the portal products. The features are given in Table 3.2.

TABLE 3.2
Features in Portal Products

Portal Feature	IBM WebSphere Portal 8.5	Oracle WebCenter Portal 11g R1	Liferay Portal EE 6.2	Microsoft Sharepoint Portal 2013
Security (authentication, RBA, SSO, authorization)	Provides in-built support for these security features	Provides in-built support for these security features	Provides in-built support for authentication	Provides in-built support for these security features
	Supports extensible security model through Trust Association Interceptor (TAI)	SSO can be achieved by integration with OIM and OID	Fine-grained and RBA is provided through robust permission model	Also supports profiles/IP-based access
	Integrates well with enterprise identity and access management suite like IBM Tivoli suite	Integrates well with Oracle identity and access manager suite	Liferay supports authentication using database, LDAP, CAS, and OpenID by default; for custom implementation of authentication mechanism, a flexible set of hooks (authentication and auto log-in pipelines) are available	
	Can be integrated with an existing enterprise IAM framework	Can be integrated with an existing enterprise IAM framework	There are various plug-ins for OpenSSO, Central Authentication System (CAS), Oracle Access Manager (OAM), SiteMinder, and Tivoli that can be leveraged	
Personalization (role-based and user attribute–based implicit and explicit personalization)	Provides full support through in-built components such as personalization rules, configuration-based interface, personalization engine, visibility rules	Provides in-built personalization support through WebCenter personalization services	Provides in-built personalization features and rules engine through Drools integration	Provides various personalization features based on user profile, account, etc.
User interface (configurable layouts, drag-and-drop portlets, responsive design, navigation, and Information architecture)	Provides full support through page layout and themes and skins	Provides full support through page layout	Provides full support through page layout and themes and support for templates through velocity/FreeMarker templates	Provides OOTB support for page layout and web part

(Continued)

TABLE 3.2 (*Continued*)

Features in Portal Products

Portal Feature	IBM WebSphere Portal 8.5	Oracle WebCenter Portal 11g R1	Liferay Portal EE 6.2	Microsoft Sharepoint Portal 2013
Enterprise search	Provides native integration with Omnifind	Supports through default Oracle Secure Enterprise Search	Supports through in-built Apache Lucene	Provides support through Microsoft SharePoint portal server search
			Plug-ins available for Apache Solr and Open Search	Provides integration with Microsoft FAST
Cache capabilities	Provides DynaCache-based capabilities	Provides wide variety of features such as Oracle coherence distributed cache	Supports Ehcache. Provides distributed caching through memcached framework	Provides caching through object cache, output cache, BLOB cache, and ASP.NET cache
AJAX/client-side components	Supports iWidget standard for widget development and gadget and provides in-built Dojo AJAX library support	Supports various client-side frameworks and support for widget/gadget	Supports AlloyUI and all popular AJAX libraries such as jQuery, YUI, GWT, VAADIN, DOJO, ExtJS, etc.	OOTB support for Web Parts available
Accessibility	Compliant with WCAG 2.0	Compliant with WCAG 1.0 AA and WCAG 2.0 standards	Partial support for WCAG 2.0	Compliant with WCAG 2.0 AA
Browser compatibility	All major browsers supported	All major browsers supported	All major browsers supported	All major browsers supported
Supported standards	JSR 168 and JSR 286	JSR 168 and JSR 286	JSR 168 and JSR 286, OpenSearch	.Net Framework
	WSRP 2.0, JAAS, JSR 170 (JCR), JSR 127, and JSR 314 (JSF)	WSRP 2.0, JAAS, JSR 170 (JCR), JSR 127, and JSR 314 (JSF)	WSRP 2.0, JSR 170 (JCR), JSR 127, and JSR 314 (JSF)	
Default Technology stack	Application server: WebSphere	Application server: OracleAS	Application server: Tomcat, JBoss, etc.	In-built application server: Microsoft portal server
	Web server: Apache Web Server/IBM HTTP Server	Web server: Apache Web Server/OHS	Web server: Apache Web Server	Web server: IIS
	Database server: Oracle, MS SQL, DB2, etc.	Database server: Oracle, etc.	Database server: Oracle, MS SQL, MySQL, etc.	Database: SQL server
	Language: Java	Language: Java	Language: Java	Language: C Sharp
Service-based integration	Support SOAP-, REST-, and WSRP-based integration	Support SOAP, REST, and WSRP-based integration	Support SOAP-, REST-, and WSRP-based integration	Support SOAP, REST, and ODATA

(*Continued*)

TABLE 3.2 (*Continued*)

Features in Portal Products

Portal Feature	IBM WebSphere Portal 8.5	Oracle WebCenter Portal 11g R1	Liferay Portal EE 6.2	Microsoft Sharepoint Portal 2013
Mobility support	Supports through responsive web design and Portal Mobile Experience theme (with mobile touch support) and mobility rules	Supports through responsive web design and provides other options such as device groups, ADF Mobile framework, responsive templates	Supports through responsive web design, device recognition plugins, and mobility theme	Supports through mobile browser view and device channels
		Allows users to create mobile sites	Also supports mobile device recognition provider plug-in, OOTB mobile device rules, mobile-specific responsive themes, Liferay mobile SDK	
Social media integration	Provides support through social media publisher	Supports through social networking services and social and collaboration services	Third-party plug-ins and adaptors, in-built facebook integration, provides various apps in Liferay Marketplace	Provides support for integration with external social networks
Collaboration (blogs, wiki, conference, community, rating/reviewing, audio/video chat, polls, surveys, bookmarks, tagging, and discussion boards)	Supports through integration with "IBM Connections" collaboration suite	WebCenter services are available for functionalities such as wikis, blogs, IM, RSS, discussions, announcements, tags, links, social networking, recent activities, worklists, mail, events, lists, analytics, etc.	Provides OOTB portlets and components for blog, wiki, community, message boards, polls, surveys, shared calendar, email, instant message activities, and plug-in for OpenSocial and SocialOffice	Provides in-built collaboration features and native support for MS Lync
		Also provides support through OWC Connect and OWC Spaces	Supports conference and video chat through WebRTC integration	

(Continued)

TABLE 3.2 (*Continued*)

Features in Portal Products

Portal Feature	IBM WebSphere Portal 8.5	Oracle WebCenter Portal 11g R1	Liferay Portal EE 6.2	Microsoft Sharepoint Portal 2013
Web analytics support	Provides Active Site Analytics (ASA) for analyzing user behavior and supports SiteAnalyzerLogService for monitoring portal usage data through server-side logging Comprehensive support using IBM Coremetrics or integration with other web analytics tools	Provides detailed reports and portal usage details	Supports in-built support for Google Analytics in themes	Provides support through Microsoft web analytics service
	Any JavaScript-based web analytics integration is easy	Any JavaScript-based web analytics integration is easy	Any JavaScript-based web analytics integration is easy	
Content management	Provides native integration with IBM WCM	Provides OOTB task flows for Oracle Content Server	Supports through Liferay CMS and Kaleo workflow	Supports through Sharepoint CMS
Development environment	Rational Application Developer IDE	Eclipse and Jdeveloper	Liferay Developer Studio	Visual Studio and Microsoft Sharepoint Designer
Localization	Provides support through language-specific WCM libraries and resource bundling	Provides localization support provided in ADF access pages using resource bundles Automatic translation of text resources into 28 languages using Jdeveloper	Liferay includes out-of-the-box support for 30+ languages through resource bundles and other components Additional languages can be easily added	Provides OOTB localization support at site and page level
Knowledge management support	IBM WCM can be leveraged for implementing knowledge management	Custom implementation with OWC content	Custom implementation with Liferay CMS and provides OOTB knowledge base portlet Achieved through Liferay integration with Moodle or OpenKM	OOTB support for document management

(*Continued*)

TABLE 3.2 (*Continued*)

Features in Portal Products

Portal Feature	IBM WebSphere Portal 8.5	Oracle WebCenter Portal 11g R1	Liferay Portal EE 6.2	Microsoft Sharepoint Portal 2013
ESB support	Supports integration with WebSphere Message Broker and other ESB products	Supports integration with Oracle Enterprise Service Bus	Supports integration with Mule ESB	Supports services-based integration
Feed support	Supports RSS and ATOM feed through OOTB portlet	Supports RSS and ATOM feed	Supports RSS and ATOM feed through OOTB portlet	Supports RSS and ATOM feed
Web frameworks	Supports frameworks like JSF and Struts and Spring	ADF needs to be used to exploit full potential of WebCenter Supports frameworks like JSF and Struts and Spring	Supports frameworks like JSF and Struts and Spring	.Net Framework
Responsive web design (RWD) Support	Supports RWD HTML5, CSS3, and touch gesture support	Supports RWD Support for HTML5 as well as support for mobile devices and touch gestures in both iOS and Android	Supports RWD Support of AlloyUI and CSS Media query for RWD	Supports RWD
Enterprise integration	Can leverage standard integration mechanisms like SOA, WOA (RESTful services), WSRP, APIs, and asynchronous integrations (MQ, etc.) Also provides various OOTB integration portlets such as web clipping portlet, iframe portlet, and webApp integrator	Provides OOTB support for services-based integration through SOAP, REST, and WSRP	Liferay can leverage standard integration mechanisms like SOA, WOA (RESTful services), APIs, and asynchronous integrations (MQ, etc.).	Provides various enterprise integration features such as link-based integration, iframe-based integration, feed-based integration, services based integration, and WSRP-based integration

(Continued)

TABLE 3.2 (*Continued*)

Features in Portal Products

Portal Feature	IBM WebSphere Portal 8.5	Oracle WebCenter Portal 11g R1	Liferay Portal EE 6.2	Microsoft Sharepoint Portal 2013
Scalability and availability	Supports clustered, cloud-based, and portal farm deployment for providing massively scalable platform	Supports clustered server farm and cloud hosting for scalability and provides WebCenter Interaction high availability features	Liferay portal can be deployed to a JEE application server in a clustered environment for high availability and scalability; it also supports cloud deployment	Provides scalability and availability through virtual machine and cloud-based deployment
Disaster recovery support	Support warm site support	Support warm site support	Support warm site support	Supports through virtual machine and cloud-based deployment
Site admin (user management, site management)	Supports through portal admin console	Supports through WebCenter portal admin console	Supports through portal admin console	Supports monitoring tools such as unified monitoring service, health analyzer
Cloud deployment	Supports on AWS cloud	Supports cloud deployment	Supports cloud deployment	Supports cloud deployment

NOTE:

- The list is only indicative and is not an evaluation or comparison or ranking of portal products or its features; it provides a brief summary of product features
- The list mentioned in the following is only for information and education purposes. A thorough evaluation needs to be carried out for finalizing the product.
- The list is neither an exhaustive list nor covers all available portal products. Features mentioned may be partial for information purposes.
- The feature set is compiled based on publicly available documentation.

Summary

- The chapter provides various portal assessment and evaluation methodologies.
- The business scenarios that mainly involve content, functionality, and data aggregation use cases, personalization use cases, security and SSO scenarios, mobility requirements, interactive UX requirements, and collaboration and social requirements are normally good fit for portal technologies.
- If the solution is mainly for static content display without any authentication and personalization or content aggregation needs, then it may not be a good fit for portal.
- Portal assessment framework consists of business assessment, technology assessment, and product and technology evaluation.
- Business assessment mainly involves business scenario and requirement analysis, business capability analysis, and vision and strategy alignment.
- Technology assessment mainly involves technology mapping, portal fitment analysis, definition of solution architecture and best practices, technology capability assessment, and technology gap analysis.
- Product and technology evaluation involves product evaluation, technology evaluation, vendor evaluation, evaluation based on product demo, and PoC-based evaluation. Most of the evaluations are carried out based on weighted scorecard.
- SWOT analysis is carried out to identify the product weakness and potential opportunities.

4

Architecting Portals

Defining a comprehensive portal architecture is a creative exercise and it involves many enterprise ecosystem elements. As a result, a comprehensive portal architecture involves various architecture views such as security view, content view, information architecture view, application architecture, deployment architecture view, integration view, etc.

We have seen the key concepts of portal technologies and the main use case scenarios in the previous chapters. In this chapter, we will build upon those concepts and look at portals from architectural dimensions such as portal capability model, portal functional view, portal architecture motivations and drivers, and enterprise challenges that will be addressed by the portal. We will also look at various portal architecture views and various steps in portal architecture process. Finally, we will also look at sample portal solution architecture built using open source technologies. Enterprise architects, portal architects, infrastructure architects, security architects will find this chapter useful.

Introduction

Portal includes a lot of things and plays various roles in enterprise domain for solving a variety of business problems. Portal plays the key role in many business transformations and enables them to embark their digital transformation journey.

Architecting a portal solution to achieve short-term goals and to realize long-term vision needs careful evaluation and analysis to develop a robust portal architecture. We will have a closer look at portal architecture views, portal road map, portal best practices, portal architecture process, and architecture principles.

Portal Capabilities

We have seen various use case scenarios for portal from multiple viewpoints. It is now time to structure this and provide a reference capability and functional view of portal.

The intent of this section is to formalize the capabilities and functionalities provided by portal technologies and the typical low-level use case scenarios where portal can be leveraged to the fullest extent.

Aligning with the theme of the book, the architecture will be portal product and technology agnostic, focusing on generic portal capabilities.

Portal Functional Capability View

Normally portal technologies provide range of in-built features to fulfill business goals. Figure 4.1 provides a list of such functionalities and details list of various components available at each layer.

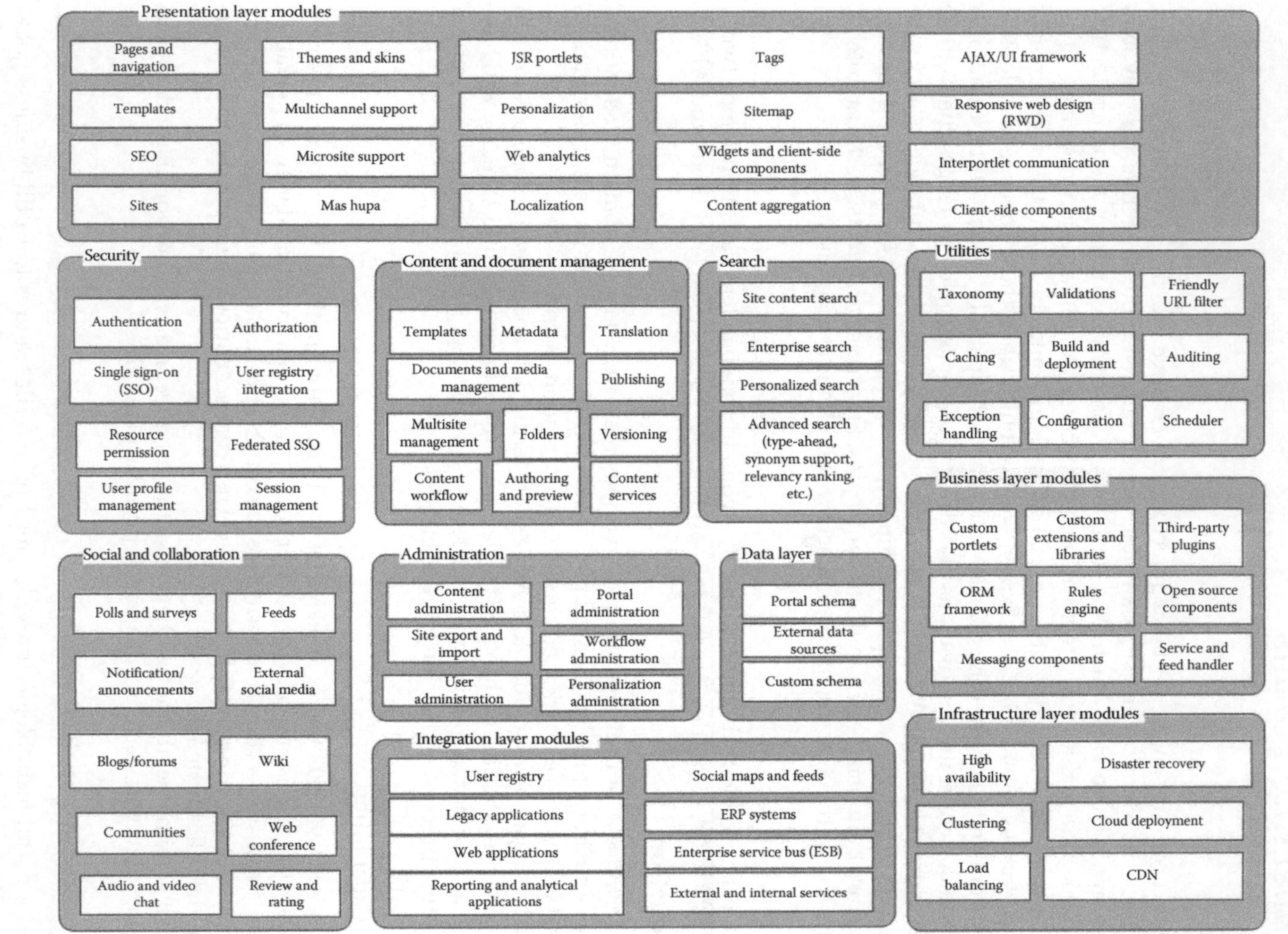

FIGURE 4.1
Portal functional capability view.

The capabilities listed in Figure 4.1 are provided either through inbuilt features or through external plugins in most portal products. The description provided here is the high-level overview of portal technology capabilities at each layer. We will have deep-dive discussions on these modules and portal capabilities in the following chapters. Let us look at each of these components and the functionality they provide.

Presentation Layer

- *Pages and navigation*: Portal pages are the key presentation components that render portlets. They offer multiple flexible features such as drag-and-drop portlets, device-based customization, consistent branding, user customization, etc. Navigation elements include breadcrumbs, left navigation elements, navigation portlet, etc.
- *Themes and skins*: Portal themes serve as a container for portal pages. They normally render header, footer, and navigational elements. We also declare global and page level variables such as styles, JavaScript libraries, web analytics scripts, and include files in themes. Themes serve the key purpose of providing the branding and layout for a portal site and have major influence on the look and feel of the overall site. We create separate themes for individual brands, devices, and geographies by reusing the same portal code. Skins are presentation elements for portlets. It provides the look and feel for individual portlets.
- *JSR portlets*: Portlets form the heart of portal technologies. Portlets are modular and pluggable web applications that contain independent rendition logic. Two main types of portlets are JSR 168 and JSR 286. Their life cycle methods and APIs are described in Chapter 5. Portlets are used as presentation components to display the content and data or to aggregate information from various data sources. Portal engine also applies personalization rules for portlets to provide highly relevant and contextual information.
- *Portal page templates*: They provide the reusable layout for portal pages. As portal is a dynamic delivery platform, the role of page templates play a key role in optimizing the page components. In most of the scenarios, templates would be equivalent to the number of unique page layouts for the site. We can create or instantiate multiple pages for each of the templates. For instance, in an e-commerce portal, all product pages will have the same layout and hence need a single template.
- *Multichannel support*: Portal site is often visited by users through various browsers and devices. Hence, it is imperative for the portal platform to render optimally in all those channels. There are various means to achieve omnichannel experience through RWD, mobile-specific site, mobility rules, etc., which are discussed in detail in Chapter 14.
- *Personalization*: This is another key feature of the portal. Personalization mainly involves customizing the user experience based on implicit and explicit user preferences. This includes things such as showing or hiding portlets, executing personalization rules, etc. Normally, personalization engine uses wide array of inputs such as explicit user-defined preferences, user's browsing history, user profile attributes, etc. Personalization also helps in targeted recommendations and promotions based on user segmentation.
- *Search engine optimization (SEO)*: This involves improving the visibility and ranking of the portal site and is focused on ranking parameters used by search engines.

SEO includes page level description, keywords, friendly URL, sitemap, portlet level keywords, etc. This will be discussed in more detail in Chapter 8.

- *Microsite support*: Portal being a presentation engine should enable business community to host and deploy microsites on need basis. Microsites are a subset of portal pages often using a different domain name or friendly URL that can be used for launching new products or for need-based promotional campaigns.
- *Web analytics*: This involves tracking the web user's behavior on portal pages, which includes drawing actionable insights from the user actions such as navigation path, downloads, exit rate, bounce rate, etc. The user experience can be optimized based on the insights drawn from the web analytics. This will be discussed in detail in Chapter 16.
- *Sites*: This component will provide features to support the creation of portal sites. Sites represent a logical grouping of portal pages catering to a group of users and provide a consistent set of functionality.
- *Mashup*: A mashup is a client-side aggregation of multiple functionalities to provide a more useful functionality. Mashup will be discussed in Chapter 6 in more detail.
- *Localization*: This involves the ability to support multiple languages. Portal technology offer implicit localization through locale passed from user agents and explicit localization specified by users. Normally, language-specific resource bundles will be used to support multiple languages. For content localization, the portal will be integrated with sophisticated translation management system (TMS).
- *Tags*: These are page level attributes that describe the key page concepts and the main content of the page. They help in making the content discoverable by internal and external search engines.
- *AJAX/UI frameworks*: This is another key element in the presentation layer. In modern portals, a portal page consists of a good number of widgets and client-side components. The widgets and client-side components are developed using AJAX toolkits such as jQuery, DOJO, Angular.js, etc. They provide all the necessary building blocks for developing a full-blown component.
- *Responsive web design (RWD)*: This involves leveraging on latest HTML5 technologies such as media queries to develop the pages so that it is optimally rendered on all browsers and mobile devices. Most of the portal products support RWD through responsive themes or Web 2.0 themes. We will discuss about RWD and AJAX toolkit in greater detail in Chapter 14.
- *Sitemap*: Sitemap provides the hierarchy of portal pages and the site taxonomy. This is often used by search engines.
- *Widgets and client-side components*: These are lightweight presentation components mainly developed using AJAX toolkits. They are increasingly becoming popular in web-oriented portals and modern applications due to their lightweight design, performance benefits, and asynchronous communications.
- *Content aggregation*: This can be done either on client side using AJAX toolkit or on server side.
- *Interportlet communication (IPC)*: This is supported by JSR 286 standard that helps in the exchange of information across portlets. It is mostly event driven. It is explained in more detail in the Appendix.

Security Layer

This layer consists of security components required for portal technologies. These components will be discussed in more detail in Chapter 9.

- *Authentication*: Most of the portal products provide inbuilt authentication mechanism for validating user credentials. As portals run in the context of application servers, native server authentication is also reused in some cases. After successful authentication, user session, security tokens, and related security cookies are created.
- *Authorization*: Authorization provides fine-grained security for portlets, services, data, and other portal resources. Fine-grained access control is achieved through authorization. Portal also provides robust permission model and role-based access control (RAC) to implement authorization rules. RAC is achieved by roles and user groups and assigning them to individual portlets and other elements within the portal.
- Single sign-on (SSO) or web SSO provides seamless navigation experience across multiple secured applications. Web SSO is achieved through security tokens that are interpreted by each of the participating applications and a centralized policy server. Most of the portal products provide security extensions to implement SSO mechanism.
- User registry integration is vital for authentication. Portals will be integrated with user registries such as lightweight directory access protocol (LDAP) or active directory (AD). Some portals also store basic user attributes locally for optimization purposes. In some other cases, portal-specific user attributes such as portal roles and portal resource permissions are stored locally.
- *Resource permission*: This is implemented through access control policy and access control list (ACL). Portal enforces coarse-grained permission at page level and site level and fine-grained access control policy at portlet, object, and service level.
- *Federated SSO*: When portal is integrated with external or third-party secured systems, federated SSO is used to enforce security policies such as role-based access control. This is often achieved through security assertion markup language (SAML)-based tokens.
- *User profile management*: This involves providing ability for individual users and administrators to edit user profile attributes and maintain password policy. This module also provides other features such as account management, profile update feature, role management feature, etc.
- Session management involves maintaining user session, session synchronization across cluster nodes, session timeout, etc.

Content and Document Management Components

Content management and content integration is one of the most sought-after features in portals. Following is the brief overview of the key components in this space. We will discuss these in more detail in Chapter 7.

- *Content templates*: Most of the portal products provide inbuilt native content management system (CMS) or seamless support for popular CMS products. This support includes support for creating content authoring templates that specify the overall structure of content, repeatable and nonrepeatable elements, file and media attachment enablers, style enablers with rich text editor, etc. This helps the authors to use the portal interface to seamlessly author the content and publish it in a quick time.

- *Metadata*: Content will be tagged with keywords. This helps in providing relevant search results for internal and external search engines. Some portal systems provide a rich taxonomy of inbuilt and customizable taxonomy of metadata. Metadata is often used to provide page level or content fragment/chunk level keywords.
- *Translation management*: Portal and its underlying CMS will be integrated with TMS to provide localized content.
- *Documents and media management*: This module provides the author the ability to manage the documents and media elements. Features include providing document storage, versioning, document life cycle management, and integration with document repositories such as SAN, media servers, etc. This component also takes care of other activities such as archiving, caching, and replication as well.
- *Publishing*: This is an integral part of a CMS system. Once the content is authored, reviewed, approved, and previewed, it will be published to targets such as web server and file server. This also sometimes includes exposing the content via JSON- or representational state transfer (REST)-based content services for upstream systems.
- *Multisite management*: This module involves managing portal pages and web content to support multiple sites. Typically, multiple sites are required for managing various brands, creating microsites, and to cater to various devices.
- *Folders*: Folders are needed for categorizing the web content and the related assets. They provide a logical grouping for related assets.
- *Versioning*: This involves managing various versions of web content to support preview, rollback, and publishing.
- *Content workflow*: This is another important element of CMS system wherein content undergoes multiple stages of approval. This normally involves content authoring, content reviewing, legal review, marketing review, and preview sign-off. Once all workflow steps are successfully completed, content will be published to the live site.
- *Authoring and preview*: This module provides authors and approvers an interface to create the web content using the templates and see the live "as-is" preview of the content. Authoring environment include features to use the predefined content templates to create the web content and tag them with appropriate metadata.
- *Content services*: In the service-oriented world, content is often consumed as simple object access protocol (SOAP)- or REST-based services by publishing platforms such as portals. This component is responsible for exposing the content through services.

Besides this, CMSs are also involved in content federation and syndication with other content systems.

Enterprise Search

Search is another important enterprise concern addressed by portal. As this is one of the crucial topics, we will discuss this in detail in Chapter 8. A high-level description of key components is given in the following:

- *Site content search*: This includes indexing all content of the portal site and providing keyword-based relevant search results from portal pages. This is the most commonly used functionality.

- *Enterprise search*: As portal aggregates enterprise-wide information, search functionality also needs to crawl and index all related structured and unstructured data. This can be done by appropriate plugins and adaptors that help the search engine to index content from various enterprise data sources such as document repositories, databases, ERP systems, reporting systems, CMSs, file stores, etc.
- *Personalized search*: This involves filtering the search results based on user's explicit and implicit preferences. For instance, if the user prefers to see the search results from a particular geography, then the results are ranked appropriately.
- *Advanced search*: This includes features such as synonym support, type-ahead support, relevancy ranking, rank boosting, guided navigation, faceted browsing, automatic result categorization, etc. Most of the features are supported by popular search engines and the portal would often use services-based integration or page redirection to serve these functionalities to the end user.

Search feature can also be used for dynamic information aggregation. We can have preconfigured search portlets to display the relevant data for the user.

Utilities

Portals need numerous utilities that are usually termed as "horizontal components" for its functionality. The key ones that are found in most of the portal products are listed here:

- Taxonomy component maintains the page hierarchy in a portal site. This is used for the construction of sitemap.
- Validations component involve validating the content, data, and user inputs and it is implemented by leveraging various open source components such as Apache Commons validator. This also involves escaping/trimming HTML-reserved characters and prevent potential malicious content to prevent cross-site scripting attacks.
- Friendly URL component is responsible for converting the cryptic portal URL to an easy-to-remember and bookmarkable URL. It also helps in better indexing by search engines. Friendly URLs can be done at portal site level as well as at individual portlet level. Since portal is a dynamic platform, it is important to provide an identifiable URL to make the pages easily accessible. This functionality is often implemented by filters that internally map the friendly URL to dynamic portal URL.
- Caching is critical in achieving high performance. It is important to provide caching at multiple layers to achieve optimal performance. Most of the portal products provide inbuilt caching frameworks and we can also leverage on open source caching frameworks such as Ehcache, OSCache, and Memcached, etc. We will discuss more about caching in Chapter 18.
- Build and deployment functionality is implemented through scripts and admin interfaces. Ant- and Maven-based build and deployment scripts help us in automating the portal release management activities. By combing build and deployment scripts with a continuous integration tool such as Jenkins, it is possible to achieve the highest level of automation in release management. We will look at this aspect in more detail in Chapter 19.
- Exception handing involves custom utilities to handle the system and user exceptions and take the corresponding action.

- Configuration-driven changes is the key element of all modern web applications. Application and server level changes are done in configuration files and the changes are reflected instantly without the need of server or application restart. Portal products support this through the hot deployment feature, custom configuration handlers and using open source frameworks.
- Scheduling tools are required to provide time-triggered actions such as file deployment, content publishing, offline batch jobs initiation, etc. In addition to portal-provided features, open source frameworks such as Quartz scheduler can be leveraged for implementing this.

Social and Collaboration

As portal is increasingly being used as a collaborative platform for internal and external stakeholders, it is natural that portal product is packed with social and collaboration features. Portal social and collaboration features actively engage end users and provide personal touch points that increases user stickiness with the portal site. It also enhances productivity by helping in the faster resolution of issues and leads to more conversion in e-commerce platforms. We will have an in-depth discussion in Chapter 10 to discuss the portal collaboration features in detail and here is a quick snapshot of the main collaboration functionality. Most of these features are realized through out-of-the-box portlets or widgets.

- *Polls and surveys*: This portlet allows the administrator to set up polls and survey questions for end users. It aggregates the opinions from all the users and provides a report based on it.
- *Feeds*: Feeds portlet allows the end user to configure REST/ATOM feeds. Additionally, portal also allows its existing content to be exposed via feeds to external systems.
- *Notifications and announcements*: This feature allows the portal to broadcast the updates to all interested subscribers. Updates such as content updates, site changes, and promotion content are most ideal candidates for notification.
- *External social media integration*: Internet-facing external portals, used by social media savvy, users expect integration with popular social media platforms. Bringing relevant conversations from social media into portal platform would enhance its usability and effectively meets the target user experience. Integration mainly happens through plugins, services and custom adaptors. Main functionality achieved through this integration are posting and creating content to external social media platforms, sharing content, social bookmarking, rating and reviewing content, etc.
- Blogs and forums portlets allow users to create meaningful conversations and help in actively engaging the end users.
- Wiki portlets help in creating the knowledge sources within portal platform.
- Communities will bring together like-minded people for the common cause. We can create product or user communities based on the business domain.
- *Web conference*: Conferencing takes the collaboration to the next level; it helps people to share their screen, do real-time joint updates, exchange documents, do co-shopping, and can perform cobrowsing.

- *Audio and video chat*: This is one of the main conversational elements. It is mainly used for issue resolution and real-time collaboration.
- *Review and rating*: This functionality is often implemented through client-side widgets. We can attach these widgets for blog content, wiki content, products, and even for pages to aggregate user ranking.

Administration

Portal's strong selling point also lies in its easy-to-use single point administration interface. We have listed some of the key admin features supported by portal technologies:

- *Content administration*: This involves activities such as setting up roles for content usage, setting up content templates and content creation process, configuring content workflows and publishing workflows, etc.
- *Portal administration*: This is the key admin functionality provided by a portal and it controls all main functionalities offered by the portal. The following are the high level functionalities within this area:
  - Workflow administration by setting up workflow roles and configuring key workflow parameters
  - Site export and import involves exporting the entire portal site along with its portal pages and portlets in an archive bundle
  - Site promotion involves moving the sites from preview environment to live environment
  - Web analytics monitoring includes configuring web analytics scripts for key pages and portlets and monitoring the site usage report and statistics
  - Search configuration includes configuring the search relevancy ranking parameters, artificial rank boosting, configuring data sources for indexing and crawling, etc.
  - Personalization configuration includes configuring personalization rules and attaching rules for pages and portlets
  - Data source management includes configuring the main portal database and other required data sources
  - Batch job configuration includes configuring the frequency and scheduling batch jobs
  - Portal administration also involves fine-tuning portal server configurations and parameters
- User administration involves creating user groups, roles, assigning roles to users, establishing permission model, establishing access controls for portal resources, user impersonation, exporting and importing users, configuring user registries such as LDAP, etc.
- Security configuration includes configuring portal with enterprise security managers and SSO configuration, configuring session time out, HTTPS configuration, configuring encryption standards, etc.

The functionalities listed here cover the main elements of portal administration. Based on the needs and business domain, other administration functionalities may be required.

Data Layer

Portals would need to connect to various enterprise data sources for aggregating data required for portlets. The main elements of this layer are as follows:

- *Portal schema*: Portals will need various database objects to persist and manage its application-specific data such as page configuration, site configuration, user details, cached session details, key portal configuration, etc. Each portal product creates its own set of database objects during initial portal setup. Portal database is often clustered for ensuring high performance and availability.
- *Custom schema*: In addition to default portal schema, portal admin users can add custom database objects while extending portal functionality. For instance, while adding custom user attributes, we may need to extend default portal user table. All these things will go in as custom schema objects.
- *Enterprise data sources*: As discussed earlier, portal needs to connect to a variety of enterprise data sources such as legacy databases, reporting databases, user databases, etc. For performance reasons, the data transfer and synchronization often happens in offline batch mode and in incremental fashion.

Business Layer Modules

There would be numerous business modules depending on the business scenario. The following list is a sample representation of typical business components found in a portal solution:

- *Custom portlets*: Based on the functional requirements, there would be numerous custom portlets based on JSR standards. Each custom portlet will be developed so that it can be used as pluggable and modular application.
- *Custom extensions and libraries*: In some cases, there would be a need to extend the core portal components to implement the requirements. Custom log-in module, custom encryption standard, and SSO integration are some scenarios where we need to use inbuilt portal extensions to fill the gaps.
- *Third-party plugins and portlets*: For some integrations, third party systems will provide pluggable adaptors and portlets that can be used within portal platform.
- *Object-relational mapping (ORM) framework*: This is one of the most commonly used frameworks to connect to data sources. Inbuilt or open source frameworks such as Hibernate/iBatis would be used for data retrieval scenarios.
- *Rules engine and business process management (BPM)*: A configurable rules engine module is required to fulfill complex business requirements. A combination of rules engine and workflow is needed for modeling complex business processes and flows.
- *Open source components*: This involves multiple open source components needed for implementing the functionality. The most commonly used open source component includes Apache components and Spring framework components.
- Messaging components include internal queue and topic destinations with a lightweight message bus. This will be used for asynchronous communication with internal and external components. Notification, information broadcast,

cache updates across cluster nodes, and event notification can be done using messaging components.

- *Service and feed handler*: This is one of the key components of a business layer. Portal products typically provide web service libraries for exposing and consuming web services. Additionally, we can also leverage open source components such as Apache Axis for this. Normally, portals also provide in-built web service and REST portlets and feed portlets.

Integration Layer Modules

Integration being one of the strengths of portal, there will be multiple modules in this category. Let us look at some of the main components with which portal will be integrated. A detailed discussion of integration components is present in Chapter 6. The list covers only the main and frequently used integrations; however, in a real-world scenario, the modules largely depend on the enterprise-wide applications and external applications that need to be integrated for implanting the solution.

- *User registry*: This is the most prominent integration and almost all portal products provide integration with popular user registries such as LDAP.
- *Social maps and feeds*: This requires integration with external map and feed services. This is often implemented through widgets and service calls.
- *Legacy applications*: This includes integration with legacy systems such as banking systems, order management systems, inventory systems, pricing system, etc. Integration is often done using APIs or services.
- *ERP systems*: This integration is normally done using services with existing legacy systems. Alternatively, a batch job can also be used for synchronizing data.
- *Web application*: Integration with existing web applications can be done in different ways such as screen scraping, clipping, portletizing, iframe, etc.
- *ESB*: Integration with ESB is one of the key elements for service-oriented architecture. This is done via services.
- *Reporting and analytical applications*: Service-based integration is often used to retrieve the report data. Other popular alternatives include widget plugins and the usage of report APIs.
- *External and internal services*: This is the most commonly used scenario wherein SOAP- or REST-based services will be integrated with the portal.

Infrastructure Layer Modules

Portal infrastructure components provide the essential components for achieving the desired scalability, availability, and performance for the portal. We will look at more details of portal infrastructure planning in Chapter 18.

- High availability is usually achieved through horizontal and vertical clustering of portal servers. This requires session and cache replication, failover strategy, and intelligent load balancing. Portal administration guide recommends the supported high availability strategies.
- *Disaster recovery (DR)*: Implementing a robust DR strategy requires creating a mirror-replica of the portal environment in a remote location.

- *Clustering*: Deploying the portal solution on multiple node in clustered configuration provides increased scalability and availability. There are multiple forms of clustering such as horizontal clustering, vertical clustering, and hybrid clustering. For best performance, clustering has to be implemented at all the layers including web server layer, application server layer, and database layer.
- Load balancing will be done at both software level and hardware level. Some of the most commonly used load balancing algorithms include round robin, weighted round robin, load-based routing, response-time-based routing, etc.
- *Content delivery network* (*CDN*): For efficient performance and scaling portal pages are often served through CDN. CDN can forward-cache static pages and static digital assets such as videos, images, and JavaScript and CSS files and will serve the request in the most optimal way.
- *Cloud deployment*: Most of the portal products can also be hosted and delivered through cloud platforms. This provides the benefit of elastic scaling and saves infrastructure investment cost.

Besides these components, portal needs other infrastructure elements such as web server, application server, and database server. Suitable capacity planning and sizing needs to be done for these servers for optimal portal performance.

Capability Solution Mapping

We have seen various portal capabilities in the earlier sections. Let us now look at sample portal solution components in Table 4.1 that can be leveraged to implement these capabilities.

NOTE:

- The capability-solution mapping is a sample mapping list intended to bring awareness about some of the commonly used portal solution components to readers. The mapping list is only for information purposes and does not cover all possible solution components to implement a capability. For actual portal engagements, careful evaluation of available solution components and products need to be done to determine the most optimal fit.
- The solution components listed in Table 4.1 are a finite subset of applicable solution components and products.
- A capability can also be realized by an open source framework or an external plugin for the portal platform.

Portal Architecture Views

Portal architecture is a combination of various architecture factors. It includes content architecture, information architecture, deployment architecture, and security architecture as a portal platform will be involved in all these areas.

Let us look at the main architecture views in a portal solution. This section will provide an overview of the main architecture views.

TABLE 4.1
Portal Capability Solution Component Mapping

Layer	Portal Capability	Sample Solution Component(s)
Presentation layer	Page template	Velocity template, FreeMarker template
	Web analytics	Google Analytics, CoreMetrics, Omniture
	AJAX toolkits	DOJO, JQuery, ExtJS, Angular JS, Backbone, YUI, Alloy UI
	Web framework	Struts, JSF, Spring MVC
Security	Authentication and SSO	OpenID, oAuth, OpenSSO
	Federated SSO	SAML 2.0
Content and document management	Native portal CMS	Liferay CMS, IBM WCM, Oracle UCM, Sharepoint CMS, Alfresco
	CMS products	Documentum, Adobe AEM, Interwoven,
Search	Open source search products	Apache Lucene, Apache Solr.OpenSearch
	Commercial enterprise search engines	Oracle Endeca, Autonomy, Microsoft FAST, Google Search Appliance
Utilities	Caching	*Open source*: Ehcache, Memcached, Apache JCS, OSCache *Commercial*: IBM DynaCache
	Build and deployment	*Open source*: Apache Ant script, Maven, *Commercial*: IBM XML access script, IBM Jython script, IBM JACL script
	Configuration handlers	Spring utilities, Apache Commons
	Validations	Commons Validator, Spring validations
	Scheduler	Apache Quartz
Social and collaboration	Social and collaboration	OpenSocial, Jive software, IBM Connections, Oracle WebCenter Spaces
	Web conference	WebRTC, Open Conference, WebEx, Microsoft Live Meeting
	Chat	Microsoft Lync,
Business layer modules	Rules engine	Drools, JRuleEngine, OpenRules
	Messaging components	Mule ESB, Tibco ESB, JBoss ESB
	ORM framework	Hibernate, MyBatis, JPA, Oracle TopLink,
	Business process management	JBPM, Activiti BPM
	Workflow	Kaleo Workflow, Aperte Workflow
Enterprise integration	SOAP- and REST-based services	Portal inbuilt service components, Apache CXF, Apache Axis2, Spring REST/SOAP services

Sample Portal Solution Architecture

Before we look at the key portal architecture views, we will look at the typical sections that go into the portal architecture definition document (also referred to as software architecture document). A sample portal solution architecture section is given in the following:

- *As-is analysis*: This depicts the existing technology ecosystem with all systems and components along with challenges and pain points.
- *Technology drivers and motivations for portal programs*: This section details the main reasons for selecting portal platform for the solution. A summary of the portal fitment and assessment analysis will be provided here. We can apply the

portal fitment scorecard, portal assessment framework we discussed in earlier chapters to finalize the portal solution.

- *High-level portal vision, strategy, and success metrics*: We will summarize the overall vision and goals of the program outlining the portal strategy. We will also specify the critical success factors.
- *Architecture constraints*: We will document any applicable constraints that have to be considered in the architecture.
- *Capability model and solution mapping*: We will map the high level requirements to portal capabilities and solution components.
- *Major portal architecture decisions*: We will document all the major architecture decisions such as technology evaluation, product evaluation, build vs. buy decisions, reusability plan, open source frameworks that will be considered, satisfying non-functional requirements, etc.
- *Architecture views*:
    - *End-to-end logical architecture*: This provides the big picture of the overall solution architecture depicting portal with all its interfacing ecosystem components
    - *Application architecture*: This view provides the portal application architecture detailing all the solution components
    - *Use case view*: This models the technical use case scenarios
    - *Security view*: This provides the security views and depicts the major security flows such as authentication, authorization, SSO, etc.
    - *Data view*: This provides the data model and data architecture along with the data flow.
    - *Process view*: This provides process flow of major and critical processes
    - *Development view*: This depicts the development view including the development elements, IDE, tools, accelerators, development systems, etc.
    - *Deployment view*: This provides the overall deployment infrastructure.
    - *Information architecture view*: This provides the structure of the portal site including the navigation elements, placement of key elements, etc.
    - *User experience architecture view*: This provides the details of user experience elements such as pages, portlets, widgets, AJAX toolkits, etc.
    - *Content architecture view*: This provides the content strategy, content workflow, content publishing, authoring, and content flows.
    - *Integration architecture view*: This provides the integration details of portal with all interfacing elements including the details such as integration type, mode of integration, implementation of service-oriented architecture, etc.
- *Architecture risks and Assumptions*: We will document all the architecture risks, assumptions, and risk mitigation plan.
- *Other architecture sections*:
    - *Reusability plan*: We will provide the details of reusability through the re-use of existing technology components, products, and any applicable external open source components.
    - *Continuous improvement plan*: This explains the improvements that can be achieved through iterations.

- *Productivity plan*: Details of all productivity improvements such as the usage of accelerators, open source tools, automated scripts, automation plans, and leveraging in-built components will be provided here.
- *Architecture best practices*: We will document all the architecture and industry best practices that are adopted in the architecture.
- *Standards compliance*: All standards related to development, testing, and deployment will be provided here.
- *Nonfunctional requirements*: This section explains how the architecture satisfies the nonfunctional requirements such as performance, security, scalability, availability, accessibility, etc.

Portal Application Architecture View

The application architecture view provides an end-to-end solution architecture depicting all the systems and integrations involved. Sometimes called the logical architecture or solution architecture, it is the main architecture view for a portal. A sample portal application architecture is given in Figure 4.2.

Portal application architecture normally uses layered model–view–controller (MVC) architecture providing separation of concerns for various layers.

- *Presentation layer*: This involves the presentation components like portlets, user experience components such as widgets, AJAX toolkits, themes, personalization components, page templates, and layout
- *Business layer*: Business layer consists of server-side components related to messaging, rules, processes, business components, and business services
- *Integration layer*: The layer primarily involves service-based integration components for integration with ESB, external and internal services such as data services, business services, report services, etc.
- *Identity management (IDM) layer*: This layer consists of authentication, authorization, and security plugins
- *Content management layer*: This layer mainly consists of content and asset management components such as workflows, templates, rules, access controls, etc.
- Monitoring and maintenance components such as real-time end-user monitoring, social monitoring, system health check monitoring, and resource utilization monitoring and maintenance batch jobs.

Portal Component View

This depicts various solution components that are used in the solution. A sample portal component view is given in Figure 4.3.

These components are basically solution components that are used to satisfy the specified functionality.

We have already seen the explanation of these components in "Portal Functional Capability View" section.

Portal Data Architecture View

The view mainly depicts the data model and the data flow and interaction across all layers.

Figure 4.4 shows the data flow in a typical portal solution.

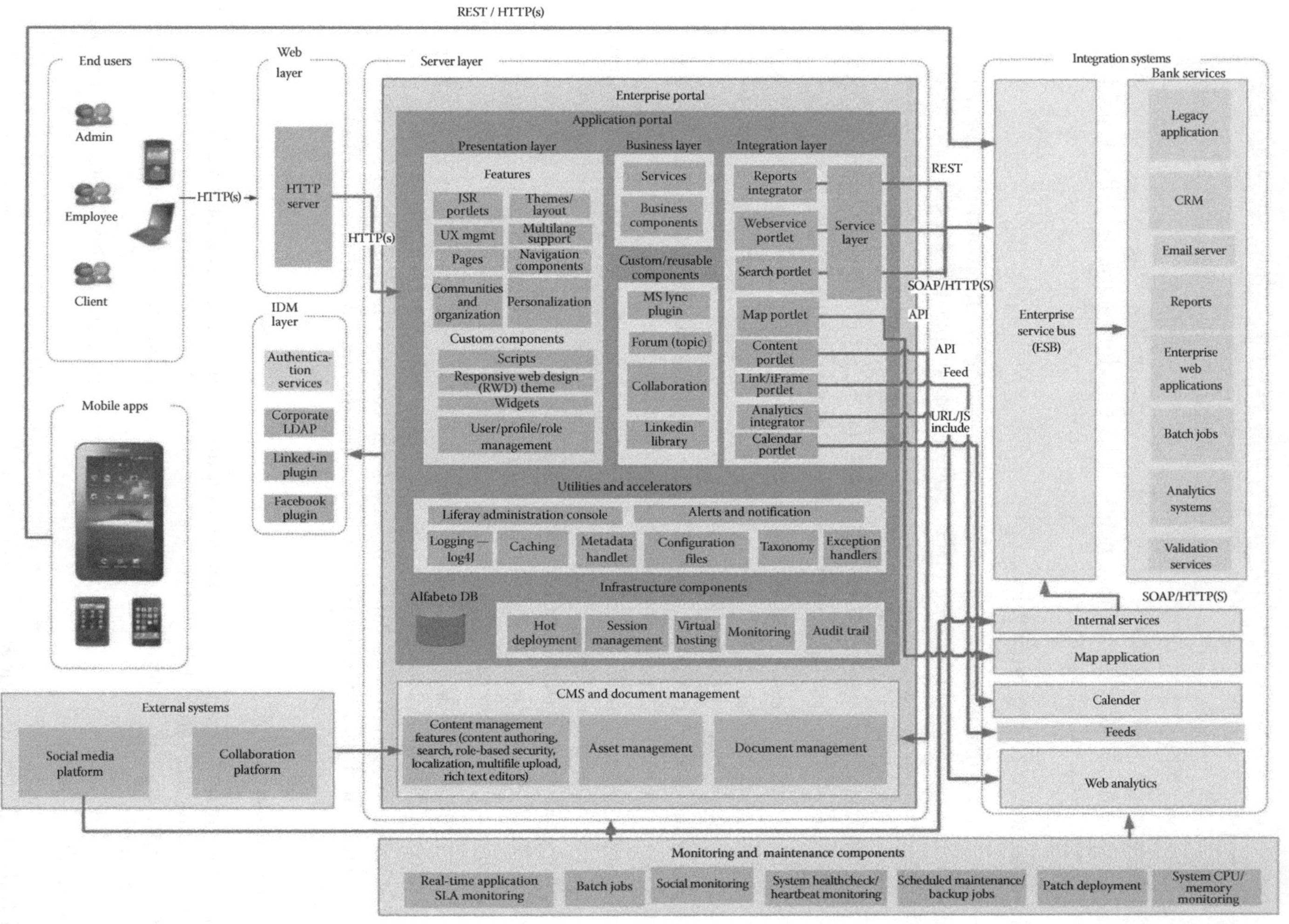

FIGURE 4.2
Sample portal application architecture.

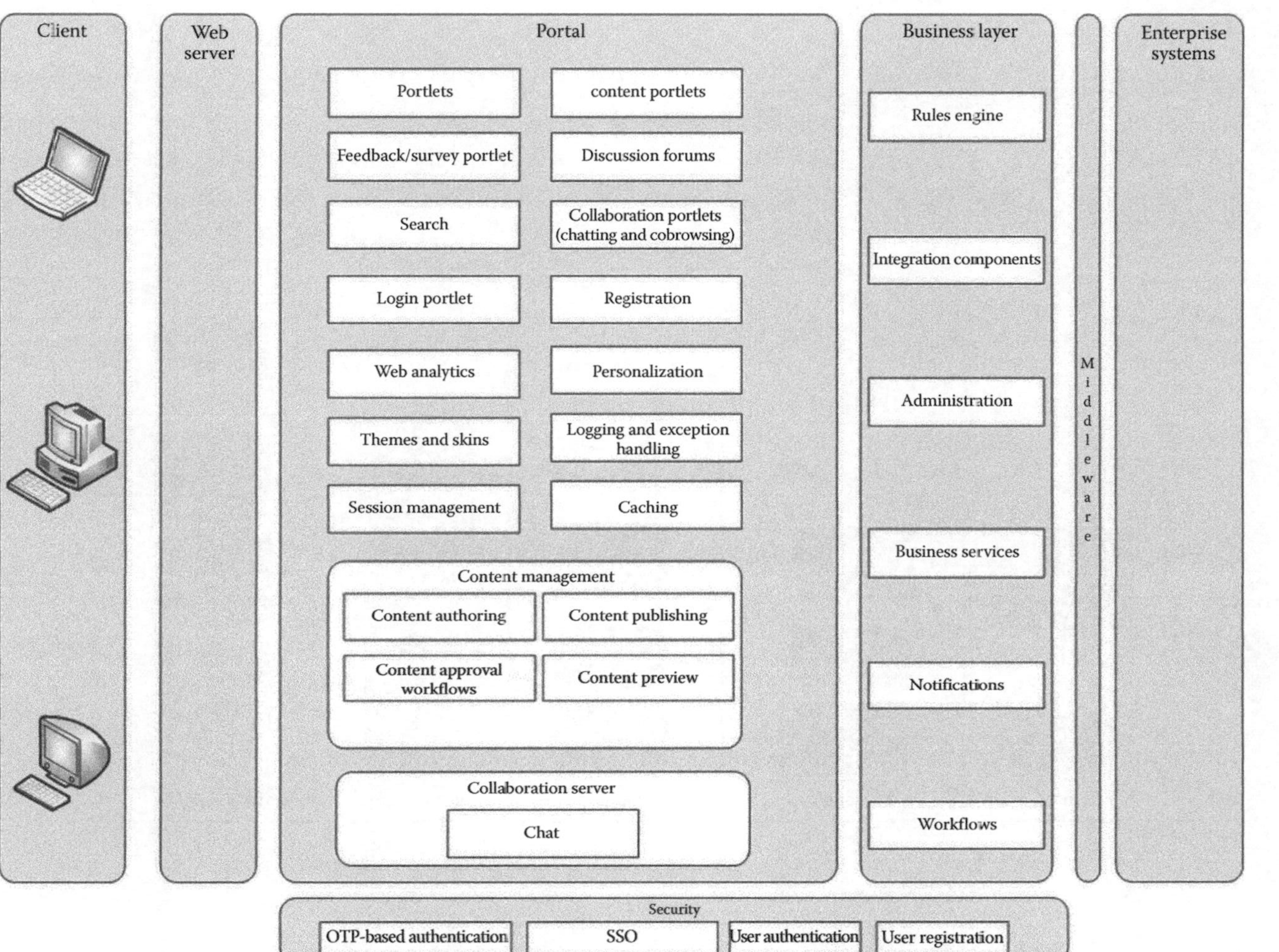

FIGURE 4.3
Portal component view.

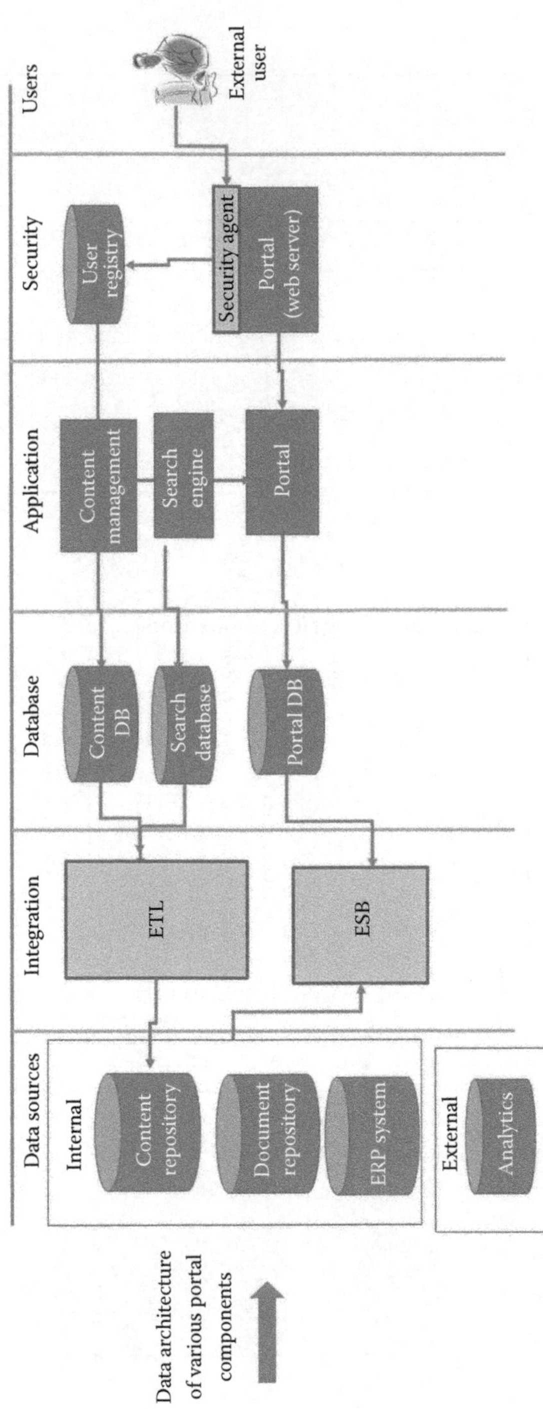

FIGURE 4.4
Portal data architecture view.

The high level steps for the given data architecture is as follows:

1. User authenticates through log-in portlet. The security plugin component in the web server uses the user registry for authentication and the creation of security tokens.
2. The portal would also interact with search and CMSs through integration portlets.
3. In the database layer, the portal persists the application and system level configuration data to portal database. Similarly, other applications use their own databases. Usually we maintain separate database schemas for storing core portal data and application data.
4. *Integration mainly happens through two systems*: ESB and ETL. The portal uses ESB using service-based integration and ESB communicates to back-end data sources. ETL tool does data aggregation and transformation from underlying databases. The ETL tool also supports data backup and synchronization jobs.
5. There is one external data source related to analytics system depicted in Figure 4.4. Data flows to this system through JavaScript APIs.

The view also provides details about other data aspects such as

- Data backup and archival details including the frequency and the type of data backup
- Data level security and how it can be achieved
- Optimizing the data flow through performance best practices
- Discussion of any applicable data integrity constraints

Portal Use Case View

This view usually depicts the core portal use cases. Though use cases are documented in functional specifications document and use case document, we provide high level details of core use cases that refer back to master requirements document to provide the high level picture. It also compliments the security view, integration view, and overall solution architecture. The main intention of the use case view is to provide a high level overview of portal scenarios depicted through use cases.

Let us check a sample banking portal from use case standpoint. Use case view would throw light into practical usages of portal capabilities and its applicability for implementing real-world scenarios. Figure 4.5 depicts some commonly used scenarios in banking portal.

One of the utilities of a use case view is to identify the portal capabilities and any applicable solution components to implement the use case scenarios. We will look at the portal capabilities that enable the use cases in banking portal:

- *Role-based access and personalization*: In Figure 4.5, there are five user roles, namely, customer, retail banker, investment banker, admin, and content author. Portal uses role-based access and personalization rules to customize the user experience based on the roles and user attributes.
- *Security and SSO*: These capabilities are used for authentication and SSO scenario. For implementing domain functionality, the portal needs to have seamless access to upstream applications. In the given case, portal needs to have SSO with core banking system, enterprise search system, and e-mail system.

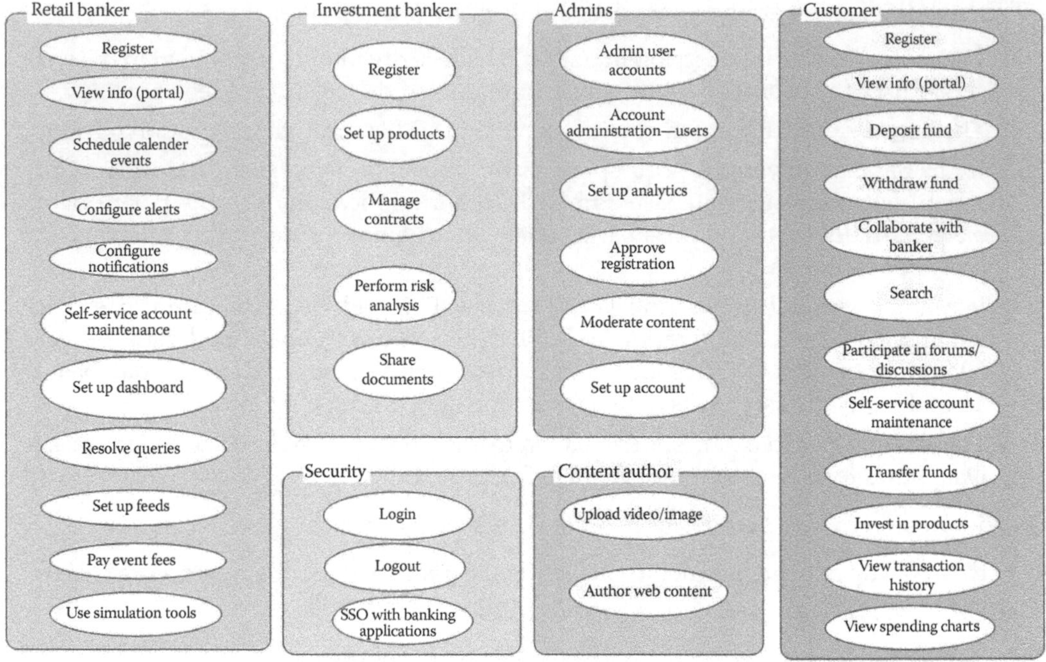

FIGURE 4.5
Banking portal use case view.

- *Enterprise integrations*: A complex application like banking portal needs to support numerous enterprise integrations. A banking portal should be integrated with user provisioning system, core banking system, security managers, e-mail system, and numerous financial services hosted internally.
- *CMS integration*: In banking portal, the portal leverages inbuilt CMS functionality for authoring content and managing documents and media. Various documents related to investment proposals and audio and video files are managed in the document management system.
- *Administration*: Portal administrator can perform various admin activities such as setting up users, impersonating users, approving registration, approving analytics, etc. Some of the admin functionalities can be implemented by leveraging inbuilt portal features.
- *Collaboration*: Banking portal customers closely collaborate with private bankers and investment bankers through real-time audio/video chat, web conferencing, and document sharing. Portal collaboration enables the self-service model and helps in resolving the customer queries faster.
- *Self-service*: There are numerous ways to achieve self-service goal. In a banking portal, there is a knowledge management module that contains solutions for frequently encountered problems and there is a real-time live chat through which customers can chat with a support representative to resolve the issue.
- *Search*: Banking portal is integrated with enterprise search engine for indexing web content and relevant documents. Customers can search for policy- and finance-related documents through search functionality.

One of the main intentions of use case view is also to identify the user personas along with their user journeys. In the given banking portal example, the main user personas are retail banker, investment banker, portal administrators, content author, and customer.

This is a simplified version of a banking portal that provides insights into usage and applicability of portal feature and functionality for a functional domain.

Portal Information Architecture View

Portal information architecture essentially consists of the following:

- Organization of site content
- Site hierarchy and sitemap definition
- Navigation model
- Information discovery strategy
- Tags, metadata, and keyword strategy
- Content hierarchy
- Effective search strategy
- SEO strategy
- Accessibility standards

The main aim of portal information architecture is to

- Enable portal user to discover the relevant information easily and quickly
- Organize the site information in an intuitive way
- Provide personalized and optimal navigation journey for user persona
- Define proper tags, metadata, and keyword to identify the relevant information easily
- Enable external users to easily reach the site through effective SEO strategy
- Provide targeted and personalized content to the users
- Leverage search for enabling optimal information discovery
- Position the key tools, functionality, and content to enable self-service model and to help users perform their tasks quickly
- Align and optimize metadata to enhance search effectiveness and information discoverability
- Enhance the accessibility and easy reach of self-service and collaboration features

A sample Level 0 information architecture for a B2C commerce portal is given in Figure 4.6.

As we can see, the content, functionality, and tools are organized for each of the personas. The functionality is obtained based on details about user personas. Common links are present in the main menu, quick links, links language selector, and my profile page.

Similar to Figure 4.6, even sitemap and navigation models are also part of information architecture.

A sample site hierarchy showing various levels of pages and content is shown in Figure 4.7.

Site hierarchy normally translates into sitemap and content hierarchy.

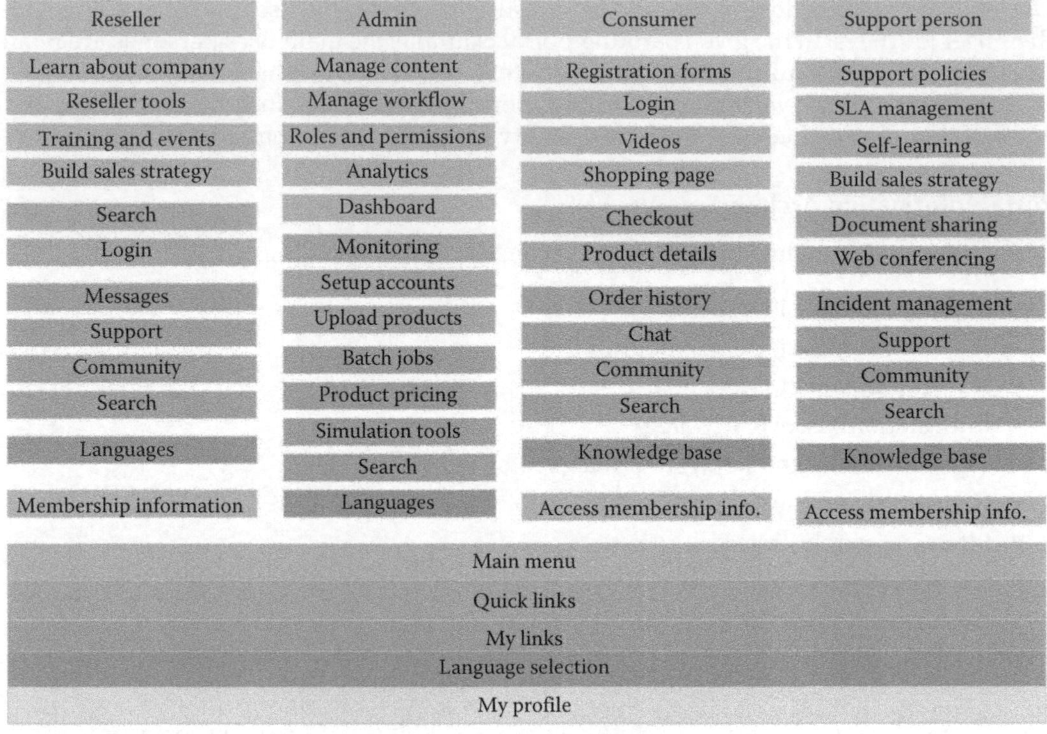

FIGURE 4.6
Sample B2C e-commerce portal level 0 information architecture view.

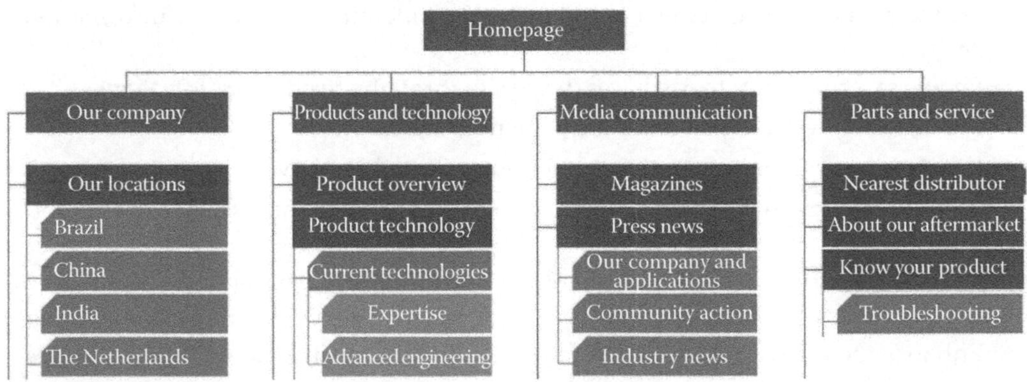

FIGURE 4.7
Sample portal site hierarchy.

Portal Deployment View

The deployment view essentially depicts the infrastructure hardware systems where the portal solution will be deployed. A sample deployment view is shown for a portal solution in Figure 4.8. The diagram shows a three-tiered portal solution deployed in an in-house deployment model.

Three tiers in the deployment view are explained here.

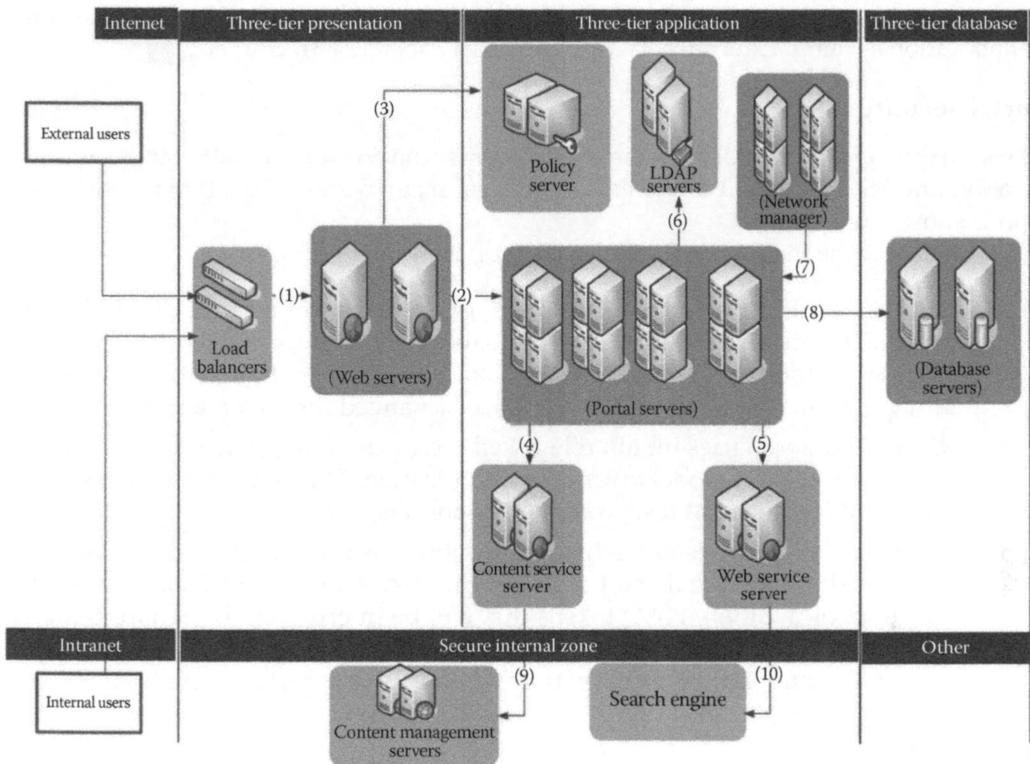

FIGURE 4.8
Sample portal deployment view.

Presentation tier:

- In the presentation tier, the enterprise load balancer distributes the load among the web servers
- Web servers will route the user request to portal servers
- Web server plugins will be integrated with enterprise security policy server for authenticating the requests

Application tier:

- Portal servers normally run on an application server. The servers will be clustered for high availability and scalability.
- Portal will also be configured with an LDAP server for authorization and enforcing role-based fine-grained access.
- Portal will be integrated with content service and search-service layer.
- CMS and enterprise search engine will be exposing service interfaces.

Database tier:

- Clustered database will be running in this tier. This will be used for persisting portal and application data.

In complex environments, we will also have dedicated file servers, middleware servers, collaboration systems, external services, third party social platforms, etc.

Portal Security View

The security view mainly depicts the key security scenarios such as authentication, authorization and SSO, federated SSO, etc. A high level security view for a typical portal solution is shown in Figure 4.9.

Let us look at the main security scenarios for portal solution:

- *Authentication*: Portal uses the enterprise user registry for authentication. Login portlet will authenticate the user credentials against the user registry. After successful authentication, a valid user session will be created and security tokens (mainly in form of browser cookies) will be exchanged for each interaction.
- *Authorization*: Portal uses inbuilt role-based access and fine-grained access control logic and permission model to achieve authorization. This fine grained access can be achieved for all portal resources such as portlets, data, etc.
- *Web/internal SSO*: For seamless communication with secured internal applications, security tokens will be used. In some scenarios, an additional security manager adds additional SSO tokens that will be interpreted by all applications to provide access to secured functionality. In such cases, the portal will be integrated with enterprise security managers and the integration usually involves adding security plugins at web server and involve HTTP header/cookie-based SSO tokens.
- *Federated SSO*: When a portal needs to aggregate data from secured external systems, one popular security option is to use federated SSO. This can be achieved through SAML tokens. When portal is interacting with secured external applications, portal acts as service provider in SAML interaction.

We have detailed all the security scenarios, best practices, and security flows in Chapter 9.

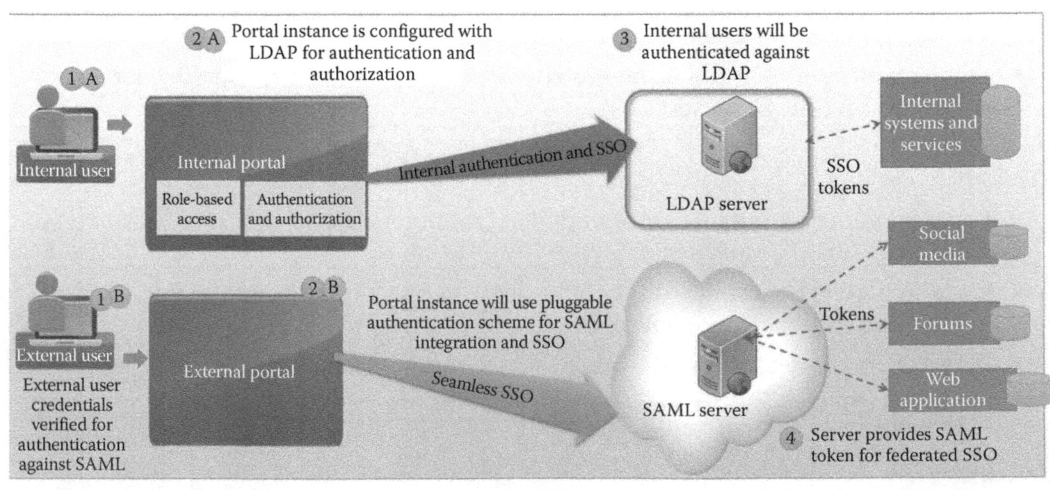

FIGURE 4.9
Portal security view.

Portal User Experience Architecture View

The portal user experience architecture depicts user personas along with their journeys through UI mockups and prototypes. The mockups should depict the main use case scenarios and journeys.

Portal architects should closely work with UX designers and UX architects to ensure that core functionality and information architecture are adequately addressed in the UX design.

UX architecture mainly consists of

- Evaluation and finalization of AJAX toolkits
- UI mockups
- Prototypes
- UI toolkit including the JavaScript libraries and style definitions and image specifications
- Refinement and implementation of information architecture
- Visual style guide to depict consisting branding
- Multidevice design

We will look at more aspects of portal UX in Chapter 14.

Portal Content Architecture View

Portal is one of the main content delivery platforms and content management is one of the classical use case scenarios for a portal. Hence, defining an optimal content management strategy is part of overall portal architecture.

Content management strategy mainly consists of defining the following:

- Evaluation and finalization of suitable CMS
- Optimizing content flows including content authoring and content publishing workflow
- Assigning suitable permissions for content owners, content reviewers, content approvers, and content administrators
- Defining tags, metadata, and controlled vocabulary and use it with relevant content to easily discover information
- Content governance
- Content delivery optimization including content caching, content update frequency, etc.
- Defining metrics to evaluate content effectiveness
- Defining omnichannel content design
- Defining content migration strategy wherever required
- Identification and definition of self-service content
- Defining content standards
- Defining content archival and retention plan
- Defining content services

We will look at portal content management in Chapter 7.

Portal Infrastructure Architecture View

This view closely aligns with deployment view. Infrastructure architecture provides greater details related to hardware specifications, interactions among server components, etc. A sample portal infrastructure architecture is shown in Figure 4.10.

As we can see, the infrastructure architecture depicts the following details:

1. All infrastructure elements of the solution including the web server, application server, database server, etc.
2. The hardware specifications of each of the servers
3. The port and protocol access details
4. Internal and external access details
5. Firewall and load-balancer details
6. Interface details

Portal Architecture Definition

Having looked at the portal capabilities, architecture views, sample solution components, sample use cases, now let us have a deep dive into the process of defining a portal architecture. This activity is usually carried out in the architecture phase.

NOTE: The phases detailed in this section are focused mainly on portal technical architecture and hence we will detail such activities. In Chapter 19 we will look at the phases from overall end-to-end program standpoint.

Establishing Portal Architecture

Portal architecture should comprehend all the factors we discussed in the architecture views.

A comprehensive portal architecture definition process is represented in Figure 4.11. This process is typically adopted in large-scale portal engagements.

At a higher level, there are three main phases in the portal architecture definition process:

1. *Portal strategy definition phase*: In this phase we consult all the business and organization stakeholder and reviews. We also do a detailed requirements elaboration, capability assessment, and current state analysis in this phase.
2. *Portal technology assessment*: This is the main phase wherein we define and establish a comprehensive portal architecture from all dimensions such as security, solution, performance, data, integration, and UX. We will also do a feasibility assessment and trade-off analysis in this phase.
3. *Portal roadmap*: We finalize the architecture and recommendations and come up with a detailed project plan for portal implementation.

Let us look at the high-level steps in each of the phases in the following. We have also detailed these activities in the following sections.

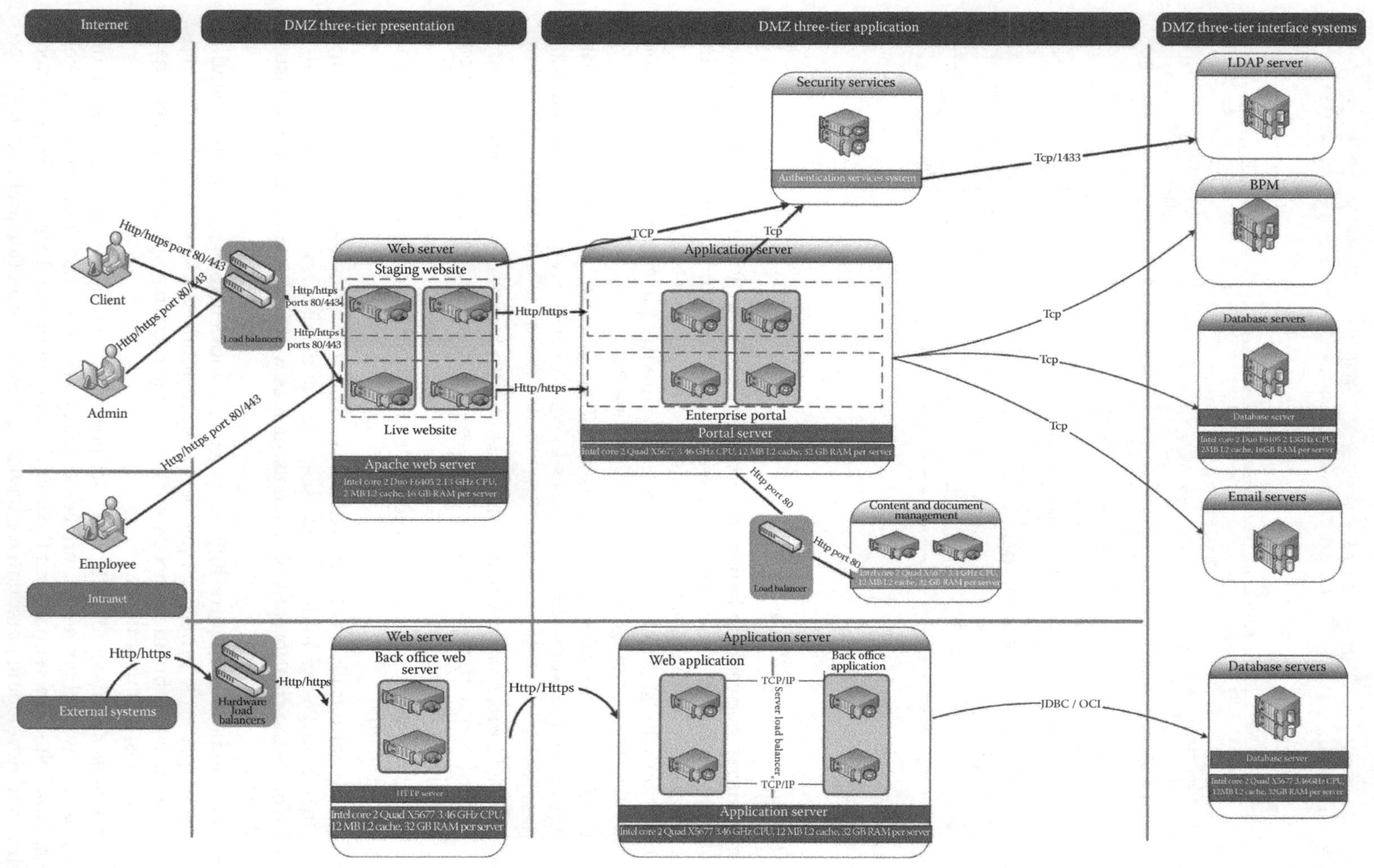

FIGURE 4.10
Sample portal infrastructure view.

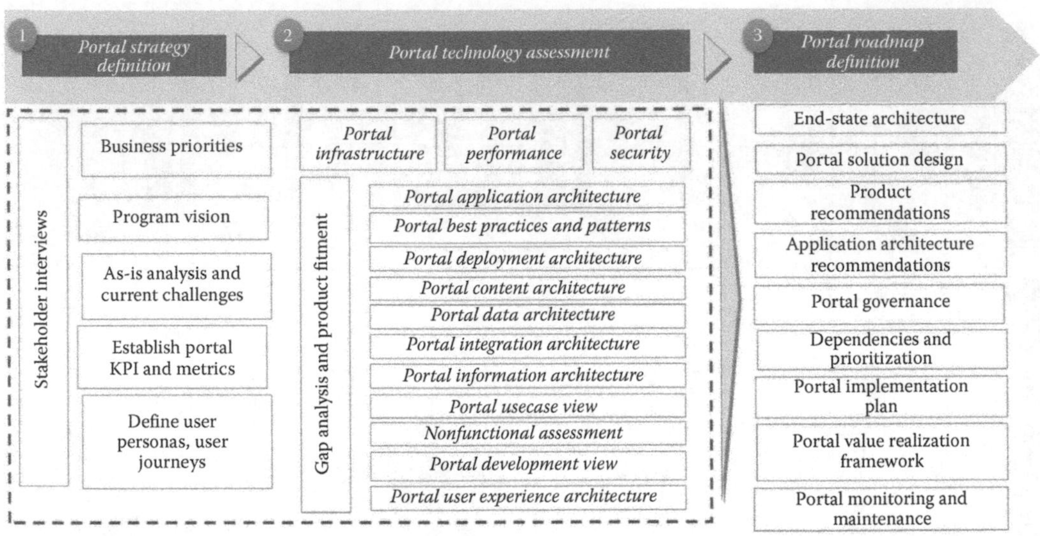

FIGURE 4.11
Portal architecture definition process.

Portal Strategy Definition Phase

- *Requirements elaboration*: Gather the requirements from various business stakeholders to get all dimensions and viewpoints of the requirements. Complex portal programs often have ambiguously defined requirements that need continuous interaction with stakeholders to create structured requirements documentation. The following are the techniques usually followed:
  - *Conduct business workshops*: This is an effective technique wherein we create high-level mockups and prototypes to walk over the requirements and business cases.
  - *Stakeholder interviews*: Conduct interviews with business team, security team, and infrastructure team to get complete understanding of functional and nonfunctional requirements.
  - Conduct focus group discussion to clarify questions and other aspects of requirements.
  - Create various views of requirements such as use case view, process view, and story board view and use case scenarios and business scenarios. This also involves the creation of UX elements such as wireframe, mockups, and visual design.
  - For portals that require high engagement with customers, we also Identify users' patterns, processes, journeys, expectations, and paths and determine customer and business needs and create user journeys built from personas, scenarios, and user flows.
- *User persona definition*: Identify key user personas and model their key user journeys along with their needs, preferences, key activities they perform, priorities, etc. This helps in personalizing the portal user experience. This also helps in modeling and developing personalized navigation and information architecture based

on user personas. Once we identify user personas, we can group them based on similarities in their journeys, priorities, access controls, etc., and this helps us to define the application roles and necessary permissions for those roles through user segmentation and grouping.

- *Prioritize requirements*: Once the complete requirements are compiled, they are prioritized based on the intended business value, implementation complexity, and time to market. The prioritized list is signed-off with all concerned stakeholders.
- *As-is architecture analysis*: This includes detailed analysis of existing technology stack, infrastructure components, business processes, and understanding the current challenges and gaps:
  - *Existing technology stack and architecture analysis*: The current-state architecture will be analyzed to check for reusability opportunities.
  - Gaps analysis is conducted to understand the gaps between current state and desired state. Gaps could be in functionality, scalability, performance, security, and also in various other dimensions.
  - Pain points across stages of the customer experience life cycle that impact each persona.
  - *Process analysis*: The process analysis is conducted for key processes specifically for portals, social, mobile, and related web technologies.
  - *Capability assessment*: We also check the maturity of the existing organization processes to support and sustain portal program. This includes both business capability assessment and technology capability assessment. Any capability gaps identified will be addressed in subsequent phases.
- *Business benefits analysis*: We will articulate the key success criteria for the portal program:
  - Define success metrics from the following dimensions:
    - Business goals such as expected growth rate, geospecific expansions, anticipated surge in user traffic, revenue increment targets, conversion rates, etc.
    - Increased online traffic by making portal engaging and retain more customers
    - Improved customer feedback and increased satisfaction index
    - Reduction in customer service requests and support calls due to enhanced self-service features offered by portal
    - Reduced time to market due to agile processes and prebuilt portal components
    - High availability and scalability
    - Performance goals such as page response times and process and transaction completion time
    - Reduced maintenance cost
    - Decreased cost for implementing enhancements and on boarding new functionality
  - *Benefits and ROI analysis*: The benefits–investment analysis provides order of magnitude budgets for initiatives identified by the capabilities, technology,

user experience, vendor relationship management (VRM), and organizational design project teams.

- Establish goals for next-generation portal in terms of performance, scalability, usability, etc.
- *Vision definition*: We create the program vision aligned to business and organization vision. This also includes the channel vision, product vision, and program vision.

Portal Technology Assessment Phase

The main activities in this phase are elaborated here:

- *Gap analysis and product fitment*: This involves technology capability assessment to analyze the organizational capabilities and determine strengths and weaknesses in the organization's ability to support existing and planned programs and operational readiness for executing and managing the program. The input to this exercise is the outcome from capabilities gap analysis and the process analysis. Opportunities for improving operation efficiency through process optimization, agility, and automation will also be analyzed.
- *Portal architecture definition*: This is the key activity that involves defining the portal solution architecture from various dimensions. The main architecture views and contributing factors for this step are given below. We have already seen the samples of various architecture views in previous sections.
  - *Technology evaluation*: Evaluate and benchmark all relevant and competing technologies for the best product and technology fit. We will also do "build vs. buy" decision analysis. Open-source alternatives will also be explored before finalizing a custom build decision.
  - *Portal architecture principals and patterns*: The main architecture principles that align to the long-term portal strategy will be created. These architecture principles form the guiding rules for solution. A list of main portal architecture principles is given in later sections.
  - *Technology workshop*: A detailed walkthrough of key architecture decisions and architecture views will be conducted with technology stakeholders of the organization to solicit the feedback and to ensure that architecture artifacts are aligned with their expected goals.
  - *Portal integration architecture*: This involves details of integrating type, integration method, ports, and protocol and development of portal interface specification document.
  - *Portal application architecture*: An end-to-end application architecture will be defined depicting all the layers and solution components.
  - *Portal data architecture*: An end-to-end data architecture showing the data flow, data model is created. A sample portal data architecture was shown in earlier sections.
  - *Portal deployment architecture*: This depicts the infrastructure components used for deployment in various environments.

  - *Portal security architecture*: This depicts all security aspects for the portal such as authentication, SSO, authorization, etc. A sample portal security architecture is shown in earlier sections.
  - *Portal development view*: This provides various elements of portal development environment such as development check list, continuous integration process, usage of IDE for development, source control plan, etc.
  - *Portal use case view*: This provides the key use case scenarios and the mapping of functionality to the portal solution components.
  - During this phase we will also document all key portal architecture decisions, assumptions, constraints, and risks along with mitigation plan.
  - *Define guidelines and checklists*: Comprehensive portal checklists, guidelines, and best practices will be used for design, development, testing, and deployment to ensure that it aligns with the overall architecture principals.
  - Portal UX architecture will be refined to fine-tune the presentation components, AJAX tool kits, visual style guide, UX prototypes, mobile architecture, and other elements. Site navigation, information architecture, and workflows will also be analyzed during this step.
  - *Nonfunctional requirement assessment*: This involves careful analysis of NFR requirements and ensuring that the designed infrastructure architecture and application architecture satisfies the specified NFR requirements. Key NFR requirements such as performance, scalability, availability, security, and accessibility are given main focus along with their testing strategy.
- Portal nonfunctional requirements obtained in earlier phases will be refined and finalized based on stakeholder feedback and our technology assessment.
- *Portal infrastructure architecture*: Based on the application SLAs, scalability, performance, and availability requirements; a detailed capacity planning; and sizing will be carried out to design the optimal portal infrastructure.

Portal Roadmap Definition Phase

In this phase we will mainly look at defining the long-term implementation plan for portal program. This phase also documents the evolution of portal to align with business vision. It consists of the following elements:

- Core roadmap elements:
  - *Core foundation platform capabilities*: This includes the main functionality that would go into the core platform release
  - *Capabilities road map*: Based on the desired capabilities and business priorities, the roadmap provides recommended capabilities, execution sequence, and precedent activities (e.g., technology updates)
  - *Governance and metrics*: Process governance provides a framework for overall and continuous improvement of the portal program. Metrics, which is an integral part of governance, help in tracking the effectiveness and success of the program
- *End-state architecture*: We will finalize all the portal architecture views and present the end-state architecture to stakeholders for sign-off

- *Solution detailed design*: Architecture assessment phase will lead to the detailed design phase wherein detailed design of the portal components will be created. The designs include portal page design, URL design, component design, integration design, and other related activities. The structure of a sample portal design document is below
  - Portal detailed design
  - Portal logical architecture
  - Proof of concepts
    - PoC1
    - PoC2
  - Solution design patterns and best practices
  - Portal product evaluation and recommendation
  - Technology evaluation and recommendation
  - Portal application design
    - Theme design
      - Header design
      - Footer design
      - Skin design
    - Portlet design
      - Portlet 1
      - Portlet 2
    - Portal performance
      - Caching design
      - Asset and content caching
      - Services optimization
    - Friendly URL design
    - SEO design
    - Web analytics design
    - Portal metadata design
      - Tags and metadata
      - Controlled vocabulary
    - Personalization design
    - Security design
      - Authentication
      - Authorization
      - Role-based access
      - Role-responsibility matrix
      - Permission model
      - Web SSO design
      - Federated SSO design

- Localization design
- Portal page design
  - Template design
  - Page hierarchy design
- Common libraries
  - Logging
  - Auditing
  - Exception handling
  - Help design
  - Configuration handlers
  - File parsers
  - Encryption utilities
  - Email client
- Integration design
  - Services design
  - Integration portlets
  - ESB integration
  - Legacy integration design
- Data design
  - Portal data model
  - Custom database design
  - Database backup
  - Database synchronization jobs
- Content design
  - Content templates
  - Content publishing process
  - Content translation
  - Content workflows
- Business process modeling
  - Rules design
- Workflow design
- Search design
  - Indexing and crawling enterprise data sources
  - Search engine integration
- Portal site design
  - Virtual portal design
  - Site taxonomy design
- Information architecture design
  - Navigation design

  - UX design
    - Widget design
    - AJAX toolkit evaluation
    - Third party plugin integration
  - NFR design
    - Scalability
    - Availability
    - Performance
  - Traceability matrix
    - Requirements—design matrix
- *Product recommendations*: The results of product and technology evaluations are shared with relevant stakeholders. The recommended products and technologies will be included in the solution architecture.
- *Application architecture recommendations*: The finalized list of architecture recommendations and principals are provided to the stakeholders. It will also be suggested to use these architecture principles for other programs within the organization to achieve uniform and smoother integrations.
- *Portal project planning*: A detailed project plan consisting of the following are provided:
  - Dependencies and roadmap
  - Phased planning
  - Release and phase-wise prioritization
  - Scope for automation and productivity improvements
  - Continuous improvement planning
  - Portal implementation plan
- *Portal value realization framework*: The framework depicts the business value realized with each phase and helps in better appreciation of ROI on portal program. We have discussed this framework in earlier chapters.
- *Portal monitoring and maintenance*: The maintenance processes and monitoring infrastructure and KPIs for the portal solution is defined.
- *Portal governance definition*: Clear roles and responsibilities for portal activities and structured processes for portal activities are established.

Portal Architecture Review

In the previous section we saw the detailed steps involved in portal architecture definition process. Sometimes we may need to do an analysis or review of existing portals and improve their efficiency. This will be a top-down approach wherein we will be analyzing the existing portal program and its ecosystem components. In this section we will look at the high level steps in portal architecture review.

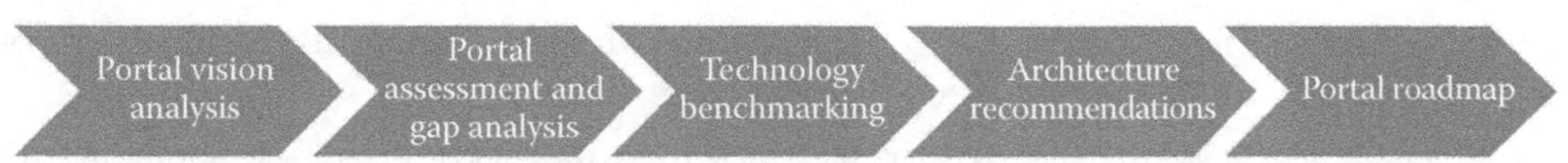

FIGURE 4.12
Portal architecture review process.

The high level steps in portal architecture review are depicted in Figure 4.12.

- *Portal vision analysis*: Understanding the vision of the overall portal program. This helps in aligning the portal strategy, portal KPIs, execution plan, and roadmap to realize the vision; it also helps in identifying the critical gaps in existing portal. For instance, if the vision of an external B2C retail portal is to "provide a unified single-stop experience to discover the products faster and transact easier," then we need to identify the gaps and metrics according to this vision.
- *Portal assessment and gap analysis*: This is the crucial step in the architecture review process. We need to analyze the existing portal program from various dimensions. We will conduct multiple stakeholder interviews and online/offline user surveys to understand overall effectiveness and end-user satisfaction. Though the assessment varies based on technology complexity, the main elements of this assessment phase is given in the following:
  - *Technology capability assessment*: We will analyze the portal technology maturity.
  - *Portal strategy assessment*: We will assess if the existing portal platform is aligned with long-term business vision. We will also review the portal application views to analyze how the platform is architected to implement the solution.
  - *Portal KPIs and metrics review*: The portal KPIs and metrics are analyzed to check if they effectively measure the success criteria and provide a good indication of user satisfaction and ROI.
  - *Information architecture assessment*: We will have a closer look at the content organization, site hierarchy, metadata strategy, navigation model, and the related metrics to understand the ease and effectiveness of information discoverability.
  - *Content strategy assessment*: This involves understanding the ease with which content can be authored and published and the effectiveness of content related to branding and information messaging. We will check if the content aligns with information architecture goals and analyze key content-related metrics.
  - *Performance assessment*: The main performance metrics such as load times and response times will be measured.
  - *NFR assessment*: Key NFRs such as scalability, availability, security, and accessibility will be tested with user loads.
  - *Portal UX assessment*: Overall user experience of the end user will be measured through usability testing. We will also check the adopted UX standards, multichannel features, and accessibility features.

  - *Portal governance assessment*: The processes around the portal solution will be examined to understand redundancy, gaps, etc.
- *Technology benchmarking*: We will benchmark the main technology elements against competitors and industry standards. The main technology elements that would be considered for benchmarking are
  - Portal performance
  - Content strategy
  - Information architecture
  - Portal site usability
- *Architecture recommendations*: Based on the gap analysis and benchmarking, we will provide the portal architecture recommendations that can be used to fill the gaps and make the portal strategy more effective. For each of the categories we saw in the assessment and gap analysis category, we will provide recommendations. Few sample architecture recommendations for each of the categories is given in Table 4.2.
- *Portal roadmap*: Based on the architecture recommendations, we will define the portal roadmap, which is aligned with the program vision.

Deep Dive into Key Portal Architecture Activities

Let us look into the architecture activities involved in the portal architecture process in detail. This gives us an idea for comprehensive portal architecture planning and finalizing end-state architecture. The core architecture activities are depicted in Figure 4.13.

We will look at the details of these activities Table 4.3.

Portal Design Considerations

The main portal design considerations are as follows:

- *Security and SSO*: Portals should leverage on inbuilt features or extensions to implement enterprise-wide SSO. Wherever required, we also need to implement federated SSO for integration with external applications.
- *Standards-based design and development*: All component design and implementation should be based on industry standards such as JSR 168 and JSR 286 portlet standard to build responsive portlets and UI standards should be based on HTML5 and other standards.
- *Services-based integration*: As integration is one of the principal motivations for the consolidated portal, it needs to be designed so as to be extensible and scalable while meeting the performance SLAs. Services-based integration approach will be prioritized over other forms of integration wherever possible, owing to the flexibility offered by this approach. This includes integration with data access services, business services, reporting system services, and others. Service-based integration includes SOAP over HTTP(S) and REST.
- *Performance, availability, and scalability*: Performance should be thought through right from the component design stage till performance-testing stage. In addition

TABLE 4.2

Sample Portal Architecture Recommendations

Category	Current Gaps and Assessment Details	Architecture Recommendation
Technology capability	Multiple technologies	Reassess and reevaluate the current technology stack
	Usage of a lot of proprietary features	Provide list of contemporary and forward-looking, standards-based products and technologies
	Tightly coupled layers and integrations	Build the platform using open-standards and service-oriented architecture for loosely coupled integrations
Portal strategy assessment	Portals built in silos	Consolidate portals to provide a unified experience
	Portal adoption challenges	
Portal KPIs and metrics review	Portal KPIs are not effectively tracking portal usage	Provide list of KPIs and portal metrics that aligns with the portal vision
Information architecture assessment	Information is difficult to find	Fine tune metadata strategy to improve content and search effectiveness
	Search is slow and ineffective	Position search as the main information discovery tool
		Provide personalized navigation features that help the user find information easily through personalized search, quick links, popular downloads, relevant recommendations, etc.
Content strategy assessment	Most of the portal content is outdated	Refine the content freshness strategy
	Content flows are complex	Automate content workflows and reduce the steps in content publishing
	Finding relevant content is difficult	Refine content metadata to improve relevancy of search results
NFR assessment	Platform not scaling for higher demands	Reassess the infrastructure and sizing
	Frequent production outages	Perform infrastructure testing to identify infrastructure gaps
	Multiple security-related issues	Build a robust real-time monitoring infrastructure
		Perform continuous security testing
Portal UX assessment	Challenges in accessing the portal site on mobile devices	Perform compatibility and multidevice testing and adopted responsive design
	Usability issues	Perform usability and alpha–beta testing to identify and fix the gaps
Portal governance assessment	No proper governance model	Establish a robust portal governance with clearly defined roles and responsibilities

to performance-based design, other performance optimization techniques will be adopted, which include the following:

- Layer-wise caching using caching framework for frequently used look-up/controlled list values and service response with appropriate cache TTL.
- Employing client-side AJAX rendering wherever applicable to improve the perceived page render time.
- The solution will also be tested iteratively to ensure that the desired performance SLA is met.
- Scalability can be achieved by using appropriate infrastructure and hardware.
- Incorporation of governance model to proactively check the heartbeat of the systems (portal and other applications) ensures system availability and uptime.
- Providing a real-time application monitoring system to check the page load time across geographies and automatic notification in the case of performance threshold violation.

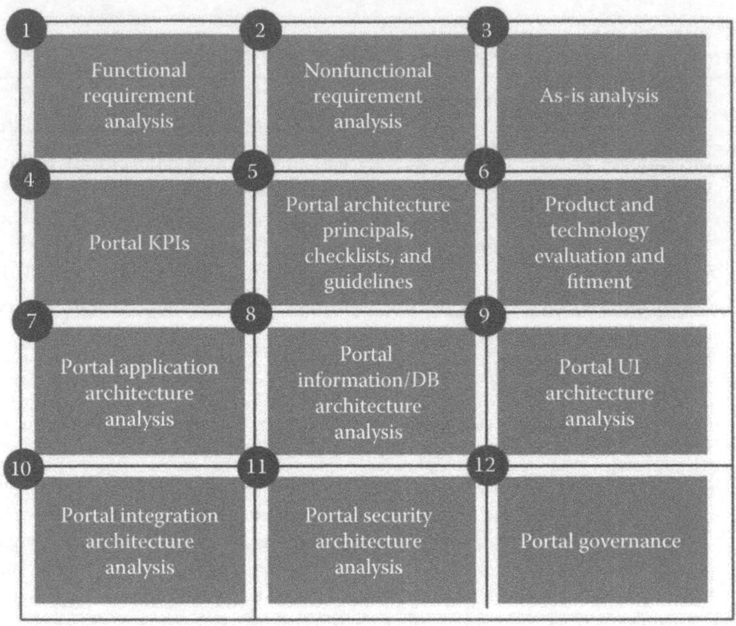

FIGURE 4.13
Portal architecture activities.

- Implementing and monitoring the key performance metrics like page load times and search result time and ensuring that they consistently meet the specified SLAs. Devise performance load test scenarios (peak load testing, endurance testing, and stress testing) to ensure that performance and scalability SLAs are satisfied during performance testing phase.

- *Reusability and automation*: Reusing the existing components and frameworks will profoundly contribute to developer productivity, faster time to market, and increase in the overall quality. Hence, based on the given business requirements, the following components are marked for reuse partially or completely:
  - Leveraging out-of-the-box portlets of the portal product
  - Development of social and collaboration features including blogs, forums, wikis, personalization features, web analytics support, message bus feature, localization support, and CMS. We need to explore the product capabilities and open source plugins and adaptors to implement these features

Portal Architecture Best Practices

We have discussed about portal architecture best practices being one of the main steps in defining portal architecture. The following are the main portal-related architecture best practices that needs to be considered while designing the portal solution:

- *Best of breed technology selection through technology evaluation*: The technology stack needs to be finalized after carefully evaluating them against the requirements. We have discussed technology evaluation frameworks and processes in earlier chapters.

TABLE 4.3

Portal Architecture Activity Details

Stage	Portal Activities
Functional requirement analysis	Compilation of portal use case scenarios, user journeys, and expected functionality in portal platform
	Create requirement-portal solution component mapping
	Identify the inbuilt portal product features that can be leveraged and the ones that need to be custom built
Nonfunctional requirement analysis	Analyze requirements for portal performance, scalability, availability, security, usability, accessibility, compatibility, etc.
As-is analysis	Current state technology stack analysis
	Existing business process analysis
	Gap and pain point analysis
	Capability analysis
Portal KPIs	Mapping business goals into portal KPIs
	Definition of portal KPIs for nonfunctional requirements such as scalability, availability, and performance
Portal architecture principals, checklists, and guidelines	Identify key portal architecture goals and principles based on industry best practices
	Identify the best practices and design checklist and guidelines
	Benchmark the metrics and architecture principles with competitor and industry standards
Portal and technology evaluation and fitment	Portal product evaluation and fitment analysis
	Technology evaluation and fitment analysis
	Identification of open source plugins, portlets, and libraries for the solution
	Architecture recommendations based on gap analysis
Portal application architecture analysis	Portal framework design and analysis
	Portlet design guidelines
	Modularity and reuse analysis for portlet and other portal components
Portal information/DB architecture analysis	Portal data model analysis
	Portal data integration design
Portal UI architecture analysis	Selection of UX framework
	Selection of AJAX toolkit
	Design of responsive and interactive design
	Navigation and user flow design
	Information architecture design
	Site taxonomy design
	SEO and web analytics design
	Establishing of UX standards such as HTML standard and accessibility standard
	Interaction and multidevice design
Portal integration architecture analysis	Service-oriented integration design
	Integration design and guidelines
	Establishing integration best practices
	Analysis of integration elements within portal platform
	Identification of custom development of portal extensions, plugins, and adaptors required for integration

(Continued)

TABLE 4.3 (*Contiunued*)

Portal Architecture Activity Details

Stage	Portal Activities
	Evaluation and benchmarking of integration options and finalizing the optimal integration method
Portal security architecture analysis	Portal security design guidelines definition
	Designing security coding and testing checklist
Portal governance	Establishing well-defined and structured process for portal release, deployment, and maintenance.
	Creating well-defined role–responsibility matrix
	Intuitive portal administration, workflow administration, and search administration interface

- *Maximum leverage of existing investment*: Wherever possible, current products and technologies should be leveraged for the new portal solution. This includes
  - Service-enabling existing legacy applications instead of retiring them
  - Reusing existing infrastructure for intranet applications that has relatively lesser traffic
- *Portal generic best practices*: The key architecture best practices in the portal domain are as follows:
  - Open- and standards-based technology and integrations. This includes using JSR standard portlets such as JSR 168 and JSR 286.
  - Leverage inbuilt portlets and out-of-the-box components provided by the portal product to the maximum extent.
  - Layered architecture using MVC pattern. This provides a clear layer-wise separation of components into various layers with distinct responsibility. MVC enables loose coupling, separation of concerns, and flexibility to change the components in each layer independently.
  - Modular and extensible component design. Each of the solution components will be designed so that it can be extended for future needs and reusable.
  - Leveraging open-source technologies wherever applicable.
  - Performance-based design.
  - Continuous build and integration approach for execution.
  - Solution should support loose coupling through layered architecture with modular and extensible design. Portal extensions and plugins can be leveraged for extensible design.
  - Portal pages and content should be based on reusable template architecture.
- *Future proof solution*: The solution should be developed using a "framework" approach wherein each the functionalities and components are designed to be extensible and reusable for future needs. This will be implemented by exposing services for the key functionality.
- *Multidevice support*: Responsive design should be adopted to support multiple devices and browsers.

- *Services-oriented integration*: All major integrations should be done via services. REST services should be preferred over SOAP.
- *User-focused design*: The portal design should keep end user in mind. It should provide an interactive and responsive user experience with intuitive functionality using lightweight, client-side components.
- *Performance-based design*: Various performance tuning techniques like the usage of client-side widgets, minification and merging, hibernate caching, etc., should be employed to improve page, transaction, and database performance.

Portal Architecture Principles

Table 4.4 is the list of key portal architecture principles that can be leveraged to realize business goals. The list maps the business goals to portal solution design elements.

TABLE 4.4

Business Goals and Portal Architecture Principles

Business Goals	Portal Solution Design Considerations
Business continuity (to ensure continuous availability of portal systems and services)	• Portal solution should use disaster recovery environment with mirror replica of the primary environment • Ensure that there are no single points of failures by using clustered architecture in portal solution • Portal infrastructure should have sufficient redundancies to sustain hardware failures, natural disasters, network failure, etc. • Portal infrastructure should factor for recoverability and maintainability
Compliance (to ensure compliance with organizations standards, policies, and applicable laws)	• The architecture standards should be in full compliance with organization standards, regulatory requirements and best practices • Portal solution should only use standard components such as JSR portlets and use standards-based integration
Best practices design (align with industry best practices)	• Portal solution should incorporate industry best practices in design, development, and testing. We will be discussing these best practices in detail in Chapter 15
Prevention of vendor lock-in (try to minimize proprietary technology)	• Portal solution should be based on open standards that will enhance interoperability, portability, and integration with diverse technologies • Service-based integration should be used to enable legacy applications to interoperate • Middleware to be used to decouple applications from specific software solutions
Ease of use (the interface should be easy to use for end customer)	• Portal UX should be designed by keeping end user in focus • Portal should provide intuitive navigation and information architecture • Portal should provide friendlier and easier information discoverable features using smart search • Portal interface should provide multichannel capabilities for omnichannel experience

Portal Road Map Strategy

As defining long-term portal strategy and roadmap is another crucial element of the portal architecture process, it is elaborated in more detail in this section.

During portal digital transformation journey we do various current-state analysis and assessment to understand existing capabilities and define a portal roadmap that aligns to their business goals. Portal roadmap normally aims to balance the business short-term needs and long-term vision. Portal roadmap provides phase-wise execution plan for rolling out portal features and functionality base on business priorities.

Figure 4.14 depicts portal roadmap phases for a B2C external portal.

Various activities and deliverables in these roadmap stages are described here.

Information Portal

- Basic portal infrastructure setup without any personalization and information aggregation
- This will be the first step in converting an existing static content into personalized dynamic delivery platform
- Portal predominantly renders static content
- Static web content from various organizations and departments will be aggregated with little or no transformation
- Most suitable for static content websites and intranet sites

Application Portal

- Functionality integration and integration of key enterprise applications
- SSO feature for enterprise applications

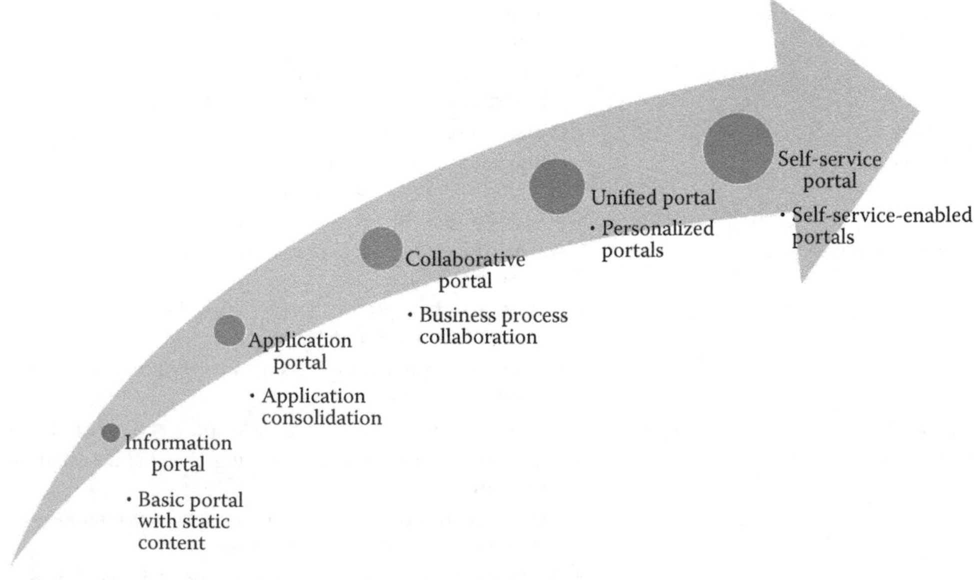

FIGURE 4.14
Portal roadmap for B2C portal.

- Consolidation of services
- Basic content management features
- Basic collaborative features such as chat
- This would be the next step in consolidating internal applications and services to move toward a truly dynamic delivery platform

Collaborative Portal

- Implementation of collaboration features such as blogs, wikis, communities, chat, file sharing, feeds, calendar, etc.
- Usage of responsive and interactive user interface such as widgets and responsive web design
- Implementation of portal personalization features and enabling of role-based functionality access
- Suitable for intranet and extranet collaboration sites
- Development of portal-based knowledge management
- Highly matured content management features

Unified Portal

- Implementation of enterprise-wide search for unified search experience
- Creation of unified portal platform for single-stop shop experience
- Leveraging web analytics to understand user behavior patterns and site tracking and monitoring
- Multichannel and multidevice enablement
- Portal as service-oriented platform for integrations
- Implementation of dashboard and unified reporting features

Self-Service Portal

- Implementation of various self-service features such as knowledge management and contextual and personalized search is done
- Business process automation, business process management, and workflow implementation is used in portal platform
- Proactive monitoring of user activities through analytics and site performance through monitoring agents
- Implementation of intuitive information architecture and site navigation for better information discoverability
- Simple and easy-to-use interface for administrators and business community to control the site features and carry out business campaigns
- Used for increased productivity, satisfaction, and to achieve self-sufficiency
- Continuous site improvement based on portal KPIs, metrics, and analytics reports

Architecture Concepts for Building Portal Solutions

We have so far seen various architecture concepts related to portal. Let us now look at application of architecture concepts and principles for two popular scenarios. This provides insights into few practical applications of the architecture concepts and best practices.

Architecture Concepts of Self-Service Portal

The principal goal of a self-service portal is to enable the end users to discover the relevant information quickly and to equip them with suitable tools, services, and processes to perform their key activities easily and efficiently.

Aligning with these goals, we will look at the main features of a self-service portal:

Eight essential features of self-service portals are given in Figure 4.15. The key technology enablers for implementing the self-service vision are information aggregation, search, and content. Let us look at the details of implementing eight self-service features through these three dimensions in Table 4.5.

Architecting Portal Using Open Source Technologies

Developing portal through open-source technologies is essential for organizations that are keen to minimize overall cost while adhering to industry standards and best practices. Fortunately, most of the portal-use cases can be implemented through open-source technologies. Let us look at a sample portal built using open source technologies. A reference open-source based portal is depicted in Figure 4.16.

NOTE:

- This is a sample portal representation based on open source technologies. All products and frameworks depicted in this section are available as open source at the time of writing this book.

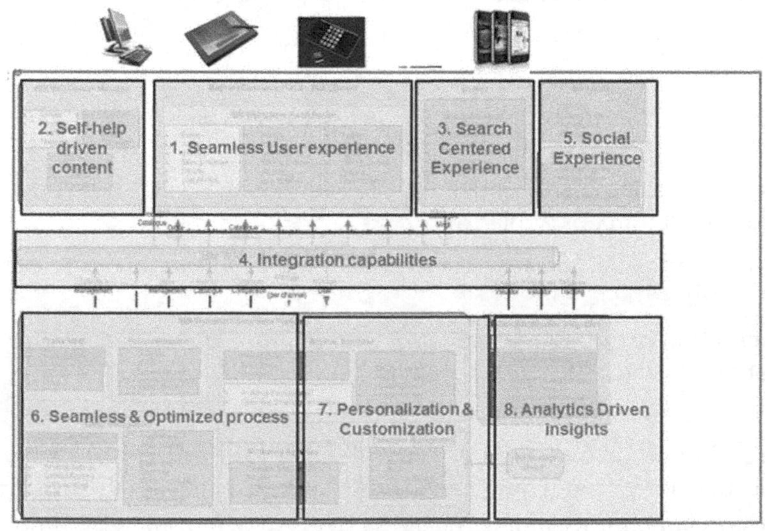

FIGURE 4.15
Features of self-service portal.

TABLE 4.5
Architecture Concepts of Self-Service Portal

Self-Service Portal Feature	Portal	Search	Content
Improve user experience	• Manage multiple branding/cobranding by templating, portal themes, and virtual portals • Provide highly personalized experience based on user preferences and behavior patterns • Use rich media, interface, Web 2.0, etc. • Enable multichannel access leveraging on built-in themes and portlets • Build intuitive portal page layouts and friendlier navigation aids • Allow user to customize page layout and rearrange portlets • Provide configurable portlets and widgets • Allow users to bookmark pages and save search results	• Leverage search engine that provides out-of-the-box integration with portal • Position search as the key tool for information discovery • Provide personalized search • Provide saved search results • Provide faceted browsing	• Define a clear strategy for improving freshness and relevance of the content • Tag content with relevant metadata to improve its discoverability • Provide immersive and engaging content
Process optimization and automation	• Automate user life cycle and process using built-in workflow engines and schedulers • Service enable portlets • Optimize process steps including the number of clicks and steps for process completion, providing alternative one-click process, process consolidation, etc. • Make generic utility portlets easily configurable for BU or customer channels	• Leverage search features such as spell-correction, auto-suggestion, guided navigation, synonym support, faceted browsing to improve the search process	• Enhance core web content manager capabilities such as templates, workflows, etc., for enabling a new experience • Enhance existing content tagging, metadata, and taxonomy framework for new customer channels for rapid integration and search • Attempt to increase reuse by designing generic authoring templates • Simplify redundant tasks like tagging, which are key drivers for personalization by automation • Simplify authoring for frequent items using batch updates and automation
Analytics and integrations	• Leverage built-in web analytics to identify, continuously monitor, and improve the user experience • Leverage built-in integration capabilities of portal for optimized integrations	• Track the most popular search terms and cache its search results • Search-enable enterprise resources and index wide variety of enterprise content	• Enhance existing integration points to support content related to new products specific to new customer channels • Track the most popular content and position it in the most prominent place
Self-help and self-service features	• Provide self-help features such as FAQ, what's this, self-approval, password reset, solution recommendations, and popular search results	• Improve search effectiveness to drive the self-service	• Provide effective content for FAQ and contextual help scenarios

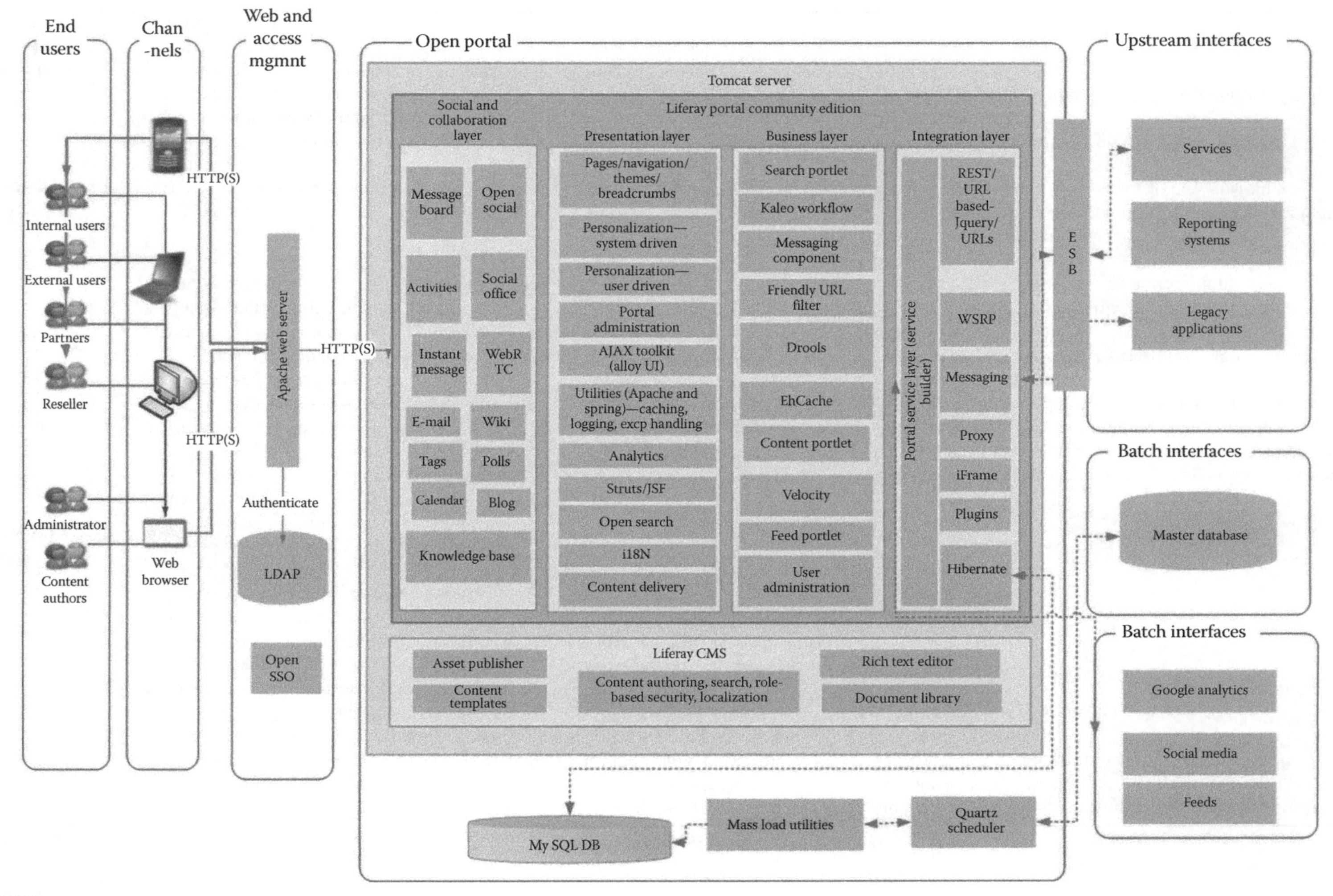

FIGURE 4.16
Open-source portal.

TABLE 4.6

Solution Components of Open-Source Portal

System/Layer	Functionality	Open Source Component
Portal software	Core portal features	Liferay portal community edition 6.2
CMS software	Content management features	Liferay CMS with document library feature or Alfresco
Presentation layer	Pages, layouts, templates, themes, skins, personalization, administration, localization, content delivery	Inbuilt Liferay features and out-of-the-box portlets (Uses Velocity and FreeMarker Templates for page layout)
	AJAX toolkit	AlloyUI AngularJS, ExtJS, or jQuery
Social and collaboration	Generic collaboration features	Integration with OpenSocial or Inbuilt support for Social Office
	Blogs, wikis, message boards, e-mails, shared calendars, polls, knowledge base, and audio chat	Inbuilt Liferay features and out-of-the-box portlets such as blog portlet, wiki portlet, shared calender portlet and various collaboration suite features
	Web conferencing and video chat Screen sharing and cobrowsing	Integration with WebRTC or Integration with Apache Open Conferencing
Security	Authentication and authorization	Inbuilt permission model and out-of-the-box access-based control
	SSO	Integration with OpenSSO
	Federated SSO	Leverage support for SAML token-based federated SSO
Business layer	Workflow engine	Inbuilt support for Kaleo engine
	Rules engine	Drools rules engine
	Caching	Ehcache framework
	Template design	Velocity template or FreeMarker templates
	Enterprise search	Integration with OpenSearch or leveraging inbuilt support for Lucene or integration with Apache Solr
	Database access/ORM	Hibernate with Spring integration or inbuilt Service Builder Framework
Integration layer	Services-based integration	Leverage Apache Axis web service runtime
	Feed integration	Leverage out-of-the-box feed portlet
	WSRP-based integration	Leverage inbuilt WSRP support
	Web analytics	Leverage inbuilt support for Google Analytics
Infrastructure components	Session management, hot deployment, logging, audit trail, and virtual hosting, web server and application server deployment	Leverage inbuilt features and out-of-the-box portlets Apache web server and Tomcat server and MySQL database used for portal deployment. Portal can be deployed on LInux OS

In the aforementioned portal logical architecture, various open source components and frameworks are used to realize the required portal features and functionality. Table 4.6 provides the details of the open source components used in the open source portal solution.

Summary

- This chapter provides various portal architecture concepts such as architecture views, portal architecture definition, portal architecture review, architecture best practices, and sample reference architecture.
- A detailed functional capability of portal is provided in the chapter. It consists of components from various layers such as presentation layer, security layer, content layer, search layer, utilities layer, collaboration layer, administration layer, data layer, business layer and integration layer, and infrastructure layer.
- A sample portal capability to solution mapping matrix is discussed in the chapter.
- Portal architecture views include application architecture view, deployment view, security view, infrastructure view, deployment view, development view, use case view, information architecture view, UX view, content view, and component view.
- Portal application architecture view provides end-to-end logical architecture for portal solution components.
- Portal component view provides various portal components in the overall solution.
- Portal development view provides development components of the solution.
- Portal deployment architecture view provides deployment servers for the portal solution.
- Portal infrastructure architecture view provides various infrastructure components involved in the portal solution across all environments.
- Portal security view provides various portal security scenarios like authentication, SSO, authorization, etc.
- Portal use case view provides main use cases scenarios and mapping of portal solution components for implementing the use cases.
- Portal content architecture view provides portal content scenarios and content strategy.
- Portal information architecture view provides portal navigation model, site and content categorization, and other information architecture–related aspects.
- *Portal architecture definition mainly consists of three phases*: portal strategy definition, portal technology assessment, and portal roadmap definition.
- Portal strategy definition phase consist of as-is analysis, defining portal KPIs, prioritizing requirements, defining program vision and user personas.
- Portal technology assessment phase consist of defining various architecture views, product and technology evaluation, and defining portal principles and best practices.
- Portal roadmap definition phase consist of providing implementation roadmap, detail design, technology and product evaluation, finalizing end-state architecture,

defining portal governance model, portal value realization framework, and defining portal monitoring and maintenance infrastructure.

- Portal architecture review consists of portal vision analysis, portal assessment and gap analysis, technology benchmarking, architecture recommendations, and portal roadmap.
- A detailed discussion of portal best practices and portal architecture principles is defined.
- A sample portal roadmap for B2C portals evolving from an information portal to application portal to collaborative portal to unified portal to self-service portal is discussed.
- Sample portal architecture for self-service portal and open source portal is detailed in the chapter.

5

Developing Portals

In this chapter we will look at the basic portal concepts, elements of portal framework, and development aspects of portal. We have seen some of the core portal concepts in the earlier chapter. We will extend it further and have a deep dive into each of the portal elements from development perspective.

This chapter lays the foundation for understanding portal elements and how it can be used. The chapter would be beneficial for students and portal developers in getting the basic understanding of the concepts.

NOTE: Most of the concepts discussed in this chapter are related to Java-based portals and wherever necessary the explanation is augmented with java code snippets and configuration files.

We have provided the code and configuration of JSR 168 and JSR 286 portlets in the appendix.

Introduction

On the development side of things, there are portal standards, APIs, and eco-system elements, which will be needed while developing portal solution. Let us look at the core concepts of portal in this section.

Portal Terminology

We will try to understand the main terms we frequently use in the wider context of portal and the ones we use throughout this book:

- *Portal*: A portal is a web-based application that provides features such as personalization, content aggregation, single sign-on, and collaboration for presenting a unified and personalized view of functionality, data, and information. It has specialized web application characteristics:
  - Aggregates data, functionality, and content from disparate sources
  - Provides a personalized view for each user
  - Enables users to customize the pages
  - Enables collaboration features
  - Enables multichannel support
  - Provides single sign-on features.

  Popular instances of public portal can be found at this website: http://www.igoogleportal.com/ and https://my.yahoo.com/.

- *Portlet*: In simple terms, a portlet is a web component that renders a fragment of page and is managed by portal container. Portlet aggregates the data and provides a personalized presentation.
- *Portal page*: It renders a complete markup from multiple portlets to render a web page. The page is an aggregation of markups generated by multiple portlets.
- *Portal container*: It provides runtime environment for running portlets. It also provides the following functionalities:
  - Manages portlet life cycle
  - Manages portlet preferences through persistent storage
  - Handles requests and routes to appropriate portlet
  - Allows portlet caching
- *Portal themes*: Theme elements control the overall look-and-feel of portal pages including navigation elements, header sections, and page layout. Themes are often comprised of Java Server Page (JSP), CSS, images, and template elements.
- *Portlet skins*: Skins provide the look and feel of the portlet including the portlet title, minimize/maximize, and help controls.

Portal Server and Ecosystem

In this section, we will look at the main portal server components and its role in the portal solution.

Portal Server/Container

Portal server or portal container is an extended service essential for the execution of a portal application.

Portal server gives the administrators and delegated administrators the facility to build portal pages and perform various administration activities. It has also strong authentication features and also can be used for the user access management system.

Portal server supports standards such as JSR 168, JSR 286, and web services for remote portlet (WSRP).

In most scenarios, portal server runs within the context of an application server. Table 5.1 provides the main differences between portal server and application server:

TABLE 5.1

Portal Server and Application Server

Portal Server	Java Application Server
• Portlets can be run in a portal server. • By default, a portal server gives features of a user profile management. • A portal server provides services for creating rich look and feel components. • A portal server provides facility for the caching mechanism that can be used by portal applications.	• JSP, EJBs, servlets and other business components can be run in an application server. • An application server doesn't provide any feature related to user profile management. • An application server in its own does not provide any rich and look feel components.

Portal Ecosystem

Portal ecosystem mainly consists of portal container and security services, application server services and integration services with enterprise interfaces. Let us look at these elements:

- Portlet container security provides run-time environment for executing server side components such as portlets, collaboration components, personalization, and server side aggregation elements.
- Services are provided by underlying application server for Java-based portal products. This includes support for infrastructure components such as JMS, web services, caching components, security components, and JCA elements. Security components include authentication and authorization services.
- Enterprise interfaces include all enterprise systems such as ERP systems, legacy systems, and web applications with which portal needs to be integrated.

Servlet versus Portlet

For Java-based portals, it is easy to understand the portal concepts from standard servlet model. It also throws insights into motivation and necessity for portlet based development.

Let us see the differences between a servlet and a portlet and the use cases that are satisfied by a portlet in Table 5.2.

As we can see from the differences, portlets help us in creating independently executable web components that can be used for developing pluggable and reusable modules. They provider greater flexibility to control sections/fragments of pages.

TABLE 5.2

Differences between a Servlet and a Portlet

	Servlet	Portlet
Rendition	Renders complete page.	Renders a fragment of the page.
Personalization	Does not support built-in personalization and persistence of user-specified attributes.	Supports personalization and stores users' preferences in preference store.
End point	Servlets are bound to URL.	Portlets are not normally bound to a URL as the URL is dynamically generated.
States and modes	Do not have predefined states and modes.	Support various predefined states, modes, and window states.
User information	No built-in access to user profile information.	Provides built-in support and access to user profile information and user preferences.
Response updates	Can update the character set of the page and set HTTP headers of the response.	Cannot set character encoding or HTTP headers of the response.
Request handling	Relatively simpler request handling.	Portlets have sophisticated request handling which handles render request and action request.
Caching	Does not support fragment-level caching.	Supports fragment-/portlet-level caching.

Portal Standards, Life Cycle, and Request Processing

In this section, we will look at various *Java Specification Request (JSR)* standards along with their life cycle methods and request processing pipeline.

Portal Standards

Portal standards are used for interoperability and portability of portlets among compliant portal servers. As portlets are independently executable and reusable pluggable components, it will be reused across multiple environments, platforms, and servers. Hence, it is important to have standards that aid in this portability and help in providing *plug-and-play* features:

- *JSR 168*: It is version 1.0 of the Java Portlet Specification that provides the requirements for core portal features such as aggregation, personalization, and security. We can specify preferences for a JSR 168 portlet; administrator can specify the preferences (which are read-only) in portlet.xml and the user can also specify the preferences in edit mode of the portlet. Preferences provide additional configuration for the portlet, thereby enhancing their reusability and personalization features. For instance, a simple weather portlet can take the zip code of the city as a user preference parameter. Each user can configure the zip code and the weather portlet displays the weather specific for the zip code for each user, thereby providing a personalized experience.
- *JSR 286*: It is version 2.0 of the Java Portlet Specification that supports client-side-aggregation, partial-page rendering through resource request method, and interportlet communication. JSR 286 provides the following features:
  - *Resource serving*: The resources can be served within the portlet context.
  - *Shared render parameters*: The feature provides portlets to specify which render parameters they can share with the other portlets.
  - *Interportlet communication* (IPC): Interportlet communication can be achieved using JSR 286 portlets.
  - *Portlet filters*: JSR 286 also specifies the filters with which portlets can transform the content of the portlet requests and responses in the runtime.
- *Web Services for Remote Portlets (WSRP)*: It provides protocols and metadata for presentation-oriented web services and means for aggregation and syndication. It allows the portal servers to expose the portlets as web services so that other systems can consume the portlet functionality as presentation services. The key distinct feature of these kind of presentation services is that the portal can provide personalization and role-based access features. Another strong use case for WSRP is that portals developed in different technology platforms can interoperate by consuming the presentation service through WSRP portlet. Other typical use case scenarios are for information aggregation across disparate web platforms without the need to data/functionality duplication and data migration.

A sample WSRP architecture is shown in Figure 5.1.

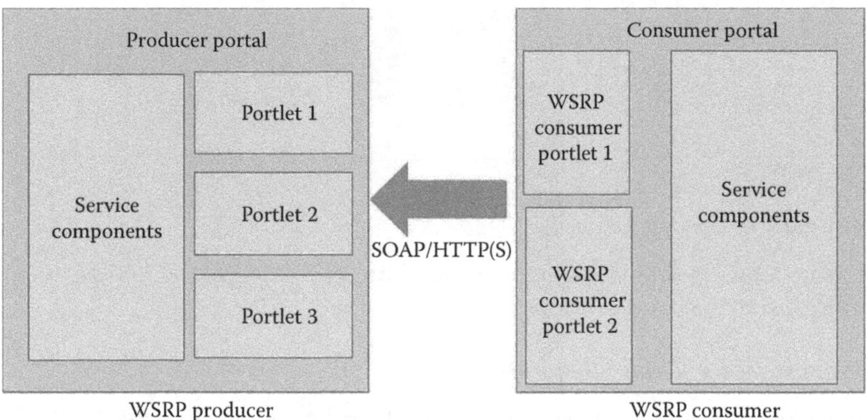

FIGURE 5.1
Sample WSRP architecture.

The main components of the WSRP architecture include WSRP producer and WSRP consumer:

- *WSRP producer*: This is the service provider that provides WSRP compliant services. Normally, portlet containers will expose the portlets as remote WSRP services.
- *WSRP consumer*: Proxy portlets consume the WSRP services. Most of the portal products provide built-in WSRP consumer portlets.

Portlet Life Cycle

Life Cycle of JSR 168 Portlet

The following are the main steps in the life cycle of the JSR 168 portlet:

1. The PortletContainer loads the portlet class and instantiates it.
2. The PortletContainer initializes the portlet object by invoking its init () method. One-time and resource-intensive activities such as resource connections and file loading will happen in this method.
3. The PortletContainer retrieves the stored PortletPreferences for the portlet object.
4. The portlet is rendered on the portal page and is ready to handle the client requests.
5. The client request can either be an action request or a render request.
6. When the request URL is generated by a portlet action such as submit action, the portlet container invokes processAction method, and for render requests, it invokes the render method.
7. The PortletContainer invokes the destroy() method when the portlet is removed from service and can release any resources and save the persistence state.

The main flow of the JSR 168 portlet is shown in Figure 5.2. A detailed step-by-step method of developing JSR 168 portlet is given in the appendix.

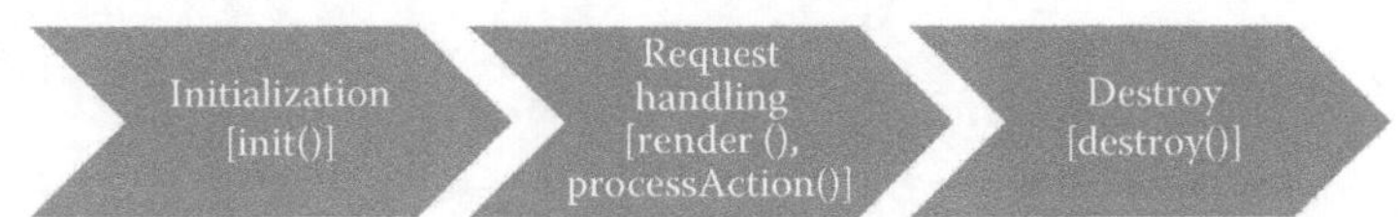

FIGURE 5.2
JSR 168 life cycle events.

Portal Request Processing

In this section, let us look at the sequence and chain of events that would occur while processing a request by a portal container.

Request Processing for Render Requests

The sequence of steps while processing a normal render request of a JSR 168 is as follows:

- A web client initiates an HTTP request for the portal page.
- A portal server receives the request and sends it to a portlet container that loads, instantiates, and initializes the portlets in the portal page.
- Upon receiving a render URL, a portlet container creates the render request and translates it into one render request for each portlet in a portal page. For each render request, a portlet container invokes the render() method on the portlet, which in turn calls doDispatch() that in turn calls doView() or doEdit(), etc., depending on the window mode. The portlet can use information such as window state, portlet mode, portal context, portlet session, and portlet preference data through RenderRequest object. The portlet produces the content using RenderResponse writer.
- If caching is enabled, a portlet container can choose to use the cached content instead of invoking render() method.
- The content fragment generated by the portlets will be aggregated on the portal page, which is served back to the requestor.

Request Processing for Action Requests

The sequence of steps while processing a normal action request is as follows:

- The HTTP request that contains an action URL is initiated. This normally happens when the user clicks on submit button or any action button on the page.
- Then a portal server sends the action request to the portlet container to process the request that loads, instantiates, and initializes the corresponding portlet.
- Upon receiving an action URL, a portlet container invokes processAction method of the portlet followed by multiple render requests.
    - A portlet can use the window state, portlet mode, portal context, portlet session, and configuration data through ActionRequest object.
    - In the processAction, method portlet can change the window state and portlet mode through ActionResponse object.
    - A JSR 286 portlet can also publish events using setEvent method in ActionResponse to publish changes and notifications.
- The content fragments generated by the portlets will be aggregated on the portal page that is served back to the requestor.

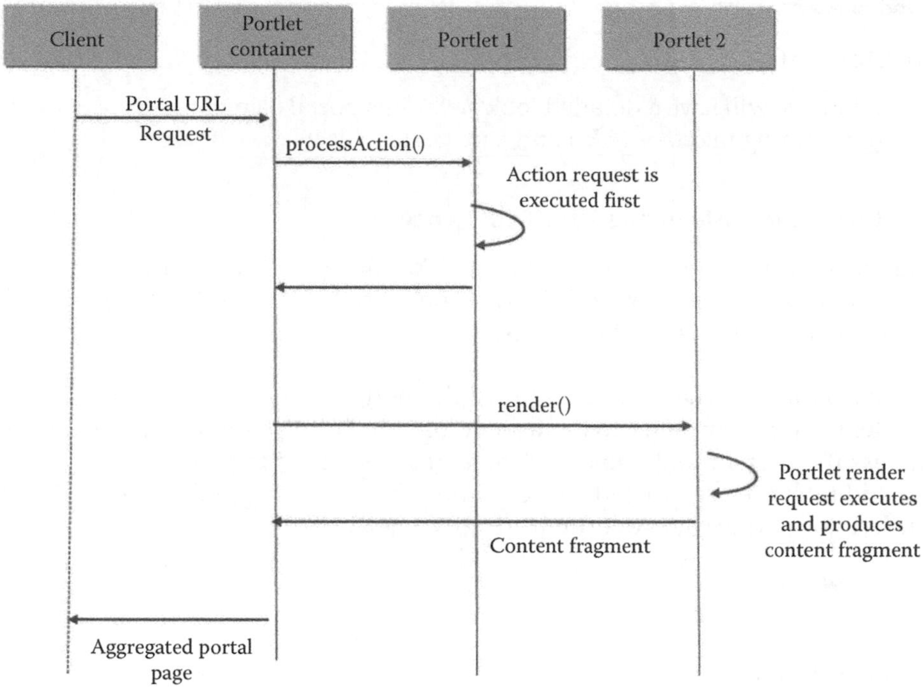

FIGURE 5.3
Sequence diagram for portlet action request and render request.

The sequence of method calls for action request and render request is given in Figure 5.3.

Request Processing for Resource Requests

The JSR 286 standard provides the additional life cycle interfaces EventPortlet and ResourceServingPortlet that the portlet can implement. JSR 286 portlets can provide link to resource in the same portlet application. A resourceRequest invokes serveResource method. The following are the sequence of events:

- A web client initiates a resource request for the portal page. Normally, this is followed by a render request.
- A portal server receives the request and sends it to a portlet container that loads, instantiates, and initializes the portlet.
- A JSR 286 portlet receives the resource request. Upon receiving a request from a resource URL, the portlet container invokes serveResource method of the appropriate portlet. The portlet can use information such as input stream, resource parameters, window state, portlet mode, portal context, and portlet session and portlet preference data through ResourceRequest object. The portlet produces the content using ResourceResponse writer.
- If caching is enabled, a portlet container can choose to use the cached content instead of invoking render() or serveResource() methods.

Portal Elements

In this section, we will have a detailed look at various portal elements such as portal application programming interface (API) and core portal objects.

Portal Objects for Customizing User Experience

Personalization is the core use case for portal. We will look at three main objects related to portal personalization here. We will look at core portal objects in the following sections. The following are the main portal objects:

- *User information*: The core strength of the portal lies in providing personalized content and functionality to the user. In order to achieve this, the portlet needs to access the user attributes such as name, role, e-mail address, and phone number. In addition, the user attribute information should be mapped in the deployment descriptor portlet.xml. An example is given here:

```
<portlet-app>
.
.
<user-attribute>
  <description>User First Name</description>
  <name>user.name.first</name>
</user-attribute>
.
.
<portlet-app>
```

  In an authenticated scenario, a portlet can get the unmodifiable Map USER_INFO from PortletRequest that has a key–value pair of available user attributes. A simple code example to get the first name attribute declared in portlet XML is given here:

```
Map userInfo = (Map) request.getAttribute(PortletRequest.USER_INFO);
String firstName = (userInfo!=null)? (String) userInfo.get(USER_
NAME_FIRST): "";
```

- *Portlet caching*: We can cache the portlet content using expiration cache by declaring the time-to-live (TTL) duration in seconds in portlet.xml. We can also programmatically update the TTL value by setting the EXPIRATION_CACHE property in RenderResponse or ResourceResponse.

  A sample portlet cache declaration of 100 s is shown here:

```
<portlet>
      ...
      <expiration-cache>100</expiration-cache>
      <cache-scope>private</cache-scope>
      ...
</portlet>
```

- *Portlet security*: The main methods in the PortletRequest interface that can be used to enforce security are as follows. We can use these methods to implement access control logic based on user security.
  - getRemoteUser returns the user name the client used for authentication.
  - isUserInRole checks if the remote user is in a specified security role.
  - getUserPrincipal method checks the principal name of the current user and returns a java.security.Principal object.

  Let us look at a simple example to understand isUserInRole method. A sample declaration in portlet.xml is given below

```
<portlet-app>
   <portlet>
          <security-role-ref>
                 <role-name>deployer-role</role-name>
                 <role-link>manager</role-link>
          </security-role-ref>
   </portlet>
</portlet-app>
```

This declaration maps the *deployer role* to the manager. So when the portlet user belonging to the *manager* security role invokes isUserInRole(deployer-role), then the result would be true.

Portlet Modes

JSR 168 portlet supports three portlet modes and one custom mode. The javax.portlet. PortletMode class provides the information about the mode of the portlet.

The modes are as follows:

- *View mode*: The view mode renders the current state of the portlet. The doView() method of the GenericPortlet class is invoked for this mode. This is a mandatory mode that all portlets are required to support. This mode can be accessed from PortletMode class as PortletMode.VIEW.
- *Edit mode*: The edit mode helps in customizing the portlet through the PortletPreferences object. The doEdit() method of the GenericPortlet class is invoked for this mode. This is an optional mode. This mode can be accessed from PortletMode class as PortletMode.EDIT.
- *Help mode*: The help mode provides the generic or context-sensitive help-related information about the portlet. The doHelp() method of the GenericPortlet class is invoked for this mode. This is an optional mode. This mode can be accessed from PortletMode class as PortletMode.HELP.
- *Custom mode*: Custom functionality can be implemented using custom portlet mode. The doDispatch() method of GenericPortlet class must be overridden to handle this custom mode.

Portlets must define the custom mode in portlet.xml.

Here is an example of defining custom mode in portlet.xml:

```
<custom-portlet-mode>
      <description>Provides configuration function</descriptions>
      <name>config</name>
</custom-portlet-mode>
```

An example code to use portlet mode in portlet class is also given here:

```
static PortletMode CUSTOM_MODE = new PortletMode("config");
            //overloaded doDispatch to call custom mode
            public void doDispatch(renderRequest request, RenderResponse
response) throws PortletException, IOException {
                  if(CUSTOM_MODE.equals(request.getPortletMode()) {
                        // Custom code to invoke custom mode
                  }
                  super.doDispatch(request, response);
            }
```

The following is the declaration in portlet.xml file for supporting all modes: three regular modes and a custom config mode:

```
<supports>
         <mime-type>text/html</mime-type>
         <portlet-mode>view</portlet-mode
         <portlet-mode>edit</portlet-mode>
         <portlet-mode>help</portlet-mode>
         <portlet-mode>config</portlet-mode>
</supports>
```

Portlet Objects and API

The core portlet objects and key portlet APIs along with their brief explanation are given as follows:

- *Portlet interface*: All the portlets should implement javax.portlet.Portlet interface directly or by extending a class that implements this interface.

  The following are the main methods used:

  - *void init(PortletConfig config)*: This method is invoked by a portlet container. It is called when the portlet application has started and is called only once per portlet object. The PortletConfig object passed contains the initialization parameters.
  - *void processAction(ActionRequest request, ActionResponse response)*: The processAction method is called in response to an action request. RenderResponse.createActionURL() or the actionURL jsp tag generates an action URL that invokes this method. This method will update the portlet state based on action request parameters. This method must handle concurrent execution from multiple threads.
  - *void render(RenderRequest request, RenderResponse response)*: This method is invoked for all the render requests. During the render request, the portlet

container generates content based on its current state. This method must handle concurrent execution from multiple threads.

- *void destroy*(): This is called when the portlet is removed from the service and can be used to release any resources. The portlet object can be garbage collected after this method.

- *GenericPortlet*: This abstract class implements the Portlet and PortletConfig interface and provides default implementations of the methods. All portlets should extend this class rather than implementing the Portlet interface.
  - *void init*(): This can be used for managing resources.
  - *void init(PortletConfig config)*: It is invoked by the portlet container when the portlet is placed into services.
  - *void destroy*(): This is invoked by the portlet container when the portlet is being taken out of the services.
  - *void processAction(ActionRequest request, ActionResponse response)*: The method is invoked for action requests for the portlet.
  - *void render(RenderRequest request, RenderResponse response)*: The method sets the portlet title and then invokes the doDispatch method.
  - *void doDispatch(RenderRequest request, RenderResponse response)*: The method is called from the render method; it invokes the appropriate method based on the portlet mode.
  - *void doView(RenderRequest request, RenderResponse response)*: The method is invoked by doDispatch when the portlet is in view mode.
  - *void doEdit(RenderRequest request, RenderResponse response)*: The method is invoked by doDispatch when the portlet is in edit mode.
  - *void doHelp(RenderRequest request, RenderResponse response)*: The method is invoked by doDispatch when the portlet is in help mode.
  - getInitParameter(java.lang.String name) returns the value of the named initialization parameter.
  - getInitParameterNames() returns the list of all portlet initialization parameters.
  - getPortletConfig() returns javax.portlet.PortletConfig.
  - getPortletContext() returns javax.portlet.PortletContext of the portlet application.
  - getPortletName() returns the name of this portlet.
  - getResourceBundle(java.util.Locale locale) returns java.util.ResourceBundle for the given locale.
  - getTitle(RenderRequest request) returns the portlet title.
- *PortletConfig*: The interface provides the global configuration information for the portlet. We will use it in the initialization methods such as init() to get the configuration parameters. The following are the key methods:
  - getInitParameterNames() returns the list of all portlet initialization parameters.
  - getInitParameter(java.lang.String name) returns the value of the named initialization parameter.
  - getPortletContext() returns javax.portlet.PortletContext of the portlet application.

- getPortletName() returns the name of this portlet.
- getResourceBundle(java.util.Locale locale) returns java.util.ResourceBundle for the given locale.

- *PortalContext*: The interface has methods to provide information about the portal server where the current portlet is running. We will use this to get the portal server level context information. The following are the key methods:
  - getPortalInfo() returns information such as vender and version.
  - getProperty(java.lang.String) returns the portal property value with the given name.
  - getPropertyNames() returns the enumeration of all the property names of the portal.
  - getSupportedPortletModes() returns the enumeration of all supported portlet modes.
  - getSupportedWindowStates() returns the enumeration of all supported portlet window states.
- *PortletContext*: The interface provides the portlet context information for the specific portlet. We will use this to get the portlet level context information. The following are the key methods:
  - *getAttribute(java.lang.String name)* returns the portlet container attribute with the given name.
  - *getAttributeNames*() returns an enumeration containing the attribute names available within this portlet context.
  - *getInitParameter(java.lang.String name)* returns the value of the named context-wide initialization parameter.
  - *removeAttribute(java.lang.String name)* removes the attribute with the given name from the portlet context.
  - *setAttribute(java.lang.String name, java.lang.Object object)* binds an object to the specified object name.
- *PortletRequest*: The interface encapsulates all the client information to the portlet. The portlet uses this to obtain information about request values.

  The following are the main methods defined by the interface PortletRequest:
  - *getParameter(java.lang.String name)* returns the value for the parameter name or null.
  - *getParameterNames*() returns the enumeration of the string object containing the name of the parameters.
  - *getParameterMap*() returns a map of the parameters; the key for the map is a parameter name and the value is the String[] corresponding to the values for the parameter name.
  - *getAttribute(java.lang.String name)* returns the value of the attribute as an object or null.
  - *removeAttribute(java.lang.String name)* removes a named attribute from this request.

- *getProperty(java.lang.String name)* returns the value of the specific property as a string or null.
- *getRemoteUser()* returns the log-in name of the authenticated user making request or null if there is no session.
- *getUserPrincipal()* returns a java.security.Principal object containing the name of the current authenticated user or null.
- *isUserInRole(java.lang.String role)* returns true if the authenticated user is included in the role else false.
- *isSecure()* returns true if this request was made using a secure channel between the client and the portal else false.
- *getPortletMode()* returns the current portlet mode of the portlet.
- *getWindowState()* returns the current window state of the portlet.
- *getPortletSession()* returns the current portlet session or, if there is no current session, creates one and returns the new session.
- *getPortletSession(Boolean create)* returns the current portlet session or, if there is no current session and the create flag is true, creates one and returns the new session.
- *getRequestedSessionID()* returns the session ID indicated in client request.

The PortletRequest request can be of two types:

- *ActionRequest*: It extends PortletRequest and represents the request sent to the portlet to handle an action. The following are the additional methods defined by this interface in addition to the ones it inherits from the PortletRequest:
  - *getCharacterEncoding()* returns the name of the character encoding used in the body of this request as a string.
  - *getContentLength()* returns the length, in bytes, of the request body that is made available by the input stream or -1 if not known.
  - *getContentType()* returns the MIME (Multi-Purpose Internet Mail Extensions) type of the body of the request as a string or null if not known.
  - *getPortletInputStream()* retrieves the body of the HTTP request from client to portal as binary data using an InputStream.
  - *getReader()* retrieves the body of the HTTP request from client to portal as character data using a BufferReader.
  - *setCharacterEncoding(java.lang.String)* overrides the name of the character encoding used in the body of this request.
- *RenderRequest*: It extends PortletRequest and represents the render request sent to the portlet. We have already seen the methods of PortletRequest earlier and they will be used by RenderRequest.

- *PortletResponse*: The interface has methods for creating and dispatching the response. The following are the main methods:
  - *setProperty(java.lang.String key, java.lang.String value)*: This sets the string property to be returned. It resets all the properties previously added with the same key. If the key is null, it throws IllegalArgumentException.

- *addProperty(java.lang.String key, java.lang.String value)*: It adds a string property to an existing key to be returned. This method allows response properties to have multiple values. If the key is null, it throws IllegalArgumentException.
- *encodeURL(java.lang.String path)*: This method returns the encoded URL of the resources. It may include the session ID and other portlet container–specific information into the URL. If encoding is not required, it returns the URL unchanged.

There are two kinds of PortletResponse:

- *ActionResponse*: The interface extends PortletResponse interface and represents response for action request. The following are the main methods defined by this interface:
  - *sendRedirect(java.lang.String location)* instructs the portlet container to send a redirect response to the client using a specified redirect location URL. The location must be either an absolute URL or a full path URI.
  - *setPortletMode(PortletMode mode)* sets the portlet mode of a portlet to the given mode.
  - *setRenderParameter(java.lang.String key, java.lang.String value)* sets the string parameter for the render request that can be accessed through PortletRequest.getParameter method.
- *RenderResponse*: The interface extends PortletResponse interface and represents response for render request. The following are the main methods defined by this interface:
  - *createActionURL()* creates a portlet URL targeting the portlet and returns a portlet action URL.
  - *createRenderURL()* creates a portlet URL targeting the portlet and returns a portlet render URL.
  - *flushBuffer()* forces any content in the buffer to be written to the underlying output stream.
  - *setContentType(java.lang.String type)* sets the MIME type for the render response.
  - *setTitle(java.lang.String title)* sets the portlet title.

- *PortletURL and ResourceURL*: PortletURL represents the URL for a portlet and ResourceURL represents a URL for resource that invokes serveResource method. It can be of two types: ActionURL and RenderURL. Portlet can use the createActionURL, createRenderURL, or createResourceURL methods of the PortletResponse interface to create the action URL, render URL, and resource URL respectively.
- *PortletRequestDispatcher*: The interface defines an object that receives client requests that are forwarded to the specified server resources. Its main method is as follows:
  - **include(RenderRequest request, RenderResponse response)** includes the content of the resources (servlet, JSPs, or HTML) in the response.
- *PortletSession*: The interface stores user profile–related information. We can bind an object to the portlet session either at the application level using

APPLICATION_SCOPE or at the portlet level using PORTLET_LEVEL. Application scope objects are available to all components that are part of the portlet application such as servlets and JSPs, whereas portlet scope objects are available to the portlet that has stored the objects and it is private only to that portlet. The following are the main methods:

- *getAttribute(java.lang.String name)* returns the attribute with the specified name.
- *getAttribute(java.lang.String name, int scope)* returns attribute with the specified name in the given scope.
- *getAttributeNames*() returns the list of attribute names.
- *getId*() returns a unique identifier of the session.
- *removeAttribute(java.lang.String name)* removes the specified attribute.

- *PortletPreferences*: The interface allows the portlet to store configuration data both for the user and for the administrator. The object contains the user-specific preference values. The value can be set by the administrator or by the user. The administrator can set the value in config mode that reflects globally for all portlet instances, whereas the user can only set the value for his or her specific portlet instance.
  There are two kinds of preferences:
  - *Modifiable preferences*: These can be changed by the portlet in any standard portlet mode. By default every preference is modifiable. This can be used by an end user for configuring the portlet.
  - *Read-only preferences*: These preferences can't be changed in any portlet mode but can be changed by the administrative modes. The preferences are read-only, if they are defined in portlet.xml as <read-only> true.

A sample entry of the portlet preferences in portlet.xml file is given here:

```
<portlet-app>
 <portlet>
   .
   .
   <portlet-preferences>
    <preference>
     <name>zipcode</name>
     <value>12345</value>
    </preference>
    <preference>
     <name>AdminKey</name>
     <value>adminvalue</value>
     <read-only>true</read-only>
    </preference>
   </portlet-preferences>
  .
  .
 </portlet>
</portlet-app>
```

In the aforementioned entry, the zip code is modifiable by the user, whereas the AdminKey preference can only be updated by the administrator.

The following are the key methods of this interface:

- *getMap*() returns an immutable map, with preference names as key and preference values as value or empty map.
- *getNames*() returns an enumeration of the keys that have an associated value or an empty enumeration.
- *getValue*(*java.lang.String key, java.lang.String defaultval*) returns the first value associated with the key as a string.
- *setValue*(*java.lang.String key, java.lang.String value*) associates the specified key with the specified value in this preference.
- *store*() commits all changes made to the preferences via the set method in persistence store.

* *ResourceServingPortlet*: This interface is specified in version 2.0 of the Java Portlet Specification that helps in linking the resources within portlet application. The main method of this interface is the *serveResource* that can access the HTTP client request headers through the getProperty or getProperties method and also can set HTTP headers for the response via the setProperty or addProperty methods.

  The implementing portlet also gets the resource ID through getResourceID method and can set the resource ID through setResourceID method.
* *Portlet filters*: They filter the portlet request and response and are modeled on servlet filter. It is declared using <filter> element in the portlet.xml. When the portlet container gets the request, it calls the doFilter() method of the first filter in the list and passes PortletRequest and PortletResponse to it. Shown here is a sample declaration of AuditFilter:

```
<filter>
 <filter-name>Audit Filter</filter-name>
 <filter-class>com.example.AuditFilter</filter-class>
 <lifecycle>ACTION_PHASE</lifecycle>
</filter>
<filter-mapping>
 <filter-name>Audit Filter</filter-name>
 <portlet-name>CustomerPortlet</portlet-name>
</filter-mapping>
```

  With this declaration the audit filter will be applied during processing of the CustomerPortlet.

Portlet JSP Tags

In this section, we will look at the main JSP tags that can be used for invoking portlet APIs. The tag library declaration for portlet specifications 1.0 and 2.0 is given as follows:

* *portlet specification 1.0*: <%@ taglib uri="http://java.sun.com/portlet" prefix=" portlet" %>
* *portlet specification 2.0*: <%@ taglib uri="http://java.sun.com/portlet_2_0" prefix=" portlet" %>

Main Portlet JSP Tags

DefineObjects Tag

The tag allows the implicit portlet objects to be used in the portlet JSP page. It is declared as follows:

```
<portlet:defineObjects/>
```

Once it is defined, these implicit portlet objects can be accessed: renderRequest, resourceRequest, actionRequest, eventRequest renderResponse, resourceResponse, actionResponse, eventResponse, portletConfig, portletSession, portletSessionScope, portletPreferences, and portletPreferencesValues.

A JSP scriptlet example of setting the cache expiration time is given here:

```
<%=renderResponse.getCacheControl().setExpirationTime(50)%>
```

–actionURL Tag

The tag creates the action URL of the current portlet and invokes the processAction method of the portlet. It accepts the following key parameters:

- *Var*: Scoped variable for the action URL
- *Secure*: Indicates whether the URL should be secure
- *portletMode*: Specifies the mode of the portlet
- *escapeXML*: Specifies whether we need to encode the HTML reserved characters
- *name*: Name of the action

The following is an example of an actionURL:

```
<portlet:actionURL windowState="maximized" portletMode="edit"
name="updateEmployee">
       <portlet:param name="empno" value="1234"/>
</portlet:actionURL>
```

The example creates a URL that brings the portlet into edit mode and maximized window state to edit the employee with an employee number 1234.

–renderURL Tag

The tag creates the render URL of the current portlet and invokes the renderRequest method of the portlet. It accepts the following key parameters:

- *Var*: Scoped variable for the render URL
- *Secure*: Indicates whether the URL should be secure
- *portletMode*: Specifies the mode of the portlet
- *escapeXML*: Specifies whether we need to encode the HTML reserved characters

– resourceURL Tag

The tag creates the resource URL of the current portlet and invokes the serveResource method of the portlet. It accepts the following key parameters:

- *Var*: Scoped variable for the render URL
- *Secure*: Indicates whether the URL should be secure

- *portletMode*: Specifies the mode of the portlet
- *escapeXML*: Specifies whether we need to encode the HTML reserved characters

Here is an example of resourceURL tag:

```
<portlet:resourceURL id="images/logo.gif"/>
```

The example creates a URL to provide a link that renders the logo.gif image using the serveResource method.

– *namespace tag*

The tag provides a unique value for the current portlet that is similar to that of the PortletResponse.getNamespace() method.

The following example adds a unique namespace for JavaScript method convert()

```
<a href="javascript:<portlet:namespace/>convert()">Convert</A>
```

– *property tag*

The property tag can be used to add property to the action URL, render URL, or resource URL and is the same as invoking the addProperty method.

The following is an example of a property tag:

```
<portlet:actionURL>
              <portlet:property name="propname" value="propvalue"/>
</portlet:actionURL>
```

– *param tag*

The tag adds a parameter to the action URL, render URL, or resource URL. An example is shown as follows:

```
<portlet:param name="paramname" value="paramvalue"/>
```

Portlet Window States

A window state specifies the amount of portal page space that will be assigned to the portlet content. javax.portlet.WindowState class represents the possible window states that a portlet window can assume.

The specification defines three window states and a custom window state:

- *Normal window state*: This indicates that a portlet will be rendered in equivalent space as other portlets. This can be accessed through PortletWindow.NORMAL variable in a portlet class.
- *Maximized window state*: This indicates that a portlet will be the only portlet on the entire page. This can be accessed through PortletWindow.MAXIMIZED variable in a portlet class.
- *Minimized window state*: This indicates that a portlet will be rendered with minimal or no output on the page. This can be accessed through PortletWindow.MINIMIZED in a portlet class.
- *Custom window state*: Custom window state can be defined in the portlet.xml using custom-window-state element.

```
<custom-window-state>
      <description>Provides 30% of the portal page</description>
```

```
    <name>custom-state</name>
  <custom-window-state>
```

Portlet class code:

```
static WindowState CUSTOM_STATE = new WindowState("custom-state");
```

Portlet Communication

In order to build an interactive presentation, sometimes it is necessary to exchange and share data across portlets; a state change in the first portlet would trigger a change in a related portlet. A simple example is that of store locator portlet and map portlet. As soon as the user provides the address in the store locator portlet, the store locator portlet provides the list of nearby store locations. When the user selects each store location, an adjacent map portlet provides the map visual from current location to selected location in the map view.

There are multiple ways to communicate the data across portlets:

- Public render parameters (interportlet communication)
- Events
- Cookies

Let us look at each of these options in greater detail.

Public Render Parameter Interportlet Communication

This feature was introduced in version 2.0 of the Java Portlet Specification (JSR 286), which allows portlets to share parameters with other portlets:

- In this case, the portlet should declare public render parameters in portlet.xml using the public-render-parameter element in portlet application section. We can use public render parameters in all life cycle methods such as processAction, processEvent, render, and serveResource.
- In the portlet section, the portlet can provide the public render parameters it would like to share using supported-public-render-parameter element.

  An example is shown here:

```
<public-render-parameter>
 <identifier>id1</identifier>
 <qname xmlns:x="http://example.com/params">x:id1</qname>
</public-render-parameter>
<public-render-parameter>
  <identifier>id2</identifier>
  <qname xmlns:x="http://example.com/params">x:id2</qname>
 </public-render-parameter>
 <portlet>
  <portlet-name>portletA</portlet-name>
  <supported-public-render-parameter>id1 </supported-public-render-parameter>
  <supported-public-render-parameter>id2 </supported-public-render-parameter>
```

```
 </portlet>
 <portlet>
  <portlet-name> portletB</portlet-name>
  <supported-public-render-parameter>id2 </supported-public-render-parameter>
 </portlet>
```

In this scenario, portlet A can share the value through id2 variable. A simple example is shown here:

We can set the id2 variable in portlet A's processAction method:

```
public void processAction(ActionRequest request, ActionResponse
response) throws IOException, PortletException {
..
response.setRenderParameter("id2"■, "id2value");......
}
```

In Portlet B we can retrieve the value through

```
portletRequest.getParameter("id2");
```

Events

Events provide a loosely coupled interaction model between two portlets. This again was introduced in version 2.0 of the Java Portlet Specification (JSR 286). The following are the main steps for event-based communication:

- The portlet must implement EventPortlet interface that provides processEvent method with EventRequest and EventResponse object.
- Declare the event at portlet application level. We need to specify the event name and object type for the sender portlet. At the portlet level, provide the qname in <supported-publishing-event> element.

```
<portlet-app>
 <portlet>
  <portlet-name>EventSenderPortlet</portlet-name>
  <supported-publishing-event>
   <qname>x:location</qname>
  </supported-publishing-event>>
 </portlet>
 <event-definition>
  <qname xmlns:x="http:example.com/address">x:location</qname>
  <value-type>java.lang.String</value-type>
 </event-definition>
</portlet-app>
```

- In the processAction method of EventSenderPortlet, we can set the event:

```
javax.xml.namespace.QName qName = new QName("http:example.com/
address", "location", "x");
response.setEvent(qName, "Event raised in EventSenderPortlet");
```

- Specify the processing event in the receiver portlet in the deployment descriptor:

```
<portlet-app>
 <portlet>
  <portlet-name>EventReceiverPortlet</portlet-name>
  <supported-processing-event>
   <qname>x:location</qname>
  </supported-processing-event>
 </portlet>
 <event-definition>
  <qname xmlns:x="http:example.com/address">x:location</qname>
  <value-type>java.lang.String</value-type>
 </event-definition>
</portlet-app>
```

- Now, we can receive the event in the EventReceiverPortlet in the processEvent method:

```
public void processEvent(EventRequest request, EventResponse
response) {
        Event event = request.getEvent();
        if(event.getName().equals("location")){
        String payload = (String)event.getValue();
        //process payload here
     }
  }
```

Cookies

Cookies are standard features for information exchange since the beginning of web applications. We can use any standard AJAX toolkit such as DOJO, ExtJs, jQuery, or even normal JavaScript code to set and get the values from cookies.

The following is a sample JSP code to add a new cookie:

```
Cookie cookieParam = new Cookie("usercookie", username);
response.addCookie(cookieParam);
```

Most of the AJAX libraries and JavaScript provide APIs to retrieve the value from a cookie.

The following is an example to fetch the cookie value in JSP code:

```
Cookie[] cookies = request.getCookies();
    if (cookies != null) {
        for (int i = 0; i < cookies.length; i++) {
            if (cookies[i].getName().equals("usercookie")) {
                uname = cookies[i].getValue();
            }
        }
    }
```

In addition to the methods discussed earlier, it is also possible to share data through portlet session.

Portlet session is private to each portlet application. Though some vendors provide a configurable global session attribute, it is not a standard and portable feature. Hence, it is recommended to use the IPC or event model for data sharing across portlets.

Portlet Packaging and Deployment Descriptor

In this section, we will look at the main portlet deployment description files and the packaging details of a portlet application. Typically, portal administrators and deployment team will take care of packaging and deploying the portlet application.

Portlet Deployment Descriptor

Portlet.xml is the main configuration file that is part of every portlet and is present in the path <app_name>\WEB-INF\portlet.xml. We will look at the main elements of the configuration file. At the portlet application level, we can declare the following deployment descriptor values:

- <portlet-app> is the main element of the configuration file. We can specify multiple portlets within this value.
- <portlet> describes one portlet.
- <description> provides a brief description of the portlet.
- <portlet-name> specifies the name of the portlet.
- <portlet-class> specifies the fully qualified class for the portlet.
- <supports> provides the supported MIME type for a given portlet mode.
- <portlet-mode> specifies the supported modes of the portlet and it occurs within the <supports> tag.
- <init-param> provides the initialization parameters that help in creating initial state of the portlet. The parameters are specified in key, value pairs.
- <supported-locale> provides a list of all supported locales.
- <resource-bundle> specifies the resource bundle that needs to be used for supporting localization.
- <security-role> provides the security role mapping information for the portlet.
- <supported-public-render-parameter> provides the list of the supported public render parameters.

In addition to the portlet.xml, each portal vendor also usually adds vendor-specific portlet configuration file that contains the details of proprietary features. For instance, Liferay portlet application contains liferay-portlet.xml in addition to portlet.xml.

Portlet Packaging

As a portlet is a web application, all resources, portlets, and deployment descriptors are packaged in one web application archive (WAR file). A typical directory structure is shown here:

- PortletApp\
  - jsp
  - htmls

- WEB-INF\
  - web.xml
  - portlet.xml
  - classes\
  - Lib\

Portal Page Layout and Construction

A typical portal page layout consists of the following elements:

- Header and footer
- Navigation elements such as left navigation and breadcrumb
- Portlets
- Contextual menus
- Link to user profile

The main steps in the construction of the overall portal page are given in Figure 5.4:

- *Portal page request*: The user requests for the portal page. In this scenario, we are assuming that the user has a valid session created after successful authentication. The portal server receives the request and other request parameters and details of the requesting device.

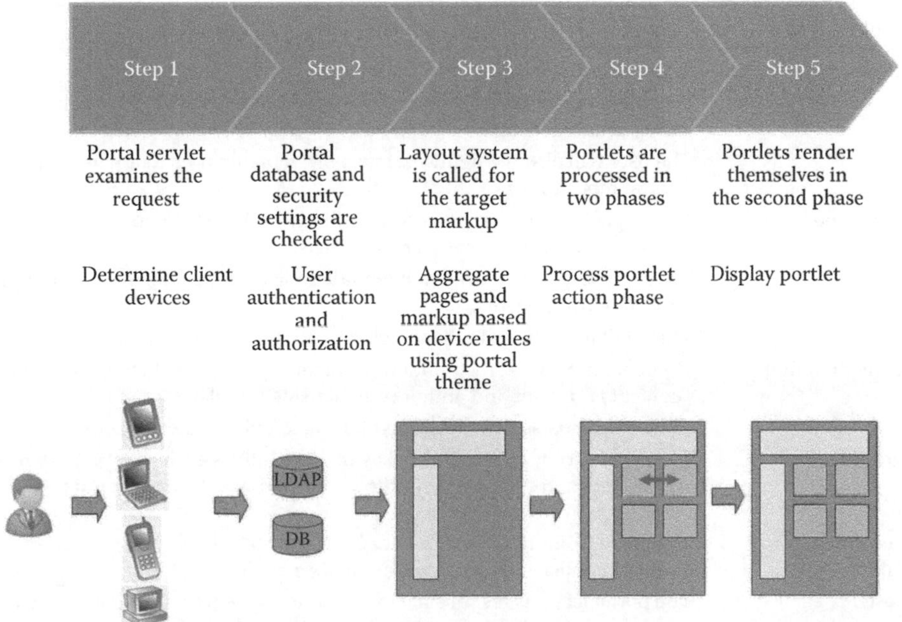

FIGURE 5.4
Portal page construction.

- *Execution of portal security rules*: As there is a valid user session, the portal container checks the applicable security rules and policies for the requesting users. This includes the access permissions to the requested page, portlets, and the other resources. At this stage all applicable personalization rules will also be executed.
- *Portal page markup aggregation*: The portal server then constructs the page consisting of a header and footer (through portal themes), navigation elements (through a combination of portal themes and navigation portlets), menus (themes and custom libraries), a link to user profile (mostly through theme JSPs), and starts invoking each of the portlets on the page. The final markup rendered is based on the device rules configured, and hence it may be optimized based on the requesting device.
- *Portlet action phase*: As we know that portlet processing has two phases for action requests, the container executes the action phase for each of the received action requests.
- *Portlet render phase*: The container invokes the render phase followed by action phase. For portlets that do not have action phase, the container simply invokes the render phase (typically doView() method) for all portlets present on the page.

Portal Roles

The key user roles required in developing a portal platform are given in Table 5.3.

TABLE 5.3
Portal Roles

Portal Role	Responsibilities and Activities
Portal user	This role is that of the primary user of the portal solution. The user accesses portal pages and executes various actions from supported devices and user agents. The user will also configure various portlet preferences that will be stored in portal repositories.
Portal developer	Developers take the primary responsibility of developing portal solution components such as themes and portlets. They will also be involved in integrating the portal platform with enterprise interface components. They will use IDE and other accelerator tools for their development.
Portal content author	Content authors use the portal web content management features to design content templates and author content using templates. They will also use the content workflows to publish the content.
Portal administrator	The administrator role handles key responsibilities such as setting up roles and permissions, configuring workflows, user administration, portal release management, and deployment.
Portal configuration controller	The configuration controller manages the portal source code, design code, and check-in policies and does release management.
Portal tester	The portal tester is responsible for executing various test scenarios such as portal functional testing, integration testing, and performance testing.

References and Further Reading

We have tried to cover the key development aspects of portal in this chapter. The chapter details the main elements, APIs, and related concepts. However, covering detailed portal specifications is beyond the scope of this book and it is recommended to go over the following official specifications:

- *JSR 168 Specification*: https://jcp.org/aboutJava/communityprocess/final/jsr168/
- *JSR 286 Specification*: https://jcp.org/aboutJava/communityprocess/final/jsr286/

We have also given sample code examples for developing JSR 168 and JSR 286 portlets in the Appendix. The Appendix provides complete details of all portlet code and configuration files that are present as part of the portlet.

Summary

- This chapter elaborates the development aspects of a portal.
- A portal is a specialized web application that provides personalized experience and aggregates data and content from various sources.
- A portal container provides runtime environment to run portlets.
- A portlet is a reusable web component that runs on a portal container.
- A portal page is an aggregation of portlets and other portal elements.
- Portal themes provide a header and footer and portal skins provide the look and feel for a portlet.
- Portal ecosystems include portal components such as aggregation components, presentation components, integration components and security, and enterprise interfaces.
- The main standards of portal are JSR 168, JSR 286, and WSRP.
- JSR 168 is version 1.0 of the Java Portlet Specification that provides the requirements for core portal features such as aggregation, personalization, and security.
- JSR 286 is version 2.0 of the Java Portlet Specification that supports client-side-aggregation, partial-page rendering, and interportlet communication.
- WSRP provides protocols and metadata for presentation-oriented web services and means for aggregation and syndication.
- The life cycle of JSR 168 portlet includes invocation of init(), render(), process Action(), and destroy() methods.
- We can specify the user information, portal caching, and security-related parameters in portal configuration file.
- JSR 168 supports three portlet modes and one custom mode. Three portlet modes are view mode, edit mode, and help mode.

- Key portlet objects include Portlet interface, GenericPortlet abstract class, Portletconfig, PortalContext, PortletContext, PortletRequest, PortletResponse, and PortletRequestDispatcher, PortletSession.
- PortletURL and ResourceURL represent the URL for a portlet and a ResourceURL, respectively.
- PortletPreferences object allows the portlet to store configuration data both for the user and for the administrator.
- Main portlet JSP tags include defineObjects tag, actionURL tag, renderURL tag, resourceURL tag, namespace tag, property tag, and param tag.
- There are three predefined windows states: normal, maximized, and minimized.
- Portlets can communicate through render parameters (also known as interportlet communication), events, and cookies.
- A typical portal page construction includes the following steps: portal page request handling, security rule execution, portal page markup aggregation and portal action execution, and render phases.
- Main portal roles are portal user, portal developer, portal content author, portal administrator, portal configuration controller, and portal tester.

6

Portal Integrations

Introduction

Integrations are at the heart of any portal platform. In fact, in most of the cases where you are going to use the portal, integrations play a major role of the use cases. Enterprise integrations are also the deciding factor for choosing a portal platform. So due to all these aspects, deep understanding of various kinds of integrations with a portal platform is quintessential for architecting an efficient portal platform.

In modern enterprise scenarios, the information is not owned by any single system; rather, it is distributed or shared across multiple systems and services. It would be inevitable to aggregate the data from all the required systems and services to build any meaningful portal platform. A classic example can be drawn from an *enterprise information portal* where we can display details about a product in the portal page. The product page contains all sorts of product information from varied sources. The pricing information is obtained from pricing enterprise resource planning (ERP) system. The core product attributes are taken from product database. Discussions about the product are obtained from public social media sites. This portal page can be built by aggregating information from at least three different internal and external systems.

We are going to see various aspects of integrations and their usage scenarios. We will also discuss various integration patterns and best practices, and lastly we will see ways to achieve optimal integrations that are scalable with high performance.

Advantages of Integrations

The main advantages of integration for a portal platform are as follows:

- Integrations enable the portal to provide a single source of information in a holistic view to all functionalities.
- It helps in information and data aggregation, which are the primary use cases for a portal platform.
- It helps in extending the portal features.
- It helps in making the portal provide seamless access to all data, thereby enhancing use experience.

As we can see, due to these advantages, implementing optimal integrations is a critical success factor for any portal program.

Challenges and the Impact of Integrations

Almost all portal implementations have integrations to some extent. Some of the main challenges due to improper integration are as follows:

1. *Performance*: A suboptimal integration can have a drastic impact on the performance. If the integration technique is not properly tested for performance, it can slow down the entire page.
2. *Scalability and availability*: The quality of integrations also impacts the overall scalability and availability of the application. Even if one of the integrated applications in the chain is not scalable, it impacts the scalability of the end application.
3. *Vendor management*: In many scenarios, it is required to collaborate with multiple vendors and subject matter experts (SMEs) for ensuring an optimal integration. Multivendor and SME collaboration is one of the operation challenges in achieving an optimal integration.
4. *User experience*: Integrations also have a profound impact on end-user experience. We have already seen that one such impact is due to performance. In addition to this, in case of a multistep transactions wherein each step requires data from the source system, the efficiency of integration influences the integrity and smoothness of the overall transaction.

Business Scenarios for Integrations

Let us look at some of the business scenarios that require integration with the portal:

- *Provide a single stop shop of all services*: This requires providing a unified view of all business functionality and services in a single interface, which requires integrating with all underlying systems to aggregate required information.
- *Provide a consistent and unified user experience and branding*: When a multistep process requires interaction with various systems, it would impact the end-user experience due to change in underlying systems and their interfaces. In order to provide a consistent user interface, uniform branding, and navigation experience in a single interface, all the underlying systems and services need to be integrated.
- *Provide a dashboard view*: Some business scenarios such as reporting applications and business intelligence applications require a dashboard view of various functionalities. This again can be achieved through information and service aggregation.
- *Enable self-service*: A primary business goal is to achieve self-service through their online interface, which would positively impact revenue and customer satisfaction. Achieving self-service is a multifaceted effort. One of the requirements to achieve self-service is to integrate all necessary systems that enable end users to complete the tasks on their own. For instance, a portal application can be integrated with underlying knowledge management to provide the solutions for the issues and help users in troubleshooting. Similarly, self-learning is another area where portal integration plays a key role.
- *Process optimization and automation*: This can be achieved by integrating all systems required in the workflow process to enable seamless process completion and also automating all possible steps in the process.

- *Productivity improvement*: By enabling easy and relevant/contextual information discovery and automating the key process steps, the overall productivity of the user will be increased. Providing the right set of tools at the right place at the right time would enable the user to complete the task in a much lesser time. One of the requirements for this is to enable proper integrations to provide the right kind of information and tools (functionality). For instance, a travel portal can provide a portal-based dashboard to provide end-to-end functionality starting from searching for an optimal route between two specified routes to booking tickets to completing the checkout.
- *Increase of revenue/conversion ratio*: Some of the aforementioned points directly or indirectly contribute to conversion ratio (i.e., number of visitors ending up in purchasing the product). Optimal user experience, availability of all relevant information, and optimized process steps are key contributors to conversion ratio.
- *Sales enablement*: By optimization of sales channel, it is possible to enable sales team to achieve their target. This includes providing sales promoting features such as targeted campaigns, real-time insights into customer behavior, multichannel enablement, and customer on-boarding process optimization. All these features require integration with various systems such as analytics systems and campaign management system.

Technical Scenarios for Integrations

The following is a discussion of some of the predominant technical scenarios that require enterprise integrations:

- *Seamless security access and single sign-on*: When navigating from one secured application to another, it is sometimes required to reauthenticate or revalidate the credentials if two applications are secured in different ways. This repeated authentication impacts user experience and comes in the way of seamless application access. To address this problem, we create an enterprise-wide single-sign-on (SSO) mechanism whereby security tokens once created are understood and accepted by all participating applications, thereby providing seamless access across those applications. This security mechanism requires integration of discrete internal applications with the portal and establishment of single-sign-on mechanism (for which the portal is one of the participating/subscribed applications). Similarly, if we need to integrate with external or third-party applications that have different security infrastructures, we can use various techniques such as federated SSO and secured services.
- *Information, content, and data aggregation*: This is an obvious scenario that requires integration with all source systems owning the concerned information, data, or content.
- *Support for adaptors and extensions*: In order to provide an extensible architecture, the portal solution should support various adaptors and extensions that can be leveraged for plugging in new functionality in the future. This scenario also requires integration with other systems.
- *Service-oriented architecture (SOA)*: A typical SOA scenario requires exposing and consuming services from various internal and external sources in a predefined format. The services form the integration mechanism in this case. We will discuss more about this in the following sections.

- *Process orchestration and validation*: A complete orchestration of a complex process often happens through a multistep workflow, and it requires invoking various systems and services. Additionally, each step also needs robust validation of complex business rules that again require invocation of validation services from source systems. For instance, a user registration process requires calls to database system, user registry system, and customer relationship management system.
- *Feature on-boarding*: If an enterprise already has an enterprise-wide content management system (CMS) or an enterprise search engine, the portal can on-board those features only through optimal integrations with such systems. Similarly, collaboration, social, and other functionalities can be enabled through appropriate integrations.

There are various other scenarios that require obvious integrations with systems such as logging, alerting, notification, monitoring, and analytics.

Integration Big Picture and Integration Types

A typical enterprise portal solution involves integration with multiple internal and external systems. Number of systems would vary based on the business scenarios and domains.

A big picture of an enterprise portal integration is given in Figure 6.1.

We are going to discuss the integration types provided in Figure 6.1 in greater detail in the following sections. Let us briefly discuss the possible integration systems given earlier:

There are mainly three broad kinds of integrations that will happen in the portal projects:

- *Integrations with core systems*: Core systems here refer to the key systems that are required for portal program implementation. Typically, a portal implementation requires systems such as content management, enterprise search engine, web analytics engine, workflow engine, rules engine, document management, enterprise database, media server, and knowledge management (KM) systems. Since many of these systems are used in almost all portal implementations, many of the portal products bundle these systems along with their main product offering. For instance, CMS, rules engine, and basic analytics are part of most of the portal products. In some scenarios, we need to integrate with existing systems available within an enterprise.
- *Enterprise application system integration*: This includes integration with all internal systems such as security system, ERP system, reporting systems, legacy systems, business intelligence systems, internal web applications, internal services, internal collaboration platforms, and other system of records (SORs). This will be required mainly for intranet portals, but even external portals will be integrated with these internal systems for aggregating information from required internal sources.
- *External system integration*: Systems such as external social media platforms, third-party system of records, and external collaboration platforms are the typical candidates for external integration. Other popular external integrations include maps, analytics, feeds, news, and external services. Security, performance, and user experience are the main concerns in these integrations.

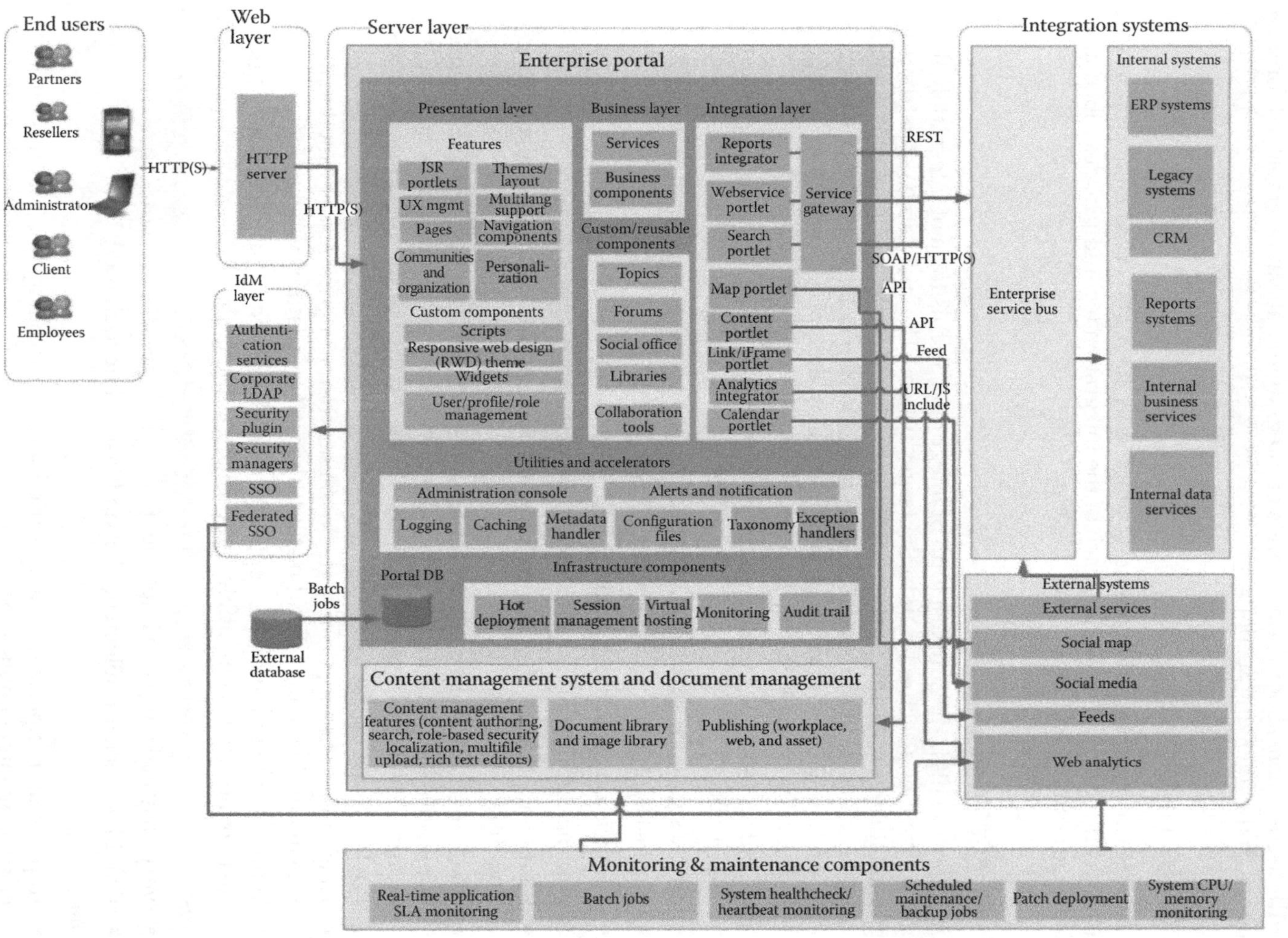

FIGURE 6.1
Portal integration big picture.

Besides integrating with these systems, a portal platform would also be expected to expose services or components for other systems. This would be in the form of web services, portlets, or widgets.

We will discuss more about various kinds of integration that can be employed for these integrations in the following sections.

Portal Integration Techniques

Let us look at various integration methods adopted in the portal solution to support various business and technical scenarios. Each of the integration technique is described along with its usage scenario and merits and demerits.

Link-Based Integration

- *Description*: This is the simplest form of integration. In this form of integration, the portal provides a secured link to the target system. The link can be constructed either statically at design time or during run time. The portal page acts as a gateway providing all the links to various applications. Some applications also need parameters that can be provided dynamically by the portal application. In modern-day portal application, this form of integration is rarely used.
- *Prerequisites*: This type of integration needs the following prerequisites for seamless experience:
  - Single sign-on with all applications
  - A consistent user and navigation experience
  - Application identified by a fixed URL pattern
- *Usage scenarios*: Typical usage scenarios are listed as follows:
  - Simple application that can provide a directory listing of all available functionalities
  - The integration with complex reporting and analytical/business intelligence applications sometimes use this model wherein we display a basic summary report and link off to the reporting tool that can then provide advanced reporting functionality such as drill-down and categorized report
  - Helps in parallel application deployment wherein partial list of functionality is available in the portal and rest is linked-off to existing systems
  - When we need to integrate applications implemented in distinct technologies that are not easily compatible and difficult to integrate
- *Pros*:
  - Very easy and simple to implement
  - Provides quicker implementation and faster time to market
- *Cons*:
  - Impacts user experience due to varied layout and navigation and has limited control on target application.
  - May require reauthentication if SSO is not implemented.
  - It will not be possible to leverage some of the core portal features such as personalization and fine-grained access control.

- *Impact on NFR (performance, scalability, availability, security)*:
    - Overall performance completely depends on the target system.
    - Scalability and availability are based on the target system.
    - SSO needs to be implemented for seamless security; otherwise, reauthentication would be required.

iFrame-Based Integration

- *Description*: An iFrame essentially embeds the target web page in the source page through standard iFrame object. Most portal products provide built-in iFrame portlets that can be configured to embed the target web page URL in portlet preference. This form of integration is seldom preferred as it has very poor user experience and has multiple security restrictions.
- *Prerequisites*: This type of integration needs the following prerequisites for seamless experience:
    - Single sign-on with target application
    - Application identified by a fixed URL pattern
- *Usage scenarios*: Typical usage scenarios are listed as follows:
    - When we quickly want to integrate with target web application on which we have minimum control
    - When iFrames are acceptable within user community (this will more likely be used internally than in external portals)
- *Pros*:
    - Very easy and simple to implement
    - Provides quicker implementation and faster time to market
- *Cons*:
    - Inconsistent user experience due to nonuniform page layout and due to potential horizontal and vertical scrolling.
    - Many browsers impose restriction on usage of iFrames, and some browsers don't support it due to security reasons.
    - Will not be able to leverage portal features such as personalization, preferences, sessions sharing, and caching.
    - Has potential security issues related to cross-domain issues, clickjacking, and cookie hijacking.
- *Impact on NFR (performance, scalability, availability, security)*:
    - Inconsistent page performance due to variation of load times across various sections of the page. iFrame may load after other portlets.
    - Scalability and availability are based on target system.
    - SSO needs to be implemented for seamless security; otherwise, reauthentication would be required.

Service-Based Integration

- *Description*: This is the most popular form of integration in modern portals. In this type of integration, the portal is integrated to systems by consuming the exposed services. Service provider should expose the business functionality as standards-based service using SOAP- or REST-based services. The portal will use built-in service components and consume services through JSR standard portlets. Most of the portals provide built-in support for exposing and consuming web service.

  This integration option has multifold advantages over other integration methods discussed earlier. The main advantage is that service-oriented integration helps in providing flexibility in integration and makes the portal platform extensible. This facilitates loose coupling, thereby allowing each of the system change independent of each other. It fits well with content aggregation use case of the portal wherein we can aggregate data and content from diverse sources through services.

  There are multiple variants of this kind of integration:

  - *Point-to-point service integration*: In this scenario, the portal provides and consumes ad hoc web services. Internal and external systems expose web services that will be consumed by web service portlets. This kind of integration will be required when we want to integrate with ad hoc external services or when we have fixed and limited set of services to be integrated with. Three key types of scenarios are SOAP over HTTP(S), REST over HTTP(S), and WSRP. While SOAP-based service invocation is the traditional way of invoking services, REST is a more popular and optimal for lightweight web scenarios. SOAP is often considered heavyweight due to exchange of XML and other standards. REST provides lightweight alternative through exchange of data in JSON (JavaScript Object Notation) format. Figure 6.2 shows three types of integration.
  - *Enterprise service bus (ESB)-based integration*: ESB is a message-oriented middleware that not only helps in centralizing the service access but also provides a host of other features. ESB is fully compliant with SOA principles with core focus on flexibility, scalability, and decoupling so that this layer can become the common layer to be accessed across all enterprise systems including the portal. ESB will facilitate data validation and transformation if needed before sending the data to downstream systems. Service bus is data format agnostic too and can handle data formats such as file, messages, and database batch jobs. ESB provides service decoupling between service consumers and providers as well through protocol translation and data transformation capabilities. This will also provide lightweight service orchestration logic. This is the centralized access point for integration platform providing adaptors and validation services and helps in business process orchestration. Workflows can be handled in the business process management (BPM) layer, and this layer can integrate with presentation layer such as the portal along with service governance and hence would most optimally serve as an integration middleware. ESB is an ideal choice when we have numerous internal and external systems to be integrated via services. It will also help us on-board other services in future with minimal effort. A typical portal-ESB integration is shown in Figure 6.3.

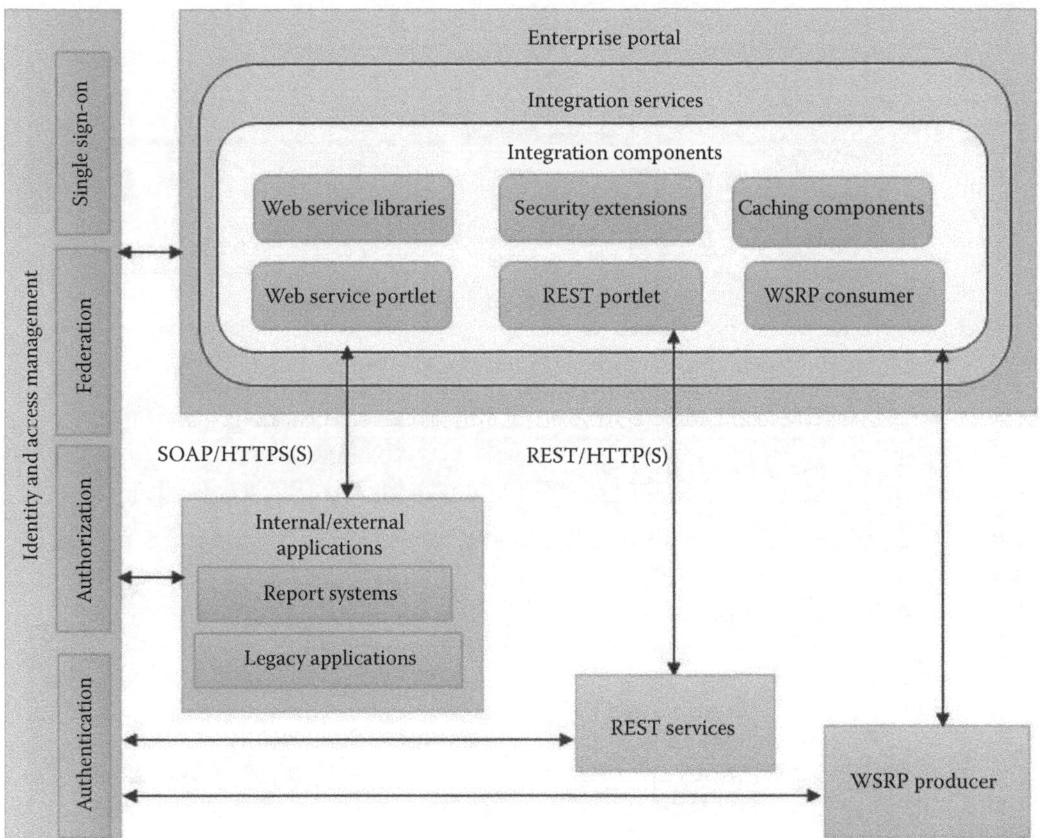

FIGURE 6.2
Point-to-point services integration with portal.

In this type of integration, the portal normally uses web services to integrate with ESB. In some scenarios, the ESB software provides native adaptors to be integrated with the portal.

- *WSRP-based integration*: WSRP option will be used if we need to integrate with an existing portal platform or with a non-portal platform exposing WSRP services using service-based integration. Most popular portal platforms support WSRP 1.0 and WSRP 2.0 to expose JSR portlets as presentation web services. This can be consumed by another portal platform that acts as WSRP consumer. This is one of the preferred options when we want to integrate two portal platforms developed in different technologies.

- *Prerequisites*: Services-based integration needs the following prerequisites for seamless experience:
  - Single sign-on with ESB
  - Support for authentication from all service providers
  - Availability of standard services
- *Usage scenarios*: Typical usage scenarios are listed as follows:
  - Integrating with any SOR through services
  - Integrating with legacy and ERP systems through services

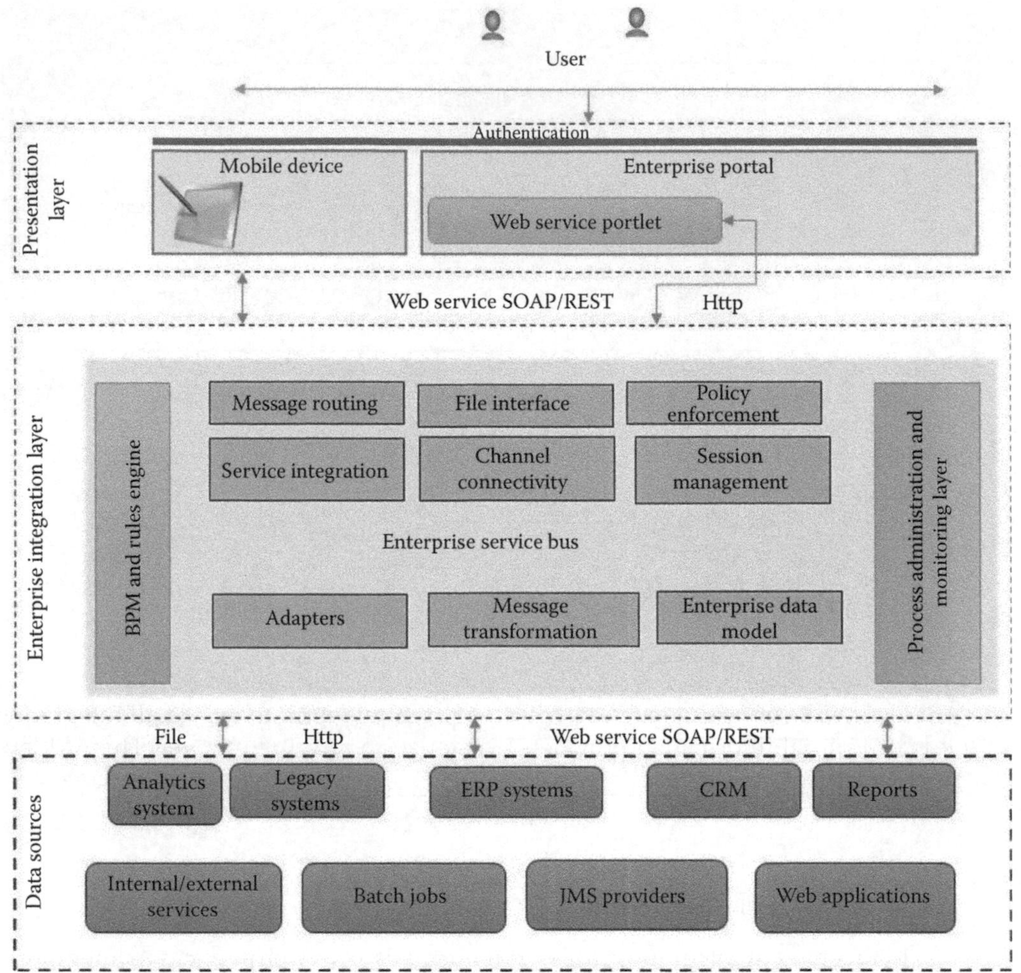

FIGURE 6.3
ESB-based integration.

- Integration of third-party and external systems through services
- Create a standards and open integration architecture platform for future needs
- Provide centralized service access through messaging middleware

- *Pros*:
  - Provides high flexibility and loose coupling architecture
  - Helps in extending the portal platform with future services
  - Enhances modularity and reusability of functionality
  - Can leverage portal features such as personalization, caching, and preference management
  - Provides clear separation of concerns
  - Helps in easier on-boarding of services in future

- *Cons*:
  - SOAP-based integration tends to be heavyweight sometimes.
  - Not well-established standards for transaction management and security in services and might require additional service gateways for complimenting services layer.
- *Impact on NFR* (*performance, scalability, availability, security*):
  - Needs careful design of service integration components to provide scalable and well-performing integration

API Gateway–Based Integration

In today's hyperconnected world, we can see that many of the external systems such as social media platforms, blogging platforms, apps, payment systems, games, and registration systems expose application programming interfaces (APIs) for integration over a variety of channels such as smartphones, TV, and kiosk. API management is one of the emerging trends in integration technologies.

An API is a gateway to connect the applications, services, and business processes with various channels and applications. APIs are the fast the becoming standard for enterprise integration, data sharing, and multichannel experience.

Portals and user experience platforms normally use API gateway layer for integration as shown in Figure 6.4.

The API layer will serve as a gateway within a portal platform to enable all integrations with internal/external information providers to happen in a secure manner. The API layer will provide the ability to expose a portal platform's capabilities to inside or outside consumer

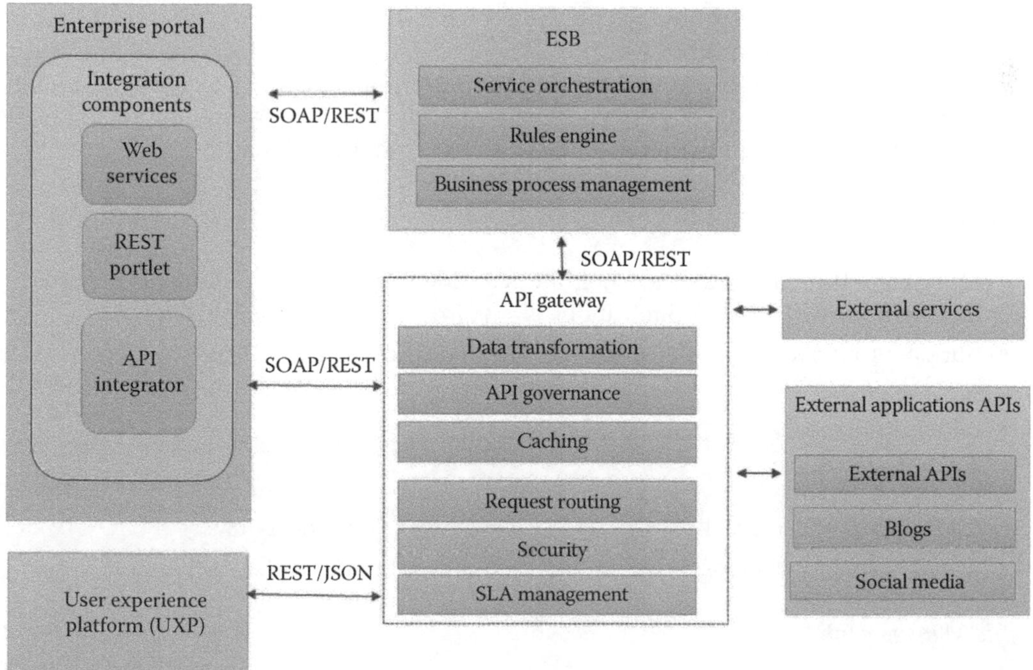

FIGURE 6.4
API gateway based integration.

in a simpler manner by providing easy-to-understand transport and message formats. Integrating external applications using APIs and exposing internal applications through APIs enable organizations to reuse the existing infrastructure to implement new applications.

The API layer will primarily include a web console and runtime gateways. The web console can be used for configuring the API integrations, defining security policies, implementing throttling of data, and managing the deployments to the gateways. The runtime gateway component handles all the integrations and API calls happening between internal and external systems.

This layer will handle the following capabilities in a portal platform:

- Reusable connectors for integrating with different external information providers and social media.
- Schedule integrations with external information providers to periodically bring data batches.
- Process data received from external information providers and store the required metadata in the CMS.
- Expose reusable APIs to web portal and back-end systems for consumption of metadata stored in the CMS.
- Manage real-time integrations to external information providers if necessary, when requests are initiated from the portal or back-end systems.
- Monitor incoming traffic and availability of APIs.
- Enable caching to improve response times.
- Provide analytical reports on number of calls made to external information providers, calls originating from back-end systems and portal.

The API layer provides a lightweight REST/JSON façade to a portal platform's WSDL-based web services. The API gateway provides out-of-the-box REST to SOAP mediation feature that will be leveraged for creating the mobile interface layer solution. The API gateway also provides many other standard features like the following:

Identity and Access Control

- Out-of-the-box connectors to integrate with identity platforms like Oracle Access Manager (OAM) and CA SiteMinder
- Support for OAuth, SAML Assertion, X.509 certificates, etc.
- Single sign-on (SSO)

Security

- JSON/XML schema validations, HTTP parameter validations, etc.
- Threat protection (cross-site scripting, SQL injection and DoS attacks, etc.)

Traffic Management

- Spike arrest to make sure that requests do not overwhelm back-end service capacity

- Response caching to reduce API latency
- Quota enforcements

Mobile Integration Features

- Push notifications
- Support for mobile streaming protocols
- Data compression

Pros

- Cache for improved performance
- Provides security for exposed APIs and services
- Manages the SLAs and API governance
- Handles required data transformation
- Handles API versioning
- Handles request routing
- Handles caching

Cons
Introduction of API gateway would introduce an additional layer of abstraction that would complicate the overall architecture. Impact on NFR (performance, scalability, availability, security):

- API Gateway enhances system scalability and availability.
- Security policies can be effectively enforced
- Performance can be optimized through caching and other techniques

API gateway can be used independently and also along with ESB. Let us look at the advantages of using it along with ESB.

ESB-Based API Gateway

The ESB layer will be used in cases where there are requirements for complex data transformations, data enrichment from multiple systems, and non–service-based integrations (MQ, JMS, FTP, legacy, etc.). The ESB layer will complement the API layer to enable integration with any internal system in any format using any protocol.

This layer will handle the following capabilities:

- Any complex data transformations and orchestration requirements before loading the data fetched from external information providers and social media into the CMS
- Any complex data transformations and orchestration requirements while handling API requests and response from web portal and back-end systems
- Prebuilt connectors and support for a wide range of systems and data formats

- Managing integrations between web portal and other internal applications
- Provision of admin web consoles to view reporting and analytics details

API gateway deployment for portal solution:

API gateway can be deploy in three modes: as a cloud proxy, on-premise or as a plugin.

Cloud Proxy: In this deployment model, the entire API gateway stack is deployed in the cloud. The service consumer directs the API call to the API manager deployed in the cloud. The API call is authenticated, authorized, and implemented in the cloud. The API implementation may call a service in the portal server. Ideally, a VPN tunnel is created between the API Manager's cloud infrastructure and portal server. The advantage of this model is the low initial capital investment needed to setup the infrastructure.

On-premise: In this model, API management stack is deployed as part of portal eco system. Deployment is usually done in the DMZ. All calls to back-end application is goes through the API manager.

Plug-in: This is a hybrid of the cloud proxy and on-premise. API calls from users are directed to a HTTP server or a service gateway hosted in the DMZ. The HTTP server/gateway then offloads the task of authentication, authorization, and metering the API call to an API manager deployed in the cloud. Once the call is authenticated and filtered, it is then forwarded to the back-end service. The vendor provides a plug-in which is installed on the HTTP server.

Feed-Based Integration

- *Description*: In this form of integration, the information is aggregated through XML feeds. Two popular formats are RSS and ATOM, which are used for content syndication. Almost all portal products provide a built-in feed portlet to consume external and internal feeds. Feed XML is formatted using XSL to suit the presentation requirements.
- *Prerequisites*: This type of integration needs the following prerequisites for seamless experience:
  - Availability of feed in standard format such as RSS (Rich Site Summary) or atom format
  - Ability to discover the feed through a unique URL
  - Ability to accept parameters that are required for personalization
- *Usage scenarios*: Typical usage scenarios are listed as follows:
  - Frequent changing of information such as news, stock market updates, exchange rates, status updates, notification, content updates, and blog entries can be exposed and consumed as feeds.
  - Requirement for asynchronous content syndication and need for automatic content updates.
- *Pros*:
  - Very easy and simple to implement
  - Provides optimal integration through asynchronous feed updates

- *Cons*:
  - This requires the target system to publish the updates in the required feed format.
- *Impact on NFR (performance, scalability, availability, security)*:
  - Provides high performance as we can optimize the feed retrieval through caching and other techniques

Clipping and Screen Scraping

- *Description*: In this form of integration, the HTML content from the target web page is *clipped* and presented in the portal page. Portlets allow us to configure the starting and ending HTML markers, which define the boundary for the HTML that will be clipped.

  A variation of this integration is to update the target web page with known beginning and ending marker HTML elements. This can be integrated using clipper portlet. This method can be adopted when we have control over target web application.
- *Prerequisites*: This type of integration needs the following prerequisites for seamless experience:
  - Target web page should contain a deterministic and static HTML start and end elements.
- *Usage scenarios*: Typical usage scenarios are listed as follows:
  - When we do not have other options of integration with target web page, we will use this technique.
  - When there are clear-cut start and end markers in the target web page.
- *Pros*:
  - Provides a decent alternative for content aggregation with minimal impact on user experience.
  - We can leverage some of the portal features such as skins during clipping.
- *Cons*:
  - Could result in security issues due to cross-domain scripting
  - Could cause inconsistent user experience
- *Impact on NFR (performance, scalability, availability, security)*:
  - Availability and scalability are directly dependent on target web page.
  - Impacts performance to some extent due to cost involved in parsing the HTML content.

Portlet-Based Integration

- *Description*: Many portal vendors and third-party systems provide JSR 168 or JSR 286 standard portlets for providing native integration. For instance, content portlet to integrate with CMS, workflow portlet for integration with workflow engine, ERP portlet for integration with ERP system, analytics portlet for integration with web analytics system, and reporting portlet for integration with report systems are some of the examples of this kind of integration.

Alternatively, developers can also custom develop portlets for the specific project and organization needs. It is recommended to use portlet standards and configurable parameters during custom development to ensure reusability of the custom portlet and to develop a lighter version of portlet such as JSR 286–based portlet or a client-side widget.

Another variant of this form of integration is that some of the existing web applications are reengineered to become JSR-compliant portlets. This portletlization is normally used in migrating existing web applications or legacy applications into a portal platform.

- *Prerequisites*: Availability of portlet for integration
- *Usage scenarios*: Typical usage scenarios are listed as follows:
  - When we are doing legacy modernization to migrate existing web applications to a portal platform
  - When the internal systems or external systems provide standard portlet mode of integration
  - Need for decommissioning back-end legacy systems
- *Pros*:
  - We can leverage all the portal features such as personalization, skins, access controls, multichannel support, layout customization, SSO, and look-and-feel customization
  - Portlet-based integration helps us in providing reusable, modular, and pluggable integration modules
- *Cons*:
  - Sometimes need custom development
- *Impact on NFR* (*performance, scalability, availability, security*):
  - Impacts performance to some extent due to the integration

Widget-Based Integration

- *Description*: This is another integration method that is gaining popularity especially in lean portals. In this scenario, a JavaScript-based client-side component such as widget will be used for integration. Widgets are lightweight pluggable alternatives to the web applications that communicate to back-end services through AJAX-based technologies and use JSON-like lightweight data formats. Widgets are popular mainly because they can be embedded into any web application portal or nonportal application and for its ability to asynchronous communicate resulting in performance optimization. A few portal containers and portlets also run widgets to ease the integration of widget with portlet.
- *Prerequisites*: Widgets should be preferably developed in standard client-side libraries such as JavaScript or using HTML standards.
- *Usage scenarios*: Typical usage scenarios are listed as follows:
  - When we are trying to integrate with third-party systems that provide widgets, it would be the preferred choice of integration.

- If the functionality needs to be integrated with various web platforms in different technologies, developing a widget along with integration services is a better choice. For instance, a chat widget or map widget would be a better choice.
- When we need to perform lightweight integration using client-side technologies.

- *Pros*:
  - Widgets are a lightweight, platform-/technology-independent way of integration.
  - Widgets support multiple technology optimization techniques such as lazy loading, asynchronous communication, and partial rendering.
- *Cons*:
  - Heavily depends on client side and hence needs browser with JavaScript enabled.
- *Impact on NFR (performance, scalability, availability, security)*:
  - Provides optimum performance benefits

Core Portal Integrations

In this section, let us look at few key integrations that are necessary in almost all portal platforms. This throws insights into optimal integration aspects of core portal integrations.

CMS Integration

Rendering personalized content and marketing web content are some of the primary use cases for all portal systems. So, it is imperative that the portal be integrated with a CMS for efficient management of the content. It is for the same reason that most of the portal products also include a native CMS system. For instance, Liferay CMS, IBM WCM, and Oracle UCM have native integration through portlets with their respective web content products.

However, in some cases, it is required to integrate the portal with an enterprise-wide CMS system for various reasons. In such cases, we need to understand the available options and ways to integrate them.

The following are various methods to integrate the portal with an enterprise CMS:

- *Native content portlets*: If the portal product is bundled with native CMS, it provides native content portlets to manage and configure the content. This is a straightforward way of integration. The native portlets provide many configurable features such as metadata-based retrieval, configuration of content path, and content fragment name.
- *CMS APIs*: Additionally, most of the native CMS systems also expose APIs that can be used to have greater control of the web content. CMS APIs provide features for content tagging, content searching, content indexing, etc. CMS systems that are compliant with open standards such as JSR 283 also provide JCR (Content Repository API for Java) to access the content from the CMS.

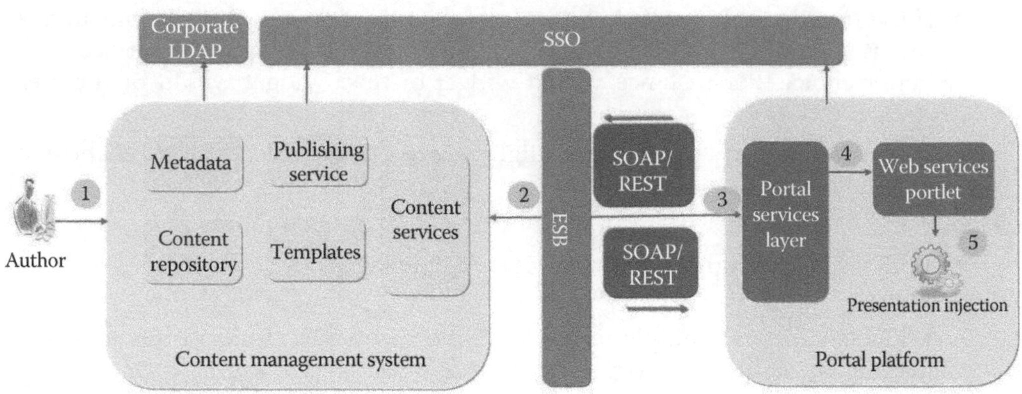

FIGURE 6.5
Portal–CMS integration.

- *Service-based integration*: Most of the CMS systems provide content services that can be leveraged to retrieve the content. The web service can be either SOAP based or REST based, but the preference is toward the latter because of its lightweight characteristic. This stands out as the most preferred approach as it complies well with service-oriented architecture.
- *Integration using JSR 170/JSR 283 compliant content repositories*: The standard specifies Java content repository (JCR) API for bidirectional access of content from a compliant content repository. This is a preferred option if the target CMS supports JCR.

A portal integration with CMS using a service-based integration is shown in Figure 6.5.

As explained in the second option, the portal uses SOAP- or REST-based service to retrieve the content through content services. The high-level steps for content management and integration are as follows:

- Author uses CMS authoring templates to author the content.
- CMS exposes content through content services via ESB or for a point-to-point integration.
- The portal's web service portlet gets the content XML through service layer and injects the presentation code such as style and layout and renders the final page. It also enforces all applicable personalization rules.

Search Engine Integration

Search is one of the key factors influencing user experience. The portal is an aggregation platform, and search is the key tool to discover the relevant information from all enterprise sources aggregated by search. The main search features used within a portal include the following:

1. Contextualized and personalized search based on user attributes and access controls
2. Faceted and categorized search features
3. Configurable relevancy ranking

4. Exposing search as a service for external systems
5. Support for advanced search features such as typeahead, synonym support, multilingual search support, semantic search, relevancy rank boosting, and ability to include all or any of the keywords
6. Using preconfigured search portlets for dynamic delivery on portal pages

Modern-day portals use search-centered experience positioning search as the primary navigation tool by placing search functionality in prominent position. This aids in faster discovery of relevant information, thereby positively impacting user experience and conversion rate.

Due to all these factors, most of the portal products provide a basic search engine with open-source products such as Apache Lucene and also provide robust support for integrating with external enterprise search engines.

Figure 6.6 shows various search features needed in portal search functionality.

The portal search normally needs these features:

- *Content search*: This includes configuring the search engine to search for matching web content. The content will be matched based on keyword, metadata, path, tags, etc. The most popular approach is to use SOAP- or REST-based services to retrieve

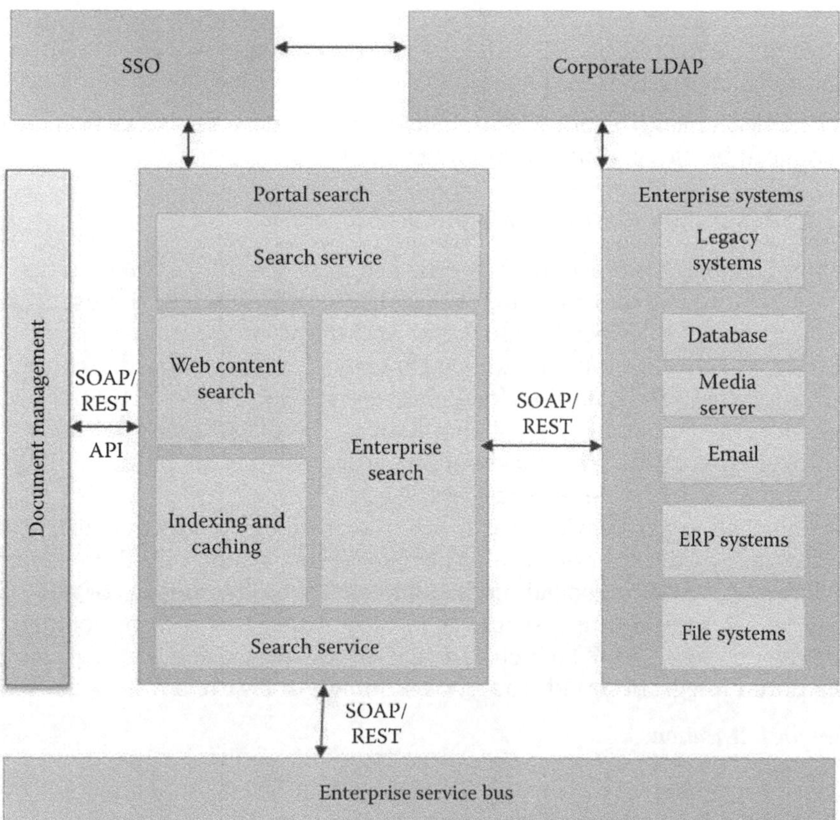

FIGURE 6.6
Portal search.

matching content from CMS. Alternatively, CMS-provided APIs can also be used for content search.

- *Enterprise search*: This includes indexing and searching matching content from various enterprise sources such as database, ERP systems, mail, file system, chats, and web/media servers. In most of these integrations, web service–based integration is used.
- *Search services*: The portal would also expose its search services to other systems via ESB or web service. On top of the search results provided by the search engine, the portal adds other value additions such as personalization, role-based filtering, and personalized recommendations.
- *Indexing and caching*: For efficient search results retrieval, the search engine should index all content sources and cache it. Caching would happen at the search engine layer as well as at the portal layer.

Though the portal provides built-in search features, in most cases, it would be very basic and may not fulfill all required search functionalities. It is therefore required to integrate with enterprise search engines. The following are the main methods of integration with enterprise search engine:

1. *Service-based integration*: This is the most popular form of integration. Most enterprise search engines provide search services that can be leveraged by the portal. Web service portlet will use SOAP- or REST-based search service from the search engine for such integration.
2. *Native portlets or widgets*: Some search engines also provide JSR portlets and widgets that can be plugged into a portal platform.

Social and Collaboration Platform Integration

One of the predominant use cases of the portal is to play the role of collaboration platform. This use case is more relevant in intranet portal scenarios wherein the users can use the portal as a single-point interface to collaborate and share information.

Some of the main collaboration features include blog, message boards, forums, user and product communities, wikis, audio/video chat, review and rating, activities, web conferencing, and document sharing. As collaboration is one of the principal use cases of the portal, all portal products provide these collaboration features out of the box. We also have an option to integrate with open-source products.

With the increase in popularity of external social media platforms such as Facebook and LinkedIn, many external portals also need to be integrated with these external social media platforms. All external social media platforms provide plug-ins or API-based integration that requires obtaining a secure application ID. They also optionally provide a software development kit (SDK) which can be used for integration.

A sample portal integration with Facebook is shown in Figure 6.7.

Prerequisites for Integration

1. The portal supports sign on using the Facebook or LinkedIn credentials by leveraging the OAuth2.0 standard.
2. For the Facebook integration, the portal site will have to be added as an application in Facebook. Facebook will create a unique application ID for portal application.

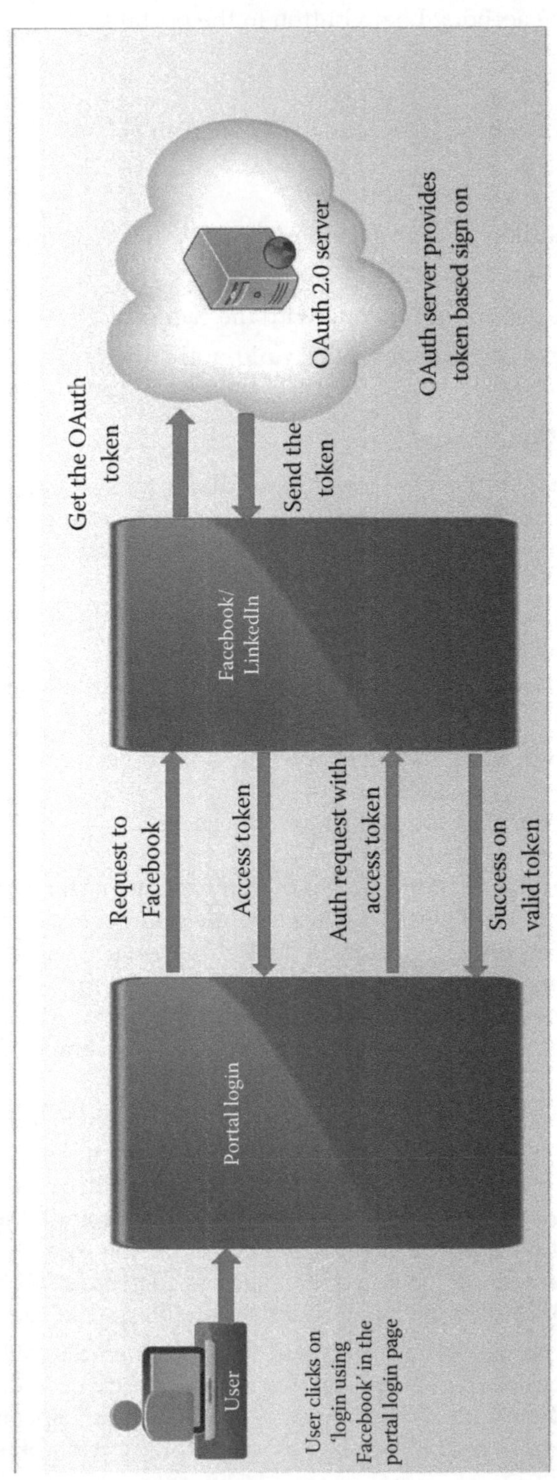

FIGURE 6.7
Portal facebook integration.

3. The application ID generated will be configured within the portal site.
4. This would add the Facebook Login button to the portal site.

Facebook Integration

High-level steps in the facebook integration flow is given below:

1. Client clicks on Login via Facebook.
2. Request is sent to Facebook, which generates an access token using an OAuth2.0 API.
3. The access token is sent to the client.
4. The client sends the access token along with the request URL to Facebook.
5. Facebook validates the access token and, if valid, authenticates the user successfully.

Security System Integration

This is the most fundamental use case for any portal. Portal systems must be integrated with the security systems of the organization and also provide single sign-on with other applications. There are mainly three types of security integration:

- *User registry (such as Lightweight Directory Access Protocol (LDAP))*: For authentication and user profile updates and for user registration
- *Internal SSO (also known as web SSO)*: For providing seamless access to secured internal applications
- *Federated SSO:* For providing seamless access to secured external applications

A typical portal security infrastructure is shown in Figure 6.8:

- For authentication and user profile access or updates, the portal must be integrated with user registry such as LDAP, which is a single point of access to all enterprise applications. It holds policy and user credential information. All portal products support built-in plug-ins for integration with various kinds of user registries. They can be configured for synchronization with the portal. Portals also provide extensible security infrastructure and APIs that can be leveraged for custom user registry integration.
- For achieving web SSO (internal SSO or web SSO), normally token-based or HTTP header–based integration is followed. The portal will be integrated with an enterprise-wide security manager such as SiteMinder, and it will be configured as a participating application. For this kind of integration, vendor-provided security plug-ins and extensions will be used on the portal end. Once the integration is done, an additional SSO token will be generated after successful user authentication, and the portal will use the SSO token with all requests with internal secured applications.
- For achieving external SSO, the portal will use federated SSO. Normally, this is done using SAML assertions. The portal will act as identity provider for achieving this kind of integration with Federation server, which runs a specialized web service that can issue, manage, and validate requests for security tokens and identity management.
- We will see the detailed flow of web SSO and federated SSO in Chapter 9.

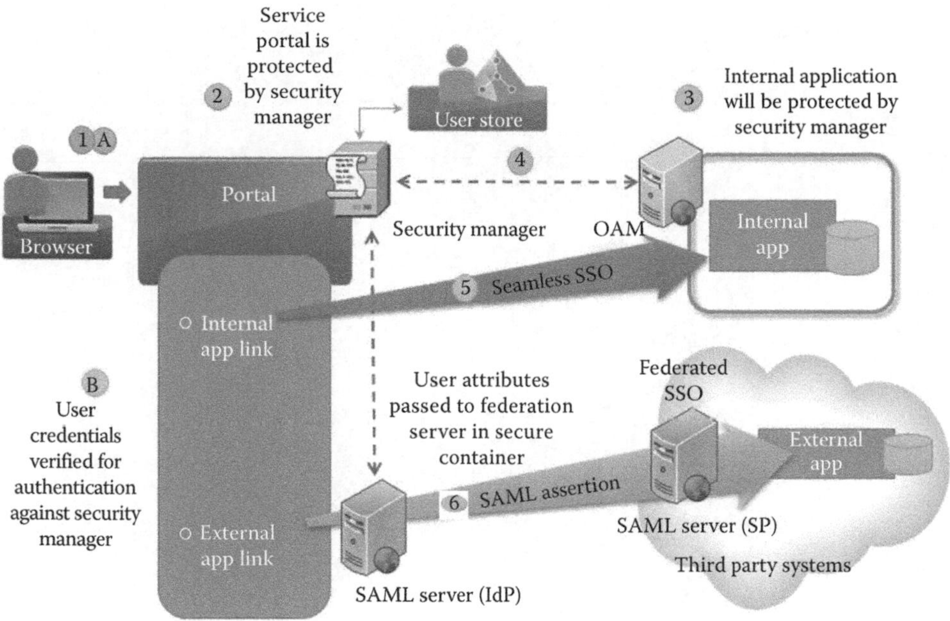

FIGURE 6.8
Portal SSO flow.

Business Process Management (BPM), Business Rules, and Workflow Integration

A configurable rules engine is required for complex business applications. It helps portal application to be easily customizable and extensible and to meet regulatory compliances. There are various kinds of rules that a rules engine would execute. Some of the prominent ones in the context of the portal are as follows:

- *Personalization rules*: Ability to customize the user experience, functionality, data, and navigation based on implicit and explicit preferences
- *Recommendation rules*: Ability to analyze user preferences, user download history, and purchase history and to recommend content or product that would be most liked by users
- *Business logic rules*: Various rules required for implementing business functionality and business processes
- *Workflow rules*: Rules to decide the sequence of workflow steps
- *Transaction processing rules*: Rules required for executing a transaction
- *Notification rules*: Rules that govern alerting and notification trigger on occurrence of a particular event or when a particular threshold is reached

Due to the importance of rules engine in the portal domain, some portal products provide built-in rules engine for these scenarios. Additionally, there are open-source rules engine plug-ins and portlets. For instance, Drools provides JSR 94-compliant rules engine Drools portlet that can be used for configuring and executing rules. As always, the external rules engine can also be integrated via service-based integration and rules APIs.

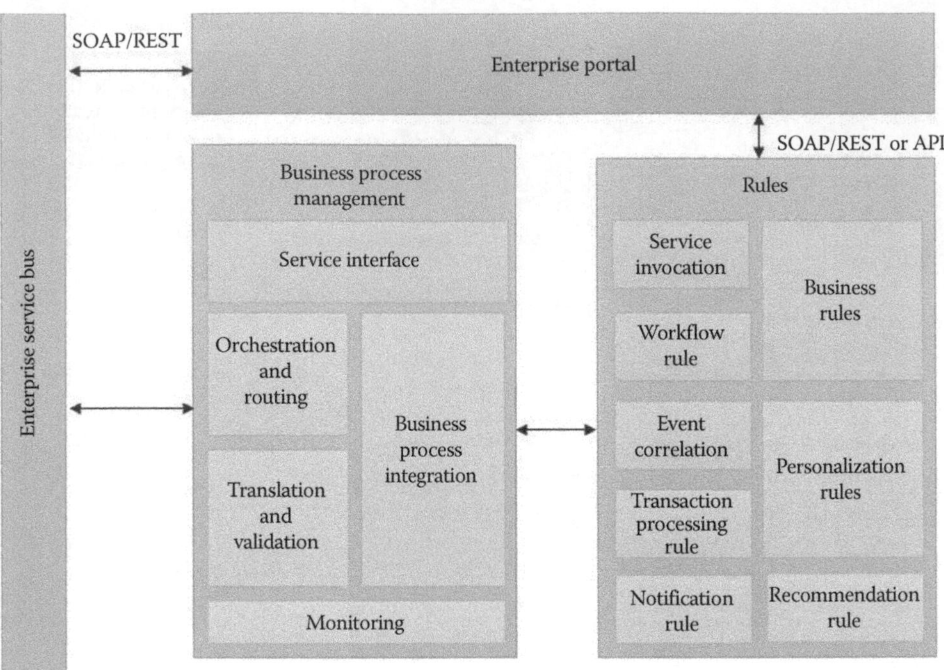

FIGURE 6.9
Portal–BPM integration.

The BPM is another popular use case scenario where portals are preferred. This includes end-to-end configuration and modeling of a complex business process such as user registration, multistep content approval, and product shopping process. BPM has close ties with rules engine as the process step execution requires lot of rules to be configured. BPM also includes orchestration of business process steps and request routing. The business process should also be customized for various domains, languages, and geographies and hence need translation and validation services. Portals are normally integrated with external BPM products or ESB that has built-in BPM capabilities.

The high-level integration of the portal with BPM and rules engine along with their capabilities is shown in Figure 6.9.

Though BPM has complex workflow capabilities and hence provides a sophisticated workflow engine, some portal products provide built-in basic workflow engines. Kaleo workflow engine is one of the popular open-source workflow engines that have plug-ins for portal products.

Knowledge Management Integration

Knowledge management portals are widely used both within organization and as an external entity. Though there are exclusive KM tools available, it is possible to build an effective KM tool leveraging portal technologies. A KM portal has the following business benefits:

1. Acts as a collaboration platform for internal and external stakeholders
2. Provides a platform for coauthoring and cocreation

3. Improves productivity of the users by reusing solution articles and troubleshooting tips
4. Enables self-service business goal
5. Acts as an effective document and asset management system
6. Compliments the social and collaboration features to actively engage the end users
7. Helps in realizing numerous business goals such as conversion ratio, cross sell/up-sell, site traffic, and enhanced user experience

Partial KM features such as solution articles management and knowledge repository are used in almost all portal applications as they augment well with intended business goals.

The core components of a KM portal are shown in Figure 6.10.

As we can see, the core components of a KM portal are already a part of portal technology stack. Workflow engine, search engine, collaboration tools, responsive user experience, feeds, intuitive navigation, knowledge repository, metadata and tag management, content and document management, and analytics are provided as part of most portal products. The gaps can be fulfilled by integrating the portal with open-source or commercial products as discussed in the previous sections. On top of these core KM components, the portal would be able to add personalization and recommendation rules and provide

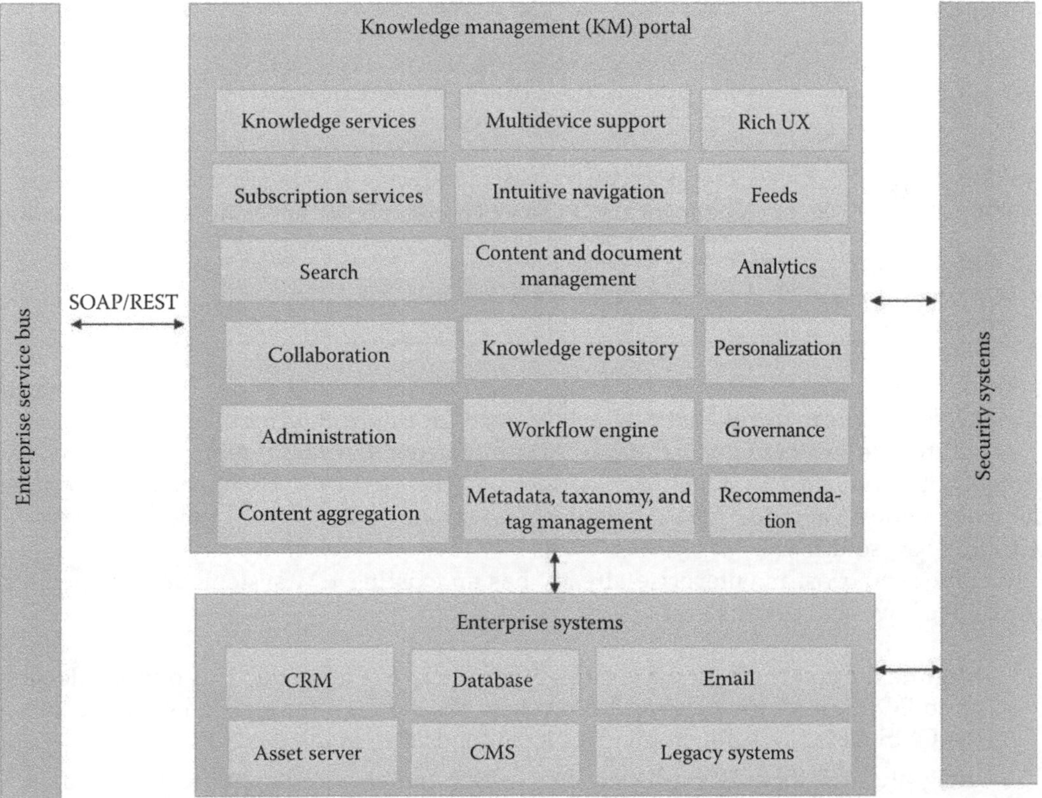

FIGURE 6.10
Portal-based knowledge management system.

TABLE 6.1
KM Capability Portal Solution Mapping

Core KM Capability	Portal Solution Component
Knowledge services	• Portal web service feature
Multidevice support	• Portal mobility theme • Portal device recognition plug-in • Portal support for responsive web design
Rich UX	• Portal support for responsive web design • Customizable layout and portal page templates • Multilingual support
Intuitive navigation	• Built-in navigation portlet • Built-in navigation features such as breadcrumb and left navigation
Feeds	• Out-of-the-box feed portlet
Search	• Out-of-the-box search portlet • Search engine integration
Content and document management	• Support for content authoring, publishing, and metadata tagging through portal CMS • Integration with content and document management systems • Support for content categorization • Built-in taxonomy support
Analytics	• Built-in web analytics support • Integration with web analytics product
Collaboration	• Built-in social and collaboration features such as blogs, wiki, articles, communities, message boards, chat, web conferencing, and cobrowsing • Integration with social and collaboration platforms
Knowledge repository	• Combination of portal database and content repository that can be used for storing knowledge assets and artifacts
Personalization	• Out-of-the-box personalization and rules engine
Workflow engine	• Built-in workflow engine or integration with external workflow engine
Content aggregation	• Numerous portlets for integration such as web service portlet, iFrame portlet, feed portlet, REST portlet, web service portlet, and content portlet
Recommendation	• Built-in recommendation engine
Metadata, taxonomy, and tag management	• Built-in support for metadata and tagging

governance to make a full-fledged KM system. Table 6.1 maps the core KM features with portal solution components that can be leveraged for implementing them.

In addition to leveraging existing portal components, the portal also needs to be integrated with enterprise systems such as ERP systems, legacy systems, email, enterprise database, content and document management systems, and asset and media servers for realizing KM solution.

In some scenarios, an enterprise already has an existing KM system, and in such scenarios, we have two options available:

1. Migrate the content from the existing KM system to the portal. This option allows us to EOL/sunset the existing KM system. We can build migration scripts using the CMS APIs to a JCR-compliant content repository in the portal.
2. Integrate with the existing KM system, which can be done when the organization needs to continue to use the legacy KM system. In such a case, the portal can act as a front end or as an aggregation platform for the KM system. KM system can be

one of the enterprise integrations with which the portal has to be integrated. There are mainly two forms of integration:

a. *Service-based integration*: If the KM system exposes knowledge services through SOAP- or REST-based interfaces, the portal can be integrated with it. If the system does not provide any services, it can be service enabled by building a service layer. The portal can directly invoke knowledge services or use ESB for better service governance.
b. Use API-based integration to directly get knowledge assets from the knowledge repository. This is not the recommended approach as it requires internal (and sometimes undocumented/unsupported) knowledge of the KM system.

E-Commerce Integration

The portal often is used as front end acting as storefront for e-commerce systems. Since the portal's main strength lies in presentation services, it will be used as the preferred presentation platform for e-commerce. The secondary reason is that the portal can also bring other context about the product such as product discussions from social media and product review/rating from social platforms and user communities to improve the user experience. The portal anyway has very robust personalization and recommendation rules engine that comes handy in cross selling and up-selling through targeted recommendations. The insights drawn from portal analytics coupled with portal recommendation engine can also be used for product bundling and packaging.

Having said these things, integration between the portal and e-commerce is not always straightforward as there are multiple touch points. Some of the important ones are given as follows:

1. For all core e-commerce functionalities such as shopping cart and checkout, the portal needs to be integrated with e-commerce engine via service-based integration.
2. Product information is often stored in product database from which the portal has to retrieve the information.
3. In some cases, order management, product pricing, and inventory management are done by separate ERP systems, and the portal has to be integrated with each of them via exposed services.
4. In addition to these, the portal also needs to be integrated with enterprise security systems for authentication and fine-grained access control and collaboration platform for forums and communities.
5. For performance reasons, we also will synchronize data to optimize the integrations:
   a. Basic product attributes are maintained locally and synched up on regular basis by offline batch job from product master database.
   b. Catalog information is cached and updated.

A simplified view of e-commerce portal is shown in Figure 6.11.

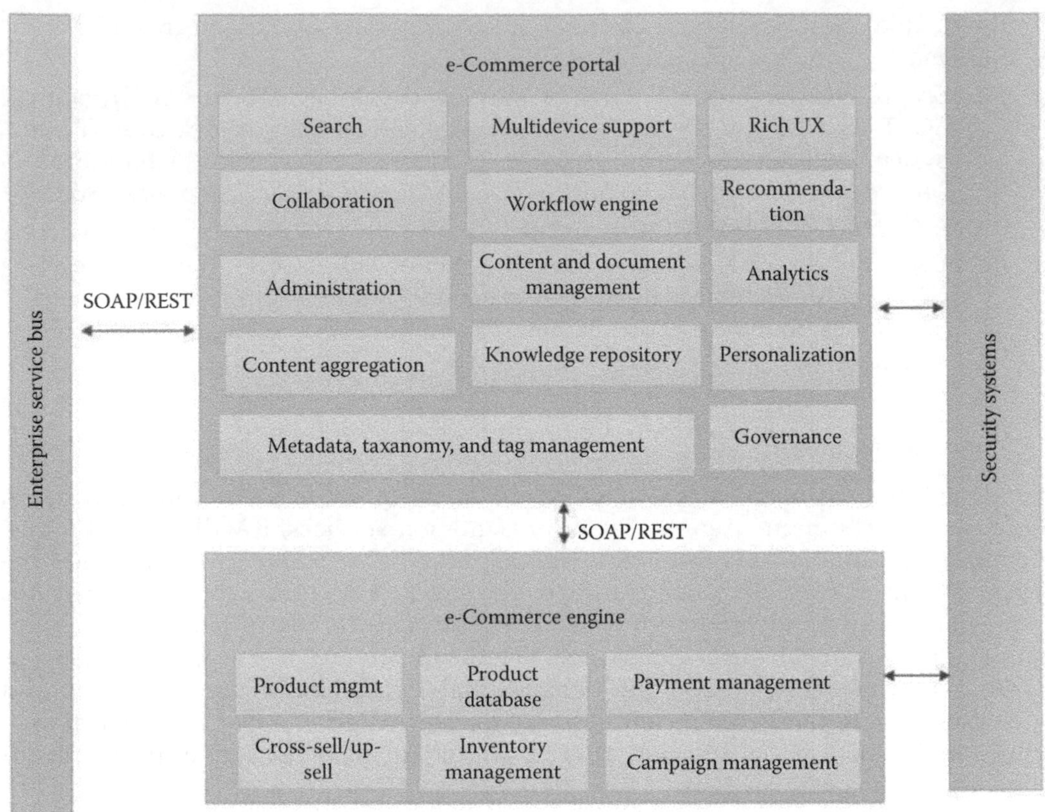

FIGURE 6.11
e-Commerce portal.

Reports and Business Intelligence System Integration

The portal is also used for building business intelligence dashboards and for front-ending reporting systems. A typical portal dashboard will aggregate data and analytics information from various analytics tools and present a summarized view of key metrics that aids the business stakeholders in taking decisions and provides insights into user behavior.

A sample flow for developing a reporting and a BI dashboard in a portal platform is shown in Figure 6.12:

- User requests for a portal dashboard page. A portal application would check for existence of security cookie. If not found, it redirects to authentication services for authentication. If found, the cookie is validated.
- Authentication service would challenge the user and validate the user credentials.
- Upon successful user authentication, the security cookie that contains all the LDAP groups like portal access group and admin group will be created.

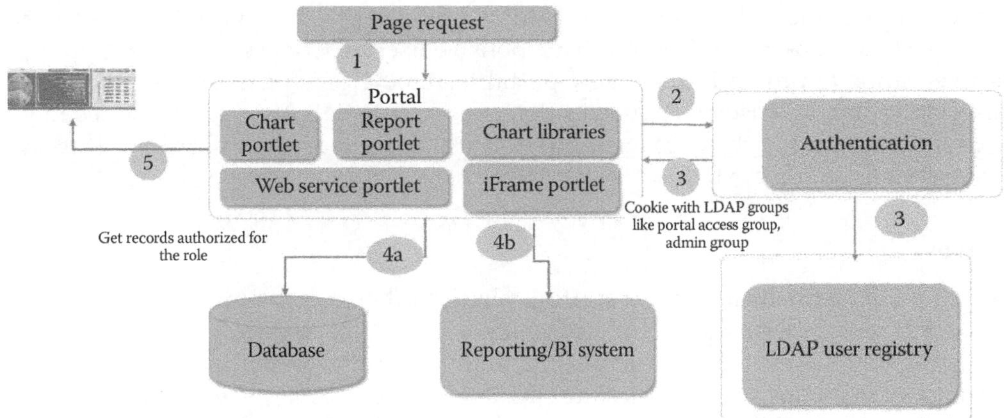

FIGURE 6.12
Reporting dashboard portal flow.

- The portal would then use the LDAP groups to filter the authorized records from the product database and construct a chart. The chart and graphs will be constructed using one of the following techniques:
  - *Using chart/graph portlet*: A JSR 168 or JSR 286 chart portlet would be developed that uses server side components to format the data required for construction of charts and graphs. There are multiple open-source chart libraries such as JFreeChart and commercial products such as High Charts, Fusion charts that can be leveraged here. Some BI tools also provide standard portlets that can be used.
  - *Using chart widget*: Client-side technologies such as JavaScript and other lightweight chart frameworks will be leveraged to construct responsive widgets that display charts and graphs. They use AJAX to communicate with server components and get the chart-related data in JSON format. While selecting an open source or commercial charting tool, we need to evaluate it based on multiple parameters such as support for various chart formats, browser support, ability to customize the charts, etc.
  - Using iFrame portlet, we can embed the original report page. This is the least preferred option.
- Both of these options use service-oriented integration to invoke the services exposed by report/BI tool.
- In addition to the data level authorization, the portal would also use the role information to hide/show the corresponding functionalities/reports to the user. The final page is rendered to the user.

Special Forms of Integration: Mashups, Widgets, Plug-Ins, and Extensions

So far, we have discussed a few traditional portal integration techniques. Let us look at some of the emerging integration methods in portals.

As we know, some of the main trends gaining popularity among portals are lightweight or lean portals, web-oriented approach, responsive user experience, mobility support, etc. The integration approach in these new portal technologies is primarily inclined toward client-side JavaScript-based components that are not only lightweight but also responsive. Let us look at some of those concepts now. These components are already discussed in earlier sections to some extent.

Mashups

A mashup is essentially a web aggregating platform that gets the information from various sources using client-side technologies (such as widgets and gadgets). Though mashups aggregate information like portals, the main difference lies in using the aggregated information: mashups primarily use the client-side APIs to combine multiple services and to provide a value-added combine functionality in a visual appealing way. For instance, let us consider a *store locator* feature in retail portal. When the user selects the address, the store locator mashup does the following things:

1. Renders map visuals and locates all the stores in that locality. This is achieved by combining the map APIs and store addresses.
2. Additionally, the mashup also gets the news feed and blog feed for each of the store location to provide feedback and rating about that store.
3. The mashup also provides the photos of the stores using the image service.

As we can see here, the mashup is not simply aggregating the information; it is converting the aggregated data into a more useful visualization that enhances user experience. Store locator mashup is aggregating the information to create a combined logical entity. In order to achieve this, the mashup mainly relies on REST-based web services and RSS/Atom feeds. Wherever necessary, it will also use APIs to aggregate the information.

The portal on the other hand primarily aggregates the information and presents without combining each of the multiple functionality into a logical entity.

In some scenarios, we will also provide mashups within a portal page to enhance user experience. As mashup is built on client-side component, it can be rendered in a widget portlet. This hybrid approach would provide us best of both worlds in customer facing web applications.

Widgets

As discussed earlier, widgets are client-side components that use AJAX-based technologies to communicate with server components. They are the lightweight alternatives to portlets and are heavily used in web-oriented architecture. Widgets provide the responsive and interactive user experience and also provide multidevice support. They are also platform independent and hence can be easily plugged into a variety of HTML-based web platforms. Most of the collaboration tools such as chat, forums, blogs, and social media are available as pluggable widgets. As widgets mostly use asynchronous communication model, the page performance is also better when widgets are used.

Many portal products provide built-in widget portlet to run the widgets. Most of the web-oriented portals and lean portals heavily use widgets as a lightweight alternative to JSR 168 portlets.

If we are building a portal platform that is heavily used by Internet users, it makes sense to leverage widgets to a large extent as they provide the intended benefits. However, if there are requirements for heavy personalization, a lot of server side processing, strict security rules, and then a JSR 286 would form a better alternative than widget.

Plug-Ins and Extensions

Plug-ins and extensions help us in enhancing the out-of-the-box portal functionality and customizing it for the required scenario. For instance, the portal provides default support for LDAP; however, a client has a custom nonstandard user registry that is not currently supported by the portal. In such cases, we can use the plug-in API to extend the portal security infrastructure to integrate with the custom user registry.

If there are any enhancements to the core portal functionality (such as login module, portal administration module, core portal interfaces), it must be done only using the extension feature provided by the portal vendor. This ensures that custom component is not overwritten during future upgrades and migrations.

Most of the open-source products provide plug-ins to portal products.

Web Frameworks

In some scenarios, portals may need to be integrated with existing web frameworks such as Struts and Spring MVC. In such scenarios, we can leverage the integrations recommended for these web frameworks. A few brief points in this regard are:

- *Struts*: We can leverage the Struts-config.xml for page flow and tiles-def.xml for defining page layout.
- *Spring MVC*: Spring framework exposes spring web MVC application framework for the portal.
- *Java Server Faces* (*JSF*): Most portal containers support JSF standards JSR 127, and we can develop a JSF portlet as well. Additionally, we can also migrate the JSF applications as portlets.

Portal Integration Patterns

Table 6.2 provides a list of most commonly used integration patterns within a portal platform.

TABLE 6.2

Portal Integration Patterns

Portal Integration Pattern	Description	Usage Scenario
Publisher/subscribe and fire and forget pattern	The portal client sends the request through a message to the ESB or target. The client will not expect an immediate synchronous response. However, it will listen to the response queue. The communication happens in an asynchronous fashion. The ESB will place the message in the JMS queue or topic. A target system that is subscribed to topic and processes message and portal listener will be notified with the response. JMS infrastructure ensures durability and guarantees delivery of the message. *Implementation*: This pattern is implemented using JMS queue, topic, and ESB. Portal products provide support for JMS APIs for message construction and listeners to receive the response.	This pattern is used when the portal client wants to send a notification to bulk subscribers, for instance, cache updates and event changes. The pattern can be used for point-to-point communication (using JMS queue) and bulk communication (using JMS topic). We can use this when target system supports message-based communication.
Gateway pattern	This is the most popular pattern in portal scenario. Client applications want to interact or need data and functionality from multiple back-end systems.	This is the classical portal scenario. When the client applications need an aggregated view of all data and functionality from various back-end systems, we can use the portal.
	The portal serves as a single point of access and as a gateway integration platform for aggregating all data and functionality from back-end systems. It will use built-in content aggregation features and portlets for this. The portal will abstract the interaction details with back-end systems and simplify the access mechanism. The portal optionally uses ESB for service aggregation and service governance. The portal gateway provides seamless single-stop-shop experience for the user. *Implementation*: This pattern is implemented using built-in content aggregation portlets such as web service portlet, REST portlet, feed portlet, content portlet, and database portlet. Service aggregation is done using ESB, which does service integration, message translation, message routing, and governance.	When we need to interact with various back-end services with a single point of access, we can use this pattern.

(*Continued*)

TABLE 6.2 (*Continued*)
Portal Integration Patterns

Portal Integration Pattern	Description	Usage Scenario
Service-oriented integration	This is another classical scenario for the portal. All required data and functionality are exposed through standard services. The service can be exposed and consumed through SOAP or REST interfaces. The pattern provides advantages like loose coupling, flexibility, extensibility, and reusability. *Implementation*: This pattern is implemented using portal-provided web service libraries or open-source web service libraries such as Apache Axis for web service consumption. In modern web applications, lightweight service consumption through REST-based service using JSON data is the preferred format. Another elegant way of implementing this pattern is through asynchronous service invocation using AJAX libraries. ESB is also another efficient way of implementing this pattern.	This pattern is the most popular way of integrating with back-end systems, and the following are some usage scenarios: When we want to integrate with internal or external applications that are service enabled, we can use this. In legacy modernization, we will build services on top of legacy ERP systems for integration. When we want to build a flexible, scalable, and robust platform to support future extensions and services on-boarding, we will use this pattern. When we have layered architecture and need separation of concerns and standards-based integration.
Message bus pattern	In this pattern, the portal client interacts with a message bus component that provides robust service aggregation features, schema validation, message routing, and validation. Message bus connects various systems that expose distinct interfaces and supports various protocols. Message bus provides various value additions such as process orchestration, routing, translation, and message policy enforcement.	This pattern is used when we need to aggregate multiple back-end services in a scalable way. Want to orchestrate a complex business process based on services and for BPM. Need robust service governance process.
	Implementation: This pattern is implemented by commercial or open-source ESB products that act as message-oriented middleware.	Need features such as process workflow, message translation, message routing, rule-based validation, and protocol validation.
Broker	The broker mediates communication directly or indirectly between client and the service provider. It locates the services, routes the requests, and establishes the communication. The broker acts as intermediary between the client and service producer. *Implementation*: The pattern is implemented by the message broker and service broker.	This pattern can be used to abstract the target service by using indirect broker. Brokers abstract the internal details of the service.

(*Continued*)

TABLE 6.2 (***Continued***)

Portal Integration Patterns

Portal Integration Pattern	Description	Usage Scenario
Proxy	Proxy pattern acts as a single point of access for implementing policies and communication to the target system. A client can use proxy for communicating with local or remote interfaces in a seamless fashion. *Implementation*: The pattern is implemented through custom development of integration interface to the target system.	Proxies such as AJAX proxy help us in establishing communication with multiple systems while enforcing security and compliance.
Service orchestration pattern	Client contacts the system that orchestrates the services for a long running transaction. Orchestration includes rule-based service invocation, proper sequencing of service invocation, transaction handling, and message correlation through an intermediate service integration layer. *Implementation*: The pattern is implemented through ESB and BPM tools. The portal will act as client for these systems.	This pattern is used for implementing complex and long running business process that is exposed as services.
Service aggregation patterns	A service aggregation pattern consolidates information from numerous applications and/or components and provides transformation and enforces business rule. The pattern provides a single consolidated and consistent view for the user. *Implementation*: The pattern is implemented through ESB and portal service aggregation functionality.	We will use this pattern when we need multiple services to be integrated from various systems and when there is a need of a common single interface.
Service wrapper	In this pattern, an exposed service wraps around the functionality of the legacy system that can be invoked by any service consumer such as portal or ESB to access legacy functionality. *Implementation*: This pattern is implemented using custom development of services on top of existing legacy functionality or using built-in service layer for legacy systems.	This is used during legacy modernization and to expose existing ERP functionality as service.

(*Continued*)

TABLE 6.2 (*Continued*)

Portal Integration Patterns

Portal Integration Pattern	Description	Usage Scenario
Request response patterns	There are multiple variants of this pattern such as the following: Asynchronous client and asynchronous back end where both request and response are asynchronous via ESB. Asynchronous client and synchronous back end where the request from the client to ESB is asynchronous, and the communication between ESB and back end is synchronous. Synchronous client and asynchronous back end where the request from the client to ESB is synchronous, and the communication between ESB and back end is asynchronous. Synchronous client and synchronous back end where both request and response are synchronous via ESB. *Implementation*: Depending on the scenario, this pattern can be implemented using JMS, AJAX (for asynchronous communication), and API (for synchronous communication).	This is another commonly used pattern in modern portal applications. When the back-end system exposes services or if we can use JMS queue or topic, we can use asynchronous communication via AJAX components. All client-side components such as widgets will use asynchronous communication with back-end services.
Data integration, functionality integration, process integration, and presentation integration patterns	These various integration patterns consolidate respective entities: Data integration: Client aggregates data from multiple data sources. *Functionality integration*: Functionality will be aggregated through APIs or service integration or through messaging middleware. *Process integration*: This involves orchestrating process steps through a process orchestration tool that includes process modeling, process workflow handling, and rules enforcement. *Presentation integration*: This includes aggregating various user interfaces from different systems to get the functionality of the individual systems. *Implementation*: Implementation is usually done by various integration portlets such as web service portlet, iFrame portlet, content portlet, clipping portlet, and other BPM tools and ESB.	This is a classical use case of portal implementation. The portal would need data aggregation and functionality aggregation for providing a single window to various functionalities. Process integration is needed when implementing a complex and multistep business process wherein each process step requires interaction with a different system.

Portal Integration Best Practices to Achieve Optimal Performance, Scalability, and Availability

Let us look at some of the best practices to achieve optimal efficiency in integration. The following list details the most efficient integration methodology that can be adopted under various categories.

Application Integration Design

- The integration should preferably be done using services to the maximum extent possible. This helps in loose coupling and helps in better scalability at either layer.
- Asynchronous service invocation should be preferred over synchronous. This helps us achieve better scalability and performance.
- Lightweight service methods such as REST should be preferred over SOAP. This would perform better in web scenario.
- Lightweight data exchange format such as JSON should be preferred over XML. Most of the JavaScript libraries provide a faster and efficient parsing of JSON.
- ESB is the preferred choice for integrating a large number of services and for providing efficient service governance.
- Design for layer-wise caching to ensure optimal performance. This also includes designing optimal cache invalidation techniques. Some of the effective caching techniques for integration are as follows:
  - Cache the service response for a fixed duration on portal end. We can design a cache invalidation service that can be invoked when the cache value is updated. For instance, we can cache the web content retrieved from content web service of CMS. When the cached content is updated, the CMS system can invoke the cache invalidation service during the content workflow.
  - For database optimization, we can create lookup tables to store the frequently used values such as user profile information and basic product attributes. We can design database synchronization jobs to update these local lookup tables from the master tables.

Application Development and Testing

- During development and testing, the integrations should be done on an iterative and continuous basis. Iterative testing helps in the early detection of integration defects.
- Scalability and performance testing of integrations should be done during early stages of testing.
- All third-party services, plug-ins, and widgets should be thoroughly tested for scalability and performance. This helps in the early detection of any potential defects.
- The user experience and performance behavior of the integrations should be tested on multiple devices and on different browser platforms.

- Automated testing tools such as Selenium should be used to the maximum extent for improved productivity.

Business Process Integration

- Business process testing should be done end to end to check the overall transaction performance and scalability.
- A faster and lightweight alternative should be provided in addition to the regular process steps. For instance, a three-step user registration alternative should be provided in addition to the three-page registration process. This enhances perceived user experience.
- Commercial or open-source BPM tools should be leveraged for implementing complex business processes.

Summary

- This chapter provides various aspects and insights into portal integrations.
- Portal integrations help the portal provide a single unified interface to users by aggregating information and functionality from multiple sources.
- The main challenges in portal integration include performance, scalability and availability, user experience, and vendor management.
- The main business scenarios that need portal integrations are providing a single stop shop of all services, providing a consistent and unified user experience and branding, providing a dashboard view, and enabling self-service, process optimization and automation, productivity improvement, sales enablement, etc.
- The main technical scenarios for portal integrations are seamless security access and single sign-on, information, content and data aggregation, support for adaptors and extensions, SOA, process orchestration and validation, and feature on-boarding.
- The main portal integration techniques include link-based integration, iFrame-based integration, service-based integration, feed-based integration, clipping and screen scraping, portlet-based integration, and widget-based integration.
- Various core portal integrations such as CMS integration, search engine integration, social and collaboration integration, BPM integration, security integration, KM integration, e-commerce integration, and reports integration are discussed. Most of these integrations are service based and help in extending the portal features and functionality.
- Special forms of integrations include mashups, widgets, and plug-ins/extensions. Mashups and widgets are client-side components that are built using lightweight architecture and rely on REST-based services in an asynchronous data aggregation.

7

Portal-Based Content Management

Content management remains one of the most significant and prominent use cases where portals are being used. The content management scenario is so popular that there are many portal products built around content management functionality. There is an increasing convergence among portal and web content management technologies. Portal products have content management features such as an in-built content management system (CMS), workflows, content authoring templates, content publishing mechanisms in addition to content portlets; web content management products have portal features such as personalization, role-based access, security and single sign-on (SSO), localization, etc. As a result, we see lightweight content-focused portals which feature portal functionality around content management. This marrying of portal and content management technologies bring the best of both worlds to business and content domains. They achieve the much required business goal of faster content turnover, personalization, business friendly content management and administration, and a lightweight platform.

In this chapter, we will look at various aspects of the convergence of portal and content management technologies.

We have also included a portal–CMS-based dynamic delivery platform architecture in the Chapter 23 which elaborates the concepts explained in this chapter. Portal architects, enterprise architects, and content architects will find this chapter useful.

Portal Content Management Scenarios and Capabilities

In portal scenario, web content plays a vital role and is used in almost all portal implementations. The main business scenarios for portal-based content management are as follows:

- Web content management for marketing campaigns in marketing- and sales-related portals
- Microsite creation for sales campaign
- Authoring the product data and promotion content for e-commerce portal
- Content intensive enterprise information portals
- Support content in support and knowledge management portals
- Content to provide self-service features such as FAQs, how-tos, solution articles, etc.
- All web content and digital media rendering scenarios within portals

Portal Content Trends

The main trends in portal-based content management are as follows:

- *Rich digital content and media*: Portal content management should support a wide array of media and static assets and immersive content.
- *Relevant content discoverability*: In a portal scenario, it is critical that the relevant content is easily discoverable to increase its effectiveness and utility. Content strategy should thus be geared toward increased content discoverability.
- Content should be available across multiple channels, across various customer touch points; it should preferably use responsive web design for achieving this.
- Content should be personalized based on users' behavior, profile attributes, and other implicit/explicit preferences.
- Content should be available in multiple languages and in multiple regions to cater to portal users in various geographies.
- Content strategy should get relevant content from external and internal social media and collaboration platforms.
- There should be content syndication to and from external systems through Representational State Transfer (REST)-based services.
- Business-friendly content management and publishing process with minimal IT involvement and quicker content publishing time should be available.
- Widgets availability through JavaScript (JS) libraries for interactive content should be made available.

Portal Content Management Capabilities

The main content capabilities required for portal content management are as follows:

- *Content Authoring*: The portal should provide re-usable and standard templates for content authoring. The templates eco system should support friendlier rich text editors (RTE), WYSIWYG (What you see is what you get) editors, repeatable elements, complex content structures, flexible structures, configurable elements, keyword/metadata tagging, image/media file section, analytics scripts tagging, workflow association, and other related features. Content authors should be able to use these presentation templates to author rich content and do a preview of the content.
- *Content Aggregation*: The portal should support aggregation of content from various sources. We have seen various integration technologies supported by the portal, which can be leveraged for this purpose. The portal should be able to retrieve the relevant content from external sources through services-based (preferably REST based) integration.
- *Content Management*: The portal should provide various end-to-end content management features such as content authoring, content lifecycle management, tagging, workflow, content translation, content categorization, content approval, and content publishing.
- *Workflow*: Content management needs workflow capabilities for modeling various scenarios such as multi-step approval, content publishing, content translation,

content promotion, asset management, etc. The portal provides an in-built workflow and a rules engine, which can be used to create content-related workflows.

- *Content Versioning*: Like any artifact, content should be versioned to preserve the historical data after each update. Versions will be useful for packaging a release and for rollback scenarios.
- *Content Archival and Retention*: For business and legal requirements, it is required to retain the content for a specified time period. The portal platform should be able to support this.
- *Content Definition and Classification*: Content authors and administrators should be able to classify the content into a logical group for easier retrieval. The platform should support a taxonomy of content categories.
- *Search Capabilities*: Portal search should be able to index the content from CMS and other content sources. It should use content tags and keywords to identify the matching content and provide it in search results. Portal search should also be contextual and personalized so as to provide the most relevant content for the search keyword.
- *Content Publishing*: The portal should support content publishing to various publishing targets such as file system, web server, content repository, etc. One of the most popular forms of portal content publishing is to expose the content in JSON (JavaScript Object Notation) or XML format through REST- and SOAP (Simple Object Access Protocol)-based services for other systems.
- *Dynamic Delivery and Presentation*: The portal should be able to aggregate the content dynamically from various content sources. The CMS is one of the main sources of content; additionally, the portal should also get the content from other enterprise sources such as database, email systems, collaboration platforms, social platforms, etc. For consumer facing portals, the content is also aggregated from external social media platforms.
- *Rich Media Support*: Portal content management should support various types of media such as images, video, audio file, presentations, etc., which will be added to content.
- *Social Media Support*: Content is not just authored by content authors. Most of the content is also aggregated dynamically from external and internal social platforms that contain relevant user generated content (UGC). For instance, a portal product page will contain authored web content with product description, but it would also get relevant posts, discussions, and reviews from social media platforms to provide a holistic picture about the product.
- *Content Administration*: Content administrators should be able to set up content sources, manage content publishing targets, create metadata and tag taxonomy, manage content categories, publishing jobs, manage content workflows, and other content administration–related activities.
- *Usability*: The usability of content is the prime factor for its success. Content templates should support all usability-related aspects such as accessibility standards, tagging, categorizing, widget support, responsive design support, multi-device layout support, multi-locale support, and all other aspects impacting content usability.

- *User Generated Content (UGC) Management*: In the web 2.0 scenario, most of the content is generated by end users through collaboration and social platforms such as blogs, forums, communities, wikis, reviews, and other external social media platforms.
- *External CMS Integration*: If an organization has already invested in core content management systems, the portal would act as a front-end for them. The portal would render the content from CMS and transform it to suit the final presentation. We had looked at the details of portal integration with an external content management system in Chapter 6.
- *Content Personalization*: Like all portal presentation, rendered content is also personalized based on user attributes. This includes role-based access to content categories, filtering based on content sensitivity, etc. Content personalization is used to manage targeted promotion content and for targeted campaign management.
- *Multi-Lingual Support*: The portal should be able to provide content in a language of the customer's choice. To achieve this functionality, the portal should be integrated with a content translation system to provide various translations of the content.
- *Content Scalability and Flexibility*: The platform should provide seamless scalability to support increase in content load. The content templates should be flexible enough so that they can re-used for authoring content of various formats and structures; the content workflows should also be flexible enough to provide content translation, multi-step complex approvals, and other business rules associated with content publishing.

Portal Content Architecture

In this section, we will look at the main components and functionality of portal-based content management systems. Like we discussed before, most popular portal products provide in-built content management functionality or provide good support for integration with external content management systems. The high-level portal-based CMS architecture is shown in Figure 7.1. The main components are detailed in this section.

Core Content Components

This is the heart of the system, which contains the following main components:

- *Content Templates*: These templates provide the authors a tool to author the content. Templates are designed to be standards based, re-usable and flexible to support all kinds of content. Template editors also provide WYSIWYG (what-you-see-is-what-you-get) and rich text functionality to facilitate authors.
- *Inline Editing*: This allows authors to edit the content in preview mode.
- *Content Repository*: It stores all the content along with its metadata and hierarchy details. A standards based content repository such as a Java content repository (JCR) compliant repository will help in easy integration and migration.

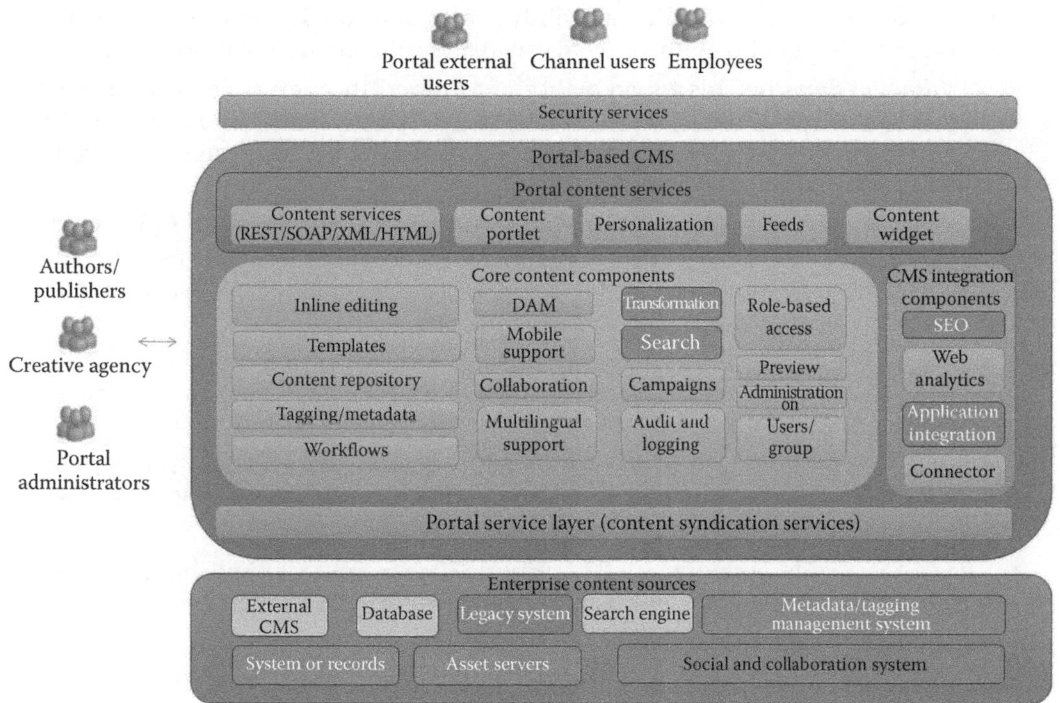

FIGURE 7.1
Portal-based CMS architecture.

- *Tagging/Metadata*: This is another key element in content authoring. Authors need to associate the content with particular tags and metadata, which will help in easy discovery and sharing of the content. Sometimes, the portal needs to be integrated with dedicated metadata management systems (MMS) to model and retrieve the metadata hierarchy. Similarly, a few systems of records (SOR) maintain controlled vocabulary values (such as customer list, country list, etc.), and a portal CMS needs to be integrated with them as well.
- *Workflows*: Complex content processes are modeled as workflows in the system. This includes multi-step content publishing and reviewing workflow, content translation workflow, and others.
- *Digital Asset Management (DAM)*: This is mainly the asset repository which stores global static assets such as images, videos, documents, media files, flash files, etc. The image selector components in the content template pick up the assets from the DAM system. Digital assets are also categorized, tagged, and maintained in a logical hierarchy for easier identification of the asset. In a few scenarios, the portal needs to be integrated with enterprise-wide DAM systems, document management systems, or media servers for retrieving relevant assets.
- *Mobile Support*: This includes mobile specific layouts and templates and mobile device rules to re-direct to a mobile specific layout. Other components in this category include responsive web design (RWD), mobile JavaScript libraries, etc.

- *Collaboration*: This functionality is mainly achieved through portal-based collaboration or by integrating with external social and collaboration platforms.
- *Multilingual Support*: This functionality is achieved through content translation workflows, which leverage translation management systems. Translated multilingual content needs to be properly tagged and stored in language-specific folders.
- *Transformation*: Content retrieved from external sources need to be transformed to suit the native content structure. A content transformation engine is used for this purpose. An extensible stylesheet language (XSL) is one of the most commonly used transformation tool.
- *Search*: This includes search services, which can be used by the portal and other systems for content search. The portal retrieves relevant content using the tagged metadata for the content.
- *Campaigns*: This includes pre-defined content and workflow, which can be used for launching campaigns in a very quick time. The component accelerates the campaign management.
- *Audit/Logging*: The system logs all key events such as content publishing, versioning, purging, translation, content promotion, etc. using these components.
- *Role Based Access*: The portal uses in-built fine-grained access to control the access to CMS functionality. The normally used roles are content author, content publisher, content reviewer, content workflow manager, and content administrator.
- *Preview*: This feature is mainly used after the complete authoring of the content. It provides the look-and-feel of the entire content and all associated assets in the context of the whole page. Authors can do an inline edit to fix any issues.
- *Administration*: Content administration includes various activities such as managing content workflows, assigning content roles to users, promoting content, content archival/purging, etc.
- *Users/Group*: The portal uses native user and group management for managing content roles as well.

Content Management System Integration Components

In addition to core features, CMS components also support other functionalities such as search engine optimization (SEO), web analytics, etc. Some of them also require integration with external systems:

- *SEO*: Content templates have a provision for adding SEO tags. The key tags are page description, keywords, metadata, content tags, title, etc.
- *Web Analytics*: Web analytics script, tags, and classes can be added to the content during authoring. This requires inclusion of web analytics scripts, which help in tracking the effectiveness of content.
- *Application Integration and Connectors*: For efficient content management, CMS has to be integrated with other systems such as translation management systems (TMS), external content systems, social and collaboration systems, metadata systems, etc. Connectors will be used for this purpose.

Portal Service Layer (Content Syndication Services)

Content syndication mainly involves surfacing external content on the portal page. The portal mainly uses REST-/SOAP-based web services to retrieve the content from external sources. Few specific systems also provide software development kits (SDKs) and application program interfaces (APIs), which can be used for integration.

As discussed in Chapter 6, portals provide lot of components, which can be used for this integration.

Portal Enterprise Content Services

In order to expose the content to other systems and services, the portal provides various components:

- *Content Services*: The portal will expose the content through REST-/SOAP-based services, which provide content in JSON or XML formats.
- *Content Portlet*: Most portal products provide JSR portlets, which provide native integration with their in-built CMS. For external CMS integration, web services portlet can be used.
- *Feeds*: Content can also be exposed as RSS (Rich Site Summary)/Atom feeds. This is mainly used for content that is frequently updated and needs notification. Content such as "featured products," "breaking news" are ideal candidates to be exposed as feeds as they change frequently and are of high interest.
- *Personalization*: The portal adds personalization features for the content by providing interest-/preference-based content and data.
- *Content Widget*: Content can also be exposed as widget components. Widgets can be plugged in as lightweight JavaScript libraries in other web applications and they internally use AJAX and REST services to consume content.

External Enterprise Content Sources

Let us look at the main content sources used by portals. The most preferred form of integration is by using REST-based services.

- *External CMS*: If an organization already has an existing enterprise CMS, we can either integrate the portal with it or migrate the content from the enterprise CMS to the portal CMS. We will look at the migration aspects in detail in the "Portal content migration" section.
- *Database*: Some enterprises store content and binary assets in the enterprise database. In such cases, the portal needs to retrieve content from the database.
- *Legacy Systems*: This includes ERP, reporting systems, and other legacy applications, which host the relevant content.
- *Search Engine*: Some content is also dynamically aggregated and requires integration with search systems. For instance, a product page will get authored content and aggregate product-related search results from the search engine.
- *Metadata/Tagging Management Systems*: An enterprise may use organization-wide metadata from a metadata management system. In such cases, the portal needs to be integrated with it.

- *Social and Collaboration System*: The portal also needs to retrieve content from external and internal social and collaboration platforms. For instance, relevant blog content and discussion content would add more details to the main content of the page.
- *System of Records* (*SOR*): A few enterprises host the controlled list of values in SORs. This includes exchange rates, pricing values, customer lists, etc. In such scenarios, the CMS needs to be integrated with SORs.
- *Asset Servers*: There are dedicated asset servers which manage and provide optimized delivery of assets. The CMS needs to be integrated with such systems to add the content level assets.

Portal Content Strategy

Portal content strategy involves managing the end-to-end life cycle of web content that will be rendered in the portal so that it translates into program success. This includes enhancing the effectiveness of content, making the portal content more usable, easing the content management processes through efficient governance models, and making the content easily discoverable. Content strategy is closely linked to the portal information architecture, portal governance model, and portal search so that the portal can render the right content at the right place at the right time.

Portal content strategy includes the following aspects:

- *Alignment with Business Objectives*: Content strategy should be in sync with long-term business goals. For instance, if the business wants a collaborative content, then the content strategy should comprehend content syndication from multiple content sources, which in turn requires services-based integration. The most commonly applicable business goals for content strategy are
  - Uniform branding, which can be achieved through re-usable, uniform, and consistent content presentation templates, style elements
  - Consistent look and feel, which needs well-defined visual style guide, re-usable content layouts, and well-defined image specifications
  - Providing coherent content by presenting all related and useful information in a single place
  - Content freshness, which needs accelerated content publishing and content update process
  - Providing high impact content through immersive experience
  - Faster and relevant information discoverability, which needs right tags and metadata for content and efficient content search
  - Providing easily accessible and optimized content for all channels
  - Efficient content authoring and publishing workflows
  - Efficient content metadata tagging strategy for efficient information discovery
  - Delivering optimized content for all channels

- *Content Life Cycle Management*: This requires end-to-end management of content life cycle stages that includes
    - Content creation through templates
    - Content review and approval through workflows
    - Metadata based content tagging
    - Content publishing
    - Content translation
    - Content versioning
    - Content retention and archival
    - Content purging

Most of these features are provided by in-built portal and CMS products as they are standard functionalities; however some of them need to be customized or configured to suit the business needs. For instance, the content approval process would vary from one organization to another and would require customizing the in-built workflow. Another classical example is that of metadata tagging. The metadata heavily depends on the industry domain and business organization. So we need to create the appropriate metadata taxonomy based on the business needs and use it for content tagging.

- *Content Freshness Management*: This includes an efficient way of surfacing the most recent content on the page with minimal IT intervention. Two ways to achieve content freshness is to
    - Define an efficient content publishing process so that content is available in the public portal page as soon as it is approved and published. The process should also take care of clearing any cache on-demand to achieve this.
    - Retrieve content from any third party site with minimal delay. This can be done through methods such as feed subscription, frequent polling, content syndication, and such methods.
- *Content Usability Management*: Usability is an umbrella term that includes many aspects which impact the end-user experience. Enhancing usability includes keeping content simple, making the content available in the user's language of choice and in users' geography, optimizing the content delivery for the user specific device, enhancing the accessibility of the content, making the content available in various formats such as HTML, XML, JSON, etc., so that it can be consumed by other systems, including intuitive and user-friendly navigation systems, making the content relevant and easily discoverable through intuitive information architecture, using visuals and graphics effectively, leveraging SEO best practices for the content, enhancing the content search, increasing content readability, and providing personalized content.
- *Content Migration*: In some scenarios, content residing in legacy systems need to be migrated to the portal eco-system. Content migration involves the following key steps. We will look at more details in the following sections.
    - Structuring the legacy content into a format that can be fitted into new content presentation templates
    - Mapping the legacy content hierarchy into the new content categories

    - Mapping the content keywords into new tags and content metadata
    - Automating the migration through scripts
    - Testing the content migration in phases
- *Content Tagging and Metadata*: Keywords, tags, and metadata are important assets for a content—they make the relevant content available to the end user and for the search engine. It also helps in dynamic delivery as the portal can dynamically aggregate the keyword-based content from internal and external systems. For instance, a portal product page can get all content authored content that is tagged with product name as well as external feeds, which have the product name as the key word. Content metadata and tags bring in the much needed structure to the content by attaching a meaning to the content. Meaning can be multi-dimensional such as "who authored the content?," "to which geography this content belongs to?," "on which page should this content appear?," "who are the likely target audience who can be benefitted from this content?," "which product does this content describe?," and "when was this content created?." All these attributes, qualities, dimensions, and aspects of content can be described by tagged metadata.
- *Content Analytics and SEO*: Analytics help in tracking the content effectiveness—we can gain insights into how the users are using the content, whether they are clicking on the prominent links, whether they are downloading media assets, which content is most often visited, which content is not used at all, are users able to reach the third level and fourth level pages, how effective is the navigation strategy, are users using top level navigation or left navigation for reaching different categories, in which step are the users most exiting?, are users playing the videos fully on the home page?, how is the page performing?, how much time does it take for a marquee image on the home page to load?, and what is the image load time in a mobile device?. We can gather all this information through web analytics scripts. This helps in improving the overall content strategy thereby enhancing use experience.
- The SEO, on the other hand, makes the content visible to external users by adopting search engine–friendly strategies. Through page level keywords, page title, page metadata, sitemap, robots file, seed list pages, SEO strategy drives the traffic to the page content.
- So an efficient content strategy should cover all the points discussed in this section. It should also clearly focus on how the content strategy aligns with the business goal and the portal strategy.

Portal Content Design, Authoring, Preview, and Publishing

This section describes the end-to-end flow in content management including content search and caching strategy. The best practices that need to be followed in this process are also discussed.

User Interface Design Elements

Before we start with content flow, we need to keep the design elements and user interface (UI) artifacts ready. Let us have a quick look at them:

- *Wireframes*: The creative agency or UX designers will create wireframes, which depict the overall layout of the page and various sections in that page. Each section (which translates into a portlet or a widget) is described and its content source is called out. Wireframes are best in conveying the page structure and its various sections. They need to be reviewed and signed-off by the business and all concerned stakeholders.
- *Mockups*: Visual mockups are normally the HTML pages which mimic a real-world web page. It contains dummy/placeholder content, uses exact styles, dummy graphics, and implements click-through and navigation functionality. The main intention of mockups is to show end user experience and navigation flow. This also needs to be finalized and signed-off by the business and all stakeholders.
- *Visual Style Guide*: Sometimes referred to as the UI toolkit, it defines all the UI elements used on the content and web pages. It specifies the page in pixels, and provides detailed styles and specifications for all UI elements such as text, graphics paragraphs, fonts, color schemes, HTML elements, etc. The visual style guide plays a vital role in defining a common framework for a uniform and consistent look and feel. It provides a clear guideline for content authors and page administrators, and specifications to which they need to adhere to. The visual style guide is often accompanied by style definitions in CSS files, JS library files and sample images, and media files. Mockups use the visual style guide specifications.
- *Information Architecture*: As part of information architecture, UX designers define the site map, page hierarchy, content hierarchy, metadata organization, and navigation elements such as left navigation, header-/footer-based navigation, breadcrumb, tagged navigation, etc. Search is also an effective tool for information discovery; therefore, the placement of search function is also defined. The information architecture also needs to be signed-off by enterprise architects and business stakeholders.
- *Metadata Taxonomy*: The completed controlled vocabulary of metadata needs to be finalized and created.
- *Content Categories*: The complete logical categories for content classification should be finalized and created. It is often directly translated into folder structure.
- *Rich Media Files*: All media files such as images, graphics, videos, flash files should be created and made available in digital asset repositories.
- *Content Templates*: Content authoring templates should be developed and finalized. The templates should be preferably based on standard technologies and should be developed so that it is re-usable.
- *Content Workflow Definition*: All content-related workflows such as content publishing, content translation, and content approvals should be finalized.

Content Management Process

Once we have these required pre-requisites in place, we can define a detailed content process. The high level steps are depicted in Figure 7.2.

- *Step 1: Selection of content authoring template*—Content authors can select predefined content templates for content authoring. Portals provide functionality to display content templates with rich text editor (RTE), image selection tools, and other content-friendly features.

  As we have seen in the "Portal content trends" section, multi-channel enablement is one of the emerging trends in content management. In order to render content optimally on mobile devices, the author can select content templates specifically for mobile devices or set device rules to route to a different content based on the device.
- *Step 2: Configuring the template for current content structure*—One of the best practices is to create content templates that are re-usable. So, content authors can author a wide variety of content structures and layout with minimal number of content templates. Content templates are usually flexible and extensible. They accommodate additional repeatable sections to suite the content needs. Authors can leverage this feature to configure the template and create specific content chunk or content page.
- *Step 3: Author content as per specifications (using visual style guide)*—Authors can use the established visual style guide to create the content chunk. They can use

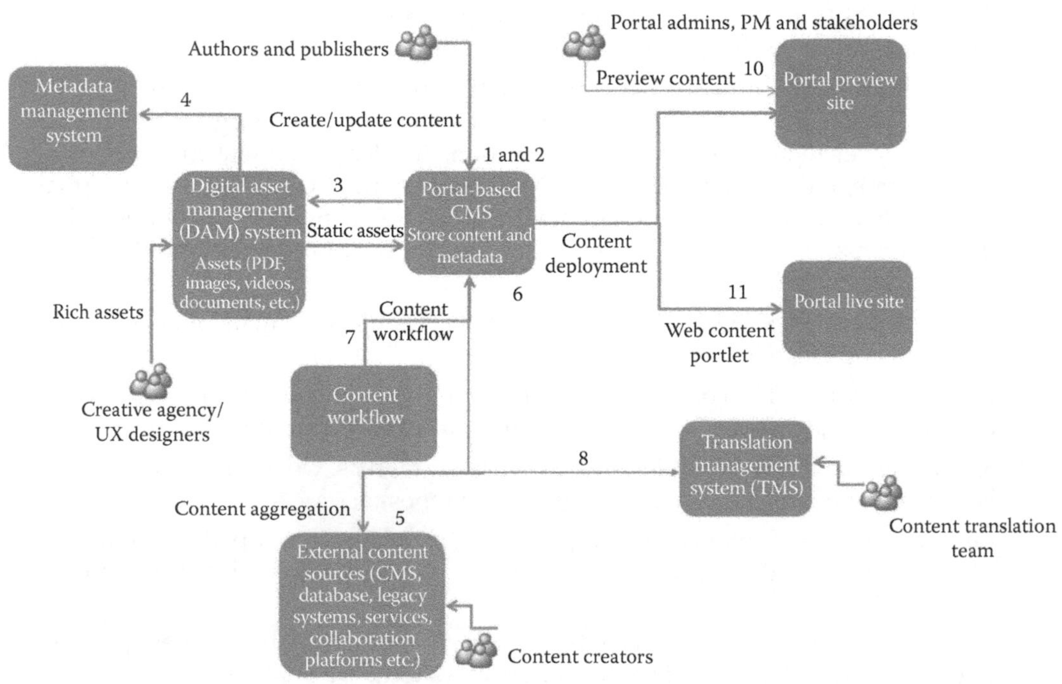

FIGURE 7.2
Portal content process.

the copy deck and update the styles and content for the requirements and leverage WYSIWYG editors. The styles related to the responsive web design (RWD) can be included to target mobile devices.

- *Step 3a: Attach the static assets*—Most of the content chunk and content pages require graphics such as images, videos, media files, flash files to create an impactful content. The structure of the content template provides fields such as "image selector" and "asset selector," which attach the images, videos, and other static assets to the content. The assets are normally maintained in a digital asset management (DAM) platform and they too will be tagged with relevant metadata. The asset selectors allow authors to browse through the metadata taxonomy or search assets by their keywords to facilitate faster and relevant asset selection.
- *Step 4: Tag content with metadata*—Once the content is completely authored along with the required assets, authors can attach the relevant page-level metadata, keywords, and tags that would appropriately describe the content. The content metadata will be selected from a metadata hierarchy, which maintains a controlled vocabulary of metadata values structurally organized in a logical hierarchy. For instance, in an e-commerce scenario, the tags are organized by the product categories and product names; authors can select the tags relevant for the subject product content and use it for tagging.
- *Step 4a: Add SEO, analytics scripts and preferred URL*—This is an optional step. Some content require addition of web analytics scripts and tags. Adding web analytics scripts normally requires two steps:
  - Adding web analytics master scripts at the bottom of the content page.
  - Attaching a CSS "class" for individual UI and content elements that need tracking; for example, if we need to track asset download, we need to add a CSS class to its hyperlink element so that web analytics software can track its download.
  - Similarly, SEO strategy requires adding page-level metadata, keywords, page title, page description, and other required values. Authoring template would provide appropriate elements for it.
  - In most of the cases, the templates accommodate for addition of web analytics and SEO elements.
- *Step 5:* [*Optional*] *Integrate from other content sources*—If we need to migrate or integrate from other content sources such as external CMS, database, legacy systems, internal/external social and collaboration platforms, services, we can use a custom/commercial off-the-shelf (COTS) content migration tool such as an ETL (Extract, Transform and Load) tool to load the content into the portal CMS. The detailed steps and process involved in content migration will be explained in the section on portal content migration.
- *Step 6: Assign the content to correct content category*—The next step is to assign the content to the correct category. The author can select the most appropriate logical category for the content from the pre-defined category hierarchy. This will be used by the content publishing workflow to publish the content into the appropriate folder.
- *Step 7: Initiate the content approval workflow*—The next step is to initiate the content approval flow. Based on the content process defined by the business, the content

may need to go through a multi-step approval from content reviewers, marketing team, legal team, business team, sales team, etc. Once all the approvals are done, the content is ready for publishing.

- *Step 8*: [*Optional*] *Initiate content translation workflow*—Optionally, the content may need to be translated into different languages for publishing in various geographies. Content translation is usually done through integration with a translation management system (TMS). Post content translation, the language/region specific metadata for translated content would be tagged to content. Translated content will be published to appropriate folders and will be published to different URLs.
- *Step 9*: [*Optional*] *Initiate multi-device publishing workflow*—In some scenarios, a different version/rendition of content that is targeted for various devices would be published. Multi-device publishing can be best achieved through responsive design.
- *Step 10*: *Preview content and inline editing*—Once the content is fully authored along with all images and metadata, the content is published to the preview site. Portal administrators, project managers, the marketing team, the author, and concerned stakeholders can preview the content. Preview provides the overall look and feel of the content and how it fits into a page. The author can make inline edits in the preview pages.
- *Step 11*: *Promote content to portal live site*—The final step in the content workflow is to promote the page content to a live production server. This usually involves copying the content and its related metadata to the appropriate folder in the production server. The step also clears any page-level cache on the production server so that the fresh content is rendered on the page.

Post publishing, the main activities include content versioning, content archiving, and content tracking through web analytics.

Portal Content Search

The portal search, by design, should index all aggregated content. So this naturally includes the web content present in the CMS. There are mainly two methods for indexing web content:

1. The search crawler can crawl all the portal pages and index them based on the page keywords and metadata. This is popularly known as "site search."
2. The portal search engine can directly connect to the CMS system through a connector and index the content in the CMS.

Each of these methods has its pros and cons. The first method wherein the portal search engine only crawls and indexes the content on portal web pages helps in efficient indexing and finding relevant content as the portal page web content is clearly associated with the page-level metadata and keywords. The drawback, however, is that if the portal is only retrieving a partial content from the external CMS, then the search engine can miss out potentially relevant content from the content source.

In the second technique, the portal search can index the complete web content in the CMS, but associating the content to its relevant metadata would require an understanding of the CMS structure and usage of CMS APIs. So in order to make better and complete sense of the content, the search engine should use the CMS adaptor, which would be able to associate the content with its relevant metadata. This is the preferred way for crawling and indexing web content.

Portal Content Caching

To optimize the performance of content delivery, we need to have a robust multi-layer content caching strategy. The following are some of the content caching techniques used:

- *Multi-Layer Caching*: The content is cached at each of the layers in the request processing pipeline—CMS layer, services layer, portal layer, and content delivery network (CDN) layer
- *Content Fragment Caching*: The page content is broken into multiple section level content fragments and cached; this helps in faster page loads without compromising on content freshness. In portal world, a content fragment/chunk corresponds to rendition output from a portlet.
- *Page-Level Caching*: Portal and browsers can cache the entire content page
- *CDN caching*: CDN systems can forward-cache and help in optimal page delivery across multiple geographies; this is mainly used for static pages

Web Content Portlet Design

As we have seen in the previous sections, content portlet is one of the primary integration touch points between portal and CMS systems. Many enterprise portal products come bundled with native CMS, which is optimized for web content management. In such cases, portals also offer in-built content portlets for retrieving content from native CMS systems. For instance, Liferay provides web content management portlet and web content display portlet for managing web content. These native portlets provide seamless integration between portal and the in-built CMS. Web content portlets also provide other features such as content authoring, content publishing, etc., from portal interface.

There are mainly two integration scenarios between portal and CMS:

- Portal uses its native CMS from where it gets all of its web content.
- Portal is integrated with a full-fledged enterprise CMS.

At a high level, we have three design scenarios to retrieve and display web content from CMS. The first design choice is used for portal-bundled CMS and the rest are applicable for external CMS integration.

- Leverage in-built native web content portlets: This is the default choice when native CMS is used.
- Leverage CMS vendor provided standards-based portlet: Some CMS vendors also provide JSR-compliant portlets. They can be configured on the portal server to connect to the enterprise CMS.
- Design custom web content portlet: In this case, we will custom develop a portlet to retrieve the content from enterprise CMS.

TABLE 7.1
Comparison of Three Web Content Portlet Options

	Native Web Content Portlet	CMS Vendor-Provided Portlet	Custom Web Content Portlet
Usage scenario	While retrieving web content from native CMS	While retrieving web content from internal enterprise CMS	While retrieving web content from internal enterprise CMS
Functionality supported	Web content display, content authoring, content publishing, content workflow	Mainly web content display and content authoring	Mainly web content display
Integration method	API based	Mainly services based	Mainly services based; CMS API can also be used
Performance and scalability	Optimal performance and scalability due to seamless integration	Good performance and scalability	Depends on type of integration used

Table 7.1 provides a high-level comparison between these three options.

Let us now look at the low-level design aspects of these three portlets.

Native Web Content Portlet

The portlet comes bundled along with the portal product and seamlessly integrates with the native CMS. Liferay's web content management portlet and IBM's Web Content Rendering portlet/JSR 286 Web Content Viewer portlets are examples of these kinds of portlets. These portlets mainly use internal content APIs for integration.

Native portlets support wide a variety of content functions such as content authoring, content viewing, content editing, content publishing, content services, content conversion, etc. Some portals also provide extension features so that portal developers can customize the behavior of the portlet. This is mainly used for customizing the presentation and rendition of the web content.

The main configuration parameters for this portlet are as follows:

- Content path: The web content path can be specified from the native CMS
- Portlet presentation format: The display format can be selected for the web content. Display format could be one of list view, summary view, detailed view, etc.
- Required workflow: The content can be added to any existing approval workflows. This is mainly used during content authoring.
- Portlet permissions: These settings specify portal roles for who can view the output from the portlet.
- Asset association: Related digital assets can be attached, such as image graphics, video, marquee image, flash file, etc.

Generally, native integration optimizes the performance of native portlets.

CMS Vendor-Provided Web Content Portlet

These are normally JSR-standard portlets provided by the enterprise CMS product vendor. They mainly use either services-based integration or API-based integration.

These portlets are mainly used for content viewing purposes, and occasionally they provide content editing function as well. Initial configuration needs to be done to connect to the enterprise CMS. The configuration options are similar to that of native portlets.

Custom Web Content Portlet

When integrating portal with enterprise CMS and if there is no vendor-provided portlet, then a web content portlet can be custom developed. The primary purpose is to display the web content.

Integration with CMS

Though we can use the CMS API or JCR API (if enterprise CMS is JCR compliant) for integration, the most preferred option is to use services-based integration (preferably REST-based services). The JSR 286 standard is preferred, or, alternatively, we can develop a JavaScript content widget using content services. The choice of integration and caching configurations has great influence on the performance and scalability. If the target CMS does not support content services, then we can develop an intermediate services layer for this purpose.

It is always recommended to fetch only the plain content through content services and portal can inject the necessary presentation code. This is required to optimize the presentation to the target device.

The main configuration parameters for this portlet are as follows:

- CMS configuration: The connection details of target CMS are provided along with details of content services.
- Content query: Here we specify the content identifiers, which can help the content services to retrieve the content. This could consist of content id or content fragment name or fully qualified content path. Portal user has to select the options from a drop-down list to ensure correctness of values. Portal can locally store or cache these look-up values for performance reasons.
    - We can also make this interface highly flexible by allowing the user to write a content query by providing a query builder option. This advanced option would be useful for filtering the content.
- Content metadata: sometimes content metadata can also act as an identifier for the content. In such cases, we will configure the content metadata. This could include the content language, content tags, content category, etc.
- Content language: This adds as additional filter criteria.
- Content presentation: Here we can specify a predefined list of presentation formats. For each presentation format, the portal will inject the necessary styles to the content. Generally, this content transformation can be done using EXtensible Stylesheet Language (XSL).
- Target client: Here we can specify the target device or client.
- Permissions: We can set the portal roles for who can view this content.

Portal Content Migration

In many scenarios, we need to migrate content from various existing sources to the portal CMS or enterprise CMS. This is seen in scenarios such as legacy modernization, application consolidation, and new capability creation or during new platform development. Since this is one of the most common scenarios in content space, let us have a deeper look at the process, steps, and best practices in migration.

Content Artifacts for Migration

The key content artifacts that need to be migrated are as follows:

- *Core Content*: This is at the heart of the migration. Source content could be in the form of HTML, XML, or in a database or present in an external CMS. We need to first transform the content into the new format to align with the new content strategy. This includes mapping the old metadata with the new one, old content category with the new category, old content structure to new structure, and old URL to the new URL. A combination of CMS APIs and content transformation tools (such as XSL) can be leveraged to automate this migration effort.
- *Images and Static Assets*: In this case, the old images and digital assets need to be re-sized as per the new visual guide specifications. For instance, a visual style guide may specify a specific height and width in pixels for a marquee image. So when we have to migrate the old marquee image, we have to either re-size the image or re-create a new one. The second aspect of image/asset migration involves migration and mapping of metadata associated with it. This mapping will move the images and assets to appropriate folders in the new asset repository.
- *Tags and Metadata*: We have already discussed mapping of old metadata to new one. This will be done along with migration of content and images.
- *URLs*: Content URLs in the new platform will be naturally different from the old ones. In this case, mapping is not an elegant strategy; the new platform should have a consistent URL, which factors the content category, region, language, and have a brief content description as part of its URL. This also works well for SEO strategy. A simple example of such a friendly URL is given here: http://localhost/en_US/commerce/product/prod1234
- *Localized Content*: Any existing localized content should either be mapped to an appropriate folder/category in the new hierarchy or it should be re-translated with the localization workflow.
- *Documents and Files*: Sometimes, the legacy systems store the associated documents and files along with content, which also need to be migrated to the portal CMS.

Content Migration Methodologies

There are various techniques to migrate the content from the old platform to the new portal platform:

- *Manual Copy*: This is the simplest way of migrating the content wherein the migration team will manually copy the content from the old system and use the content templates to publish them to the new platform. The method is neither scalable nor preferred and should be used only when it involves less amount of content.

- *Usage of CMS APIs/Services and Transformers*: If the source content system exposes the content through APIs or through services, it can be leveraged to extract the content, transform, and bulk load it into the target CMS platform. The end-to-end sequence of steps can be automated through custom scripts. This is one of the preferred and efficient methods for migrating large-scale content.
- *Usage of ETL Tools*: There are many content migration tools and ETL tools that can be leveraged for migration. We need to configure them with source and target systems and other functionality like content transformation, metadata mapping, etc. will be executed through the tool.

Content Cut-Over Strategy

During migration, we need to decide on how we want to surface the new content. We need to decide when to retire old content platforms, the strategy for co-existence, etc. Let us look at some of the strategies for this:

- *Big-Bang Content Migration*: In this plan, all the content from the source content systems will be migrated in a single shot. The old systems are retired and the new system made active. The disadvantage is that there could be potential issues related to content incompleteness, incorrect mapping, and user experience. Customers may not like the content in the new format or may need changes to the information architecture or navigation elements. There may not be enough time to incorporate the feedback from end users. Also, if the new platform needs to be rolled back for some reason, there may not be any fallback platform for business continuity.
- *Phase-wise Iterative Migration*: This is the most efficient method of content migration wherein the content is migrated in phases. The phases will be logically partitioned based on geography-specific content roll outs, languages-specific content roll outs, customer segments–specific content roll outs, site sections, etc. For example, all the content in the products pages of the site will be migrated in the first phase, followed by the home page, etc. The least risky section will be chosen for the initial migrating phase. This gives more room for thorough content testing and incorporating user feedback. In the process, ways to improve and optimize the migration process can be identified. The flip side of this approach is that we need to maintain multiple platforms (which require a platform co-existence strategy) and users may face inconsistent user experience till the complete migration is completed. In spite of these challenges, this is the most preferred content migration strategy.

Content Migration Process

The main steps involved in end-to-end content migration process is shown in Figure 7.3.

FIGURE 7.3
Content migration steps.

The high level steps are explained here:

- *Identify Content Sources*: In this step, all the enterprise sources from which content has to be migrated to the new portal platform are identified. This could include file system, legacy database, legacy web application, database, old CMS systems, etc.
- *Content Analysis*: After identifying the content sources, the content is analyzed and the various content types, mapping details, extraction method, etc. are identified.
- *Content Cleansing*: Before the start of migration, the content has to be cleansed. This includes removal of duplicate content, outdated content, and unnecessary content; conforming to new naming conventions, content validation, and standardization; and mapping content category and content metadata to the appropriate new categories and metadata. This step keeps the content ready for migration.
- *Content Extraction and Loading*: This is the main step in the migration where the actual content is loaded from the source system to the target system. Any of the migration methodologies discussed under the section on content migration methodologies can be adopted. Migration will usually be done in batches and is automated.
- *Content Transformation*: Migrated content is transformed into the new structure. The XSL and related technologies can be leveraged for content transformation. The transformation makes the old content compatible and compliant with the new CMS structure.
- *Content Enhancement*: In some cases, the content needs to be enhanced to suit the new platform requirements. For instance, it may involve adding new metadata values, changing content structure, adding web analytics scripts, SEO values, service enabling the content, adding RWD for the content, adding widgets to the content, etc.
- *Content Validation and Publishing*: Post migration, the new content is validated for its completeness and correctness. Once the content is signed-off by all relevant stakeholders, it will be published to all publishing targets.

Portal Content Best Practices

The main portal content–related best practices are explained in this section. They are categorized based on content lifecycle stages.

Content Authoring

- Create standards based, flexible and extensible content templates so that they can be re-used to create various kinds of content.
- During authoring, focus only on core content. The injection of presentation elements such as associating styles, positioning, etc., can be done by the presentation engine such as the portal. If the content is exposed as JSON data to external systems, consuming systems will be responsible to add the presentation elements. In other words, it is recommended not to mix presentation and core content.
- All content must be associated with metadata. Metadata such as keywords and tags should be the preferred way to identify the content.
- Content templates should have provision for web analytics and SEO tags.

Content Workflows

- Create a fallback and exception flow to handle the unavailability of content reviewers. For instance, the review workflow should be time bound and should automatically re-route to a backup reviewer if the original reviewer does not respond within a specified time period.
- Keep the content workflows simple enough and business friendly to satisfy the business models. Increase in workflow complexity and number of steps in the workflow would lead to poor adoption and usage of the workflow.

Content Testing and Migration

- Leverage the automated tools to perform content testing and migration. If no tool fully satisfies the needs, develop the migration and testing script to automate these two activities.
- Always migrate content in iterations. This provides an opportunity to fully test an iteration and ensure that content is fully and correctly migrated.

Content Publishing

- The content publishing workflow should be flexible enough to publish to various publishing targets and in various languages.
- The publishing workflow should be easily manageable and configurable.
- There should be well-defined content rollback strategy to rollback the published content in case of publishing failure.

Content Presentation

- The portal presentation should leverage the uniform visual style guide for consistent user experience.
- Create a content re-usable strategy to re-use the entire content or a portion of it across multiple pages. This will reduce the content management overhead.
- Only use metadata to identify the relevant content.
- Adopt multi-layer caching to optimize the performance of content delivery.

Summary

- Content management is one of the main scenarios for portals.
- Content management is required for marketing campaigns, web content rendering, self-service features, portal page content, etc.
- Main portal trends include rich digital content and media, relevant content discoverability, multi-channel content, personalized content delivery, business-friendly content management processes, self-service content delivery, and interactive content.

- The main content capabilities required for portal content management are support for content authoring, content aggregation, content management, workflow, content versioning, content archival and retention, content definition and classification, content search, content publishing, dynamic delivery and presentation, rich media support, social media support, content administration, user generated content (UGC) management, external CMS integration, content personalization, multi-lingual support, content scalability, and flexibility.
- Portal content architecture includes components in the core content layer, services layer, CMS integration component layer, and enterprise content source layer.
- Core content components include templates, content repository, metadata, workflows, multi-lingual support, collaboration, mobile support, DAM, search, translation, campaign management, role-based access, and content preview.
- CMS integration components include SEO, web analytics, and other application integrations through connectors.
- Enterprise content sources include external CMS, database legacy system, search engine, metadata system, assets servers, system of record, and social and collaboration system.
- Portal content strategy includes comprehensive design for content design alignment with business objectives, content lifecycle management, content freshness management, content usability management, content migration, content tagging and metadata, content analytics, and SEO.
- The main UI design elements are wireframes, mockups, visual style guide, information architecture, metadata taxonomy, content categories, rich media files, content templates, and content workflow definition.
- Content management process includes steps such as selection of content authoring template, configuring the template for current content, content authoring, attaching static assets, metadata tagging with content, SEO/analytics specification, content categorization, content workflows, content translation, multi-device renditions, content preview, and content promotion.
- The main elements involved in content migration are core content, images and static assets, tags and metadata, URLs, localized content, and documents and files.
- *Content cut over strategy are of two main types*: Big-bang content migration and phase-wise iterative migration.
- *Content migration involves these steps*: Identification of content sources, content analysis, content cleansing, content extract and load, content transformation, content enhancement, content validation, and content publishing.

8

Portal Search and Search Engine Optimization (SEO)

Search plays a vital role in implementing core portal use cases. Most portal products provide an in-built search engine due to its importance. Portal search is essential for indexing and discovery of relevant information from all aggregated content. Search makes the relevant information discovery possible, which greatly impacts user experience. It is also an effective tool in dynamic information aggregation.

In this chapter, we will explore various search use cases in the portal scenario and other aspects related to portal search. We have already seen the integration of the search engine and the portal in Chapter 6. Portal architects and enterprise search architects would find this chapter useful.

Portal Requirements of Search

Portals provide a unified and personalized view for the user. Providing targeted and aggregated content and functionality through portlets is one way to achieve this unified view. Let us say that the end user wants to customize the "unified experience"; the user can achieve this by selecting a specific set of portlets/widgets on the page; each of the portlets and widgets are then configured with user-defined preferences.

An effective method for user preference–based information aggregation is by using search portlets. For instance, if the user has configured a particular product name in the product search portlet, then the portlet would search for the specified product information from all enterprise sources such as database, ERP systems, social and collaboration platforms, and will render product-specific information on the search results page. This process effectively makes a search portlet into a product information display portlet by dynamic content aggregation.

To summarize, the following are the main requirements for search in a portal platform:

- *Dynamic Content Delivery*: The example of product search across various enterprise sources is a classical instance of dynamic content delivery. This is a more effective strategy than authoring the product content (sometimes referred to as "static content delivery"). Unlike content authoring, dynamic delivery does not actually need manual content authoring effort; instead, it leverages existing content in enterprise sources such as database, ERP, social forums, discussion forums, etc., to collect the required information and transform it into a pre-defined presentation format.
- *Information Discovery*: Search is one of the most efficient navigation and information discovery tool. Users can search for a keyword and navigate to the required page from the search results page. This avoids multi-page navigation that happens in regular context menus.

- *User Experience Impact*: An optimized and personalized search feature such as type-ahead feature, synonym support, saved search, spell-check, Boolean operation support, proximity search, faceted and categorized search will all enhance the end-user experience.
- *Information Aggregation*: Search can fulfill this core portal use case most efficiently. A search engine will have connectors for most of the enterprise sources and can crawl, index, and cache the content from all those sources. The portal can add personalization and presentation rules on top of those search results for optimal user experience.
- *Enhanced Accessibility*: Search can increase the accessibility of relevant information to all end users with minimal effort.
- Due to the vast potential of search, search platforms are sometimes used as alternatives to horizontal portals as search can aggregate the information as effectively as portal. For the same reason, most enterprise search products are also bundled with a lightweight presentation portal that can be used for enterprises where search is needed most. However, search products lack some of the core portal strengths such as personalization, responsive presentation, etc. in such cases horizontal portal can compliment enterprise search.

Portal Search Attributes

The main attributes required for a portal search are as follows:

- Portal search service should be easily integrated through standard interfaces such as REST/SOAP services.
- Portal search should be scalable to index huge amount and varied type of enterprise content.
- Search engine should support in-built or pluggable connectors to crawl and index a variety of enterprise content from various sources.
- Secured search should be supported for sensitive information.
- Basic search operation should be executed efficiently; it should support caching and other performance enhancing features.
- Customization of search results pages (such as adding portal theme and portal style guide) is preferred, if possible.
- Search should be able to index various file types such as pdf, html, and various data sources such as database, CMS, ERP systems, web application, and external web sites.
- Advanced search features such as type-ahead, synonym support, wild card search, secure search, faceted search, related searches, guided navigation saved search, and result teaser is preferred.
- Search engine should support result filtering based on meta tag values, which will be used by the portal for personalization

Portal Search Architecture

The main search components in a portal are shown in the logical architecture depicted in Figure 8.1.

The key search components of a portal platform are explained here.

- *Search Services*: These expose the search results from portal platform to external systems and services. Portals would also add additional personalization rules to filter and format the search results.
- *Web Search*: This component is responsible for crawling internal and external web pages. The search engine can leverage many web site features such as site map, robots.txt, and seed list for crawling and indexing web page content. This will be discussed in more detail in the section on portal search process.
- *Database Search*: A dedicated database search can be done through database connectors.
- *Content Search*: Content in CMS systems are crawled and indexed through CMS connectors.
- *Crawler*: This is the main component that crawls all enterprise content sources.
- *Indexer*: The search documents are indexed, cached, and stored in a dedicated index location.
- *Web Service Portlet*: This can be used to integrate with any web service that exposes content through SOAP/REST based web services.
- *Search Portlet*: If a portal needs to be integrated with an external search engine, this portlet can be used for services based integration.
- *Connectors*: In some scenarios, the product vendors provide plug-ins and connectors, which can be used to connect to those systems such as ERP systems, legacy systems, etc.
- *Advanced Search Components*: These components implement functionality such as type-ahead search, faceted search, wild card search, secure search, guided navigation, synonym support, saved search, and spell-check; search administration will be used by the portal. Portal search administration normally involves configuring search content sources, configuring saved search criteria, search alerts and notification, relevancy ranking configuration, synonym configuration, black listing search terms, artificial rank boosting, etc.

A search engine normally stores the indexed content in a search index store. Large content indexing requires a clustered search index architecture for efficient index storage and retrieval.

A really large complex and vast enterprise content and social media platform needs to be indexed by big data search engines due to the high volume of data.

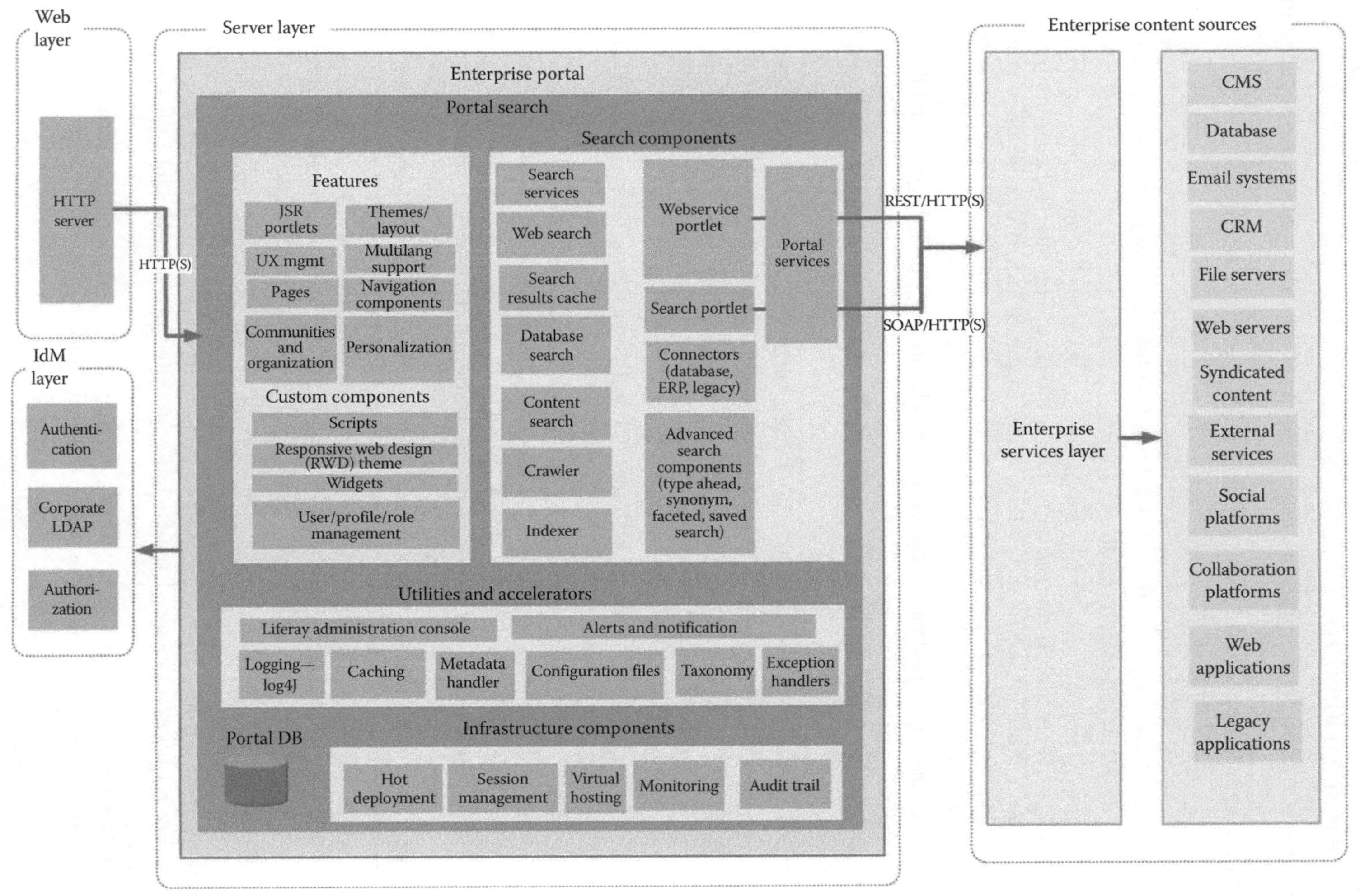

FIGURE 8.1
Portal search architecture.

Portal Search Process

As search needs to index a variety of structured and unstructured content from various internal and external content sources, let us look at some of the commonly used techniques for achieving the same. There are mainly five ways of crawling and indexing enterprise content:

1. *Services-Based Integration*: A search engine will consume the services from content sources for indexing the content. Some of the legacy systems for which we do not have any other alternative for indexing (such as web site crawling, connectors) can employ this technique.
2. *API-Based Integration*: Some product vendors provide Software Development Kit (SDK) or connecting APIs, which can be used to connect to the source systems. Database systems and CMS systems are good candidates for this kind of integration.
3. *Web Crawling*: This is one of the most commonly used techniques for crawling and indexing the web content. Any application that has web interface can be used as a source for crawling. The crawling spiders usually "follow" the links from the main page to reach all the pages. In this case, the web application needs to provide the following:
    - "Follow" instruction as part of page metadata
    - All site pages reachable directly or indirectly through main page
    - Site map file
    - Robots.txt file specifying the follow/no follow instructions
    - Minimal orphan pages (which cannot be reached from the links)
4. *Vendor Provided Connectors*: Similar to APIs, few product vendors provide pluggable connectors for popular search engines which connect to their systems.
5. *Seed List–Based Crawling*: In some cases, the web site or the content source has content that is not reachable by traditional crawling techniques such as link-following, sitemap, etc. One example is a dynamic list of product content which is not present in any web page or in the site map file. In such cases, a seed list page can be created that contains the link to all such content so that the crawler can index that content. Through explicit configuration or linking it to one of the crawlable web links on the site, it can be ensured that the search crawler reaches the seed list page.

Indexing Process Using Seed List

The sequence of creating and indexing content using the seed list page is shown in Figure 8.2.

The high level steps shown in Figure 8.2 will help us understand how a search engine can use the seed list details to index the content.

In the sequence diagram shown in Figure 8.2, we have taken an example of a content management system (CMS), which provides us the seed list details. Normally, the content within a CMS resides in a proprietary structure that cannot be fully and efficiently crawled by a search engine. So, the seed list page containing links to all crawlable and indexable content within the CMS will be used. For this scenario, a "crawler helper" component will

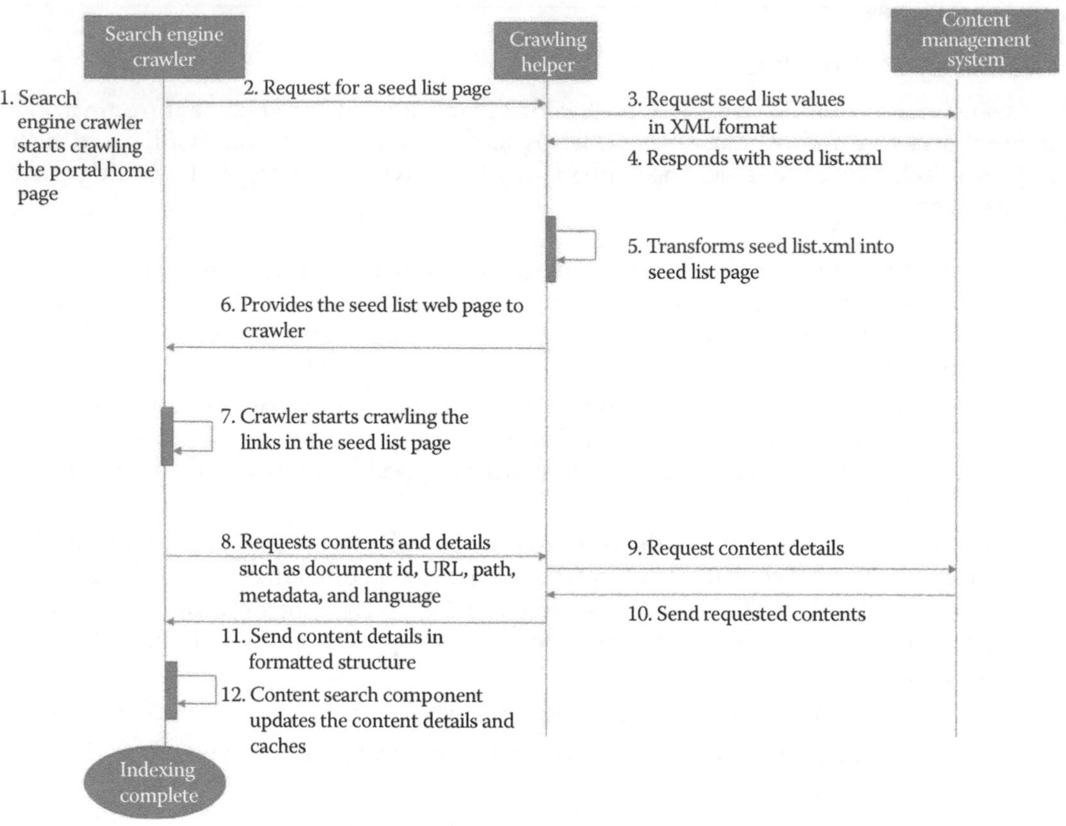

FIGURE 8.2
Indexing using seedlist page.

be used, which will transform and format the seed list values received from the CMS into a format that the crawler understands. It is also assumed here that the portal home page links off to this seed list page. Here are the high level steps:

1. The search engine crawler starts with the portal home page following all the links. The crawler reaches the seed list page link on the home page.
2. The crawler requests for the seed list page.
3. The crawler helper requests the CMS for seed list values in XML format.
4. The CMS responds back with an XML file containing the list of contents.
5. The crawler helper formats the XML into a web page, which it can easily crawl.
6. The seed list page is now provided to the crawler.
7. The crawler starts following each content link in the seed list page.
8. For each of the content links, the crawler needs details such as document id, URL, metadata, path, and the content language. This is later used for identifying the content and associating the crawled content to its identifiable metadata.
9. The crawler helper forwards this request to the CMS.
10. The CMS provides the requested details for the specific content.

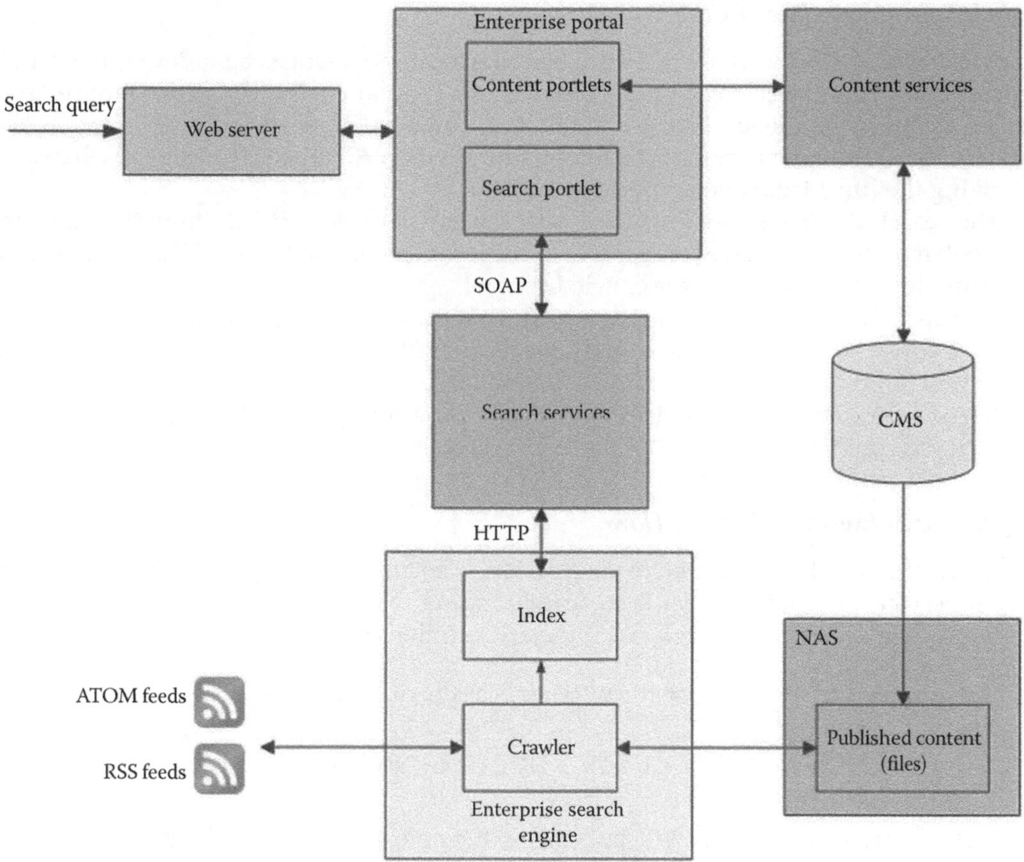

FIGURE 8.3
Portal search process.

11. The crawler helper formats the details in a format, which is easy for the crawler to understand.
12. The content search component of the crawler indexes each of the content and associates it with the metadata values.

NOTE: We can further optimize this by including the content details such as document id, URL, path, language, and metadata as part of the seed list XML in Step 3.

End-to-End Portal Search Process

Let us now look at an enterprise portal search scenario. In Figure 8.3, the search engine crawling and indexing of CMS content and feed is shown. The integration of the enterprise search engine with the portal is also depicted. Figure 8.3 is used to explain the search crawl process and indexing process of various content formats.

Search Crawling and Indexing Process

The main search crawling techniques for various content sources are explained here.

Search Engine Crawling of CMS Content

Crawl is the process by which the search engine locates content to be indexed. It is a pull process where the search engine pulls content from the content location. The search engine can also crawl a relational database to obtain metadata. The start URLs, follow URLs in the search engine can be configured to initiate crawling. All content must be reachable by following the links from one or more start URLs.

If the search engine is crawling a web site, the crawler issues HTTP (hypertext transfer protocol) requests to retrieve content files in the locations defined by the URLs and retrieve files from links discovered in the crawled content.

In Figure 8.3, the content chunks obtained from the CMS will be dumped into a shared network drive (NAS). This shared folder or drive will be available for the search engine and it will be configured as one of the crawling targets.

Alternatively, the crawler can directly connect to the enterprise CMS through connectors to crawl the content.

Portal Search Execution Process Flow

In Figure 8.3, portal is integrated to enterprise search engine through search services. The search service internally connects to search engine for retrieving the content and feed results. The main steps in search execution are as follows:

1. The search portlet will use the web services client to interact with the search web service.
2. The search web service will use the HTTP client implementation to open a connection with the search server.
3. The search parameters will be sent as a request parameter along with other parameters that define the results set format and properties. We can also send other access control and personalization rules such as user role, data/result filtering parameters along with search query term.
4. The search engine locates results in the index and provides the results in XML format.
5. The XML output from the search server will be parsed and the results will be rendered by applying appropriate styles using content transformation tools such as XSLT (Extensible Stylesheet Language Transformations).

Search Engine Crawling of Feeds

Feed data can be provided to the search engine through a push process by configuring the feed URL within the search engine.

Search Engine Crawling of Documents

The search engine uses the content/document repository as the data source that holds the digital assets such as documents, pdfs, images, audio, and the video contents along with their metadata. The portal indexes the document along with its metadata. Portal search would fetch the metadata from the content management repository, and display them on the portal as search result lists. Search can be based on keyword, text, category or attribute and search queries are executed as per the request to fetch the search results from the response.

Search Engine Crawling of Web Applications

The start URL can be used to specify the location of the web application that needs to be crawled.

Portal Meta Tags and Personalization

We have seen in Figure 8.3 an example of crawling and indexing web content and feed content. In order to make the crawled content meaningful, it needs to be associated with identifiable metadata.

Content source is the best place to add the metadata as it knows more about the content. Let us look at ways of adding metadata and how search engines can use the metadata for portal personalization and filtering results.

Portal Meta Tags

We can leverage the portal page-level metadata tags for efficient content categorization and identification. Search engines index metadata from the crawled documents and use it for filtering search results. Metadata describes the data that can be used for retrieving relevant and filtered search results. Let us look at some sample portal meta tags:

```
<meta name=portalurl content="home/reseller/desktop">
<meta name=usergroup content="customer">
```

Search engines also store the metadata associated with the document during indexing. Let us now discuss how these meta names can be leveraged for portal personalization.

Personalization

Every piece of content chunk is tagged with appropriate target audience and also other personalization criteria. In the metatag example discussed in the section on "portal meta tags", meta values for portal URLs and user groups were added. The meta tag name "usergroup" provides the relevant target audience/user group for the portal content. The search engine provides meta tag filtering to include only those search results that contain specified meta tag values of the usergroup. Based on the metadata for the target portal page, it will be extracted by the search engine and sent in the form of a result to the user as per the user credentials for the particular usergroup. Thus, personalized search results based on user groups can be obtained.

Portal Search Best Practices

The following are some important tips on how to use search effectively in a portal platform:

- *Optimized Search*: As search is a prominent feature of a portal, we need to optimize the end-to-end search features in all layers:
  - *Presentation Layer*: Create a lightweight search widget or search portlet that provides optimal experience on all devices. Provide intuitive features like type-ahead, synonym support, wild card match, spell-check, full text search, auto suggestion, etc. Create a user-friendly search results page that provides faceted browsing, relevancy ranking, search results pagination, and allow the user to configure the relevancy criteria. Also, provide other features such as saved search, popular search, personalized search and related search features.

    - *Server Layer*: Explore the feasibility of leveraging portal in-built search engines or use open source search tools such as Apache Solr or Lucene. Integrate with external search engines only when it is absolutely required. Provide layer-wise search results cache mechanism for optimal performance. Trigger search cache invalidation when the source content changes; for instance, a content publishing flow can invalidate the server side search cache that caches that content in its search result.
    - *Integration Layer*: Always use services-based integration for integrating with external search engines and with all enterprise content sources.
- *Personalized Search*: Add personalization features such as user preference–based search rank boosting, user defined search criteria, customized search experience, customizable search results page size, configurable search results relevancy ranking, and customizing search results page to enhance user's search experience.
- *Prime Positioning of Search*: Provide a prominent position for search in portal pages. It is preferred to place global search in the header of a portal theme so that users can utilize the search in all portal pages. Additionally, a dedicated search portlet can be placed in a prominent location of the portal page to provide contextual and advanced search features.
- *Search Centered Experience*: Many portal platforms now provide search centered experience. The global gateway pages feature search as the primary tool for information discovery and navigation. Another innovative usage of search is to use multiple instances of search portlet on the product page each having a pre-configured search keyword. For example, the first search portlet is pre-configured with a keyword such as "product features," which will dynamically aggregate the product features from multiple sources, and a second search portlet will be pre-configured with a keyword such as "product feed," which will get feeds from all social and collaboration platforms. In this technique, the portal product page can be dynamically aggregated with minimal content authoring effort.
- *Search Friendly URLs*: Portal URLs tend to be cryptic containing ids, path, navigation state, and other information. This poses challenges for SEO (search engine optimization) and for search indexing. To address this problem, we need to create a friendly URL, which meaningfully describes the page (though it is dynamic). We will look at this point in more detail in the next section on SEO.
- *Search Services*: As portal search is a combination of search along with personalization, portal as a platform can expose search as one of its main services to external systems.

Search Engine Optimization (SEO)

The SEO is an important aspect of external web applications. It involves techniques to improve the discovery of web pages from popular search engines thereby increasing the internet traffic of potential customers.

Advantages of SEO for Portal Platform

A portal application can derive the following advantages from an effective SEO strategy:

- A good ROI and revenue due to effective marketing
- Higher ranking from popular search engines
- High visibility for the portal site, organization brands, and the overall digital strategy
- Increased site traffic and potential increase in revenue
- Achieving the portal KPIs (key performance indicators) related to conversion ratio, page visits, etc.

Portal SEO Strategy

Let us look at the ways we can effectively implement SEO techniques in a portal platform.

Keyword Optimization

Page level keywords should provide the most accurate description of all portlets on the page. They should be carefully chosen based on content analysis, competitor analysis, and market and customer analysis. Since portlets are dynamically aggregated for a given page, it is necessary to provide a meaningful description of all the portlet content in the keywords section that is usually defined in portal theme. An effective way to have a meaningful keyword for the portal page is to aggregate the keywords from all its page-level portlets after they are loaded. This ensures that keywords and metadata do not miss any portlet level information.

It is also necessary to ensure that the keyword values specified occur with higher frequency and with good proximity in the portal page. Few search engines also look for the occurrence frequency and high keyword density for ranking the page.

Portal Page SEO Optimization

Let us look at some of the main SEO related optimizations that need to be done on a portal platform. The main portal SEO elements include page level SEO tags, link optimization, site map optimization, URL optimization, etc.

Page Level Metadata Optimization: The main metadata tags that the portal site needs to take care of are the following:

- *Title*: The page title should meaningfully describe the portal page
- *Header*: The h1 and h2 headers should be tagged for high level titles
- *Meta Tags*: Various page level meta tags such as description, keywords should appropriately describe the contents of the page
- *Image Tags*: These tags should properly describe the images through "alt" attributes

Link Optimization: The authority and quality of inbound links play a key role in deciding the page rank of the portal page. Social marketing and collaboration tools such as blogs, wiki, forums, communities, customer review links, analyst review pages, partner sites, affiliate sites can be leveraged to link to key portal pages.

Additionally, the anchor links in the page should contain appropriate keywords that accurately describe the target page.

Site Map Optimization: The portal site should provide a site map file that defines the entire hierarchy of the site and all the pages. The search engine spider uses it for traversing the entire site.

URL Optimization: There are multiple aspects for optimizing the portal URL:

- *Sanitizing URL*: Like mentioned before under the section on search-friendly URLs, default portal URLs are not user friendly. They contain the session information, page id, portlet information, source, path, navigation state, and all such details which make the URL long, cryptic, and difficult to remember and bookmark. Besides, the URL is dynamic; it cannot be bookmarked or remembered as it changes with each login. All these aspects pose challenges for both the end users and for search engines. To address this problem, most portal products provide multiple techniques. The following are some of the commonly employed methods:
    - *Friendly URL Mapping*: Portal administrators can specify a fixed friendly URL for a portal page. This fixed URL will serve as a static value irrespective of user state or other dynamic parameters. However, internally, the portal will map it to the portal specific URL.
    - *URL Filters*: Portals provide an extensible URL filter framework wherein the URL creation process can be customized. The state information can be extracted from the default URL and re-directed to the custom URL. Business-friendly and user-friendly URL patterns can also be constructed. For example, in an e-commerce site, the URL can be constructed depicting the category and sub-category level products in a URL path.
    - *URL Patterns*: We can specify the friendly URL pattern in the portal framwork. For instance, the URL can be specified to be http://host/category/subcategory/** wherein the "**" will be substituted by the product name at run time. This will be very useful for dynamic pages.
- *URL Depicting the Hierarchy Structure*: The URLs should depict the proper hierarchy of the portal pages. For example, http://portal/home/product/productdetails mimic the hierarchy in the site map page. Similarly, for a global portal site, the URL contains the geo name followed by the country name followed by the language.
- *URL Depicting the Navigation Structure*: When the user traverses the portal site, the bread crumb portlet creates the friendlier bread crumb trial of the navigation path. The URL should also match the bread crumb style pattern, which provides an easy-to-remember and navigable URL.
- *Prominent Keywords in URL Structure*: Providing a descriptive keyword-based URL would also help the search engines to discover the information better. For instance, featuring a product name in the URL of its page is the best way to describe the page.

Quick Links

Providing quick links such as site map, feeds, contact us, FAQs, social apps, seed list page, and about us on all pages (through portal theme footer) will ensure that the search engines will reach the prominent links by following these links from the home page.

SEO-Friendly Content Strategy

Various aspects of content strategy are discussed in Chapter 7. Beside those points, the content strategy should also be SEO friendly. This can be achieved by having an optimal content update frequency and content containing the page level keywords with relatively higher density.

Minimize SEO Blockers: There are known SEO blockers such as broken links, duplicate content, URL redirects, and canonical tags that need to be fixed. This again can be taken care of in the content strategy and during UI testing.

Monitoring and Tracking SEO Effectiveness

Finally, the effectiveness of SEO has to be continuously monitored. Once the portal site goes live, page rankings have to be constantly checked in various search engines, tool-based link analysis have to be done, the site traffic obtained from the search engines have to be monitored, and SEO monitoring tools have to be leveraged. All the findings from this monitoring and tracking activity should be used to further optimize the SEO tags, and refine the content.

Besides these techniques, search engines also use other parameters such as page size, page loading times, page freshness, page performance, etc. for ranking site web pages. Page size and load time need to be carefully analyzed to ensure that they are optimal.

Summary

- The chapter explains various portal search scenarios and various touch points between portal and search.
- The main portal requirements for search are dynamic content delivery, information discovery, user experience, information aggregation, and enhanced accessibility.
- The main portal search attributes are availability of easy and standard-based service integration, scalable search, pluggable and extensible connectors, support for secured search, search optimization, meta tag based search result filtering, ability to index various content types, and support for advanced search features.
- Portal search architecture mainly involves search services, web search, database search, content search, crawler, indexer, search portlet, connectors, and advanced search components.
- The main methods for search crawling are through service calls, API calls, web URL crawling, vendor provided connectors, and seed list-based crawling.

- The search crawler requires the start URL or feed URL to be configured for crawling the target content.
- Portal meta tags can be used for search results filtering and portal personalization.
- The SEO helps the portal site to get more visitor traffic, increased revenue, and high visibility.
- The main ways to achieve SEO in portals are through page level metadata, link optimization, URL optimization, URL depicting the hierarchy structure, URL depicting the navigation structure, quick links, SEO friendly content strategy, and by minimizing SEO blockers.

9

Securing Portals

The portal platform is used to deliver many applications for which security is of prime importance. Applications related to e-commerce, finance, banking, retail all require robust security. This automatically requires comprehensive security enforcement on its host platform which is the portal.

On the technical side of things, the portal has to manage content, services, functionality, data, and applications from various sources. More often than not, these data sources and external applications are protected and hence it becomes a natural requirement to provide a robust security feature that allows seamless access to all these applications and content to the portal user. In addition to this, the portal has to manage its own security such as role-based functionality and portlet access rules, page access rules, personalization rules, resource permission model, user administration, fine-grained data access, etc.

In this chapter, we will look at various security aspects of the portal. We will also look at a few special security scenarios such as external secure service integration, secure content integration, and user registration, which fall under the realm of portal security.

Portal architects and enterprise security architects would find this chapter useful.

Portal Security: An Introduction

In this chapter, we are mainly concerned about key security-related scenarios in the portal. We will also see security-related best practices in Chapter 15 and we have also seen some of the main security-related portal integrations in Chapter 6; similarly, will look at security-related testing aspects in Chapter 11. This chapter complements these concepts by detailing the core security scenarios and elaborating various techniques and best practices related to portal security.

Portal Security Assessment

Let us look at the main steps involved in the overall security assessment of portal applications. Portal security assessment primarily involves the following elements:

- *Portal Security Reviews*: This involves employing early and iterative security code reviews, enforcing of secure coding best practices, and leveraging security checklists during portal development. Additionally, applicable security compliance and regulatory checks will be conducted such as compliance to ISO27001, PCI standards. We can leverage open source security scanning tools such as PMD, FindBugs, and Open Web Application Security Project (OWASP) models and tools for automating security code review. We will see a security checklist in Chapter 15. Security code review and security compliance should be one of the key gating criteria for portal release.

- *Portal Application Risk Assessment*: Internal security teams and external security SMEs can be engaged to assess the risk of the portal application. They perform the risk profiling of the application and do a threat modeling. Risk profiling provides details of potential risks for the portal and a threat model details the exploitation approach. Threat modeling identifies vulnerable user scenarios, dependent systems, attack surface, and models the threat. More targeted security test cases and scenarios can be designed based on risk profiling and threat modeling.
- *Portal Application Security Scan*: Security tools can be used to do vulnerability scanning of the portal application. The tools simulate exploitation scenarios such as SQL injection, buffer overflow, cross-site scripting, and others to identify any existing vulnerabilities of the portal system.
- *Portal Security Testing*: This includes executing application security tests such as penetration testing, risk-based testing, ethical hacking, denial-of-service testing, and white and black box testing, etc.

Portal Security Architecture

Portal security mainly relies on two things: the portal's in-built security model along with its extensions, and external enterprise security infrastructure. The portal's in-built security model mainly consists of the authentication module, authorization controls such as role-based access, portal access control, portal resource permission model, portal SSO (single sign on), etc. These will be discussed in detail in the coming sections. Enterprise security infrastructure consists of a security proxy/security manager that handles SSO, user registry such as Lightweight Directory Access Protocol (LDAP), user provisioning systems, identity management (IdM) systems, and other infrastructure level security elements such as firewalls, networks, etc. In this section, let us look at the overall security architecture of an enterprise portal.

A high level security architecture of a B2C (business to customer) portal is shown in Figure 9.1. We will look at the main components of the security infrastructure.

Portal

The portal server normally runs on an application server. For instance, a java-based portal server runs in a java enterprise application server and hence depends on the application server security features. This includes user session management, security tokens, security extensions features, etc. The application server runs in host OS and is protected by OS level security features such as file ACLs, OS services, etc.

The portal also has various in-built security features such as:

- User authentication modules, which authenticates user credentials against the configured user registry. Many portal products provide in-built connectors to various user registries.
- Authorization modules, which provide fine grained access to individual pages, porlets, and portal resources.

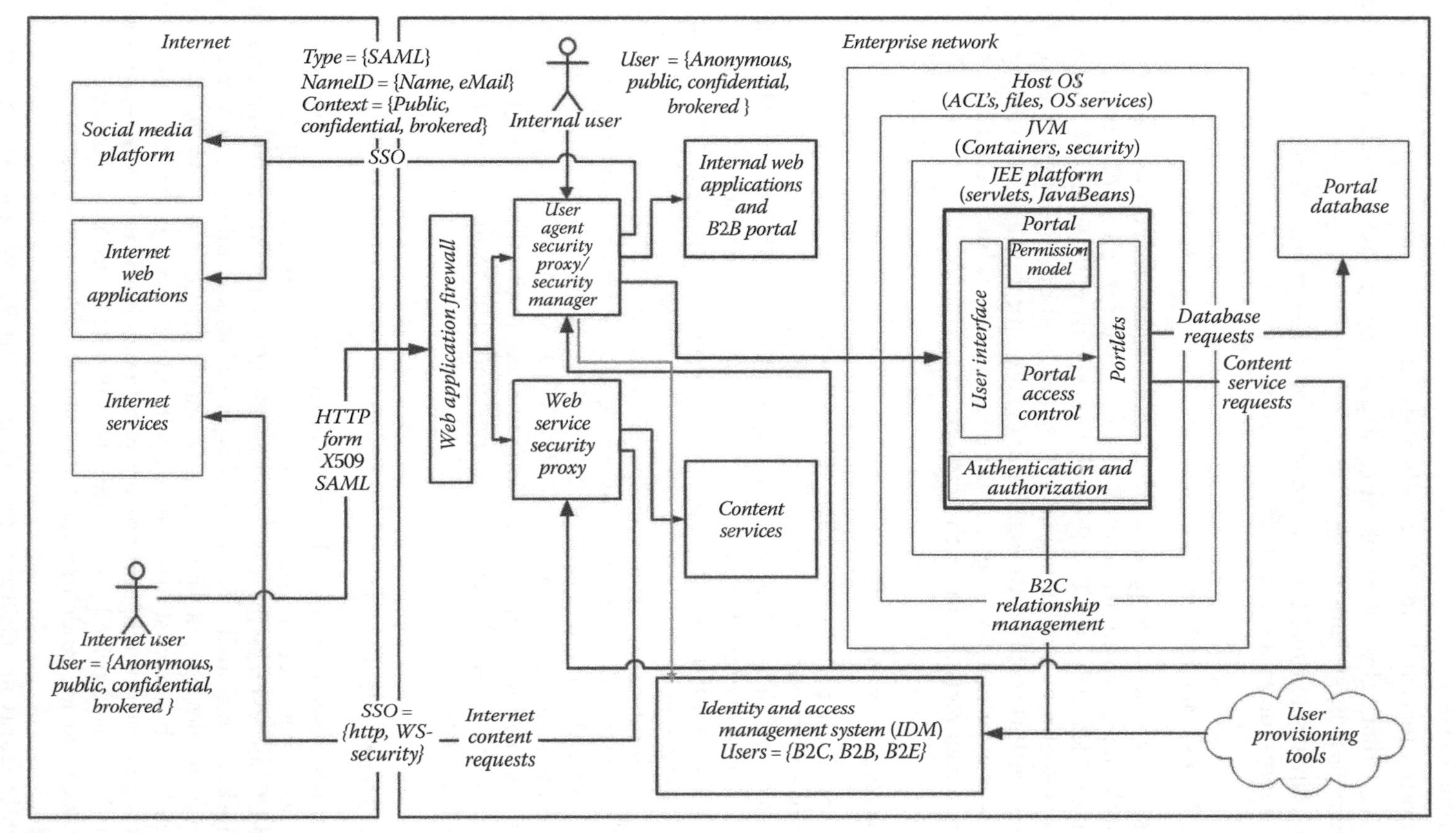

FIGURE 9.1
Portal security infrastructure.

- Portal access control and permission models that consist of role based access to portal functionality.
- Login portlet that can be used for authentication.
- Portal SSO that helps in establishing single sign on functionality with other secured enterprise systems.
- User administration that helps in creating and assigning various roles to users and portal resources and updating user profile.

Identity and Access Management System

The IDM systems provide enterprise-wide user management and maintain user policies and user entitlements, which are applicable to enterprise-wide applications. They consist of user registries such as LDAP, SSO servers, Security Assertion Markup Language (SAML) servers, security token management systems, user provisioning systems, etc. They also provide modules to support various kinds of authentication and store enterprise-wide roles for a given user identity. User provisioning tools synchronize portal user details from enterprise user registries through sync jobs.

Security Proxy/Security Manager

They help in providing enterprise-wide web SSO across all internal applications. User agent plug-ins and proxies will intercept portal requests and establish the SSO with internal applications such as internal web application and B2B portals. They also provide policy-based authentication and authorization. The security proxies in the web server help the administrators to configure a variety of security and routing rules. These proxy agents also pass user context information and entitlements information, which can be used by portals for personalization. In some cases, the security proxies also interact with the policy server to get user entitlement and policy related information. We will see the details of this in the coming sections. Tools such as CA SiteMinder, Oracle Access Manager (OAM), IBM Tivoli Access Manager (TAM) will perform some of the functionality mentioned above. In the security architecture provided in Figure 9.1, internal web applications and B2B applications are secured by security manager systems.

Web Service Security Proxy

This proxy provides security for web services invoked by the portal. The proxy ensures that web service messages are secured and their integrity and confidentiality is not compromised. They leverage the web service security standard to transparently secure messages. The key functionality of the services proxy include authentication (mainly using SAML assertions), message filtering, message encryption, certification verification, processing of WS-S (web service security) message headers, and maintaining message integrity. It plays a key role in mitigating security vulnerabilities such as message sabotage, denial-of-service, unauthorized access, etc. OWASP's XML Security Gateway Evaluation Criteria (XSGEC) provide guidelines for evaluating the XML gateways used for securing web services.

In the portal security architecture provided in Figure 9.1, content services that provide web service–based access to enterprise content is secured by web services security proxy.

Web Application Firewall

The firewall mainly restricts access on pre-configured ports by specified protocols. It enforces various security policies related to enterprise applications and enterprise network. Specialized web application firewalls also guard the portal applications against critical vulnerabilities such as SQL injection, cross-site scripting, cookie hijacking, CSRF, etc.

External System Integration

In the above architecture given in Figure 9.1, we can see that external systems such as external social media platforms and external web applications use the security proxy for communication through SAML assertions. External web services use web service security proxy for integration.

Portal Authentication and Access Control

After having looked at high-level portal security architecture, we will now look at core portal security scenarios in detail.

Authentication

Portal authentication mainly consists of a login portlet, which authenticates user credentials against the configured user registry. The portal will be configured with the enterprise user registry; the portal will then leverage it for user authentication. A typical authentication process pipeline consists of the following events:

1. The user provides authentication details in the login portlet. Login portal page should be served over HTTPS (HTTP over SSL) to enable transport level security.
2. The portal authenticates the user against user registry such as LDAP.
3. Upon successful authentication, the portal fetches the user profile attributes and roles for the user.
4. The portal creates the user session and necessary security tokens.
5. The portal then executes the authorization rules, which render the portal page level components such as portlets based on the applicable roles. Portal also executes any profile-based personalization rules.

We have seen the regular authentication mechanism above. Due to the varied and complex nature of enterprise systems, there are other forms of authentication mentioned below:

1. Authentication by enterprise security managers: In some scenarios, there would be an enterprise-wide centralized authentication system such as CA SiteMinder that acts as single entry point for all secured enterprise systems. In such cases, portal would be integrated with enterprise authentication systems. Integration is usually done through vendor-provided adapters and the authentication process leverages security tokens at run time.

TABLE 9.1
Portal Permission Matrix

Role	Read Content	Update Content	Delete Content	Create Content
Content author	Yes	Yes	No	Yes
Content reviewer	Yes	No	No	No
Content admin	Yes	Yes	Yes	Yes

2. Some enterprise follows propitiatory authentication mechanism. In such cases, we need to use portal provided and application server provided security extensions to develop security adapters for the enterprise authentication systems. Most of the java application servers support Pluggable Authentication Module (PAM) framework such as Java Authentication and Authorization Service (JAAS) that can be used as a standard while implementing security extensions.
3. Due to the popularity of emerging social media platforms such as Facebook, Linkedin, Google, Twitter, etc., some of the consumer portals would also provide social media–based authentication mechanisms. This helps the end user to login with an existing Facebook account instead of creating a new account with portal system. In such cases, portal needs to be integrated with those social media platforms. We have already seen the integration details in Chapter 6.

Portal Access Control

Enforcing role-based security access is an in-built feature in most portal products. Portal permission model is usually a 3-level mapping of user/resource to roles to permissions. Table 9.1 provides a simple permission matrix of roles and permission for portal content management functionality.

Once the roles are mapped to the permissions, the portal administrator can assign roles to individual users. The users will automatically inherit the permissions through the assigned roles. In some permission models, the inherited access control can also be overridden by directly granting or denying the permission at user level; this should be used only on exception scenarios.

Permissions and access control can also be provided to secure and control access to various portal resources such as portal page templates, portlets, portal admin activities, portal services, etc.

Portal Single Sign On

Portal single sign on helps the portal to aggregate content from multiple protected data sources such as CMS content, data from secured web application, data from protected web services, etc. When the user navigates from the portal page to an external web application, it should be fully seamless. All this will be possible with the single sign on feature.

Web SSO or Internal SSO

This SSO is achieved between internal applications hosted within the organization. For instance, a portal, which needs to have seamless access to the internal enterprise resource planning (ERP) system or an enterprise reporting application, would need a web SSO.

We have already seen the high-level integration details of achieving web SSO in Chapter 6. Let us elaborate on it now. The detailed steps of the web SSO with portal is given in Figure 9.2.

- *Step 1: User request*—The portal user requests for a resource. The resource can be a secured/unsecured portal page or a document or a file.
- *Step 2: Web agent processing*—The request reaches the portal web server. The portal web server will be configured with a security manager plug-in. The security manager plug-in forwards the request to the security manager for authentication and policy evaluation.
- *Step 3, 4, and 5: User authentication and SSO token creation*— The security manager does the following things:
    - Checks policies to determine if the resource is protected or not. Normally, protected portal resources are differentiated from unprotected/public portal resources through URL pattern.
        - If the request is for an unprotected or public resource, the requested public resource is served to the user.
        - If the request is for a protected resource, the security manager checks for the existence of an SSO cookie or token.
            - If a valid SSO cookie exists, security manager forwards the request to portal server to process the request. Portal request processing is detailed in step 6. If the SSO cookie does not exist or if the SSO cookie is expired, then the security manager redirects the user to the login form.

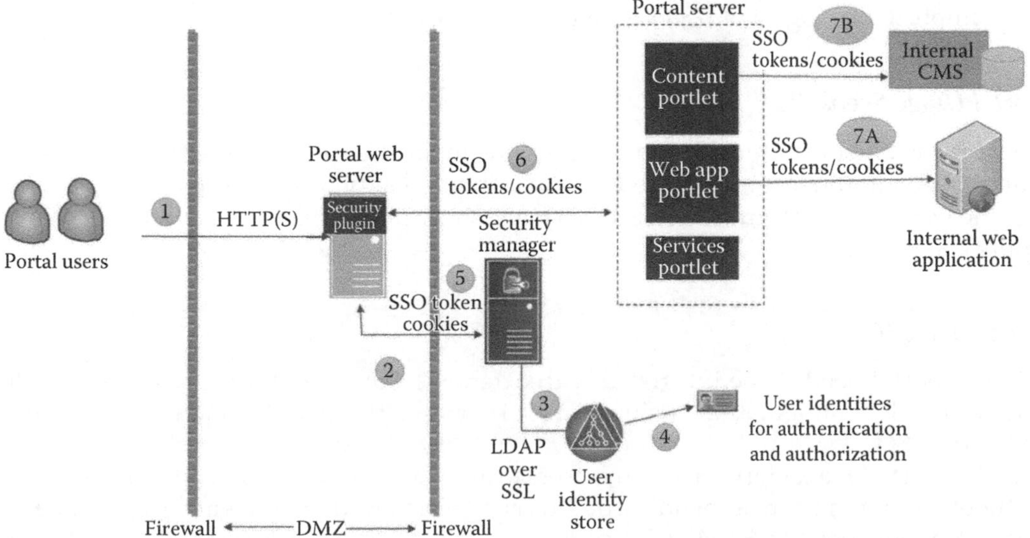

FIGURE 9.2
Portal web SSO.

  - User authentication process begins by the user sending credentials.
  - The security manager verifies user credentials from a user identity store such as LDAP.
  - The security manager also checks for roles and applicable policies for the authenticated user.
  - Upon successful authentication, the security manager creates SSO tokens/cookies, which contain user information, role information, policy information, and timestamp, etc. in encrypted format. The SSO token/cookie will be assigned to the user session.
  - User request will be forwarded to portal server for further processing.
- *Step 6: Portal authorization*—The portal will be configured with the security manger to interpret the SSO tokens/cookies. It will check the applicable roles/policies and authorization rules for the user role/user group present in the SSO cookie. If the user role has required resource permissions then the portal allows access to the requested resource.
- *Step 7a and 7b: Web SSO in action*—Now let us assume that the portal user clicks on the link in a web application portlet, which has aggregated the links from an internal web application. The user will be redirected to the internal web application that is also protected by the same security manager. Once the security manager re-verifies the validity of SSO security tokens which are sent along with the portal request, the user would get seamless access to the internal web application. The same flow is applicable for web content or documents stored in the internal CMS.

SSO Session Termination: The SSO token or cookie will be destroyed upon these scenarios:

- *Explicit SSO Logout of User Session*: This functionality is provided by the security manager.
- Implicit SSO logout of user session due to time out or inactivity.

Portal Usage Scenarios

Web SSO is one of the most common scenarios in an enterprise eco-system wherein the portal needs to interact with various secured internal applications. The portal can leverage the web SSO to integrate with ERP systems, aggregate content from other internal web applications, etc.

Federated SSO

When a portal needs to be integrated with external secured applications, we can employ federated SSO configuration. Using SAML is one of the popular methods to achieve federated SSO.

Federated SSO capability enables the users to move across partner and affiliated websites, without having to be re-authenticated. This can be achieved by implementing standards-based technologies like SAML. The portal is normally the identity provider (IdP) which does the user authentication and produces a SAML assertion for the service provider (SP), which consumes the SAML assertion to achieve federated SSO.

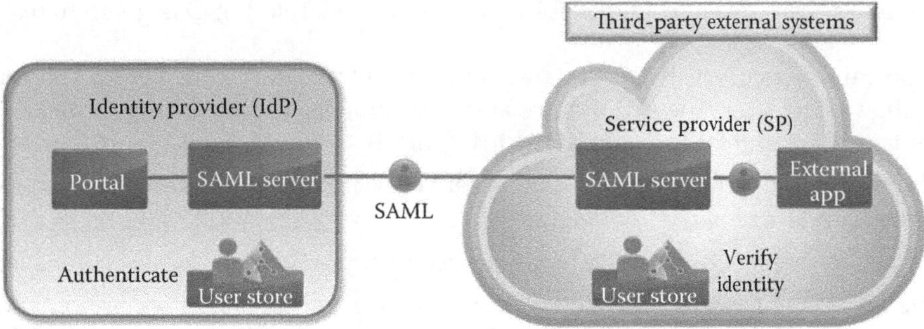

FIGURE 9.3
Portal acting as IdP in federated SSO.

The SAML server generates the SAML assertion when the user is successfully authenticated by the policy server.

When the request goes to the external affiliated/partner application, which is using SAML complaint federation security services as the service provider, it intercepts incoming SAML assertions and disambiguates the user. The user experiences single sign-on across the Internet and secure access to the portal at the external application.

Let us look at the various components and the flow in detail.

Figure 9.3 shows the role of the portal as the identity provider (IdP) in the federated SSO flow.

External secured applications are service providers (SP). Both IdP and SP rely on SAML assertions to achieve single sign on. A SAML 2.0-based flow is depicted in Figure 9.4.

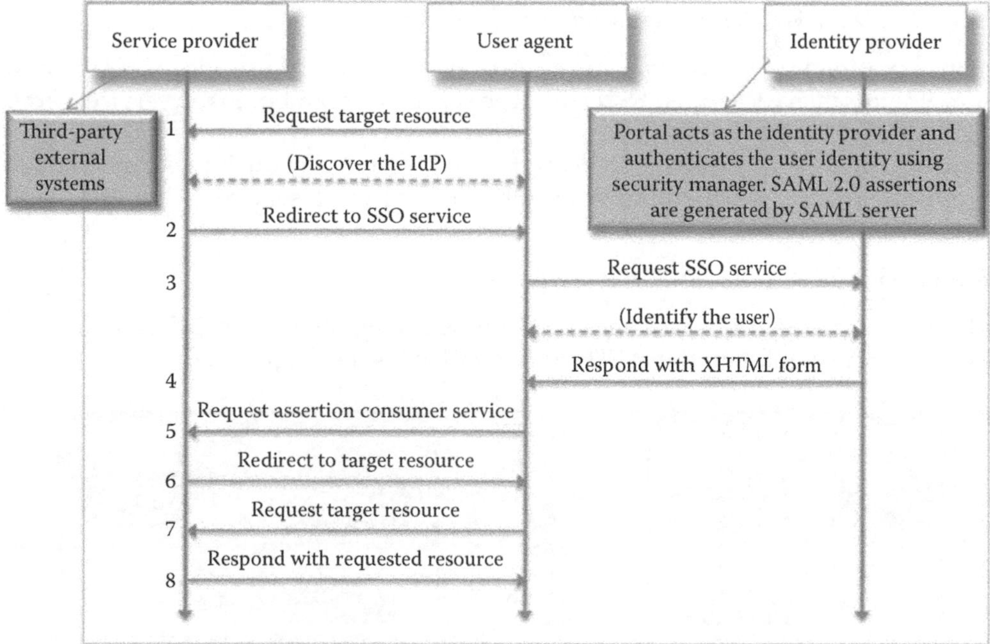

FIGURE 9.4
SAML assertion–based flow for achieving federated SSO.

The detailed steps given in Figure 9.4 for achieving federated SSO is given here:

1. A portal user accesses the portal by providing authentication credentials. The user is allowed to access the portal once authentication is successful and local security context is created for the user at the IdP (portal).
2. The user selects a hyperlink to the target application that happens to be an external secured third party application.
3. An SSO request is generated and a request is sent to the identity provider service.
4. The IdP SSO service should determine if the user has provided valid credentials. If the credentials are not valid, the IdP should challenge the user for login credentials. After successful authentication, the IdP service should process the request, build the digitally signed SAML assertion response containing the authentication attribute, and send to the user.
5. The user requests the service to the service provider (SP) with HTTP(S) response containing the SAML assertion.
6. The SP redirects the user to the target application if it successfully validates the response.
7. The user now requests for the target resource.
8. The target resource is served to the user.

In order to do a federated SSO logout, the user has to logout from both IdP and SP sessions. The previous example shows the external link scenario for a federated SSO. Let us now look at two more popular portal scenarios that require federated SSOs.

Federated SSO for Web Services–Based Portal Integration

User information will be added as an SAML token in the web service message header (Figure 9.5) to achieve federated SSO with web services integration. Web services security header can be leveraged for this.

In order to achieve fine grained authorization, additional user attributes can be added as part of the SAML token, which can be used by the target web service.

Federated SSO for APIs-Based Portal Integration

Just like services-based integration, for API-based integration, user information can be added as an SAML token in the HTTP authorization header (Figure 9.6).

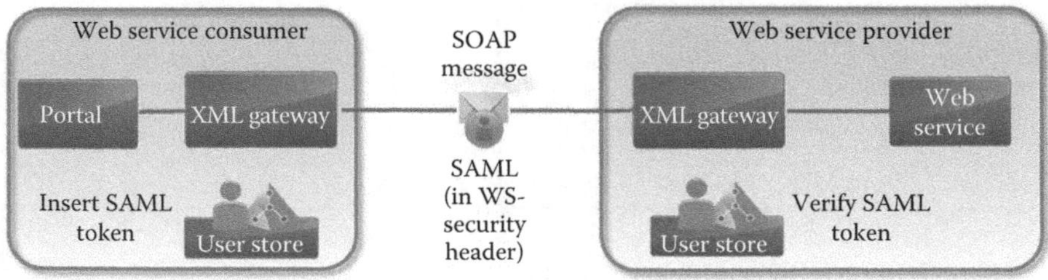

FIGURE 9.5
Federated SSO for web services–based portal integration.

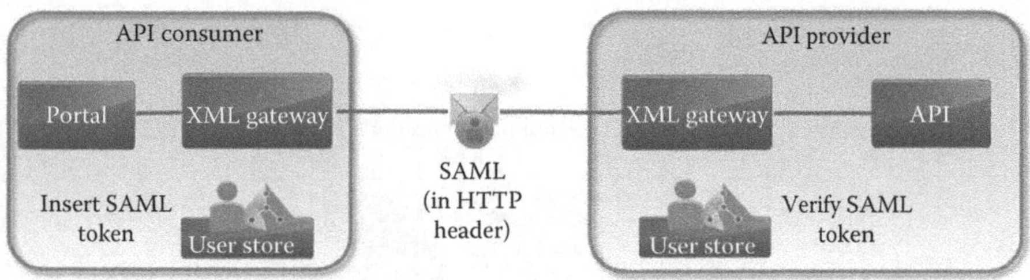

FIGURE 9.6
Federated SSO for API-based portal integration.

Fine grained authorization can be achieved by additional user attributes in the SAML token.

Portal Usage Scenarios

Federated SSOs are mainly used for integrating with cross-domain applications and external secured applications such as social media platforms, external web services with portal.

Portal User Management

Portal user administration includes activities such as user role management, user registration and provisioning, account creation, etc. We have already seen a sample role-permission matrix in the "Portal Access Control" section. We will look at user provisioning now.

User Registration and Provisioning

Many customer facing portals provide user registration functionality. This serves the dual purpose of enabling customer self-service and efficient customer on-boarding due to optimized workflows.

There are multiple ways in which a portal user registration can be implemented. Two popular techniques are given here.

1. *Using Registration Web Services*: In this option, the portal constructs the user registration user interface and the registration portlet invokes the registration services in the back end. A complex registration process spans multiple portal pages and is often implemented using portal workflow to model the multi-step approval and registration-related business rules. The back-end services store the user details in the user registry pending verification and approval.
2. *Leveraging Business Process Management (BPM) Tool*: Some organizations have sophisticated BPM tools, which model the registration workflow and all associated business rules. The BPM tool uploads the user data to a centralized user repository. In this scenario, there will be multiple registration applications, which leverage the BPM tool. The portal will be integrated with the BPM tool in the user registration scenario and BPM will take the responsibility to orchestrate the registration workflow and enforce the business rules.

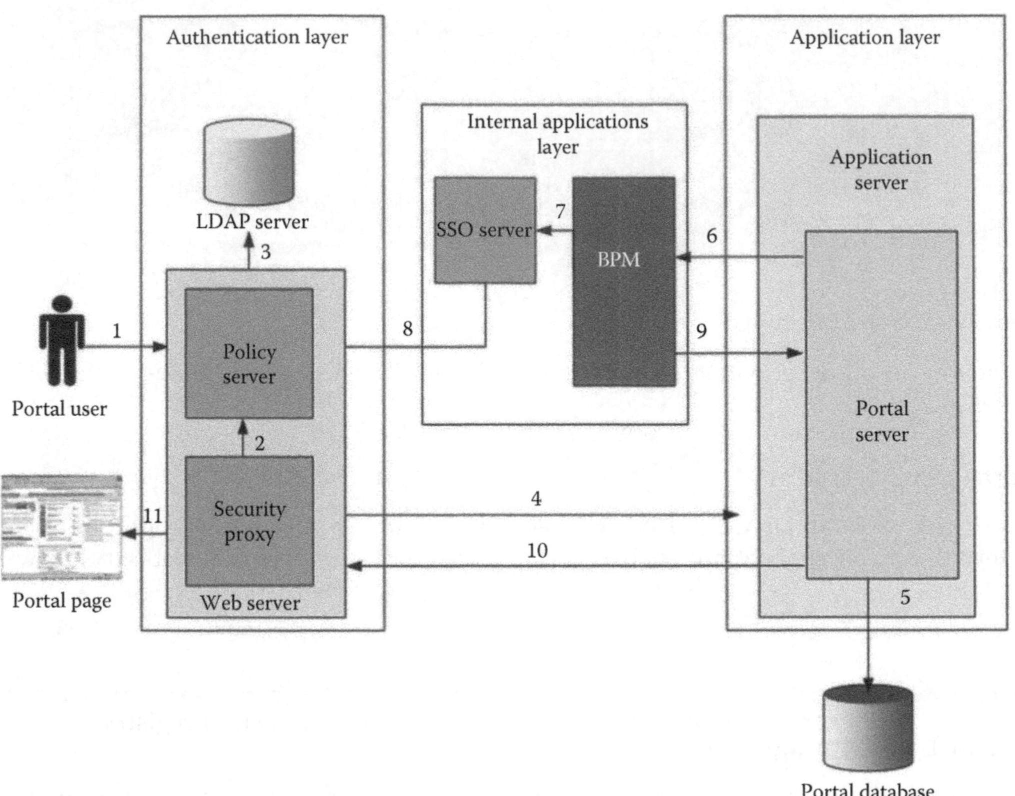

FIGURE 9.7
Portal–BPM integration for user registration.

In both the scenarios, the user details will be stored in a centralized user repository and optionally provisioned to various data sources. A subset of user attributes may also be provisioned to the portal server for performance optimization.

Figure 9.7 is a depiction of portal leveraging the BPM tool.

For this scenario, portal invoking registration service of secured internal BPMs is considered. Few BPM tools also provide customizable interface that can be used in portals. The main points and pre-requisites that need to be noted in are given here.

- In steps 1, 2, and 3, user authentication would happen. This scenario is required when an account manager wants to register his/her organization's employees and hence authentication and role verification of account manager is required. If it is for end-user registration, there is no need for authentication and user would be served with a public registration form.
- In Step 4, the portal would store/track the registration status in its portal repository. In step 5, all data required for user registration form would be fetched from portal database. This includes country list, language list, geo list, etc.
- In Step 6, the portal would invoke BPM registration web services to initiate the registration flow. Entire registration flow would require multiple BPM service invocations as required by business rules and process steps.

- In steps 7, 8, and 9, after user registration is complete, user details are validated and approved in the BPM tool, the data will be stored in the BPM repository.
- The newly registered user data will be provisioned to the centralized enterprise user repository on a regular basis through sync jobs.
- Optionally, a subset or minimal amount of user data can also be provisioned to the portal repository. The portal can use this for performance optimization purposes.

The detailed steps in the portal registration flow is given below:

- Step 1: Web request

  Portal user requests for a portal page that is formed of multiple portlets aggregating content from various sources. This use case mainly deals with aggregating content from internal web application.
- Step 2: Request interception

  As the security proxy is configured as the authentication agent with portal server, all the web requests to the portal page will be intercepted by the security proxy. The security proxy will check the user credentials in the request and will forward to policy server.
- Step 3: Authentication

  The policy server will verify the user credentials against the user registry.
- Step 4: Forwarding to application server

  Once the user is successfully authenticated with LDAP system, a SSO token is created and the request is forwarded to the Application server which is running portal server.
- Step 5: Authorization

  The access control privileges are checked for the authenticated user. The portal access permissions like the role type, resource permissions are stored in the portal database. Once the access permissions are verified, the user is allowed to access the required portlet. Personalization rules are also applied in this step.
- Step 6: Internal application integration

  During the server side aggregation, the portal connects to the internal BPM application (configured with security proxy) through services.
- Steps 7 and 8: Achieving single sign-on

  The security proxy configured with the internal application uses the policy server for verifying the validity of user session and the SSO tokens.
- Step 9: Allowing the internal integration

  After the user session and SSO tokens are validated, the content from the internal application is aggregated through services.
- Step 10: Serving the aggregated content

  The portal server now renders the aggregated content to the Web Server.
- Step 11: Portal Page display

  The portal page will be displayed to the requested user.

Portal User Administration

The portal also provides a user administration page wherein the user can update his/her profile. The portal administrator can also update roles for the portal user. In such a case, user updates will be stored in the portal repository, which will then be synched with the centralized enterprise user repository through regular synch jobs. Alternatively, the portal may also invoke user profile update web services, which directly update the centralized enterprise user repository.

Security-Related Portal Scenarios

Apart from the core security scenarios mentioned in previous sections, the portal is also a popular platform for developing applications, which require a high level of security such as banking portals, finance portals, e-commerce portals, etc. Some self-service features such as user registration, self-registration, and password reset also rely heavily on security infrastructure. In this section, we will look at some of those use cases in detail.

Secured Integration

If a portal needs to retrieve the content from an internal content management system, then there are three popular integration options: content services, content links, and content APIs. In all three scenarios, the web SSO can be leveraged to retrieve the secured content. The main pre-requisite for this is that the CMS should be protected by the enterprise-wide security proxy/security manager, which acts as an SSO server. While getting the secured content through content services, the user information can be embedded through SSO tokens in the service header; alternatively, service security proxy (XML services gateway) can be leveraged for seamless integration. For API-based integration, SSO tokens can be added to the authentication header during session creation.

A sample flow for secured link-based integration to an internally hosted web application (Figure 9.8) is shown here. For this flow, we have taken internal BPM as the web application, which provides user registration forms. (*Note*: In our earlier example in Figure 9.7, we had used BPM services for user registration; in this example, we are providing link-based access to internal BPM to demonstrate the flow.)

- *Step 1*: Web request
    - The portal user requests for a portal page, which is formed of multiple portlets aggregating content from various sources. This use case mainly deals user registration through a link to secured internal BPM tool
- *Step 2*: Secured link display
    - Portal presents the registration form link
- *Step 3*: User access of registration link
    - User clicks on user registration link. Before the user is transferred to BPM tool, seamless SSO happens due to security proxy, which is configured as the authentication agent with portal server and BPM. The security proxy will create the SSO tokens and these tokens will be a part of all portal requests. In this case, SSO tokens will be passed to the BPM tool, which successfully authenticates the user details.

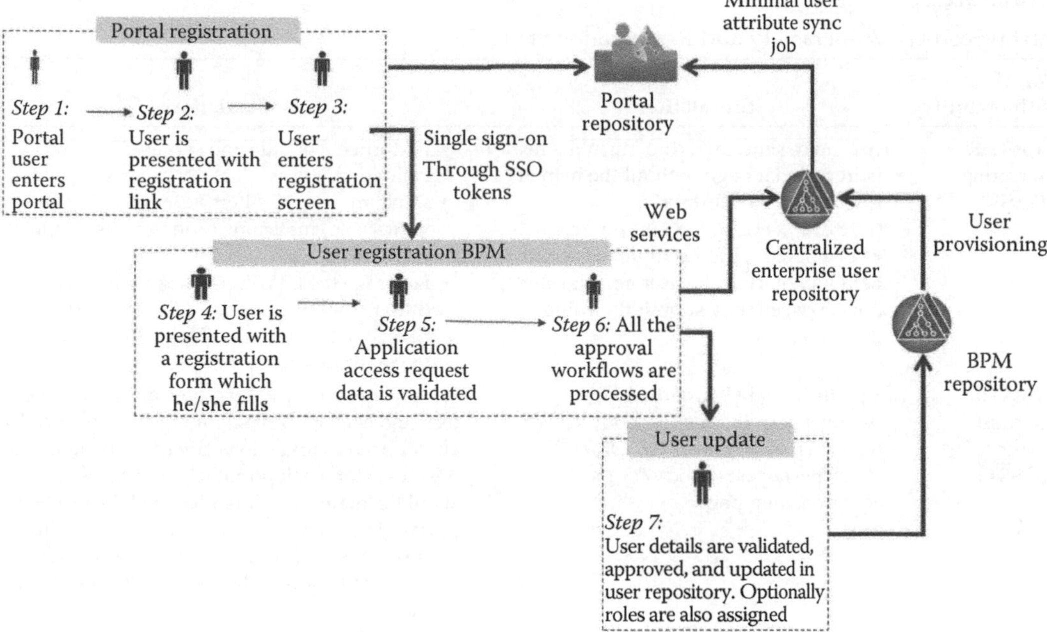

FIGURE 9.8
Secured portal integration.

- *Step 4*: Forwarding to internal BPM tool
    - BPM tool generates the registration form
- *Step 5*: Request validation
    - BPM tool validates the request and form data.
- *Step 6*: Registration workflow
    - In this step, all necessary steps required for user registration is complete. BPM would also use validation services to complete user registration.
- *Step 7*: Repository update
    - After successful registration, user details are stored in BPM repository, centralized user repository and are optionally provisioned to portal repository as well.

Secure Service Invocation

We have seen that services security proxy is one of the most efficient ways to integrate with secure services. For internal services, SSO tokens can be added to service headers and for external services, SAML assertions can be added to the security header.

Portal Security Vulnerabilities and Prevention Techniques

Listed in Table 9.2 are some of the common vulnerabilities found in portal platform and the remediation steps.

TABLE 9.2

Portal Security Vulnerability and Remediation Steps

Portal Vulnerability	Simulation	Remediation
Cross site scripting (XSS)	This can be simulated directly in the text field of portal page without the help of tools. Input the alert script (`<script>alert('XSS attack') </script>`) with the value of the text field and check if the user gets the alert pop-up when they submit the value to the server.	• Perform client-side and server-side validation. • Develop security filters to remove the vulnerable/malicious code from user input fields. • Leverage the OWASP AntiSamy Project (https://www.owasp.org/index.php/Category:OWASP_AntiSamy_Project) to filter the malicious code.
Cross site request forgery (CSRF)	Copy the portal URL and add the parameters in the request body. Check the HTTP response for 200 OK and check the response body for the corresponding page.	The server should validate the request from the user and each request should include an encoded authentication token to verify the authenticity of the requestor. Each portal resource request should contain the authentication token so that portal server can verify the authenticity of the request. Most portal servers provide an in-built mechanism to add authentication tokens to the request.
Predictable resource location	Knowing the directory pattern, the hacker tries to browse the portal admin page or tries to list the resources on the portal server.	• All admin and private pages should be protected and should be accessible only upon authentication. • A more secure way is to expose admin URL only for internal users and never over the Internet. • Leverage web server settings to prevent directory listing.
Portal request tampering	This issue can be simulated using Firefox plugin TamperData. 1. Start the Tamper data plugin. 2. Access the portal URL in the Firefox and the request and response would be captured in TamperData. 3. During the submission of request click the "start tamper" tab. 4. Post parameter fields would be displayed and tamper the parameter value. Check the server response to see if the parameter value tampered gets validated in the server side or not.	If the request to the server is manipulated the response should be HTTP 404 Not found or HTTP 500 Internal server error with redirection of the page to the customized application error page.
Abuse of functionality	Hacker can upload a malicious file.	Steps to protect a website from file-upload attacks: 1. The application should impose on file types that can be uploaded. This includes file names, file size, file extension, etc. Uploaded file folder should not have "execute" permission. 2. Use client-side and server-side validation for file types against white list values. 3. Portal should not store the uploaded file to any of the system folders. 4. Once uploaded, the files should be scanned by an antivirus software.

(*Continued*)

TABLE 9.2 (*Continued*)

Portal Security Vulnerability and Remediation Steps

Portal Vulnerability	Simulation	Remediation
Man-in-the-middle attack	Hacker can intercept the traffic and communicate with portal user and portal server.	• Always use secure transport layer such as HTTPS while serving personalized or business-sensitive information. Use SSL certificates for securing portal web server and portal application server. • Encrypt sensitive data during transmission.
Distributed denial-of-service	Portal server can be flooded with requests which overload the portal server resources.	• Leverage web application firewall policies that filter out suspicious HTTP traffic. We can set the packet filtering rules in the firewall. • Portal proxy servers also provide various options to minimize the risk of DDoS. Setting related to buffer size, timeouts can be leveraged for this purpose. • CDN networks and cloud providers also provide various security measures against the attack.
Injection attacks	Hacker can use tools like ZAP to launch SQL injection attacks on portal form fields.	• Use JDBC prepared statements or an open source ORM tools to minimize the risk from SQL injection attacks. • Validate all the user input values and remove all blacklist values.

Summary

- Security being one of the main concerns of a portal is discussed in this chapter.
- Security features such as authentication, SSO are essential for information aggregation and seamless access of secured applications.
- Portal security assessment includes portal security reviews, portal application risk assessment, portal application security scan, and portal security testing.
- High level portal security architecture include core portal security–related modules such as user authentication modules, authorization modules, portal access control and permission model, login portlet, portal SSO, and user administration. It also includes enterprise security eco-system components such as IDM, security manager, security proxy, application firewall, etc.
- Portal web SSO is mainly achieved through SSO tokens and HTTP header values.
- Federated SSO is mainly achieved through SAML assertions. The portal acts as an identity provider (IdP) in the federated SSO flow. This can be used for both external service invocation and API-based integration with external applications.
- User registration can be achieved through registration web services or through BPM tool integration.

10

Portal Collaboration, Knowledge Management, and Personalization

Collaboration brings people, process, and technology together. Collaboration plays a crucial role in actively engaging the target audience and hence plays a key role in digital strategy. Portal-led collaboration has multi-fold impact such as information sharing, productivity improvement, active user engagement, and content co-creation, reduced process turn over times and also promotes a self-service model. Though it is a popular trend for intranet portals, it is also extensively used for external portals. Enterprise collaboration mainly aims to foster enterprise social networking and leverage crowd wisdom. They empower stakeholders and help them in professional development and provide streamlined workflows.

Knowledge management is another popular utility of portals. A portal is well suited for implementation of knowledge repositories, and knowledge management for internal and external stakeholders. As this is one of the prominent usage scenarios of portals, we will look at this aspect as well. Both collaboration and knowledge management harness the collective intelligence of the portal user community for the benefit of both end users and the business.

Personalization, as we know, is one of the core use cases of portals. It enhances user experience by providing custom functionality and content based on explicitly and implicitly provided user preference values.

Personalization combined with collaboration and knowledge management would provide a unique value addition to both the portal user and for the organization.

This chapter discusses these three aspects of a portal in greater detail. Portal architects, business analysts, and portal developers would find this chapter useful.

Requirements and Benefits of a Collaborative Portal

There are numerous ways to digitally collaborate on the portal platform. Collaborative tools are part of the portal product and most portal products provide plug-in support with third party collaboration software. The main collaboration tools are audio and video chat, messengers, blogs, wikis, communities, internal and external social media platforms, activity streams, on-demand feeds, podcasts, web conferencing and document sharing tools.

Requirements

The key requirements of a portal-based collaboration platform are as follows:

- Portals should provide easy-to-use collaboration tools such as chat, wiki, blogs, communities, preferably through in-built features.
- Portals should provide collaboration-based knowledge management.
- Collaboration platforms should enable users to share knowledge assets such as document, solution articles, files, and media files.

The main collaboration tools used in the portal platform are given here. Most of these features are provided by in-built portlets.

- *Blogs*: Users can author blogs. It allows users to provide ratings, comments, social bookmarks.
- *Message Boards*: It allows users to ask questions and answers; users can also add categories, permissions, subscriptions, mailing lists.
- *Calendar*: It allows users to add events and other features such as scheduling, adding resource, export/import, etc.
- *Chats*: Users can do audio and video chat in real-time using this feature. Though it is mainly used for customer service, it can also be used by the general-purpose user for user communication as well.
- *Mail*: This feature help users to draft, send, and receive mails.
- *Wiki*: This feature provides wiki features such as content wikis, page imports, permissions, attachments, feeds, page templates, etc. It helps in information/content co-creation.
- Communities allow users to create groups to align with like-minded people, and gain from their insights. It provides a channelized way of communication; thus, people will be able to get only the required information.
- *Feedback*: This feature provides an opportunity for customers to provide feedback on specific products and services, and helps customer representatives to gather specific output.
- *Web Conferencing*: It helps in real-time sharing of information through screen-share, co-browsing and other related things.
- *Polls*: Polls provide an avenue to gather targeted customer opinion on specific services. They can help organizations to come up with statistics that can help in decision making.
- *Survey and Questionnaires*: These help organizations to gather intelligence from existing customers, which can be utilized for designing and development of new products or services.
- *Content Review, Rating and Tagging*: Content rating and tagging help customers provide the feedback on the content, thus helping the organization improve the quality of the portal content exposed.

Besides these features, other collaboration features include social bookmarks, idea management, ask and answer feature, feeds, etc. based on organization needs.

Benefits

The main benefits of collaborative features in the portal are as follows:

- It enables collaboration among all internal and external portal users. In the intranet portal scenario, employees and support teams can collaborate and share information. For extranet portals, channel users, partners, resellers can collaborate seamlessly in real-time to optimize business processes and the supply chain.
- The collaborative platform improves the accessibility and availability of the information to all users. It provides an in-built knowledge management process.

- It enhances collective knowledge through knowledge co-creation. Users can contribute to knowledge assets in the repository and businesses can get views and insights from the end user.
- It helps in word-of-mouth social marketing through customer blogs and feedback and engages the users actively. It makes their contribution count.
- Users can use the knowledge repository in their daily activities, improve their productivity, and optimize process completion time. Internal and external users can contribute and leverage solution articles and knowledge artifacts to complete their day-to-day activities more efficiently.
- It contributes to business goals such as cost optimization and self-service models. A classic example is the reduction of customer support calls or customer incidents due to re-use of knowledge assets. Similarly, self-paced e-learning and web-based trainings also provide a self-service model.

All portal products provide native support to basic collaboration features such as chat, wiki, blog, document sharing, etc. They also provide in-built CMS that can be used to build a robust collaboration platform. Additionally, there are various open-source collaboration frameworks that can be integrated with portals to fill the gap.

Trends in Portal Collaboration

Let us have a look at some of the emerging trends in portal collaboration space.

- *Strong Focus on Self-service*: There is an increased focus on achieving self-service through collaboration tools. Pro-active solution recommendations, easy accessibility of collaboration tools, enabling auto-approvals through collaboration platforms can be used to achieve a self-service model.
- *Social Media Collaboration*: Users are increasingly adopting social media-based collaborative features like content sharing, article review and rating, importing connections from social media, social media based login, etc. Demand for intranet social platforms is also on the rise.
- *Business Enablement*: Social collaboration was earlier considered as a main tool for consumers and end users. However, business is now actively using these channels for social marketing and other means for directly connecting with their customers and engaging them actively.
- *Mobile Support and Responsive Web Design*: This is a generic trend noticed across all technologies. Users are now increasingly using mobile devices to access the portal platform. Responsive web design (RWD) is a technology that allows "write-once-render-anywhere" model.
- *Collaborative Commerce*: Trends such as co-browsing, co-shopping, products recommended by your connections, social recommendations, trending products bring the searchlight on collaboration tools in commerce and retail business domains.

Challenges in Achieving Collaboration

The key challenges usually faced and common best practices to address those challenges while implementing collaborative features are as follows:

- *Incentive Management*: Users might not be motivated to contribute in some cases. There should be reward/recognition to provide incentive for the contribution. Points for each contribution, gamification, regular recognition of contributors are some of the incentives that can motivate users to share and collaborate.
- *Security Issues*: When portals are integrated with external social platforms, maintaining information privacy and preventing accidental information leakage are some of the security concerns. In order to address this, robust data security and sharing policies are needed.
- *User Profile Management Across Multiple Platforms*: When multiple collaboration platforms are used, user attributes are distributed across different platforms. Each platform has a different interpretation of roles and responsibilities. So a centralized user profile management platform (preferably through centralized enterprise security management tools) is needed to have a uniform and consistent security profile across all platforms.
- *Inconsistent User Experience*: While collaboration features are rolled out and the portal is being integrated with external social and collaboration platforms, users may face disjoint and inconsistent user experience (UX). This challenge needs to be addressed through proper UX planning and by using uniform visual style guides.
- *Continuous Improvement*: Key performance indicators (KPIs) need to be defined to continuously monitor and track the effectiveness of collaboration tools. These metrics provide insights into the effectiveness of the platform and how it can be improved.
- *End User Adoption*: If the collaboration platform is not adopted and effectively used by the target audience, it leads to failure of the program. Hence, user experience, functionality, and design should be customer-centric.
- *Organization Culture Challenges*: In a few organizations, the culture of information sharing and collaboration is not part of the regular business processes and hence users may find it challenging to adapt to the new collaboration culture. In such cases, the collaboration culture can be imbibed through incentives and rewards programs.

Defining Best Practices–Based Collaboration Strategy

In order to effectively address the challenges mentioned in the previous section, a strategy for establishing a robust long-term collaboration platform need to be defined. High level steps for establishing collaboration strategy are given here.

- Understand the critical business process, user touch points, collaboration needs, and get insights into the tasks people do in their daily routine; focus on tasks and activities that involve information sharing and collaboration opportunities

- Conduct collaboration focused workshops and interviews with various business stakeholders, employees, and a subset of end users to understand the ways to increase their productivity
- Based on the inputs from the above activities, identify collaboration requirements and objectives
- Map the collaboration objectives to the fulfillment strategy and identify specific collaboration tools and technologies in the portal product; if there are gaps, identify the open source and commercial collaboration tools which can be used to fill the gaps
- Define the collaboration metrics and KPIs, which track the effectiveness and success of the collaboration platform
- Continuously, monitor the metrics and KPIs and fine tune the collaboration tools accordingly.

Knowledge Management in the Portal

The portal is also widely used as a knowledge management platform, which provides a centralized knowledge repository and the management processes around it. A knowledge portal provides a structural framework for maintaining and enhancing the collective knowledge within an organization.

Portal Knowledge Management Architecture

The key elements of portal-based knowledge management are shown in Figure 10.1.

Portal Services Layer

A portal provides core services such as personalization, fine-grained access control through role-based access, knowledge workflows content management services, and presentation components. It provides a platform upon which knowledge management services can be developed. Portal content management is mainly used as a knowledge and document repository and portal workflows can be used for modeling knowledge processes such as solution contribution and document management processes. Analytics-based tracking can be leveraged to track the user behavior and usage of knowledge content.

Knowledge Management Layer

This is the core element of the system and contains the following key components:

- *Collaboration Tools*: An efficient knowledge management (KM) portal should provide collaboration tools such as wiki and blogs, which serves the dual purpose of collaboration and knowledge management. User pages, product pages, user communities and product communities are other instances of such tools.
- *Content Taxonomy*: Since a KM portal aggregates various content types from multiple content sources, it is important to maintain a uniform and consistent taxonomy to classify the content based on uniform metadata.

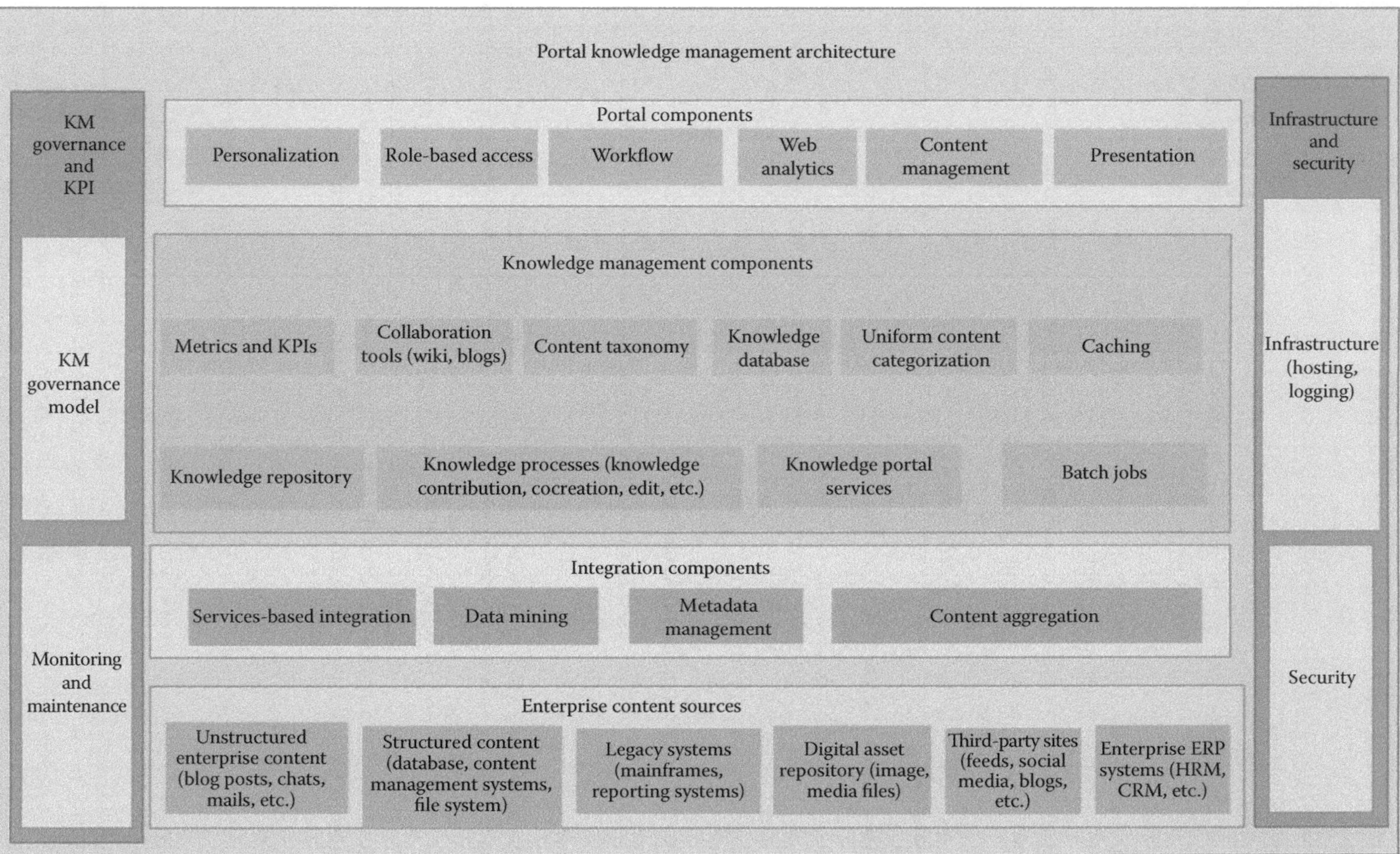

FIGURE 10.1
Portal-based knowledge management.

- *Knowledge Database*: This maintains all the knowledge management–related configuration information.
- *Uniform Content Categorization*: Using content taxonomy and metadata, the content is categorized into a pre-defined list of content categories. This helps in eliminating duplicate content and provides the most relevant content (based on category and metadata) to the user.
- *Caching*: This component is used for caching frequently accessed knowledge artifacts for optimal performance.
- *Knowledge Repository*: This mainly contains solution articles, web pages, and managing documents and assets.
- *Knowledge Processes*: It defines easy-to-use and secured processes related to knowledge creation, review, approval, and update.
- *Batch Jobs*: If real-time synching of content from content sources has performance issues, then offline batch jobs will be created to synch the content on a regular basis.
- *Metrics and KPIs*: The main metrics and KPIs to determine the success of a knowledge management system will be established. Some KPIs will be discussed in the "Best Practices and Critical Success Factors in Knowledge Management" section and in Chapter 16.
- *Knowledge Portal Services*: Knowledge content has to be exposed as services to other systems through knowledge services.

Integration Layer

The integration layer leverages the integration capabilities of the underlying portal platform. Though the main form of integration uses services-based integration, other content aggregation techniques such as API-based content retrieval can also be leveraged. A centralized metadata management system also needs to be integrated for tagging the knowledge content with relevant metadata.

Enterprise Content Source Layer

This contains the entire enterprise content source such as file systems, ERP systems, database, CMS, legacy systems, collaboration platform, asset servers, and document management systems, internal and external services from which the knowledge management system aggregates the knowledge assets. The data from these systems could be either unstructured or structured. Before loading or migrating the content from these systems, the data must be cleansed and properly tagged.

Besides these main layers, portal horizontal components such as infrastructure, monitoring and maintenance components, governance model, and security components will be re-used for the knowledge management system as well.

Strategic Goals of a Knowledge Portal

- Essentially, a knowledge portal should provide structured access to the collective knowledge of an enterprise. It should reduce dependency on people and provide a unified access to knowledge artifacts such as solution documents, best practices, process and policy documents, etc.

- It should provide a platform for users to share the knowledge, artifacts and search for artifacts. Processes should be developed to submit, update, and discover the knowledge artifact efficiently.
- It should aim toward improving the productivity of employees, support team, and end users through efficient and timely discovery of relevant knowledge assets, thereby providing a competitive edge for the business.
- Knowledge portals also should promote the self-service model by helping users solve issues on their own and improving customer satisfaction.
- Knowledge portals should reduce the process cycle time; for instance, it should reduce the learning curve through self-training and help in continuous innovation.

Challenges to Knowledge Management Portals

There are challenges from various quarters in developing and maintaining a robust knowledge portal. Let us look at some of the key challenges and high-level best practices to address them:

- The knowledge portal needs to provide a single point of access to both structured and unstructured content from various sources such as CMS, document repository, and file systems. Each of the content sources may follow various content and metadata classification formats and there is also a possibility of duplicate content across multiple systems. So the knowledge management portal needs to sanitize the content metadata/classification into a uniform classification scheme, eliminate content duplicates, and provide a common structure for accessing and contributing the content.
- The users need to actively contribute and share the knowledge assets for the long-term success of the knowledge portal. In the absence of a proper incentive and rewards system, users may lose motivation to actively contribute to the knowledge management portal.
- Some knowledge portals lack governance processes leading to maintenance issues. The knowledge portal should establish a consistent and user-friendly process for accessing and contributing knowledge assets. The processes should be consistent across all channels and all user roles.
- Knowledge portals also face challenges in integrating with various content sources such as legacy systems and ERP systems as it needs to manage heterogeneous technologies. Sub-optimal integrations may lead to scalability, availability, and performance issues. In order to address this challenge, offline batch load of documents and content from content sources into knowledge portal is performed; using asynchronous services-based integration is another effective integration technique in such cases.

Best Practices and Critical Success Factors in Knowledge Management

In order to address the above challenges, the following best practices for developing a knowledge management portal can be adopted.

- Identify all content sources and content types that will be aggregated by the portal. For each content source, define an optimal integration strategy and for all content types provide a centralized content classification scheme. Convert all structured and unstructured content into a common content format. Provide a common taxonomy for content metadata classification. This enables consistent and relevant search results in the knowledge portal.

- Develop a robust incentive system to reward active contributors to the knowledge portal. Classify the contributors into various levels such as "knowledge contributors," "knowledge expert," and "knowledge champions" based on the number and quality of their contribution. Provide a point-based reward framework to encourage and sustain knowledge contribution.
- Track the usage and effectiveness of the knowledge portal. Some of the key metrics are "number of solution articles accessed," "number of solution articles added," "percentage reduction in customer requests through solution articles," "percentage productivity improvement due to the knowledge portal," and "percentage quality improvement due to asset reuse."
- Develop a robust governance process for knowledge management. Cleary define the roles and responsibility for content creation, review, approval, and usage of knowledge artifacts. Define a process for knowledge sharing, knowledge access, knowledge storage, knowledge update, and deletion.
- Portal administrators and business communities should provide long-term commitment and actively involve users to enhance adoption and conduct awareness campaigns. They should continuously monitor and fine tune the knowledge portal by tracking KPIs.
- Design the knowledge portal so that it can be utilized by users for their daily activities and for completing the processes.

Portal Personalization

Personalization is one of the core strengths of a portal. It has many dimensions. In a nutshell, personalization involves customizing the user experience based on the user's implicit/explicit preferences, user attributes, navigational behavior, and other activities.

Personalization lets portal sites customize their content, data, and functionality automatically for each user. It can customize the user experience based on profile attributes, preferences, purchase history, products or pages viewed, and so forth. Personalization then selects content that is most appropriate for that profile. The page is assembled with the proper personalized information, and the user sees his/her personalized page.

The main aim of personalization is to enrich user experience, keep users engaged, and increase customer's loyalty. It can also be used for targeted marketing, personalized sales promotion, and such activities.

As personalization is one of the core features of a portal engine, let us examine the various aspects of personalization in this section.

The complex user interface and experience can be personalized based on personalization attributes. A sample personalized user interface is shown in Figure 10.2.

The personalized portal home page depicts some of the main utilities of portal personalization: personalized content, services, social interactions, links, portlets, support, and personalized search can be seen. In the coming sections, we will see how to employ various personalization techniques to achieve these.

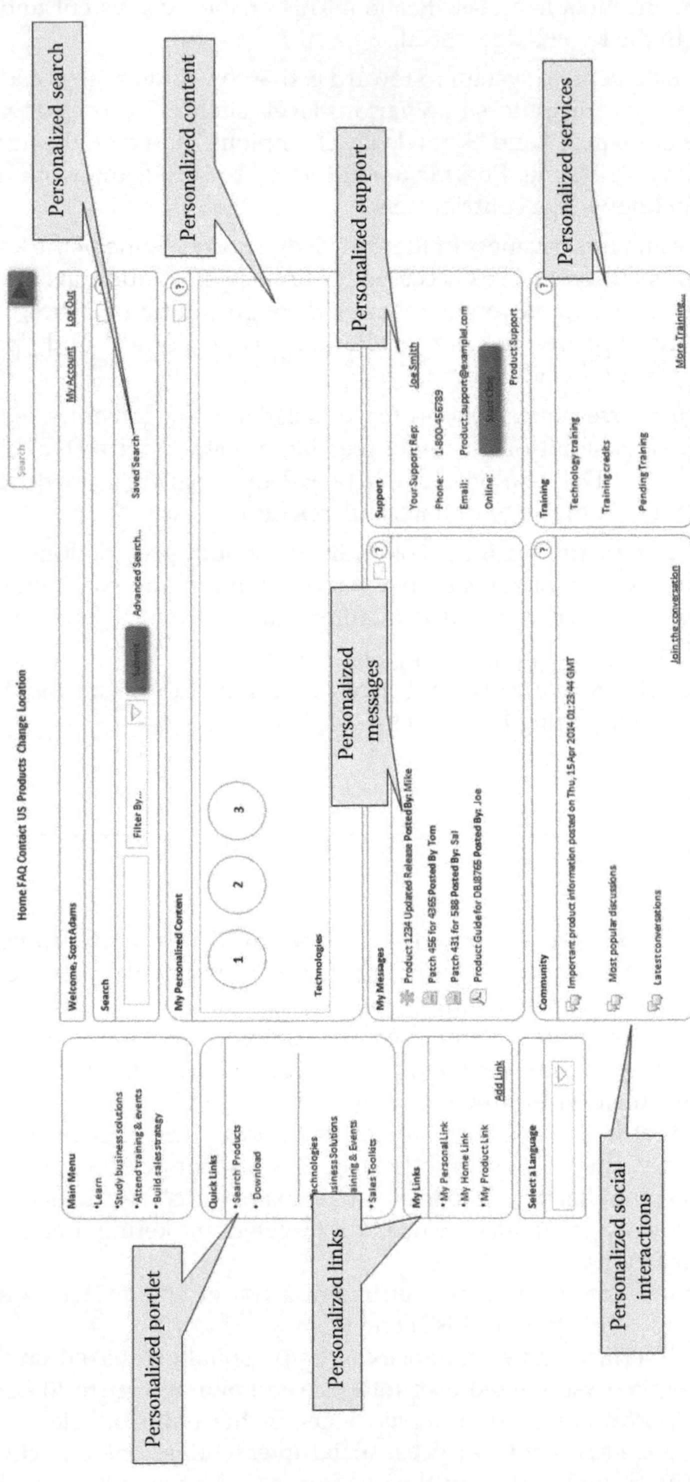

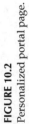

FIGURE 10.2
Personalized portal page.

Personalization Concepts

While personalization is an important aspect in all portal platforms and business domains, it has huge monetary benefits especially in retail and e-commerce domains as it can directly influence the user's purchase behavior and loyalty, and lead to a higher conversion ratio.

Various attributes will be used by the personalization engine to personalize the user experience. We will see details in the coming sections. Let us look at the key factors and user profile attributes which can be considered for personalization:

- Demographics such as user profile attributes, location, language, etc.
- User's browsing history and web activities on portal pages
- Implicitly or explicitly expressed interest and preferences, which can be used for both personalization and for recommendations
- Social connections, which can be leveraged for social recommendations
- User's transaction and purchase history
- Cross-device activities, which the user performs across various devices and across sites (such as affiliate sites) to get holistic insights into user's behavior
- User segments based on user roles, groups, communities, etc.
- Rating and reviews done by the user
- Insights drawn from web analytics tracking

In addition to personalizing user experience, these attributes also help in providing highly effective recommendations such as:

- Product packages and bundling
- Personalized search results
- Personalized recommendations on top picks, best sellers, and products
- Cross-sell and up-sell suggestions
- Popular products and activities popular within the close social circle of the user
- Target emails, content, news, customized promotion, and sales campaigns

Personalization Logical Architecture

The key components of a personalization engine within a portal are shown in Figure 10.3.

A description of each of these components is given here:

- *Personalization Editor*: User interface to configure personalization rules. The portal administrator can use this interface for configuring and setting up various personalization rules for data, content, and functionality personalization
- *Rules Engine*: Executes rules created in the personalization editor; normally, the rules engine provides an interface to configure the rules
- *Recommendation Engine*: Evaluates recommendation rules based on various implicit and explicit parameters

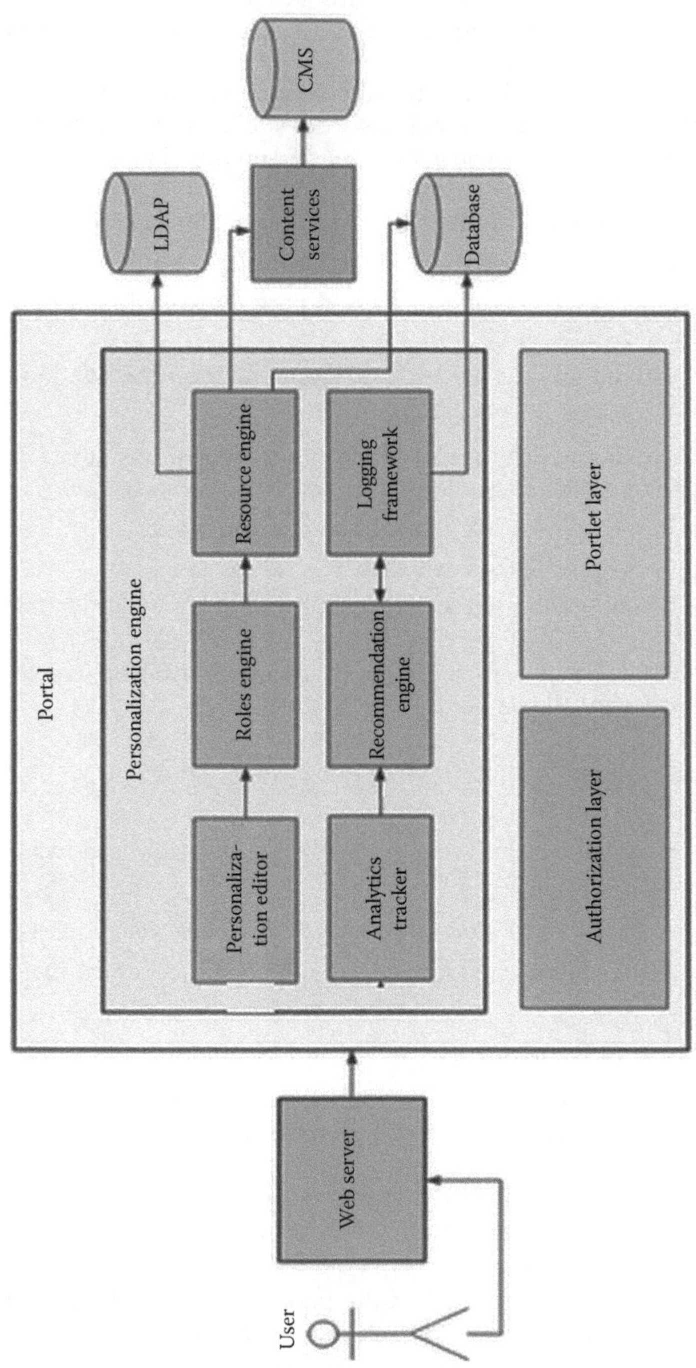

FIGURE 10.3
Portal personalization engine.

- *Resource Engine*: Resolves the queries produced by rules into content pieces to be returned; mainly used for content personalization
- *Logging Framework*: Records information about execution of personalization rules
- *Portlet Layer*: The portlet layer consists of portlet and related library components
- *Authorization Layer*: The authorization layer is responsible for providing access control privileges for the logged in user; it resolves user groups, inheritance of privileges from parent resources, page permissions, and others
- *Web Analytics Tracking*: This component tracks user behavior on the portal pages and feeds the analysis to the personalization engine
- *Implicit Personalization*: This includes understanding the user interests/likes/preferences through user actions and personalizing the content based on it. Collaborative filtering is normally used for understanding the user interests.

Personalization Types

There are various techniques to achieve personalization. Let us look at some of the most popular ones.

Rules-Based Personalization

Rules-based personalization relies on having an admin person to define a set of business rules that determine which content and functionality is displayed for a given user.

To this end, rules-based personalization requires three kinds of resources: users, content/functionality, and rules to map users to content and functionality. These three resources are detailed below.

The basis for personalization is collecting and maintaining information regarding users. The collection of all the pieces of information relating to one user is referred to as a user profile. User information can be collected either directly from the user (via a user profile attribute) or from other sources such as tracking the user's online activities. Users can be grouped into categories to facilitate personalization (which is sometimes referred to as "user segmentation").

Web content consists of the full array of data delivered through the portal such as static HTML, CMS content or XML pages. It is important to note that on a typical portal page, only a portion of the page need be personalized. In other words, some parts of the page are static, and rest of the page can be personalized at portlet level or content fragment level.

Personalization rules allow portal admins to specify the content to be shown in a given section or on entire page based on a user profile. Personalized content and personalized service in Figure 10.2 is an example for this.

Demographics-Based Personalization

Let us look at a technique to achieve user personalization (this technique automatically changes the portal page language based on the browser locale).

The portal home page will have a JSR portlet delivering the content in U.S. English. Initially, on load of this portlet, the user's preferred language is obtained through browser settings or from HTTP header and user country is obtained through IP address. The JSR portlet then delivers the content in an appropriate language. Personalized social interaction and personalized messages in Figure 10.2 is an example for this.

Look and Feel Personalization by Show/Hide of Portlets Based on User Group

Another popular usage of personalization is in displaying only a specific set of portlets on the portal page based on personalization rules.

Personalization by showing or hiding portlets based on user group can be achieved by creating rules. User profile related rules can be set using the personalization editor. The show/hide rules can be implemented both at the client side and at the server side. For implementing the visibility rules on the client side, we can leverage JavaScript libraries, which execute post page load can hide the portlets and widgets. On the server side, the page aggregation engine can suppress portlets based on rules; the rendered output does not contain portlets that are not applicable for the user. Personalized portlet in Figure 10.2 is an example for this.

It is also possible to personalize the look and feel based on the device type. This includes changing the page layout, which is optimized for the user device and this is usually implemented through mobile and device rules mapping to page layout on the portal end. In this case, a separate page layout optimized for mobile experience is created and mapped to the mobile device while configuring the rules. At run time, when portal servers determine the requesting device, it will execute the device rule which automatically choses the mobile-optimized page layout.

Providing custom theme (header, footer and navigation) is another kind of look and feel personalization. A user may explicitly prefer a particular type of theme that will be used for personalization.

Personalized Content and Data Retrieval Using Web Services

Content can be retrieved from content services using web services. Rules configuration will be used to retrieve personalized content based on the rules defined by the personalization editor. The rule would select the content based on the current user group, and other configuration parameters. This is achieved by filtering the content retrieved through content services based on user role and other applicable attributes. These user profile values would be obtained from the session. Personalized content in Figure 10.2 is an example for this.

Using User Session Attributes for Personalization

User session attribute values can be used to create personalization rules. Alternatively, user profile attributes in the portlet code can be used to customize the content/information/data retrieval. This is often used for fine-grained personalization scenarios such as content and data filtering.

Anonymous Personalization

Even the experience of guest users who chose not to register with the portal site can be personalized. The portal will leverage browser cookies and IP information for this kind of personalization. For instance, based on browser locale, the user can be redirected to locale specific portal pages; user selections can be stored in browser cookies and used for personalization.

Recommendation-Based Personalization and Collaborative Filtering

Recommendation-based personalization uses a technique called collaborative filtering, implemented in a recommendation engine. The recommendation engine uses complex statistical models and other techniques to learn the usage patterns of the portal site in order to personalize without providing explicit rules. This is sometimes referred to as implicit personalization. An example of collaborative filtering can include a site visitor rating a product, and those ratings are compared with the ratings offered by other visitors to identify any similarities across user segments. Collaboration filtering algorithms detect similarities and patterns to provide personalized recommendations.

Summary

- The main collaborative features provided by a portal are chat, wiki, blogs, communities, knowledge base, web conferencing, calendar, polls, rating and reviewing, document sharing, etc.
- Collaboration portal helps in increasing information availability and sharing; it enhances collective knowledge, social marketing, improves productivity, and provides cost optimization and a self-service model.
- The key trends in portal collaboration include focus on self-service, social media collaboration, business enablement, mobile support and responsive web design, and collaborative commerce.
- The key challenges in collaboration are incentive management, security issues, user profile management across multiple platforms, inconsistent user experience, continuous improvement, end user adoption, and cultural issues.
- A successful collaboration strategy includes understanding the critical business process, user touch points, collaboration needs, conducting collaboration focused workshops, mapping the collaboration objectives to the fulfillment strategy, metrics-based monitoring.
- Portal knowledge management architecture consists mainly of portal layer, knowledge management layer, and enterprise content sources layer.
- The portal layer consists of personalization, role-based access, workflow, analytics, content management, and presentation components.
- The knowledge management layer consists of collaboration tools, content taxonomy, knowledge repository, content categorization, knowledge processes, batch jobs and services.
- The enterprise content sources layer consists of structured and unstructured content from various enterprise sources such as chat, blog, mail, ERP, database, social platform, etc.
- The main goals of the knowledge portal are providing structured access to the collective knowledge of an enterprise, providing a knowledge sharing platform, promotion of self-service mode, process optimization, and cost optimization.
- The key challenges for a knowledge portal are content variations, content duplicity, scalability, dependency on upstream systems, challenges in pursuing users

to share the knowledge and adopt the knowledge portal, and lack of governance processes.

- Personalization lets portal sites customize their content, data, and functionality for portal users.
- Personalization can be done based on user demographic details, browsing history, implicit/explicit parameters, tracking metrics, etc.
- The main portal personalization components include the personalization editor, resource engine, rules engine, recommendation engine, and analytics tracker.
- The key types of personalization are rules-based personalization, demographics-based personalization, look and feel personalization, user session–based personalization, anonymous personalization, and collaborative filtering.

11

Portal Testing

An effective testing strategy plays a quintessential role in the quality and overall success of any project. This is true in portal scenario as well. The portal platform addresses multiple concerns and is a composition of multiple technologies and integration with varied systems. This warrants a robust as well as multidimensional testing that can effectively test all portal usage scenarios. The portal testing complexity further increases due to the numerous delivery channels and vast diversity in the end user environments. Just because a portal system works fine in a controlled quality assurance (QA) environment, it does not necessarily imply that the end user will experience the same. There could be many variations between the QA environment and the end user environment and there could be multiple layers in the delivery pipeline that could impact the end user experience. The key motive of this chapter is to explore portal testing from these dimensions and see how the gap between experience at the testing environment and the end user environment can be minimized.

Portal testing can be most effective when it is done iteratively and as a continuous process.

Portal developers, portal testers, and project managers would find the information in this chapter useful.

Challenges in Portal Testing

Let us first look at the main challenges in testing portal applications.

- *Lack of Comprehensive Test Views*: Traditional testing methods fall short of a few testing aspects/dimensions which are critical for the success of a portal project. This testing dimension is known as "test view." Some of the key test views required for portal applications are functional testing, integration testing, security testing, client side widget validation, localization testing, process testing, end user testing, and multivariant testing. These test views analyze the portal application from various dimensions and can throw light on the potential challenges an end user may face with the portal application.
- *Comprehensive Portal Performance Verification*: It is very challenging to properly assess all possible performance scenarios faced by the end user. This could be due to various factors such as variety of end user devices, diversity in accessing network, geo-specific variations, accurate assessment of perceived performance, performance impact due to external systems with which the portal is integrated, performance variations due to variance in end user load, post-production issues, etc. In the light of these variations, all possible performance scenarios need to be simulated during portal testing. A real-time performance monitoring infrastructure should also be set up for continuous monitoring.

- *User Interface Testing*: This dimension in testing is another challenging aspect due to variation in end user device and user agent. Other aspects like usability, accessibility, language variations, and widget performance all fall under this umbrella.
- *Infrastructure Testing*: A comprehensive and successful infrastructure testing needs an accurate picture of end user load and other details such as peak traffic, maximum transactions for a time period, seasonal trends and variations, etc. In many scenarios, these details are not available during the initial testing phases. So there could be challenges in scalability and availability of portal application during initial portal releases.
- *Business Effectiveness Verification*: This testing is more from a business point of view. How can we accurately assess the effectiveness of a portal program? Some portal success factors such as user satisfaction and self-service enablement cannot be quantitatively measured accurately. The assessment is also not a one-time activity that can be completed during the testing phase of the project. These are some of the challenges that are faced in this category.
- *Multi-Geo and Localization Testing*: For a globally deployed portal application, the application's performance, availability, scalability, and user experience need to be tested for each of the geographies. Local variations may affect the perceived performance and usability of the application. This again cannot be accurately done in QA environment especially for the initial release.
- *Integration Testing*: A portal normally has multiple enterprise integrations with various internal and external systems. With these integration comes various testing challenges such as accurately testing performance and scalability of the interfaces. These interfaces also need to be tested for multilingual support, multi-geo support, service performance, availability, fault tolerance, etc.
- *Business Process Testing*: Many test cases are authored at granular levels such as component functionality or use case or for a scenario. However, in the case of a portal, complex business processes are modeled using workflows and services. If test cases which test these processes end-to-end do not exist, the performance, user experience, and usability issues of these business processes cannot be accurately assessed. So test cases should be designed to test all critical business processes and transactions.
- *Defects Detection and Traceability*: Due to the complex nature of portal applications, it is important to detect defects in the early stages of the project. To ensure completeness of requirement, it is also needed to trace the requirements till the test case.
- *Security Testing*: This involves testing role-based access, SSO use cases, fine-grained and course-grained access, etc. As there could be potentially numerous user roles and testing each of the possible security scenario would be challenging.

In the following sections, we will look at a portal testing framework to address these challenges and study the critical success factors for portal testing.

Portal Testing Framework

A testing framework for portal application should provide a framework for comprehensive testing of a typical portal application. It should provide testing methodologies and techniques that can be used to close the gaps between controlled testing and real-world portal scenarios. In this section, we will discuss such a framework and its constituent test views.

The principal aim of a portal testing framework is to provide comprehensive testing methodologies so as to effectively validate all portal use case scenarios and ensure high-quality portal deliverables.

The main elements of a portal testing framework are shown in Figure 11.1.

Let us look at each of the constituent elements of the testing framework.

Regular Testing Activities Layer

The test activities in this category include the regular resting activities carried out for regular web applications. The main test activities are described in the Table 11.1.

Portal Testing Governance

This includes testing governance processes that ensure the proper execution of all test scenarios. The main components of portal testing governance are as follows:

- *Iterative and Continuous Testing*: As a project management best practice, iterative testing needs to be adopted to carry out testing for each small iteration on a continuous basis. Automated testing tools and continuous integration tool can be used for implementing this strategy.
- *Portal Testing Automation*: During test planning and design stages, automation opportunities have to be actively considered. Automating the test execution has multifold impact such as enhanced productivity, increased quality, reduced testing duration, etc. A few testing tools that can be used to automate portal testing are explained in Chapter 15. Some open source test tools are given in the Table 11.2.
- *Portal Testing Metrics and KPIs*: Metrics and key performance indicators (KPIs) are the surest way to ensure the testing effectiveness. The first step in this process is to define the portal testing metrics and execute the test cases to get the values for these metrics and KPIs. These metrics are then baselined and benchmarked with testing best practices and industry standards. The refined values will be used for further test iterations. The key test metrics are detailed in the next section.
- *Test Environment and Data Setup*: A dedicated QA testing environment will be setup for conducting functional and system integration testing. For accurate and comprehensive data setup, data from the production environment will be used (after masking confidential information).
- *Test Monitoring Dashboard*: Most testing tools and continuous integration tools provide test reports and dashboard views that provide insights into critical test metrics such as code coverages, percentage of passed/failed test cases, test execution rate, etc. A detailed test metrics that can be monitored in the dashboard is described in the next section.
- *Testing Best Practices*: With each testing iteration, the lessons learnt and the proven best practices that will be documented in a centralized knowledge repository. These learnings can be leveraged for subsequent test iterations. The best practice also includes the tools and methodologies that helped in automating the testing and productivity improvements.

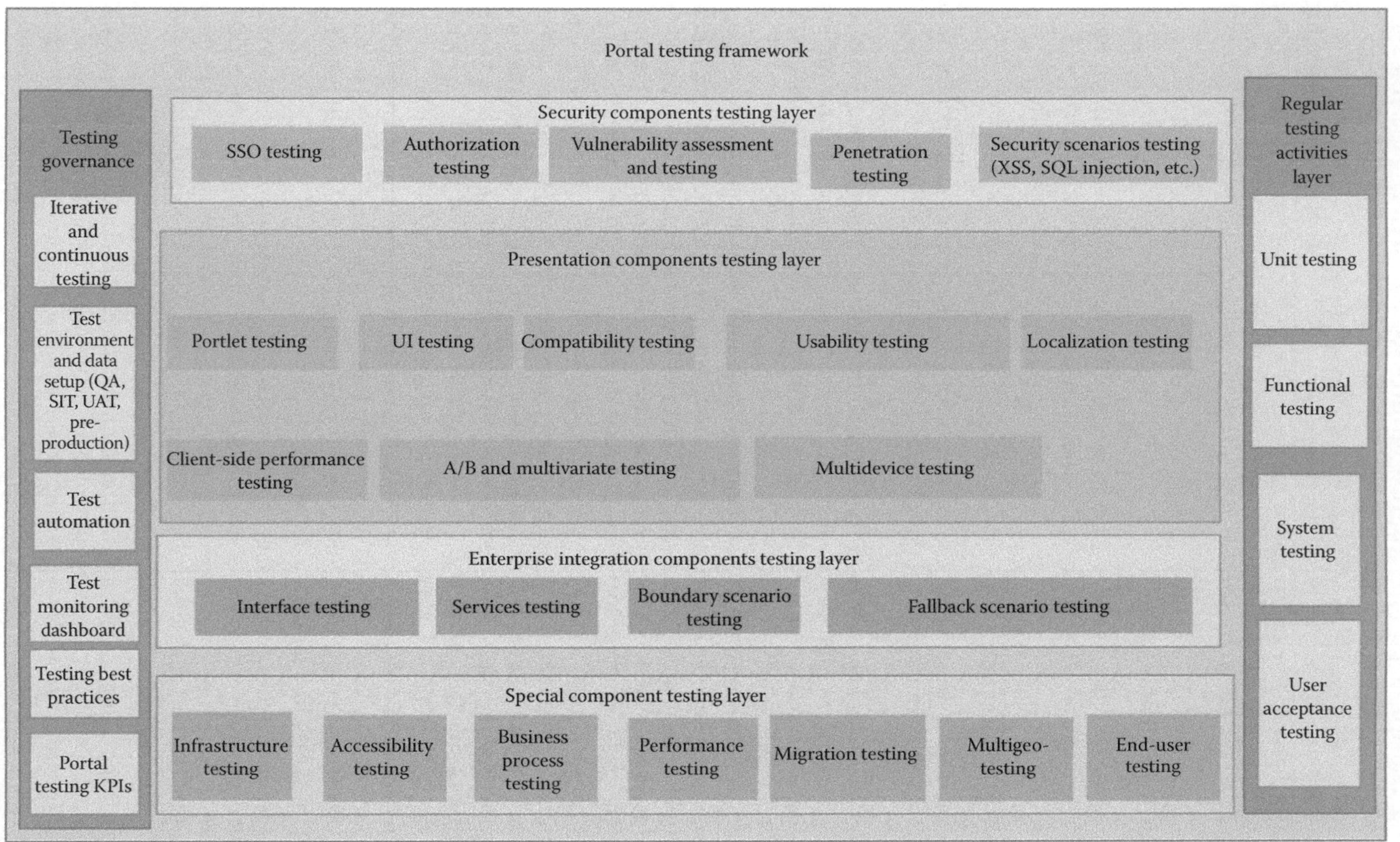

FIGURE 11.1
Portal-testing framework.

TABLE 11.1
Portal Regular Testing Activities

Testing Phase	Testing Activities
Test planning	• Analyze the use case, functional specifications, and other requirement-related documents • Compile the list of portal testing tools that can be used for automating testing • Compile the list of key testing metrics • Create a system test plan and functional test plan
Test design and development	• Design the test cases for all in-scope portal scenarios and use cases • Develop test cases and test scripts • Test data identification and creation of test environment
Unit testing	• Execute unit test for each of the portlets and its dependent components • Unit test the portal pages and templates • Perform unit testing for supporting library components and integration components
Functional testing	• Testing the functional use cases and scenarios along with boundary and exception cases • Regression testing • End-to-end business scenario and business process testing • Create traceability matrix for functional specifications and their corresponding test cases
System integration testing	• Perform end-to-end integration testing; test the integration of the various systems involved in the solution to validate whether they work cohesively to provide an integrated solution for specified functionality • Execute test cases to uncover integration related issues
User acceptance testing	• Testing business scenarios from business stakeholders • Business feedback review analysis

TABLE 11.2
Portal Testing Tools

Portal Testing Tool	Purpose
Junit	Can be used for unit testing portlets and library components
Selenium	Can be used for automating the portal web testing
Jenkins CI	Most popular continuous integration tool that can be leveraged in a portal project
Cucumber	Can be used for testing portal behavior
SoapUI	Can be used for portal services testing; can also be leveraged for testing service interfaces integrated with the portal
Jira	Can be used for portal issue tracking

Portal Presentation Components Testing Layer

UI Testing

User interface (UI) testing is one of the main activities of web testing. It involves testing the user interface components such as portal pages, navigation portlets, etc., on all supported platforms. Tools such as Selenium will be used to record and automate the page flows, UI elements and transactions.

Usability Testing

This involves testing the usability of the portal interface that includes the accessibility and compatibility of the portal application. A/B, which creates multiple variants of the application, is a popular testing method for testing usability.

A/B testing can be used for validating simple portal page changes, whereas multivariate testing has the ability to test several combinations of changes in one run. The typical changes would include the following:

- Look and feel changes such as button's wording, size, color, and placement changes
- Content changes such as content positioning, inclusion of media with content
- Layout changes
- Images/button/video position changes
- Text size changes

Success metrics and effectiveness such as conversion, click-to-action usages, time-on-site changes, etc., will be tested and analyzed. The changes that had maximum impact and influence on end-users will be retained.

Accessibility Testing

Portal site accessibility is a key nonfunctional requirement that enables all users to access the key functionality. Few geographies and countries also include accessibility standards as part of regulatory compliance checks. Web content accessibility guidelines (WCAG) defines the accessibility standards that are widely adopted. Though there are different compliance levels specified by WCAG, the following are the commonly followed guidelines and accessibility best practices for portal applications:

- Portal pages to provide text alternatives for media files
- Plug-in WCAG checker tools during content authoring in portal content editors to perform instant accessibility validation
- Provide various versions of CAPTCHA (completely automated public Turing test to tell computers and humans apart) such as audio/text version to assist all users
- Keyboard accessible functionality for all main features
- Portal content strategy to include readable, understandable, and structured content creation
- Portal site should provide adjustable font sizes and shapes
- Portal should provide consistent and predictable navigation
- Portal should provide context sensitive and detailed help
- In case of exceptions or failures, portal should provide descriptive and localized error messages and the detailed next course of action

There are various accessibility checker tools listed at http://www.w3.org/WAI/ER/tools/, and w3c validator service (http://validator.w3.org/) can be leveraged for testing the accessibility compliance level of the portal site.

Broken Link Testing

Broken links on a portal page not only affect the user's navigation but also impact the page load times due to HTTP 404 issues. As part of UI testing, link validator tools have to be used to identify any broken links. Link validation is normally done for href links. Open source tools such as W3C link validator (http://validator.w3.org/docs/checklink.html, http://validator.w3.org/) can be leveraged for this purpose.

Compatibility Testing

This includes testing the end user experience of the page site on all supported browsers and devices. Web testing tools such as the Selenium Web Driver can be leveraged for cross-browser testing; testing can also be carried out on different versions of the same browser. The cross-browser and multidevice testing report contains details such as response times, pass/fail scenarios, and sample screenshots. This can be used for further analysis to fix the identified issues.

Client Side Performance Monitoring and Testing

As portal platforms are increasingly adopting widget-driven lean models, it is important to monitor and test the client side components such as JavaScript based client side modules, widgets, gadgets, etc. In order to monitor and test the performance of these components, the user load can be simulated through the Selenium web testing tool; tools such as the DynaTrace Ajax edition or Yahoo YSlow or Google PageSpeed can be used to monitor and analyze the performance of these components. The tools would also provide remediation steps to address performance issues. The main metrics that will be monitored in this category are

- Page DOM (document object model) load time
- Perceived page load time
- Page size
- Asset load time

Portlet Testing

This mainly includes testing the core portlet functionality, user experience on various devices and browsers, boundary conditions, and usage of portlet preference. Wherever required, complex scenarios such as inter-portlet communication, portlet caching, portlet preference handling, portlet exception handling, and localization scenarios will also be tested.

Localization Testing

This involves testing the locale specific features of the portal application. As a prerequisite for this testing, localized data required by the application need to be populated; for instance, the availability of localized web content and localized assets in the CMS, activating all locale URLs, availability of all locale specific resource bundles, etc. Main testing activities focus on testing the locale specific variations and its impact on expected portal functionality and user experience. Few sample scenarios is given here:

- Testing automatic content and label localization based on URL change
- Locale specific search testing

- Testing locale specific functionality and business rules
- Testing the format, layout changes as per the changed locale
- Testing the behavior of input fields and forms for localized content
- Testing localized file parsing that contains double-byte characters
- Testing the behavior of integrated interfaces with localized content as input parameters
- Testing input encoding functions and filters for localized content
- Testing content translation accuracy and consistency
- Localization testing of social and collaboration components

Multidevice Testing

While implementing mobile-first approach, the portal user experience needs to be tested on various mobile devices. The main activities in multidevice testing are

- *Functional Testing*: This involves testing the core portal application features and use cases in mobile devices. As the user experience is optimized for a mobile device, the process steps, page flows will be tested in this category.
- *Device Compatibility Testing*: Device simulators will be used to test the user experience on all the devices.
- *Device Accessibility and Performance Testing*: WCAG accessibility guidelines and MWBP (mobile web best practices) guidelines and checklist will be used to test the accessibility and mobile best practices. The portal page performance on mobile devices will also be tested.

Portal Enterprise Integration Components Testing Layer

In this section, we will look at the testing aspects of the portal integration layer.

Service Testing

As a portal predominantly uses services-based integration for interacting with external interfaces, it is necessary to perform thorough testing of services. First, let us look at the main challenges encountered in services testing:

- *Multilayered Architecture and Multiple Points of Failure*: Services-based integration adopts a multilayered architecture that involves multiple systems and services. For instance, a portlet would invoke the portal services layer, which in turn would invoke the enterprise services gateway or enterprise service bus which in turn would invoke an external service. Due to the involvement of multiple systems in this service invocation pipeline, we need to have test cases to validate service invocation calls at each of the layers as there could be multiple points of failure.
- *Performance Testing of Services*: Calculating the accurate performance, load metrics, and SLAs for services would be challenging as well. For example, a portal page SLA expected is 3 s and the expected site traffic is 20,000 visitors per hour. This is translated into performance SLA and load value for the underlying services of upstream/dependent systems. These metrics can then be used for testing services.

- *Testing Boundary Scenarios*: There could be numerous boundary conditions such as timeout handling, exception handling, providing proper error/fault codes, localization handling, fallback handling, disaster recovery scenarios, etc. We need to devise test cases to check all these scenarios.
- *Services Security*: Testing security aspects for services would involve identifying role based data access, user authentication, data encryption, and authorization scenarios.

So in order to conduct a comprehensive portal services testing, we need to adopt the following services testing methodology:

- *Isolated Services Testing*: Automated services testing tools have to be leveraged and each of the services involved in the invocation chain have to be tested individually. The services test cases should include positive functional scenarios, boundary conditions, and security scenarios. For subsequent releases, regression tests should be carried out to check the compatibility of the latest version of services with their specification.
- *End-to-End Services Testing*: This involves testing all the services that are involved in a single invocation call end-to-end. For instance, if a portal service call pipeline involves invoking portal services layer, Enterprise Service Bus (ESB) and an external service, all three services will be tested in combination end-to-end. Positive and negative functional scenarios, boundary scenarios will be tested in this case to also check if they conform to specified functional and nonfunctional requirements.
- *Business Process–Based Services Testing*: A portal often models complex business processes that internally depend on services. Orchestration of these processes requires invocation of services in a particular sequence with specific business rules. As a part of this testing, the business processes execution will be simulated so that the services are invoked in the same order. In this particular case, functional testing and business rules handling will be validated.
- *Service Performance Testing*: The performance KPIs need to be first translated from the portal page to the underlying service. The various performance and load related testing such as stress testing, load testing, response time testing, scalability testing, etc., can then be done.
- *Interoperability and Regression Testing*: Interoperability tests will check if the services conform to the open standards. For instance, a web service interoperability testing validates if the specification complies with WS-I (web services I) standards. Regression testing of services validates if the services are backward compatible. This testing needs to be executed for services exposed by the portal.

Boundary Scenario Testing

This category includes exception conditions such as

- Entering numeric values outside the specified range
- Testing the application behavior for special and multi byte input characters
- Simulating interface timeout scenarios and testing the application behavior

- Uploading a large file through UI or from a batch program and checking for application behavior
- Configuring the portal page to display huge data in pages such as portal search results page and checking for its performance
- Checking the behavior of the application after disabling the JavaScript in the browser
- Entering malicious script, reserved characters, special characters, blacklisting characters in the portal text area, and checking for validation

Fallback Scenario Testing

During the requirements elaboration phase, fallback will be designed for handling the unavailability of the dependent systems or applications. This testing aims to test these fallback related scenarios. Some fallback scenarios are given here:

- Fallback handling during portal content translation when the master content file is not available
- Graceful degradation of functionality when the back end systems are not available
- Transaction rollback when the upstream services are not available
- Fallback handling when portal primary node or primary site is down

Interface Testing

This is testing the enterprise interface through their APIs or exposed services. Services testing will be leveraged for this activity. The interfaces will be tested for performance, scalability, and availability.

Special Component Testing Layer

In this layer, components and scenarios that are very specific for portal solutions will be tested.

Portal Infrastructure Testing

This testing is mainly carried out to check if the portal infrastructure components (such as server hardware, portal database, network devices, and file servers) are optimally sized to handle adequate load and meet the performance SLAs. The main test scenarios in this category are listed in Table 11.3.

Performance Testing

Portal performance testing is one of the key elements for the success of a portal program. It directly impacts the end user experience. The main aspects of portal performance will

TABLE 11.3
Portal Infrastructure Testing Activities

Infrastructure Test Category	Testing Activity
Load testing	Simulate the normal user, transaction, and data load for the portal application and test the performance, scalability, and availability of the application
Endurance testing	Conduct load testing for extended duration (normally done continuously for 72 h)
Scalability testing	• Test the overall system scalability primarily through load tests to check the scalability limit of the system • Incrementally increase the load to check the limits of system scalability • Load test on individual servers of the solution; this includes individual testing of the portal web server, portal application server, portal database server, and all servers involved in the overall solution
Availability testing	• Running the normal load test for an extended duration through endurance testing will help in identifying the availability of the applications • Real-time monitoring of all systems involved in the application will also help in accurately assessing the system availability

be explained in Chapter 20. Performance testing involves performance modeling, infrastructure testing, cache testing, and performance monitoring:

- *Performance Modeling*: This is an important exercise that is essential for performance based design. As a part of this exercise, the following steps are carried out:
  - *Identify the critical portal use cases and scenarios*: Business critical and complex technical scenarios need to prioritized and identified. Additionally, use cases that consume lot of resources and use cases that invokes multiple services and use cases that are frequently accessed by the user will be included in this list. The objective is to model the most important scenarios from the business and end user perspective. A product checkout process or a complex services–based integration would be included in this list.
  - *Identify the goals of performance modeling based on established metrics and KPIs for each of the scenarios mentioned*: For instance, a 5 s process completion time for product checkout process and a 2 s SLA for portal search in an e-commerce portal would serve as a baseline metric for the modeling.
  - *Model the workload for each of the scenarios*: The workload could be in the form of average user load, peak user load, maximum number of page loads, volume of input data, maximum number of files to be processed, etc.
  - *Analyze the portal design*: With the given workload and performance objectives, the design has to be analyzed to validate if it meets the specified performance metrics. This happens in an iterative basis after fine-tuning the design and infrastructure design.
- *Infrastructure Testing*: We have already seen various aspects of infrastructure testing in the previous section. Basically, the resource utilization, network bandwidth usage, and response time are tested by loading the portal application under various scenarios such as load testing, stress testing, peak load testing, etc.

- *Cache Testing*: For optimizing performance, caching will be implemented at various portal layers such as client layer, server layer, and database layer. In order to ensure that the cache is appropriately used, each of the caching components need to be tested individually as well as in combination. The effectiveness of cache is measured through important cache metrics such as response time, cache hit percentage, cache access, etc.
- *Performance Monitoring*: A robust internal and external performance monitoring infrastructure needs to be setup for early identification of performance issues. The main internal systems and parameters that will be monitored is given here:
  - Resource Utilization
    - Portal resource utilization (CPU, disk, memory, network)
    - Throughput of critical transactions
    - Response time for key portal pages
    - User load
  - Portal Web Server
    - Threads count
    - Keep alive connections
    - Asset caching parameters
    - Server throughput
  - Portal Application Server
    - Active threads count
    - Connection pooling parameters
    - Garbage collection activity
    - Heap size and utilization
  - Portal Database Server
    - Query execution time
    - Buffer cache hit ratio
    - Indexes usage
    - Buffer waits
  - Portal application monitoring metrics
    - Total page load time
    - Time for first byte
    - Total time in executing client side JavaScripts
    - Total asset download time
    - Number of HTTP request
    - Number of XHR requests

The main performance testing activities can be tabulated as given in Table 11.4.

TABLE 11.4
Portal Performance Testing Activities

Portal Performance Testing Phase	Activities
Performance test planning	• Identify the main portal performance SLAs related to response time, throughput, resource utilization, etc. • Identification of critical business and technical scenarios related to portal platform.
Performance test scripting	• Create portal performance test scripts and automated scripts • Create performance test data and test environment to model various load scenarios
Performance test execution and reporting	• Conduct various performance tests such as normal load test, peak load test, stress test, endurance test, process testing, etc. • Monitor resource utilization and portal server logs during test execution • Perform performance testing on portal services, individual components in each layer and also for end-to-end scenarios. • Report performance test results for further analysis such as bottleneck analysis and performance fine-tuning.

Migration Testing

In a few scenarios, portal implementation requires data and content migration from legacy systems to the new portal platform. In such cases, it is important to test the migrated content and data. The main data and content-related test cases include the following:

1. Test cases to check the completeness of data and content migration
2. Test cases to check for duplicity of data or content
3. Test cases to check for inconsistent or incorrect transformation of data during migration
4. Test cases to check for proper re-categorization of content and proper re-tagging of content with proper metadata post migration.

Process Testing

Test cases should be designed to test the end-to-end functionality involved in a business process. This includes testing the portal pages involved, portlets required for execution, navigation flow, workflow involved, and the execution of business rules. This process-centric testing can uncover the challenges faced by the end user while completing a business process or transaction. The main candidates for this kind of testing include

- Critical and complex business process
- Most frequently executed business process
- Business process or transaction that involves multiple steps
- Multistep approval business process
- Business process which rely on availability of external services

Multi-Geo Testing

For globally deployed portal applications, we can leverage geo-based tools that monitor and test the portal application for performance and availability. This can be employed after the initial portal release. Web analytics scripts can also provide geo-specific performance information for the portal site. Real user monitoring tools and end user monitoring tools can also be used for this purpose. Multi-geo testing provides the actual performance perceived by end user.

End User Testing

For portal projects where end user adoption is one of the critical success factors, a selected set of end user communities will be involved in beta testing of the portal application. The application will usually be allowed to be tested by a selected subset of end users on their environment and the feedback is gathered. End user experience related to usability, navigation, compatibility, ease of use, performance will be compiled from beta testers and priority issues will be taken up for fixing before the final release of the application.

Security Component Testing Layer

The main security testing areas include authentication and authorization testing, vulnerability checks that include remote command execution, cross-site scripting, accidental information disclosure, denial of service attacks, SQL injection attacks, etc. There are three stages where we can conduct a security testing for portal application.

1. *Portal Source Code Scanning*: Source code scanning for security issues can be done manually and through security scanning tools. This needs to be part of the code review process. Open source tools such as FindBugs (http://findbugs.sourceforge.net/), PMD (http://pmd.sourceforge.net/), OWASP SWAAT (https://www.owasp.org/index.php/Category:OWASP_SWAAT_Project) can be leveraged for detecting vulnerabilities in the portal source code. Additionally, portal developers should also use the portal security checklist as a guideline for developing and addressing security issues at the source. A portal security checklist is provided in Chapter 15.
2. *Portal Application Scanning*: This scanning is done at run time. Open source vulnerability assessment and scanner tools such as Zed Attack Proxy (https://www.owasp.org/index.php/OWASP_Zed_Attack_Proxy_Project), SQLMap (http://sqlmap.org/) can be used to scan the portal web application, obtain a report of the vulnerabilities, and address the issues.
3. *Continuous Security Monitoring*: Once the portal application is deployed to production, a continuous security assessment is done. The most important techniques in this category are
   - Log file monitoring and analysis for security incidents
   - Iterative security testing of code enhancements and patches
   - Ethical hacking to proactively identify any security holes
   - Updating the portal product, OS, and other infrastructure systems with regular security patches

The main portal testing activities in this phase are as follows:

- *Authentication Related Tests*: In this portal functionality, test cases for SQL injection, bot-based authentication attempts, password policy, account policy checks, etc., can be designed.
- *Authorization and Fine-Grain Access Control Related Tests*: Test cases for role based access controls on portlets, personalization related test cases, data security policy validation, and other functionality can be designed.
- *Vulnerability Testing*: A risk analysis and vulnerability assessment for the portal application will be done to identify the potential risk factors. Security test cases will be designed based on these assessed threats.
- *Penetration Testing*: This testing is done to break the portal application by mimicking sophisticated security attacks. Two primary types of security testing for portal applications are as follows:
  1. *Black box testing*: Penetration testing will be done once the system is ready for deployment. Vulnerabilities based on the initial model will be used to create penetration scenarios. The scenarios normally used for an external facing portal include buffer overflow, SQL injection, cookie hijacking, cross-site scripting, cross-site request forgery, etc. Collaborative portals include lot of components such as reviews, feedback, blogs, wiki, comment, and such features that result in user-generated content (UGC) and black box testing would be crucial in testing security vulnerabilities in such cases. Security tools such as OWASP ZAP and others can be leveraged for this kind of testing.
  2. *White box security testing*: In this testing category, the security test cases will be designed after understanding the intricate details of portlet code and portal architecture. The main security testing scenarios in this category include:
     - Creating a REST service request to list the portal directory or content structure after analyzing the service details exposed by the portal
     - Trying to exploit the user profile details of other users by exploiting the personalization and user profile service exposed by the portal
     - Scenarios to mimic the JSR 286 serveResource calls with dummy data to the server to store malicious content on the server or to retrieve sensitive information.
- Portal security testing: Security scenarios testing that includes test cases related to input validation, cross-site scripting, SQL injection, blacklist input tests can be tried for user generated input content. This also includes the following test scenarios:
  - *HTTP parameter testing*: Test cases can be designed to manipulate HTTP request parameters, state information, HTTP headers, and cookie information.
  - *Session management*: Test cases related to session time out, exploiting multiple parallel sessions, idle session time out values, session hijacking, and cookie management can be designed in this category.
  - *Encryption and transport level security*: Test cases can be designed to check for transport layer interception and snooping of confidential data such as user profile information, business confidential information and other sensitive data.
  - *Impersonation related tests*: Test cases related to automatic elevation of privileges and accidental information leakage.

- *Log file scanning*: Portal log files can be tested for exposure of critical information such as user profile details, password details, server details, and the access controls for log files.
- *Error handling*: The portal handling of validations and exception scenarios can be tested and checked for accidental information leakage.

Critical Success Factors of Portal Testing

Test Automation

Automating test cases would help in faster execution of test scenarios. Especially in regression testing, automation is the most effective way to ensure backward compatibility and for catching regression issues. The main test automation techniques are as follows:

- Create unit test scripts and functional test scripts and integrate it with the build process using continuous integration tools (such as Jenkins CI). In this way, every time a build happens, the unit and functional test cases are automatically executed and issues are reported.
- Web testing can be automated through web testing tools that record and playback through scripts. This again can be plugged into the build process for continous testing.

Test Metrics

The key portal test metrics are as follows:

- Requirement traceability completeness
- Defect categorization (usability, UI, functional, integration)
- Percentage of duplicate defects found
- Code coverage percentage
- Regression test automation level
- Number of days defect (defect age)
- Number of defects in system testing and UAT (user acceptance testing)
- Number of defects missed out in functional testing
- Defect density
- Defect severity index (defect categorized by severity)
- Number of regression defects
- Percentage of test automation

We can monitor these metrics in the project management dashboard and ensure that metrics are in healthy state. Notifications can be triggered in case any of these critical metrics move below the benchmark threshold value.

Agile Approach for Portal Testing

As more and more portal projects adopt agile-based execution, the testing should also be agile. Agile testing involves continuous and iterative testing on a working set of portal code in parallel to development. The testing happens in close collaboration with the business and development team to incorporate any feedback. Testing happens in iterations.

Agile methodologies mainly involve user story-based iterations and heavily adopt test driven development. The iterative and continuous nature of testing adopted in agile execution will help in early detection of issues. The high-level testing phases and activities in agile testing are given in the Table 11.5. All the phases are executed in an iterative manner along with each release.

The key benefits of adopting an agile testing approach for portal projects are as follows:

1. Reduces defect fixing and release effort, and increases code quality due to early detection of the defects
2. Increased productivity due to continuous and automated test execution
3. Helps in absorbing feedback and change requests suggested by stakeholders by just-in-time testing
4. Ensures that requirements are fully implemented and helps in regression testing; this is done by a technique called test-driven development wherein the code is developed incrementally to pass the test cases.

Continuous and Iterative Testing

Continuous and iterative testing is the most critical success factor for the success of a portal project. This strategy can be implemented through continuous integration tools and test automation. It can provide the following benefits:

- Early detection of errors
- Productivity improvement of the overall project due to test automation
- Increased quality of the deliverable
- Faster turnaround for portal releases

TABLE 11.5

Portal Agile Testing Activities

Agile Testing Phase	Testing Activities and Output
Test design and planning	• User story review with story-based test approach • Test automation analysis and design • Creation of manual and automation test scripts • Story traceability matrix creation • Creation of test data *Output*: Traceability matrix, test plan, automation analysis
Test execution	• Manual and automated testing • Iterative and continuous functional testing • Iterative and continuous integration testing • Iterative nonfunctional testing (performance, scalability, security, availability) • Conducting iterative testing using continuous integration tools such as Jenkins *Output*: Test results, test score card, code coverage report
User acceptance testing (UAT)	• Testing acceptance criteria specified by business and users *Output*: Acceptance test results

Summary

- This chapter explores various dimensions of portal testing and the main components of a portal testing framework.
- The key challenges in portal testing are lack of comprehensive test views, comprehensive portal performance verification, user interface testing, infrastructure testing, business effectiveness verification, multi-geo and localization testing, integration testing, business process testing, defects detection and traceability.
- Portal testing framework consists of regular testing activities layer, portal testing governance, portal presentation components testing layer, security components testing layer, enterprise integration components testing layer, and special component testing layer.
- Regular testing activities layer includes testing activities such as unit testing, functional testing, system testing, and user acceptance testing.
- Security component testing layer consists of security testing scenarios such as SSO testing, authorization testing, vulnerability testing, penetration testing, and testing various other security scenarios.
- Portal presentation components layer testing includes portlet testing, UI testing, compatibility testing, usability testing, localization testing, client side performance testing, A/B and multivariate testing, multidevice testing.
- Enterprise integration components testing layer consists of interface testing, services testing, boundary scenario testing, and fallback scenario testing.
- Special component testing layer consists of infrastructure testing, accessibility testing, business process testing, performance testing, migration testing, multi-geo testing, and end user testing.
- Testing governance consists of horizontal components such as test environment setup, test automation, iterative and continuous testing, test monitoring dashboard, testing best practices, portal testing KPIs.
- Critical success factors of portal testing are test automation, presence of relevant test metrics, agile approach for portal testing, and continuous and iterative testing.

Section II

User Experience Platforms and Advanced Portal Topics

12

Introduction to User Experience Platforms (UXPs)

The user experience platform (UXP) also referred to as the customer experience platform (CXP) is the next step in the evolution of user-centric presentation platforms. It is one of the fastest emerging trends in UI Space. A UXP strives to provide a highly personalized and engaging user experience at all digital touch points for the end user. In the presentation and integration side of things, we need to clearly understand the role of portal, lean portal, and UXP so that we can use them in the most appropriate fashion.

Due to increased focus on customer engagement, customer-centric portals are adopting UXP-like features such as lean model, agility, web-oriented design, etc. In a few cases, UXPs are preferred over portals for deeper user engagement. We also notice many overlapping features and concerns addressed by portals and UXPs. In light of all these points, it is essential to understand the role each of these platforms play in an enterprise ecosystem and use them optimally in implementing digital strategy.

In this chapter, we will explore various concepts of UXP, the interconnection between UXP and portals, components of UXP, etc. Digital architects, portal architects, and UX architects will find this chapter useful.

Introduction

Importance of Managing User Experience

Studies have shown that a well-managed user experience is more likely to result in tactical and strategic benefits; tactical benefit through conversion of a user visit into a sales and strategic benefit through long-term user relationship leading to customer retention and increased loyalty. Hence, an investment in customer experience management capabilities of the platform is strategically important for all customer facing online channels. On similar lines, a personalized customer service also goes a long way in reducing customer churn probability.

A UXP plays a vital role in the digital strategy of an enterprise due to these reasons.

What Is UXP?

A UXP is essentially a user-centric platform that provides pre-integrated capabilities to deliver exceptional user experience through a variety of delivery channels for all user touch points. The principal aim of the UXP is to facilitate high user engagement features through an integrated set of components such as search, collaboration, e-commerce, recommendations, analytics, document management, mash-ups, portal, etc. At the heart of the UXP is seamless customer experience and active engagement; all other features and technology enablers revolve around this central theme. The UXP provides a convergence of various technology and functional capabilities so as to provide a unique value proposition to end users, business, and IT communities, and plays a vital role in providing a differentiated digital experience.

As we can see, there is a high degree of overlapping features and use cases between UXPs and horizontal portals; UXPs highly resemble the features of lean portals that will be discussed in Chapter 21. Horizontal portals perfectly compliment the UXP through its built-in capabilities, integration components, and personalization features. In addition to this, UXP also adds other accelerators (based on the business domain), which help customers, business, and IT folks to efficiently use the platform.

Case for UXP

Let us look at a sample scenario to understand the effectiveness and usage scenarios of UXP.

An organization wants to build a next-generation customer-centric platform and leverage a UXP for building its e-commerce platform. Let us navigate through a few customer journeys to see how the UXP offers a differentiated experience.

As part of the marketing campaign, the UXP sends out an email to known customers with a link to sign up customer emails ids are obtained based on their expressed interest, purchase history, user comments, likes, etc. gathered from analytics tools. One of the customers decides to register and the UXP offers a pre-built registration form to register quickly. The registration process is optimized with lesser steps and self-approval features. The registration widget also provides an option to link the customer's social profile with the application. Customers can check out the products, offers, and promotions in the site; they can search for products through the site search widget. The customer then uses the product comparator widget to compare the features of different product brands to make information-based decision and selects the product. The UXP's recommendation engine pulls up other relevant products that complement the selected product based on user purchase patterns and the social recommendations. Finally, the UXP provides a combo offer of two products, which the customer decides to buy. The customer then uses 1-click checkout to purchase the product. Post purchase, the customer decides to expedite shipping by changing the order's shipping method. The customer uses a real-time chat to connect to a support agent who would change the shipping method of the order. E-commerce UXP also provides customers an ability to track the order and view order status reports from any device.

The next time the customer logs in, UXP provides the promotional content related to the previous purchase and related category in the landing page. The user will also be presented with a small feedback survey widget to rate the experience of the previous purchase.

In this journey, we saw how UXP optimizes the main customer journey across all channels through personalized and responsive interfaces. The key differentiator of an UXP platform is to provide a highly responsive and interactive interface (in this example search widget), accelerators (such as user registration widget), decision making tools to influence customer behavior (product comparator widget in this example), collaboration (such as real-time chat), targeted recommendation (such as combo-offer for product bundle) along with optimized business processes (such as one-click checkout, optimized registration).

UXP Core Capabilities

The UXP is still evolving and the technology stack of an UXP can vary across business domains/verticals. A high-level overview of UXP capabilities is shown in Figure 12.1.

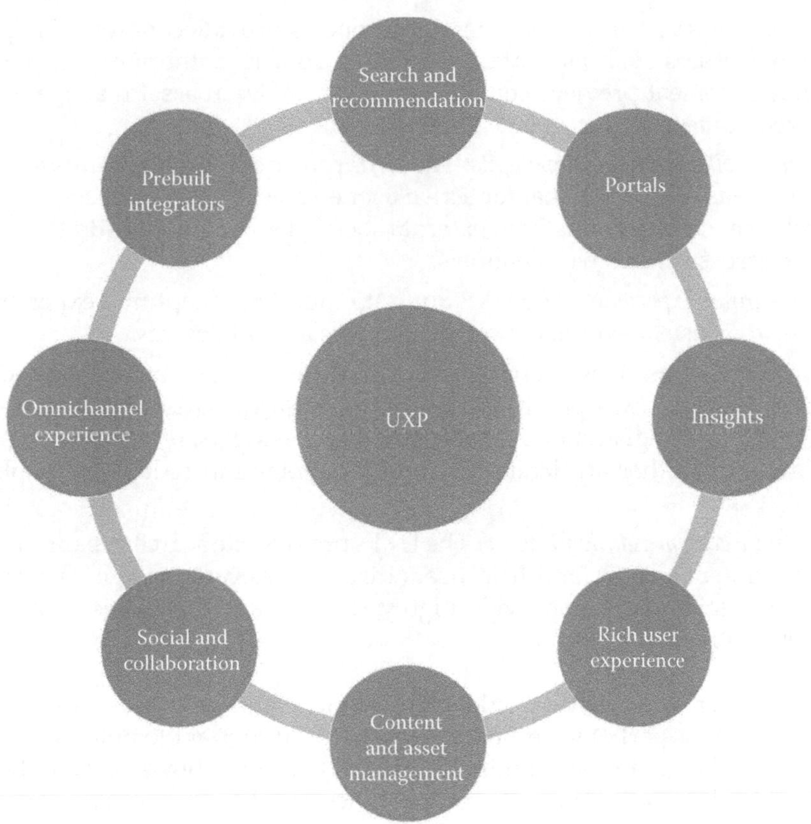

FIGURE 12.1
UXP platform capabilities.

The core capabilities are geared toward improving overall user experience and engagement of end user while fulfilling business goals. Let us have a look at the UXP capabilities shown in Figure 12.1.

- *Portals*: We have already seen horizontal portal capabilities at length in previous chapters. The portal is one of the core components for UXP. It provides information aggregation, single sign on and personalization which can be leveraged by UXP. Other portal capabilities such as self-service features, workflow, collaboration, security, information architecture, etc., can be leveraged for building a UXP.
- *Insights*: Web analytics and other analytics driven customer insights can be used to provide increasingly positive and engaging customer experience. The insights and personalization features can be used for recommendations and for providing targeted content.
- *Rich User Experience*: User design elements and other rich Internet application capabilities such as interactive widgets, gadgets, web 2.0 components, HTML 5/CSS 3, lean models, responsive web design (RWD), adaptive design, and web-oriented architecture, mash-ups, coupled with usability testing components are part of the UXP to provide an immersive user experience.

- *Content and Asset Management*: These components provide core web content management features such as content templates, content authoring and publishing workflows, content preview, content localization, digital asset management, personalized content delivery, content services, etc.
- *Social and Collaboration Components*: The UXP provides inbuilt features for collaboration such as blog, wiki, chat for active user engagements. Social connectors also pull relevant conversations from external social platforms and unify the customer identity across various web channels.
- *Omni-Channel Experience*: The UXP aims at rendering an optimal experience and seamless/consistent experience on all channels and all devices.
- *Pre-Built Integrators*: This is one of the main differentiators of UXP: based on the business domain, UXPs provide various pre-built accelerator components such as dashboard, user registration forms, e-commerce widgets, reporting components, etc. This will further accelerate the time to market and reduce the deployment time.
- *Search and Recommendation Engine*: The UXPs provide site search capabilities across various content sources and help users discover relevant content easily. In-built recommendation engines provide highly relevant and context-sensitive content and product recommendations.

UXPs are still evolving and hence would include other common capabilities such as digital commerce, API, etc. as part of its technology stack. It is important to note that the capabilities of UXPs vary based on the solution domain. Figure 12.1 shows commonly seen UXP capabilities; as UXPs evolve, a new set of capabilities based on the solution domain may be found. For instance, a UXP designed for a B2C e-commerce would provide many pre-built e-commerce features such as shopping cart widget, cross-sell/up-sell components, APIs across integration and extensions, etc., whereas an employee UXP would provide pre-built collaboration suite and in a telecom domain, the UXP would provide a predictive analytics module to predict the customer churn rate. So in order to enhance user experience for a specific solution domain, the features and capabilities provided by the UXPs would vary.

Web Application versus UXP

As a customer engaging platform, UXP has unique technology stack for providing superior and differentiating end-user experience. Table 12.1 looks at some scenarios which differentiate UXP from regular web application.

Business Drivers and Motivations for UXP

There are numerous web platforms in the current market and what differentiates UXP from those needs to be understood. Let us look at some of the main business drivers to select UXP:

- *Agility and Faster Time-To-Market*: Existing web platforms and horizontal portals provide a good development framework for solution development. A few integration components need to be custom developed based on solution needs. However, few scenarios demand faster time-to-market and nimble processes especially in the B2C space to maintain competitive edge. This requires out-of-the-box

TABLE 12.1

UXP vs. Web Application

Category	Web Application	UXP
Primary purpose	Solution implementation and mainly information display or realizing specified functionality	Establishes deeper relationships with customers through active engagements and aim for longer customer retention
Delivery channel	Primarily web channel with support for mobility	Supports all delivery channels to provide seamless experience across all channels; highly optimized for mobile
Usability	Aimed at implementing the specified usability features	Provides multiple user design and UI testing and analytics-driven customer insights to arrive at superior usability. Additionally, provides intuitive information architecture and social and collaboration features.
User Experience	Traditional look and feel which heavily relies on server side components.	Rich user experience leveraging forward looking features such as lightweight, web-oriented architecture using widgets, HTML 5 and other contemporary technologies to delivery highly engaging and immersive experience
Development and deployment model	Mostly custom development for solution implementation Possible reusability of open-source components	Provides in-built integrated components and accelerators which can be used for quicker development and faster deployment
User interaction	Mostly transaction based	Actively engaging and relationship based

integrators, solution accelerators that can be deployed quickly. The UXPs fill these gaps through solution and domain-specific accelerators that enable the business to deploy the solution quickly to the market. They provide much needed agility in development and testing. Operational agility can be enhanced through improved and automated processes and workflows.

- *Usability*: While it is possible to achieve usability in all web platforms, it needs involvement of multiple SMEs, UX designers, and custom integration efforts. The UXPs provide an inbuilt UX design and management capabilities along with usability testing tools such as A/B testing and multivariate testing which provide rich user experience.
- *Engaging and Interactive User Experience*: User experience is one of the core strengths of UXPs. They provide the best UX features and best practices out-of-box eliminating the need for a dedicated UX team and integration/testing team. User experience can be continuously improved through real-time analytics and in-built UI testing features. Customer engagement directly translates into a multitude of business benefits such as increased online revenue, increased customer retention, faster penetration of new markets, higher customer loyalty, reduced customer churn, etc.
- *Control and Governance*: Business gets higher control through configurable widgets and pre-built accelerators. They can perform many business critical tasks such as campaign management with minimal IT involvement. This further enables marketing and sales functions by providing greater control over cross-channel brand management.
- *Competitive Advantage*: It can be achieved through differentiated marketing, increased customer retention and loyalty that can be achieved through UXPs.

Portals and UXPs

UXPs overlap with portals in terms of capabilities, functionality features, etc. In fact, many UXPs are built on top of portal platforms. The UXPs extend the portal experience and focus primarily on the user. Many of the best practices of portal design such as user-centric design, accelerators, and lightweight models are incorporated as part of an UXP. While horizontal portals provide a robust development and integration platform, UXPs provide a pre-built platform (which forms a partial solution) that is easier and faster to deploy for a specific target audience and business domain. Let us have a quick look at the focus areas of both portals and UXPs. This helps us to understand the role of the portal in UXP development.

Figure 12.2 shows one of the evolution steps in presentation/front-end technologies which are used for B2C platforms.

The diagram depicts a very high level evolution of presentation platforms. The main observations are

- Horizontal portals are more of a development platform; they provide all the APIs, standards, libraries, reusable portlets, navigation components, pages, execution environment and supporting eco-system components such as security, infrastructure, etc. Whereas the UXP is more of a pre-built partial solution which fulfils most of the domain-specific/vertical-specific requirements out-of-the-box.
- Horizontal portals compliment UXPs as they fulfill the core features of the UXP such as information aggregation, personalization, infrastructure, security, etc.
- Portals being a platform can be used for the development of a solution to any solution domain or business vertical; on the other hand, UXPs specialize in a particular domain—though UXPs can be reused, they will not provide equivalent/seamless benefits across other business verticals or solution domains.
- Horizontal portals traditionally are considered heavy in terms of development effort, time-to-market, etc., though lean portals and portal accelerators address this problem to a great extent. On the contrary, UXPs are designed to be lightweight

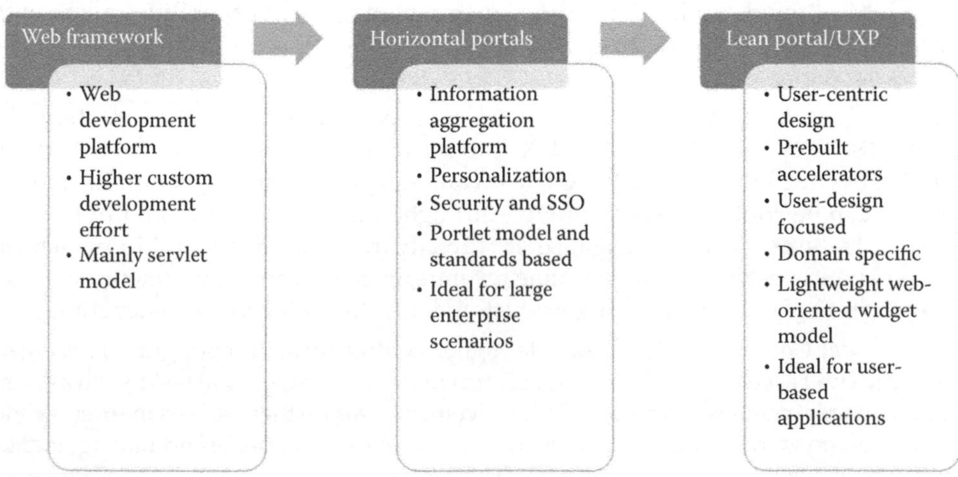

FIGURE 12.2
Evolution of presentation technologies.

customer platforms that are coupled with a lot of pre-built integrators and accelerators that bring in a lot of agility and faster time-to-market.
- A UXP is essentially a lean portal platform with vertical-specific accelerators. It uses all presentation layer best practices.

In a nut shell, portals and UXPs are complimenting technologies in the digital strategy. The portal's core strength lies in robust enterprise integrations, personalization, enterprise security, and infrastructure, whereas UXPs focus on end user and experience enhancing technologies and processes. Due to this factor, horizontal portals and its services can lay the foundation for a UXP solution.

Views of UXP

In this section, we will look at UXPs from various dimensions. This will help in understanding the impact of UXP from various perspectives and how effectively the UXP fulfils the business drivers and motivations discussed earlier.

Business View of UXP

Some of the key business views of UXPs are mentioned in this section. We will also look at the main business value derived from UXPs (Figure 12.3).

- *Digital Marketing*: This is the key business function that will be greatly benefited from UXPs. The main usage scenarios are
  - Effective customer segmentation for targeted and differentiated marketing and campaign management using web analytics features in UXP
  - Business-friendly customer management features such as authoring, publishing flows, and other workflow capabilities provided by UXP can be used by the digital marketing team
  - Effective email marketing can be done for targeted groups
  - Personalized campaign management and targeted content to carry-out multichannel campaigns
  - Fine-tune the campaign through real-time cross-channel actionable intelligence drawn from analytics
  - Brand management through social listening
  - *Social marketing*: UXPs provide many features to launch social campaigns, social listening, sentiment analysis, and establishing integrated identity and customer digital footprints.
  - Provide personalized loyalty and reward programs to enhance customer retention
  - Context aware recommendations, content, and functionality based on user behavior, access device, location, and interests.

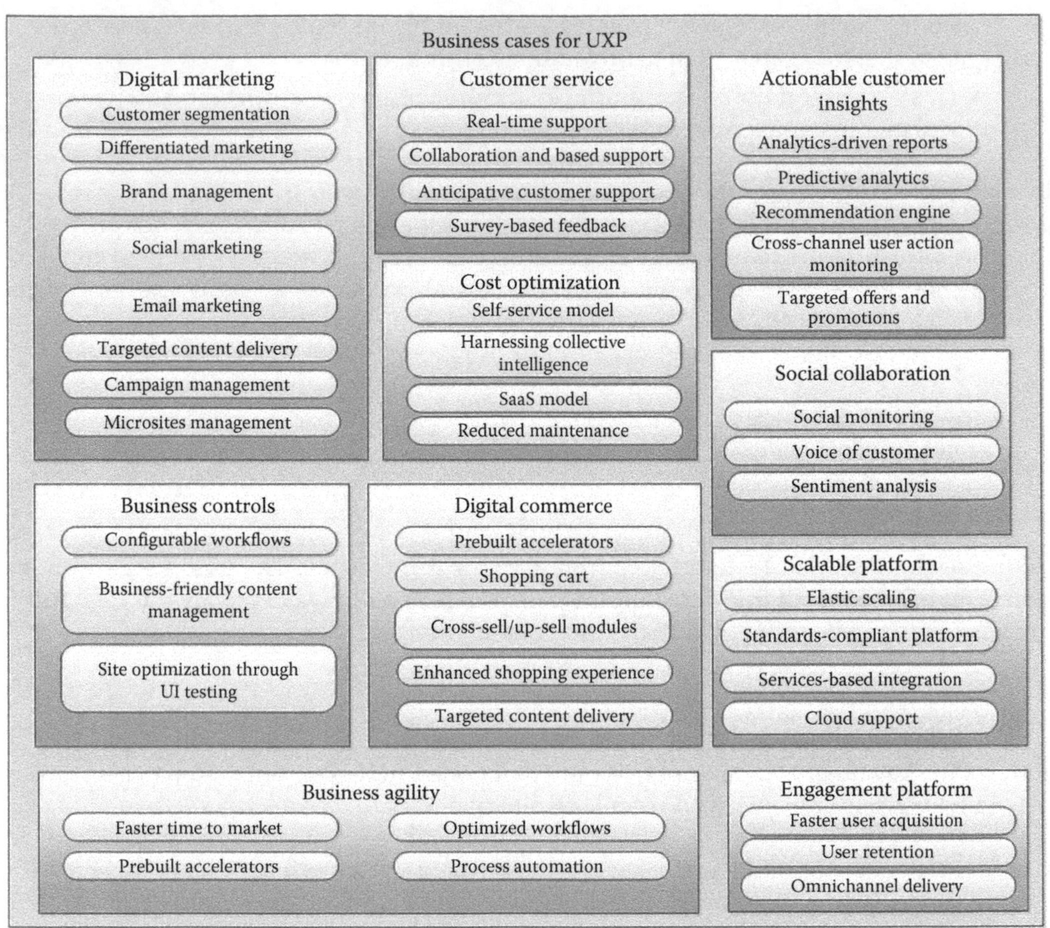

FIGURE 12.3
UXP business scenarios.

- *Digital E-commerce*: This business domain greatly benefits through the use of UXPs. E-commerce UXPs
  - Have pre-built e-commerce modules and accelerators that can provide the best of both commerce and content management
  - Provide highly effective and personalized offers and promotions for the target audience based on insights drawn from UXP analytics
  - Effectively use the recommendation engine for relevant product recommendations and best sales/promotion offer
  - Identify effective cross-sell/up-sell opportunities based on customer behavior and order history
  - Leverage content management features to store product content management and product catalog
  - Provide integrations with enterprise systems through pre-built integrations

    - Provide immersive and social shopping, co-shopping, personalized shopping experience
    - Increase customer loyalty and customer retention through personalized touch points, pro-active collaboration and anticipative customer support.
- *Next Generation Customer Support*: The UXPs help to provide interactive and real-time support through collaboration features along with anticipative customer support features.
- *Engagements Platforms*: The UXPs provide compelling user experience platforms that enable easier customer acquisition and retention. They enable anytime-anywhere platforms optimized for all delivery channels.
- *Business Controls through Configurable and Business-Friendly Functions*: The UXPs provide greater control to business to carry out their main activities such as campaign management, micro-site creation, user onboarding, website optimization, layout customization, etc., through configurable interfaces with minimal dependency on IT teams. This enables an internal self-service model. The UXPs provide easier and friendlier site creation and management features. Coupled with web content management and digital asset management capabilities, business teams get greater control over the web content management with minimal dependency on IT and support teams. Marketing efforts, campaign effectiveness, and user activities can be monitored at a single place through reports and dashboards.
- *Cost Optimization*: The UXPs drive the self-service model and provide easier maintenance and deployment options such as SaaS model that reduce the total cost of platform ownership. They also provide knowledge management and collaboration features that harness the collective and social intelligence to further drive the self-service model.
- *Increased Agility*: Optimized processes, automated workflows, pre-built accelerators all help in making the UXP more agile and brings the solution faster to the market. Rules-based process automation and business process management optimizes the overall user experience with key business processes.
- *Actionable Customer Insights*: Real-time analytics provide insights into customer activities. They help to provide a synchronized cross-channel view of user actions. This can be used to provide targeted offers and promotions to increase the conversion ratio. Social analytics will also be leveraged to understand and analyze the user's social activities. The insights drawn from these analytics initiatives can be used for predicting and optimizing customer behavior, and can be used for minimizing customer churn, providing relevant recommendations, optimizing conversion rates, enhancing satisfaction scores, etc.
- *Social Collaboration*: In this category, UXPs aim toward creating a consolidated identity of the user from all social platforms and use it for personalization and recommendations, for instance, content recommendations based on interests drawn from social media platforms and social recommendations–based product suggestions. Social listening and monitoring for assessing user and brand sentiments is also part of this component. Social customer service or "voice of customer" platform wherein social media platforms are leveraged for customer service is one of the important aspects of this component.

- *Scalable Platform*: The standards compliant UXP would support business growth through the elastic scaling offered by SaaS model/cloud hosting. Besides this, the layer-wise components are loosely coupled and built around service based integration for future extensions. Web-oriented technologies, widget-based interface, and asynchronous services–based integration model further enhances the platform scalability. Business can provide a unified experience for all internal and external stakeholders such as vendors, partners, resellers, employees.

End User View of UXP

Most of the business goals mentioned in Figure 12.3 can be realized by active end user engagement. The success of UXPs is largely attributed to end user participation. The primary purpose of a UXP is to provide an enriching experience to the end user. Let us look at the UXP from the end user's standpoint.

- *Rich, Deep and Immersive Experience*: The UXPs provide an enriching and compelling user experience with the following distinct features.
    - High level of interactiveness through responsive and interactive widgets
    - Single view holistic and synchronized cross-channel experience through dashboards
    - Guided navigation through a personalized navigation model
    - Optimized digital touch points to provide pleasant and engaging user journeys
- *Easy Discovery of Relevant Information*: This is through optimized site search, intuitive information architecture, and innovative features such as single-page application, etc.
- *Higher Usability*: The principal aim of the UXP is to enhance the usability for the end user through user-friendly features, high accessibility, and increase the overall user satisfaction index. It has an optimized content strategy to display relevant and compelling content to make the platform more usable.
- *Easy to Use Interface*: The UXPs provide friendlier interfaces through:
    - Drag-and-drop widgets
    - Easy to personalize interface
    - Configurable page layouts
- Highly contextual and relevant content and tailor-made product recommendations based on usage trends, purchase patterns, and social interests/connections.
- Personalized and next-generation customer support through first-call resolution, real-time collaboration based support, etc.
- Self-service features such as
    - Decision support tools and do-it-yourself (DIY) tools such as product comparators, converters, etc.
    - Knowledge base to search for relevant solution articles
    - Availability of right tools at the right place
    - Easier, faster, and automated process workflows
- *Multichannel Availability*: The UXPs provide optimal experience on any device and any platform through a combination of responsive design and mobile apps.

- *Collaborative Environment*: Hyper personalized experience, knowledge management features, and collaborative tools offered by UXPs would benefit the end user in leveraging the collective knowledge.
- *Optimized Content*: The UXP content strategy provides compelling and inspirations content that provide easily discoverable content.

IT and Operations View of UXP

From the development and maintenance standpoint, UXPs have the following main usage scenarios and advantages:

- Pre-built integrators and synergized/harmonious technology stack for vertical domain to help in accelerated development, testing and deployment of the solution, and reducing development overhead. This guarantees higher degree of deliverables while keeping the release timelines short.
- Reduction of total cost of ownership (TCO) due to self-service features such as automated processes, self-service, collaboration and knowledge management features. The UXPs make it easy to extend and enhance functionality reducing the support, maintenance, and enhancement costs.
- Best-of-breed and forward-looking and contemporary features such as web-oriented architectures, widget model, multichannel enablement, lightweight components, and REST service models will make the UXPs a preferable choice for customer-centric platforms and to make it future proof.
- In-built UI testing and site optimization features such as A/B testing helps IT and operations teams to continuously fine-tune the platform and enhance its effectiveness.
- *Easier extensions and maintenance*: Due to the usage of standards-based platforms and integrations, it would be easier to onboard new features, perform new integrations with minimal maintenance effort.

UXP Architecture

The UXPs are predominantly built on web-oriented architecture where widgets play a key role in the presentation layer. They have a range of technical components to provide optimal user experience.

A high-level architecture view of a typical UXP platform is shown in Figure 12.4.

Let us look at the core components in different layers.

Interacting Systems

A UXP can be accessed from many systems such as browsers, mobile devices, PDAs, tablets, kiosks, etc. As UXPs expose APIs for external systems, external web applications and social media platforms can consume those services or embed the reusable widgets provided by UXPs. Other access channels include call centers for customer support team and through emails.

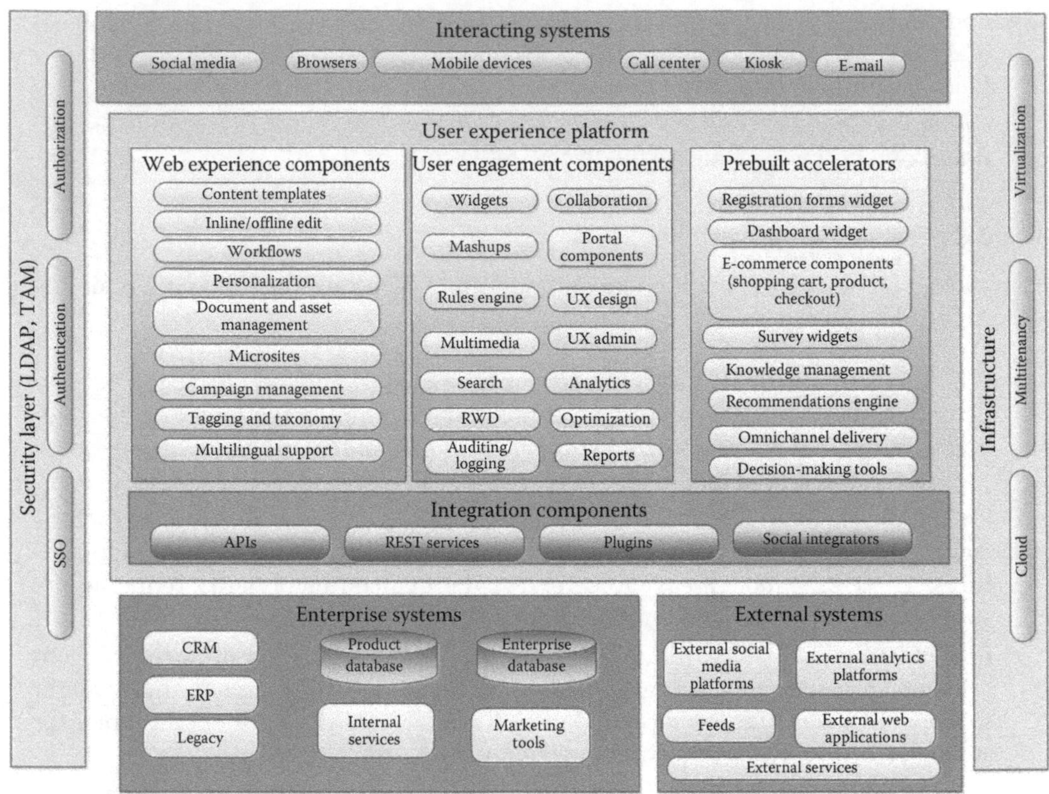

FIGURE 12.4
UXP architecture.

Core User Experience Platform

The modules and components depicted in this section are normally found in most UXPs. The accelerators and pre-built integrations may vary based on the target audience and the solution domains. Let us look at these modules.

Web Experience Components

All components required to deliver an optimal site experience are available in this module. Core content management components such as content templates, content authoring and publishing workflows, content localization, SEO/web analytics components, personalization components to provide highly relevant content and metadata tagging for content are part of this module; they help in building an engaging rich media content. Besides these components, UXPs also provide in-built campaign management and micro-site management that would enable business to quickly deploy/optimize seasonal campaigns and micro-sites.

Most of the components in this category are ready-to-be used for off-the shelf deployment in the solution with only configuration changes. For instance, content templates, workflows, campaign and micro-site management features require only configuration or minimal customization to be deployed as part of the solution. This optimizes time-to-market while providing a high-quality end user experience.

User Engagement Components

The UXPs are predominantly built around lightweight widgets that are essentially client side components. Portal capability such as content aggregation, personalization, and security form the core of UXPs. A UXP also uses mash-ups to aggregate the content on the client side. The user experience design and administration components provide in-built design and administrator interfaces to configure layouts, styling, designing, etc. They also provide other flexible features such as widget configuration, drag-and-drop, configurable page layout, do-it-yourself tools, decision making tools, etc. Responsive web design (RWD) is used for presentation component development and to provide an omni-channel experience. The search component mainly provides site search features. The UXPs also include website optimization features such as rules based targeted content, UI testing through A/B testing and multivariate testing to optimize the impact of content delivery. Auditing, logging, and reporting features help administrators to keep track of site usage statistics. User interface testing and real-time insights obtained from web analytics help in continuously improving the user experience.

Prebuilt Accelerators

Pre-built integrators and accelerators are the core strength of UXPs. They help to get the solution up and running quickly. Pre-built accelerators are most commonly the components used by end users with minimal customization for integrations. These include mainly the following:

- Forms that can be used for user registration and onboarding
- Dashboard widgets for intuitive visualizations to provide a single view of various data sources
- Pre-built e-commerce components such as shopping cart widgets, payment gateway integrators, cross-sell/up-sell modules, etc.; these can be readily deployed in an e-commerce UXP
- Survey widgets for getting user feedback
- Pre-built knowledge management system for information sharing and collaboration
- In-built recommendation engine to provide context-relevant and personalized recommendations
- Domain specific decision-making tools such as product comparators, "what-if" analyzers that aid and influence in decision making and influence user behavior
- Omni-channel delivery tools using RWD for developing hybrid and native mobile apps

Integration Components

The UXPs mainly expose functionality through APIs and services. In addition to in-built integrators, they also provide service-based, API-based, and plug-in-based integration with external and internal systems.

External and Internal Systems

This mainly involves the system of records that is used by UXPs for implementing business logic. They include enterprise ERP, CRM, legacy systems, enterprise database, product database, internal services, marketing systems, etc.

External systems mainly include external social media platforms, external feeds, services and web applications and analytics platform.

Security

This layer is responsible for providing authentication, authorization, and single sign-on services. The UXPs also leverage underlying servers, such as application server and web server, features to establish seamless SSO. Authorization services are used to implement role based access controls within the UXP.

Infrastructure

Many UXPs have adopted SaaS model as they are hosted on cloud. They can also be deployed in-house and support multi-tenancy. Since UXPs mostly cater to Internet audience, they should be built to provide elastic scalability which can be provided through cloud or clustered model or virtualization model. Built on web-oriented architecture, lightweight components further help in performance and scalability.

TABLE 12.2

UXP Capabilities for Various Solution Domains

Solution Domain	Capabilities of UXP	Pre-Built Integrators of UXP
Internet-facing retail UXP	• Omni-channel experience to provide optimal rendition on all devices • Personalized content delivery • Search for faster product discovery • Videos content for product demos • Content management for product content • Usability testing capabilities using A/B testing to test the effectiveness of page variants and maximize conversion ratio • Collaboration features for user engagement and customer support	• In-built social integrators to bring in social conversations and discussions under a single platform • In-built shopping cart widget and payment integration for providing digital commerce experience • Recommendation engine component to provide relevant recommendations • Pre-built analytics for providing customer insights about user transactions. Pre-built form widgets for user registration • In-built social listening to hear "voice of customer" and monitor social trends and sentiment
Intranet employee UXP	• Security services for achieving SSO with internal applications • Document management for employees to share documents • Collaboration features such as blogs, wiki, forums, communities	• Pre-built customer dashboard to show all main employee-related functions • Pre-built integrations to internal enterprise CRM and ERP systems • In-built knowledge management for increased employee productivity
Internet banking UXP	• Personalized offers • Digital collaboration office to virtually interact with banker • Integrations with core banking systems	• Pre-built customer and admin dashboard to provide view of all account and transaction data • Pre-integrated rules engine to calculate credit and risk score • Pre-built decision making tools for risk profiling, fraud detection

UXP Capabilities Based on Scenarios

Let us have a look at key capabilities offered by UXPs based on the solution domain.

UXP for Various Customer-Centric Scenario

As discussed earlier, some of the core capabilities and pre-built integrators in UXPs vary based on the solution domain. Let us look at some of the UXP capabilities for various solution domains in Table 12.2.

Summary

- This chapter provides an introduction to user experience platforms covering various views of UXP and UXP architecture.
- The UXP is a user-centric platform that provides pre-integrated capabilities to deliver exceptional user experience through a variety of delivery channels.
- The core capabilities of UXP include portals, insights, rich user experience, content and asset management, social and collaboration components, omni-channel experience, pre-built integrators, and search and recommendation engine.
- The UXPs differ from regular web application by deviating from transaction-based services to experience enhancing and relationship enhancing services.
- Key business drivers and motivations for UXP are agility and faster time-to-market, usability, engaging and interactive user experience, control and governance, competitive advantage.
- Main business cases for UXP include digital marketing, digital ecommerce, next generation customer support, engagements platforms, business controls through configurable and business-friendly functions, cost optimization, increased agility, actionable customer insights, social collaboration, and scalable platform.
- End user view of UXP includes rich, deep, and immersive experience, easy discovery of relevant information, higher usability, easy-to-use interface, highly contextual and relevant content and tailor-made product recommendations, personalized and next generation customer support, self-service features, multi-channel availability, collaborative environment, optimized content.
- The IT and operations view of UXP include pre-built integrators and synergized/harmonious technology stack, reduction of total cost of ownership, best of breed and forward-looking and contemporary features, in-built UI testing and site optimization features and easier extensions and maintenance.
- UXP architecture mainly include interacting systems layer, core user experience platform layer, integration components layer, external and internal systems layer, and security and infrastructure layer.
- Core user experience platform layer includes web experience components, user engagement components, pre-built accelerators.

13

Designing User Experience Platforms

Designing a user experience platform (UXP) is a creative challenge. We need to model various customer touch points and user journeys, identify experience enhancement opportunities, and engage customers actively to align with strategic business goals.

UXP design is slightly different than designing user interface (UI). UI is one part of the overall user experience. We will see the detailed process of a portal user experience (UX) design in Chapter 14. In this chapter, we will look at the main design aspects of designing a UXP.

Introduction

An end user experience is a mix of different factors such as content organization, ease of use, information discovery, and sum total of all user touch point experiences.

Designing an effective UXP primarily needs thinking from an end-user stand point. The usage scenarios, usability needs, key touch points, potential challenges, business process, customer support, collaboration, and social touch points all need to be carefully evaluated from the user lens.

With the increasing popularity of social channels, mobility, and word-of-mouth publicity, the user experiences can quickly amplify, influence, and propagate to a huge audience; this has potential to impact positively or negatively on branding, online revenue, and site traffic and customer retention. The impact of the user experience on product branding would be huge for customer-centric organizations. This requires us to carefully understand, analyze, evaluate, and improve the user experience for the user journeys.

We need to explore all opportunities to convert customer touch points and journeys to provide engaging, immersive, and relationship-enhancing experiences.

In this chapter, we will explore these topics. We will also look at a sample UXP design for a banking domain.

Design Principles of UXP

Any UXP design should adhere to the following key design principles. Though the solution components and accelerators vary based on the solution domain, the design of UXP components should adhere to these design principles:

- *Web-oriented model*: The presentation components should be predominantly based on web-oriented architecture consisting of widgets, gadgets, and HTML 5 components. This helps us in designing lightweight model using asynchronous JSON services with service producers.

- *Lean model and lightweight architecture*: The presentation components, integrations, data exchange formats, and media files should all preferably be kept lightweight to align well with omni-channel experience.
- *Standards-based platform*: The components should be based on HTML and web standards such as HTML 5 and CSS 3 so that it is easy to extend the functionality and create a plug-and-play architecture.
- *Service-based integration*: REST services based integration is preferred during integration with external interfaces. This provides a loosely coupled model providing enhanced flexibility.
- *Context-aware components*: The front-end components should provide context-aware content based on accessing device, access location, and any implicit/explicit customer preferences. This makes the content more relevant and engaging for the end user.
- *Configuration-driven components*: The widgets, workflows, rules, and page layouts should all be configurable so that they provide business-friendly interfaces.
- *Usability*: This is the prime requirement for all UXP components. The individual components and the end-to-end business process should be assessed for usability. Usability aspects include accessibility, relevance, information discovery, simplicity, and multichannel access.
- *Self-service focus*: Enable end users with "do-it-yourself" tools and functionality to positively impact user experience. This involves process optimizations, process automation, availability of decision-making tools, personalized navigation, contextual recommendations, etc.
- *Multichannel experience*: UXP platforms will be accessed from multiple devices and channels such as mobile devices, tablets, TVs, kiosks, third-party systems, web applications, and portals and provide interfaces to interact with all the channels in an optimal fashion. REST services and APIs are some of the most popular forms of integration with other systems.
- *Enhance conversion*: Create customer-centric model to convert a visitor to a loyal customer through proactive engagement and touch point enhancements.
- *Synchronized and optimized processes across all channels*: The business processes should be integrated across all channels to provide consistent and seamless user experience. This also avoids disconnected user experience.
- *Cross-channel integrated architecture*: The UXPs specialize in providing vertical or solution-specific tools, features, and processes with end-to-end integration. This avoids silo architecture for each channel (such as mobile, web, and kiosk).
- *Vertical-specific accelerator*: UXPs should provide pre-built accelerators that make the platform easy to integrate and deploy for a specific business scenario. This usually includes pre-built widgets, out-of-box integration adapters, easy-to-configure workflow engines, in-built dashboards, configurable visualizations, etc.

UXP Trends

The concept of UXP is emerging and is based on target audience and solution vertical. However, there are few key trends that influence the design of UXP, which are given as follows:

- Rich, immersive, and inspiring content leveraging graphics, text, and multimedia content
- Highly optimized search engine optimization (SEO) strategy to drive user traffic
- Hyperfocus on user's social persona, activities on social platforms, and unified user identities
- Seamless and consistent user experience across multiple channels and devices
- Listening to customer's opinions and feedback through official forums and social media platforms and proactively engaging them in their preferred platforms. Using voice of customer (VOC) and social customer support systems to address the customer's problems
- Social customer engagement through a consolidated view of user's activities in all social platforms
- Touch- and mobile-enabled interfaces
- Natural human interfaces to interact with systems and devices
- Delivering highly contextual, relevant, and personalized content and functionality based on insights drawn from web analytics

User Experience Strategy

The main focus of user experience strategy is to look at the business functionality from an end-user standpoint and deliver value at all touch points.

At a high level, devising an effective user experience strategy consists of steps depicted in Figure 13.1.

- *Empathize*: In this stage, we understand the user personas, model user journeys, users' touch points, etc. The main activities in this stage are as follows:
  - Identification of the existing organization's user experience capabilities
  - User persona identification and user segmentation, which include identification of main activities done by each persona, their interests, access channels, likely preferences, etc.
  - Modeling all user journeys and prioritizing the journeys that are most frequently used and the ones that have direct impact on revenue and end-user experience
  - Modeling business processes that are used in user journeys
  - Creating an experience map for all user personas
  - User touch point analysis

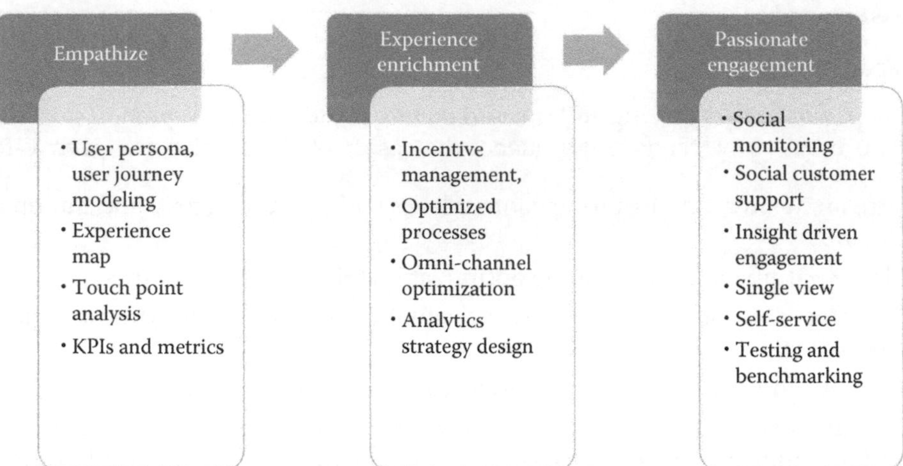

FIGURE 13.1
User-experience strategy.

- High-level definition of experience key performance indicators (KPIs)
- Identifying SEO strategy to enhance the visibility of the platform
- Identifying all opportunities to automate and optimize workflows and business processes

- *Experience enrichment*: This is the crucial stage wherein we identify all opportunities to enhance end-user experience. The main activities in this stage include the following:
  - Designing an effective collaboration strategy at various user touch points, which includes providing chat, product forums, user communities, etc.
  - Designing user reward opportunities such as loyalty programs and incentives based on content contribution and active participation
  - Designing relation-enhancing features across all user channels and devices
  - Designing campaigns that suit user personas identified in the previous step
  - Designing an easier user on-boarding process such as intuitive registration forms and optimizing registration process
  - Designing multichannel customer support tools
  - Designing analytics strategy and metrics to understand user activities, pain points, and behavior across all touch points and across all channels
  - Designing an experience-enhancing content strategy that includes placing the right content at the right place, recommending context-sensitive content, and designing immersive content
  - Designing intuitive information architecture to enhance information discoverability
  - Designing tools and features to collect explicit user feedback through forms, surveys, etc.

    - Designing an optimal UI strategy includes prototyping, designing wireframe and visuals, defining UI standards, user research, and defining information architecture and guidelines and style guides
- *Passionate engagement*: In this stage, we will actively seek out all opportunities for user engagement across channels and platforms. The key activities include the following:
    - Social monitoring and listening to understand VOC, brand-related sentiments, product discussions, and opinions
    - Social customer support to engage and address customer issues in social channels through social customer relationship management systems
    - Using single view of analytics report to gain insights from user activities and continuously optimize the UXP, marketing campaign, and content based on the insights
    - Using hyper collaborative features such as cobrowsing, coshopping, video/conference chat–based customer support, and personalized collaboration
    - Promoting and optimizing self-service features based on insights from analytics and explicitly expressed user feedback
    - Continuously testing and benchmarking the user experience and using it as one of the inputs for feedback loop for improving the user experience

Deep Dive into UXP Design Activities

We will have a detailed look at some of the key activities we discussed in the earlier section. We will look at two main activities that can be used to actively engage end users. User-experience mapping and touch-point analysis are popular techniques to identify, quantify, and enhance end-user engagement factors. We will look at these two points in detail in this section.

Though both these techniques follow slightly different approaches, their ultimate goal is to provide differentiated end-user experience; both these techniques take user-centric approach to discover the "moments of truth" and bring business closer to customer. Both techniques compliment each other: touch-point analysis can be a substep in user-experience mapping and vice versa. Customer research, surveys, inputs from web-analytics reports, user interviews, brainstorming sessions, workshops, business documentation, and process flow analysis will all be used as inputs for these two techniques.

Understanding of these techniques helps us in identifying experience-related gaps with existing applications and to design efficient user-centric platforms.

User Experience Mapping and Enhancement

This map essentially identifies all customer interactions (touch points) and areas where we can add value to user experience. We start by taking the inventory of all user touch points and use it to improve quality of interactions to provide a differentiated experience. The touch points and journey may vary for each of the user personas and user segments, and hence the experience, pain points, and experience enhancement measures would also vary in the process.

The main steps are as listed in the following sections.

Inventory of Touch Points and Experience Mapping

This requires modeling user journeys for various user personas and user segments and identifying various touch points. Let us look at a simple e-commerce scenario to understand this further. A user experience mapping and touch points for e-commerce are given Table 13.1.

This inventory will be used for further analysis and optimization.

Experience Impact Analysis

After compiling a touch point inventory, we will assess the user experience at each touch point using the following parameters:

- *Overall satisfaction*: How satisfied is the customer with the touch points?
- *Value of the touch point*: How does the touch point address user's goals, objectives, needs, and expectations?

TABLE 13.1

User-Experience Mapping

Channel \ Touch Point	Product Research	Shopping Cart	Product Purchase	Order Management and Postpurchase
Web	Product search. Product compare. Product browser.	Shopping cart feature.	Check out flow. Payment gateway. Gift coupon/ voucher flow.	Track order. Track shipping.
Mail	Mail customer support about queries.	Mail the products for ordering.		Mail customer support about order updates.
Mobile device	Call on-call support for feedback. Use mobile app for research.	Call customer support for or use mobile app for shopping.	Call customer support for purchase or use mobile app for checkout.	Call customer support for order updates or use mobile app for order tracking.
Collaborative customer support (chat, IVR)	Chat with customer support.	Chat or co-browse with customer support for shopping. Resolve shopping cart issues with customer support.	Chat with customer for purchase. Resolve purchase-related issues with customer support.	Chat with customer support for order- or shipping-related issues.
Social media	Solicit feedback from friends. Read product review comments. Compare product ratings. Follow product-related trends and conversations.	Coshopping. Cobrowsing. Social product recommendations. Review social reviews, ratings, and feedback.		Postpurchase experience on social platforms. Recommend the brand and product to social connections.

- *Popularity of the touch point*: How often/frequently is the touch point used by various user personas?
- *Experience challenges*: Are there any challenges that the customer faced at those touch points?
- *Business impact of the touch point*: How do customer interactions at those touch points affect the overall business goals?

This analysis helps us to assess the overall user experience at all channels.

Experience Improvement Plan

We would come up with a plan to improve the overall experience at all the touch points; touch points are prioritized based on the impact analysis done in the previous step. Some of the most effective techniques for this are as follows:

- *Enable self-service*: Wherever possible, implement the self-service model and enable end users to perform the task themselves with least dependency. For instance, automated password reset, self-help tips for tasks, guided navigation, and knowledge-based support are some of the self-service opportunities that can be explored.
- *Improve effectiveness of the experience*: Improve the efficiency and effectiveness of the experience. This can be done through process automation, process optimization, and proactive and anticipatory customer service to deepen customer relationship and loyalty.
- *Provide enabling tools and content*: Equip users with the right tools at the right place to enable faster decision making. Search, comparators, converters, calculators, planners, translators, and social connectors positioned at strategic places help in providing an engaging experience.
- *Incorporate user survey feedback*: Address any explicitly mentioned pain points by the end user.
- *Analytics-driven improvements*: Carefully evaluate the analytics report to understand customer exit rates and usage patterns and optimize the experience accordingly.
- *Add experience differentiators*: Provide value differentiators that keep the customers engaged. Loyalty points, personalized offers, hypercollaboration, smart search, guided navigation, and multichannel enablement are some of the examples of differentiators.

User Touch Point Analysis and Improvement

A user touch point is any interaction between the end user and product or offered service. The touch point analysis identifies the areas of customer experience improvement and provides the details of improving the experience. For instance, when a customer logs a service incident, the customer support executive would be presented with all the details of the customer including the past activities, customer segment, and a prediction of probable churn. All this information can be obtained through a customer interaction system after touch point analysis. A customer support representative can then use one of the suggested offers to improve the user experience and user retention.

At a high level, user touch point analysis consists of these steps:

Identifying Cross-Channel Touch Points

We need to identify all possible user touch points with the platform across all channels. This includes web, customer support, email, phone, and online knowledge base. Within the web channel, we also need to identify predominant touch points. We have seen this step as part of user experience mapping, and we can leverage the inputs from that exercise for this.

Analyzing User Expectations across All Channels

Once we have identified cross-channel touch points, we need to understand the needs, goals, and expectations from various user segments for each of the touch points. For instance, an average resolution time lesser than 2 days would be a common expectation from a customer support touch point. These data can be collected through offline customer surveys, online feedback forms, etc.

Insights gained from user experience mapping and experience impact analysis are some of the crucial inputs for this step.

Prioritizing and Planning for Touch Point Experience Enhancement

Each of the customer touch points is then prioritized based on its impact on the end-user experience. The touch points that highly impact the user experience and the ones that are most frequently used across channels across user segments are given higher priority.

After prioritizing, we plan for improving each of those touch point experiences. For instance, since customer support is one of the critical touch points we can explore and improving the service experience through knowledge-based service, solution recommendations, automated process tasks, hypercollaboration-based support, social customer support, etc., is highly necessary. Experience improvement plan from user experience mapping will be leveraged in this step. In this phase, we will also device KPIs to measure the overall experience for each customer touch point transaction. For instance, an explicit rating post issue resolution or identification of the positive sentiment in the user feedback reflects upon the enhanced quality of customer support.

Measure, Monitor, and Improve

We then continuously monitor the KPIs for all touch point across all channels and use the metrics to iteratively improve the user experience.

Figure 13.2 shows customer journey across various touch points for the entire lifecycle of a product purchase experience. This gives us the touch points, which can be optimized. In the following sections, we will deep dive into reference designs for UXP.

UXP Presentation Design

We have seen in the previous sections that core design principles of a UXP are web-oriented architecture, lightweight presentation and integration, RWD-based UI, standards-based development, services-based integration and Omni-channel experience. We will design the presentation layer for UXP based on these design principles.

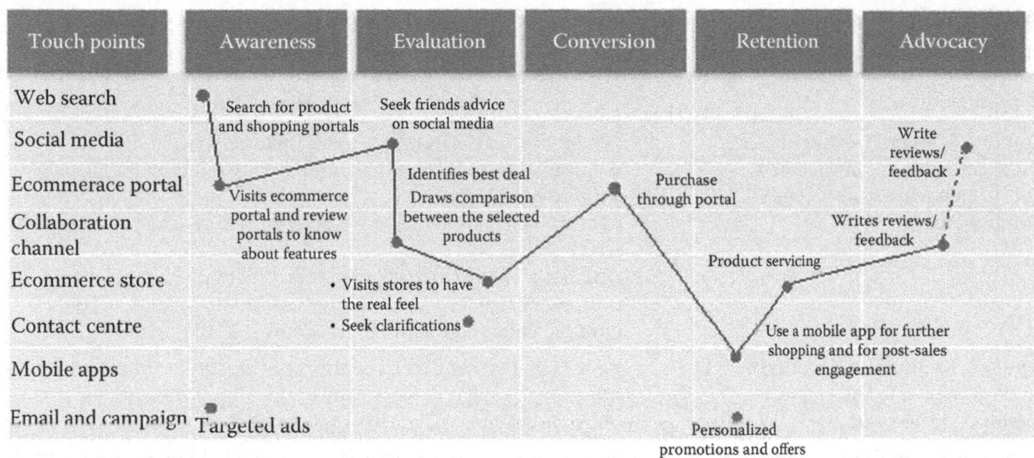

FIGURE 13.2
Customer touch points during product purchase.

The presentation layer chosen for this design is a pure-RWD-based technology. This design ensures that the design is web oriented, lightweight, and uses REST-based services.

NOTE: The UI technologies shown in the reference architecture are for educational purposes. There are many competing and alternative frameworks that can be used to implement the reference architecture.

A reference architecture for RWD-based presentation is shown in Figure 13.3.

Pure RWD consists of single codebase to cater to all web channels. It adapts to the user's screen layout and provides a rich and interactive experience through widgets. This architecture style offers single page application (SPA), which provides a SEO-friendly

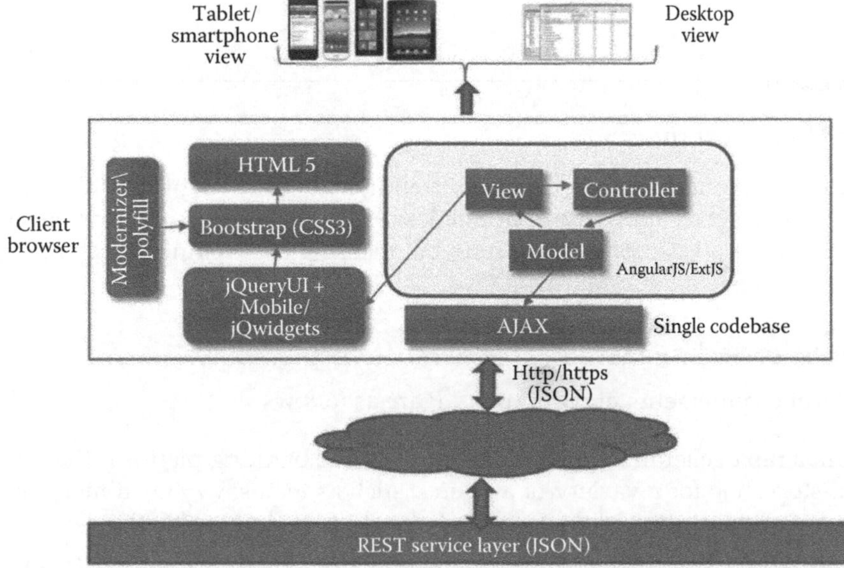

FIGURE 13.3
Presentation design for UXP.

TABLE 13.2

UI Frameworks for RWD-Based Presentation Design

UI Frameworks	Description
jQuery + jQueryUI + AngularJS Single codebase for all channels, 100% open source, moderate GUI components	• jQuery is used for DOM traversal/manipulation, CSS manipulation event handling, animation, and is an excellent support for AJAX. • jQueryUI enables interactive web applications and provides rich UI controls. • AngularJS enables rich client-side interactivity but is a more comprehensive JavaScript framework. It supports MVC, data binding, validation, routing, directives, templates, testing, etc.
jQuery + KendoUI + AngularJS Single codebase for all channels, KendoUI is licensed	• KendoUI provides rich UI controls developed in jQuery and a framework similar to KnockoutJS and AngularJS with features like data binding using MVVM, validation, themes, templates, etc.
Bootstrap + Angular UI + Angular JS Single codebase for all channels, 100% open source	• Bootstrap provides UI controls and RWD helpers to build mobile-first front end. • Angular UI provides UI components that works well with Angular JS. Angular JS supports MVVM, two-way data binding, validation, routing, templates, etc.

consistent URL. There are other variants of this architecture wherein we maintain separate codebase for mobile and desktop browsers and optimize the mobile experience through mobile services.

UI frameworks such as AngularJS use the MVC model in the presentation layer to provide clean separation of concerns. Let us look at other UI frameworks that can be used to implement this reference architecture in Table 13.2.

NOTE: Table 13.2 provides an indicative list of UI frameworks that can be used for implementing the reference architecture. However, there are many other UI frameworks, such as Sencha Touch and ExtJS, that can be leveraged as well.

Banking UXP Design

We had a look at the main design principles, trends, and UXP design activities in the previous sections. Now let us apply those principles to design a next-generation omni-channel banking UXP. In this case study, we are re-engineering an existing legacy banking platform to the next-generation banking UXP.

Requirements of Banking UXP

The high-level requirements of banking UXP are as follows:

- Design a next-generation customer-centric online banking platform that provides a one-stop shop for a variety of audience such as tech-savvy customers, bankers, partners, support staff, and prospects (who are first-time visitors).
- Support all the core online banking functionalities currently supported by legacy banking application such as transaction handling, account statements, reporting, and funds transfer.

- Enable access to the various new banking platform channels such as mobile devices, kiosk, ATM, social platforms, bank branches, and web.
- Allow other web applications and systems to interact with the new banking platform to leverage its services.
- Provide next-generation customer support to enhance customer experience and reduce customer churn.
- Integrate with core banking systems, HR systems, risk management systems, and in-house marketing systems.
- Optimize existing business processes and workflows to make them more agile and nimble and adopt next-generation and forward looking UI technologies to provide responsive and immersive user experience.

Challenges with Legacy Online Banking System

- No active customer engagement
- Absence of multichannel access
- New product launch taking 3–4 months
- Absence of real-time reports and financial portfolio positions
- Absence of a 360° view of customer activities and profile
- Tight integration of online banking with back-end core banking systems
- High cost of maintenance and enhancement

Banking UXP Solution

Aligning with the customer-centric approach, the banking UXP will be designed to enable and enhance the experience of all customer touch points. High-level user and functionality research and analysis provide these details:

- *User personas*: There are mainly four user personas, namely, prospect, customer, banker, and administrator.
- *User journey*: The key user journeys are user registration, account opening, funds transfer, and online payments.
- *Touch points*: The main user touch points are user registration form, customer service section, account dashboard, and digital bank branch process.
- *Potential experience enhancements*: Optimize new user registration, provide a unified view of all account activities, enhance real-time support, provide lightweight service-based integration with back-end systems, and enhance new product launch process.

Features and Capabilities of Next-Generation Banking UXP

Based on the design principles and best practices we discussed earlier, the capabilities of next-generation banking portal are depicted in the Figure 13.4.

Let us look at various features of the UXP and how it not only addresses current problems but also enables business to build a next-generation customer-centric platform.

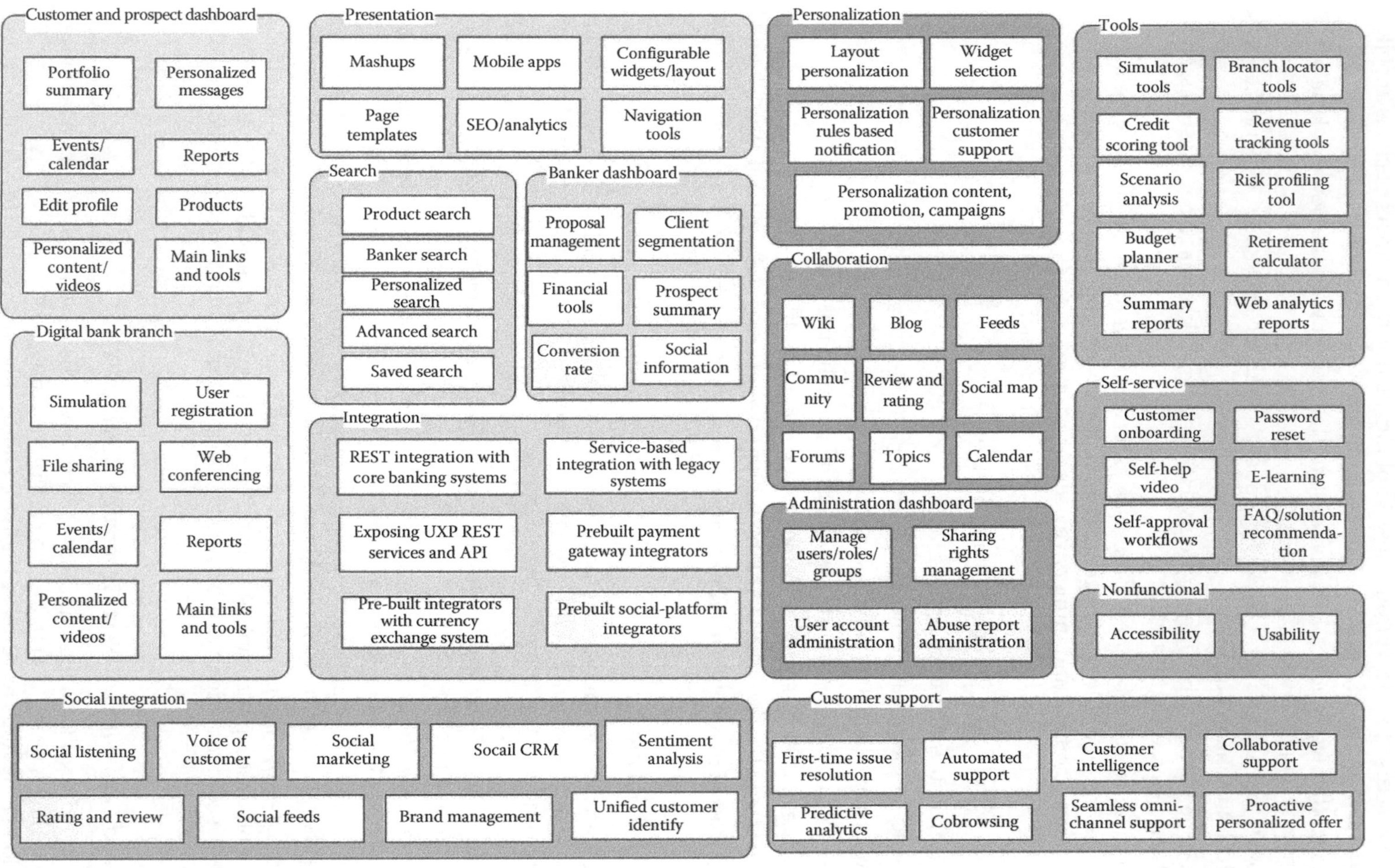

FIGURE 13.4
Banking UXP architecture.

Unified Dashboard View

The next-generation banking UXP provides a unified view of all information and activities through intuitive dashboard and visualizations. The dashboard will be personalized for each of the user personas. Customer and prospect dashboards can view the summary of their portfolio and products through intuitive visualizations such as summary reports, drill-down reports, and categorized reports. They can also see any scheduled events through a shared calendar in their dashboards. Personalized content and videos will be pushed to their dashboard by administrators based on their profile and financial activities.

A banker dashboard provides a single customer view through a summarized view of his/her prospects and customers categorized into various segments along with their holistic financial activities that can be used by the banker to recommend and propose new products. Bankers can also access financial tools for product recommendation, conversion rate calculation, production performance comparison, etc.

An administrator dashboard mainly consists of features to manage users, accounts, and user permissions and to moderate the user-generated content.

Flexible and Engaging User Experience

Highly intuitive and engaging presentation components will be built for banking UXP. This includes configurable widgets required for account and product information, personalized and customizable page layouts and page templates optimized for all channels, and services and mobile apps to cater to a wide variety of devices and user channels. Personalized rules-based push notifications and targeted content will be used to ensure customers get relevant content at the right place. Administrators and bankers will also use the social activities and spending patterns of the customer to provide personalized offers, coupons, and financial products. Context-aware mobile app will also push location-based branch information and any applicable discounts on transactions.

The UXP also contains several other interactive features such as configurable decision-making tools, client-side social map mashups, and intuitive and personalized navigation.

Search plays a key role in banking UXP by helping customer search for relevant content/policy/process information and applicable finance products. Customers can reach relevant bankers and products and can save the search results for future use.

Digital Bank Branch

This is one of the main features of a banking UXP that not only helps in active engagement with customers but also plays critical role in converting prospects into loyal customers. This feature is a virtual branch that provides most of the features that a customer can experience at a physical bank branch. Prospects and customers can register and sign up for services, do a web conferencing with screen sharing with the bankers of their choice to discuss the product proposals, evaluate products and proposals with decision-making tools, view the reports of their portfolio, share the files with bankers, and collaborate with customer support executives in real time.

This module of UXP helps in quickly on-boarding the customers and converts a prospect or leads into customers in quick time. For existing customers, digital bank branch provides a hypercollaborative platform to interact with bank executives virtually anytime anywhere.

Self-Service Features and Decision-Making Tools

The banking UXP is equipped with numerous self-service features to enable users to do the tasks faster, easier, and in an efficient manner. This includes features like self-registration, password reset, self-approvals in key workflows, e-learning, self-help videos, FAQ, and solution recommendations.

UXP also enables various user personas with relevant tools that help them in taking information-based decisions in real time. Tools such as financial returns simulation tools, scenario analysis tools, risk profiling tools, credit scoring tools, budget planning tool, and retirement calculator help customers and bankers to arrive at the most optimal decisions.

Web analytics plays a vital role in understanding user behavior and helps bankers and administrators to provide highly relevant and contextual product recommendations and offers to the prospect and customer.

Prebuilt Integrators and Services and API-Based Integration

A built-in integrator is one of the strong unique selling points of vertical UXPs. The banking UXP comes with built-in integrators such as payment system integrator, social platform integrator, and currency exchange integrator. In addition, UXP provides REST- and API-based integration for both exposing and consuming services.

Omni-Channel Collaboration

Customers, prospects, and bankers can collaborate through multiple features such as blog, wiki, chats, communities, forums, and topics. Customers can also leverage the social map and share calendar features.

Next-Generation Customer Support

Synchronized cross-channel insights into customer activities and customer intelligence that can be gathered through web analytics can be used for providing highly personalized customer support; collaborative customer support includes cobrowsing, web conferencing, and real-time chat. This helps in pitching for personalized and relevant proactive product offers and anticipatory customer support through predictive analytics. A collaborative solution knowledge base and personalized customer support help in a first-time issue resolution. Search and solution recommendation can be leveraged for automating the support.

Social Integration

Though financial applications traditionally rarely use social media, due to increasing influence of social platforms, banking UXPs rely heavily on social platforms to enhance user experience and effectively manage brand image.

Using prebuilt social integrators, a banking UXP has features such as social listening, sentiment analysis, and VOC to proactively identify customer complaints on social media platforms and address it before it impacts the brand image of the organization and the financial product.

A unified customer identity will be created by the UXP combining the profile within the banking application and the attributes obtained from the social platforms. This helps in further providing social media–based recommendations and mining further prospects.

TABLE 13.3

Banking UXP Touch Point Enhancements

Touch Point	Scenario before Banking UXP	Banking UXP Improvement
User registration process	Multistep registration that took about a week for completing registration	• Self-approval and three-step self-registration that completes registration in 1 day
Customer service	Reactive, disjoint customer support experience across multiple channels	• Cohesive and synchronized cross channel collaborative customer support to enhance first-time resolution • Anticipative customer support based on predictive analytics • Personalized product offers and recommendations based on analytics-driven insights
View of financial activities	Silos of application architecture	• Unified view of all user activities in dashboard view
	Users needing to navigate to multiple pages and applications to get information	• Intuitive visualization consisting of drill-down reports • Real-time customer insights through web analytics
Prospect, customer, and banker interaction	Unstructured interaction that often required prospects and customers to visit physical bank branches	• Digital bank branch platform that provides a virtual branch with all intuitive features where prospects and customers can collaborate with bankers • Hypercollaborative features such as blogs, wiki, chat, and knowledge base that increase information sharing
Online interactions	Transaction based	• Customer centric focusing mainly on long-term relationship enhancing
	Commoditized services	• Active engagement–based services

Touch Point Analysis for the Banking UXP

Let us look at the improvements for each of the user touch points in the next-generation banking UXP in Table 13.3.

Summary

- This chapter provides various aspects of designing a UXP.
- Planning an efficient UXP requires carefully evaluating usage scenarios, usability needs, key touch points, potential challenges, business process, customer support, collaboration, social touch points, etc.
- The main design principles of UXP include web-oriented model, standards-based platform, service-based integration design, context-aware components, configuration-driven components, and usability.

- A high-level strategy of an effective user experience includes empathize, experience enrichment, and active engagement.
- User experience mapping identifies all customer interactions (touch points) and areas where we can add value to user experience.
- The main steps in user experience mapping include inventory of touch points and experience mapping, experience impact analysis, and experience improvement plan.
- User touch point analysis identifies the areas of customer experience improvement and provides the details of improving the experience.
- User touch point analysis includes identifying cross channel touch points, analyzing user expectations across all channels, prioritizing and planning for touch point experience enhancement, and measuring, monitoring, and improving.
- The key UXP trends are rich, immersive, and inspiring content, highly optimized SEO, seamless and consistent user experience across multiple channels, customer listening, social customer engagement, touch and mobile enabled, and natural human interfaces.
- The design of a next-generation UXP is discussed. The main features and capabilities of the banking UXP included unified dashboard view for each user persona, flexible and engaging user experience, digital bank branch, self-service features and decision-making tools, prebuilt integrators and services and API-based integration, omni-channel collaboration and next-generation customer support, and social integration.

14

Portal User Experience and Omni-Channel Enablement

A user experience of a portal platform has a great influence on user adoption, retention, usage, and ultimate success of the portal site. An interactive, responsive, and multichannel-enabled platform is the key to achieve overall user satisfaction.

Front-end technologies are changing in a fast pace to keep up with user expectations. Since a portal is used as a presentation platform in a vast majority of cases, it should keep up with changing trends and disruptions happening in front-end and presentation technologies. A portal has to either provide built-in support for the latest technologies or provide easy integrations through plug-ins for supporting it. Aligning with latest UI trends makes the portal future-proof.

This chapter explores these aspects from various dimensions. We will look at the portal user interface (UI) architecture, latest UI and web technology trends, main challenges in UI layer, and UI best practices. Portal developers and user experience (UX) designers and UI developers would find this chapter useful.

Portal Responsive UI Architecture

One of the main focus areas of this chapter is to discuss the emerging trends in portal UI area. A responsive portal UI is a pre-dominant trend which is the key enabler for portal omni-channel and mobile first strategy. Let us first understand the main elements of a responsive UI architecture. The UI elements can be easily integrated into portal to support the responsive design.

The main elements of a responsive UI architecture within portal are shown in Figure 14.1. A responsive web design (RWD) provides fluid layout and UI elements to portal so that the user experience is optimized for all browser and mobile devices. An RWD can be implemented using standard technologies, and most of the portal products provide built-in support for RWD technologies. Let us look at each of these components:

- *Themes and skins*: Portal themes provide the headers and footers for all portal pages. A portal header is a centralized location to put the header menus, context menu, global search, user profile link, welcome message, and similar UI elements that need to be in the site header. A theme component also provides access to the user profile information to display the welcome message and place the minified cascading style sheet (CSS) file. A portal footer contains links to contact us, FAQ, copyright statement, expanded popular links, and minimal sitemap elements, and the footer JSP includes minified JavaScript libraries such as web analytics scripts

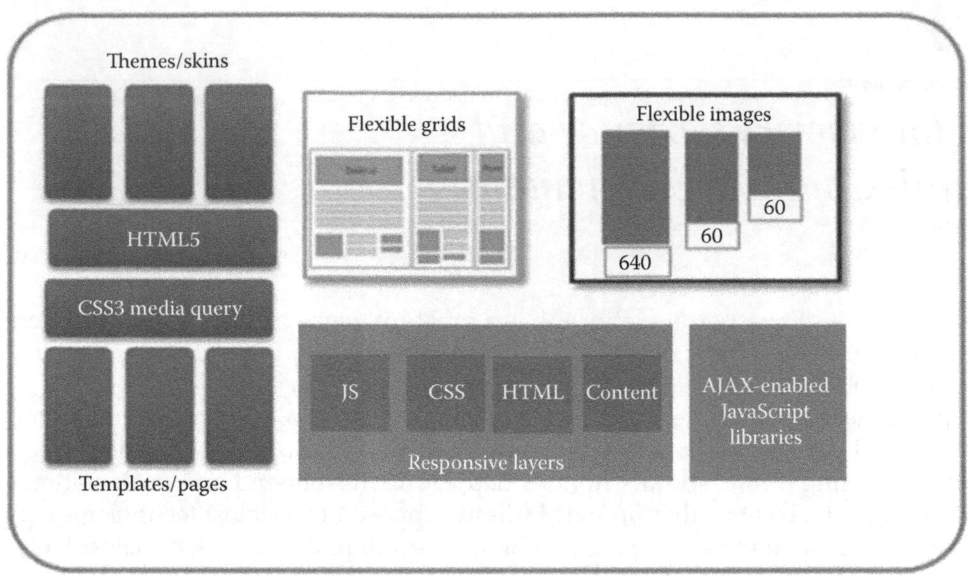

FIGURE 14.1
Portal responsive UI architecture.

and AJAX toolkit libraries. The theme serves the main function of presenting the consistent and uniform brand experience across the portal site. Organizations use a distinct theme for each of their brands sites. Users can also choose themes from the available set of themes. Portals provide built-in responsive themes such as "Responsive theme" or "Web 2.0 theme" that can be leveraged for building responsive portals. In some portals, themes also play a major role in rendering the navigation elements. A left navigation, breadcrumb are included as part of themes in some portal products. Portal provide policies and rules to administrators to configure variants of theme based on requirement.

- Skins are the presentation elements for the portlet. It contains the links to minimize, maximize, help text, and link to various portlet modes.
- *HTML 5*: This is the latest version of HTML standard that provides many built-in UI components and standards for rendering videos and other crucial components. It is one of the key elements of RWD.
- *CSS 3 Media query*: Another element of RWD that helps in creating a fluid layout that suits to multiple devices and user agents. CSS media queries provide device-specific styles based on aspect ratio, resolution, and orientation of target devices. Media queries in CSS are used to alter the layout at various breakpoints in the design. They allow the page to use different CSS style rules based on target device characteristics by feeding different CSSs.
- *Portal templates and pages*: Portal templates provide the reusable page layouts for rendering the portal pages. They specify the page layout and size for each of the page sections where we can configure portlet and navigation components. Portal also allows us to configure additional parameters such as user-friendly URL, search engine optimization (SEO) tags, web analytics tags, device and mobility rules, and theme configuration.

- *Responsive layers*: Using HTML 5 and CSS 3 and other technologies, we will create a responsive UI that has the following distinct advantages:
    - Provides omni-channel enablement through autoadjustment of layout
    - Provides clear separation of presentation, content, and device-specific styles
    - Helps in easier debugging and graceful functionality degradation
- Four layers form the responsive layers: JavaScript, CSS, HTML, and content. One of the main advantages of RWD is a clear separation of presentation logic from the actual content, which can be achieved through these layers. Here is how that separation of concerns works:

  The presentation logic mainly resides in HTML, CSS, and JavaScript (JS) components. HTML decides the page layout and high-level markup, CSS injects the style to the content, and JavaScript adds behavior to the content. This model provides a greater flexibility for us to reuse the same markup and content for a variety of devices with minimal code change.

  The content is obtained from AJAX calls, service calls, and server-side components in the *JSON* (JavaScript Object Notation) or XML format. The pure content will be transformed (usually through XSLT) so that it now contains the HTML markup elements and the required style definitions.

  This design not only provides us the flexibility to render on multiple devices but also provides high level of extensibility to add any new device without changes to the core content.
- *AJAX-enabled JavaScript libraries*: These are the technical components that enable the behavior changes to the content. Most of the JavaScript libraries such as jQuery, DOJO, AngularJS, and ExtJS also provide built-in UI elements such as panels and gird elements that can be readily configured for the solution needs.
- *Flexible images*: The flexible images are required for optimal rendition on various devices that have different screen resolutions and form factors.

Portal Omni-Channel Solution Tenets

An omni-channel portal should be designed to with following key solution tenets:

- *Multichannel capability*: Create and optimize web content for all channels and languages. Leverage portal platform features to launch and manage campaigns across geographies. Also, enable other required capabilities such as cross-channel collaboration, responsive user experience, multichannel work flows to provide seamless experience across all channels.
- *Contextualize the engagement*: Use in-built portal personalization engine to provide targeted content and personalized promotion. Content can be personalized based on user's device, location, purchase history, etc. Bring in relevant social conversations and listen to customer's opinion and interests across various channels to further customize the experience. Provide contextual self-help, decision aiding tools, collaboration support.

- *Multichannel user experience*: Optimize the end-user experience for all supported devices leveraging responsive and adaptive designs. Portal should provide single-view of customer journey through dashboard view.
- *Measure and improve*: Leverage cross-channel analytics, social analytics, multivariate testing, and other techniques to measure the success and continuously improve the user experience.

Trends in UI and Web Technologies

The main trends and forward-looking features noticed in portal UI technologies are as follows:

- *Mobile-first strategy*: Target mobile devices first is the critical element of this strategy. The focus on RWD enables the code to run on any device. Adaptive and device-agnostic content that provides a single code base running on any browser or device.
- *Interactive content strategy*: Easily accessible, fresh, and immersive content that provides a lot of interactiveness to the end user.
- *Intuitive information architecture*: This provides friendlier and easier navigation through a simple sitemap, helping the user to discover the relevant information quickly and easily. Expanded footer, fixed/static navigation elements, search-based information discovery, and one-click task processing widgets all help in creating an effective information architecture.
- *Flat and simple design*: A simple UI with easy-to-use and easy-to-navigate interfaces with minimal page hierarchy is another emerging trend.
- *Touch and natural UIs*: This is mainly due to the growing popularity of smart devices that allow the touch functionality and gesture-based interaction.

The main trends noticed in web technologies are as follows:

- *Single page applications* (SPA): Here, the entire site consists of single page with intuitive page navigations. The content for page sections is fetched on demand asynchronously. This is suitable for launching campaigns and information-heavy portals.
- *Hybrid and RWD-based applications*: These are gaining traction using standards such as HTML 5 and CSS 3. This follows the model of "write once, run anywhere" where there will be a single code base that will serve for all devices and browsers. Hybrid applications (sometimes referred to as "partial RWD") are a combination of RWD and functionalities to leverage native device features.
- *Lightweight and lean design*: Lightweight is seen in all aspects of web application: page size, JSON-based data exchange, asynchronous AJAX-based integration, lighter widgets, lighter integration, quicker deployment and smaller JS/CSS libraries are all part of the lightweight theme that the industry is adopting.
- *High scalability* expectations: Due to the proliferation of mobile devices and improved online access in developing economies, elastic scalability is a natural expectation. The web application should be able to support a sudden traffic spike without any functionality or performance degradation.

Challenges in Portal UX

The main challenges faced in the portal user experience are listed as follows:

- UX is a rapidly evolving field. Portal has to keep up the pace by supporting and integrating with the latest UI technologies.
- A multitude of devices with various form factors poses challenges in ensuring optimal user experience.
- A poorly implemented portal UX that has not adapted to the latest UI technologies poses business challenges such as poor end-user adoption, lesser conversion rates, decreased user traffic, poor transaction and process success rates, reduced user retention and loyalty, and reduced usability.
- Traditional portals come bundled with JS and CSS libraries that are sometimes "heavy" and this is not in-line with emerging UI trends.

Portal UX Strategy

The portal UX strategy should consider the following factors:

- *Market*: The market where the portal will be operating. Perform a competitive analysis to benchmark the solution stack, performance, security, scalability, and availability with the best-in-class products and solutions. Try to match the relevant parameters. Some business domains and markets, such as the retail industry, demand high-performance UX whereas some domains, such as the B2B domain, require robust integration and transaction management. Portal UX design should factor in all these factors.
- *Technology*: Portal UX should be flexible and adaptive so that it can be used on any browser and on any device. We should also continuously monitor the usage of the portal UX and its accessibility metrics and constantly watch the trends in UI space and adopt the relevant ones. All technology components should be standards compliant, which enables the site administrator to easily migrate and switch over to a different UI technology with minimal effort.
- *Target audience*: We need to clearly understand and profile the target audience. This includes the likes/interests/preferences of the end users so that we can design the interface accordingly. For instance, if the target audience is made up of social media savvy, then the portal UX should contain the best-in-class social and collaboration features that match or exceed the industry trends. User surveys, user feedback analysis, feature requests can be used to understand the target audience.

Portal UX Definition Process

Let us now have a deep dive into various activities involved in creating the overall user experience in portal.

The high-level steps are depicted in Figure 14.2:

- *Portal strategy and user design phase*: Sometimes referred to as envision phase or empathizing phase, the UX and portal architects engage with client stakeholders through interviews and workshops and conduct focused grouped discussions with other concerned teams. The objective is to understand the UI-related requirements, to understand the main business and technical drivers for the UX changes, and to analyze the current pain points to come up with an action plan to fill the gaps. During this phase, the UX architects and designers define the UX strategy, conduct user surveys, define the main user personas, perform usability evaluation, define key performance integrators (KPIs), model the user journey, and perform the industry and competitive benchmarking. The main deliverables from this phase are as follows:
  - UX requirements document covering all UI-related requirements such as use cases and persona. A sample persona definition table for an e-commerce domain is given in Table 14.1.
  - UX strategy document that includes multichannel UX strategy, market study, target audience analysis, UX roadmap, UX framework analysis, etc.
  - Usability gaps analysis document and identifying the problems faced by users based on logged defects and incidents. During this analysis, we will also identify opportunities to enhance usability and make the portal more easy to use. Few key usability enhancement scenarios in portal are
    - Displaying the top downloads, trending topics, most discussed topics, and top search results in a prominent place of the portal page
    - Providing access to saved search results
    - Providing relevant recommendations to user
    - Providing easier access to frequently asked questions
    - Providing automatic adjustment of UI based on user device
  - Displaying UI-related KPIs that are mapped to business objectives
  - Providing industry and competitive benchmarking against identified competition in the market and identification of desired features based on competition and industry best practices
- *Information architecture phase*: Information architecture establishes the navigation requirements in terms of task and information organization and is based on user persona analysis. In this phase, we define the main information architecture for the portal site, which includes the following:
  - Portal navigation model that details various navigational elements like header-menu navigation, left navigation, breadcrumb navigation, and quick links
  - Sitemap and site taxonomy showing the hierarchy of pages in the portal site
  - Navigation model, taxonomy, page flows for mobile devices

  The main deliverables from this phase are
  - Information architecture document that contains details about the navigation model
  - Sitemap document depicting the site hierarchy and menu structure

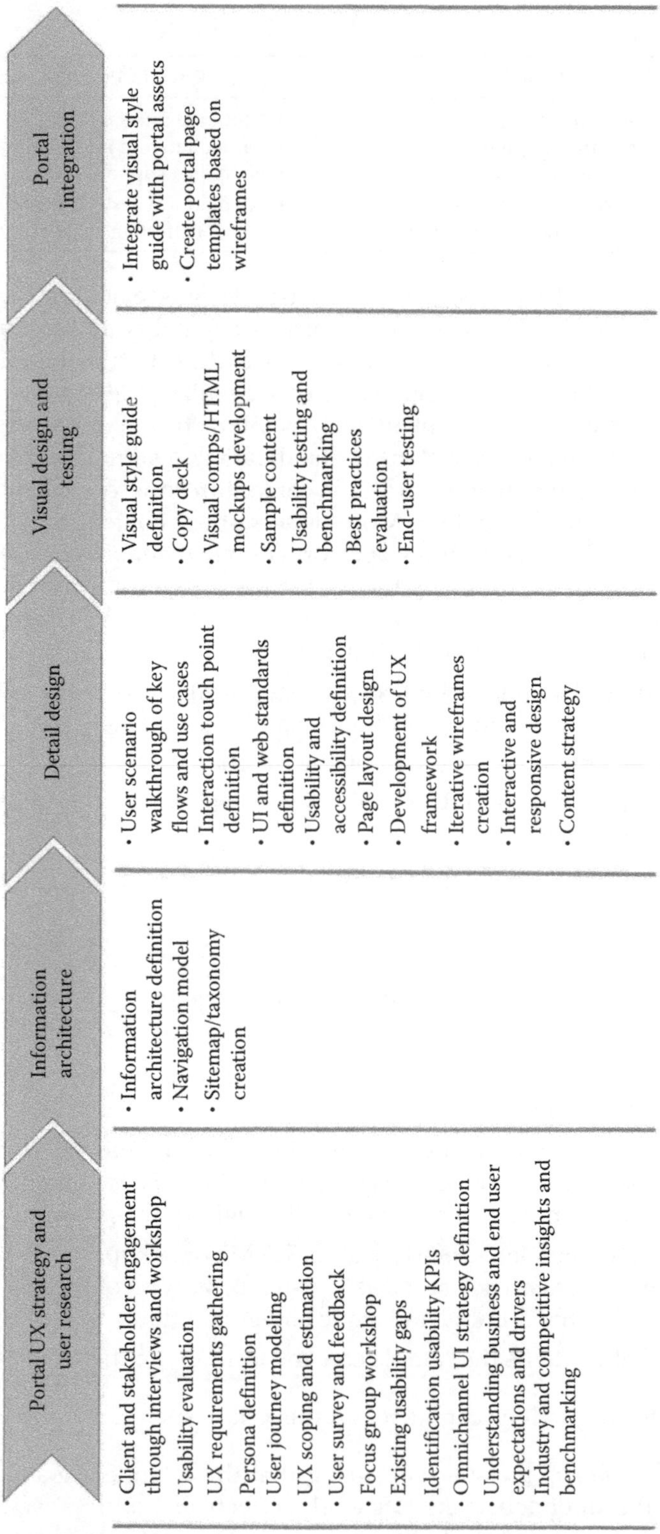

Portal UX strategy and user research	Information architecture	Detail design	Visual design and testing	Portal integration
• Client and stakeholder engagement through interviews and workshop • Usability evaluation • UX requirements gathering • Persona definition • User journey modeling • UX scoping and estimation • User survey and feedback • Focus group workshop • Existing usability gaps • Identification usability KPIs • Omnichannel UI strategy definition • Understanding business and end user expectations and drivers • Industry and competitive insights and benchmarking	• Information architecture definition • Navigation model • Sitemap/taxonomy creation	• User scenario walkthrough of key flows and use cases • Interaction touch point definition • UI and web standards definition • Usability and accessibility definition • Page layout design • Development of UX framework • Iterative wireframes creation • Interactive and responsive design • Content strategy	• Visual style guide definition • Copy deck • Visual comps/HTML mockups development • Sample content • Usability testing and benchmarking • Best practices evaluation • End-user testing	• Integrate visual style guide with portal assets • Create portal page templates based on wireframes

FIGURE 14.2
Portal UX definition process.

TABLE 14.1
User Personal Definition

Personal	User Scenario	Current Pain Points
Customer	• Find products. • Purchase products. • Log an incident.	• Cluttered interface • Difficult to find information • No online support
Support executive	• Resolve customer queries. • Document the solution.	• No platform to document the solution • Lack of effective collaboration tools

- *Detailed design phase*: In this phase, we will do user design–related activities such as defining UI and web standards, defining portal accessibility and usability guidelines, and selecting UI framework libraries. UX architects translate information captured from usability analysis and use cases to finalize UX Framework. The key activities in the UX strategy document such as interactive and responsive design will be detailed with elaborative steps in the detailed design document. We also define the content strategy that includes the content freshness, content placement, and visual elements in the content. More details about content strategy are discussed in Chapter 7. UX architects also perform detailed analysis of user scenarios to understand the ways to optimize the user experience in key user journeys. As a result of these analysis activities, the designers will create the wireframes iteratively. Wireframes serve the following purposes:
  - Provide an overall layout and all constituent elements such as navigation elements, header, footer elements, and portlets.
  - Provide placement and positioning of key functionality.
  - They aid in design of portal page design. Portal page layouts are modeled based on wireframes.

  The main deliverables from this phase are
  - UI design document
  - Wireframes
  - UI, accessibility, and web standards definition
  - Reusability analysis of UI artifacts
- *Visual design and testing phase*: This phase includes design and development of key artifacts such as the following:
  - *Visual style guide*: This includes specifications of UI elements such as fonts, color, size, image resolution, and page specifications. These specifications help in achieving uniformity and consistency throughout the portal page.
  - Visual design comps also referred to as HTML mockups provide the static presentation elements. They serve as a visual prototype of the UI design, and they also provide the dummy and static navigation flow.
  - Copy deck that contains the sample content adhering to the visual style guide.

Various kinds of UI testing will be conducted in this phase such as the following:

- *Usability testing from end users*: For ensuring that the intended users of a system can carry out the intended tasks efficiently, effectively, and satisfactorily. It is about carrying out experiments to find out specific information about the design.

The primary objective of usability testing is to assess the user experience of the application through user feedback, observations, and discover usability issues. Usability testing includes

- Standards compliance check
- Accessibility testing through tools
- Browser and device compatibility testing
- User feedback collection can be done through
  - User experience tracking and monitoring while performing the most frequent and important business transactions and processes
  - User perception tracking and monitoring about the design in terms of ease of use and navigation
  - User reviews and ratings collection

The key deliverables from this phase are as follows:

- Visual style guide and definition
- UI toolkit comprising of all required CSS and JS files
- Copy deck
- HTML mockups/front-end code/visual comps

- *Portal integration phase*: This is the final phase wherein we integrate the UI elements into the portal framework. Most portal products provide seamless and built-in support for the UI integration. The main integration touch points are given in the following:
  - *Portal themes*: As themes render the header and footer for all portal pages, we include the merged and minified version of master CSS and JS files in portal themes. Also, the navigation elements identified in the previous activities will be modeled in the themes.
  - *Portal page layouts*: These will be modeled based on agreed page wireframes and HTML mockups. Focus will be given to ensure reusability of the layouts.
  - *Portlet skins*: These contain the visual style guide elements related to each of the portlets.
  - Portal site hierarchy will be modeled based on reviewed sitemap and site taxonomy.

The main UI/UX deliverables are shown in Figure 14.3. This figure also shows how we develop the UI artifacts based on industry best practices and brand guidelines.

Implementing Mobile-First Strategy through Portal

Many consumer-facing websites are increasingly adopting the mobile-first approach that to their mobile audience for initial rollouts.

In this section, we will have a deep dive into mobile-first concepts. We will look at the key technology enablers and portal-based reference architecture for implementing this strategy.

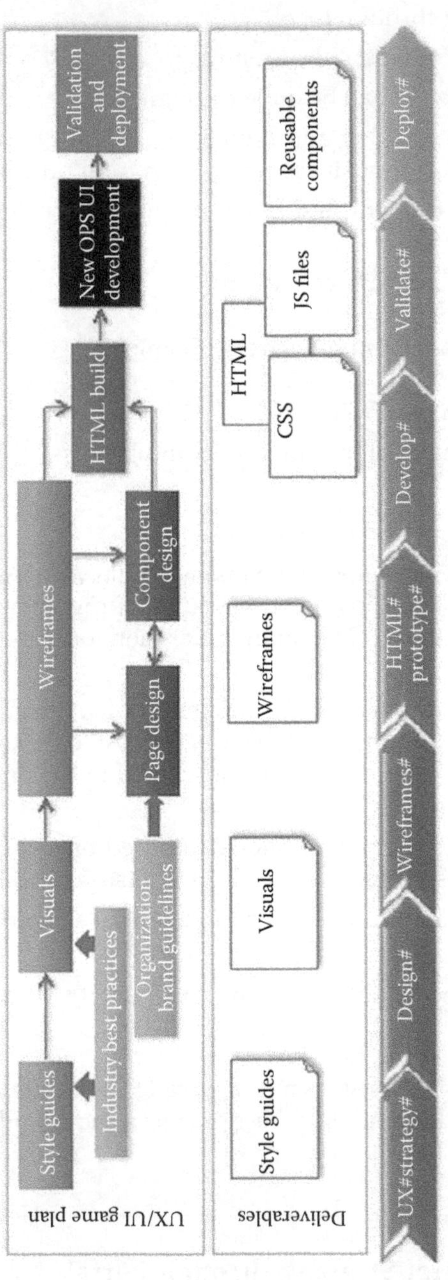

FIGURE 14.3
UI/UX deliverable.

Mobile Portal Design

Traditional portal applications were built for desktop browsers; screen size, number of portlets, page flows, and site taxonomy were all designed for desktop browsers in which mobile experience was playing a secondary role. A mobile experience was created by a dedicated mobile site based on the amount of mobile users. As the web is now increasingly being accessed through mobile channels, organizations are adopting the mobile-first strategy to primarily target the mobile devices.

Let us now look at the main design elements for implementing the mobile-first user experience.

A mobile portal can be built using multiple techniques: leveraging a portal's built-in mobile support and leveraging cutting-edge open-source and COTS frameworks by integrating with them or using mobile accelerator plug-ins. In general, there are mainly three options for creating a mobile experience:

- *Native mobile apps*: Here, we develop the mobile apps specific for a mobile OS such as Android and iOS. Native apps are built for a specific mobile platform using software development kit (SDK) provided by the platform vendor. These apps can efficiently utilize the OS-specific capability and are highly optimized for the OS platform.
- *Hybrid apps*: A hybrid application also runs on the device but is written with standards web technologies. A web-to-native abstraction layer enables access to device capabilities such as the accelerometer, camera, and local storage.
- *Mobile web application*: Mobile web applications are server-side apps built mainly using RWD and/or adaptive design. These render HTML that has been styled so that it renders well on all the devices.

The most popular option in portal context is to use RWD in a mobile web application, and the next best option is to go for hybrid apps. We are going to discuss sample reference architectures for these options in the next section.

The following design considerations are required for building mobile web application and hybrid mobile apps:

Adaptive design: This design enables a single code base to run on any device or browser. The user experience detects the target device and its capabilities and constraints and adapts itself to deliver the optimal experience for the target device. It heavily uses the progressive enhancement technique that we are going to discuss shortly and many other techniques such as media queries and CSS3. One adaptive technique involves creating predefined page layouts for popular mobile device specifications and using scripts to identify the device and using the most appropriate layout for the layout. Media queries will be designed for low-, medium-, and high-resolution mobile viewports, and adaptive images will be used. A sample media query for various resolution viewport is shown as follows:

```
/* Low resolution viewport */
@media (min-width: 321px) {
/* Styles for smartphones*/
}
/* Medium resolution viewport ----------- */
```

```
@media (min-width: 768px) {
/* Styles for tablets*/
}
/* High resolution viewport----------- */
@media (min-width: 1224 px) {
/* Styles for desktop and laptop*/
}
```

Technology enablers: The key technology enablers are HTML 5, CSS 3, and RWD, which help us in implementing standards-based mobile-first portal. It is always recommended to rely on industry standards to ease future extensibility and portability.

Lean and lightweight: The mobile portal should use lean architecture for the entire end-to-end processing chain. This includes leveraging lightweight widgets implemented using client-side technologies, using lightweight data exchange formats such as JSON, reducing number of HTTP requests by minimizing asset, reducing the size of JS/CSS files through minification process, using optimized and adaptive images, and adopting on-demand and lazy loading for assets.

Responsive design: This involves using HTML 5, CSS 3, and related technologies to create a user experience optimized for all mobile devices. We have already seen the details of an RWD in Figure 14.1.

Mobile business prioritization: During the requirement elaboration phase, we discussed about omni-channel strategy. This strategy involves the following key elements:

- Analysis of business-critical and user experience touch points with the application
- Identifying the key user journeys on mobile devices and optimizing the mobile-based flow for the same.
- User-centric focus and understanding the areas of frequent usage, user needs, user expectations, and ways to optimize their omni-channel experience on those areas
- Profiling the user segments and the target device segments who will be using this portal and using a device profile information to build the responsive design
- Building the mobile experience prototypes during the UI design phase
- Analyze the mobile limitations and devise graceful degradation or fallback mechanisms.

Perceived performance: Some of the points discussed before such as lean architecture, JavaScript-based mobile app development, and responsive and adaptive design all have one thing in common: they all help us to achieve optimal page performance on mobile devices. To improve the perceived mobile performance, we also need to use adaptive and optimized images.

Progressive enhancement: In this design, we deliver more and more styles progressively as the device size and/or the connection quality increases. For instance, we can start with basic content and graphics that contain the key message for basic mobile devices. Next, we add additional styling elements in CSS that beautify and add interaction features with portal. Based on device capabilities, we will also add highly interactive touch capabilities.

Mobile information architecture: This includes the information organization and page flow design optimized for mobile experience. Due to limited real estate and potentially challenging bandwidth issues, the mobile information architecture should be simple with minimal navigational depth. The key best practices in mobile information architecture are providing summarized view (to provide a high-level statistical summary of the data), simple dashboard view, tabbed view, etc. Each of them helps users to get the relevant information faster on the device and to complete the task quicker.

Device rules: Like discussed before, most of the portal products support mobile device rules wherein we can configure the rules based on mobile device specifications. These rules will be used for automatic device detection and can be used to request redirection to the configured mobile portal page template and other mobile-specific functionalities.

Mobile portal accelerators: Few more portal products provide mobile accelerators as product plug-ins. These accelerators provide a built-in support for mobile page layouts, mobile-optimized images, and other features. They also provide end-to-end supporting environment for mobile portal development such as IDE plug-ins, mobile portal management features, and deployment plug-ins to improve the productivity of the mobile portal development team.

Native mobile apps through portal mobile services: Few portals also provide presentation services and mobile SDK for developing native and hybrid mobile apps. Portal exposes the core functionality as service; this includes portlets as service, personalization rules as services, and other presentation services.

Mobile capabilities: The mobile-first experience can leverage the mobile-specific capabilities to provide immersive and interactive features in the web applications to actively engage the audience:

- Location information to push any location-specific notification such as sales deals, social connections, map information, etc.
- Multitouch feature to design touch friendly interfaces
- Browser acceleration for optimal media rendition
- Device-specific sensors and capabilities

Adapting to constraints: Mobile devices come with a lot of diversity: OS platforms, device-specific capabilities, mobile network variations, etc. All the constraints and challenges posed due to these variations need to be factored into the app design. The mobile experience should gracefully degrade if a specific feature is lacking in the target device or in the operating environment. Similarly, due to network issues, the data transfer rate should be minimal to guarantee optimal performance.

Mobile content strategy: Content strategy plays a crucial role in optimizing mobile experience. A generic thumb rule about mobile content is that we should add progressively more context to the content based on the available real estate. For instance, for a smartphone with 320px × 480px dimension rendering a news portal, we can just display the top five headlines in the "Featured news" section. The same news portal, when accessed from a 960px × 700px viewport, can render the top five headlines with a brief teaser abstract for each of the headlines. And when the portal is accessed from a tablet, we can provide a photo/video tagged with each headline and its extended summary. Mobile content strategy also focuses on showing the most relevant content; placing appropriate amount of content and visuals; increasing findability, understandability, and usability; and maintaining consistency in content format. The click-to-action buttons should be prominently placed and should be persuasive to increase conversion rate.

Quality Considerations in Mobile Portal

Let us look at some technology enablers to achieve the key quality criteria in a mobile portal solution in Table 14.2.

Sample Responsive Design–Based Reference Architecture for Mobile-First Strategy

We have seen three popular flavors of implementing the mobile-first strategy (i.e., native mobile app, hybrid app, and mobile web application portal). In this section, we will look at two sample architectures for mobile portal application and for hybrid application.

NOTE:

- As with any sample reference architecture, the technology components and framework are for information purposes only and do not recommend any particular technology or framework. The architecture provides a framework for desired capabilities.
- A particular architectural capability can be realized by numerous technology components and frameworks. We are not providing the exhaustive list of all those technologies and frameworks as it is beyond the scope of this book.

Mobile Portal Based on Responsive Design

We will see the lean portal architecture in Chapter 21. The mobile portal architecture borrows the same concepts and extends it by adding mobile features to it.

A sample mobile architecture based on RWD is depicted in Figure 14.4.

Let us look at the key components of this architecture and focus on the mobile-specific features.

TABLE 14.2

Mobile Portal Quality Considerations

Quality Consideration	Technology Enabler in Mobile Portal
Usability	• RWD based on HTML 5/CSS 3 can be leveraged to provide a highly interactive and usable mobile application. • Hybrid app can be built using portal services. A hybrid mobile app would further enhance usability by utilizing the device-specific features as well.
Maintainability	Solution should be built on HTML 5 standards that make it easy to maintain and extend.
Extensibility	In order to extend the features, third-party libraries such as PhoneGap or Sencha Touch can be leveraged to utilize the device capabilities.
Device diversity	Usage of RWD and HTML 5 standards can address various mobile devices.
Performance	Lightweight and lean portal design coupled with features such as on-demand and asynchronous loading would minimize the number and size of server request.
Interactiveness	Touch features can be enabled using third-party and hybrid mobile libraries. This would help us build highly interactive and immersive mobile portals.

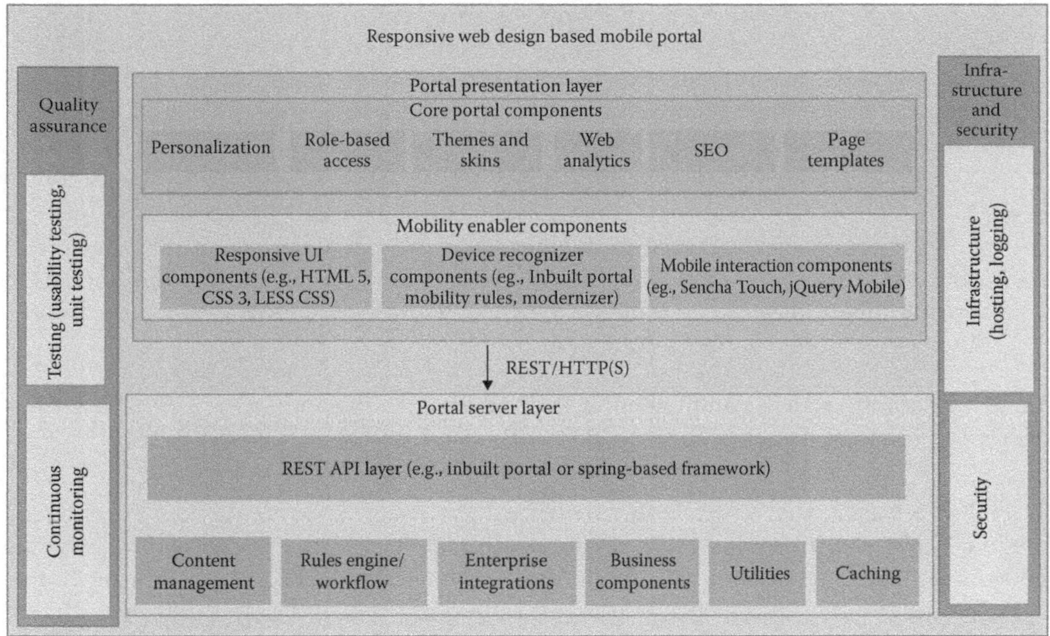

FIGURE 14.4
Mobile portal architecture.

Portal Presentation Layer

This layer contains the core components and mobile enabler components.

Core portal components include the following:

- *Personalization engine*: This provides a custom experience for the portal site on all devices based on user preferences and profile attributes.
- *Role-based access*: This enforces the fine-grained security by securing the access to pages and portlets based on user access privileges.
- *Themes and skins*: The Web 2.0 and responsive themes support the responsive libraries and also provide the navigation features. Skins provide the look and feel for individual portlets.
- *Portal page templates*: These provide a reusable layout structure for portal pages. Mobile-specific page layouts can also be designed.
- *SEO and web analytics*: These are implemented through SEO tags and keywords and web analytics scripts.

Mobility enabler components include the following:

- *Responsive UI components*: The RWD is implemented using standard HTML 5, CSS 3, and LESS CSS frameworks. The responsibility of these components is to provide a device-agnostic uniform user experience through the usage of media queries and other supporting features.
- *Device recognition components*: These components provide browser and device detection capabilities and abstract the developer from the underlying details. We can

leverage the portal built-in mobility/device group rules for this or use portal device recognition plug-ins or use third-party JavaScript libraries such as modernizer for this purpose. They provide seamless feature detection capability and handle the incompatibilities to provide a consistent functionality. In some scenarios, a mobile-specific portal page variant will be used for optimal mobile experience. Device rules route the requests to the appropriate template based on the requesting device.

- *Mobility interaction components*: These components provide the core mobile interaction features such as touch enablement and provide unified handling of both touch and mouse inputs. There are multiple external JavaScript libraries such as Sencha Touch and jQuery Mobile that can be leveraged for this. Some of these libraries also provide the UI components that can be optionally used.

Portal presentation layer components interact with the server through REST-based services and exchange data in a JSON or XML format.

Portal Server Layer

The main component on the server layer is the REST API layer, which can be built by using the built-in portal capability or using an open-source framework such as Spring framework. Presentation components use asynchronous REST model to communicate with portal server components.

The main portal server components include

- Content management that provides content services for update and retrieval of content
- Rules and workflow engine for modeling and executing business workflows
- Enterprise integration layer to communicate with all required portal interfaces
- Core business components that implement the business logic and functionality
- Utilities such as exception handlers, auditing, and encryption
- Caching services for performance optimization

Besides these two main layers, we also have an infrastructure layer that takes care of handling security and hosting.

Quality assurance components take care of conducting UI-related testing such as usability testing and unit testing to ensure delivery quality. Continuous monitoring is required to identify and address any production issues.

Portal-Based Hybrid Mobile App

Another flavor of the mobile portal is the development of hybrid mobile application. A hybrid mobile application tries to achieve the "best of both worlds" by providing a uniform programming interface to developers and also leveraging the native device-specific capabilities.

A revised version of earlier mobile web architecture can be used for implementing hybrid mobile application as depicted in Figure 14.5.

As we can see, the only difference between the hybrid applications is the presence of native bridge/wrapper component.

This native bridge provides the capability to access the device native features. This is the combination of the core mobile platform and JavaScript. There are many hybrid frameworks such as PhoneGap that can be leveraged for implementing this feature.

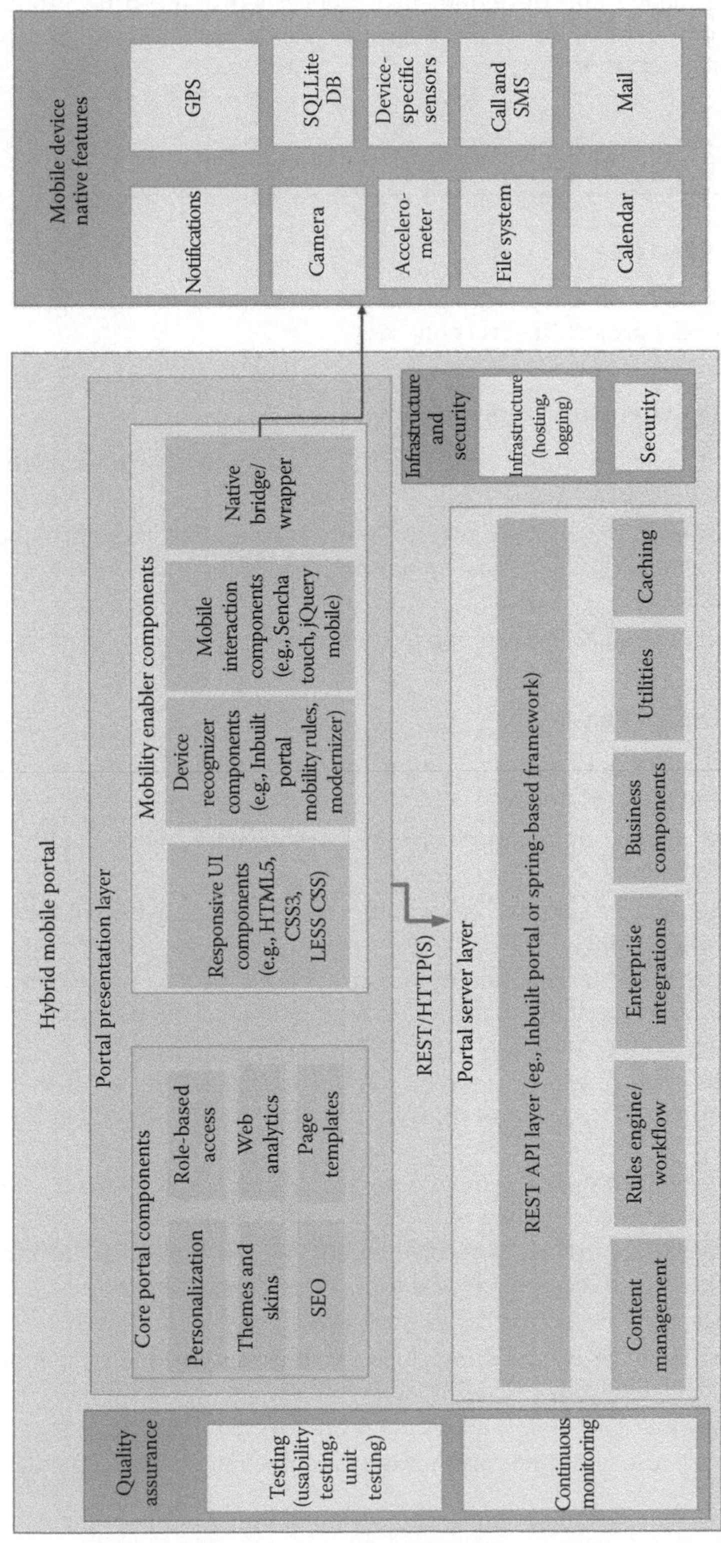

FIGURE 14.5
Hybrid mobile portal architecture.

As far as native mobile app development is concerned, few portal products expose mobile services and provide mobile SDK that can be leveraged to build the native mobile apps using the portal services.

Portal UX Best Practices

The key best practices in portal UX design are as follows. We have categorized the best practices for each of the project life cycle phases.

Best Practices in Requirements Elaboration Phase

- Engage with all relevant stakeholders early and often. Review the understanding and deliverables iteratively.
- Have early screen and prototype reviews with stakeholders to confirm the understanding of business functions and navigation model and to identify any potential usability issues.
- Clearly identify the UI KPIs that map to the business goals and objectives.

Best Practices in Design Phase

- Design the UI artifacts iteratively. For instance, first iteration contains low-fidelity wireframes and the next iteration contains high-fidelity wireframes.
- Always follow a user-centric approach while designing. Provide quality and consistent UI touch points.
- Keep the design simple yet interactive so that users can easily find out the relevant content and functionality.
- Involve end users and target audience in early iterations to solicit feedback about the user experience, navigation, and effectiveness of UI. This would be highly relevant when designing external facing portals.
- Keep up with emerging and popular trends in UI such as touch-enablement, single-page application, responsive and adaptive UI, RWD, and omni-channel enablement.
- Create separate wireframes for mobile devices and for web browser so that it is easy to understand the target user experience and navigation flow.
- Make an inventory list of all reusable components such as page layouts and JS component libraries that can be reused for further development.
- Ensure the following best practices in web accessibility are followed:
  - Provide text alternatives and image/video tags to make the page more accessible and readable from a screen reader software.
  - Provide keyboard accessible shortcuts for main functionality.
  - Provide easy-to-use, simple, and understandable interface and navigation.

- Test and ensure the compatibility of the solution on various browsers and on mobile devices.
- Develop web content accessibility guidelines (WCAG) for implementing accessibility, and test the end portal page with an accessibility tool.

Best Practices in Development and Testing Phase

- Establish the UI standards that will guide the developers while creating UI artifacts.
- Accessibility is one of the main concerns of the UI. Test and ensure that the UI implements WCAG accessibility guidelines and provides graceful degradation in functionality.
- Test UI validation separately from that of functional testing. This will create a laser-focus on UI elements and validations. Ensure UI-related testing activities such as A/B testing, user interactivity testing, and user perceived performance testing are conducted.
- Perform multidevice testing and geospecific performance testing to understand the user's perceived page performance and to ensure the web page works consistently on all devices and on all form factors.
- Leverage the UI testing tools such as Viewport Resizer, Responsinator, and performance analysis tools such as Google PageSpeed, Yahoo YSlow for testing.

Summary

- A portal UI architecture mainly includes responsive themes, templates, adaptive/responsive design, and responsive layers consisting of JS, CSS, HTML and content, flexible images, and supporting JavaScript libraries. HTML 5 and CSS 3 are key enablers for a responsive design.
- In the responsive layers, HTML provides markup, CSS injects the style, and JavaScripts injects the behavior. This provides a clean separation between content, presentation, and behavior aspects.
- The main trends in UI technologies are mobile-first strategy, interactive content strategy, intuitive information architecture, flat and simple design, and touch and natural UIs.
- The main trends in web applications are single-page applications, hybrid and RWD-based applications, lightweight and lean design, and high scalability expectations
- The main challenges in portal user experience are rapidly changing front-end technologies, multiple devices and form factors, and outdated portal presentation components.

- A portal UX process includes these steps: portal UX strategy definition, information architecture definition, detail design, visual design and UI testing, and portal integration.
- The portal UX strategy definition phase includes working with business stakeholders to elaborate UX requirements, user persona and journey modeling, identification of usability KPIs, and identifying any existing usability gaps.
- The information architecture definition phase defines the key navigation elements, search, and sitemap.
- The detail design phase includes defining UI, accessibility and web standards, page layout and template design, wireframe development, and UX framework development.
- The visual design phase includes defining visual style guide, developing visual comps, benchmarking, and usability testing.
- The portal integration phase includes integrating the UI elements within the portal platform.
- The main design considerations for a mobile portal are adaptive design, HTML 5/CSS 3-based responsive design, lean and lightweight architecture, mobile business prioritization, optimal perceived performance, progressive enhancement, mobile information architecture, device rules, mobile portal accelerators, native mobile apps through portal mobile services, mobile capabilities, constraints adaptation, and mobile content strategy.
- A sample architecture mobile portal architecture based on responsive design consists of mobile enabler components such as responsive UI and mobile interaction components using a service layer to asynchronously interact with server-side components is discussed in the chapter.
- For developing a hybrid mobile portal, we can leverage native bridge to use a device-specific functionality.

15

Portal Best Practices

Adopting the general rules of thumb and industry standard best practices and being aware of common pitfalls and antipatterns will always provide an edge to the developers and architects. They can identify the lead indicators of the failure and provide them an opportunity to fix the issues before the issues snowball into a major incident.

This proactive approach to quality also has additional benefit of productivity and quality improvement. Adopting best practices would create fewer defects and hence lesser time in defect fixing and testing. We have already looked at some of these best practices in various chapters within the context of that chapter such as integration, performance, security, and infrastructure. Here, we will look at a more comprehensive and overall list of best practices in portal.

In this chapter, we will explore various aspects of portal best practices, common pitfalls/antipatterns in portal programs, and ways to avoid them. We will also look at this topic that would be of high interest to portal developers and architects.

Common Pitfalls and Antipatterns in Portal Programs

We have noticed some commonly occurring pit falls in portal programs. We have categorized them based on the project life cycle phase of their occurrence.

Requirements Related

- *Incomplete requirements*: As portal caters to a wide variety of audience and provides a large set of functionality, requirements need to be elaborated from all the dimensions. Especially the nonfunctional requirements related to performance, security, and scalability should be defined unambiguously. In many portal programs functional requirements are not fully defined and nonfunctional requirements (such as performance, security, scalability) are ambiguously defined. This will lead to lot of gaps during later phases of the project.

Architecture Related

- *Misfit portal product*: It is important to carefully evaluate the business scenarios and use cases to ensure that the scenario warrants portal. We have given the details of assessing portal scenario in Chapter 3. Positioning portal for nonportal scenarios would result in cost overrun and expectation mismatch.
- *Absence of portal roadmap and success metrics*: Long-term portal strategy and roadmap should be properly defined along with key success metrics.

Project Management Related

- *Lack of portal adoption*: If the portal is not adopted by the end user community, it will ultimately fail to realize the intended business benefits. The user adoption failure could be due to various factors such as UX challenges, lack of proper communication, incorrect positioning of portal, lack of key features in portal, and not adopting user-centric approach.
- *Ambiguous ROI metrics*: If the proper portal key performance indicators (KPI) and success factors mapped to business objectives are not defined, then it would be challenging to quantify the benefits and ROI from portal program.
- *Lack of portal governance*: Absence of robust portal governance would result in issues on maintenance and cost overruns.

Infrastructure Related

- *Absence of disaster recovery infrastructure and business continuity processes*: This impacts the availability and business continuity in data center failures during unexpected natural disasters and during unexpected hardware failures.
- *Nonscalable portal applications due to insufficient hardware*: This impacts the portal from scaling during peak load and high demands.
- *Absence of real-time server health check monitoring infrastructure*: If the portal is designed for global audience, then the monitoring infrastructure should be devised to handle that as well using geo-specific monitoring tools.

Testing Related

- Absence of multidimensional testing and real-usage scenario testing.
- Security testing such as vulnerability assessment and penetration testing is often compromised or skipped.
- Absence of usability testing, performance testing, scalability testing, and omnichannel testing would lead to poor adoption and scalability challenges post production.

Portal Best Practices in Project Phases

In this section, we will look at various portal best practices that can be followed in project lifecycle stages:

Requirement Phase

- Ensure that we capture the requirements related to the following:
  - Geo-specific performance requirements and workload pattern
  - Expected load details including normal load and peak load
  - Performance metrics

- Metrics and requirements for nonfunctional requirements such as scalability, availability, and security
- Accessibility- and usability-related requirements
- Create a complete and detailed functional specifications with requirements traceability matrix

Architecture Phase

- *Appropriate fitment and positioning of portal product*: One of the most costly mistakes that can happen is to position the portal solution where it is not appropriate. This will create unnecessary expectations and ambiguous ROI and ultimately leads to the failure of the program. Use the techniques given in Chapter 3 to check if the business scenario needs the portal product.
- *Robust governance model*: Establish and define proper processes for portal activities such as release management, defect fixing, product patches and updates, and portal maintenance. The standard operating procedures help in the clear identification of roles and responsibilities and in the efficient execution of processes.
- *Self-service features*: As the desire for self-service is increasing in the business community, the portal architecture should comprehend this during architecture stages. The information architecture, collaboration platform, content strategy, portal search, user administration, and knowledge management should all aim toward achieving the self-help model wherein customer can complete the tasks and processes with minimal external help. Self-service features vary across business domains, the common ones are self approvals, customer payment services, password reset, product renewal service, and lead and referral generation for sales team.
- *Business enablement*: Portal architecture should enable the business community to use and configure the portal platform without any help from IT or maintenance team. The most commonly used business functions such as content workflows and campaign management should be business friendly.
- *Configurable portal components*: Portal components such as portlets, workflows, administration interfaces, and rules engine provide configuration features. The design should leverage this feature to reuse these components through those configurations instead of customization or extensions.
- *Robust caching strategy*: Cache is the primary enabler for achieving performance. In portal scenario, we need to devise the caching strategy for caching content for individual portlets and also devise appropriate cache invalidation procedures. The caching strategy should do a fine balance of performance and content freshness. Since portlets render fragments of content, we need to devise caching strategy around caching content fragment and the invalidation strategy for the same. The caching best practices mentioned in Chapter 18 should be adopted.
- *Layer-wise separation*: The portal framework should be based on the architecture pattern that provides layer-wise separation of responsibilities and concerns. The most popular pattern is the usage of model-view-controller (MVC) pattern, wherein the portal Java Server Pages (JSP) is the view, the portlet code is the model, and the portal servlet is the controller.
- *Multisite management*: In many scenarios where the portal needs to be rolled out globally, the user experience, business rules, business processes, and branding

would be based on the target geography. However, the underlying portlets and code base would be predominantly the same. For efficient code management and maintenance, we can leverage the built-in multisite management feature and virtual portal feature that allows us to create the variations (UX, URL, themes, locale, content) while using the same underlying portal code base.

- *Future readiness*: The portal platform should be architected based on forward-looking technologies and provide suitable extensions so that it will be easy to customize and extend the platform for future business needs. Front-end technologies undergo changes at rapid pace, and hence the portal platform should be able to switch or accommodate any new UI framework without much disruption. This would be possible through layered architecture and separation of presentation logic from content. Similarly, the portal platform needs to be integrated with internal enterprise systems and portal platform should support all necessary integration components.

Design Phase

- *Standards-based design*: The development and integration should be based on open standards. This includes Java Specification Request (JSR) standards for portlets, standards-based enterprise integration, standards-based content template design, and standards-based widgets. This avoids lock-in with proprietary technology, product and vendor and enhances interoperability, extensibility, and integration with diverse technologies.
- *Focus on reusability*: While designing portlets and libraries, the focus should be given to make them reusable in various scenarios. We can leverage the portlet configuration mode to enhance portlet reusability based on user preferences.
- *User-centric design*: The end user should be kept in mind when designing the UX, portal functionality, navigation, information architecture, content, search, and other processes.
- *Performance-based design*: Use performance guidelines in all lifecycle stages of the project. A sample portal performance checklist is given in the next section, which can be used for portlet development. Conduct iterative performance testing on incremental builds of the project.
- *Lightweight portlet design*: Make lightweight portlets by using client-side technologies and client-side aggregation.
- *Proof-of-concept-based design validation*: All complex portal integrations and other technically complex functionalities need to be validated using proof of concepts (PoCs). This will help us to accurately assess the feasibility and performance of those technical features.

Development Phase

- *Simplistic UX design*: Due to omni-channel access, it is important for the portal user interface and information architecture to be developed so that it is easy to use and easier to discover relevant information.
- *Portlet session*: Minimize the data stored in a portlet session. Use event-based model or interportlet communication to share data instead of using a portlet session.

- *Portlets per page*: Having too many portlets not only would clutter the portal page but also could also make the user interface complex. This could also have an impact on the performance. The general rule of thumb is to have it anywhere between four and six portlets on regular portal pages and still lesser portlets on home page and landing pages. Client-side aggregation and widgets should be leveraged to improve the performance.
- *Focus on automation*: We can leverage available open-source and commercial tools to automate the repeatable tasks during portlet development. Activities such as static code analysis, build, deployment, testing, release management, and monitoring can be automated using existing tools. Chapter 19 discusses the methods and corresponding tools in this regard.
- *Configuration-driven localization*: The portal should use resource bundles and configuration-driven approach to perform localization. Essentially, the core code artifacts such as portlet code and library code should be abstracted from localization changes.
- *Portlet user experience*: The portlet rendition should be tested on all target browsers and devices to ensure that the intended functionality works as expected. Usage of iframes should be avoided as they would impact the user experience.
- *Best practices and code checklist*: Portlet best practices and coding guidelines should be used during development, and it should be enforced through code analysis tools as a key gating criterion.

Integration Phase

- *Service-oriented architecture*: We need to leverage the rich services support given by portal technologies and employ it to the maximum extent while integrating with enterprise interfaces. This also helps us to achieve loose coupling and have a clear separation of concerns.
- *Lightweight services*: The focus should be to achieve integration based on lightweight services such as Representational State Transfer (REST) instead of SOAP (Simple Object Access Protocol).
- *Asynchronous invocation*: Use JSR 286 standard portlet and leverage the serveResource method to perform the server-side invocations asynchronously.

Testing Phase

- *Code coverage*: Portal testing should be aimed toward achieving at least 80% code coverage.
- *Continuous and iterative testing*: Testing should be done after each phase in iterative way.

Deployment Phase

- *Server configuration*: Portal server needs to be properly configured to ensure optimal performance, scalability, and throughput. This includes connection pool configuration, memory and cache configuration, and cluster settings. Most portal product vendors provide optimal server settings and benchmarking numbers which can be used.

Postdeployment Phase

- *Robust business continuity planning*: We need to have software and hardware designs to ensure continuous availability of the application. This includes eliminating all single point of failures, providing enough component redundancy, designing for proper scalability and availability testing of infrastructure components, and establishing a dedicated disaster recovery environment.
- *Continuous monitoring and notification infrastructure*: The postproduction deployment and portal application should be continuously monitored using real-time monitoring tools. This helps in the early detection of portal performance issues and production outages and in addressing them quickly. We also should develop the internal server monitoring infrastructure to keep a close watch on the portal server CPU and memory utilization.

Portal Checklist

We have seen high-level best practice guidelines that can be used as rule of thumb during various lifecycle stages of the portal project. In this section, let us go a level deeper to look into how the guidelines translate into specific portal coding checklist/gating criteria. This checklist can be used manually or it can be configured in existing IDEs/static code analyzers to enforce portal quality. Checklists are normally used as quality gating criteria before the code check-ins or during portal code reviews. Continuous integration tools such as Jenkins can be used to monitor the code quality based on these checklist criteria. The checklist details are given in Table 15.1.

Best Practices in Portal Security and Performance

The portal being an external facing web application needs to take utmost care to fix security vulnerabilities. It also has to handle various security scenarios such as role-based access, resource permission model, SSO, and enforce business-specific security policies.

Portal Security Best Practices

The main aspects of portal security are discussed in the Chapter 9. In Table 15.2 we will look at security-related best practices and guidelines.

TABLE 15.1
Portal Checklist Details

Best Practice Category	Portal Checklist Criteria
Layer-wise separation	• Review the portlet architecture to ensure that it follows MVC architecture. • Check if the modules in individual layers are strictly following the specific concerns. For instance, view modules such as portlet JSP should only address the presentation concern and should not execute any business rules.
Standards-based design	• Check if the portlets are based on JSR 168 and JSR 286 standards. • Check if the enterprise integration is using open standards such as REST or SOAP.
Configuration-driven localization	• Check if the portlets are using resource bundle for localizing the labels and other values. • Check if the relevant locale content is automatically picked up for the locale page. • Check if the portal URL accommodates variation for geo and locale variations and all other supporting components such as portlets, navigation components, search, and integrated services will automatically accommodate the locale variations. • Check if the content localization is handled through the content translation workflow. • Check if all supported locales are defined in the portlet deployment descriptor.
Optimized portlet packaging	• Check if common functions such as encryption, logging, file parsing, and service invocation are available as common external libraries to the portlet. • Group all portlets that connect to same back-end systems under one packaged application. This allows them to cache the connection details and configuration.
Appropriate usage of portlet preferences	• Check if the customizable configuration parameters are available as writable portlet preferences. • Check if the noncustomizable configuration parameters are available as read-only portlet preferences.
Optimal usage of portlet session	• Check if portlet session usage for sharing data is minimal. • Check if portlet JSPs are not creating any temporary portlet sessions. • Do not use portlet session for anonymous sessions. • Check if the key session configurations such as session time-out value and idle session time-out are optimally configured. The general rule of thumb is to set the session time-out value of 30 min.
Portlet view JSP best practices	• Check if the HTML elements and JavaScript names include portal namespace. • Use external JavaScripts for injecting behavior and external cascading style sheets (CSS) for injecting style instead of using inline styles and inline JavaScript code.
Automation and productivity improvement best practices	• Check if the portal development process leverages static code analysis tools such as PMD, CheckStyle, FindBugs, and SonarQube. These open-source tools can be included as part of build process and plugged into continuous integration tool so that the static code analysis can be automated. • Check if the portlet build and deployment process is automated through build and deployment scripts.
Portlet development	• Check if there are any local or instance variables used within portlet methods. Instance variables should be avoided to make the portlet methods thread safe. • Document the portlet classes, methods, variables, input/output, and flows. Follow Java naming conventions while naming methods and variables.
Testing	• Check if the WCAG accessibility standards and HTML standards and JS and CSS standards are adhered to using tools.

TABLE 15.2

Portal Security Best Practices

Security Vulnerability Category	Portlet Best Practice
SQL injection	• All portlet form input fields should enforce blacklist validations. • Portlets should preferably use container-based data source and ORM framework for database connection and ensure the usage of prepared statements instead of direct JDBC calls. • Most portal products provide built-in filters that will sanitize the input data through proper encoding. These filters should be leveraged to filter and encode malicious content.
HTTP request and cookie validation	• Leverage built-in portal-provided filters for validation. • Leverage open-source tools such as HTTP validation engines such as OWASP Stinger validation engine to enforce the HTTP request and cookie validation. • Preferably, personalization and user-related information should not be stored in cookies. If it is stored, the cookie should be encrypted and should be expired upon session logout/time-out.
Client-side validation	*Cross-site scripting* • Perform validation and encoding of special characters for all user-generated content (UGC). This is especially relevant for collaboration portlets such as blogs, wiki, chat, message boards, and communities. • Leverage both client-side and server-side validations to encode the special character. We can also use the open-source tools such as Spring Framework's HTMLUtil.escapeXML for avoiding XSS. • Use filters that remove or encode the malicious code when received from a user and when rendered to a portlet. • Portlet developers can also leverage AntiSamy libraries (https://www.owasp.org/index.php/Category:OWASP_AntiSamy_Project) for preventing XSS. • Additionally, web server modules such as mod_security of Apache server can also be configured for enhanced security. *Cross site request forgery* • These kinds of attacks exploit an existing user session to carry out attacks transparently through link clicks or image clicks. • Provide an additional layer of security for secure transactions such as password change and funds transfer. This includes reauthentication or two-factor authentication. • Use a unique exchange token that can only be authenticated by the portal server; the unique encrypted exchange token should be transmitted for every request. This eliminates unauthorized or duplicate requests.
Portal authentication and authorization	• Preferably, portal's a built-in log-in module should be leveraged or extended for authentication. • If the organization has a different authentication mechanism that is not provided by a portal, then we must extend the pluggable security model of the portal to perform authentication and authorization instead of custom coding. The portal's pluggable security module ensures that authentication and authorization is in compliance with all security standards. • A portal's built-in fine-grained access controls such as role-based resource access, permission model, and portlet-level security rules should be leveraged instead of building custom authorization modules.
CAPTCHA for user forms	• An external portal that provides user registration or form submission functionalities should preferably use CAPTCHA (Completely Automated Public Turing test to tell Computers and Humans Apart) to prevent automated form submission and bot-based attacks.

(Continued)

TABLE 15.2 (*Continued*)
Portal Security Best Practices

Security Vulnerability Category	Portlet Best Practice
Secure transport layer	• Use HTTPS-based communication for all portal pages containing personal and business confidential information.
Input validation	• As portal collaborative features include a lot of UGC and other portal forms, input fields need to be thoroughly validated for blacklist characters, reserved characters, and malicious content. We can employ client-/server-side validators and request validating filters for this activity.
Portal session management	• The session auto time-out and inactive time-out values need to be configured appropriately to have minimum possible values; this reduces the attack surface area. • Multiple portal sessions for a single user ID need to be avoided unless it is absolutely needed. • It is recommended to leverage portal session management feature for the generation of session IDs and session tokens as it provides optimal encryption and security.
Data exploitation and information disclosure	• Classify portal data into appropriate security category and enforce security policies for each type of data category. • All secure and confidential data should follow specified encryption standards and should be transported over secure transport layer such as HTTPS. • Proper logging and audit mechanisms along with good error handling features should minimize this vulnerability.

Security Best Practices Related to Server and Host Security

In addition to adhering to best practices for portal server, we also need to secure the underlying portal hardware and host systems. The following are the key best practices in this area:

- Antivirus software
  - Ensure that an antivirus software is installed on all portal servers and fully enabled.
  - An antivirus software should be regularly updated.
- Portal server hardening
  - Create a network deployment architecture to identify all interactions of portal production servers with other systems and enable only the required ports and protocols.
  - Remove or disable unnecessary services and software from portal production servers. Provide minimal resource permissions to production server users. Request should be granted only on needed basis with sufficient business justification.
  - Enable frequent vulnerability scan on the servers.
- Regular patch management
  - Periodically install the portal patches released and recommended by a portal product vendor.
  - Verify the impact of patch in preproduction before moving it to production.

- Firewall enablement
    - Enable the firewall to allow only the particular ports and protocols.
    - Allow filtered access to IP and TCP ports required for portal application.
    - Block the external access to portal production servers unless absolutely required.
- Host intrusion detection
    - Enable host intrusion detection system to monitor changes to portal configuration files and log files.
    - Monitor other events such as failed log-in attempts and buffer overflow.
- Logging of security events
    - Log all key security events such as remote logging, impersonation, number of failed log-in attempts, and terminal logging.

Portal Performance Best Practices

In a performance-based design, portal program needs to adopt these key performance-related guidelines:

- *Design and adoption of performance guidelines*: We have given the performance-related best practices in Table 15.3 that can be used as checklists or guidelines during portal development. This can be one of the review criteria during manual review. This avoids the potential performance issues at the source.
- *Early and iterative performance validation*: Performance testing should not be done at the final stages of testing; on the contrary, it should be done at very early stages of the development. During functional testing and integration testing, we need to test the performance aspects of the individual module as well as end-to-end calls.

TABLE 15.3

Portal Performance Best Practices

Performance Category	Portlet Best Practice
Portal page performance	• All JavaScript and CSS files used by portlets should be merged and minified. • The merged and minified JS and CSS files should be included in the portal themes so that it is accessible to all portal pages and portlets. Preferably, the minified JS files should be included in the footer JSP files and minified CSS file in the header JSP file that improves the perceived performance. • The images are optimized through number of techniques such as CSS sprites, on-demand loading, and CDN caching.
Service invocation	• All the portlets should preferably invoke external services through a centralized portal service layer. • A portal service layer should optimize the service invocations through caching and batching calls. • Lightweight RESTful services with JSON data format should be preferred over XML-based SOAP services.
Caching best practices	• Frequently access files and content should be stored in global cache that is accessible to all portlets. Suitable cache invalidation procedures should be designed to refresh the cache when the source data change.

- *Definition of performance metrics and KPIs*: During portal requirement elaboration phase, the performance metrics and KPIs should be clearly defined. The main performance metrics are response time, process/transaction completion time, geo-specific page load time, asset download time, etc.
- *Accurate infrastructure planning based on performance metrics and load requirements*: The portal hardware infrastructure should be thoroughly planned based on the performance metrics and load requirements. Most of the portal products provide benchmarking numbers and hardware specifications that can be leveraged for hardware planning. Portal product vendors also provide a questionnaire-based hardware sizing specification that can be used for accurate infrastructure planning. Once the infrastructure is set up, it should be tested to ensure that it scales up to the specified load by conducting tests such as peak load testing, stress testing, endurance testing, and performance testing.
- *Fine-tuning portal server performance*: Most portal servers provide best practice recommendations and configuration parameters for optimal performance. Parameters related to cluster configuration, JVM heap size, connection pool settings (minimum pool size, maximum pool size), thread pool settings, cache settings, and load balancing options need to be fine-tuned and configured based on product recommendations and based on the analysis from performance test.
- *Continuous performance monitoring*: We need to perform mainly two kinds of monitoring: external portal application monitoring and internal server health check monitoring. External monitoring includes real-time, cross geomonitoring of portal application that serves as early warning system for detecting any performance and outage issues. The monitoring infrastructure normally provides a way to configure the performance threshold values and notification mechanism. This helps us to reduce the availability issues. Similarly, portal log files and resources such as connection pool and thread pool should be monitored as well. Internal monitoring includes monitoring the health check of portal infrastructure such as CPU/memory utilization, network utilization, uptime of all portal services, and availability and performance of all enterprise interfaces. In case of any performance or availability issues, appropriate system administrators need to be notified.

Best Practices in Portal Program Management

We have seen the key best practices in Chapter 19. Given here is an extended list of the best practices:

- *No big bang approach*: More often than not, portal projects tend to get complex due to enterprise integrations and due to mix of multiple technologies. Additionally, the user and business expectations would need to be carefully managed. In order to address this, we need to adopt iterative or agile execution methodology wherein we can execute releases quickly and incorporate the feedback.
- *Continuous integration and dashboard monitoring*: Leverage continuous integration tool such as Jenkins and monitor the key project quality metrics through the dashboard.

We will look at other best practices of program management such as portal governance model, continuous integration, productivity improvement, continuous improvement, etc. in Chapter 19.

Tools and Frameworks for Ensuring High Quality

Some of the useful tools and frameworks that can be used for portal solution are given in Table 15.4. Most of the tools and frameworks given in the table are open source.

TABLE 15.4

Tools and Accelerators for Portal

Project Lifecycle Stage	Tool/Framework	Brief Description and Purpose
Portal development	CheckStyle (http://checkstyle.sourceforge.net/), PMD (http://pmd.sourceforge.net/), FindBugs (http://findbugs.sourceforge.net/), SonarQube (http://www.sonarqube.org/) Cobertura (http://cobertura.github.io/cobertura/) CVS (http://www.nongnu.org/cvs/), Git (http://git-scm.com/) Ant (http://ant.apache.org), Maven (http://maven.apache.org)	These open-source tools can be used for static code analysis of portal code base. Cobertura tool can be used for testing code coverage. CVS and Git open-source tools can be used for portal source control management. Ant and Maven are build tools which can be used for portal builds.
Portal testing	Apache Junit (http://junit.org/), TestNG (http://testng.org/) Selenium (http://www.seleniumhq.org/) SOAPUI (http://www.soapui.org/) Grinder (http://grinder.sourceforge.net/), Apache JMeter (http://jmeter.apache.org/)	Junit, TestNG open-source frameworks can be used for unit testing portlet code. Selenium tool can be used for automating the portal web testing and for executing browser compatibility testing. SOAPUI can be used for web services testing and debugging. Grinder and JMeter can be used for load testing and performance testing.
Portal release management	Jenkins CI (http://jenkins-ci.org/)	The open-source tool can be used for continuous build, integration, and deployment and as CI dashboard.
Portal debugging and performance assessment	JavaMelody (https://code.google.com/p/javamelody/), Spring Insight (http://static.springsource.com/projects/tc-server/6.0/devedition/cinintro.html), Memory Analyzer (http://www.eclipse.org/mat/)	These open-source tools provide insights into the performance of APIs, end-to-end transactions, database calls, service calls, etc., and help in analyzing the memory heaps, bottlenecks and performance issues.
Portal performance monitoring	Bucky (http://github.hubspot.com/bucky/), moskito (http://www.moskito.org/)	This tool can be used for performance monitoring.

Summary

- This chapter provides the common portal pitfalls and key portal best practices from all project lifecycle stages.
- The common pitfalls seen in portal projects are incomplete/ambiguous requirements, in appropriate portal positioning, absence of portal roadmap and success metrics, lack of portal adoption, ambiguous ROI metrics, lack of portal governance, absence of disaster recovery infrastructure and business continuity processes, nonscalable portal applications due to insufficient hardware, absence of real-time server health check monitoring infrastructure, absence of multidimensional testing, and lack of security testing.
- Requirement-phase portal best practices include complete elaboration of all NFR requirements and requirements related to accessibility and usability.
- Architecture-phase portal best practices include appropriate fitment and positioning of portal product, robust governance model, self-service features, business enablement, configurable portal components, robust caching strategy, layer-wise separation, multisite management, and future readiness.
- Design-phase portal best practices include standards-based design, focus on reusability, user-centric design, performance-based design, lightweight portlet design, and proof-of-concept-based design validation.
- Development-phase portal best practices include simplified UX, minimized portal session values, appropriate number of portlets per page, focus on automation, configuration-driven localization, optimized portlet user experience, best practices, and code checklist.
- Integration-phase portal best practices include service-oriented architecture, lightweight services, and asynchronous invocation.
- Testing-phase portal best practices include appropriate code coverage and continuous and iterative testing.
- Deployment-phase portal best practices include optimal server configuration, robust business continuity planning, continuous monitoring, and notification infrastructure.
- Portal security best practices include using best practice to avoid SQL injection, HTTP request and cookie validation, client-side validation, portal authentication and authorization, CAPTCHA for user forms, secure transport layer, input validation, portal session management, data exploitation, and information disclosure.
- Portal performance-related best practices include design and adoption of performance guidelines, early and iterative performance validation, definition of performance metrics and KPIs, accurate infrastructure planning, fine-tuning portal server performance, and continuous performance monitoring.

16

Portal Analytics, KPIs, and Localization

We have discussed the critical success factors, metrics, and to some extent key performance indicators (KPIs) to measure the success of portal solutions in the previous chapters. Since tracking the success metrics and constantly improving the portal experience are an important aspect of portal governance model, we will discuss these aspects in detail in this chapter. Analytics play an important role in tracking user behavior and portal effectiveness. KPIs are the portal success metrics that reflect the usage and return on investment (ROI) of portal strategy. Portal localization is required for globally deployed portals that cater to audience who expect portal available in their preferred language.

We will look at the various aspects of portal analytics, the KPIs, and what and how these metrics are measured in typical portal implementations. This chapter would be beneficial for analytics team, portal developers, portal architects and business community.

Portal Analytics Introduction

Analytics is used to get actionable insights. Portal analytics is all about collecting, processing, and reporting the portal usage data for the continuous improvement of the portal platform. Based on the purpose and domain of the portal, the exact tracking metrics may vary but the primary intent of the analytics strategy remains the same: continuously monitor and improve the business impact of the portal.

The key high-level objectives of portal analytics are as follows:

- Understand user actions such as click-through navigation, bounce rate, asset downloads, most accessed pages, frequently visited pages, and frequently accessed content. This helps in obtaining implicit feedback from customer actions.
- Understand the customer demographics, customer category, and the entire customer journey on the portal site.
- Understand portal performance parameters such as page load times across geographies, process and transaction completion time, asset download time, and availability time.
- Understand the client environment details such as accessing device, OS, browser version, geography, and screen resolution.
- Quantitatively measure the overall success parameters of the portal program and campaigns against the defined success metrics.

- Help the business and infrastructure team to plan for the demand and needs for the customer.
- Effectively help in continuously improving the portal platform to align with the customer needs and business goals.

Portal analytics provide the answers to questions such as the following:

How many people are viewing my campaign video on the portal home page?

Which asset is the most downloaded?

Is the portal page loading within 2 s in all geographies?

Do users use global header search or the search portlet most?

What is the percentage increase in the new user visits and registration last month?

How many people who visit the portal site first time end up buying the product?

Which is the most traversed navigation path in my portal site?

Overall the prime purpose of portal analytics is to gain insights into end-user behavior and portal usage metrics.

Types of Portal Analytics

There are mainly two types of web analytics:

1. Log file–based analytics
2. Page tagging–based analytics

Log File–Based Analytics

In this category, the portal's built-in analytics engine will intercept and log the portal usage information such as portal page access, portlet access, navigation portlet usage, and user interactions. These details will be recorded in the server-side log file. The log file will be read by the analytics engine for providing portal analytics report.

One main drawback in this approach is that the client-side actions and customer behavior that does not reach server will not be recorded. For instance, client-side component actions and user actions in JavaScript widgets that do not invoke server-side component will not get recorded in the server log files. As the portal is becoming more and more client centric and as widgets are increasingly get used, log file analysis may not yield complete analytics data. Also if any actions fetch the data from the cache, they will not be recorded as well.

Page Tagging–Based Analytics

In this case, the analytics data is collected through client-side JavaScript libraries by tagging the portal pages with the JavaScript include files. This provides the flexibility to track both page-level activities such as page load, site traffic, and user load and also page component–level activities such as link clicks, button clicks, menu changes, video access, and asset download statistics. The component-level events can be tracked by assigning and populating predefined JavaScript variable values and event values at runtime. The analytics statistics are sent to the web analytics server through an image request for further processing. The web analytics server then creates the report for business users.

TABLE 16.1

Log File Analysis vs. Page Tagging

Category	Log File Analysis	Page Tagging
Analytics technique	• Portal activities are logged in the server log file. • Analytics engine processes information from log files and creates report. • Primarily server-side activity.	• Portal pages are tagged with web analytics JavaScript. • User and portal activities are sent to web analytics server in real time. • Primarily client-side activity.
Analytics data	On enterprise servers.	On third-party web analytics servers.
Setup and configuration	Portal server–level configuration.	Mainly through JavaScript include files and JavaScript variable population.
Drawbacks	• Cannot track client-side activities. • Cannot track activities on cached data.	Cannot track if JavaScript is disabled. Analytics data are stored in third-party servers.

The main drawback in this method is that page tagging relies completely on JavaScript. If the user device/user agent does not support JavaScript or if JavaScript is restricted/disabled, then the page tagging would not work properly.

A high-level comparison of log file analysis with page tagging in Table 16.1.

Challenges in Establishing Portal Analytics

The following are the primary challenges in establishing robust web analytics for a portal:

1. Portal analytics has the potential to collect and track various portal events and user activities. We need to clearly understand the business objectives and KPIs and translate them into the web analytics metrics.
2. In some scenarios, setting up and configuring web analytics is disruptive and quite involved especially for page component–level tracking. For instance, to track a new button click, we may need to edit the page code or portlet code. This comes in the way of seamless operations of portal and poses maintenance overhead. To overcome this, we need to have a portal analytics framework that is extensible, nonintrusive, and configurable for accommodating new requirements.
3. The portal analytics scripts and variables need to be configured so that it creates minimal performance overhead on the portal page performance. The generally followed thumb rule is to include the web analytics JavaScript files at the end of the portal page (such as footer JSP in portal themes) to optimize the perceived page load time.

Portal Analytics Architecture

Most portal products provide in-built support for server-side log-based analytics tracking. Portal admin consoles provide the basic portal usage metrics and configurations to log the portal usage data to server-side log file. Page tag-based analytics is more widely used as it is more effective and provides more comprehensive analytics information than server-side logging. Let us look at the architecture of client-side portal analytics, which uses page-tagging technique. Though there are various web analytics software like Google Web analytics and Omniture, most of them require the same setup.

A high-level web analytics–portal architecture for page tagging–based analytics is shown in Figure 16.1.

As we can see, that portal analytics architecture consists of the following elements:

1. One-time setup activities that include embedding the web analytics code in portal pages. This normally involves including few JavaScript libraries at the end of the portal page
2. Runtime analytics activities that send the tracking information (such as page navigation, site traffic, and click path) to the web analytics server that processes the analytics data and presents the intuitive reports. This is achieved through tagging the portal elements such as portlets, forms, buttons, etc. with special tags and JavaScript variables understood by web analytics engine

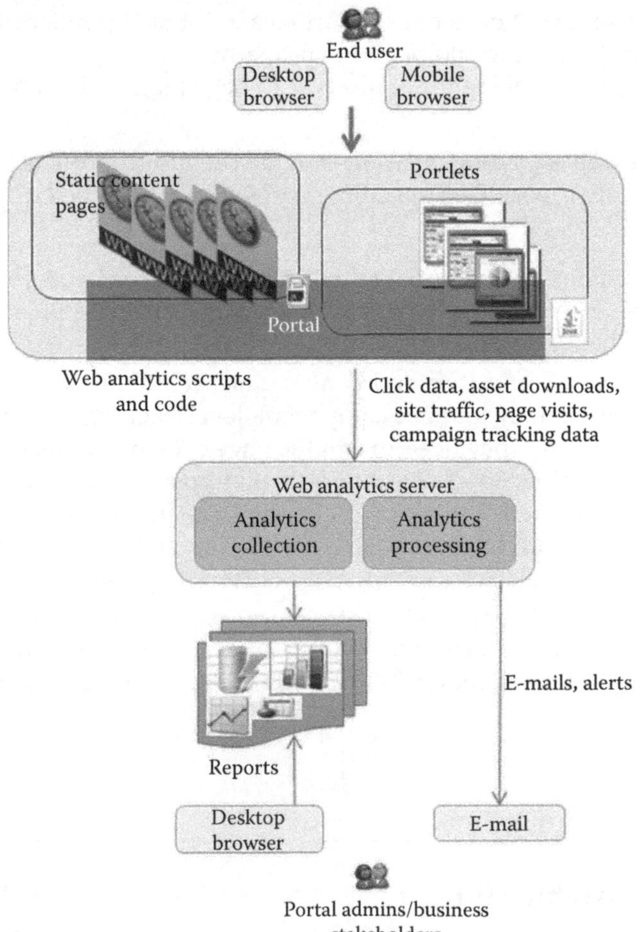

FIGURE 16.1
Portal tag-based web analytics architecture.

3. Analytics collection and processing activity will be done at web analytics server. Analyzed data will be generated into intuitive reports

One-Time Configuration Setup

Most of the web analytics software include the core JavaScript libraries hosted on web analytics server site. The following are high-level one-time setup steps:

1. *Page-level script setup*: The JavaScript code (which is main JavaScript files or a JavaScript snippet) needs to be placed in each page. In the portal, we can achieve this in portal theme that renders the header and footer for each of the portal pages. We can copy the code into the footer of portal theme. Some portal products provide dedicated placeholder element in portal pages for web analytics scripts.
2. *Presentation component–level setup*: The web analytics framework provides few specific JavaScript variables that need to be embedded within page components such as within portlets, buttons, links, images, videos, marquee flash files, and widgets. The value for these variables needs to be dynamically populated at runtime either from a server side or at a client side. For instance, a variable related to user-profile attribute can be populated from the server side, whereas a user click action variable can be populated from the client side.
3. Additionally, the portal admin also has to configure the reports in the web analytics site. Most web analytics software provide prebuilt reports (such as site traffic report, user flow report, Geo-specific report, etc.) that can be customized to meet the business needs.

Given here is an example for setting up Google Analytics web analytics with Liferay Portal. These concrete steps provide insights into the way web analytics is integrated into the portal:

NOTE: The following steps are applicable for Liferay Portal 6.2 EE.

Setup and Configuration of Google Analytics with Liferay Portal

- To start with, we need to sign up with Google Analytics service, which provides Google Analytics IDs.
- Liferay Portal provides built-in support for Google Analytics. This can be leveraged to configure the JS scripts required.
- Go to Control panel → Actions → Manage pages → Settings → Monitoring tab and input the Google Analytics ID.
- Add the Google Analytics code to Liferay Portal page. This includes adding the core Google Analytics JS files and configuring the Google Analytics ID for tracking the pages.

Tracking Page-Level Events with Google Analytics on Liferay Portal

After configuring the page-level web analytics scripts on the portal, we can track activities such as page visits and navigation. We can leverage this for top N page visits, mostly visited/used pages, pages per visit, bounce rate, page views, unique visitors, etc., in a portal application.

Runtime Web Analytics Flow

- At runtime, the web analytics framework collects the values that are populated statically and dynamically. These values will populate the web analytics JavaScript variable values.
- The JavaScript include files then create a web beacon or image request to pass the values to the web analytics server in real time.
- The invisible image is usually a 1 × 1 pixel dimension and request happens for each page load.
- The web analytics server software interprets the variable values and creates the dashboard reports to display the collected statistics that business can access in real time.

Let us look at the concrete steps for setting up a component-level analytics in Liferay Portal.

Tracking Component-Level Events with Google Analytics on Liferay Portal

In order to track the events within a page such as asset downloads, link clicks, and media access, we can define five components and associate it with events. The five categories include category, action, label, value, and implicit count. This can be used to track low-level event tracking.

The following is a sequence of steps for tracking the click of all download buttons on the home page:

1. Go to Manage → page → JavaScript for the page
2. Add the JavaScript code to track individual components such as buttons, links, images, videos etc. We normally use _gaq.push API to generate the event.
3. The analytics report will capture the details once the event has occurred.

Process to Identify Portal Analytics Metrics

We have seen that identifying the appropriate analytics metrics is key in making the effective usage of portal analytics. In the absence of such metrics, either we will be leaving out the business-critical transactions or we will be looking at wrong metrics. We will now see how to establish such tracking metrics.

The main steps involved in this process are given in Figure 16.2:

- *Business priorities*: We will identify the business objectives to measure in this stage. Each business has a list of strategic long-term goals and vision. We need to derive the key business objectives from those goals. For instance, if the business vision is to create a self-service portal platform, the business objectives would be to
  - Enhance user experience
  - Reduce support incidents
  - Improve customer satisfaction
  - Reduce process completion time

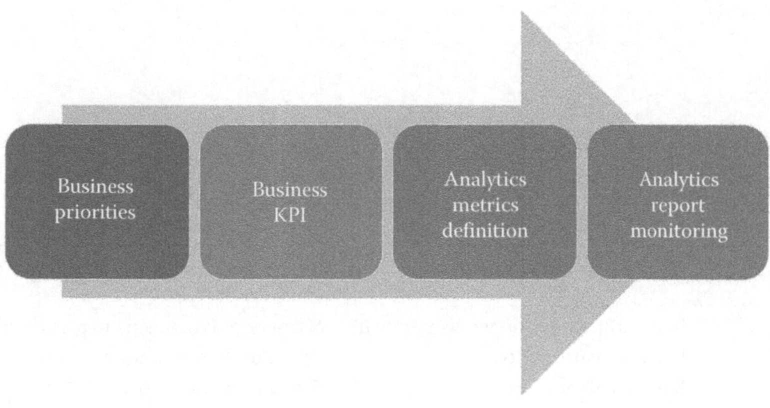

FIGURE 16.2
Establishing portal analytics metrics.

TABLE 16.2
Business Objectives: KPI Mapping

Business Objective	KPIs
Enhance user experience	Average time on site
	% increase in site traffic and new visitor rate
Reduce support incidents	% reduction in the volume of support tickets
	% reduction in the volume of support calls
Improve customer satisfaction	Average customer feedback rating
	Customer satisfaction index
Reduce process completion site	Average process and transaction completion time
	% reduction in process completion time

- *Business KPI*: In this stage we will identify how to measure the identified business objectives. Once we identify the main business objectives, we will then come up with KPIs, which are the markers to measure those objectives. Table 16.2 shows a sample mapping of business objectives to KPIs:
- *Analytics metrics definition*: The identified KPIs can then be mapped to the web analytics tool metrics. Each web analytics software has a way to track and measure the KPIs. We need to map the KPIs to the web analytics software–specific metrics and JavaScript variables. Once they are identified, they will be configured on the portal page.
- *Dashboard report monitoring*: Business stakeholders, portal administrators, and other concerned stakeholders can continuously monitor the web analytics metrics in the real time. They can use this to fine-tune the user experience and understand the effectiveness of their digital strategy.

Portal Key Performance Indicators

Let us now look at the KPIs that are used in portal programs in Table 16.3. These KPIs are compiled from portals built for various business domains.

TABLE 16.3
Portal KPIs

Category	KPI	Description
Business revenue impact	Conversion ratio	It is the ratio of the number of visitors to the number of sales.
	Site traffic and page views per visit	Number of page visits in a particular duration.
	Unique visitor ratio	Total number of unique visitors.
	Repeat visitor ratio	Total number of repeat visitors.
	% increase in user enrollment	Number of users registering to the site.
	ROI (Return on Investment)	It is the ratio of the net profit on a portal program to the total investment cost.
	Revenue per visit and revenue per order	The monetary value of each order.
Customer satisfaction impact	Customer satisfaction score	The explicit feedback score or rating given by a customer through customer surveys and other feedback channels.
	Average process and transaction completion time	Total time taken for completing a business process or transaction.
	Site abandonment/drop rate/exit rate	Number of visitors dropping in the middle of a process.
	Number of log-ins per week	Total number of log-ins per week.
	Time on portal site	Average amount of time spent on the site.
Self-service effectiveness	% reduction in customer support call, e-mail, and incident volume	Reduction in ticket/call volume.
	Average incident resolution time	Average time taken for complete resolution of the support ticket.
Collaboration impact	Number of chat sessions	Total number of chat sessions.
	Blog traffic	Total number of blogs authored and edited.
	Number of wiki articles accessed	Total number of wiki articles read, authored and edited.
	Number of user and product communities	Total number of communities.
	Perceived load time	Load time perceived by the end user.
Performance-related metrics	Page load time for each geography	Total HTML DOM load time.
	Asset load time	Time taken to download assets such as documents and images.
	Portal availability	Total availability time of portal platform per year.
Partner portal effectiveness	Earnings per click	It is the average earnings per click sent by partners to the main sales site. It helps partners understand the profit they would obtain by traffic routing to the main web site.
	Impression rate	It represents the total number of times a partner program is accessed.

Portal Localization

Localization involves customizing the user experience based on the specific needs related to the user's language, geography, country, etc. Various aspects of portal localization include the following:

- *Portal site localization*: This mainly includes customizing the following elements:
    - Look-and-feel customization such as the properties (e.g., size, color) of user interface, icons, dialog boxes, and UI component labels based on the user's geography
    - Layout customization such as page template changes, support for right-to-left layouts, and navigation changes
    - Site accessibility so that portal pages are easy to use for all users
    - URL changes based on country, geography, and language changes
    - Support for multibyte character set to support various languages
- *Controlled value localization*: In a few scenarios, we store the controlled list of values, such as country list, and restricted list of values, which also need to be localized. For this, the portal uses resource-bundle files that contain the translated values for each language.
- *Content localization*: For this, we normally use automated or manual translation and portal CMS will be integrated with translation management system. We have seen the details in Chapter 7.
- *Culture-specific attributes*: This category includes elements that are more impactful and meaningful based on the culture of the target audience:
    - Color combinations
    - Tone of error/warning messages
    - Localized audio messages
- Localization testing includes testing the localization aspects:
    - Usability testing needs to be tested by representatives/native speakers from that country and geography to catch any language or culture-specific issue.
    - *Multilanguage testing*: We need to test the portal site page layout, formatting, and other elements related to look and feel for all required languages.
    - Error message testing for all supported languages.
- *Regulatory compliance customization*: Different countries have various rules and regulations that portal platform needs to adhere to. There are some common portal scenarios:
    - Content archival period varies from county to country.
    - Accessibility standards are stricter in some countries.
    - There are regulations related to data storage locations. This is normally handled through rules engine integrated with a portal.
- Value formatting changes based on the language used:
    - Date formats
    - Currency values

- Unit of measure
- Time format

- *Integration support for localization*: Some of the commonly faced integration-related challenges for localization are as follows:
  - Few enterprise integrations use text-based values as flags, markers, for instance, using a string value as a flag to the service or function call. This will break during localization scenario where the string value will be localized. It is better to consider a language-independent or a static value as a flag for service or function calls.
  - Some enterprise interfaces do not support all languages required for portal; in such case, we need to design for the fallback to the master or default language. First-level and second-level fallback handling rules need to be designed.
  - *Character reading and file parsing challenges*: Custom-built file parsers (on the client side and server side) need to be designed for multibyte characters and all various encoding formats. Hence, these components need to be thoroughly tested with all languages.
  - *Content transformation issues*: The content transformation scripts and utilities need to be tested for all supported localized content types.
  - *Content editors*: The content editors need to support all required languages and formats.
- *Search support for localization*: The portal search engines should be tested for multilingual search and indexing to ensure that the search process is working consistently for all supported languages.
- *Ease of language addition*: The portal should be able to easily support and test addition of new languages without any code changes. This can be achieved by leveraging built-in language support and using resource-bundle-based configuration files for language-specific values.

Portal Localization Design Considerations

Given below are the main design considerations and best practices while designing the portal localization features:

- *Locale Independent User Interface*: All textual elements, such as status messages and GUI component labels, should be displayed in end-user's locale. This can be done by using the resource bundle keys as labels for UI elements and using the target locale-specific message at run time. Portlet labels and strings should also be fetched from resource bundles. Essentially all portlet view JSPs should be independent of the languages. This prevents the tight coupling of UI elements from localized labels.

We can leverage JavaServer Pages Standard Tag Library (JSTL) internationalization tags for localization. Locale specific resource bundles will be stored under WEB-INF/classes.

A sample code to declare the resource bundle and set the message key for "Submit" label is shown below:

```
<fmt:setBundle basename="nls.header"/>
<fmt:messagekey="submit"/>
```

Language specific resource bundles are stored as follows:

```
WEB-INF/classes/nls/message.properties
WEB-INF/classes/nls/message_en.properties
WEB-INF/classes/nls/message_ja.properties
```

- *Culturally Independent Data Format*: Data format, such as dates and currencies, should conform to the end user's region and language. Most of the UI date elements supports all variations of data formats such as locale specific date format, currency format, etc. This can be leveraged during localization.
- *Language Independent Data Storage and Processing*: Portal should be designed for storage and processing of data originating from different locales. Portal database schemas and portlet preferences should be designed for this.
- *Common portal codebase*: Portal code, libraries should not be changed for each locale. With the addition of localization data, the same portal code base should run globally. Multiple instances of the same codebase could be deployed depending on scalability requirements of the application.
- *Easy support for adding new language*: Most portals provide good support for adding new languages. They also provide in-built support for popular international languages.
- *Testable*: Portal solution should be easy to test its internationalization features with or without translated localization files.
- *Ease For localization*: Portal should reduce time, cost, and impact for localization.
- *Geo-specific business rules and flow*: In some cases local regulations require a customization to the existing business rules. Similarly, the page flow may different slightly to accommodate geo-specific variations. In such cases, portal should provide easily configurable interfaces and components to accommodate the changes. We normally use configurable rules engine and configuration-driven page flows to support such requirements.
- *Usability guidelines*: The usability requirements would vary across countries. For instance, the accessibility requirements are more stricter in few countries. For all the usability requirements, it is recommended to adhere to standards (such as WCAG accessibility standard) and test all locale-specific variations during testing.
- *Fallback handling*: Portal should use fallback language and resource bundle if the specified language or resource bundle is unavailable. For instance, portal can display English language labels instead of displaying a blank content when a locale is not defined.

Summary

- Portal analytics is all about collecting, processing, and reporting the portal usage data for the continuous improvement of the portal platform.
- The main aim of portal analytics is to understand the user actions, customer demographics, portal performance, and the client environment details and help in continuously improving the portal platform and measurement of portal success parameters.
- Portal analytics can be obtained from log file–based analytics and page tagging–based analytics.
- In log file–based analytics, the analytics engine will intercept and log the portal usage information such as portal page access, portlet access, navigation portlet usage, and user interactions.
- In page tagging–based analytics, the analytics data are collected through client-side JavaScript libraries by tagging the portal pages with the JavaScript include files.
- The main challenges in establishing portal analytics are creating accurate KPIs, intrusive methods of tracking, and performance impact.
- Page tagging–based portal analytics involves including the analytics scripts and JavaScript variables on portal pages and runtime tracking of user actions.
- The processes to identify appropriate portal analytics metrics include business priority identification, business KPI mapping, analytics metrics definition, and dashboard report monitoring.
- Portal localization involves customizing the user experience based on the specific needs related to the user's language, geography, country, etc.
- The various aspects of portal localization are portal site localization, controlled value localization, content localization, culture-specific attributes, localization testing, regulatory compliance customization, language-based value formatting, integration support for localization, search support for localization, and ease of language addition.

17

Portal Operations

A robust portal governance framework involves optimized portal operations. The main portal operations–related activities include build and release management, portal maintenance, incident handling, portal administration, and troubleshooting. Once the portal application is deployed to production environment, an efficient operations team with well-defined standard operating procedures backed by automated tools and robust governance can ensure smooth portal maintenance and high portal availability.

In this chapter, we look at the main operational elements related to portal programs. Portal administrators, project managers, and infrastructure team will find this chapter useful.

Portal Release Management

Portal production release management includes building and deploying all portal components to the production environment for the feature rollouts. It includes several checks to ensure a successful rollout in an optimized way. In this section, we have given typical activities that will be carried out in portal release management and a production readiness checklist that can be used for the production portal release.

Portal Release Activities

As a portal consists of lot of components from different layers, the release management tends to be complex and needs careful planning. Given in the following are the typical activities involved in portal release management. We have used Java-based portal server for explaining the release activities. Before the product release the portal functionality should be thoroughly tested and signed off in preproduction environment. We have given a detailed readiness checklist in the next section that can be used for the release management.

One-Time Setup Configurations and Activities

The activities given in the following are normally done one time during initial setup:

- Configure the application server that is running the portal. This includes configuring data source, memory, and heap size fine-tuning, JNDI setup, etc.
- Open-source utility libraries used by portal such as commons-beanutils.jar, commons-codec.jar, commons-collections.jar, commons-configuration.jar, commons-digester.jar, commons-lang.jar, commons-logging.jar, log4j.jar, Xbean.jar, etc. should be copied to appropriate library folders

- Configure the portal web server. This includes installing security agent/plugin, copying required portal images to the appropriate folders, setting up the redirection rules, setting up web server caching, etc.
- Execute these activities in Portal server:
  - Install theme and skins required for the application.
  - Configure all portal interfaces such as CMS, search engine, user registries, etc. and test the integrations.
  - Configure all portal users, roles, permissions, and access control policies.
  - Install any application-related plugins and extensions,
  - Configure the server-specific settings recommended by portal vendor.
- Install all custom data objects in production database.
- Install all content templates in the production content management system (CMS).
- Configure the content source and collections in the search engine.

Repeatable Activities

The activities given in the following are done for each of the releases:

- In clustered deployment, we usually perform a node-by-node rollout deployment wherein we deploy the code one node (starting with primary node) at a time and then synchronize all the nodes. So we need to isolate the node for deploying the latest code base.
- *Build activities*: Using build tools, build portlet war files, library JAR files, and configuration files from the source repository.
- Deploy portal pages on the production servers. In some portal servers, we can also promote the pages from preproduction to production environment.
- Deploy and install portlet war files through deployment scripts.
- Copy all the required web content and documents/assets from preproduction environment to production CMS. Activate all the web content and assets.
- Activate all pages and portlets.
- Restart portal server cluster.

Production Smoke Testing and Checkout

- Perform a smoke test of key pages, flows, and transactions to ensure all release functionalities are working as expected.

Portal Production Readiness Checklist

Since portal solutions involve many technical components and impacts many systems, we need to have a comprehensive checklist to ensure that all prerequisite actions are performed before production rollout. The checklist plays a crucial role in the smooth rollout in a quick time.

The checklist mainly consists of the following elements:

- Hardware:
  - Hardware specifications are given to support groups for resource allocation
  - The portal server hardware is hardened to meet security requirements
  - All required ports are enabled in portal production servers and protocols are enabled
- Portal performance:
  - Performance service level agreement (SLA) on portal performance is defined, tested, and communicated to the customers
  - Infrastructure and capacity planning and testing are done to meet the performance SLAs
  - All portal servers are configured and fine-tuned to meet the performance SLAs
- Portal Support:
  - Portal support governance is defined and appropriately staffed with clearly-defined roles and responsibilities
  - L1, L2, and L3 support teams are formed and equipped with appropriate resources
- Portal availability:
  - Availability SLAs are defined and communicated to all appropriate groups
  - The point of contacts are identified and staffed for round-the-clock support for all systems
  - Downtime handling procedures are defined
  - Communication procedures are defined for notifying in case of outage and scheduled maintenance
  - Ensure the disaster recovery (DR) environment is setup and all synchronization jobs between primary site and DR site is fully tested.
- Portal architecture:
  - Architecture review is complete and signed off
- Portal security:
  - Security review is complete
  - Security testing is complete; vulnerability assessment, penetration testing, ethical hacking, simulated injection attacks, etc. are all executed successfully
  - Production systems are tested for vulnerabilities and account access have been setup with appropriate privileges
- Portal testing:
  - Detailed testing report is available, which satisfies code coverage criteria
  - All specified types of testing such as functional, integration, multidevice, and performance testing, scalability testing, compatibility testing, endurance testing, UI testing, and load and stress testing are successfully completed and signed off by the testing team
  - Failure recovery testing is completed to ensure continuous portal availability
  - User acceptance and business testing is completed and signed off

- Documentation and training:
  - Appropriate amount of support documentation is available to aid the portal support
  - Documentation related to portal architecture, flow, environment setup, and configuration is available
  - Portal troubleshooting documentation is available
- Portal implementation plan:
  - Portal build and deployment scripts are ready and fully tested in preproduction environments
  - Steps to promote the portal from preproduction to production is fully documented
  - Post deployment smoke testing steps are available
  - Back out and contingency plan is available to handle release failure scenarios
  - All internal and external portal dependencies are fully documented
- Communication plan:
  - A detailed communication plan and a list of key stakeholders who need to be notified is ready
- Portal operations guide:
  - Detailed troubleshooting guide to help the portal support team is ready and the same is communicated to support team
  - All offline and online batch jobs are documented in detail
  - Backup and archival requirements are documented
  - Disaster recovery plan is in place
  - Remote and real-time continuous monitoring infrastructure and plan is ready and in place

Portal Administration

In this section, we will see the key portal administration activities. These activities are typically managed by user with admin or super admin role. Key portal administration activities include portal content management, portal roles management, portal workflow management, portal search management, portal infrastructure management, etc.

Portal Content Administration

One of the predominant portal admin activities is to manage the portal content. This includes setting up the templates; assigning author, reviewer, and publisher roles to appropriate users; setting up the content workflows; managing content archiving jobs; managing content metadata taxonomy and appropriate content categorization; and such content-related activities. If the application uses in-built portal CMS, then the native portal administration interface can be used to manage these admin activities. If the portal

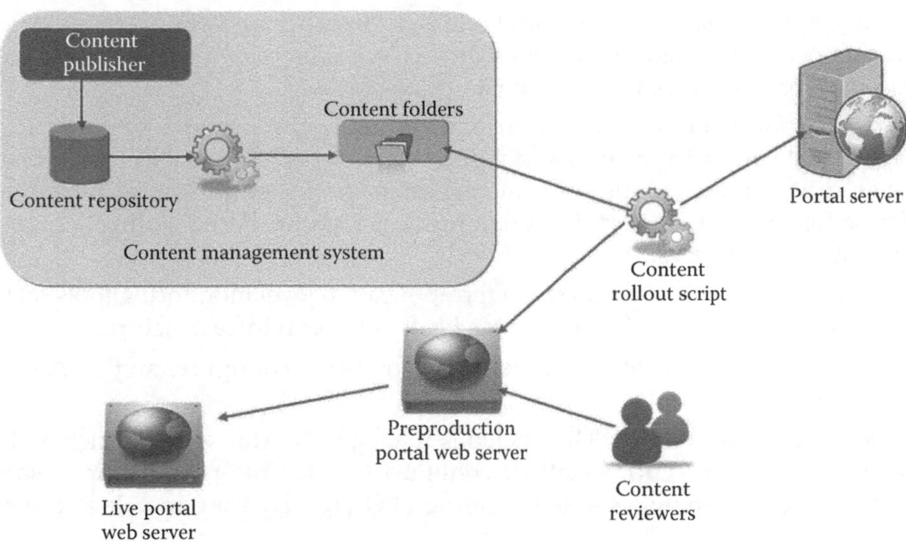

FIGURE 17.1
Portal content publishing workflow configuration.

is using an external CMS, then a custom admin interface has to be built or native admin interface has to be customized to manage the content.

Let us look at a content-publishing flow and the administration-related activities for this in Figure 17.1. For this example, we have considered portal integrated with external CMS. We will try to detail the activities of a portal administrator in detail through this example.

The portal administration interface will set up the content publishing workflow that basically invokes the content publisher module in the CMS to push the reviewed content to content folders. After this, it will invoke content rollout script that copies the content from content folders to preproduction web server. Content reviewers and marketing department will look at the content on preproduction environment and provide their approval. As a final step, the content will be moved to a live portal server. As we can see, this workflow has multiple steps that include invoking an automated rollout script and content approval step. This content publishing workflow is one of the main portal administration activities. Portal admin will configure the workflow, assign the approver, and execute the workflow steps manually in the case of exceptions. For instance, in the case of one-off content chunk publishing or emergency patch release, portal admin will manually invoke the content rollout script to directly push the content to live server.

Other Portal Administration Activities

Following are the other administrative activities related to portal:

- *Portal site administration*: This includes creating the site hierarchy, defining the taxonomy, creating and configuring portal pages, configuring portlets in the page, specifying search engine optimization (SEO) for the page, creating custom layouts for devices, assigning themes to the pages, etc.

- *Portal workflow administration*: Portal admins can setup and configure workflows that are primarily used for content management. They can also look at the workflows in progress and can start/stop any workflows.
- *Portal security*: User administration portlets allow the portal admins to set up users, create and assign roles and permissions to users, create security policies, create and map resource permissions, and manage user admin pages. Admins can also setup SSO within portal through header or cookie-based settings and other authentication policies.
- *Portal monitoring*: Admins can setup the application level monitoring tools on portal servers to continuously monitor the health of portal infrastructure.
- *Virtual portal management*: Portal admins can create, configure, and manage the virtual portals.
- *Portal settings management*: This includes managing portal settings such as URL mappings, friendly URL creation, configuring and fine-tuning portal server, configuring web analytics scripts, adding SEO tags, creating mobile and device rules, etc.
- *Portal search administration*: This includes configuring search sources and setting up search collections and indexes.
- *Portal plugin management*: This includes installing and configuring external plugins that are required for the portal.

Portal Postproduction Monitoring

We have seen in previous chapters that continuous and real-time portal monitoring is essential for maintaining the performance and availability SLAs and hence monitoring activity forms one of the main portal operations post production deployment. In this section, we will look at various aspects of portal monitoring.

Given below are various types of portal monitoring commonly employed:

- Internal monitoring of portal infrastructure to monitor the portal server and all dependent systems
- External monitoring of portal to monitor the deployed portal application in real time
- Portal application monitoring to monitor the portal application components and resources

Internal Monitoring of Portal Infrastructure

In this category, we will use tools or custom monitoring components to monitor the health check of portal servers and infrastructure components. The internal monitoring tool monitors the portal servers in this methodology:

- The main endpoints used by portals are configured in the internal monitoring tool. This includes the main portal URLs, service endpoints used by portal, external web applications URLs that are used by portlets, etc. Some systems such as portal database and lightweight directory access protocol (LDAP) may not have an exact endpoint that indicates its uptime and availability. In such cases, a separating monitoring mechanism will be devised for each of these systems.

- Internal portal monitoring tool polls the configured URLs in preconfigured frequency to check its availability and performance. Additionally, for the systems that do not have an endpoint, special scripts or commands that indicate their availability and performance will be executed. For instance,
  - A dummy query execution on portal database indicates its performance and availability
  - A dummy user profile query for LDAP to check for its availability and performance
- Scripts and commands will be designed to check for the uptime of network-attached storage (NAS) drives, network connectivity, and CMS and other dependent systems.
- For the URL endpoints, the HTTP response code/content of the response will be used to interpret its availability. Normally HTTP 200 response code within a pre-specified time will be considered as success and HTTP 404/HTTP 500 or a very slow response is considered as failure. Similarly, for other special commands there will be a predefined success and failure criteria: for instance, a successful query execution is considered as success factor for portal database availability.
- In the case of failure scenarios, a mail will be sent to the configured list of support personnel to take further action.
- The internal monitoring tools also should provide availability, performance, and health check reports and enable support teams to monitor the overall system health in a dashboard view.

External Monitoring of Portal Applications

This is sometimes referred to as "end-user monitoring" or "real user monitoring" wherein the portal application is monitored for performance perceived by end users. The external monitoring tool typically works as follows:

- The external monitoring tool has different nodes spread across the various geographies.
- The external monitoring tool provides admin interface where we can configure the node and the URL for each node. We can leverage this feature to configure the geospecific portal URL for each of the geo nodes. The admin interface can also be used to configure the failure threshold and performance SLA threshold values.
- The monitoring tool polls the portal URLs from the corresponding node in a predefined frequency. This ensures that a Geo-specific portal site is monitored by a monitoring agent in that corresponding geography to provide an accurate assessment of perceived response time.
- The tool sends notification in the case of server error like
  - 500 internal server error for portal application URL
  - If the response time is more than the configured time (e.g., if the response time is consistently greater than 6 s for configured portal URLs)

- If the page content size is less than the configured size (e.g., if the response content size is less than 100 bytes)
- If a document or asset download time is higher than the configured time (e.g., if the document consistently takes more than 20 s for download)

- Similar to the internal monitoring tool, dashboard reporting can be leveraged for real-time monitoring.

As portal applications are being deployed globally and as end-user experience is increasingly influenced by perceived performance, external monitoring tools play a crucial role in ensuring the high availability and performance of the portal application.

We can also leverage the external monitoring tools for simulating end-user testing scenarios and for geospecific load testing.

Portal Application Monitoring

Application monitoring provides a detailed view of portal application performance and helps in debugging and analyzing the issues. There are multiple ways in which the portal application monitoring can be done:

- Portal already provides in-built support for web analytics which can be leveraged for application monitoring as well. This serves the purpose of real-time end-user monitoring providing crucial metrics from end-user perspective.
- Another popular technique in application performance monitoring (APM) is leveraging code instrumentation. This helps in providing in-depth code-level performance report and call tracing support.
- Application monitoring agents installed on each of the portal servers can monitor the target servers and applications. This provides details on application and component availability and performance.

The main application monitoring metrics are as follows:

- Portal page metrics:
  - Page availability
  - Active portal sessions
  - Page response time
  - Asset download time
  - Page throughput
- Portlet metrics:
  - Portlet response time
- Server metrics:
  - CPU usage
  - Heap/Memory usage
  - Garbage collection rate
  - Active threads
  - Active database sessions

Portal Support and Maintenance

Support and periodic maintenance are ongoing activities in portal lifecycle. In this section, we will look at the key activities and best practices in this area. The main activities in portal support and maintenance are as follows:

The main aspects of portal support and maintenance are shown in Figure 17.2. It primarily includes the following:

- *Release management*: Portal releases and deployment is one of the main activities of the portal support team. It includes deploying major/minor releases, ad hoc and one-off patches, and any defect fix releases. We have given a production readiness checklist in the previous section that can be used as a guideline for portal releases. We need to explore all possible opportunities for automation of release and deployment activities. Build and deployment scripts and continuous integration tools can be leveraged for achieving automation in portal release.
- *Change management*: Managing changes include analyzing the change request details, doing impact analysis, and deploying the change. Change management process is detailed in Chapter 19. Normally a change control board (CCB) is responsible for managing and deploying all the changes. Portal operations team works closely with CCB in deploying the changes to production environment.
- *Availability and performance monitoring*: We have seen various ways to monitor the availability and performance of the portal application. A dashboard view tracking main performance and availability metrics is maintained by portal support team to regularly check the metrics and take appropriate action. Portal support team will also be notified by monitoring agents in case of SLA violations.
- *Infrastructure management*: This includes regular health check monitoring of resource utilization and the health check of the portal infrastructure. Based on the resource utilization, application growth and usage patterns, the capacity of infrastructure components needs to be fine-tuned for optimal scalability and load handling.
- *Configuration management*: The portal server settings and other configuration parameters will be fine-tuned based on the inputs from server and application monitoring tools. Vendor recommended product and application patches will be applied on regular basis for the optimal performance of portal server.
- *Incident management*: Another important responsibility of the portal operations team is to handle production incidents related to production outage, performance issues, etc. The best practice is to creating a standard operating procedure (SOP) to handle the incidents based on its criticality. We have described a detailed incident management process in the coming sections.
- *Continuous improvement*: One of the key to operations efficiency is to have a framework for continuous improvement. Gradual and iterative improvement in productivity, quality, turnover time, incident volume reduction, and creation of knowledge base are some of the attributes of continuous improvement. We will look at these in greater detail in the following sections.

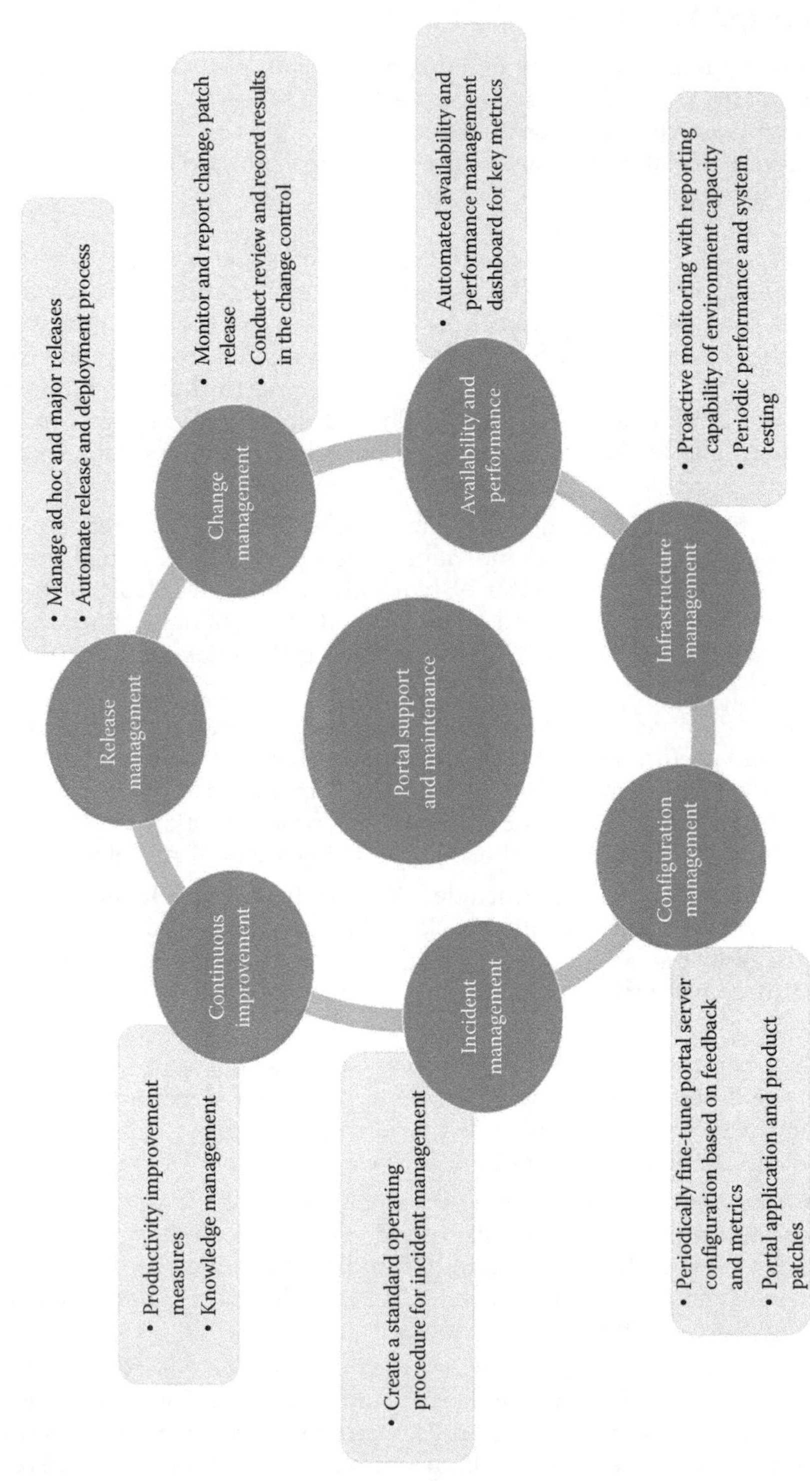

FIGURE 17.2
Portal support and maintenance activities.

Portal Operations Best Practices

Let us look at some of the effective and time-proven best practices that can increase efficiency in portal operations in Table 17.1.

Portal Maintenance Dashboard

Portal support and maintenance team will greatly benefit from a dashboard that provides the information about key metrics, KPIs, and monitoring data. It provides a high-level view of overall health of portal application. The dashboard mainly consists of four views related to portal incident metrics, portal infrastructure metrics, portal monitoring metrics, and proactive maintenance metrics as shown in Figure 17.3.

TABLE 17.1

Portal Operations Best Practices

Portal Operations Best Practice	Key Benefits
Proactive maintenance	
• Perform root cause and trend analysis for high priority production incidents and proactively improve the code quality in modules that have higher defect density	• Reduces number of production issues • Reduces maintenance cost and overall cost
• Employ static code analysis tools to improve the code quality during development stage	• Improves code quality and reliability
• Engage portal development team to add self-help features such as context sensitive help, improved navigation, and improved search	• Improve portal performance
• Analyze web analytics report and send feedback to the development team to fix any identified perceived performance issues, navigation problems, and issues with information discovery	
• Engage portal development team to add collaboration and self-service features such as chat and knowledge-based search	
Automation of frequently executed activities	
Automate operation activities such as code deployment; health-check monitoring; application patching; notification; build, deployment, reporting, and release activities; and other frequently executed tasks	• Improves turnover time and quality • Improves productivity
Development of standard operating procedures and process standardization	
• For all maintenance activities we can develop a SOP that details step-by-step execution details of the activity. Scenarios like portal cluster restart, incident handling, code deployment, and cache clearance are ideal candidates for which SOP can be defined	• Provides consistent response to an incident
• A standard and optimized support process needs to be established to handle portal production incidents	• Helps the nontechnical and support staff to perform the task easily
Efficient knowledge management for support activities	
Create a dedicated knowledge base for support and operations that contains the best practices, SOP, solutions, templates, checklists, policy, and process details based on past experience	• Enables the portal support and operations team to leverage the previous learnings and best practices • Increases productivity of support and operations team • Faster turnover time • Enables self-service model

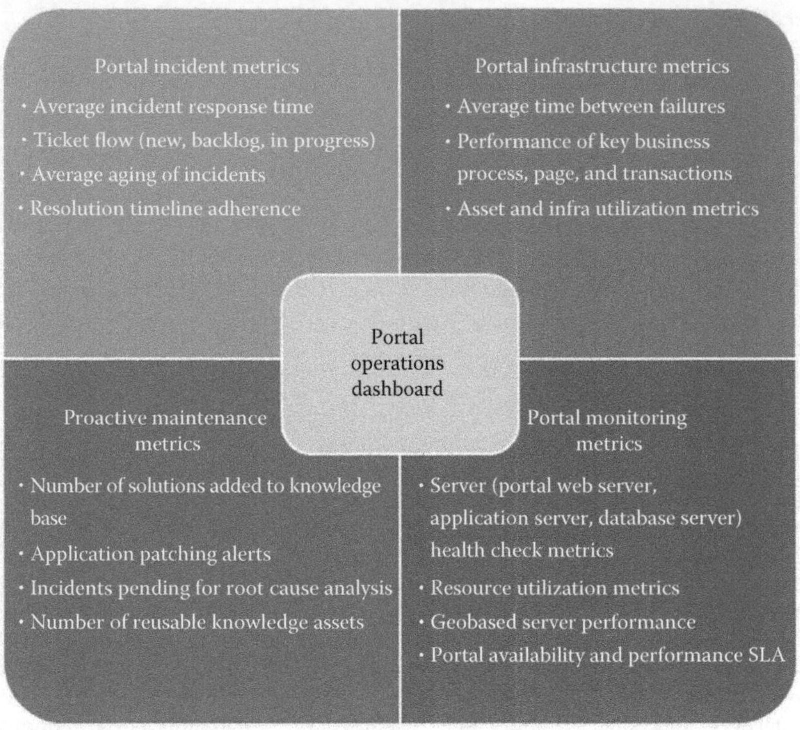

FIGURE 17.3
Portal operations dashboard view.

The metrics tracked in each of the four categories is given in the above diagram.

Continuous Improvement Process

The key continuous improvement measures and best practices are described in Chapter 15. In Table 17.2, we will focus on portal support and operations-specific continuous improvement measures.

Productivity Improvement Measures

Some of the continuous improvement initiatives we discussed earlier also contribute significantly to the productivity improvement:

- Reusable solution artifacts will improve the incident first-response time and overall issue-resolution time.
- Automation of key support activities leveraging tools and accelerators reduce the overall manual effort and, hence, the turnaround time.
- Knowledge base to store the reusable artifacts and the structured knowledge would reduce dependency on subject matter experts (SMEs) and enables support teams to reduce the turnaround time drastically. It creates a robust and scalable support framework that helps in self-service and improves service metrics. It also serves as a collaborative tool among support community to share the knowledge and increases the accuracy of the solution response.

TABLE 17.2

Portal Continuous Improvement Measures

Portal Continuous Improvement Initiative	Details
Root-cause analysis	For each incident logged and for each production outage happened on portal site, the support team needs to do a thorough root-cause analysis. This helps us to identify the problematic code areas and modules upon which we can proactively act and address any potential issues. We can reduce the incident volume and call volume through analysis of logged incident and defect patterns and proactively address the problem areas. Special care should be given to root-cause analysis of frequently occurring and high-priority issues.
Self-service initiatives	Some of the support and operations related self-service features include knowledge-based search, adopting incident avoidance architecture through proactive code maintenance, and providing contextual help. Other initiatives include real-time chat and leveraging other collaborative features. How-to documents and FAQ documents will aid in defect and incident avoidance.
Continuous process improvement	One of the key goals of support governance is to iteratively fine-tune and optimize the support processes to improve the overall efficiency. This includes process standardization, automating the key process steps, incorporating the learnings and best practices, and eliminating the redundant or unnecessary steps in the process.
System and incident monitoring	Portal monitoring infrastructure can be leveraged to create a custom dashboard view focusing on support and operation metrics such as system performance, availability, system load, etc. This helps the support and operations team to take remedial actions at the earliest. Similarly, incident monitoring can provide insights into incident ageing, SLA conformance, average issue resolution time, and average first response time.
Support training and self-learning	Cross-skill the support team to handle multiple portal topics. Provide e-learning and training platform to enable support team to address varied range of issues.

- Self-service initiatives reduce incidents volume. Initiatives such as e-learning and self-paced training for support staff also helps in quickly onboarding new team members by reducing dependency on SMEs.

Portal Support and Incident Management Process

Supporting portal site and handling incidents is one of the main portal operations activities. This includes handling customer queries, support incidents, and handling any production issues. The process is outlined in the Figure 17.4.

The main steps in the support and incident management process flow are as follows:

- *Incident logging*: Portal users can log the incidents requesting for support or for reporting any problems while using the portal site. Production issues such as production performance issues and production outage issues can also be logged as incidents. End user may also request for enhancement through incidents.

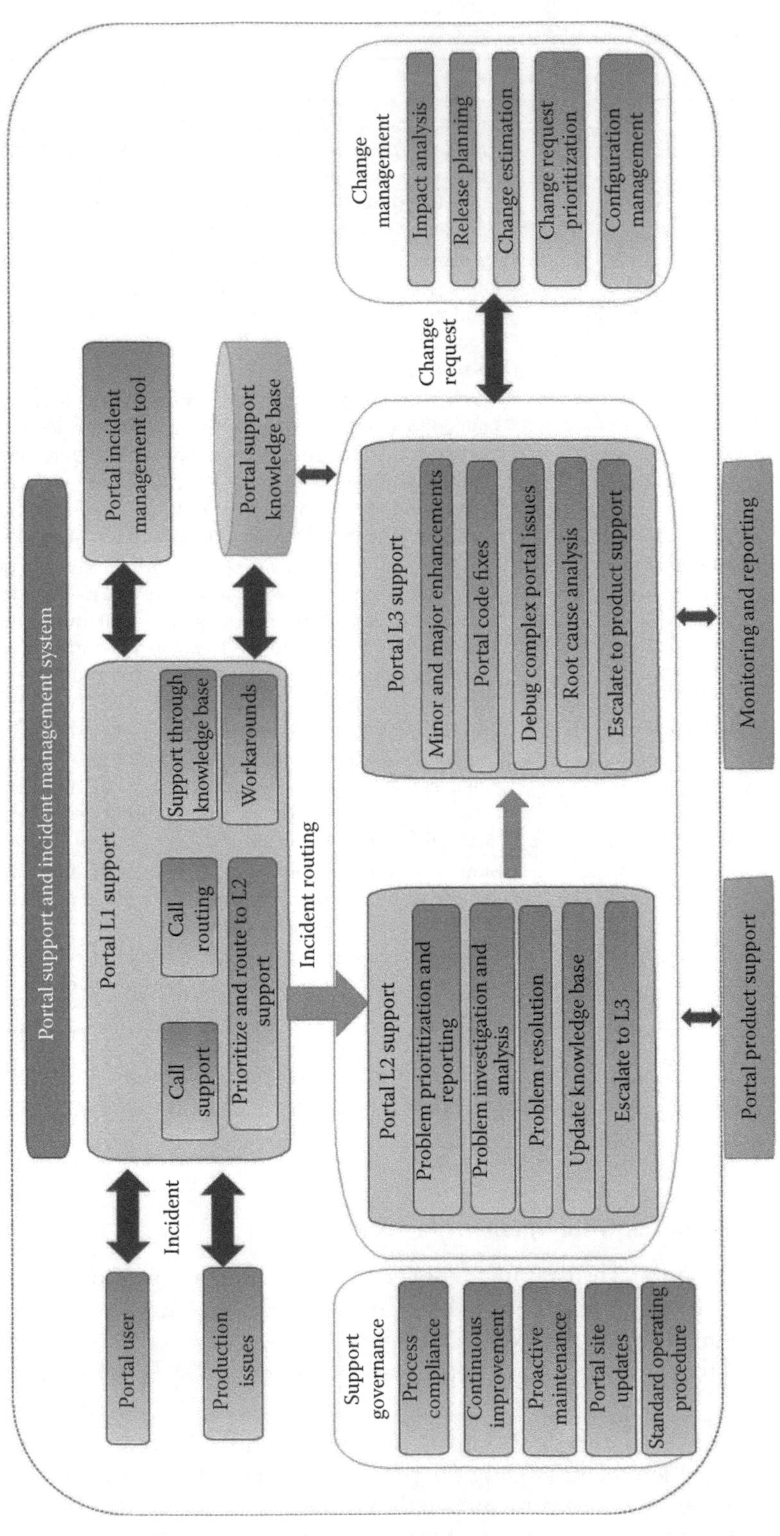

FIGURE 17.4
Portal incident management process.

- *Portal L1 support*: This support team mainly consists of on-call support that handles customer calls and will be the first point of contact for logged incidents. They use the portal support knowledge base to resolve any easy queries and use available best practice documents or standard operating procedures available in the knowledge base. They also provide all known workarounds for the commonly encountered problems. The objective is to address majority of customer issues at this stage. L1 support team heavily relies on portal support knowledge base and incident management system. All queries that cannot be resolved at this stage will be prioritized and routed to L2 support.
- *Portal L2 support*: This consists of a team with portal knowledge and they work closely with portal development team to resolve the issues. They investigate the problems and resolve issues taking help from system administrators. Medium complex issues such as intermittent outages, application patching, portal upgrades, portal backup, and minor configuration changes will be handled by this team. Once the issue is fixed, they will update the knowledge base with the solution details. Unresolved and high complexity issues will be escalated to portal L3 support.
- *Portal L3 support*: This team consists of core portal technical team members who can do the root-cause analysis of the problem and fix any portal code-related issues. The team is responsible for handling highly complex technical issues that require portal code updates. They will also be responsible for addressing minor and major enhancement requests. If the issue is traced to the portal product, the team will engage the portal product vendor support team.
- *Change management*: All code updates go through change management process that will be discussed in Chapter 19. Change control board will do the impact analysis, the estimation, and the release planning for deploying the release. It will also be responsible for prioritizing the incoming change requests and configuration management.
- *Support governance*: All support activities are governed by predefined processes, using a SOP for executing the activities. The governance also includes continuous improvement and proactive site maintenance. We will discuss about continuous improvement in the coming sections.

Business Continuity Management in Portal

The business continuity process mainly consists of establishing the processes to handle the scenarios when portal servers and data centers are down due to unexpected events. In order to ensure continuous availability, we need to set up the disaster recovery (DR) portal environment, preferably in a different geographic location.

DR essentially involves creating a mirror site (updated with exact portal code and configuration) in a different geographic location and using the site in the case of a disaster.

The details of DR setup are explained in Chapter 18.

Portal Troubleshooting

Production issue analysis and troubleshooting are important aspects of portal maintenance. As portal solution consists of various enterprise systems, services, layers. Troubleshooting an issue involves careful analysis of all systems and layers involved in the solution. In this section, we will provide a sample troubleshooting flow and portal troubleshooting tips.

The troubleshooting flow is for a portal integrated with an enterprise CMS through content services layer. Detailed steps of the flow are given in Figure 17.5.

The main points about the troubleshooting flow depicted in Figure 17.5 are as follows:

- There are mainly three application layers in request processing considered in this example: portal → content services → enterprise CMS (portal-invoking content services to fetch content from enterprise CMS). The trouble shooting steps can be mainly followed by portal L1 support team.
- The first step is to ensure that the problem is due to portal platform and then categorize the problem based on its severity. We have given sample categorizations in the following sections.
- The next step is to isolate the problem to portal application layer or to portal infrastructure layer.
- If the issue is traced to portal infrastructure, detailed infrastructure analyses such as log file analysis, resource utilization analysis and analysis of memory dump and network issues will be done. Once the infrastructure issue is identified, it will be addressed and tested leading to the closure of the issue.
- If the issues are traced to portal application layer, we need to debug the issue layer by layer. In this scenario, we need to look out for themes, problem patterns, and markers to identify the exact layer among portal, content services, and enterprise CMS layers. In the subsequent section, we have given a few common problem patterns that help us isolate the problem to a particular layer.
- Once the exact layer and system is identified, support team can look up in the support knowledge base to identify any related solutions for this. If the problem can be fixed through a known solution, the support team will execute the fix and close the ticket.
- If the problem cannot be resolved from the knowledge base, the support team will escalate the ticket to the next level of support.
- If the issue is due to different systems (such as content services or CMS), the support team will route the incident to the corresponding teams.

Sample Portal Issue Categorization

We have seen that one of the first steps in the troubleshooting is to categorize the problem into known severity so that we can prioritize them as per the specified SLAs. Here are some sample categorizations of issues:

- *Critical-priority issues*: Issues such as server outages, very slow page response, internal server error on home pages, production outages, and the loss of key functionality qualify for this category. Usually these issues have SLAs within an hour as it impacts the business revenue.

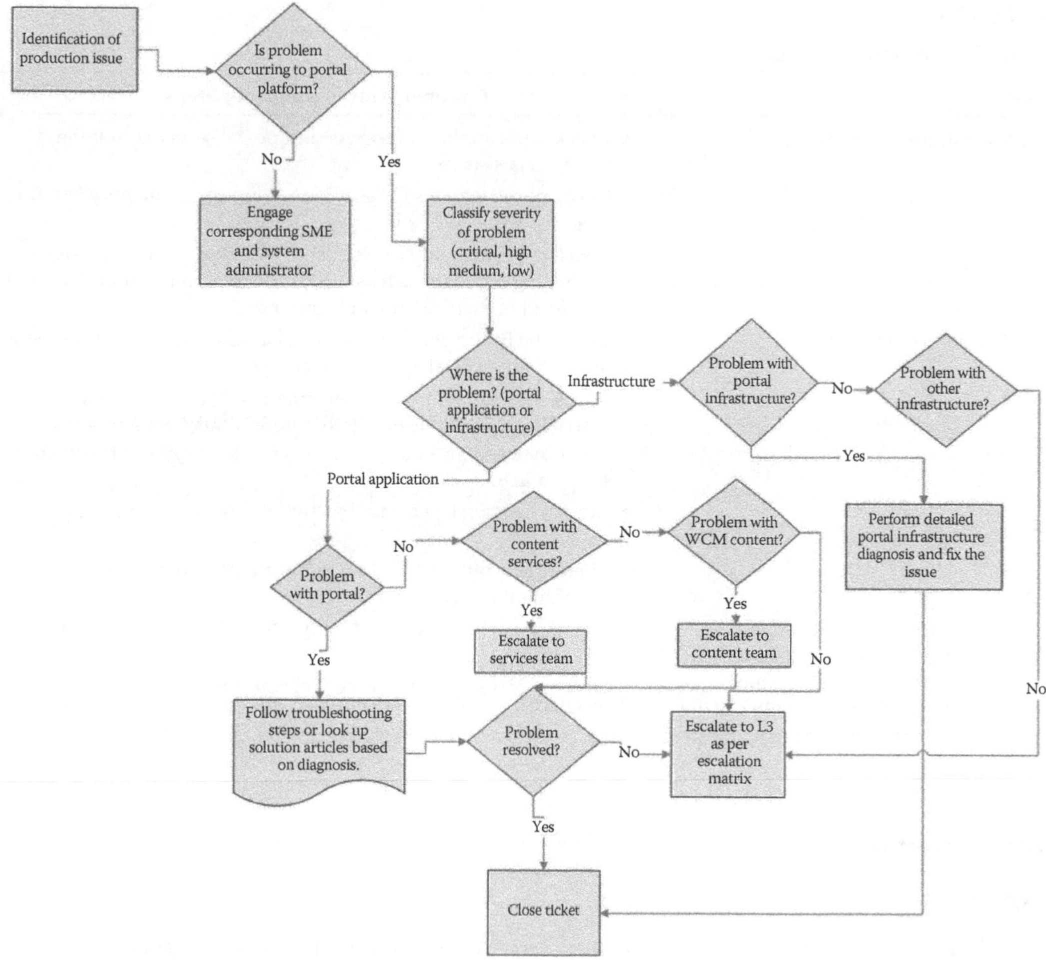

FIGURE 17.5
Portal troubleshooting process.

- *High-priority issues*: If the portal site is working but if multiple pages are not rendering or if we are getting HTTP 404 or HTTP 500 internal server issues, they would qualify for high-priority issues.
- *Medium-priority issues*: Incorrect positioning of portlets and incorrect branding that can be fixed through configuration would come under this category.
- *Low-priority issues*: Very low-impact items and cosmetic issues such as content style issues, typos, and image-specification issues would come under this category.

Portal Troubleshooting Tips

Let us look at some tips in isolating commonly occurring portal issues and some recurring problem patterns in Table 17.3.

TABLE 17.3

Portal Troubleshooting Tips

Issue	Common Troubleshooting Steps
Portal application down	• Check if the application server and portal server is running; if not, restart server • Check portal log files for any connection issue, memory issue, or access issue and fix it • Check the availability of all portal components in the request-processing pipeline such as web server and application server to ensure all of them are up and running
Portal application is slow	• Check the health check monitoring dashboard for resource issues on any of the portal application components • Check the availability and performance of all dependent systems to which portal is integrated. If there are any performance issues on back-end systems, engage corresponding support team • Isolate the issue layer-wise by checking the performance of all the layers • Check the health of all portal infrastructure components including the network
Content issues such as style issues causing incorrect display, grammatical errors/misspellings, broken links, images not displaying correctly	• The issues are most likely due to incorrect web content authored in CMS • Find the corresponding content chunk and fix the issue in the CMS.

Summary

- This chapter provides the portal support and operations related insights.
- Production release readiness checklist consists of hardware checks, portal performance checks, portal support checks, portal availability checks, portal architecture, portal security checks, portal testing checks, documentation and training checks, portal implementation plan, communication plan, and portal operations guide.
- Portal administration activities include content administration, portal workflow administration, portal security configuration, portal site administration, virtual portal management, portal settings management, portal search administration, and portal plugin management.
- Portal postproduction monitoring includes internal monitoring of portal infrastructure, external monitoring of portal, and portal application monitoring.
- Key portal support and maintenance activities include release management, change management, availability and performance monitoring, infrastructure management, configuration management, incident management, and continuous improvement.

- Portal operations best practices include proactive maintenance, automation of frequently executed activities, development of standard operating procedures and process standardization, and efficient knowledge management for support activities.
- The main steps in portal support and incident management process include incident logging, L1 support, L2 support, L3 support, change management, and support governance.

18

Portal Infrastructure and NFR Planning

This chapter mainly deals with the infrastructure aspects of the portal. As we have seen from earlier chapters, an optimal infrastructure plays a vital role in portal performance, availability, and scalability. A portal platform can accommodate the business growth only with a proper infrastructure planning.

We will look at the infrastructure planning, clustering, and testing aspects of a portal infrastructure here. A sample disaster recovery (DR) setup for portal for business continuity is also given. We will also look at various nonfunctional requirements in a typical portal project and ways of achieving it. Portal architectures, enterprise architects and infrastructure architects will find this chapter useful.

Portal Infrastructure Planning

Portal-Sizing Questionnaire

Portal product vendors publish a sizing questionnaire that can be leveraged in arriving at accurate and recommended sizing requirements for the portal. Though the exact set of questions would slightly vary across portal products, given below is the common set of factors considered in the sizing questionnaire. This provides insights into the details that needs to be gathered during portal infrastructure sizing exercise.

- Load-related factors:
  - Total number of registered portal users
  - Maximum number of anonymous portal users
  - Maximum number of concurrent user sessions for a specific time period
  - Peak load requests
  - Average portal session time
  - Availability, scalability SLAs
  - Performance SLAs
- Portal-related factors:
  - Maximum number of portlets
  - Maximum number of portal pages
  - Average number of portal pages accessed per user session
  - Maximum number of service integrations
  - Average memory required by portlet

  - Average session size
  - Maximum storage requirements for portal objects
  - CPU requirements for background jobs and services
- Content-related factors:
  - Total content volume
  - Maximum number of content templates
  - Maximum number of concurrent authoring sessions
  - Content volume required for migration if required
- Infrastructure-related factors:
  - Server topology (2-tiered, 3-tiered, n-tiered architecture)
  - Network topology
  - Requirement of secure transport layer
  - Considerations for cloud hosting
  - Clustering requirements
  - Disaster recovery SLA (RPO, RTO, etc.)
  - Cloud requirements

Portal Sizing

Portal infrastructure sizing and capacity planning requires careful planning and should consider multiple factors that contribute to the overall load on portal systems. Most of the portal product vendors provide sizing guides and benchmark infrastructure/server settings that can be used for calculating the optimal infrastructure capacity of the portal.

The main load factors that will be used for designing the optimal portal infrastructure are

- Total number of anonymous and registered users
- Peak user load
- Maximum number of concurrent users per hour
- Maximum transactions per hour
- Total content volume

In addition to portal vendor recommended sizing values, we can fine-tune the CPU and memory sizing by considering a few more aspects. We have given sample CPU and RAM sizing in the following, which can be used to fine-tune the values wherever required.

NOTE: The sizing formulas given in the following are indicative, which covers the main aspects of CPU and RAM sizing. The formula may need to be fined-tuned based on the application complexity and load factors. Preferences should be given to portal vendor–recommended values and the given formulas can be used for fine-tuning the sizing values.

CPU Cores

The total number of CPU cores required can be obtained from the benchmarking numbers and sizing recommendations given by the portal vendor. It normally depends on the

- Average number of portal transactions for specified time period
- Average CPU processing time for a single transaction
- Application complexity
- CPU required for OS
- Expected page response time
- Peak load

While calculating the CPU size, we must also calculate the CPU requirements of other applications running on the same server as they too would consume the CPU cycles. For instance, in the case of vertical clustering, we will be running multiple server instances on a single machine and hence will need to include that in our CPU-sizing calculation.

The sizing factors mentioned above can be input to vendor-recommended sizing questionnaire to get the recommended CPU sizing numbers. Alternatively, we can also use the benchmarking numbers published by portal vendor to arrive at the closest matching CPU configuration for a given load.

RAM Sizing

A sample formula for calculating the RAM size for a single portal server is as follows:

$$\text{RAM Size} = (\text{Sum}(\text{PM1}, \text{PM2}) * \text{MCU} * (1 + \text{GR})) + \text{OR}$$

where

PM1 and PM2 are the total memory required for each of the portlets; We need to identify the total memory consumed for all portlets

MCU is the maximum number of concurrent user sessions or concurrent transactions

GR is the expected growth rate

OR is the OS memory requirement

PM1 and PM2 can be calculated by determining the application cache size and application session size required by each portlet.

NOTE: The formula given is for a single portal server running on the machine. If multiple portal applications are running on the same machine, then the aforementioned function should be calculated for each of the portal servers and the total RAM size would be the sum total of all the values from individual portal servers.

As a sample calculation, let us consider the portal requires the following memory requirements:

- Total memory requirement of all portlets = 200 MB
- MCU = 100
- GR = 20% (0.2)
- OR = 2000 MB

Using the earlier formula, we get RAM size = 26,000 MB or 26 GB. We can round it off to the next higher configuration (in this case 32 GB).

NOTE: The sizing recommendation assumes that portal is the only application running on the server. However, if we run multiple portal instances on portal server as in case of vertical clustering, then sizing calculation has to be done for each of the portal server instances and the overall server configuration should be based on sum total of all sizing requirements of the portal servers running on that server.

Portal Virtualization and Cloud

Virtualization can be done at various levels such as OS virtualization, platform virtualization, cloud hosting, usage of virtual machines, etc. In this section, we will look at the two main aspects of virtualization related to the portal.

Installing Portal on Virtual Machines

Virtual machine provides an abstraction of underlying hardware resource that can be spread across multiple machines. This enables us to provide high scalability by transparently increasing the hardware capacity such as CPU, memory, etc. Virtual machines are one of the most preferred options to set up DR environment. Virtual machines help in the optimal resource utilization and provide best performance and high scalability.

Cloud Hosting

Most of the portal products support cloud deployment that can be used to provide elastic scalability. Cloud vendors provide key infrastructure elements such as web server, application server, and database server used by the portal.

In portal scenario, sometimes the portal might have dependency on various internal enterprise systems such as enterprise interfaces, chat systems, email systems, file servers, etc. Let us look at one such integration in the Figure 18.1.

As we can see in Figure 18.1, the portal deployed on cloud uses an integration layer to communicate with internal enterprise systems. There are other connectivity options for cloud-based portals:

- *Cloud direct connect*: Some cloud providers expose private network services using a dedicated private line, outside Internet. This will provide dedicated ports that will be opened on the cloud through which the communication can happen. This connectivity being private is a secure option.
- *Third-party Tools*: Third-party tools provide readily available interfaces to create the connectivity between cloud apps and on-premise systems.
- *Custom layer*: A custom layer can be created for connectivity.
- *Enterprise service bus* (*ESB*): Multiple ESB products provide connectors for cloud connectivity, which can be utilized to expose the internal applications to the portal on cloud.

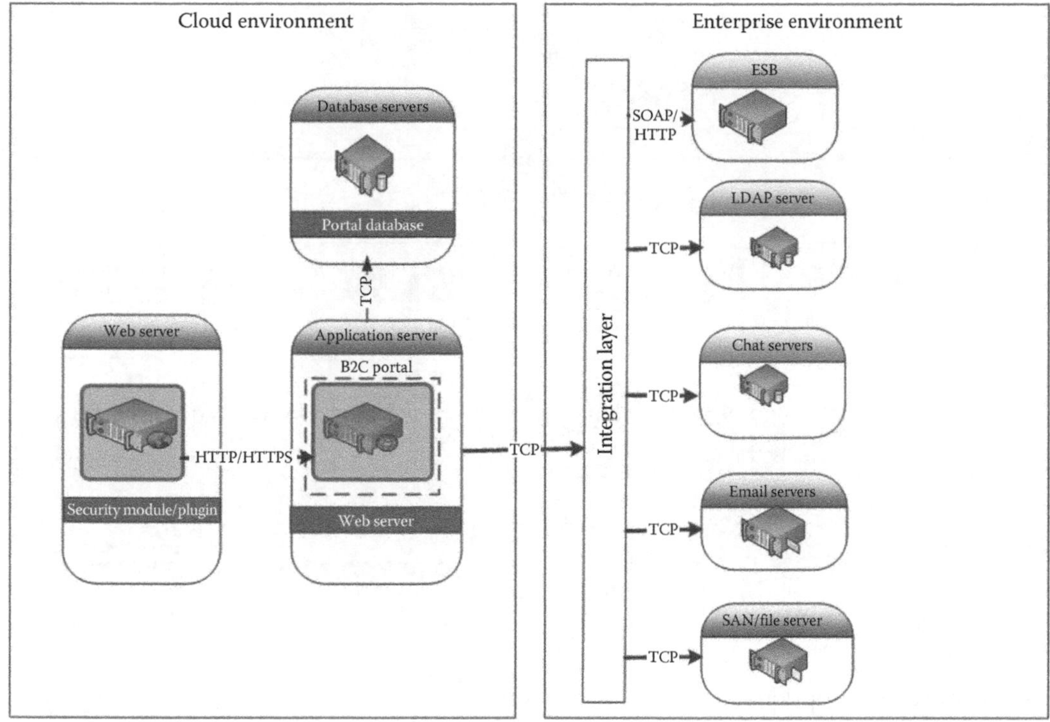

FIGURE 18.1
Portal cloud hosting.

Preferably portal production and pre-production environments should be deployed in high available mode by having the servers deployed across multiple availability zones. Below are the vital points for portal architecture in this regard.

- *Multiple availability zones*: Key components of the architecture—including portal web server, portal application server, and database servers are deployed across multiple Availability Zones of the cloud.
- *Load balancing*: In the event of a web server instance failure, the Load Balancer (LB) will automatically route traffic to healthy instances across Availability Zone (Datacenter).

Let us look at details of high availability, disaster recovery, and fail-over in cloud hosting scenario

- *High availability and DR*: The portal application will be deployed across multiple cloud availability zones and will be load balanced using load balancer (LB). All the application traffic to the servers will go via LB. This will ensure that the application continues to be available in case of a server failure or entire availability zone failure; thus providing high availability to the application. In Figure 18.2, we have used cloud server in two different regions for DR setup. The primary region has two availability zones for ensuring high availability.
- *Disaster Recovery*: Portal Application will be deployed in a standby/running server mode with-in a separate DR region. A new application release/code release will be

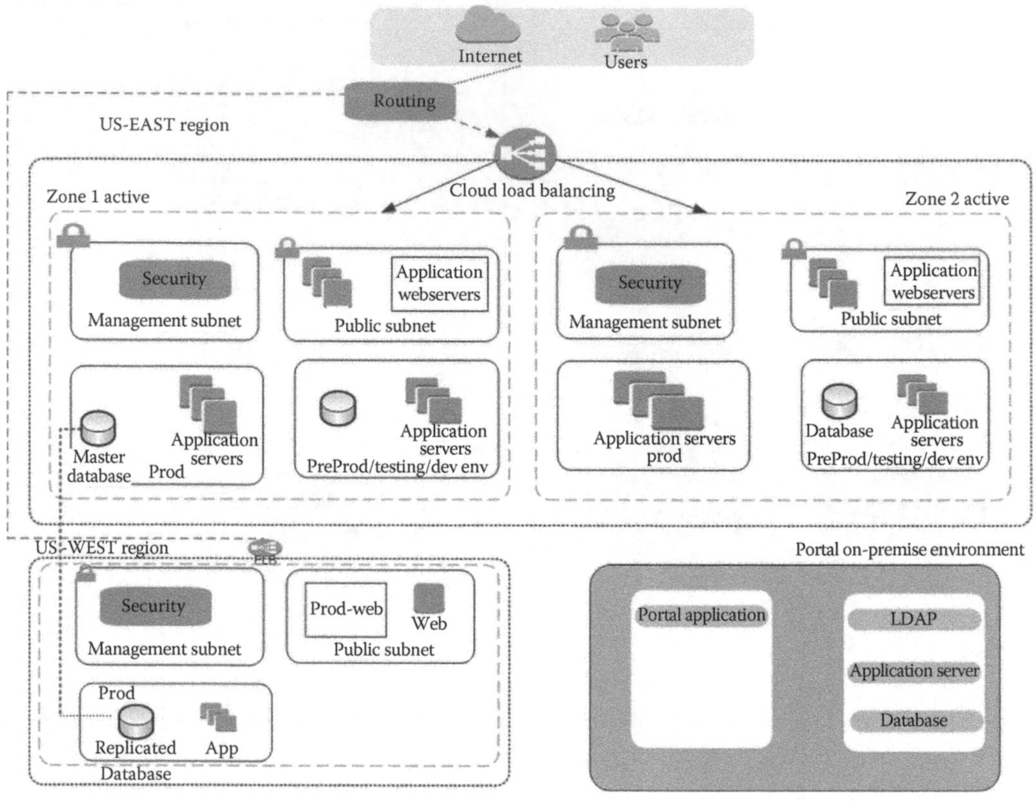

FIGURE 18.2
Portal cloud deployment across multiple zones.

applied to both DR and primary server thus ensuring that DR and primary are in sync using scripts.

- *Database replication and backup*: Most cloud vendors provide database replication option that can be used for this purpose. For instance, Amazon Web Service (AWS) provides Mysql Read Replica option, which can be leveraged for building the DR, and scale the read operations in DR region. Scripts can be used for scheduling file backups across primary and DR regions.

Figure 18.2 provides conceptual architecture view for hosting portal application.

Portal Clustering

Portal cluster consists of multiple managed servers that help in uniform workload management. Clusters can be created on a single physical machine or it can involve multiple machines with latter being the most efficient one.

A portal cluster consists of multiple server instances (sometimes referred to as nodes) that are managed by a cluster manager. The server nodes can run on the same machine or on different machines. The cluster manager is responsible for synchronizing the code, configuration, data, session, and cache on all its member nodes. It also takes care of routing the requests based on the performance and availability of its member nodes and, hence, helps in achieving high availability. There are mainly two types of clustering: vertical and horizontal clustering.

Vertical Clustering

In this configuration, multiple portal server nodes are defined and run on the same physical machine and this helps in vertical scaling. Vertical clustering requires high server configuration to support multiple server instances. Since the cluster runs on a single machine, the availability of the application depends on the machine.

Horizontal Clustering

In this configuration, the portal server nodes are distributed across multiple physical machines.

This helps in effectively leveraging server resources and is more reliable.

Portal horizontal cluster configuration is shown in Figure 18.3.

Live cluster consists of node 1 and node 3 that are defined on two separate physical machines. Similarly, portal staging cluster consists of node 2 and node 4.

The cluster manager is responsible for managing the configuration and synchronizes state of all its member nodes. It constantly monitors each of the member nodes and if any node failure is detected, it routes all subsequent requests to available nodes thus ensuring high availability.

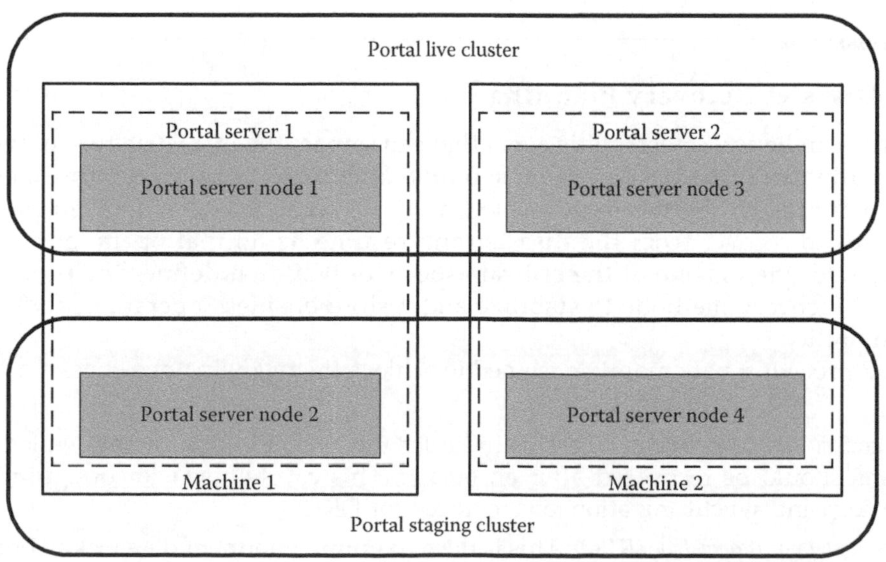

FIGURE 18.3
Portal horizontal clustering.

Multitenancy Model and Virtual Portals

Portal supports creation of multiples sites on a single portal instance. We can configure a different look and feel, theme (header and footer), content, user role, and access permissions for each of the portal sites. Under the hood, all these portal sites would still use the common portal code base and the variations can be implemented through configurations. This can be achieved through the "virtual portals" feature.

Most portals provide the "virtual portal" feature that have the following characteristics:

- Virtual portals allow us to run multiple virtual portal sites with a single portal code base.
- The URL and the domain can be varied for each of the virtual portals.
- We can employ different themes and skins for virtual portals.
- Each virtual portal can also be configured with a different user registry.

Virtual portals are very useful feature for supporting

- Geospecific branding and geospecific URLs
- Microsites
- Seasonal campaigns
- Brand-specific site for a single organization

Portal Disaster Recovery Planning

A disaster can be any catastrophic event that can impact the infrastructure of the organization and can bring down its entire online operations. As a part of business continuity planning (BCP), the organization needs to come up with detailed plans and procedures to recover from the disaster and resume its normal operations. Disaster recovery (DR) plan is one of the critical aspects of BCP that defines the process, systems, and recovery methods to stabilize and restore business operations for continuous availability.

The DR procedures are mainly designed to achieve the following objectives:

- *Recovery time objective* (*RTO*): This indicates the period of time within which systems should be recovered after an outage. This can be used for designing the backup and synchronization jobs required for DR.
- *Recovery point objective* (*RPO*): This is the maximum amount of data loss an organization can sustain during the outage.

Critical Success Factors for DR Strategy

Implementing a DR solution is a complex task involving significant cost and implementation time. Hence, it is imperative that any DR solution that is implemented must comply with the enterprise DR strategy and satisfy the following minimum success criteria.

- The DR strategy must comprehend business requirements, business criticality of the application, business justification for the project, cost–benefit analysis, and RPO and RTO approved by the business.
- DR solution normally involves regular sync jobs to fetch data from master site that has potential to add additional overhead on primary production site. Impact of DR solution on the current production system performance level must be minimal. Any performance impact must be highlighted during the design phase and verified during the proof of concept (POC) phase.
- The replication, backup, and synchronization components should be designed to satisfy the laid out RTO and RPO.
- Dry runs and simulations need to be conducted to ensure that DR scenarios, failover, and RTO/RPO objectives are fulfilled by the DR environment.
- DR site when enabled as the production site should provide the same performance level as the primary production site.
- DR solution must allow for trials without affecting the production operations and/or compromising the solution capabilities in meeting the RPO and RTO requirements.
- Recovery of application platform should be transparent to the users, that is, no recovery steps are required to be carried out by the users or other applications.
- Production support team must be involved in all phases of DR planning and implementation. Production support team should take ownership of the DR solution when activated. Training in appropriate technology area must be provided to the production support team.

Portal DR Strategy and Setup

To provide disaster recovery capability, secondary data center is introduced into the architecture in addition to the default primary data center.

- Primary portal data center is capable of handling all traffic at peak and is used exclusively for normal operations. All of the components such as firewalls, load balancers, database servers, and so on are fully clustered so that there is no single point of failure.
- The secondary (DR) data center hosts exactly the same hardware, software, and application stack as the primary portal environment.
- The secondary (DR) data center is replicated with data from the primary data center. In the event of a disaster, traffic will be routed to the secondary (DR) data center. Updates from the DR data center will be replicated back to primary data center when it becomes operational. This will keep the application databases in sync.

- In normal operations, the enterprise load balancer will route the portal to the primary site. In the event of a disaster, the load balancer will route them to the secondary (DR) site.

The key points about the portal DR setup shown in Figure 18.4 are as follows:

1. Both production environment and DR environment have the same set of hardware, application code, data, and configurations. In some cases, virtual machines are used in DR environments for optimal resource utilization.
2. Periodic synchronization jobs and replication will happen from portal database, CMS, search index, user repository, and file servers present in production environment (primary site) to DR environment. The replication and synchronization jobs can be automated and are scheduled to run on regular basis. The main replication activities are as follows:
   a. Replication of portal server configuration and pages, portlets, and other portal components in portal server
   b. Replication of portal database
   c. Scripts to copy the files from primary NAS file server to file server in the DR environment
   d. Replication of content from production CMS to DR CMS
3. Portal site load balancer monitors the availability of primary environment and in the case of disaster it automatically routes the traffic to the DR environment

Portal Infrastructure Testing

Portal infrastructure testing helps ensure optimal performance, scalability, reliability, and predictable functioning of critical business systems related to portal. It helps to validate any changes and overall capacity of enterprise IT Infrastructure encompassing all underlying hardware, network, and/or software components and processes that govern them; it helps in mitigating business risks while a system or a group of systems undergo infrastructural changes of different scales and increase the infrastructure reliability.

Infrastructure testing is normally carried out after building the infrastructure for the new capability to test the system scalability. It is also carried out during infrastructure consolidation or migration.

Challenges in Infrastructure Testing

The main challenges in this category of testing are

- Accurately assessing the performance impact at various geographies
- Rapid changes in infrastructure technology landscape
- Lack of exact user load and site traffic details

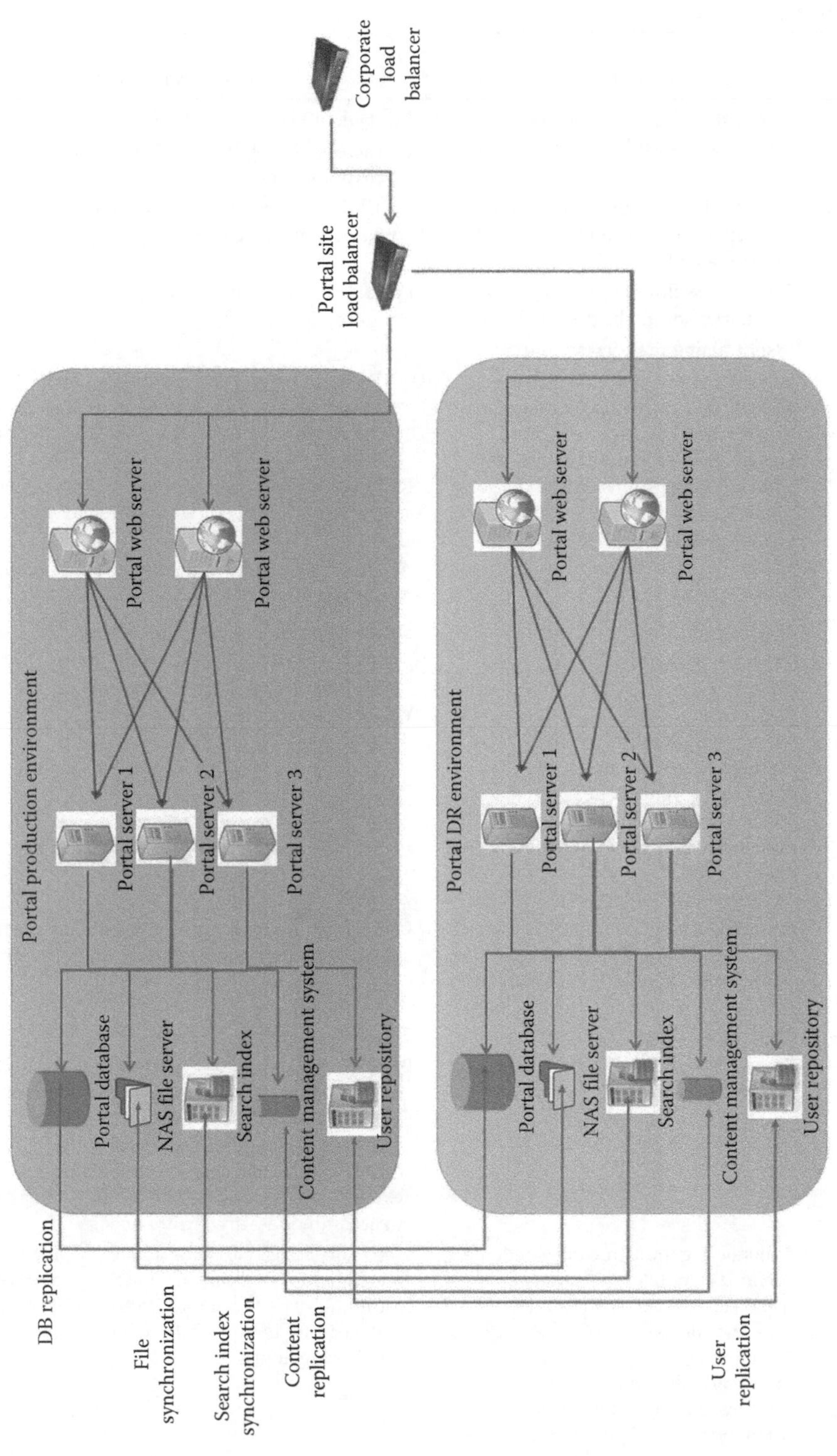

FIGURE 18.4
Portal DR setup.

TABLE 18.1
Portal NFR Strategy

Portal NFR Category	NFR Details	Approach to Fulfill NFR
Accessibility	Portal should allow the site to be easily usable and navigable for all users	Implement WCAG standards Use accessibility testing tools to ensure accessibility compliance
Documentation and training	All portal functional components and dependencies should be properly documented	Portal developers should create the documentation of various portal modules.
	The process flows and debugging scenarios should be documented	Portal team can work with content team to create training material
	User training material should be created	
Availability and scalability	Portal platform with all its dependent components should have high availability to support continuous business operations. Portal platform should also be able to scale to support the peak load	Portal can leverage high availability clustered configuration, cloud hosting and DR environment to support high availability. Redundancy configuration should be designed for each of the critical software and hardware components. Additionally appropriate infrastructure planning is also essential for optimal scalability and availability
Security	Portal platform should satisfy all security requirements	Security based design and security testing needs to be done to ensure security compliance. The details are elaborated in Chapter 9.
Logging, reporting and auditing	Portal application should audit the core events such as security events, configuration changes, content publishing events, page promotions, deployment, versioning, system changes, role/user details, etc. Wherever required, portal should also provide the information in report format.	We can leverage the portal in-built audit features.
	Portal should log the related high level actions including Date/Time, problem context, and Action/Function and code source. Levels (severe, warning, info) and it should be configurable	Logging framework can be used during portal development to satisfy the logging requirements.
Extensibility	Portal platform should be extensible for future needs and integrations	By adopting standards based integration and development we can make the portal platform extensible. Key features such as security components, integration modules and collaboration modules should be designed to be extensible through external plugins and adaptors to accommodate any future needs
Monitoring	A monitoring infrastructure should be defined to monitor the portal application and system at various levels. This include real-time user activity monitoring, application performance and availability monitoring, system resource utilization and health check monitoring, multi-geo monitoring, etc.	Web analytics is one of the key tools which can be leveraged for real-time user activity monitoring. Additionally real-user monitoring (RUM) tools can be leveraged for application performance monitoring across geos.

(*Continued*)

TABLE 18.1 (*Continued*)

Portal NFR Strategy

Portal NFR Category	NFR Details	Approach to Fulfill NFR
Portability	The application should be easily portable to different platforms and environments	If we develop portal application using standards such as JSR, WSRP, etc. we can deploy and run those components on any compliant portal server. Another aspect of portability can be achieved through usage of HTML standards by building client-side AJAX components which can run on any web platform and hence is easily portable.
Compliance to standards	Portal application should be compliant to various portal standards such as JSR 168, JSR 286, WSRP and HTML standards such as HTML 5, CSS 3, etc.	Compliance to open standards should be one of the key design goals during portal architecture and design phases. Standards compliance checks should also be validated during code reviews.
Usability	Portal platform should be easy to use on all supported platforms by wide variety of audience	Portal can use standards-based design, compatibility testing, usability testing, and localization to enhance usability.
Compatibility	Portal application should run on all supported browsers, devices and platforms	Most portal products provide in-built support for various browsers and mobile devices. Browser and device compatibility testing should be carried out to ensure that end application works as expected across all supported user agents, devices and platforms
Discoverability	Portal platform should allow the user to easily discover the relevant information in a quick time	Information discoverability can be enhanced through intuitive portal information architecture, smart search and friendlier navigation features Portal personalization also be leveraged to provide the most relevant content for the user
Performance	Portal platform should satisfy the specific performance SLAs related to response time, load time, transaction completion time, etc.	Performance best practices and checklists such as lightweight design, caching, UI optimizations can be done in portal to meet the performance SLAs. More details are covered in Chapter 20
Archival/ backup	Portal platforms should support data archival and backup for business and regulatory purposes	Backup and archival jobs can be designed to take periodic backups. The backup frequency is fine-tuned to satisfy the RPO
Disaster recovery (DR)	Portal platform should enable the business continuity through DR plan	This can be achieved through a DR site and regular content/data replication across primary and DR site. We have seen the details in previous sections
Maintenance	The portal platform should be easy to maintain	Portal governance process provides elaborative details of maintenance activities and related roles and responsibilities. The details are provided in Chapter 17
Release and deployment requirements	Portal platform should support frequent and iterative releases for quicker time to market. Portal solution should support automated and scheduled deployments	Agile project execution methodology backed with automated release management process helps in iterative portal releases. Custom deployment scripts and continuous integration (CI) tools such as Jenkins to schedule and automate deployments.

Infrastructure Test Types

The main tests conducted for testing infrastructure are as follows:

- Load testing to test the scalability of various infrastructure components during normal and peak loads. Portal page response time and resource utilization are monitored.
- Stress testing to test the system's error-handling capability by putting higher than expected loads.
- Endurance testing to test the reliability and availability of the infrastructure components during endurance scenarios.
- Volume testing to test the server throughput while handling large volumes of data.

Portal Nonfunctional Requirements and Planning

Portal nonfunctional requirements (NFR) are an important aspect of portal solution. They help in increasing the success and adoption of the portal program. Given in Table 18.1 are the important portal NFRs and approaches for fulfilling those NFRs.

Summary

- The chapter details about portal infrastructure concepts such as hardware sizing, clustering, DR planning, and NFR planning
- Any portal infrastructure sizing should factor user load, transaction load, and content volume
- Portal product vendors will provide sizing recommendations that should be given priority for portal infrastructure planning
- CPU sizing should factor in an average number of portal transactions per user session, average CPU processing time for single transaction, SSL factor, application complexity, and CPU required for OS
- Memory sizing should factor in total memory required for each of the portlets, maximum number of concurrent user sessions or concurrent transactions, expected growth rate, and OS memory requirement
- Portal installation can leverage virtual machine hosting and cloud hosting
- The main forms of portal clustering are horizontal clustering and vertical clustering
- In vertical clustering, multiple server nodes are defined and run on the same physical machine and in horizontal clustering, the portal server nodes are distributed across multiple physical machines
- Portal virtual host helps in defining multiple portal sites on the same portal server with variations in look and feel, URL, user registry, etc.

- DR planning should be done to achieve RTO and RPO
- RTO indicates the period of time within which systems should be recovered after an outage
- RPO is the maximum amount of data loss an organization can sustain during an outage
- The critical success factors for DR strategy are complete compilation of DR requirements, minimal performance impact of DR solution on production environment, DR site with same performance as primary site, and transparent recovery for end user
- Portal DR setup includes creation of portal DR environment that mirrors all application components from the primary site. Periodic synchronization jobs and replication happens from portal database, CMS, search index, user repository, and file servers present in production environment (primary site) to DR environment.
- Key portal nonfunctional requirements are accessibility, documentation and training, availability, security, logging and auditing, extensibility, monitoring, portability, compliance to standards, usability, compatibility, discoverability, performance, archival/backup, DR, maintenance, and release requirements.

19

Portal Governance and Program Management

A proper program governance is required in portal programs which usually consists of numerous tracks with lot of internal dependencies. While successful portal program management ends up winning business confidence in portal technology, a failure would lead to questions about portal capabilities. Despite its multifold advantages and promises offered by portal, we have witnessed various challenges (some of which are of large scale) for a variety of reasons. We have witnessed a recurring pattern and common themes across various portal program failures. This chapter aims to identify those themes so that portal program managers, portal architects, and business stakeholders can be cognizant of the common pitfalls and antipatterns and address them early in the game. We will also look at some of the practically proven and adopted best practices to identify the issues and address them.

Common Portal Project Management Challenges

Portal projects face some common challenges during execution and other phases of the project lifecycle. Given in the following are some of the prominent challenges that we will address in subsequent sections:

- *Cross-functional team coordination*: More often than not, portal project involve multiple functional teams for building a holistic solution. This includes search team, security team, subject matter experts (SMEs) of various interfaces, infrastructure team, product vendors, content team etc. A lack of proper coordination leads to schedule slippages, performance issues, and incompatible interfaces.
- *Lack of governance process to handle complex activities*: Many of the complex portal-related activities such as code deployment, production checkout, portal site promotion, production bug fixes, etc., need to be properly structured with clear roles and responsibilities. Lack of governance processes result in a lot of manual effort and loss of time.
- *Change request handling*: Portal applications are of common interest for many stakeholders. As a result, after the initial release or during the user acceptance testing (UAT) we would get a good number of enhancement requests. If they are not handled efficiently it would result in poor adoption, effort/cost overrun, schedule slippage, and expectation mismatch.
- *Managing multiple roles and environments*: An end-to-end portal project execution needs multiple roles such as SMEs, developers, testers, business analysts, integration architects, infrastructure specialists, etc. It is required to closely work with all these roles across environments for the success of the project.

Project Management Stages

In this section, we will look at various stages in end-to-end portal program management. We have already seen the portal architecture related activities in these stages in Chapter 4. Here we will look at other project management activities in each of the phases.

At a high level, the following are the key phases in the end-to-end project management:

- *Program envision and assessment phase*: Program vision, portal strategy, solution requirements, and program objectives are defined in this phase
- *Portal architecture and design phase*: Portal solution architecture and design artifacts are defined in this phase
- *Portal solution development and testing phase*: Portal solution is developed and tested in this phase
- *Portal maintenance and evolution*: This is an ongoing phase wherein we maintain the deployed portal solution and do iterative releases as defined in the portal roadmap strategy

Let us look at each of these phases in detail and look at the project management activities in those phases:

Program Envision Phase

In short, we will elaborate the requirements and set the direction for portal program in this phase. The portal project manager along with portal architects gets view points from various dimensions to build the holistic picture. The project manager is responsible for facilitating and organizing the necessary meetings with all concerned stakeholders and ensures the participation of all relevant stakeholders.

The main activities involved in this phase are as follows:

- *Business requirements elaboration*: Through stakeholder interviews, questionnaire, AS-IS analysis and requirements workshop the business analysts will gather and elaborate the requirements.
- *Feasibility assessment studies*: We will conduct various assessment studies such as organization readiness, capability assessment, process maturity study, and technical feasibility.
- *User experience–related activities*: Creative agency and user experience designers will come up with wireframes, mockups, visual comps, style guides and UI prototypes, and conceptual UI blueprints based on the discussions. These UI artifacts can be used to understand the requirements, navigation, and overall user experience. Portal project manager needs to get these reviewed and signed-off from business.
- *High-level project plan*: During this phase, the project manager also identifies all high level activities and the timelines and resources for the same. All the high-level tasks, ownership, and timelines will be part of project implementation plan which will be shared with Project Management Office (PMO) and relevant stakeholders. Resource planning, estimation, and communication plan will also be done during this phase.

- *Requirements prioritization and release plan*: Each business scenario and use case will be assigned priority based on its business value and impact. This helps in the prioritization of the requirements based on which the project manager can plan the iterative releases. We also will identify candidates for "quick-wins" that can be deployed quickly.
- *Initial architecture analysis*: As we have seen in Chapter 4, portal architects can conduct initial technology feasibility and as-is analysis to understand the architecture gaps and existing technical capabilities. Candidates for proof-of-concept and potential portal products are selected as candidates for further evaluation.
- *Persona definition*: Various user personas that use the portal platform will be identified and their user journeys will be modeled as flow diagrams and in the UI prototypes.
- *Portal strategy definition*: Portal architects will define the overall portal strategy along with portal objectives and key performance indicators (KPIs) that align with the overall vision of the program. KPIs also help in tracking the effectiveness and success of the program and solution. A portal strategy document should address the following concerns:
  - How the portal strategy aligns with overall program vision
  - Impact of the portal program on existing ecosystem
  - How the success of the portal program can be measured?
  - What are portal KPIs?
  - What are the long-term and short-term benefits of the portal program?
- *Portal roadmap strategy*: Portal architects will define the detailed roadmap for the portal program that is aligned with the business and organization vision. We will look at the details in further sections.

Risks and Mitigation

The main risks in this phase are as follows:

- Incomplete understanding of business requirements from all dimensions
- Ambiguous nonfunctional requirements related to performance, scalability, and performance
- Improper requirements prioritization
- Business stakeholders and program sponsors not being able to fully appreciate the value/ROI of the portal program and its impact on their business
- Incorrect resource estimation

In order to address these risks, the commonly followed best practices are as follows:

- Create multiple views of requirements and have a joint workshop with all business and other stakeholders to walk them through the requirements. For instance, create a process view, use case view, scenario view, and explain the captured requirements.

- Create a requirements checklist to ensure the completeness of requirements from all dimensions. The following is one sample checklist for requirements gathering:
  - Portal functional requirements
  - Omni-channel requirements
  - Collaboration requirements
  - Integration requirements
  - UI requirements gathering
  - Web analytics requirements gathering
  - Gather portal documentation requirements
  - Gather operating environment requirements
  - Gather portal installation/deployment requirements
  - Gather portal data migration/cleansing requirements
  - Gather portal data retention requirements
  - Gather portal solution QoS (quality of service) requirements (performance, security, availability, scalability, usability, manageability, and accessibility)
  - Gather portal security/user profile requirements
  - Gather portal standards requirements
  - Gather portal compliance/statutory/audit requirements
  - Gather portal backup/recovery requirements
  - Define portal acceptance criteria and acceptance test plan
  - Validate the portal solution assumptions with all stakeholders
  - Gather the risks associated with the requirements
  - Gather portal architectural constraints
- Establish a change request process to absorb any new enhancements or additional scope items.
- Establish a clear review and sign-off process to get the buy-in from all stakeholders on the captured requirements.
- Use the UI prototypes and mockups for explaining the captured requirements. They are most effective tools to communicate the flow and navigation to business and nontechnical stakeholders.
- Create an agile portal release plan for iterative releases. This helps us to incorporate the feedback from all the stakeholders in subsequent releases.
- Use the portal value realization framework we discussed in Chapter 2 to clearly quantify the ROI and the tracking metrics for the same.
- Use a proven portal estimation technique after identifying all project activities.

Portal Architecture and Design Phase

We have seen the activities in this phase in detail in Chapter 4. Essentially we will define various architecture views, and finalize the technology stack after detailed product and technology evaluation. Portal architects will also define the infrastructure architecture, integration architecture with interface definition, user experience architecture, and other architecture-related artifacts. Inputs from previous phase such as technology assessment, technology gaps, and detailed functional specification will be used to develop the solution architecture. All opportunities for technology reuse and open source adoption will be explored.

Architects will hold joint workshops to develop solution architecture and joint reviews with all concerned stakeholders. Additionally, we will do a detailed design of the solution and document it in the detailed design document.

Once the solution architecture is finalized, portal team will come up with a detailed design of the overall solution. Detailed design includes component design, UI element and page design, security design, interface design, and test case planning. We have also seen a sample detailed design template in Chapter 4.

Risks and Mitigation

The main risks in this phase are as follows:

- Suboptimal solution design and architecture
- Missing architecture views that does not cover all dimensions such as security and infrastructure

In order to address these risks, the commonly followed best practices are to

- Have a comprehensive solution architecture template that covers all applicable architecture views
- Conduct joint workshops to review the architecture with all SMEs and stakeholders to ensure that all view points and concerns are factored in the architecture
- Plan for proof-of-concept to validate major architecture and design decisions

Portal Solution Development and Testing Phase

In this phase, portal developers, leads, and QA team will be involved in portal development activities such as

- Portal site development
- Portal page development
- Portal content development
- Portal library and extensions development
- Performing any required portal or content migrations
- Portlet development
- Portal component development
- Unit testing of all modules
- Portal integration with all enterprise interfaces
- Security implementation

This phase also involves periodic reviews and iterative and continuous testing.

Risks and Mitigation

The main risks in this phase are as follows:

- Code quality issues due to poor execution
- Lack of coordination with various teams impacting effort, cost, and schedule
- Incomplete or incorrect implementation of functional specifications

In order to address these risks, the commonly followed best practice is to

- Perform continuous and iterative code review and quality checks by leveraging continuous integration (CI) tool
- Conduct regular synch and status meetings involving all teams
- Continuous and iterative testing
- Leverage open-source static code analyzers to automate code review process
- Use portal coding checklists and best practices to ensure optimal code quality

Portal Maintenance and Evolution

Once the portal solution is released into production environment, a governance process is set up for its maintenance and for handling ongoing operations. The activities in this phase include

- Deploying subsequent iterative portal releases as per the defined portal roadmap
- Defect fixes and applying patches and enhancements
- Closely monitoring the portal KPIs and taking corrective actions
- Providing operations support
- Monitoring the performance and availability of portal application across all geographies and handling any outages within specified SLAs
- Handling portal production incidents

Risks and Mitigation

The main risks in this phase are as follows:

- Lack or absence of monitoring process
- Lack or absence of success metrics to measure effectiveness

In order to address these risks, the commonly followed best practices are as follows:

- Set up a robust and automated monitoring infrastructure leveraging web analytics and cross-geomonitoring tools. The monitoring process should notify the operations team during performance issues or when outage happens.
- Portal success KPIs should be clearly defined during envision phase and it should be tracked on continuous basis. The KPIs should also be used for the constant improvement of the portal solution.

- Automate portal maintenance activities such as resource monitoring, patching, code deployment, etc.
- Create and use a knowledge base to store the root-cause analysis of all production incidents.

Portal Implementation and Roadmap Process

Let us look at the sample activities and deliverables in each of the phases for a portal program:

A sample portal activities plan for various phases is shown in Table 19.1.

A sample portal-execution plan with key milestone is shown in Figure 19.1.

Portal Roadmap Definition

We have seen that portal roadmap will be defined during the program envision and assessment phase. Portal roadmap strategy should have the following attributes:

- The portal roadmap should be aligned with overall business vision and long-term strategy
- Portal roadmap should define a path to incrementally add portal capabilities to reach the desired end state.
- The releases defined in portal roadmap should align with business priorities
- The roadmap should also account for quick wins
- The roadmap should enable quicker time-to-market strategy

Let us look at a sample portal roadmap exercise in the following example to make these concepts clearer.

Defining employee portal roadmap: Let us assume that we are building an intranet employee portal for an organization whose vision is as follows:

> Employee portal should be a unified information platform that should drive the employee productivity and satisfaction. It should empower employees with all right set of tools, information, and services to complete their tasks efficiently

The main business priorities are as follows (in the order of importance):

- *Business priority—1*: Employee focus
  - Employee portal should improve user efficiency and productivity
  - Employee portal should be useful in the daily activities of employees
- *Business priority—2*: Long-term strategic importance
  - Business can use intranet portal for launching new employee initiatives and policies
  - Employee portal should be a single place for discovering all employee information and provide a collaborative platform for employees to share information

TABLE 19.1

Phasewise Portal Activity Plan

Phase	Portal Activities	Portal Artifacts
Envision and assessment	• Compile requirements through workshops, interviews, and focused discussions • Requirements prioritization with business and IT stakeholders • Define scope and project plan • Understand key constraints and establish dependency and issues tracking • Establish processes, templates, and tools for development • Identify and establish PMO for governance and change management • Define NFR and establish benchmarks for system requirements • Establish necessary infrastructure for development/SIT/UAT environment • User profiling to validate UI requirements and determine ease of navigation • Map all the requirements to use case and identify any missing links • Interaction with stakeholders and business end users to understand end user requirements • Model user journeys, navigation model, and interaction model • Develop a requirements traceability matrix to ensure faithful and accurate conversion of customer requirements to final deliverables. Requirement traceability matrix is a cross reference table linking every stage of the application lifecycle with the previous and next stages • Prepare integration specifications based on interface requirements • Review all requirements-related documents from client stakeholders • Identify development resource requirements	• Portal requirements specification documents • User persona definition • Use case document • NFR requirements document • Portal strategy document • Project plan • Infrastructure requirements specification • Infrastructure planning document
Architecture and design	• Develop portal architecture views • Create detail solution design • Perform design validation through PoCs • Product and technology evaluation • Define standards for the portal design and development activities • Define all architecture views including application architecture, information architecture, security architecture, UX architecture, integration architecture, infrastructure architecture, content architecture, etc.	• Portal solution architecture document • Portal detailed design document • PoC outcome document • Interface specification document • Security design document • Validated UI standards and specification
Development and testing	• Develop the portal solution • Conduct code review • Explore the possibility of making reusable components • Defect prevention activities to identify causes of defects, thereby taking action to prevent recurrence • Portal integration • Perform end-to-end testing	• Portal code artifacts and packages • Test scripts and test reports
Evolution and maintenance	Perform continuous monitoring and do maintenance releases	Iterative portal releases

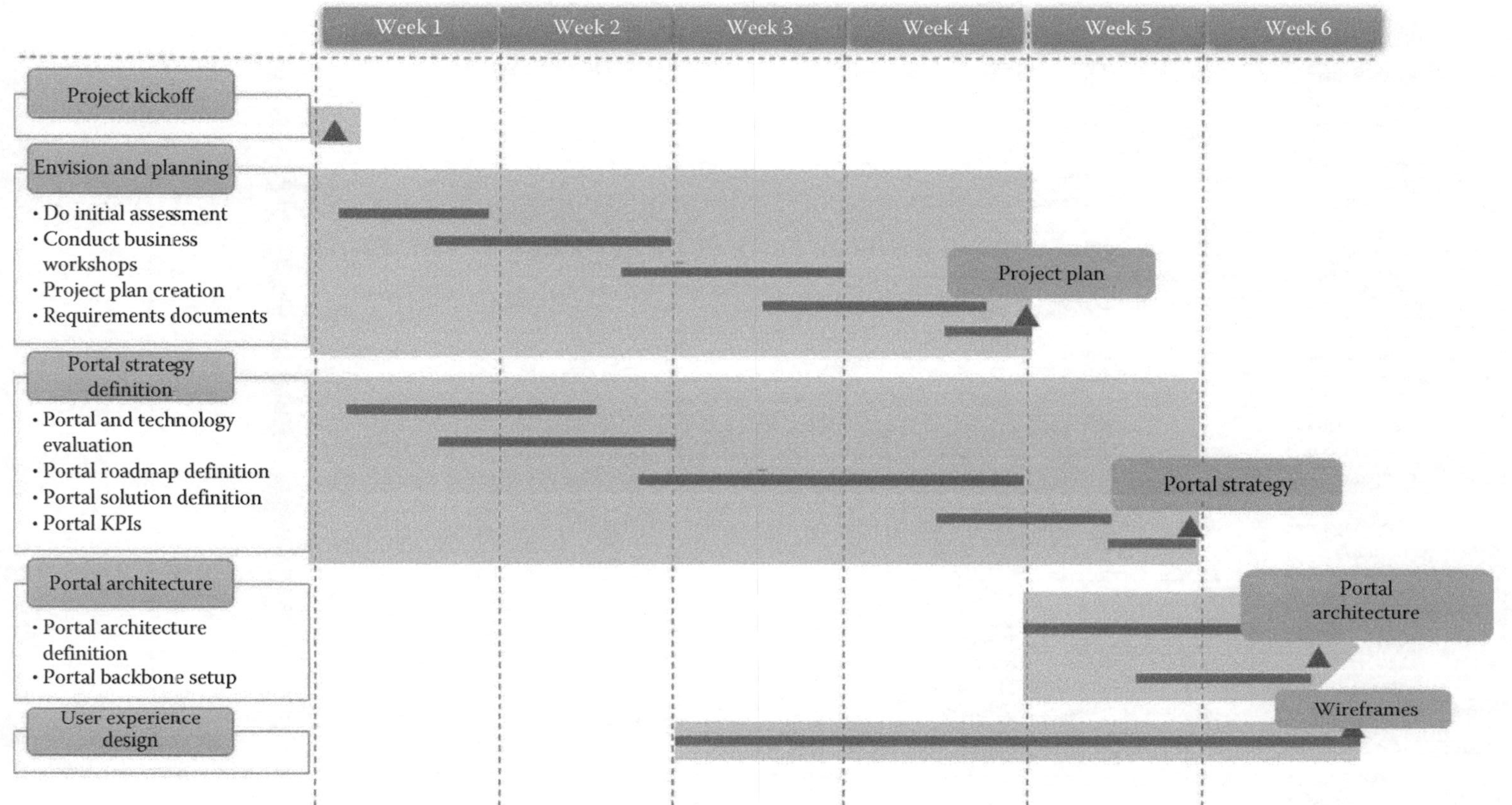

FIGURE 19.1
Sample portal execution plan.

Business priority	Portal capability	Information portal features Initial release	Collaboration portal features First release	Unified portal features Second release	Self-service portal features Third release
Employee focus	Portal content management	• Personalized content from CMS	• Internal CMS processes: content creation, publishing	• Document and asset management • Content migration	• External content integration • Content syndication
	Portal-based productivity improvement in daily tasks	• Personalized search • Employee applications integration	• Automated workflows for procurement	• Productivity reports • Intuitive information architecture	• Personalized suggestions and notifications
	Portal-led collaboration	• Blogs • Employee chat • Email	• Wiki • Employee community	• Discussion forums • Web conferencing	• External social media integration
Long-term strategic importance	Self-service features	• FAQ • Guided navigation	• Smart, contextual, and personalized search • E-learning	• Self-training • Portal rollout in all languages	• Personalized recommendations • Portal for all geos
	UX and knowledge management	• KM portal • Responsive design	• Policy portal • Multichannel enablement	• Solutions management	• REST-based external service integration
Cost optimization	Automation and accelerators for portal	• Reusable portlets • Branded theme	• Leveraging open-source tools in testing, development	• Scripts development for automating code review, deployment	• Plug and play architecture development
Robust governance and scalable digital platform	Project management and infrastructure management	• Continuous and proactive project management with continuous improvement • Infrastructure setup | continuous monitoring | metrics tracking			
	Portal governance	• Governance process for content management	• Governance process for change management	• Governance process for search and collaboration	• Governance for infrastructure management

FIGURE 19.2
Portal roadmap for employee portal.

- *Business priority—3*: Cost optimization
    - Employee portal should reduce employee on-boarding cost
    - Employee portal should reduce operations and maintenance cost
    - Employee portal should support self-service initiatives
- *Business priority—4*: Robust governance and scalable digital platform
    - Employee portal should be easy to maintain and should support faster release cycles and upgrades
    - Employee portal should enable improvised, automated, and efficient processes for employee tasks

In order to fulfill this business vision and prioritized business objectives, we will come up with following portal roadmap depicted in Figure 19.2.

The following are the important points to note from the given multidimensional roadmap:

- The business priorities are mapped to portal capabilities and they are implemented based on the business priority
- Each of the portal capability is implemented in iterative releases through various portal features.
- The portal releases are aligned to the roadmap strategy discussed in Chapter 4. Initial release will provide the information portal capability and subsequent releases enable collaboration portal, unified portal, and self-service portal features.

Portal Governance Model

A robust governance model should clearly define all the required roles and responsibility required for an end-to-end management of portal program throughout its lifecycle.

A sample portal program governance team structure is given in Figure 19.3.

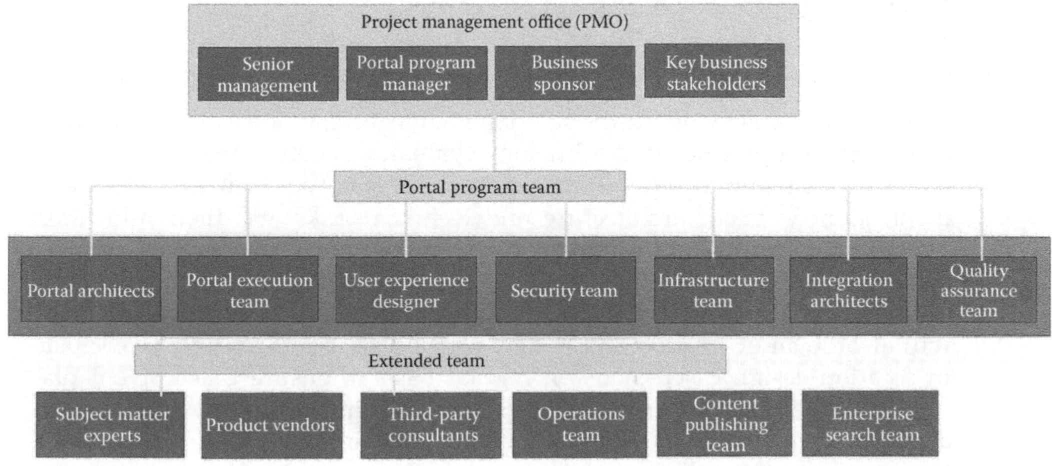

FIGURE 19.3
Portal governance team.

The key roles and responsibilities of main entities in the given governance team structure is explained in the following:

- *Project management office* (*PMO*): This is sometimes referred to as "steering committee" that consists of portal program manager, executive program sponsor, key business stakeholders, and representation from senior management. On need basis the PMO also involves other people such as CTO, COO, etc. PMO is mainly responsible for the following:
  - Owning up the entire portal program, sponsorship, and associated risks. Portal program manager communicates with all members of the PMO on a regular basis.
  - Steer the strategy and direction of the portal program. They align the program with strategic goals and objectives.
  - PMO ensures that portal program goals are aligned with the overall vision of the organization and the portal program objectives are in line with the high-level organization goals.
  - PMO does high-level project tracking and monitoring and other high-level quality assurance activities.
  - The lead members of the PMO also ensure that portal program capabilities are communicated to wider audience to enhance user adoption.
  - PMO handles high-level escalations and other issues related to schedule slippage, effort overrun, etc.
  - PMO is also responsible to ensure availability of all key functional leads and SMEs for requirements elaboration sessions and interviews.
  - PMO uses executive authority to resolve any conflicts and address any inter-track dependencies on time.
  - PMO participates in program-level risk assessment and mitigation activities.
  - PMO helps in leveraging organization-wide resources and take bottom line responsibility for the entire portal program.
  - Enforces organization policies and procedures.
- *Core portal program team*: This team takes the delivery and execution responsibility for the portal program. The team consists of portal experts and developers.
  - *Portal architects*: They define the solution architecture, guide architecture principles, conduct product and technology evaluations, define architecture view, identify open source frameworks and accelerators, perform impact assessment, identify major architecture and technical risks and their mitigation plan and provide architecture recommendations, and define portal roadmap. They actively engage with all business users to obtain the detailed functional specifications, approvals, and the verification of architecture scenarios. They will also do an evaluation and review of the project and actively participate in solution design discussions on regular basis to ensure that implementation is in line with the laid out architecture principles. We have seen various architecture-related activities in Chapter 4. Within architecture community, there could be specialized architect roles such as portal infrastructure architects, portal data architects, and others and each of them will own their

areas of expertise; for instance, portal infrastructure architect will perform a detailed sizing and capacity planning. Portal architecture community takes the ownership of the portal platform architecture and architecture decisions. They closely work with other stakeholders to apprise them about the solution benefits and obtain required sign-offs.

- *Portal execution team*: This team consists of portal developers and portal technology leads who will be mainly involved in creating design for the overall solution and in the development of the project. Developers will be responsible for developing individual modules and unit testing and leads will conduct code reviews and development of complex integrations and modules.
- *User experience designer*: They develop the user-experience specifications, visual style guide, UI mockups and prototypes that depicts the overall look and feel, navigation flow, and overall user experience. These artifacts will be reviewed with business and other concerned stakeholders and will be used for portal development.
- *Security team*: They take the bottom line responsibility in integrating the portal with existing and new security systems such as LDAP, SSO products, etc., and also define the user synchronization, user provisioning, security standards, encryption standards, setting up HTTPS and certificates on server, security testing, and other related activities.
- *Infrastructure team*: They are responsible for setting up and configuring the servers as per the required sizing and capacity specifications in all environments (development, testing, UAT, preproduction, and production). They will also be involved in infrastructure testing phase. This team includes system administrators, Database Administrators (DBA), network administrators, etc. They also report the metrics such as resource utilization reports and outage reports on regular basis to all concerned stakeholders.
- *Integration architects*: In some cases, the technology ecosystem of the organization consists of multiple integration products such as Enterprise Service Bus (ESB), API gateways, and Java Messaging service (JMS) products. In such scenarios, we require specialized integration architects who define the integration architecture and ensure optimal portal integration with existing systems.
- *Quality assurance team*: The team conducts various forms of testing such as functional testing, integration testing, performance testing, load testing, etc. We discussed more about this in Chapter 11.

- *Extended team*: These are optional teams that will be used for specific needs:
  - *Subject matter experts*: If the technology ecosystem includes a niche product or technology, then we need to take the help of the corresponding subject matter experts for optimal integration. For instance, when we are integrating a portal with a sophisticated web analytics tool, it is better to get the expert opinion from the corresponding expert to ensure that we are integrating and setting up the tool in the right way. They also provide testing data and testing support during end-to-end testing.
  - *Product vendors*: For any product-related issues or for obtaining product support or patches and one-off fixes, we can get the help from product vendors.

- *Third-party consultants*: If we are integrating with external systems such as chat or social platforms or CDN systems, we may need to involve those consultants for optimal integration with portal platform. They are also responsible to ensure that their product or component adhere to the specified performance SLAs and provide testing data and testing support.
- *Operations team*: We involve them during release and deployment activities for deploying the portal artifacts and for patching and maintenance activities.
- *Content publishing team*: For publishing new web content and content authoring, publishing team will use portal solution.
- *Enterprise search team*: For integrating the search product with portal platform, we will leverage the expertise of search team to ensure optimal integration. We will setup the crawling and indexing for portal data sources and obtain the search results in an optimal way.

Governance model should also clearly articulate and structure the key business processes along with roles and responsibilities. The main processes in a portal scenario are

- Content management (authoring, approval, and publishing) process
- Portal administration process
- Portal build, release, and deployment process
- Production outage handling process
- Product defect fixing process

Let us briefly explain the two key related to portal requirement prioritization and brand management processes of portal governance model.

Portal Requirements Prioritization Process

The process flow for the portal release management is shown in Figure 19.4.

As we can see that business will provide the business requirements (BR) that will be analyzed by portal team and they provide the feasibility to core project management team who will prioritize the requirements. Finally, the PMO validates and finalizes the priority. The prioritized list will be implemented by the portal team.

Portal Brand Management Process

Let us look at portal brand management and user experience design process in Figure 19.5.

Marketing team provides the key branding inputs and messaging elements, which will be used by core team, and incorporates them into site policies, look and feel elements, portal templates, content templates, etc., and it will be finally approved by the PMO.

Portal Governance Elements

Portal governance essentially addresses three important aspects of the portal program:

- What will be governed? This aspect covers the main focus areas, business processes, and program success elements.

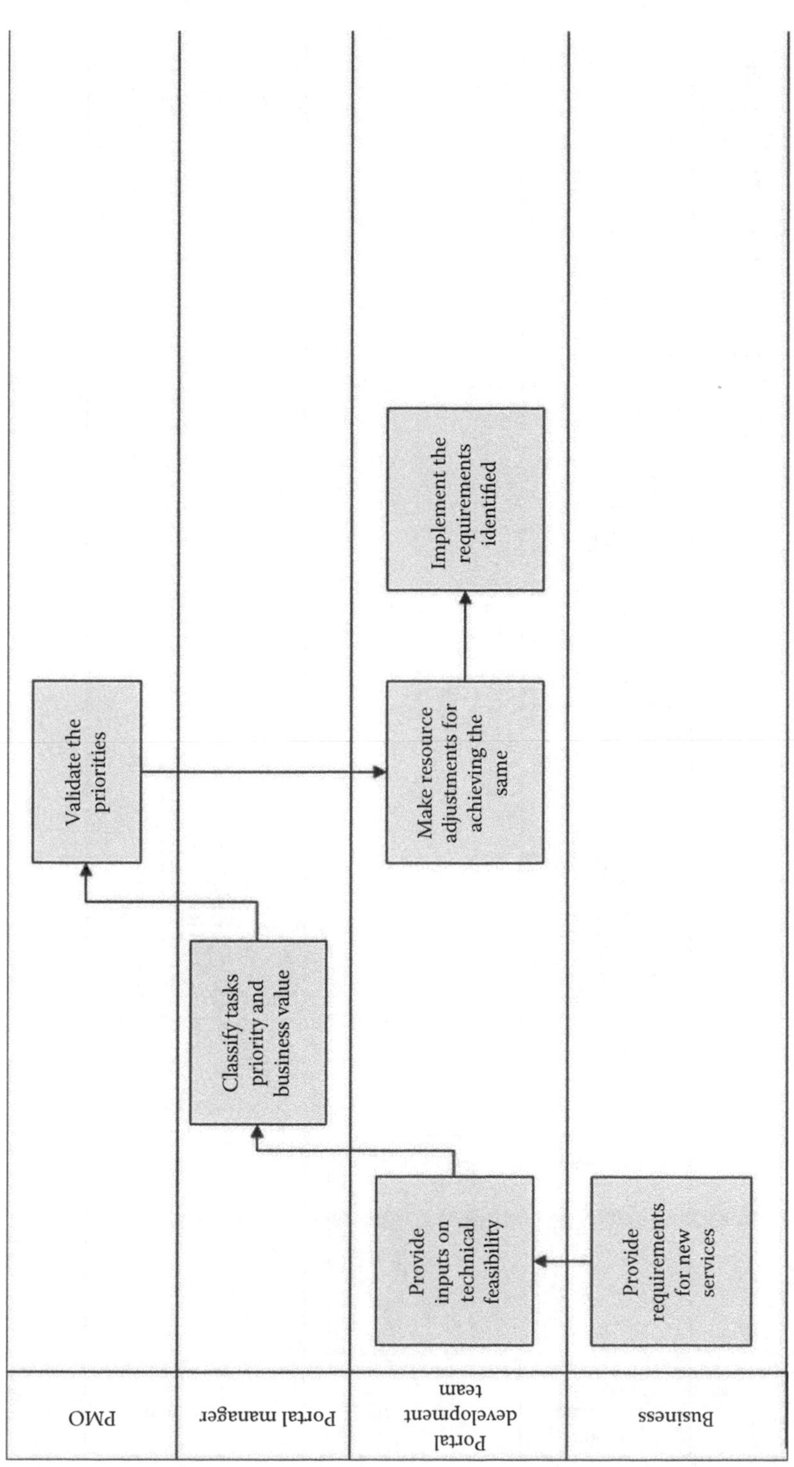

FIGURE 19.4
Portal requirement prioritization process.

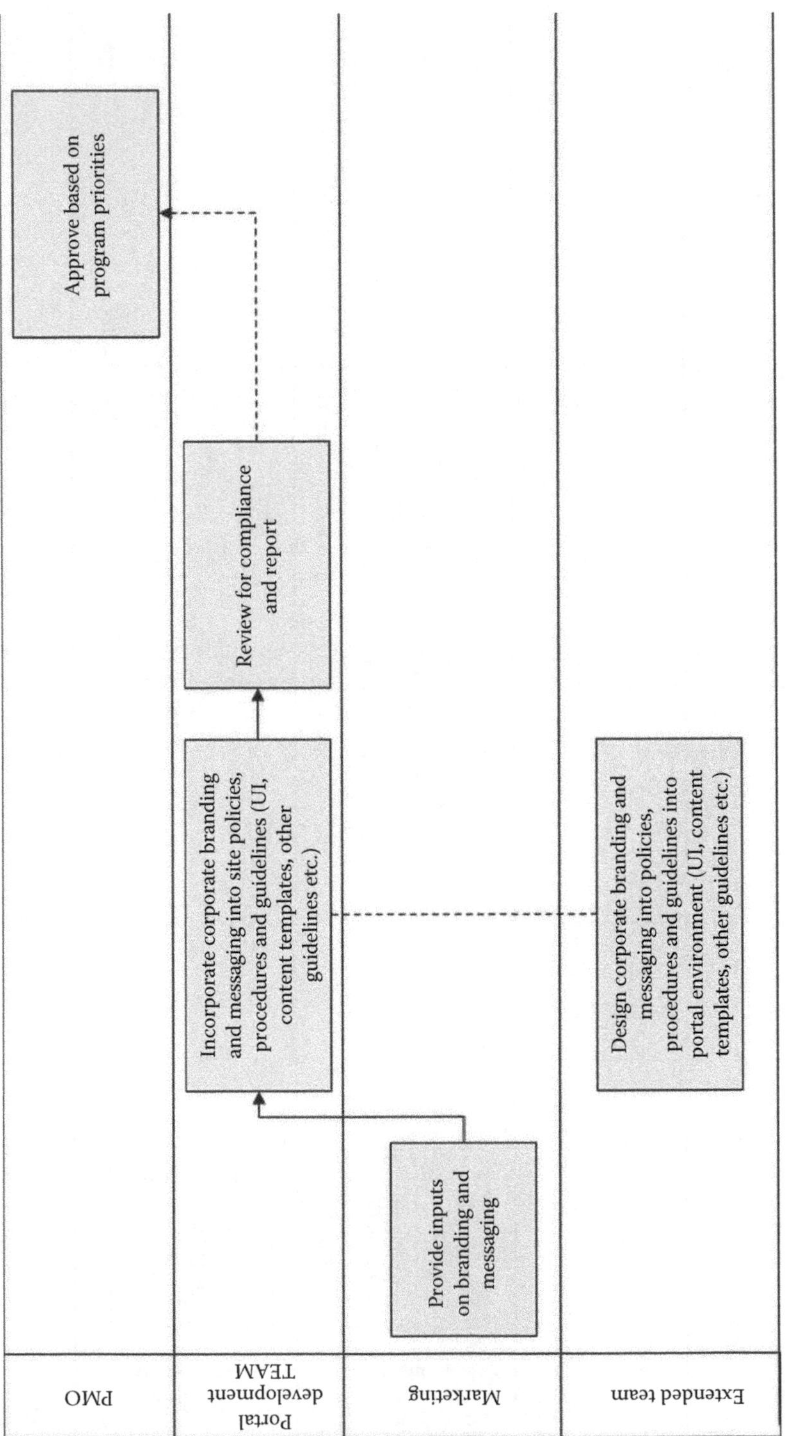

FIGURE 19.5
Portal UI brand management process.

- How will it be governed? The exact process steps, tools, and resources used for governing will be defined in this aspect.
- Who will govern it? The roles and responsibilities will be defined in this aspect. We have already seen the roles and responsibilities in the previous section.

Portal program governance should cover these important aspects as depicted in Figure 19.6:

- *Portal solution*: Manage the portal roadmap, evolution, and the releases of the portal solution. We should also govern the program vision and technology changes.
- *User experience*: Governance should be provided for UX design process, information architecture, tracking, ensuring usability, etc.
- *Enterprise integration*: This includes identifying enterprise interfaces for portal integration, defining framework, and services for integration, SME, vendor management processes, etc.
- *Content management*: Identifying and integrating various content sources would be part of this category. This also includes processes for content migration, assigning and defining content related roles and responsibilities, metadata tagging process, etc.
- *Portal security*: This includes identification and defining the security-related roles and responsibilities.
- *Portal administration*: This includes various processes such as user management, user migration, user provisioning, workflow management, defining and assigning roles, entitlements for users, etc.

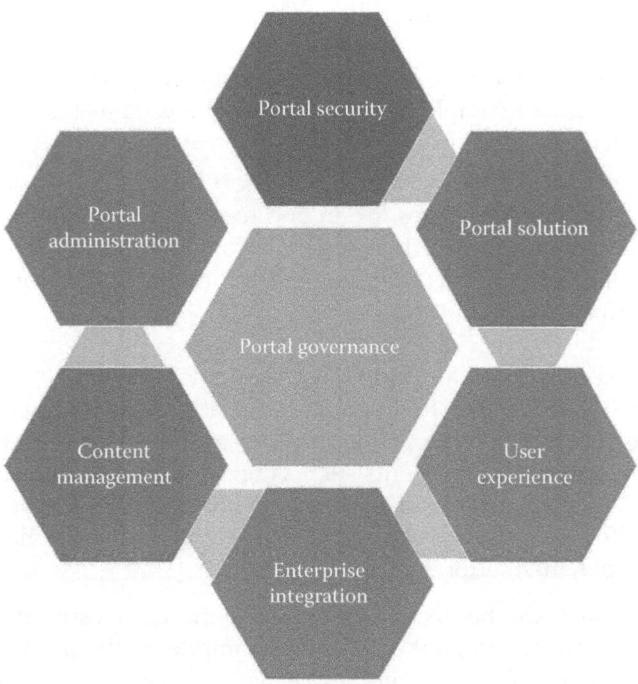

FIGURE 19.6
Portal governance elements.

Portal Estimation Model

Project managers need to provide estimation for the entire program during envision and assessment phase. This further helps in costing, resource staffing, and timeline planning for the entire program. Before starting estimation exercise, it is necessary to have the baselined and signed-off requirements specification document. All use cases, nonfunctional requirements, and exact scope items should be reviewed and finalized.

Given in the following are some of the popular estimation techniques followed in estimating portal activities. In each of these estimation techniques, the functional specification is translated into a form that is suitable for structured estimation.

- *Function point estimate*: This is one of the popular estimation techniques, wherein estimation is based on the number of functions required for implementing a specific requirement. Then, each of the functions is estimated based on the complexity. This is mainly used for business and enterprise application estimation.
- *Simple medium complex (SMC)–based estimation*: This is one of the simple estimation approaches wherein each of the functional specification is mapped to a portal use case and a component. Once we translate the requirement into a known portal component or a portal use case, we can assign a complexity value (which is one among simple, medium, or complex) for each of those portal components. For instance, if the portal provides in-built feature to support a given use case, then it is assigned a simple value, whereas if we need to completely custom build the functionality, then it gets a complex value.

This estimation technique requires the following:

- A framework or guideline to classify a portal component or a use case into simple, medium, or complex effort. This will be used as reference to carry out project-specific estimation.
- Each of the simple, medium, or complex effort should include various activities across project lifecycle stages for an end-to-end implementation of a requirement. This includes build effort, testing effort (for all kinds of applicable testing), documentation effort, deployment effort, training effort, and all other kinds of efforts required.

A sample SMC-based estimation for portal is shown in Figure 19.7.

As we can see in Figure 19.7, the functional specifications are mapped to portal components and they are classified as simple, medium, or complex based on their known complexity. Some of the complex components such as home page development are mapped to multiple functional specifications as it implements multiple functionalities. Also, we can see that the total effort is the sum total of various efforts such as build effort, test effort, document effort, deployment effort, etc.

Use case–based estimation: Another technique for estimation is to estimate the portal project effort using use case-estimation method. We will compile all the prominent use cases for the portal scenarios along with their complexity; we will also identify the actors for all the use cases. We have given the steps in Figure 19.8.

No	Requirement specification No.	Portal component	Effort complexity (simple/medium/complex)	Build effort	Design effort	Testing effort	Documentation effort	Deployment effort	Total effort
1	NA	Portal environment setup	Medium						
			UI design						
2	F1.5, F1.6	Designing portal interface for home page and search page	Complex						
3	F1.7	Design the portal admin interface	Medium						
4	NA	Development of portal theme	Medium						
			Security						
5	F2.2	Portal integration with LDAP	Medium						
6	F2.4	SSO implementation	Complex						
7	F2.8	User and user group creation	simple						
			Integration						
8	F4.3	Portal integration with ERP	Complex						
9	F4.4	Portal integration with reports system	Medium						
			Core portal functionality						
11	F5.2, F5.3, F5.4	Search portlet for search use cases	Medium						
12	F5.6	Content portlet configuration for content features	simple						
13	F5.7, F5.8, F5.9	Portal personalization rules	simple						

FIGURE 19.7
Portal estimation based on SMC method.

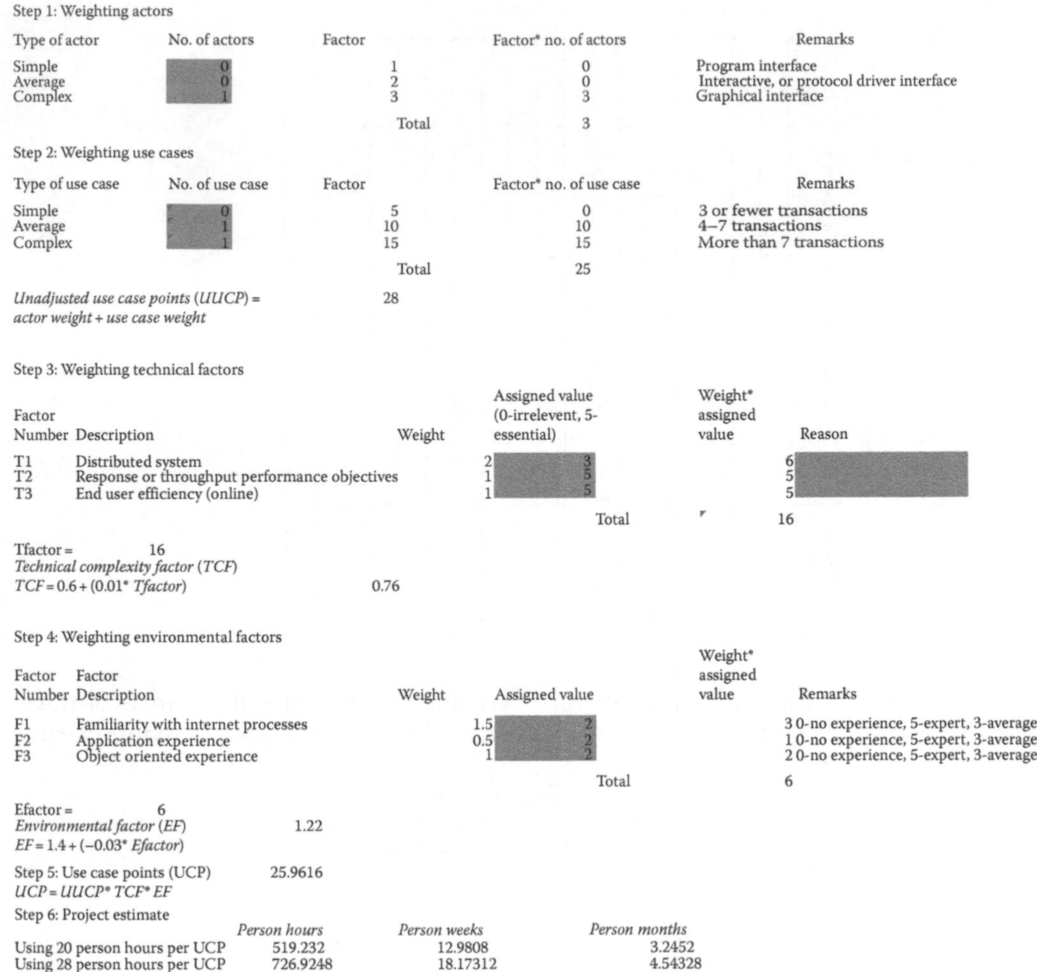

Step 1: Weighting actors

Type of actor	No. of actors	Factor	Factor* no. of actors	Remarks
Simple	0	1	0	Program interface
Average	0	2	0	Interactive, or protocol driver interface
Complex	1	3	3	Graphical interface
		Total	3	

Step 2: Weighting use cases

Type of use case	No. of use case	Factor	Factor* no. of use case	Remarks
Simple	0	5	0	3 or fewer transactions
Average	1	10	10	4–7 transactions
Complex	1	15	15	More than 7 transactions
		Total	25	

Unadjusted use case points (UUCP) = actor weight + use case weight 28

Step 3: Weighting technical factors

Factor Number	Description	Weight	Assigned value (0-irrelevent, 5-essential)	Weight* assigned value	Reason
T1	Distributed system	2	3	6	
T2	Response or throughput performance objectives	1	5	5	
T3	End user efficiency (online)	1	5	5	
			Total	16	

Tfactor = 16
Technical complexity factor (TCF)
TCF = 0.6 + (0.01 Tfactor)* 0.76

Step 4: Weighting environmental factors

Factor Number	Factor Description	Weight	Assigned value	Weight* assigned value	Remarks
F1	Familiarity with internet processes	1.5	2	3	0-no experience, 5-expert, 3-average
F2	Application experience	0.5	2	1	0-no experience, 5-expert, 3-average
F3	Object oriented experience	1	2	2	0-no experience, 5-expert, 3-average
			Total	6	

Efactor = 6
Environmental factor (EF) 1.22
EF = 1.4 + (−0.03 Efactor)*

Step 5: Use case points (UCP) 25.9616
UCP = UUCP TCF* EF*

Step 6: Project estimate

	Person hours	*Person weeks*	*Person months*
Using 20 person hours per UCP	519.232	12.9808	3.2452
Using 28 person hours per UCP	726.9248	18.17312	4.54328

FIGURE 19.8
Portal use case point estimation.

Use case point (UCP) based estimation is followed in Figure 19.8. For this calculation, we have considered two use cases. Once we got the UCP, we have calculated effort using 20 person hours per UCP. An alternate effort estimated by considering 28 person hours per UCP is also shown in Figure 19.8.

Estimation Risks and Mitigation

The main risks while estimating portal programs are as follows:

- *Exact estimation challenge*: Due to the complex nature of portal programs, many niche technologies and enterprise integrations are involved. If there is no prior experience in such technologies or if the enterprise integration has not been tried before, it would be difficult to accurately estimate for that. This would impact the effort and timelines.

The best practice to mitigate this kind of risk is by validation of the design, implementation and integration approach through a proof of concept (PoC), which gives a fair idea of complexity and effort required. For all complex functionality and integrations, a PoC-first strategy is the best way to approach.

- *Nonfunctional requirement (NFR) estimation*: The requirements related to nonfunctional elements such as security, performance, availability, scalability, etc., are often unstructured and ambiguously defined. For example, a performance requirement such as "The portal page should load fast" does not provide the complete (like how many portal pages) and exact scope (how fast in seconds) of performance requirement. The requirement should provide the exact list of pages, the exact response time, or the range of response time and the geography that makes it more specific: "Portal landing pages should load within 2–3 s for North American region" is better than earlier specification. If NFRs are not specified properly, it would not be possible to estimate accurately for it. Hence, it is important for project managers and business analysts to work closely with business and concerned stakeholders to accurately define the NFR.
- *Testing estimates*: Estimation for portal testing is another tricky thing. Due to the conglomerate of technologies, we need to devise test cases from multiple dimensions. Test cases related to usability, accessibility, multidevice compatibility, load testing, stress testing, performance testing, availability testing, multigeotesting, A/B testing, security testing, penetration testing, and vulnerability assessment testing are required when there are explicit or implicit requirements around those areas. So during estimation, project manager has to thoroughly think-through the requirements and all necessary elements for implementing it and include it in the estimation.
- *Estimation for all phases*: A single requirement specification will require multiple project phases for its complete implementation. Right from requirement elaboration in envision phase, it spans to architecture and design phase for design and implementation and testing phase for development and testing it. So when a single functionality or use case is estimated, it is important to estimate it in its entirety, which spans across various project lifecycle stages. Or in other words, the estimation number should factor the effort and time spent for that requirement in various phases. Also, we need to account for other items that consume effort such as documentation, user training, change management, vendor management, review meetings, client coordination, feature deployment, etc.

Portal Release Plan

A portal release plan should comprehend all the portal release–related activities. A well-planned portal release document helps in accurately assessing the release rollout time and can help in effective communication to the concerned stakeholders. The portal release plan provides the details of the following:

- Detailed list and sequence of portal activities required for the release
- Approximate time, dependencies, and other resources required for performing each activity

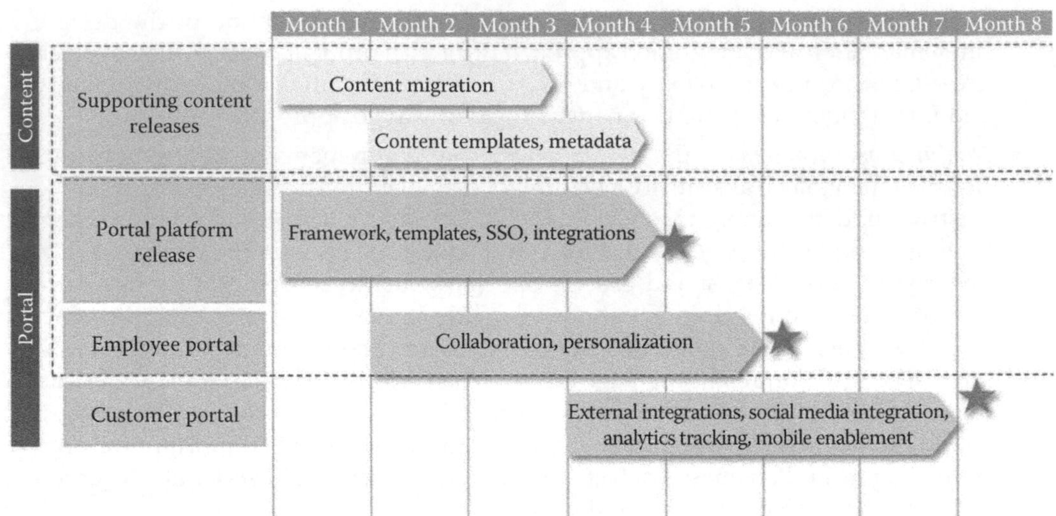

FIGURE 19.9
Portal releases.

- Ownership for each of the activity
- Impact of the rollout on any existing functionality and existing systems
- Fallback plan for rolling back the release
- Testing details for successful verification of the rolled out functionality

Figure 19.9 provides a snapshot of various portal releases of content release, portal platform release, employee portal release and customer portal release. All these 4 portal releases constitute portal road map to realize portal vision.

After having looked at a high-level release plans in Figure 19.9, we will look have a detailed microscopic look at a portal release. In order to explain the things in detail, we have considered a release having the main portal home page and we have explained all the associated release activities.

Portal Home Page Release Plan

- *Brief details of the functionality featuring in the release*: The release includes the production deployment of portal home page featuring web content portlets and search portlets. Web content portlet fetches the web content from the CMS and the search portlet can be used to search the web content artifacts based on their tags and metadata. The functionality is available for both internal and external users.
- *Role restriction if any*: None. Public users can access the content without authentication.
- *URL details*: https://host:port/portal/home
- *Target audience*: Internal employees and external public users.
- *Prerequisites*:
  - CMS should be configured with portal and sample web content should be available. (Home page content chunks should be authored, reviewed and signed-off by all stakeholders.)

- *Communication plan*: The deployment time is communicated to all business stakeholders. A marquee notification campaign is run on old home page from past 1 week.
- *Production outage time*: None. The home page will be refreshed automatically and users can access the new page once the cache is cleared.
- *Brief testing steps*:
  - Access the portal URL mentioned earlier.
  - Check the content under "Latest features" and "Announcements" section. We should see an updated content chunk with the details.
  - Search for "features" in the search portlet and we should see the "latest features" content chunk in the search results page.
- *Rollback plan*:
  - Restore the old code base from backup.
  - Deactivate the portal home page in production portal environment through portal admin console.
- Detailed portal activities for the release is provided in Table 19.2.

TABLE 19.2

Portal Release Activities

Activity	Owner	Approximate Time Period (min)	Details and Impact
One-time setup activities:			
Configure data source in the application server to point to portal database	Production operations team	50	Data source is needed to fetch the portal configuration data from portal database
Configure portal CMS it with portal server			CMS setup and configuration is needed to fetch web content chunks
Take the backup of existing code base in production environment			
Portal theme deployment	Portal operations team using Deployment script	5	Portal theme creates a consistent header and footer
Search portlet deployment	Portal operations team using Deployment script	5	The portlet executes content search
Web content portlet deployment	Portal operations team using Deployment script	5	The portlet fetches content from CMS
Portal home page promotion	Portal operations team using Deployment script	5	The page displays web content portlet and search portlet
Portal page and portlet activation	Portal operations team using Deployment script	5	The portlets and page will be ready after being activated

Portal Project Management Best Practices

Let us look at the main project management best practices in a portal project.

Agile Execution Approach

Agile is being increasingly adopted in portal projects as it effectively mitigates the risks related to project complexity and enables faster time to market. Some of the agile methods include Scrum, Extreme programming (XP), test driven development (TDD), Dynamic system development method, and adaptive software development. Agile execution approach involves user stories for a given sprint, requirements elaboration, design, testing, and deployment for sprint-based iteration. Agile methodology provides a framework for incremental solution development through sprint-based iterative releases. Each sprint is an incremental addition to the business functionality from its previous sprint. Product backlog items provide the desired features that are of value to the users. Some of the complexities of a typical portal program make the agile approach best suited:

- *Complexity in integration*: Agile enables iterative sprint-based execution wherein we can rollout integrations phase-wise. All complex and failure scenarios will be discovered early, thereby helping us to draft a mitigation plan. We can evaluate the feasibility of complex functions and integrations through proof of concepts and prototypes in agile manner to mitigate the risk caused due to complex integrations.
- *Improved productivity*: Agile practices will enable the team to perform to its fullest potential.
- *Release and deployment timelines*: Agile enables quicker time to market through sprint releases.
- *Management of dynamic and fluid requirements*: It is possible to absorb feedback from end users and business community in subsequent sprints. This provides flexibility to incorporate changes and enhancements without major disruptions. This would be useful during complex/ambiguous/evolving requirements.
- *Faster execution*: Agile allows us to have faster requirements elaboration, design, development, and testing cycles as they will be carried out for a sprint.
- *Agile best practices*: The key agile best practices are given below:
    - *Prioritize requirements*: The business-critical and user-focused requirements need to prioritize for the iterative sprints. We follow many techniques for requirements prioritization. User stories is one key requirement prioritization technique. In this technique, each user story provides user perspective of performing a business process. User stories which are independent, small, coherent, testable, and valuable to users form ideal candidates. Minimum marketable feature (MMF) is another technique used for requirement prioritization. MMF identifies set of features which provide adequate business value which can be a part of a release. Another technique used is MoSCoW which categorizes requirements into "Must have," "Should have," "Could have," and "wont have." Cost of Delay (CoD) technique uses opportunity cost of not having a feature in a release.

- *Design best practices*: The main design principles of agile methodology are as follows:
  - Keep the interface simple which is easy to use
  - The code should be self-explanatory
  - Minimal duplication of functionality
  - Highest test coverage: Test driven development (TDD) is one such technique which aims to provide highest code coverage functionality
  - Follow single responsibility principle wherein a code component addresses only one concern
  - Open/closed principle which states that software entities should be open for extension but closed for modification
  - Dependency inversion principle wherein the class should depend on abstractions rather than concrete implementations
- *Coding-related best practices*: The main code related best practices are as follows:
  - Continuous code refactoring by removing duplicate code, making the code cohesive, modular and reusable and adopting best practices and design patterns
  - Adopt test driven development to ensure completeness of all functionality
  - Check-in code iteratively and fix any broken build immediately

In addition to the above agile methodologies also include communication-related best practices such as real-time communication, Virtual collaboration, etc.

Productivity Improvement

There are multiple dimensions to productivity improvement. With each successive release, if the project manager can improve the quality, cost, and timelines without significant variation in project resources, then it will be termed as an improvement in overall productivity. The following are some of the productivity improvement measures:

- Identifying and leveraging tools to automate the project activities such as code review, release and deployment, testing, etc. Project managers can leverage the portal coding checklists, best practices, and open source tools listed in Chapter 15.
- Cross-training the portal resources so that they can perform various roles and handle multiple responsibilities
- Developing scripts and components to automate the frequently encountered activities in the portal project such as backup, migration, deployment, etc.
- Enabling faster information discovery and knowledge management tools can improve the productivity of the development team
- Adopting industry standard best practices and portal-coding guidelines and checklists help the team to achieve higher quality and this improves the overall productivity of the team

Usage of Tools and Accelerators

Project managers need to constantly seek better ways of executing the portal project. Usage of tools, scripts, and accelerators are efficient ways to achieve productivity improvements across all phases of the project. The following are some the tools and frameworks that can accelerate portal development and testing:

- Open source tools for portal static code review such as PMD, Checkstyle, and Findbugs
- Continuous integration (CI) tools such as Jenkins and Hudson that are discussed in detail in the next category
- Automatic code deployment tools and scripts faster release cycles

Requirement Traceability Matrix

Tracing the requirements from envision phase till the production deployment phase would ensure that there are no gaps during implementation and testing. Project managers can create a detailed traceability matrix that map each requirement, use case scenario to the component that implements it, and the corresponding test case.

The traceability matrix will also help during impact assessment while we are fixing any defect or estimating for an enhancement during change requests.

Continuous Integration (CI)

The concept of CI is becoming a standard for project execution due to its high potential of positive impact on quality and schedule. CI provides a single platform that can help the project managers to perform, manage, and track a lot of project management activities. CI makes efforts in small parts and is integrated daily, multiple times a day to maintain quality control. This greatly reduces time and effort and the problems faced during integration. This tool is useful in continuously building and testing projects and scheduling jobs and keeping track of them. CI tools can automate a lot of activities such as build, deployment, code review, testing, and reporting; it can trigger notification in the event of build failure or upon occurrence of any configured event; it provides dashboard view of important project statistics like code quality, defect rate, build failures, test reports, etc. As we can see, CI plays many roles and it can seamlessly connect to version control system through plugins and automate many of the project management and quality-related activities.

There are multiple open-source tools such as Hudson, Jenkins, and CruiseControl that can be leveraged for setting up a CI platform. Jenkins is one of the most popular CI tool due to its rich set of plugins.

Some of the main advantages of adopting CI tools for portal project are as follows:

- They automate some of the main activities such as unit testing, web testing, deployment, code review, code coverage, performance testing, and file copy through plugins
- They provide significant reduction in overall time due to automation
- Project managers can implement the industry standard best practices, tools, and accelerators through CI platforms
- They greatly improves the quality due to continuous and early testing

- They provide a holistic picture and overall health of the project through comprehensive dashboard
- Project managers can achieve better control over quality and timelines through CI tool

Let us look at a small case study of using Jenkins CI for a portal project. Listed below are portal project activities which can be automated through Jenkins CI.

- *Portal source control integration*: Jenkins can connect to source control CVS system through its in-built feature.
- *Portal builds*: We can configure Maven build script with Jenkins so that Jenkins can perform nightly builds in an agile methodology. Jenkins provides out of the box (OOTB) support for Maven and Ant build scripts.
- *Portal code review*: We can leverage on PMD, Checkstyle, Sonar, and FindBugs plugins of Jenkins for automating the static code analysis of portal code base. We can also use these plugins for duplicate code detection and security violations.
- *Portal code deployment*: Jenkins also has plugins to automate the file copy and portlet WAR file deployments for various application servers.
- *Portal testing*: We can automate unit testing through JUnit plugin and web testing through Selenium Jenkins plugin. We can also load test the portal application through Apache JMeter plugin.
- *Reporting and notification*: Jenkins provides plugins to report the build failures in a user-friendly dashboard and notify to the configured email addresses.

Continuous Improvement

Portal roadmap strategy provides clear guidelines for portal release along with their features and timelines. Project managers should aim to achieve all-round improvement with each release. The following are some of the improvement opportunities in portal programs:

- *Knowledge repository*: We need to build a knowledge base consisting of solution artifacts. The solution knowledge base should help address the frequently encountered problems and define best practices that act as guides during crisis situations. We can use the portal knowledge repository to store portal best practices, portal coding checklists, business processes, troubleshooting tips that can be used by portal community. Additionally, we can also expose the knowledge repository to end users and collaborate with them to create the solutions applicable for wider audience. This improves productivity and issue resolution time. Portal provides in-built CMS in and adaptors to open source KM systems that can be leveraged to build the knowledge repository.
- *Process automation*: Project managers need to proactively identify the processes that are repetitive, and that require lot of manual effort. These are the best candidates for automation. A few classical scenarios in portal programs are
  - Portal Release and deployment process, which can be fully automated through tools and scripts
  - Portal code review through IDE plugins and open source static code review tools

- Portal testing scenarios such as functional testing, web testing, load testing, and stress testing, which can be done through open source tools
- Portal content and data backup and archival activities can be automated through scripts

- Process automation not only reduces manual effort but also helps improve quality and greatly reduces overall process time. Additionally, the tools and accelerators that can be used for automation will also be used.
- *Process standardization*: Project managers can create standard operating procedure (SOP) for complex portal process. Activities such as production outage handling, one-off patch application, production testing, portal page promotion, content publishing, and portal maintenance all are multistep processes that also require approvals from multiple stakeholders. A standard set of instructions to perform these activities and the ownership (with role responsibility matrix) will help in completing these processes within the agreed SLAs.
- *Self-service model*: With each portal release, focus needs to be given on self-help features that enable the end user to complete the required task with minimal outside support. Portal features such as contextual search, FAQ, guided navigation, contextual help, e-learning, solution repository, web-based training, and solution knowledge base will go a long way in helping end user to complete the intended activities without the help of support personnel. This not only reduces the support incidents/calls but also helps in greatly improving the customer satisfaction, loyalty, and retention.
- *Increased collaboration*: Collaboration features such as chat, blogs, wikis, communities, etc., have multifold impact on end user satisfaction. An effective collaboration platform will actively engage the end users by harnessing collective intelligence and help them to share the knowledge thereby promoting self-service model. Most of the portal products provide in-built collaboration tools and plugins for external collaboration frameworks that can be leveraged to meet this end.
- *Preventive maintenance and monitoring*: After the initial portal release, preventive maintenance activities should be followed for proactive defect prevention. This category includes root-cause analysis and proactively identifying the issue before they occur and addressing them. The portal application will be continuously monitored in real time to get early warnings of performance issues and outage scenarios. The health check of portal systems and servers are conducted and corrective actions should be taken when problem patterns are noticed. Portal problem patterns include consistent high CPU utilization (more than 90%), consistent memory usage, frequent garbage collection activity, frequent cache flushing, degrading performance, frequent exceptions in log files, frequent time outs with external interfaces, internal server issue errors, etc.
- *Skill development*: Portal resources are continuously cross-skilled through trainings so that they can play various roles and carry out multiple responsibilities.
- *Reusability*: Identify the opportunities to reuse existing portal components and portlets and develop the components in modular way to enhance reusability. This will improve the productivity and accelerate the release timelines. Some of the most commonly employed reuse portal opportunities are
  - Script-based portal content migration
  - Reusable content portlets

    - Content presentation templates
    - Portal page templates
    - Database and service adaptors
- *Defect prevention*: Continuous code review, manually and through automated means, would help us to proactively uncover defects. Additionally, regular monitoring and analysis of identified defects will help to identify problem areas and patterns that would lead to potential defects in near future. Proactive code refactoring and code-quality improvement in those areas will avoid the defects.
- *Continuous code quality improvement*: Iterative code reviews should be conducted to improve the overall quality of the code. Leveraging tools such as PMD can identify the duplicate sections of the code and can eliminate the duplicates to make it more modular and reusable. Standard portal coding checklists, design patterns, and guidelines should form one of the main gating criteria before code check-in. Additionally, CI tools should be configured to automatically do the static code analysis post checking and the code quality reports should be published.

Risk Management Process

Risk management process involves continuous risk-handling activities. Figure 19.10 depicts high-level steps involved:

- *Risk identification*: Risk could occur in any project lifecycle phase. So at each phase, the project manager has to list the potential risks and quantify its impact. Risk profiling is done to identify the risk acceptance and tolerance level for each of the identified risks.

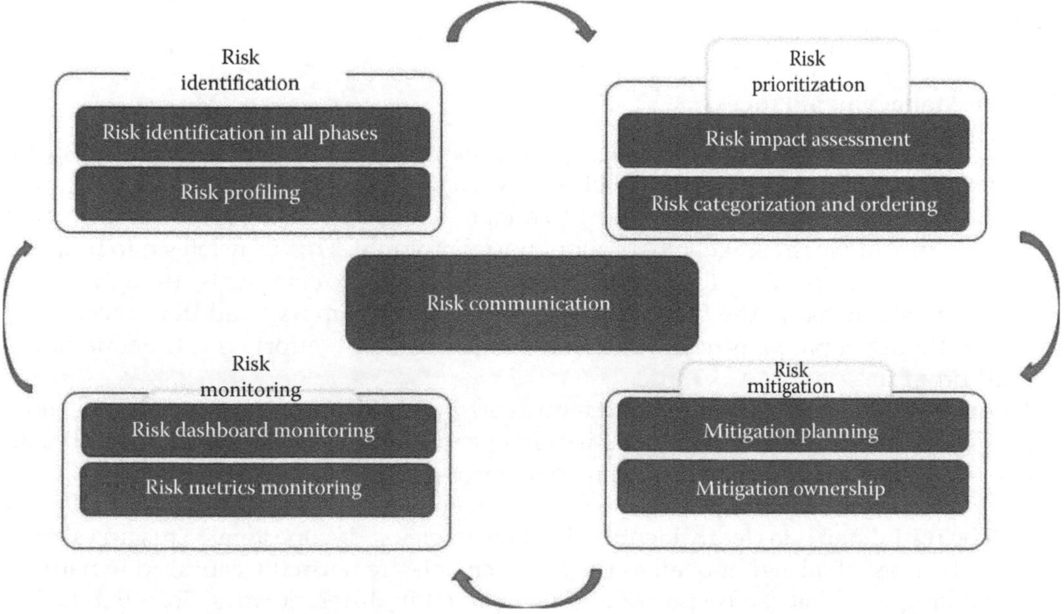

FIGURE 19.10
Portal risk management process.

- *Risk prioritization*: Once we identify the risk and its business impact, we can prioritize it based on its overall impact. Risks are also categorized as business risk, technical risk, operation risk, and security risk so that it will be easy to assign the owner. We can start drafting the action items and next steps based on this prioritized list. All business critical risks are strictly time bound and needs immediate attention. The risk quantification can be done based on the impact of the risk on business and end users. A quantifiable risk score is calculated based on risk probability, business impact, and mitigation cost. An approximate monetary value attached to the risk impact would also act as quantifying measurement.
- *Mitigation plan*: For each of the prioritized list of risk items, project managers have to come up with detailed risk mitigation plan by discussing with all SMEs and architects. The mitigation plan should be well structured and assigned an owner with an ETA for implementing it.
- *Risk monitoring*: The prioritized list of risks should be monitored on continuous basis till the risk is fully addressed. Also, we need to constantly look out for other potential risks in each project phase. Risks can be monitored through risk dashboards, regular reports, and risk metrics.
- *Risk communication*: Portal project manager need to send regular risk updates and risk monitoring reports and mitigation plan to all stakeholders in the PMO. Any long-running and critical risk should be escalated to the attention of concerned authority.

These five steps need to happen in cyclical fashion for each project phase. A comprehensive risk management dashboard should be created to have complete control on risk and mitigation plan.

We have given some commonly occurring risks in portal program in each of the project management stages earlier; the risk mitigation plan is also detailed that can be used to address the risks.

Change Management Process

Scope creep is one of the key challenges that project managers need to manage during the portal programs. Since portal solution involves many stakeholders spanning multiple domain areas and is of key interest to a lot of users, it is quite natural to have high expectations from many stakeholders about portal program. This translates into frequent reviews and accompanying feedback. Some of the feedback comments, though useful, may not be estimated in the baselined program scope. Attempts to address those comments without proper planning would have impact on cost, effort, and timeline of the overall program.

A change is anything that impacts the estimated and signed-off effort, cost, and timelines. Given in the following is an effective change management process that project managers can adopt to manage any scope creep items or change requests:

- The initial step is to clearly identify the deliverables and scope items. This first step is the most challenging of all as the requirements are normally captured in natural language that can be potentially interpreted in different ways. So, a detailed functional specification document should clearly articulate the requirements in an unambiguous manner and define the steps, process, deliverables, and business rules. We can have functional specification document for each iteration or sprint. Use case document, business requirements document (BRD), functional specifications document provide structured format to capture the requirements unambiguously. Requirements from various perspectives should be captured in these documents and should be thoroughly reviewed and signed-off by all concerned stakeholders.

- Once the requirements are finalized, it needs to be baselined and the project manager should get them signed-off from the PMO and all relevant stakeholders. Once signed-off, the requirements should be frozen for that release iteration and it should be baselined.
- During the course of project execution, all review comments and feedback should be compiled. The comments that deviate from the baseline requirements are termed as "change requests." Project managers should also clearly articulate why a given review comment is categorized as a change request by comparing it with the baselined scope item.
- The portal execution team would perform a detailed impact analysis of the requested change. The analysis includes the effort required for implementing the change, impact on other modules, and timeline required to implement the change.
- PMO reviews the change request and its business value and importance. Based on the discussion it will be submitted to change control board (CCB).
- CCB will come up with detailed plan to implement the change request. The implementation plan has the details of additional effort, exact timeline, impact on existing modules, the release and deployment plan, and testing methods.
- Once the change request is implemented, it is tested and released to the business owner for further testing and verification.

Key Performance Indicators of Technical Project Management

The critical program KPIs to measure the success of technical project management process are as follows:

- *Code quality*: There should be standard code quality governance process at all levels
- *Degree of automation*: Automated tools and components need to be employed to the best possible extent
- *Continuous build and monitoring*: Builds should be frequent and continuously monitored for success and failures, testing metrics, etc.
- *Notification/alerting mechanism*: Proper notification mechanism should be established to notify all stake holders about the overall project status and project health
- *Productivity improvements*: There should be a framework for continuous productivity improvement by leveraging best practices, learning, and the usage of automated tools

We have discussed more about these KPIs in Chapter 15.

Summary

- The chapter discusses various project management aspects of portal.
- Common portal project management challenges are cross-functional team coordination, lack of governance process to handle complex activities, change request handling, and managing multiple roles and environments.
- Main project management stages are program envision and assessment phase, portal architecture and design phase, portal solution development and testing phase, and portal maintenance and evolution phase.
- *In project envision phase, we perform these activities*: Compile requirements through workshops, interviews, define scope and project plan, define requirement traceability and requirements, and define NFR requirements.
- *In architecture and design phase, we do the following activities*: Portal architecture definitions, design validation, PoCs, product evaluation, etc.
- In development and testing phase we develop portal solution, we do portal integration, and perform end-to-end testing.
- In evolution and maintenance phase, we perform continuous monitoring and maintenance release–related activities.
- Portal governance model defines all the required roles and responsibilities required for an end-to-end management of portal program throughout its lifecycle.
- Key entities in portal governance model are PMO, core portal program team, and extended team.
- Popular portal estimation techniques are function point estimate, use case–based estimation, and SMC-based estimation.
- Portal release plan should comprehend all the portal release–related activities.
- Main portal project management best practices are agile execution approach, productivity improvement, usage of tools and accelerators, requirement traceability matrix, CI, continuous improvement, risk management process, and change management process.

20

Portal Performance Engineering

Performance is a key ingredient for the success of any online platform. It impacts user experience, site traffic, conversion rate, user loyalty, and other key elements that are directly associated with the success of the program. In a portal scenario, performance is of prime importance as portal eco-system involves multiple layers, multiple systems and hence multiple points of failure. During information aggregation, the portal depends on various content sources and it becomes challenging to maintain optimal performance.

We have already seen some of the performance best practices and checklists in Chapter 15. As performance is one of the critical success factors for portal applications, we have dedicated this chapter to focus on the key aspects of portal performance such as caching, performance testing, and other aspects related to portal performance engineering. Portal developers, portal architects, performance engineering team, enterprise architects, and quality team will find the content of this chapter useful.

Introduction

The principal judge of the portal performance is the end user as most of the portals are predominantly targeted for Internet audience. Users expect a good page response time and transaction completion time. A page-load time within 1 s across geographies is considered to be a decent response time for today's audience. However, as there is lot of diversity in the target environment, we need to factor the network latency across geographies, performance on various devices, performance during personalization scenarios, performance challenges during integration/information aggregation, etc.

Critical Success Factors for Portal Performance

We have seen some of the performance best practices in previous chapters. Let us look at the key success factors for optimal portal performance:

- Establishing well-defined performance service-level agreements (SLAs) for functional and nonfunctional requirements. This also includes collecting all related performance requirements such as user load details, portal usage trends, geo- and device-specific performance SLAs, etc.
- Comprehensive performance testing to simulate all major portal scenarios and use cases from end-user stand point. This includes load testing, endurance testing, multidevice testing, process testing, stress testing, peak load testing, multigeo-testing, etc.
- Factoring-in performance as one of the criteria during infrastructure design and testing.

- Adopting a "bottom-up" approach during portal development. This includes performance-based component design, caching, using performance checklist for code reviews and gating criteria, etc.
- Performing continuous and iterative performance validation from early phases of the portal development. This includes leveraging automated performance testing tools and continuous integration.
- Building a comprehensive performance monitoring infrastructure that monitors the health check, resource utilization, and performance of internal portal systems and external portal applications in real time. The monitoring infrastructure should also notify the admins during performance issues.

Caching

Caching frequently accessed information on the portal page improves performance of the portal site, delivers enhanced user experience, and reduces resource consumption on the web server, application server, and database server. Information can be cached at various layers depending on the level of dynamism of the information and access control restrictions. The closer the information is cached to the requestor the better the user experience will be. The aim of caching in the portal is to increase the cache hits and at the same time to ensure that dynamic or personalized content is delivered to the user to ensure content freshness.

Caching optimizes content retrieval by storing frequently accessed data in the closest possible location. As caching plays a major role in portal performance optimization, let us look at it in greater detail in this section.

Content Types and Portal Caching Scenarios

One of the key aspects to achieve success in caching is to decide "what to cache," "where to cache," and "how long to cache." "What to cache" is a question of content type that needs to be cached; it is all about choosing the appropriate cache candidates. "Where to cache" is related to the layer where the cached data needs to be stored and "how long to cache" is essentially the cache period. In order to answer the questions related to caching candidates and cache period, we need to understand the content served by the portal. Let us look at it in the following.

Portal Content Type

Portal mainly serves two types of content—static and dynamic:

1. *Static content*: Portal serves various types of information in the form of pages and portlets. Some of this information does not change over a period of time (in some cases for extended duration) and is shown to public users who access the site. This type of public information is referred to as static information. Static information does not change over a considerable period of time and is shared across multiple users as it is not personalized. For example, the "about us" and "contact us" information rarely changes and qualifies for static information.

2. *Dynamic content*: Certain information shown on the portal varies based on the personalization or access control logic and hence is categorized as dynamic content. For instance, search results portlets are based on user-configured values, personalized feed content is dependent on the user-configured feed URL, etc. The main attributes of dynamic content are that it is heavily dependent on user context and underlying content changes frequently.

As far as "what to cache" is concerned, static content is the most natural choice and the starting point for caching.

Portal Caching Scenarios

As web content and authored content form a major chunk of information portals, let us look at the types of caching options available for content caching. Portal page content can be cached at a page level, content fragment level, or object level.

- Page caching provides maximum benefit, but it is useful only if all entire information on the page is static.
- If any information on the page is dynamic (due to personalization or access control), it leads to a cache miss. In such a scenario, caching the various fragments (portlet level content) that form the page will be a more effective caching strategy.
- In cases where the fragments can also be dynamic, caching the information retrieved from the backend systems in an object cache will be an effective design leading to maximum cache hits.

Portal Page Caching

We can improve the performance considerably by caching entire portal pages. The entire page that has been constructed from different portlets can be cached on the edge server or on the portal web server. This technique is used for portal pages that are static containing content that changes rarely.

Cache invalidation: If the portal page is cached at the edge server layer (CDN Layer), then it can be invalidated under three circumstances:

1. An expiration timeout occurs.
2. A cache item is purged to make room for newer entries.
3. The portal server sends an explicit invalidation for a group of cache items. Usually the invalidation is done through an application program interface (API) or service call using the page URL as the cache key. Invalidation is triggered when the portal content changes through content updates or by content publishing.

Content Fragment Caching

We can cache the individual portlet outputs that constitute the page. We can improve its performance by caching the output of portlets into memory. The cache key is constructed using the content id or metadata (using a unique value generated through hash function) constructed from content identifiers. We can leverage on object caching to cache content fragments.

Cache invalidation: The portlet content fragment in the cache has to be invalidated whenever the content is updated and published by the author. An invalidation service can be

TABLE 20.1
Portal Cache Candidates

Portal Object	Caching Layer and Type	Caching Duration
Static assets (images, PDFs, documents, video files, CSS, JS, etc.)	Best cached at CDN layer followed by web server layer	Can be cached for an extended duration ranging from day to a week based on the frequency of change, as it is mainly static content. TTL (time-to-live)-based cache invalidation can be used
Portal page content: static content (FAQ, contact us, etc.)	Page level cache, which can be cached at CDN layer or at portal web server layer	Can be cached for an extended duration ranging from day to a week based on frequency of change, as it is mainly static content. TTL (time-to-live)-based cache invalidation can be used
Portal page content: dynamic content (personalized portlets, search results, role-based access content, etc.)	Combination of fragment level caching and object level caching	Cache invalidation tied to user session On-demand caching when the source content changes
Portlet level content	Combination of fragment level caching and object level caching	Cache invalidation tied to user session On-demand cache invalidation when the source content changes
Search results	Object caching: search results cached with search query keyword as cache key for fixed duration	The caching duration is configurable and determined based on the frequency of update in source content
Information retrieved from backend Information such as the following: • Data obtained from database • Content retrieved from content services • External feeds (RSS/ATOM) • Data retrieved from web services	Object cache: data from external systems is cached at portal layer using object caching with the query string/data identifier as the cache key	The caching duration is configurable and determined based on the frequency of update in source content Additionally on-demand cache invalidation triggered when source content changes

called whenever the content is updated or published. The invalidation service will necessarily take the content ID of all the modified contents and invalidate the cache that has the specified content ID as the key.

Portal Caching Candidates

The main portal elements that are ideal for caching are given in Table 20.1.

Portal Caching Layers

When using portal and other integrated products like reverse proxies and edge caching products, information can be cached at different layers depending upon the level of dynamism and sensitivity. Layer-wise caching is also one of the most effective techniques to achieve optimal performance in multilayer systems. A simplistic representation of layer-wise caching in a portal environment is given in Figure 20.1.

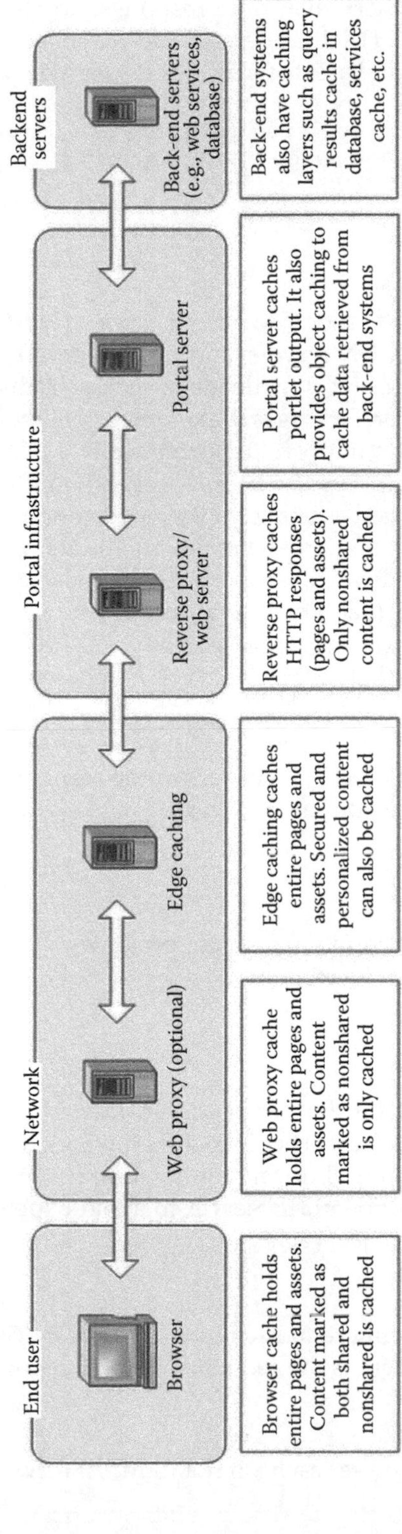

FIGURE 20.1
Portal layer-wise caching.

Browser Cache

Browsers have built-in cache where they store responses to HTTP request based on the caching parameters set in the HTTP headers of the response. A sample instruction in Apache web server to cache digital assets for 2 days is given below

```
<FilesMatch "\.(ico|pdf|txt|jpg|jpeg|png|gif|js|css|swf|json)$">
 Header set Cache-Control "max-age=172800, public"
</FilesMatch>
```

Edge Caching

Portal assets like images, PDFs, videos, JavaScripts, stylesheet (CSS) files, and Flash files can be cached by edge servers (CDN servers) and can be served from the server closest to the end user. This will provide faster downloads as well as reduce the load on the origin web server and application server. For pages that require personalization or access control, prefetching option can be used to improve performance.

Additionally, static portal pages can also be fully cached on the edge server. Edge server serves the portal pages and related assets from the nearest node and provides other optimizations such as asset caching, on-demand cache invalidation, etc.

Some edge servers also provide features like optimal routing and SSL acceleration features that improve portal site availability and performance.

Web Proxies

User request might be passing through intermediate proxy servers that can cache information. This again is controlled by HTTP headers in the response. Portal provides mechanism to control the HTTP headers on the response.

Reverse Proxy

Shared information can be cached by the reverse proxy web server. This again is dependent on the HTTP headers set in the response.

Portlet Caching

Portlet caching is a local cache on the portal server. Dynamic, personalized, or access-controlled content generated by the portlet is cached locally on the portal server through object caching or fragment caching. Information retrieved from portal database or backend servers is cached locally on the portal server to avoid expensive calls across the network. This can be cached in an object cache.

Example Scenario

Let us consider a portal page being requested by an end user. The portal page consists of themes and multiple portlets. Here is the sequence of steps involved:

1. User hits a portal page URL
2. The browser checks the browser cache. If not found, it forwards the requests to the edge server (CDN).

3. If the content is cached by edge server, it serves the cached content from nearest geographical server; if the content is not cached on CDN it forwards the request to the web server/reverse proxy.
4. The web server/reverse proxy checks the local cache and if not found, forwards the request to the portal server.
5. The portal server pulls up the themes and various portlets on the page.
6. For each portlet, the portal server checks local cache to see if the portlet output has been cached. If not, the portlet code is executed.
7. If the portlet requires backend information, it checks local object cache. If not found, it calls the backend systems to retrieve and cache the content in the object. Optionally, the back-end servers can use their own caching layers for further optimizations.
8. The portal server caches the portlet output if it is configured to be cached.
9. The portal collates the responses from each portlet and theme.
10. The response is sent to the web server/reverse proxy.
11. The response is sent to the edge server. It caches the page if the page is configured to be cached.
12. The response is sent to the browser. It caches the page based on cache header directives.

Portal Caching Methodologies

Let us look at the various caching techniques that can be used in a portal scenario.

HTTP Cache Headers

This caching is based on HTTP headers set in the response. Portal provides options to specify the caching configurations at a page level using portal theme. While creating the response, portal checks the configuration of all elements of the page and identifies the correct caching headers to set in the response. We can also specify the cache TTL (time-to-live) in the HTTP cache headers.

Object Caching

Portal can leverage in-built object caching or use open-source caching frameworks (such as Ehcache, OSCache) for providing object caching feature. Object cache is essentially a sophisticated Map that can store the key-value pairs. Object caching frameworks provide configurations to specify the cache TTL, cache size, priority, and other options.

Example of Content Fragment Caching Using Object Caching

Each individual content portlet retrieves the content from content data source (such as CMS). Content web service will return content ID along with the content chunk in the response. Content chunk fragment will be stored in object cache with the key as Content ID; this is the second level of cache.

Similarly, content portlet will maintain a cache that resolves the content ID from the content query parameters (which are configured in content portlet preferences). This object cache will have the value as list of content IDs and hash code of the query parameter will

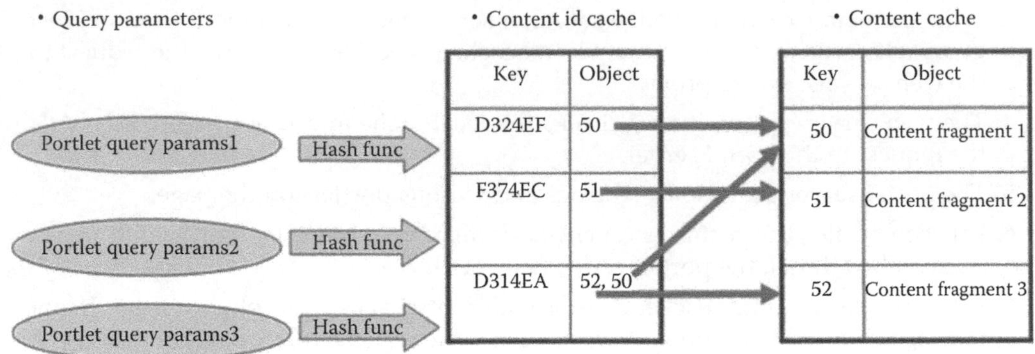

FIGURE 20.2
Two-level content fragment caching.

be used as cache key; this is the first level of cache. Content portlet will be configured with values such as content metadata, content path which form the content query parameters. A hash function of these query parameters will be used as cache key and content ids will be mapped against these key values.

Two-level caching implemented using object cache is shown in the Figure 20.2.

Cache Candidates

Portlet content fragments, frequently used objects, controlled list of values (such as country names, language names), data retrieved from database call and service call, and files are ideal candidates that can leverage on object cache.

Portal Server Settings

In addition to optimal infrastructure planning, we also need to fine-tune the portal server configurations for optimal performance.

Some of the key server parameters for a Java-based portal server are as follows:

- *JVM heap size*: The minimum and maximum heap size can be configured based on the load- and vendor-recommended values.
- *Thread pool settings*: We can adjust the maximum and minimum thread pool size.
- *Connection pool settings*: We can adjust the maximum and minimum connection pool size.
- *Cache settings*: We can fine-tune the native portal server cache framework settings. This includes cache memory settings, clustered cache settings, cache replication settings, cache invalidation algorithm, disk offload options etc.
- *Cluster settings*: We can configure the cluster configuration, cluster synchronization, and clustered caching options in this settings.

Portal Performance Testing Essentials

In this section, we will look at the key elements of portal performance testing.

Portal Performance Testing Process

Figure 20.3 shows the high-level steps in the performance testing process.

The main steps in the performance testing process are as follows:

- The nonfunctional requirement (NFR) for the portal site in general and the key business transactions and processes needs to be identified. NFR requirements includes performance SLAs for performance, security, scalability, availability, and other nonfunctional requirements. NFR gathering can be done from following sources:
    - Existing application logs
    - Volumetric requirements given by the client
    - User survey feedback
    - Stakeholder interviews
    - Business performance SLAs
    - Industry and competitive benchmark
- Performance test design and strategy to create all applicable performance test case scenarios for captured non functional requirements.
- Application setup and test script preparation, which includes setting up test data and development of all necessary test scripts.
- Repetitive performance test execution, which includes load tests and bottleneck tests
- Scalability testing of infrastructure and projecting the infrastructure capacity: Once the performance test scripts are executed, we will recheck the infrastructure scalability and provide the capacity projections for the infrastructure.
- Preparation of performance test report to provide results of performance testing. These reports indicate whether the existing infrastructure satisfies the specified performance SLAs.

Next, we will look at some the core activities in the portal performance testing process.

Key Steps in Portal Performance Test Execution

The main activities in performance test execution are as follows:

- Simulator-based test case preparation, which includes identifying interfaces for each simulator, building simulator, and load testing the simulator.
- Portal server setup, which includes configuring the portal server with appropriate values for thread pool, heap size, connection pool, etc.

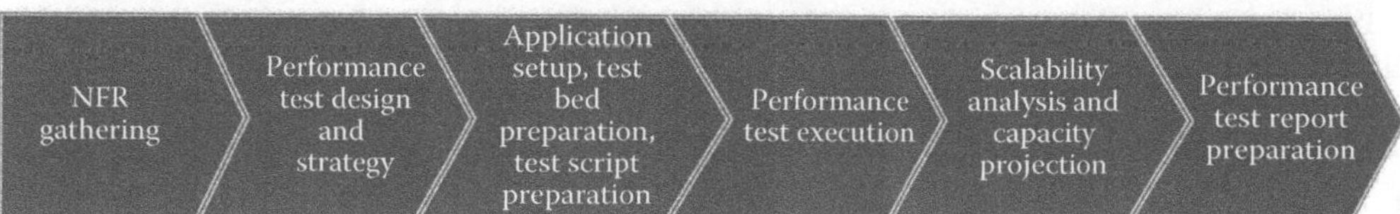

FIGURE 20.3
Portal performance testing process.

- Test Bed preparation:
  - Setting up the data for application testing
- Performance test script development:
  - Analyzing various transactions and processes based on performance metrics
  - Analyzing different types of upstream enterprise interfaces that need to be tested
  - Building scripts for each interface
  - Building the script data

Performance Load and Stress Testing

This includes testing the portal system under normal and peak loads and checking the performance. Key steps in this testing are as follows:

- *Ramp-up and mixed load test at different loads*: Maintain user load for some duration and then gradually step-up the user load and check the portal performance.
- Load system with average concurrent users over a specified period and analyze system behavior.
- Test each transaction with varying loads in an isolated way.
- Mixed load testing by combining all the business transactions of a process and conduct multiple tests with increasing load.
- Concurrent user testing by loading the portal system with maximum allowed concurrent user load.
- Conduct endurance testing through normal load testing for an extended duration of time ranging from 48 to 72 hours. We can check for system performance, memory leaks, transaction integrity, etc.
- Monitor system performance and resource utilization for each iteration.

Portal Performance Testing Types

The main testing types in the overall performance testing are specified as follows:

Web Component Testing

Page Load Times and Page Size Testing for Key Pages

It involves testing the load times and page size for key portal pages such as the home page, gateway page, and landing pages. We can benchmark them against industry standards and best practices. Performance testing and benchmarking needs to be done on all supported browsers and devices.

Static Asset Performance Testing

This includes testing the performance impact of static digital assets (images, JavaScript, CSS, videos, JSON, etc.) on portal pages. The number of web requests for digital assets and size of each of these component's impact the performance of portal pages.

Server Side Analysis

Following are the main activities in server side analysis:

- Performance testing of business components such as portlets and integration components
- Database call performance testing
- Enterprise integration performance testing
- Service testing

Infrastructure Testing

In this phase, we will use load testing tools to understand the following key performance parameters of various infrastructure components:

- System availability
- Transaction throughput
- Response times
- Resource consumption
- Data volumes

Portal Performance Testing Checklist

During portal performance testing, we can follow these guidelines to ensure a comprehensive coverage of all scenarios:

Critical Transaction and Process Identification

- Identify the key transactions and processes that are critical for business and identify frequently executed transactions and processes, and ensure that they are covered in test scenarios.
- Create the workload model for the critical transactions and processes.
- Execute the test cases based on the workload model.

Data-Intensive and Scheduled Jobs

- Identify the online and offline batch jobs, volume-intensive replication or synchronization jobs, lengthy transactions, and multistep processes and prepare test data to simulate the data load and test these scenarios.

Server Monitoring and Reporting

During the performance test execution, we need to monitor the following parameters:

1. Generic parameters:
    a. CPU utilization—user, system, and idle
    b. Memory utilization

   c. Page level values—number of HTTP requests, page size, and page load time
   d. Physical disk—read, write, and total
   e. Disk queue length
2. Server side parameters such as thread pool size and connection pool size
3. Client side parameters—response time, throughput, and hits/sec
4. Network monitors

The test execution report should include the following values:

1. Response times at different load values
2. Throughput at different load values
3. Transactions per second
4. Hits per second
5. Errors
6. CPU utilization at different load values
7. Memory utilization at different load values

Performance Metrics

The key performance related metrics for portal components that need to be monitored are as follows:

- *Time to first byte*: The time taken by the user agent (browser) to receive the first byte of the response from the server.
- *Total DOM load time*: This includes the total time taken for the page DOM to load with all markup, applying CSS styles, DOM parsing by browser, executing the scripts, rendering the page, and ready for user interaction.
- *Perceived load time*: The load time perceived by the end user. This often is the total page DOM load time excluding the time to execute the page scripts.
- Total number of web requests per page including all the requests sent for images, JS/CSS files, JSON/XML files, media files, XHR requests, etc.
- Total size of global static assets (media files and binary files) per page.
- Load time of global static assets per page.
- Total portal page size.

Summary

- Portal performance plays a key role in impacting end-user experience. This chapter explores various aspects of portal performance engineering.

- Critical success factors for portal performance are well-defined performance SLAs, comprehensive performance testing, performance-based design, performing continuous and iterative performance validation, and building a comprehensive performance monitoring infrastructure.
- Portal performance testing process includes NFR gathering, performance test design and strategy, performance test setup, performance testing, scalability and capacity analysis, and performance test reporting.
- Caching the frequently accessed data in the nearest temporary location improves the performance.
- A full-page caching is suitable for static content type whereas content fragment caching would be suitable for dynamic content. Frequently used objects can be cached in object cache.
- The main caching layers in portal infrastructure are browser caching, edge caching, web server caching, portal server caching, and service layer caching.
- Portal performance testing includes static asset performance, web component testing, server side analysis, and infrastructure testing.
- The key performance metrics are time to first byte, total DOM load time, perceived load time, total number of web requests per page, total size of global static assets, load time of global static assets, and total portal page size.

21

Next-Generation Portals and Portal Trends

In the previous chapters, we have looked at various scenarios and use cases where a portal would help a business in achieving their business goals. We have also seen the main strengths of portal technologies. Portal is predominantly used in the presentation tier of the model–view–controller (MVC) architecture. As we know, the presentation tier technologies undergo changes in rapid pace. With the popularity of Web 2.0 technologies, social media focus, and a huge number of lightweight AJAX toolkits, the expectations from presentation components are changing from time to time. Coupled with this is the penetration of mobile devices that are becoming the primary access mechanisms for online access. All these have their impact on portal as well.

In this chapter, we look at the some of the main challenges with existing traditional portals, portal trends seen across various industry domains, and features of next-generation portals. Enterprise architects, business analysts, UX designers, and front-end engineers would find this chapter useful.

Quick Recap of Portal and Its Utility

We have so far seen portal from various dimensions. Here is a quick snapshot of the predominant portal scenarios:

- Portal provides highly personalized and contextualized user experience, thereby increasing the user satisfaction and loyalty.
- Portal's core strength lies in the aggregation of data, content, and functionality to provide a unified (dashboard-like) interface.
- Portal has strong security features to provide seamless single sign-on (SSO) with all aggregated applications and functionality. Besides, portal also provides role-based access control and fine-grained permission model.
- Portal provides a pluggable, reusable, and modular platform through portlets, which would be easier to extend to suit future needs.
- Portal supports multiple features for providing intuitive user experience such as drag-and-drop portlets, mobile enablement, inbuilt navigation components, web analytics support, and search engine optimization (SEO) support.
- Portal can also be leveraged for building a robust collaboration platform and a knowledge base platform.

Though portal does much more than this, the given list covers the key utilities of portal technologies for business scenarios.

Organizations usually use an existing portal product (open source or commercial off the shelf [COTS]) to realize the portal solution. Though it is possible to build a custom portal platform using individual components such as SSO adaptor, rules engine, personalization engine, template engine, AJAX toolkits, etc., it is seldom done because of increased build and testing effort.

The aforementioned summary covers majority of portal scenarios and ecosystems.

Traditional Full-Featured Horizontal Portals and Challenges

Looking at the benefits of portal, it will seem like portal platform is a "one-size-fits-all" solution wherein a single portal platform would solve almost all business problems. In reality, it is not the case. We have seen some of the common pitfalls and challenges in portal programs in Chapter 2. Those points are more related to process, governance, operations, and positioning of the portal in business context, which can be addressed through appropriate business processes and robust governance.

There is another key dimension to this portal challenges. This portal-related challenge is due to a combination of technological factors, changing business expectations, and recent trends in presentation technologies. Let us look at those challenges.

Traditional horizontal portal products are mature and have strong technology-enabling factors to satisfy the core portal use cases and scenarios we discussed in previous sections. The following list provides few insights into few challenges faced by the organization in some cases:

- *Heavyweight technology stack*: Most of the traditional portal products tend to be relatively heavyweight when compared to modern AJAX toolkit–based web technologies. Hence, they require high-end hardware and server, which also means higher cost. However, some portal products address this challenge by providing a *lighter version* of the portal product.
- *Longer release cycles*: This is a byproduct of the above-mentioned problem. If the portal platform involves multiple components with a wide array of technology capabilities, building, testing, releasing, and deploying would also be impacted. Again, we can fix this problem by adopting agile methodologies.
- *Unused portal features in the selected solution*: We have noticed that in some cases, even though organizations have invested in robust portal products, their business functions do not warrant a full-featured portal product. A worst-case scenario would be that the organization uses only a very few portal features for their solution. This has multifold impact such as expectation mismatch, performance issue due to unnecessary background jobs, complex deployment processes, etc.
- *Heavy technology focus*: Though it is understandable that portal development needs specialized technical skills, business expects minimal IT involvement in activities such as setting up new campaigns, launching new microsites, content reviewing and publishing, user set up, core administration activities, etc. Though some of these capabilities were initially in the realm of IT team, due to competitive and market pressures, business is involved in these activities in recent days. Though traditional portal products provide robust administration features and intuitive interfaces for this, it is still evolving and sometime requires intervention from IT teams.

- *Product-driven business processes*: In some other cases, a process or workflow is heavily dictated by the product that would require a lot of customization to customize to business needs. For instance, a workflow engine in a portal product may need to be heavily customized to support complex content publishing and localization process. The more the customization, the more would be the development and testing cost.
- *Management cost*: This again is a manifestation of heavyweight technology stack challenge. The heavier the product is, the more difficult it would be to maintain and manage it.

This list is not applicable in all scenarios and hence is relevant only in some specialized cases. We will now look at the trends that are driving the business and market expectations that have direct contribution to the aforementioned challenges.

Portal Trends

Let us now look at the emerging trends that impact portal technologies from various dimensions. A deeper understanding of these trends and their importance is critical in creating a next-generation, future-ready portal platform. Some business scenarios (such as mobile-centric consumer-based sites) would also necessitate the need for next-generation portal platforms. For the sake of better understanding and analysis, the trends are categorized into the following categories:

- Presentation technology and user experience trends
- Business-specific trends
- Operations-specific trends
- Integration related trends
- Other technology trends

In each of these categories, we will look at the trends that have a potential impact on how the portal platform is built.

Presentation Technology and User Experience Trends

Presentation technologies undergo rapid changes. Web 2.0, mobile-first platforms, responsive web design (RWD), lightweight AJAX frameworks, and location-based services are some of the changes that are happening in this area. As portal is a predominant player in presentation space, these trends have a natural impact on portal as well. Let us look at the main trends in presentation and user experience areas:

- *Web-oriented architecture*: The presentation platforms are increasingly adopting this architecture style wherein lightweight protocols such as Representational State Transfer (REST) and JavaScript Object Notation (JSON) are used to pass message and manipulate resources. Though most of the portal products provide REST interface for their services, the architecture in itself is not fully web-oriented in those cases.

- *Widgets and gadgets*: In modern presentation platforms, AJAX-based widgets are preferred more than portlets. Widgets and gadgets are built using client-side AJAX technologies that provide fully plug-and-play architecture. They act as lightweight alternatives to portlets.
- *Responsive design*: The web pages are built using RWD concept wherein the page and page components auto-adjust optimally to the requesting device leveraging media queries, HTML5, and CSS3. RWD is a primary technology enabler for implementing mobile-first strategy.
- *Mobile-first strategy*: Traditional presentation platform is mainly targeted toward desktop browsers and it provides alternate pages/site for mobile devices. However, in mobile-first strategy, the primary target is mobile device and this enables increasing the reach of the website. This strategy involves device recognition, flexible layout, mobile touch support, mobile-optimized presentation components, mobility rules, cross-device analytics, and ability to reuse UI code for mobile apps either directly or through services, etc.
- *Intuitive user experience*: For taking customer engagement to the next level, organizations are providing intuitive information architecture, search-based navigation, guided navigation, contextual search results, enhanced information discovery, and enhanced SEO and search engine marketing (SEM) to make the web pages more usable.
- *User-centric platforms*: The platforms are designed by keeping end user in main focus. Design, testing, enhancements, all are oriented toward end user. The feedback explicitly given by the end user and the insights gathered from analytics will be used in enhancing the user experience. We have discussed the user experience platforms in Chapters 12 and 13.
- *Lightweight UI*: Enterprises and customers are inclined toward keeping the web pages light, integrations light, and having a plug-and-play architecture using AJAX frameworks (such as Angular JS and Backbone JS) instead of server-heavy components. Single-page application (SPA), RESTful services, JSON-based data exchange, mobile centricity, single UI code for all channels, and RWD are some of the common themes noticed.

Enterprise Integration Trends

- *Lightweight integrations*: Traditional Simple Object Access Protocol (SOAP)-based and XML-based integrations tend to be heavy in terms of data exchange. Especially for web, lightweight integration options using REST with JSON or using ATOM/RSS feeds is the option that is more preferred.
- *Service-enabled layers*: Even a product that has components for multiple layers communicate across layers through services. In some of the traditional products, the intra-layer calls were happening through APIs and they are now replaced by services. This has the dual advantage of providing loosely coupled architecture and exposing the key functions as services for external consumption.
- *API gateway-based integration*: Enterprises are using API gateways (sometimes coupled with ESB) for integrating with internal and external platforms.

Other Technology Trends

In this category, we will look at the other technology trends that impact portal.

- *Prebuilt accelerators and portlets*: In order to enhance productivity and improve time to market, the portal should offer prebuilt portlets and related functionality. For instance, common scenarios such as user registration, content authoring, page layouts, release and deployment, and registration forms should come along with the portal product and it should be easily customizable to suit the business needs.
- *Hypercollaboration platforms*: Customer-facing websites such as B2C and retail websites are actively involved in providing social and collaboration features such as social marketing, social listening, and targeted campaigns. They enable and encourage users to author content, share content, co-create content, and rate content through various collaboration features such as blogs, wikis, communities, forums, etc. This harnessing of collective intelligence not only improves productivity but also keeps the users actively engaged. Social media is the new distribution channel as word-of-mouth/peer influence is preferred over a paid advertisement.
- *Cloud hosting option for elastic scalability and high availability*: Products are available as services in clouds through SaaS model. Businesses are leveraging this to reduce the infrastructure and maintenance costs. Appropriately addressing the security concerns and integration complexity would make the cloud option more preferable than the traditional in-house deployment option.
- *Open source adoption*: Organizations are also inclined toward leveraging on open source frameworks and components based on open standards wherever it fits the overall solution strategy. This not only reduces the overall cost of ownership but also saves them from vendor lock-in to enable future migrations.

Business-Specific Trends

- *Portal of portals for single view across business chain*: Instead of having a silos of numerous vertical portals within an organization such as HR portal, CRM portal, etc., organizations are moving toward creating a consolidated multichannel portal experience. This will reduce duplicate data, provides consolidated view of functionality, ease the cost and maintenance effort, and provides an opportunity for robust governance. The consolidation also provides a single view of data across various channels and a holistic view of the activities of customers across various geographies.
- *Building high-performance workplace through intranet portals*: This requires highly collaborative portal platform and an efficient knowledge management system enabled by the portal to improve employee productivity.
- *Seamless, channel-agnostic, consistent, and personalized experience across all digital channels and touch points*: This functionality provides an opportunity for user to seamlessly access the process from all digital channels.
- *Continuous connectivity*: The platform should be available round the clock and should be accessible anytime, anywhere, with optimal performance.

- *Self-service model*: Identify the operations that are having high service cost and transition them into a self-service model to optimize the cost and operations. Portal can play the role of knowledge management system and collaboration system to implement this model.
- *Business-friendly administration*: For business-critical activities such as campaign management, web marketing, site management, user on-boarding, business process management, the platform should provide easy-to-use administration for the business community without intervention from the IT team.
- *Active customer engagement*: Organizations do it through various means such as soliciting explicit feedback, surveys, polls, collaborating with customers, active social listening, sentiment analysis, customer profiling, customized loyalty offers, targeted content/email, real-time user behavior analysis, etc. All these lead to higher conversion and increased customer retention and loyalty.
- *Extreme personalization*: This is enabled by providing highly relevant content, customized user experience, location-based services, targeted recommendations based on the user's past behavior, tailor-made promotions, persona-based content and programs, etc.

Operations-Specific Trends

Operations involve platform maintenance, management, platform patches and updates, enhancements, release and deployment, monitoring, support, and such activities.

- *Agile development methodology*: This is gaining traction across all industry domains and enables faster releases, quick enhancements, faster time to market, and early feedback.
- *Actionable insights and enhancements*: Business needs real-time insights into customer behavior and actions to improve the user experience. The user actions can be monitored from multiple geographies across all channels to closely understand the user experience and these are presented through intuitive and sophisticated dashboard-style reports. The technology enabler for this is web analytics.
- *Proactive customer service*: The service industry is moving toward proactive and anticipative service suggestions. A customer service portal should analyze the customer behavior and provide proactive services such as highly contextual recommendations, relevant search results, live chat, solutions-based knowledge repository, etc., in order to serve the customer better. The platform should enable the organization to directly establish connection with the customer using push notifications, real-time customer communications, one-click chat, click to call, and similar features.
- *Easy-to-use administration*: Portal should provide easily understandable, navigable, and intuitive administration features so that administrators with minimal technical knowledge can quickly learn and use these administration features.
- *SaaS adoption*: More enterprises are embracing the cloud-hosted deployment model to optimize cost and for rapid deployment.

The main trends explained here are summarized in Figure 21.1.

Portal driver	• Functionality fulfilment • Predominantly single channel • Business-driven model • Siloes of vertical portals	• Multichannel access • Synchronized and seamless experience across all touch points • Customer and user-centric platform • Consolidation of all portals to get unified view of all channels, departments, and users
Portal-based customer service	• Servicing customer in reactive mode	• Predicting customer needs and selfservice • Providing anticipatory services • Proactive service • Effective usage of social and collaboration • Active engagement through information cocreation
Portal presentation	• Traditional portlets • Predominantly webservice (SOAP) based • Primarily aimed toward desktop	• Web oriented predominantly using widgets • Light weight REST and JSON-based services • Pre-dominantly based on mobile • Responsive and adaptive design • Pre-built components and accelerators
Portal infrastructure	• Mainly in-house based • Heavier technical and IT involvement in administration	• Increasingly moving toward cloud • Continuous monitoring • Real-time analytics for effective tracking • Business-friendly administration • In-built monitoring and analytics infrastructure
Portal operations	• 3–6 month release cycles	• Cloud based deployment and SaaS model delivery • Mainly agile with quick release cycles • Focus on faster time-to-market

FIGURE 21.1
Emerging portal trends.

Trends in Intranet and External Portals

If we look at the trends from internal and external portal standpoint, the following scenarios standout.

Intranet Portals

Intranet portals are mainly used for internal users like employees and internal stakeholders who use intranet portal as a communication channel, collaboration platform, and for their daily activities:

- *Services-based integrations*: Intranet portals provide unified view of all data, applications, and services through enterprise integrations that include ERP systems for HR and finance applications, reporting applications, and integration with database and CMS systems.
- *Security*: As the intranet portal often interacts with discrete systems, security assumes greater importance. This includes SSO experience, authentication and authorization, service access, role-based functionality access, deploying security gateways, etc.
- *Collaboration*: The main collaboration features include
  - Engaging the user community through collaboration tools like blogs, chats, communities, and wiki
  - Providing a knowledge base for internal community
  - Allowing a single platform for users to learn, share, and interact
- *Process improvements*: Internal policies and tools often involve multistep process and manual involvement. Emerging trends in process optimization are as follows:
  - Minimizing process steps and reducing the overall transaction time
  - Focus on self-service model
  - Focus on automating process steps
  - Providing intuitive user interface
  - Enabling search-based information access
  - Well-defined information architecture
  - Intuitive navigation structure

External Portals

Extranet or external portals form online digital gateways for external users for the organization. The scope and complexity of external portals are naturally high as they need to be accessible across various geographies and in different languages with strict SLAs.

- *Business Function Focus*: External portals achieve many of the goals of sales and marketing business functions such as
  - Portal platforms should ease business operations (mainly related to sales/marketing)
  - Portal platforms should enable users with greater control for content authoring and publishing operations

  - Portal platforms should support business users, should be able to manage campaigns and microsites effectively
  - A lightweight platform is preferred to reduce the time to market and realize return on investment (ROI) in quick time.
  - Easy integration with CMS, enterprise search systems, and other enterprise systems are preferred.
  - Enable the user with relevant information discovery with ease and convey consistent user experience.
- *Search-centered experience*: Search has great potentials to provide relevant content and is an important tool in information architecture. In order to leverage the full potential of search, we need to
  - Provide easy access to search from all pages
  - Optimize search experience by providing optimized search function, context-based and personalized search results and improving relevancy of search results
  - Expose search functionality as a service
  - Search content within all enterprises systems including web, database, CMS, etc.
  - Have dynamic page aggregation based on preconfigured search terms.
- *Analytics enablement*: Web analytics is playing a key role in providing deep customer insights and optimizes the user experience based on it. The following are the key steps involved:
  - *Acquire* the key analytics information including site usability data (page views, downloads, click maps, click paths, etc.), understand the visitor profile (user segments, geos, languages, etc.), and the conversion statistics (new visitors, returning visitors, leads exit rate, visit duration, etc.).
  - *Analyze* the information obtained to understand the site usability (information discoverability, site interactivity, information architecture effectiveness), conversion statistics (visitor stickiness, exit rates, etc.), and sources (campaign effectiveness, SEO effectiveness, and external ad effectiveness).
  - *Act* on the information by making necessary improvements to site design, information discoverability, and navigation changes and provide targeted content and effective campaigns.
- *Social media integration*: To engage customers actively, we need to integrate portal with social media channels and provide features such as content sharing, rating, and review; pulling conversations from social platforms; social customer support, etc.
- *Multichannel integration*: As mobile devices and tablets are increasingly becoming popular channels for web access, the portal site should support access over all these channels. Mobile enabling the sites and providing native mobile apps is gaining momentum. In addition, the information should be consistent and integrated across all the channels.

Next-Generation Portals

Once we look at trends from various perspectives, we can identify the recurring themes that are expected in a next-generation portal platform. The main tenets and attributes of next-generation portal are summarized as follows:

- Lightweight web-oriented architecture
- Highly responsive UX
- Omnichannel portals
- Hyperpersonalization
- Simple and robust platform with continuous improvement
- Accelerators and prebuilt components
- Social and collaboration enabled
- User experience platform
- Vertical focus

The key elements of each of these tenets are depicted in Figure 21.2.

Let us see each of these attributes in greater detail.

Lightweight Web-Oriented Architecture

This is one of the primary attributes of next-generation portal that is based on lean philosophy. The architecture should be lean in all aspects. This can be achieved through web-oriented architecture elements such as widgets, gadgets as the primary presentation elements, and communicating with server side components through RESTful services and using lightweight data exchange formats such as JSON. In many scenarios, it is not necessary to use all the portal features of a portal product; in such cases, we can also customize the portal product to operate in a project-specific mode wherein only the necessary services are running. Lean or lightweight architecture is aimed at deriving maximum ROI and to make full use of portal components for meeting the business objectives.

As this is a critical aspect of next-generation portal, we will look at a sample lean portal architecture in the next section to elaborate this concept.

Highly Responsive UX

The user experience should be highly responsive and interactive. Rich user experience, widgets, Web 2.0 features, touch-enabled features, friendlier navigation features, intuitive information taxonomy, and search-enabled information discovery are some of the primary tenets of the user experience.

Omnichannel Strategy through Mobile Portal

Enabling mobile-centric features in portal or implementing mobile-first strategy through portal requires understanding of the following:

- Deeper understanding of target audience and the content they would be accessing on mobile. This will help us to position the content strategically on a mobile layout.

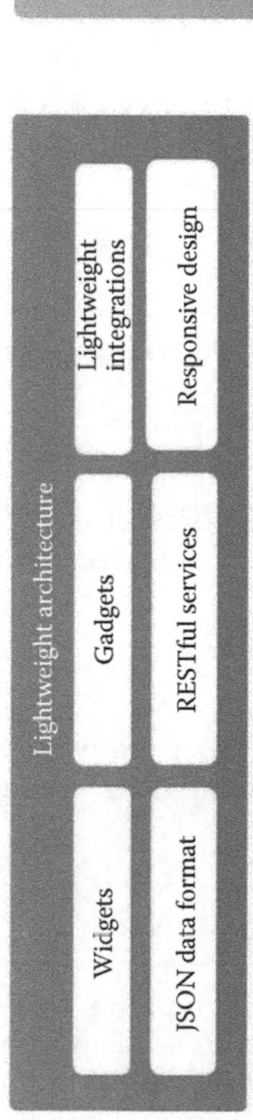

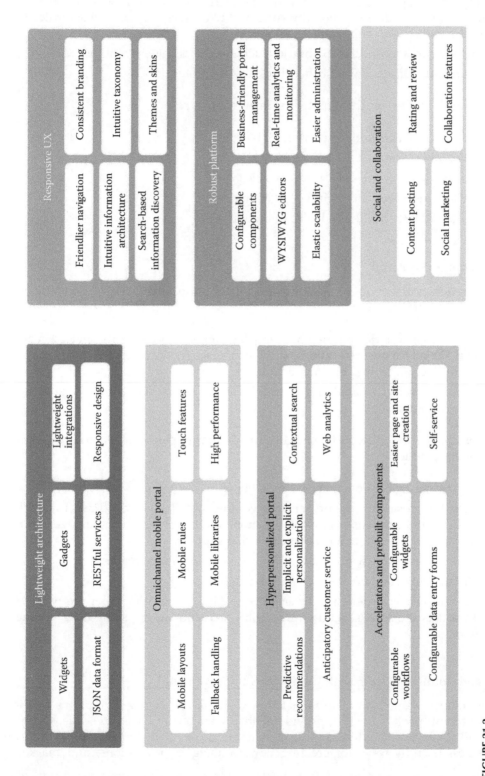

FIGURE 21.2
Components of next generation portal.

- Comprehending for all mobile layouts, network challenges, mobile limitations, and form factors through mobility rules and RWD techniques. Fallback rules to comprehend device limitations.
- Leveraging mobile-specific JS libraries such as Sencha, jQuery mobile, etc.
- Building only on standards such as HTML5, CSS3, etc.

So the portal should enable the mobile-first features such as

- Mobile page layouts with responsive web design
- Touch-enabled features
- Device recognition rules and mobility rules
- Faster loading pages with lightweight components
- Graceful fallback to address device limitations

Hyperpersonalized Portal

Next-generation portal should take the personalization to next level. This can be done mainly through the following:

- Having a holistic understanding of user behavior and actions across devices, geographies, applications, transactions, and web pages. This can be achieved through web analytics and other tracking techniques.
- Leveraging predictive analytics to anticipate the user's next action or effective recommendations.

Using these techniques, the portal should provide highly personalized user experience such as the following:

- Predictive content/product recommendations.
- Anticipatory customer support services. For instance, if a user continues to search with different keywords or navigates to more number of search result pages, then the portal can prompt for a real-time live chat support.
- Fine-tune self-service features based on its usage and effectiveness.
- Contextualized and personalized search results.
- Personalized user experience for each device. Portal can remember the widgets and portlets the user has chosen in earlier interaction and display them during next visit.

Simple and Robust Platform with Continuous Improvement

The user interface and administration features should be kept as simple as possible. Next-generation portals should provide features such as what-you-see-is-what-you-get (WYSIWYG) content editors, configurable workflows and data/registration forms, and business-friendly ways for creating new campaigns, promotions, and marketing content—A simple yet robust administration interface that enables business to manage the portal activities with least assistance from IT team.

The portal platform should provide extensions and plugin architecture so that it can be easily adopted to future integration needs and it should be scalable to support the intended business growth and high traffic and data volume. One of the ways to achieve elastic scalability is through cloud deployment and exposing the portal functionality as a service to ensure that the platform is available anytime on any device anywhere.

Real-time web analytics and monitoring services should provide insights into customer behavior and enable business to continuously fine-tune the user experience based on it. For instance, if the customers are exiting portal consistently in a specific form in registration flow, business can relook at the page and make improvements to prevent the exit rate.

Accelerators and Prebuilt Components

Next-generation portal should provide the core portal services as prebuilt widgets and presentation components that can be easily customizable to suite the business specific needs. Customization should be mainly done through configuration with the least amount of custom coding.

The following are some of the most commonly used portal components that are ideal candidates for inbuilt components:

- Easily configurable workflow tasks and process engines that can be used for modeling complex business processes with minimal customization
- Configurable data entry forms with inbuilt validations and business rules support
- Easier process for page and site creation and portlet/widget configuration, which enables to launch new pages without any help from IT team
- Marketing-friendly content creation, templates creation, and publishing process
- Out-of-the-box self-service features such as knowledge management integration, search integration, inbuilt enterprise search, etc.

Social and Collaboration Enablement

Next-generation portals should provide an ecosystem to support various collaboration features and integrators with popular social media channels. Businesses should be able to leverage these features to effectively launch social marketing campaigns and gather a unified profile and social graph of the user.

Platforms should also support publishing content to various social platforms, expose and consume feed-based content, review/rate content, collaborate with personal and business connections, location specific services, mobile, social, and other social features.

As far as collaboration is concerned, some of the main features include real-time web conferencing, co-browsing, social shopping, screen and document sharing, content cocreation, etc. Portal platforms should provide inbuilt features or plugins to support these functionalities.

User Experience Platforms (UXP)

Sometimes referred to as customer experience platforms (CXP), these are platforms that are mainly focused on end user. Their principal aim is to enhance user experience and provide responsive and active engagement features. They include portal technologies for information aggregation and additionally they also provide prebuilt accelerators such as widgets, forms, commerce modules, etc., which provide positive user experience and accelerate development.

We have discussed more about this in Chapters 12 and 13.

Vertical Focus

Another feature of the next-generation portals is that portals are designed specifically for a business domain or for providing a key technology capability. For instance, the next-generation banking portal specifically provides all tools, functionality, and accelerators that can help organizations to quickly deploy the banking solution to market. Let us look at a sample next-generation portal and its features and solution components in the following section.

Next-Generation Banking Portal

In this case study, we will look at features of a next-generation portal for a specific business scenario. All the trends, features, and attributes of next-generation portals, we discussed earlier can be seen in this case study; the components are contextualized for banking domain. The next-generation banking portal aims to provide a holistic user experience platform for the banking domain. It should have functionality, tools, and interfaces that help all the portal user roles such as customer, banker, and system administrator. Let us look at some of those features:

- Customer dashboard:
  - Customer dashboard provides customer interaction across financial application
  - Consolidated view of cash flow, risk details, account details, cash position, and other related financial data
  - It provides the interactive visualizations for information such as transactions, spend reports, etc.
  - Dashboard is developed using widgets and interactive visual graphs
- Admin dashboard:
  - Portal should provide various admin modules such as account setup, security configurations, etc.
  - Portal should provide proactive cross-sell modules based on cash flow
  - Admin should be able to provide personalized products such as bonds, investments, etc.
- Security:
  - Portal should provide multifactor authentication
  - Multiple level approvals and authentication for high-value and high-risk transactions.

- Customer engagement and support functionality:
    - Portal should provide rich marketing features through videos, one-click call, etc.
    - Provide intuitive support features such as chat, video calls, web conference, etc. This can leverage the collaboration features.
    - Portal should link the customer's social persona with bank account through portal social plugins.
    - Portal should provide close collaboration tools with banker such as, chat, cobrowse, web conference, etc.
    - The portal should provide multichannel availability through hybrid or native mobile app.
- Information architecture:
    - Easier accessible menus and tabs for most popular features such as reports, payments, accounts, etc.
- User experience:
    - The portal should provide consistent and coherent branding.
- Rich toolsets:
    - Admin should be able to use simulators to analyze risk and evaluate what-if scenarios
    - Portal should provide payment monitor tools
    - Portal should provide tools for fraud detection
    - Portal should provide tools for credit risk management

Reference Architecture of Next-Generation Portal

We have so far seen the challenges with traditional portals, portal-related trends, and main attributes of next-generation portals. With this background, let us now look at building a sample next-generation portal.

NOTE:

- The architecture, frameworks, and components given here are for information purposes only.
- The intention of this architecture is not to recommend any particular technology or product but to provide concrete details of the next-generation portal attributes along with a reference architecture.
- There are other competing frameworks and components that are equally capable as the components shown in this architecture. It is beyond the scope of this book to have an exhaustive list of all those competing AJAX frameworks and technologies.

Portal Architecture

A conceptual architecture for the next-generation portal is shown in Figure 21.3. The components in each of the layers is technology/product agnostic so that any technology-of-choice can be used to implement the reference architecture. However, for the sake of concrete explanation we have chosen a sample technology and mapped the component to technology elements.

The main architecture principles that are followed while developing this architecture are as follows:

- The next-generation portal architecture should implement the mobile-first strategy.
- The architecture should be based on lean model and provide lightweight solution components and lightweight integration.
- Commonly used portal solution elements should be provided as prebuilt components.
- The architecture should be web oriented with focus on widgets and client-side components.
- Lightweight service integration using REST and JSON is preferred during integration and for exposing the services.
- Architecture layers and components should be technology and product agnostic.
- The architecture should provide extensions and provisions for plugins so that we can extend it for future integrations.
- The implementation solutions should be easily deployable on cloud platform to enable SaaS model.
- The architecture should provide provisions for business-friendly administration and critical function management through configurations.

Let us look at each of the layers in detail.

Portal Client Layer

The next-generation portal is mainly geared toward web-oriented architecture. There are mainly three high-level categories of modules identified in the aforementioned architecture.

- *View components*: This mainly consists of AJAX-based widgets, mashups, and gadgets that are lightweight and communicate to server components via lightweight REST services. Theme elements provide prebuilt page header and footer that provide a consistent look and feel for the pages. The entire presentation modules are built using HTML5 and CSS3 along with RWD support so that we can have write-once-run-anywhere models that cater to a wide variety of devices.
- Service components consist of components that expose the service from the portal platform for consumption of external applications. This is for implementing "portal-as-a-service" model. Feed and service producers provide portal presentation data through XML and JSON data formats. Mobile services

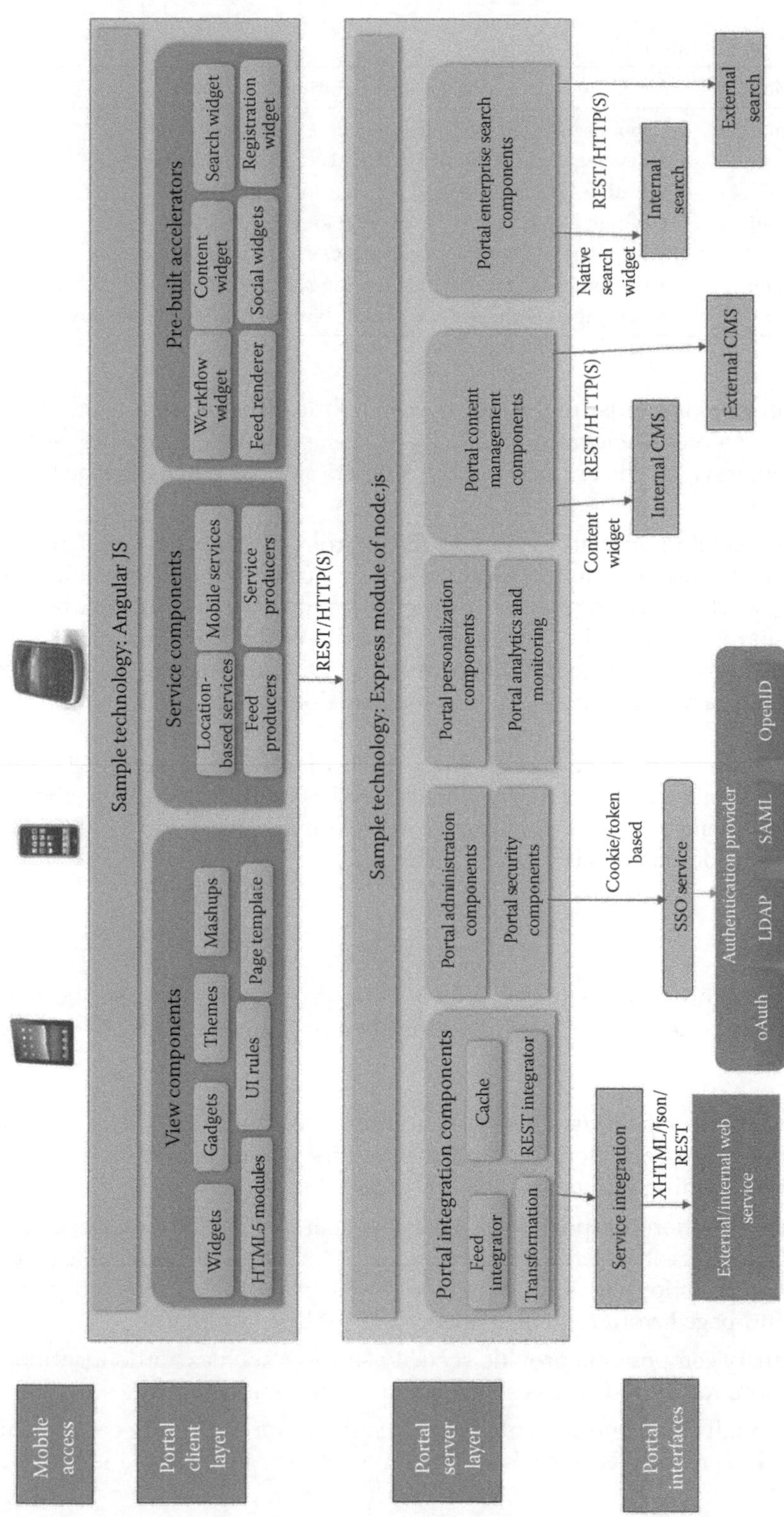

FIGURE 21.3
Reference architecture of next-generation portal.

TABLE 21.1
Presentation Layer Solution Components

Architecture Module	AngularJS Solution Component
View components	• Inbuilt AngularJS view and template components • Leverage inbuilt AngularJS modules and directives feature • Native AngularJS controller scripts for routing
Service components	• Inbuilt AngularJS service support for REST and Feeds • AngularJS model components (JSON or JavaScript objects)
Prebuilt accelerators	• Custom widget development using AngularJS • Leveraging AngularJS native data binding elements, filters, and validations

provide services for consumption of native mobile app consumption. Location-based services provide location-sensitive services such as location-based event notification, navigation services, social connections updates, and other relevant notifications.

- Prebuilt accelerators aim to minimize the custom development and maximize productivity for faster time to market. The key portal scenarios such as content rendering, workflow configuration, user registration setup, social media integration, and search functionality will be provided out-of-the-box through widgets. In most of the cases, it needs to be configured to suit the solution needs. The prebuilt component library also depends on the solution domain.

For the sample solution, we have chosen AngularJS, a JavaScript-based MVC framework as the implementation technology. It provides an extensible lightweight JavaScript-based framework for implementing the solution. A sample mapping of the main modules to AngularJS solution components is given in Table 21.1.

Portal Server Layer

The server layer mainly consists of components that provide required services for client layer. The high-level categories of modules identified in the aforementioned architecture are as follows:

- *Portal integration components*: This set of components mainly provides integration with external feeds and services and the required transformation. For optimal performance, caching will be used.
- Portal administration components consist of a business-friendly interface that provide easily manageable configuration interface for efficient management of key portal tasks. Functionalities such as workflow configuration, site setup, content updates, and page layout management are part of this module.
- Portal security components provide security services such as authentication, SSO, authorization, role-based access control, and session management.
- Portal personalization components provide services for providing contextual and customized user experience such as widget, visibility rules, personalized search results, etc.

TABLE 21.2

Server Layer Solution Components

Architecture Module	Node.js Solution Component
Portal personalization components	Custom feature to provide rules-based access
Portal integration components	• Leverage REST-based service creation feature of express.js
Portal security components	• Leverage session management features of express module
Portal administration components	• Custom administration interface for managing workflow, security, and content
Portal content management components	• Provide lightweight solution specific CMS or integrate with open source lightweight CMS • REST-based integration with external CMS
Portal enterprise search components	• Provide lightweight solution specific search or integrate with open source lightweight search component • REST-based integration with external search

- Portal analytics and monitoring components provide efficient and real-time tracking of user activities and provide insights into the effectiveness of the portal site, pages, and components. These tracking components provide a dashboard report view of click-stream, asset downloads, bounce rate, etc. Businesses can also configure it to track the business-critical flows and processes.
- *Portal content management components*: As content management is one of the predominant use cases of portal, the content services provided by these components are critical to the success of the portal. The architecture supports both inbuilt lightweight CMS integrated through native content widgets and external CMS integrated through REST services (assuming that external CMS exposes REST-based content services). Inbuilt CMS should also support intuitive content templates and WYSIWYG editors, content workflow configuration and such features so that the marketing team can easily and quickly push promotion and campaign content.
- *Portal search components*: Similar to content management, enterprise search can also be provided as an inbuilt feature or through external integration. External search integration is preferably through REST-based services.

The sample solution uses the express module of node.js and other node.js functionalities for implementing the architecture. Node.js provides powerful features for writing server-side code and provides an event-based model for better scalability. Express module is used to implement web server in node.js for efficient request handling and request routing. A sample mapping of main functional modules to AngularJS solution components is given in Table 21.2.

Portal Interface Layer

The interface layer consists of all internal and external interfacing systems such as security modules, CMS systems, search systems and external services, and websites. As mentioned before, the preferred way of integrating them is through REST-based services. Additionally, widgets and vendor/plugins can also be used for integration.

Alternate Scenarios for Next-Generation Lightweight Portals

We have seen a full-blown portal reference architecture for a next-generation lightweight portal. There are other alternate ways where we can realize portal solutions:

- *Single-purpose minimal lean portal solution*: We can custom build a minimal lean portal using AJAX frameworks such as AngularJS, Backbone JS, and Bootstrap, etc., for serving a specific purpose. Since the custom portal will be built for a single purpose, it might not contain all portal features such as full-fledged content aggregation, personalization, single-sign-on, etc. We can build a subset of features that is just enough to realize the solution for given a business scenario. This is sometimes efficient as the solution may not need all the features offered by a full-blown portal product. However the solution should adhere to the main architecture principles laid out in the beginning of this section such as lightweight design, lightweight integration, mobile-first approach, extensible and plug and play architecture, etc. A few examples of single-purpose minimal portals include document management portals, process portal, media portal, knowledge portal, etc. A special case of content portal is discussed in the next point.
- *Lightweight WCM-based portals*: This approach is similar to that of a minimal single-purpose lean portal we discussed earlier. In this case, the specific purpose is content management. Since web content management is one of the widely used scenarios, we can either custom build a content management portal or leverage a commercial lightweight WCM products (such as Adobe AEM, SDL Tridion, Sitecore, Oracle Content management system, IBM Webcontent manager, etc.). Even traditional horizontal portals provide a leaner version of portal specifically targeted for web content management or for user experience management. These tools (sometimes referred to as user experience management tools or customer experience platforms) provide accelerated development, rapid content and site deployment, personalization features, workflow features, rules engine, and service-based integration which all revolve around content management. So it is possible to achieve best of both worlds: core portal features in lightweight fashion and content management.
- *Leveraging commercial lean portal products*: There are many commercial lean and web-oriented portals available in the market that can be leveraged for this purpose. Some of the examples include Backbase portal, Liferay portal, and numerous AJAX framework-based tools.

Comparison of Next-Generation Lightweight Portals with Traditional Horizontal Portals

A sample comparison of traditional horizontal portal with-generation lean portals is given in Table 21.3.

TABLE 21.3

Traditional Portal vs. Lightweight Portal

Category	Fully Featured Horizontal Portal	Lightweight Portal
Main attributes	• Predominantly portlets based on presentation markup rendition • Portlet container provides runt-time environment for running portlet • JSR 168 and JSR 286 standards for portlet development	• Predominantly widgets using AJAX calls to communicate with back end • Web-oriented architecture and widget-container model relying mainly on standard web technologies such as HTML5, CSS3 • Lean, portal-less portal model
Portal features	• Personalization • Access control • Reusable page layouts • Content management • Collaboration • Localization • Support for RWD • Support for mobile web • Security • Search • Web analytics • Customization • Enterprise integration through both server-side and client-side aggregation • Scalability and availability	• Personalization • Localization • Inbuilt RWD • Inbuilt mobility support • Security • Search • Basic web analytics • Customization • Enterprise integration • Scalability and availability • Information aggregation mainly through client-side widgets
Mobility support	• Supports mobile web through responsive design • A few portal products provide mobile services and mobile SDK for developing hybrid mobile apps	• Out-of-the-box mobility support due to responsive design and HTML technologies • Supports both mobile web and hybrid mobile app
Data aggregation	• A mix of server-side and client-side aggregation • Native portlets for data aggregation	Predominantly client-side aggregation using lightweight services such as REST and JSON data exchange format
Portlet rendering	Container-based portlets	Lightweight client-side components such as widgets and AJAX-based components
User experience	• Traditional look and feel targeted for desktop browsers • Multidevice support through plugins and other third party libraries	• Built-in mobile supports to implement mobile-first strategy • Contemporary user experience based on RWD and other modern web technologies such as HTML5, CSS3, etc.
Main usage scenario	• For scenarios requiring robust enterprise integrations • When we need to build an enterprise-wide platform catering to a wide variety of audience hosting/aggregating large number of applications and services	• For implementing mobile-first strategy • For building lightweight-focused vertical portal applications
Deployment Model	• In-house development and cloud deployment	• Cloud-based hosting • On-demand services
Extensibility	• Mainly through hooks, extensions, and plugins	• Mainly through REST APIs and widgets

Summary

- The chapter captures the trends, features, and architecture of lightweight portal and emerging portal trends.
- Some of the common challenges in full-featured horizontal portals are heavy-weight technology stack, longer release cycles, unused portal features in the selected solution, heavy technology focus, product-driven business processes, and management cost.
- The main presentation tier trends are web-oriented architecture, widgets and gadgets, responsive design, mobile-first strategy, intuitive user experience, user-centric platforms, and lightweight UI.
- The main enterprise integration tier trends are lightweight integrations and service-enabled layers.
- Other portal technology related trends are prebuilt accelerators and portlets, hypercollaboration platforms, cloud hosting option for elastic scalability and high availability, and open source adoption.
- Business-related trends are consolidated portal view, building high-performance workplace through intranet portals; seamless, channel-agnostic, consistent, and personalized experience across all digital channels and touch points; continuous connectivity; self-service model; business friendly administration; active customer engagement; and extreme personalization.
- The main operation-specific tier trends are agile development methodology, actionable insights and enhancements, proactive customer service, easy-to-use administration, and SaaS adoption.
- Trends in intranet portals are service-based integrations, security, collaboration, and process improvements.
- Trends in external portals are sales and marketing focus, search-centered experience, analytics enablement, social media integration, multichannel integration, and digital marketing.
- The main attributes of next generation portals are lightweight web-oriented architecture, highly responsive UX, omnichannel portals, hyperpersonalization, simple and robust platform with continuous improvement, accelerators and prebuilt components, social and collaboration enablement user-centered focus, vertical focus, and user experience platform and vertical focus.
- A reference architecture based on custom next-generation portal is given, which is implemented using AJAX toolkits.

22

Why Do Portal Programs Fail?

Despite its multifold advantages and promises, we have witnessed various failures (some of which are of large scale) for a variety of reasons. The failures can be attributed to multiple reasons. We have witnessed a recurring pattern and common themes across various portal failures. We have already seen some of the anti-patterns and portal challenges in previous chapters in context of the chapter topic. This chapter aims to identify most of the problem patterns so that portal architects and business stakeholders can be cognizant of the common pitfalls and antipatterns and address them early in the game. Portal architects can take proactive measures to adopt the best practices and identify the common pitfalls in portal programs. Guidelines provided in this chapter can be used to take course correction actions in the early stages of the project. We will also look at some of the practically proven and adopted best practices to identify the issues and address them. Portal developers and portal architects will find this chapter useful.

Portal Problems Categories

At a high level, we can categorize the reasons of failures into these categories:

- Business-related reasons that can be mainly attributed to business-related activities. This category of reasons need not be specific to portal program but is generic for any digital project.
- Technical reasons include portal technology–specific reasons.
- Operations and execution-related reasons include all the reasons involved in the execution of portal program and its operations such as maintenance and management.

Business-Related Challenges

Given below are some of the main challenges that fall under business category.

- *Lack of proper and comprehensive vision*: Sometimes, organizations do not have clear long-term vision of their digital strategy and portal programs. Ambiguous or constantly changing business goals or nonalignment of business goals with the industry trends would contribute to inconsistent business visions. As a result, the portal program will be designed to address business goals that are not complete and that change constantly. Hence, it is necessary to have a clearly defined long-term vision for the organization so that all programs can be aligned to it.

- *Challenges in organization readiness and capability gaps*: In a few other scenarios, the organization may not be ready to carry out programs such as portal-led transformation. They lack the required process maturity, required operation readiness, portal supporting ecosystem, right skilled people and project management and execution experience. This leads to heavy dependency for all aspects of program management. We have seen in the previous chapters that a capability assessment phase to assess the organization readiness to undertake portal initiatives. Based on the outcome of such assessment studies, corrective measures and steps need to be taken before commencing the portal project.
- *Lack of portal strategy*: A clear business vision should be converted and articulated into a comprehensive portal strategy. The strategy should define how portal program would realize the business long-term strategic vision; it should also provide how short-term tactical goals can be achieved through the portal; this includes identification of portal target audience user persona definition, portal roadmap definition, identification of supporting projects, building portal ecosystem, resource alignment, and team formation. If the portal strategy lacks these points, then it would lead to improper program execution and impacts the solution adoption from end-user community.
- *Lack of proper backing and executive sponsorship*: Like any program, portal projects should get complete buy-in and support from an executive management. All concerned stakeholders such as IT team, infrastructure steam, security team, and business sponsors should endorse the program and fully support it. The project management team should actively involve all the concerned stakeholders in defining the portal program strategy and governance process. The portal project management team should proactively reach out to all concerned stakeholders and keep them updated about the program updates. The executive team should champion for the program and drive the end-use adoption.
- *Lack of portal adoption planning and cultural issues*: We have seen many instances where a good portal solution was not successful mainly due to the end-user adoption. It could be due to a variety of reasons such as the portal failing to meet the end-user expectations, absence of end user focus, and inconsistent user experiences. Most importantly, portal program should be designed in such a way that it should be of use in the end user's daily activities. Portal-based collaboration platforms and knowledge management systems face another type of problem: cultural differences. A few users will not be willing to share the information and contribute to the knowledge repository. In order to address this, there should be a reward-based incentive system that encourages contributions from the users to the knowledge repository. All efforts should be made to position a portal as an indispensable tool for their daily activities that encourage active participation of the end users.
- *Program cost*: In some scenarios, the overall portal program cost would be relatively higher due to the inherently complex nature of the engagement. If the cost is not managed properly, it would spiral into overrun of effort, time, and overall program cost.
- *Lack of tracking and monitoring*: This is one of the important reasons for failure. We have seen that a robust portal strategy is required for the long-term success of the program. One of the critical components of an effective portal strategy is the

clear definition of success metrics. The portal strategy should clearly identify the success metrics and map it to the program goals; it should clearly articulate what success means and how it can be measured through metrics and what the short-term and long-term portal program objectives are and how they align with business goals and vision. Such metrics should be collected on continuous basis and use it for continuous improvement. For instance, we can leverage web analytics to understand the unused page sections, ineffective content, and poor campaigns and improve the user experience accordingly. Portal KPIs therefore are not only important for understanding pain points but also helpful in achieving continuous improvement. In addition to the collection of tracking metrics, it is also important to proactively solicit user feedback through online/offline surveys and gauge the user satisfaction index. Some portals provide built-in feedback and survey portlets that can be leveraged for this purpose.

- *Lack of clear focus of the portal program*: Right from the beginning, the portal strategy should clearly define the principal focus of the portal: should it be focused on end users or should it be developed to solve business problems? Should we employ mobile-first strategy or should we target desktop browsers and then transition to mobile? It is recommended to clearly understand the expectations from the target audience and their common interests so that we can design the portal for optimal adoption and usage.
- *Improper communication planning*: The project management office should involve all stakeholders and have a clearly defined communication plan about the program updates and communicate any potential program risks and issues. Once the portal solution is rolled out, the project management team should also carry out adoption campaigns to spread the awareness about the new portal capability and its utilities. Users should be clearly made to understand how portal can be put to use for fulfilling their demands and daily activities.

We have briefly discussed the solutions to these challenges; a detailed discussion of the solution is also given in Chapter 19.

Portal Technology–Related Challenges

The reasons given in the following are mainly applicable for the traditional portal products and technologies that tend to be heavyweight in nature. Also, it is important to note that portal programs failures are generally caused by a combination of multiple reasons and seldom by a single reason. In some other times, a single reason would also manifest into multiple pain points. We will look at all these aspects here:

- *Complexity of portal technology stack*: Generally, any enterprise solution stack is complex due to a variety of reasons. An enterprise includes an infrastructure and technology ecosystem consisting of security servers, database, file servers, content servers, ERP, and legacy systems. A portal, which is usually positioned as the gateway to unified interface, often takes the responsibility to weave all the technologies, services, systems, and applications. In such scenarios, the portal technology stack tends to become complex due to presence of multitude technologies and due to integrations it has to perform with internal and external systems. The organization that has a good track record of handling complex solution and technology stack can pull it off successfully and maintain the portal in long runs; however, the organizations that are not exposed to complex technology stack and that are executing the portal program for the first time are more prone and vulnerable to failure due to increased complexity. As aforementioned, technology stack complexity results in other issues such as

- Increased maintenance and operations cost
- Increased release and deployment timelines
- Increased development and training cost
- Challenges in bug fixes and enhancements rollouts
- Potential performance issues

An effective way to handle the complex technology stack such as portal is to adopt agile methodology in all phases of the project execution. Identify quick wins and execute the initial release quickly in a span of 4–6 weeks. Incorporate the feedback in subsequent iterations. This "fail early" concept will uncover the issues faster and help us to address it quickly. Though portal stack is complex, it provides seamless integration and accelerators across layers that can be leveraged by right-skilled team for efficient execution.

- *End-to-end performance challenges*: In many cases, end-to-end performance is always a tricky issue. There are many systems, technologies, layers, and infrastructure elements that play vital roles in the end-to-end performance chain. Assuming all other things being equal, portal technology itself has many internal layers such as presentation, business, and database layer components. Obviously, all portal products provide best practice guidelines and performance recommendations that can reap high performance from the stack; recommendations such as server configurations, API usage, development checklists, and caching guidelines form crucial aspects of this list. However, from our experience, these performance recommendations and guidelines are sometimes overlooked by portal execution team due to a variety of reasons such as project timeline pressures, inefficient project governance and process issues, and lack of experience and skillset of the execution team. A bad performance can have a ripple effect on

  - User experience
  - Site traffic and retention/loyalty
  - Service level agreement (SLA) slippage
  - Site availability and scalability issues
  - Data loss

  The best way to address the performance issues is through early and iterative testing. An end-to-end performance testing should be done along with functional testing iterations very early in the game. This helps us to uncover potential performance bottlenecks and issues and take corrective actions. Performance testing and engineering should never be an afterthought and should not be taken up after issues are identified; the cost of fixing performance issues is high in the later stages of the project. Rather, performance-based designs should be adopted to ensure that the solution meets the performance SLAs and tests to detect any issues early in the game. We can leverage the portal performance engineering concepts discussed in Chapter 20 for this.

- *Insufficient infrastructure*: Though this seems like an obvious issue, many times people overlook the infrastructure-related exercises such as capacity planning, sizing, and infrastructure estimation for the solution requirements. Portal product vendors usually provide the optimal sizing values and benchmarking numbers for the best performance of the portal. This can be used as a guideline and further optimizations need to be done on top of it. Right-sized server hardware, memory, CPU, and network bandwidth is crucial in achieving the expected performance and right scalability and availability. Additionally, all infrastructure-required tests should be carried out such as scalability testing, performance testing, peak load testing, stress testing, and endurance testing with the planned hardware configuration to check if the infrastructure is sufficient enough for proper scalability and performance. We have discussed the portal infrastructure concepts in Chapter 18, which can be used for optimal infrastructure planning.
- *User experience issues*: As the portal is used as the main presentation layer in vast majority of cases, it naturally takes the responsibility of delivering exceptional quality user experience. The user experience space is highly competitive with the advent of new web frameworks, AJAX toolkits, and responsive and interactive user interfaces (UIs) and such. The portal needs to constantly match and support the industry-leading UI frameworks to meet and exceed end-user expectations. Some of the common portal UI–related issues are as follows:
    - Development of traditional user experience (UX) though portal platforms, which provides partial support to Web 2.0 features
    - Lack of interactive, immersive, and responsive features
    - Usability and performance issues
    - Inconsistent branding, visual appeal, and navigation features
    - Minimal widgets and client-side components leading to frequent full-page loads
    - Minimal usage of JSR 286 portlets affecting page performance

  It is not surprising to note that a portal UX plays the principal role in creating the first impression of end users and ultimately affects the site traffic, repeat customer rate, customer loyalty, conversion ratio, etc. A responsive and interactive UX goes a long way in ensuring high customer satisfaction, which later translates into the success of digital strategies.

  In order to achieve the exceptional user experience, the best practice is to engage the UX architects and design team in creating visual mockups, visual elements, navigation flows, and other UI elements and reviewing user interface design with all the stakeholders. Once the final version is signed-off, they can be easily integrated into the portal platform as most of the portal products provide built-in support for the latest UI technologies. The branding elements along with the header and footer can be used to build the portal theme and other related portal components. UX best practices and frameworks are discussed in Chapter 14, which we can leverage for optimal portal user experience.

- *Information architecture and information discovery challenges*: Lack of intuitive information architecture acts as an irritant in the user experience. Users would be struggling to navigate the site, find the right information, or browse unnecessary pages or would take longer duration to get the relevant information. In the long run, users tend to abandon the site and look for better alternatives that can do the job quickly and accurately. So it is also important to design the information architecture intuitively so that it enables the users to discover the right information in the right place at the right time. There are numerous ways for building an intuitive information architecture:
  - Providing search-centered navigations
  - Using smart search features such as type ahead and synonym search
  - Requiring friendlier navigation elements such as expanded footers
  - Having smart navigations through widgets such as product selector widgets
  - Providing quick links, saved search results, expanded footers, context menus, etc.
- *Not having user-centric approach*: The end-user focus should be kept in all stages of the project including design, development, and testing. This strategy would lead to adopting the latest trends in the user experience such as lean model, faster time to market, self-service, multidevice support, and responsive design.

We have discussed other thumb rules and best practices to address these issues in Chapter 4.

Operations- and Execution-Related Challenges

The main operations and program execution related challenges are given here.

- *Team skillset and composition issues*: As portal technology is often a mix of a variety of technologies that require skillsets of presentation and server-side components, sometimes it is challenging to find people with right skillset who have thorough understanding of all involved technologies. Even while onboarding a new team member or training a new team member, the learning curve and training time are relatively higher due to the complexity and variety of technologies involved. This has an impact on overall execution and program schedule. It also impacts critical bug fixes and enhancement rollouts.
- *Lack of proper program governance structure*: In the absence of a proper governance structure, role–responsibility matrix, accountability, and standard operating procedures are largely undefined throughout the organization. As a result, the portal team suffers from smoother execution and maintenance of the portal.
- *Big bang approach*: Though agile execution is increasingly adopted these days, there are still some instances that would go for big bang execution with long release cycles. Normally, portal programs have relatively higher complexity due to the amount of integrations and due to the involvement of multiple technologies. Adopting big bang execution style for such complex programs would result in

the late identification of performance and functional issues. We will also lose the competitive edge due to longer release cycles.

The best practice usually followed in complex implementation is to adopt agile or iterative methodology wherein we release the features in smaller and quicker iterations. We will also carry out the proof of concept during the design phase to validate and ensure the feasibility of product features and integrations. We have elaborated the agile execution methodology in Chapter 19.

- *Poor implementation*: This is another obvious point for project failure. If the portal project execution is not properly managed and controlled, it would naturally lead to effort, time, and cost overrun failing the project. Poor execution would occur due to multiple reasons such as improper staffing, nonvalidated technologies, big bang execution approach, heavy custom coding, and minimal usage of in-built product features. We had detailed discussion on this in Chapter 19.

Summary

- This chapter explores some of the common pitfalls, antipatterns, and problem patterns that lead to the failure of portal programs.
- The main business-related reasons for failures are lack of proper and comprehensive vision, challenges in organization readiness and capability gaps, lack of portal strategy, lack of proper backing and executive sponsorship, lack of portal adoption planning and cultural issues, program cost, lack of tracking and monitoring, lack of clear focus of the portal program, and improper communication planning.
- The main technology-related reasons for failures are complexity of portal technology stack, end-to-end performance, insufficient infrastructure, user experience issues, information architecture and information discovery challenges, and not having user-centric approach.
- The main operations and execution-related reasons for failures are team skillset and composition issues, lack of proper program governance structure, big bang approach, and poor implementation.

Section III

Case Studies

23

Portal Case Studies

We have seen the major characteristics and utilities of portals in various chapters. We have also examined the optimal portal fitment, business transformation scenarios, and portal scenario assessment in the previous chapters. Here, we will look at few case studies that reinforce those concepts. Each case study details the main business drivers that warrant the usage of portal technology and the required portal solution. Wherever required, we have also detailed the challenges addressed by the portal and the benefits realized by portal solution.

The case studies are agnostic to any particular portal product or technology and mimic the real-world portal scenarios.

The key intents of these case studies are to

- Provide common use cases, business scenarios, themes and problem patterns where the portal can be used in real-world scenarios
- Provide a portal solution approach to address the problems
- Identify the key business drivers and scenarios where portal can be put to use
- Understand the business, technical, and operational benefits of portals

NOTE: The case studies capture the essence of portal usage scenarios and are closely modeled based on commonly encountered business scenarios.

Intranet Portal Case Study

Creating a productive intranet platform is one of the main usage scenarios for portal. Let us look at a case study about this.

Unified Employee Portal Case Study

This case study is about the development of new intranet platform for employees based on portal technology.

Background and Business Scenario

The organization has multiple business units such as HR, sales, marketing, and IT spread across geographies. Currently, each of the departments has its own employee web applications that depend on multiple other systems such as ERP and CRM. The organization is facing challenges to maintain and scale the current ecosystem to new geographies, and employees are finding it hard to use the current platform. The organization decides to address these issues through a technology transformation.

Key Business Drivers

- Provide a consolidated and unified view of all applications and functionality belonging to all business units in a single place for organization employees.
- Build a framework to provide a consistent and relevant access to related business information to employees.
- Enhance productivity and self-service through collaboration and other features.
- Provide a consistent user experience, brand identity, visual design, navigation and intuitive information architecture, and easy-to-use digital platform so that employees can effectively use the intranet site for their daily activities.

Key Technology Drivers

- Build a scalable and reliable platform that is easy to maintain and extend.
- Simplify enterprise integration and enhancement process.
- Provide seamless user access across multiple secured applications.

Key Operational Drivers

- Reduce operational and maintenance costs.
- Reduce employee on-boarding timelines through process optimization.
- Increase platform availability through robust monitoring infrastructure.
- Ease the process to reuse the platform for new geography.
- Consolidate the data from internal systems for operational efficiency.

Current Challenges

- An employee has to sometimes login to multiple web applications to complete a task, and in the process, he/she may need to relogin multiple times.
- Disjointed and inconsistent user experience and varied navigation and search features across web applications.
- Minimal collaboration features among employees of different departments.
- Data duplication across multiple systems and web applications.

Portal Solution

- A new intranet platform was built using a portal technology that provided multi-device access.
- Back-end internal applications such as ERP and CRM and services were integrated with portal to provide a single-stop-shop experience for the employees. Service-based integration was adopted for integration.
- Portal consolidated the functionality and migrated data from a back-end system to enhance consistency and reduce data/functionality duplication.
- A single-sign-on feature was used to provide seamless access to all protected applications.

- A new portal had redesigned user experience to provide a consistent and uniform user experience.
- Portal search was leveraged to enhance relevant information discovery.
- Built-in portal workflows were used to model the complex business process.
- Portal provided a personalized access of information and functionality.
- Access control was restricted based on unit and role.
- Portal localization features were used to enable multilanguage access various geographies.
- Various portal built-in features coupled with plug-ins were leveraged to build robust collaboration features such as chat, employee communities, wikis, and blogs.
- Multiple self-service features were introduced through automated processes and process optimization.
- The high-level conceptual architecture is shown in Figure 23.1.

Solution Benefits

- Increased employee productivity through self-service and collaboration features.
- Reduced times for on-boarding new employee.
- Easy to expand the platform to new geographies.
- Employees can perform the task anytime and anywhere though mobile-enabled portal and with increased availability.

Internet Portal Case Study

Retail Portal Case Study

This case study is about technology transformation for a retail organization.

Background and Business Scenario

The existing online channel for the retail organization was facing challenges from multiple fronts. It lacks the contemporary and forward-looking user experience and navigation features. With the increase in product inventory, customers often find it difficult to find the relevant product. The business wants to do a visual redesign and perform technology transformation to the new platform that can help the business grow.

Key Business Drivers

- Drive the sales opportunities through relevant product recommendations, personalized campaigns, and targeted content and intuitive cross sell, up-sell, and product bundling options.
- Provide better self-service experience for the customers.

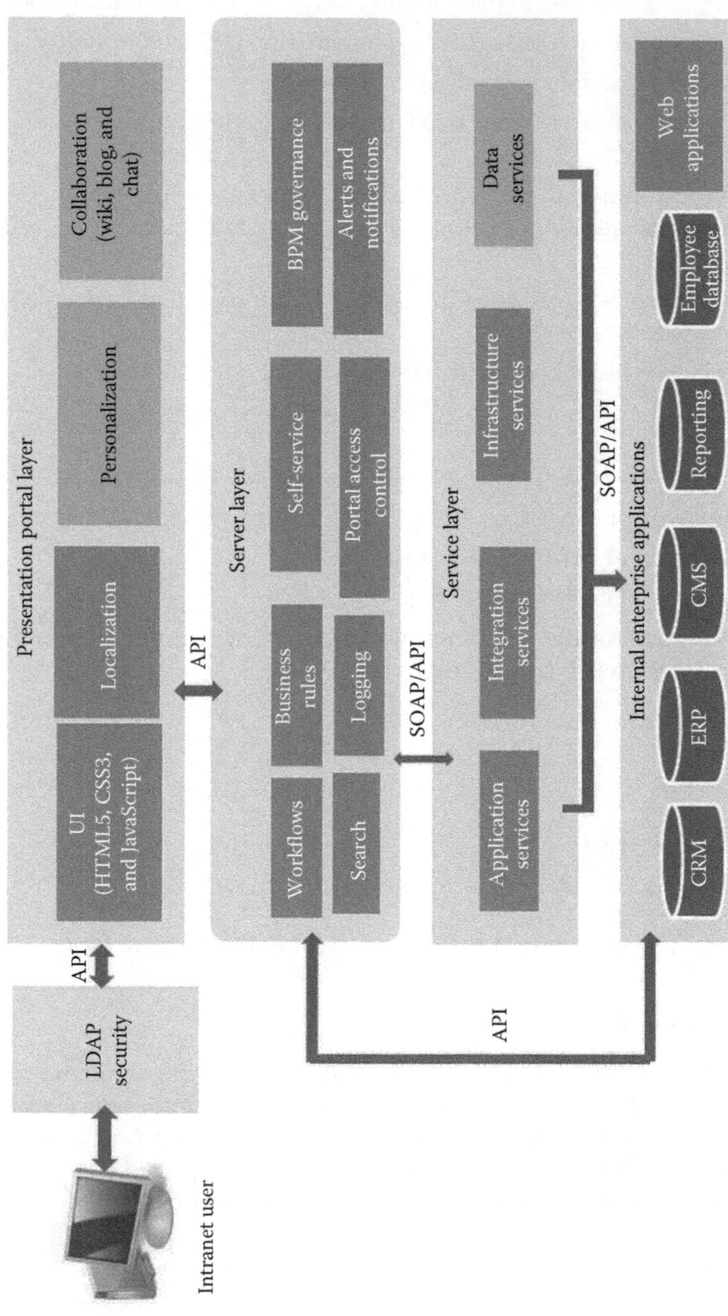

FIGURE 23.1
Intranet employee portal conceptual architecture.

- Revamp the information architecture to make the site easy to navigate and enhance information discoverability.
- Build a platform to enable future needs such as expansion to different geographies and to scale to support business and customer growth.
- The platform should also support nonlinear growth through easy on-boarding of new systems, services, and applications.

Key Technology Drivers

- Remove the outdated technologies and consolidate multiple complex technologies through service-based integration.
- Effectively use the potential of search and recommendation technologies.

Key Operational Drivers

- The new platform should enable the business to launch the marketing and sales campaigns with minimal intervention from the IT team.
- The new platform should support the launching of brand-based microsites.
- Empower users to make purchase decisions easily.

Current Challenges

- The marketing and sales teams have a huge dependency on the IT team for publishing marketing content and for launching sales campaigns.
- Multiple products and technologies making it difficult to maintain and scale.
- No effective monitoring mechanism for understanding customer behavior and activities.

Portal Solution

- A responsive and interactive next-generation retail platform was built with portal technologies. Retail portal enables end-user to customize the portlets and user experience through portlet preferences and configure dashboard page.
- The new retail portal provides intuitive features such as customer dashboard that provides information at a single source that is simple to understand and simple to use, enabling members to make key decisions.
- Retail portal provides intuitive features such as product comparator that enabled customers to make purchase decisions easily.
- Portal search was optimized to leverage the full potential of search to realize business goals. Advanced features such as typeahead search, product categorized search, faceted search, guided navigation, and synonym support were provided to enhance search experience.
- Portal was integrated with a recommendation engine to understand the customer's purchase history and current trends to provide highly relevant product recommendations. The recommendation engine was also used to bundle and package the related products for cross-selling and up-selling.

- Search engine optimization (SEO) best practices were followed on the new retail portal to enhance its visibility and to drive the Internet traffic.
- Service-oriented architecture was implemented by integrating the portal with enterprise service bus that formed a single interface for all interactions with all upstream services. This helped to service-enable all back-end systems and consolidate their functionality through services. The functionality carried out by outdated technologies was replaced by portlets and widgets.
- The content management process was made business friendly by providing an easy-to-use content templates and efficient content publishing process. The sales and marketing team can use the content features to publish the marketing content and campaigns with minimal IT intervention.
- Retail portal provided personalized experience through relevant and targeted content and personalized offers.
- Portal was integrated with web analytics tool to track the key customer activities such as navigation paths, conversion ratio, exit rate, popular downloads, and popular content. Through web analytics, portal platform was able to collect data across channels and helped in behavior tracking and customer profiling and customer segmentation. The content strategy and information architecture were continuously fine-tuned based on the insights drawn from customer behavior.

Solution Benefits

- Guided navigation and relevant search increased customer satisfaction and loyalty.
- Personalized offers and sales promotion resulted in increased conversion and online revenue.
- Continuous improvement of user experience was possible through web analytics reports.
- The service-based infrastructure enabled easy on-boarding of multiple systems and services.
- The marketing team was able to provide highly targeted content, campaigns, and promotion offers through portal personalization and recommendation features.
- Business-friendly content process enabled business to quickly launch marketing campaigns.
- Virtual portals reduced the time to launch microsites and multi-geo sites.

Customer Service Portal Case Study

Next-Generation Customer Service Portal Case Study

This case study is about the development of a next-generation customer service platform based on portal.

Background and Business Scenario

An organization has an existing web-based support application that is the main channel for customers to get product support. The organization has various internal applications that are used for customer support such as solution knowledge base, CRM, incident management system, and collaboration system. Factors such as increased product sales, competitive pressures, and entry into new geographies have forced the organization to revamp their customer service platform to stay ahead in the race. The organization hired a consultancy firm to review their online strategy and also did an online survey and solicited feedback from its customers about the expectations from next-generation customer service. The organization came up with the specifications for the next-generation service platform based on the customer feedback and recommendations given by the consultancy firm.

Key Business Drivers

- Develop next-generation customer-service platform with enhanced self-service features.
- Provide a relationship-enhancing and engaging features through a personalized user interface through a customer-centric platform to drive customer satisfaction.
- Improve content on-boarding and easier content publishing process for knowledge articles.
- Provide a cohesive delivery of solution and support content.
- Consolidate redundant business systems.
- Simplify customer touch points with the new service platform.
- Provide easier information access and increased consumer engagement.

Key Technology Drivers

- Provide a standard integration interface in the new platform for efficient integration.
- Improve the search function through configurable and efficient relevancy ranking features.
- Provide a monitoring tool to track user activities on the service platform and intuitive reporting features.

Key Operational Drivers

- Reduce functionality complexity and improve operational efficiency.
- Provide enhanced maintenance and production support.
- Reduce support costs by making information easier to find.
- Enhance content publishing process with minimal interference from the IT team.
- Reduce support call volume and incident volume.

Current Challenges

- The organization has a large, dynamic, and distributed IT landscape with multiple interfaces and a mix of advanced and legacy systems with evolving architectural guidelines.

- Customer churn rate is high due to lack of customer engagement features.
- Inefficient search leading to poor user experience.
- Poor performance from existing platform.
- Existing support platform provides obsolete content and inefficient workflow for support features.

Portal Solution

- A new customer service portal was developed using lean portal technologies that provided a single dashboard view of relationships across product and services for the customer. The service portal adopted service-based integration with back-end IT systems.
- The new service portal had many forward-looking features such as lean architecture using widgets and lightweight component model and adopted responsive web design for omni-channel enablement.
- Portal also provided an easy-to-use content management tool for managing marketing and support content.
- Content authoring and publishing processes were optimized, and the dependency on the IT team was removed. Many steps in the content publishing were automated and provided self-approval features to make it business friendly and to lessen the time taken for content publishing.
- Portal was integrated with a search engine to provide enhanced and search-driven navigational guidance.
- Portal was integrated with existing knowledge management system to provide easy access for customers and support staff to access and contribute to solution knowledge base.
- Web analytics tool was leveraged to track and gain insights into customer activities.
- Portal collaboration features were introduced in phases. This included real-time chat with support staff, web conferencing, and information sharing through product communities and wikis.
- Reusable widgets and portlets were created as part of new portal, which has configuration features for future extensibility.

Solution Benefits

- Search-driven self-service greatly enhanced information discovery. Customers were able to find the relevant solution articles quickly and easily.
- New portal provided enhanced levels of usability and functionality.
- Reduction in operational overheads due to efficient content publishing process.
- Real-time analytics reports helped business to identify the customer pain points quickly and take corrective actions.
- Reduced customer calls due to collaboration and self-service features.

Portal Content Management Case Study

Given in the following is a case study of a dynamic delivery platform developed using portal integration with external content management system (CMS).

Scenario before Portal Transformation

The organization used online strategy primarily for information display purposes. The main business driver was to help the customers to discover the relevant information in quick time.

The following were the pain points in various categories:

- Online platform:
  - Existing online platform was built on an outdated technology that displayed static content.
  - Users were finding it difficult to find the right content.
  - There were multiple sites for consumers, partners, and resellers.
  - There was no personalization and analytics.
  - Only web channel was supported.
- Infrastructure:
  - The site was built on a non-clustered environment.
  - Static pages served through a web server.
  - Nonexistent page monitoring and disaster recovery environment.
- Search:
  - An outdated search technology was used. Search engine was not indexing all enterprise content sources.
- CMS:
  - There were multiple CMS systems without any centralized access system leading to a lot of duplicate contents.
  - Content publishing was a cumbersome process; it took more than a week to publish a new content. The content publishing process required the involvement of the IT team.
  - Most of the site content was authored that required a lot of manual effort.
  - There was minimal content reuse.
  - There was no metadata or tagging system.
  - Content publishing was happening at page level requiring an entire page publish even for small changes.

Dynamic Delivery Platform Based on Portal and Enterprise CMS

An enterprise portal platform was used to do the technology transformation. A high-level solution architecture is shown in Figure 23.2.

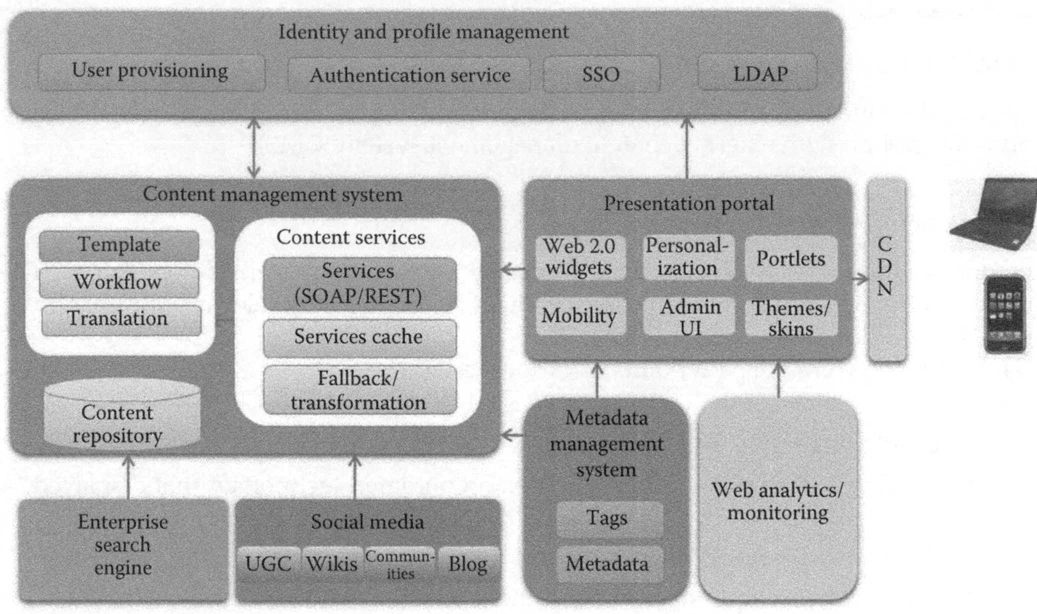

FIGURE 23.2
Portal-based dynamic delivery platform.

Portal Delivery Platform

- Highly configurable portal was developed providing personalized content delivery.
- Enterprise portal was integrated with consolidated CMS and enterprise search.
- Portal supports multiple channels including web, mobile, and tablets through responsive web design (RWD).

CMS Consolidation

- All CMSs were consolidated through content migration.
- Publishing was done at content chunk level enhancing content reusability across multiple portal pages.
- Template-driven authoring and metadata-driven delivery.
- CMS integration through dynamic web services.
- Content was dynamically aggregated minimizing the content authoring effort.
- A centralized metadata management system was used to manage the content metadata.
- Metadata was used for tagging the content.

Infrastructure

- Portal infrastructure was built using clustered servers.
- Real-time monitoring tools and web analytics were used along with the portal.
- End-to-end setup of disaster recovery environment.

Main Benefits of the Portal Solution

The key benefits realized from the portal transformation are as follows:

- High amount of content reuse due to dynamic content aggregation.
- Better site management leveraging portal's site management utilities.
- Portal provided a single view, providing holistic view of all user activities.
- Highly scalable and available dynamic delivery environment due to cluster deployment.
- Portal pages uptime and availability can be monitored in real time.
- Infrastructure to support business continuity through disaster recovery environment.
- Added features like guided navigation and parameterized search-enhanced user experience.
- A user-friendly search to reduce call center costs by making information easier to find.

Appendix: Detailed Steps for Development of JSR Portlets

In the first section of the book, we discussed various development aspects of portals, mainly in Chapter 5. The sections in this appendix complements those concepts through discussion of sample code, flow, and deployment descriptors. Portal developers and portal testers would find these sections useful.*

JSR 168 Portlet Development

In Chapter 5 we discussed about the main APIs, code snippets, deployment descriptors, and the lifecycle methods of JSR 168 portlet. Here, we will discuss about the sample code and detailed steps for developing a simple JSR 168 portlet.

Context

We will develop a simple Hello World portlet that supports view mode and edit mode. We will look at the JSP code, portlet.xml file, and the portlet class code. This describes end-to-end steps in the development of JSR 168 portlet.

Flow

The example uses a simple flow:

1. The user configures a guest name in edit mode (edit.jsp)
2. The processAction method of the portlet stores the entered guest name in the portlet preferences
3. The view mode (view.jsp) gets the stored guest name from portlet preferences and displays it on the view.jsp

JSPs

Hello World portlet supports view mode and edit mode and hence we have two JSPs for each of the modes.

* For discussion of development concepts we have taken JSR standards for code example.

Edit.jsp

Edit.jsp collects the guest name from the user and submits to process action via action URL.

```
<%@ taglib uri="http://java.sun.com/portlet_2_0" prefix="portlet"%>

<form action="<portlet:actionURL/>" method="post"
        name="<portlet:namespace/>guestEntryForm">
        Name:<input name="<portlet:namespace/>name" type="text"/> <br/>
        <br/> <input type="submit" value="Provide Guest Name"/>
</form>
```

View.jsp

View.jsp displays the guest name collected from the request parameter.

```
<%@ taglib uri="http://java.sun.com/portlet_2_0" prefix="portlet"%>

<portlet:defineObjects/>


Hello World Portlet

<p>
       This is a simple portlet which just echoes the guest name. The
name should be first configured in the edit mode
</p>
<%
       String name = (String) request.getAttribute("GUEST_NAME");
%>
<p>    Hello <%=name%>!
</p>
```

Portlet Class

The portlet gets the guest name from the request parameter in the processAction method and stores the value in portlet preferences. The preference value is specified by the user.

```
package com.sample;

import java.io.IOException;

import javax.portlet.ActionRequest;
import javax.portlet.ActionResponse;
import javax.portlet.GenericPortlet;
import javax.portlet.PortletException;
import javax.portlet.PortletMode;
import javax.portlet.PortletPreferences;
import javax.portlet.PortletRequestDispatcher;
```

```
import javax.portlet.RenderRequest;
import javax.portlet.RenderResponse;

public class HelloWorldPortlet extends GenericPortlet {

       public void init() {
       }

       public void processAction(ActionRequest request, ActionResponse
response)
                        throws IOException, PortletException {

              //Get the value of guest name from the edit jsp
              String name = request.getParameter("name");
              PortletPreferences prefs = request.getPreferences();
              //Store the guest name in preferences
              prefs.setValue("GUEST_NAME", name);
              prefs.store();
              response.setPortletMode(PortletMode.VIEW);
       }

public void doEdit(RenderRequest renderRequest,
                     RenderResponse renderResponse) throws IOException,
PortletException {

              PortletRequestDispatcher portletRequestDispatcher =
getPortletContext().getRequestDispatcher("edit.jsp");
              if (portletRequestDispatcher != null) {
                                    portletRequestDispatcher.include
(renderRequest, renderResponse);
              }
       }

       public void doView(RenderRequest request, RenderResponse response)
                     throws IOException, PortletException {
              PortletPreferences prefs = request.getPreferences();
              String defaultValue = "";
              //Get the guest name from preferences
              String name = (String) prefs.getValue("GUEST_NAME",
defaultValue);

              //Set the request attribute for use in the view.jsp
              request.setAttribute("GUEST_NAME", name);

              PortletRequestDispatcher portletRequestDispatcher =
getPortletContext().getRequestDispatcher("view.jsp");
              if (portletRequestDispatcher != null) {
                                    portletRequestDispatcher.include
(request, response);                }

       }

}
```

Portlet Deployment Descriptor (Portlet.xml)

The deployment descriptor provides the following details about the portlet:

- *Portlet class*: The tag *portlet-class* provides details about the main portlet class.
- *The supported modes* (*view and edit*): The tag *supports* specifies all the supported modes of the portlet. In this example the Hello world portlet supports only view and edit modes.
- *Portlet description*: The *portlet-info* tag provides the title and keywords for the portlet.
- *Security role mapping*: The tag *security-role-ref* specifies the roles that can access the portlet. Hello world portlet can be accessed by users with "guest" or "user" role.

```
<?xml version="1.0"?>

<portlet-app xmlns="http://java.sun.com/xml/ns/portlet/portlet-app_2_0.xsd"
xmlns:xsi="http://www.w3.org/2001/XMLSchema-instance"
xsi:schemaLocation="http://java.sun.com/xml/ns/portlet/portlet-app_2_0.xsd
http://java.sun.com/xml/ns/portlet/portlet-app_2_0.xsd" version="2.0">

        <portlet>
                <portlet-name>helloworldportlet </portlet-name>
                <display-name>Hello World Portlet</display-name>
                <portlet-class>
                        com.sample.HelloWorldPortlet
                </portlet-class>
                <expiration-cache>0</expiration-cache>
                <supports>
                        <mime-type>text/html</mime-type>
                        <portlet-mode>view</portlet-mode>
                        <portlet-mode>edit</portlet-mode>
                </supports>
                <portlet-info>
                        <title> Hello World Portlet</title>
                        <short-title>HelloWorldPortlet</short-title>
                        <keywords></keywords>
                </portlet-info>
                <security-role-ref>
                        <role-name>guest</role-name>
                        <role-name>user</role-name>
        <role-name>user</role-name>
                </security-role-ref>
        </portlet>
</portlet-app>
```

JSR 286 Portlet Development

In Chapter 5 we discussed about the main APIs, deployment descriptors, and the lifecycle methods of JSR 286 portlet. Here we will discuss about the sample code and detailed steps for developing a simple JSR 286 portlet. As we know, JSR 286 portlet specification supports event model and interportlet communication. We are going to look at these features in this example.

Context

This sample code has an event producer that adds an employee name to a specific queue and an event consumer that receives the event through the same queue.

Flow

The example uses a simple flow:

1. The user provides an employee name in view.jsp of the event producer portlet
2. The processAction method of the event producer portlet sets an event with the employee name on a specific queue
3. Event consumer portlet gets the employee name from the event from the same queue and updates the portlet session variable
4. The view.jsp of event consumer portlet gets the employee name variable from the portlet session and displays it on the page

Event Producer Portlet

view.jsp

The JSP gets the employee name from the user and invokes the processAction method via action URL. This component is the first one that will be invoked during this even processing chain.

```
<%@ taglib uri="http://java.sun.com/portlet" prefix="portlet"%>
<portlet:defineObjects/>
<form action="<portlet:actionURL/>" method="post"
       name="<portlet:namespace/>Emp Name Entry Form">
       Name:<input name="<portlet:namespace/>empname" type="text"/> <br/>
       <br/> <input type="submit" value="Provide Employee Name"/>
</form>
```

Event Producer Portlet Class

Event producer portlet gets the employee name from the request parameter and sets the event with this value in the processAction method. This will produce the event on the specified queue and the consumer portlet that supports event processing on that queue can then start processing the event.

```
package com.sample;

import java.io.IOException;
import java.util.HashMap;
import java.util.Map;
import javax.portlet.ActionRequest;
```

```
import javax.portlet.ActionResponse;
import javax.portlet.GenericPortlet;
import javax.portlet.PortletException;
import javax.portlet.ProcessAction;
import javax.portlet.RenderMode;
import javax.portlet.RenderRequest;
import javax.portlet.RenderResponse;
import javax.xml.namespace.QName;

public class EventProducerPortlet extends GenericPortlet {
       public void processAction(ActionRequest request, ActionResponse
response)
                     throws IOException, PortletException {
              //Get the value of employee name
              String empname = (String)request.getParameter("empname");

              // Send the event using the appropriate QName
              response.setEvent(new QName("http:example.com/events",
"empname"), empname);
       }
}
```

Portlet Deployment Descriptor

The deployment descriptor specifies the publishing event and the qname. As we can see from the deployment descriptor, the event producer portlet only supports view mode and supports event publishing on the qname *x:empname* with *java.lang.String* based event value.

```
<?xml version="1.0" encoding="UTF-8"?>
<portlet-app version="1.0" xmlns="http://java.sun.com/xml/ns/portlet/
portlet-app_2_0.xsd">
<portlet>
 <portlet-name>EventProducerPortlet</portlet-name>
 <portlet-class>com.sample.EventProducerPortlet</portlet-class>
       <supports>
              <mime-type>text/html</mime-type>
              <portlet-mode>VIEW</portlet-mode>
       </supports>
       <supported-locale>en</supported-locale>
       <supported-publishing-event>
              <qname xmlns:x="http:example.com/events">x:empname</qname>
       </supported-publishing-event>
</portlet>
       <event-definition>
              <qname xmlns:x="http:example.com/events">x:empname</qname>
              <value-type>java.lang.String</value-type>
       </event-definition>
</portlet-app>
```

Event Consumer Portlet

View.jsp

View.jsp collects the employee name from the portlet session variable and displays it on the page. The session variable value will be set by event consumer portlet.

```
<%@ taglib uri="http://java.sun.com/portlet" prefix="portlet"%>

<portlet:defineObjects/>

<%
//retrieve the object from the session
String empName = (String) renderRequest.getPortletSession().
getAttribute("empname");

if (empName != null) { %>
       <div>
              Employee Name:
                            <td><%=empName %></td>
       </div>
<% }
%>
```

Event Consumer Portlet Class

Event consumer portlet processes the event it gets from the queue and obtains the employee name and sets the portlet session variable that will be used by view.jsp.

```
package com.sample;

import java.io.IOException;
import java.util.HashMap;
import java.util.Map;

import javax.portlet.EventRequest;
import javax.portlet.EventResponse;
import javax.portlet.GenericPortlet;
import javax.portlet.PortletException;
import javax.portlet.ProcessEvent;
import javax.portlet.RenderMode;
import javax.portlet.RenderRequest;
import javax.portlet.RenderResponse;

public class EventConsumerPortlet extends GenericPortlet {
       // This method processes the event from the specific qname and
updates the portlet session
       public void processEvent(EventRequest request, EventResponse
response) throws PortletException, IOException {
              String empname = (String) request.getEvent().getValue();
```

```
            //Store the value obtained from event in the portlet session
            request.getPortletSession().setAttribute("empname",
empname);
        }
}
```

Portlet Deployment Descriptor

The deployment descriptor specifies the processing qname and the supported mode of the portlet. The deployment descriptor shows that the Event consumer portlet processes events publishing on the qname x:empname.

```
<?xml version="1.0" encoding="UTF-8"?>
<portlet-app version="1.0" xmlns="http://java.sun.com/xml/ns/portlet/
portlet-app_2_0.xsd">

<portlet>
    <portlet-name>EventConsumerPortlet</portlet-name>
    <portlet-class>sample.EventConsumerPortlet</portlet-class>

        <supports>
               <mime-type>text/html</mime-type>
               <portlet-mode>VIEW</portlet-mode>
        </supports>
        <supported-locale>en</supported-locale>

        <supported-processing-event>
               <qname xmlns:x="http:example.com/events">x:empname</qname>
        </supported-processing-event>
</portlet>

        <event-definition>
               <qname xmlns:x="http:example.com/events">x:empname</qname>
               <value-type>java.lang.String</value-type>
        </event-definition>

</portlet-app>
```

Further Reading

Gothelf, J. (2013) *Lean UX: Applying Lean Principles to Improve User Experience*, 1st edn. O'Reilly Media, Beijing, China.

Krug, S. (2013) *Don't Make Me Think, Revisited: A Common Sense Approach to Web Usability (Voices That Matter)*, 3rd edn. New Riders, Berkeley, CA.

Minter, D. and Linwood, J. (2004) *Building Portals with the Java Portlet API (Expert's Voice)*. Apress, Berkeley, CA.

Sarin, A. (2011) *Portlets in Action*, 1st edn. Manning Publications, Shelter Island, NY.

Sullivan, D. (2003) *Proven Portals: Best Practices for Planning, Designing, and Developing Enterprise Portals: Best Practices for Planning, Designing, and Developing Enterprise Portals*, 1st edn. Addison-Wesley Professional, Boston, MA.

Index

A

Accelerator, 272, 278, 279
Access control, 216–218
Adaptive design, 309, 318
Administration, 71, 82, 349
  content, 348–349
  plugin, 169, 350
  search, 71, 350
  security, 350
  site, 71, 349
  virtual portal, 350
  workflow, 71
Adoption challenges, 22
Agile approach, 262–263
Agile execution, 404
Analytics, 333–335, *see also* Web analytics
Anti-patterns, 319–320
Appendix, 471–478
Application architecture, 77, 96
Application integration design, 174
Application program interface, 122
  ActionRequest, 125
  ActionResponse, 126
  GenericPorlet, 123
  PortalContext, 124
  PortletConfig, 123
  PortletContext, 124
  PortletPreferences, 127
  PortletRequest, 124
  PortletRequestDispatcher, 126
  PortletResponse, 125
  PortletSession, 126
  RenderRequest, 125
  RenderResponse, 126
Architecture best practices, 77, 100, 102
Architecture definition, 88–96
Architecture principles, 103
Architecture review, 96–98
Architecture views, 74–75
Assessment and gap analysis, 97
Assessment framework, 40–54
Authentication, 217, 219
Authorization, 216, 220

B

Best practices, 319–330
  performance, 328–329
  phases, 320–324
  program management, 329
  security, 324–328
Boundary testing, 255
Business assessment, 41–43
Business benefits analysis, 91
Business continuity management, 359
Business controls, 20
Business domains, 30–31
Business drivers, 15–16
Business enablement, 17
Business specific trends, 431–432

C

Cache, 414–420
  browser cache, 418
  candidates, 416, 417
  edge cache, 418
  invalidation, 415
  layers, 416–418
  methodologies, 419–420
  portlet caching, 418–419
  reverse proxy, 418
  scenarios, 414, 415
  web proxy, 418
Cache headers, 419
Cache testing, 258
Caching type, 415–416
  fragment caching, 415
  page caching, 415
Capability solution mapping, 74, 75
Case studies, 459–469
  content management portal, 467–469
  customer service portal, 464–466
  dynamic delivery portal, 467–469
  internet portal, 461–464
  intranet portal, 459–461
  retail portal, 461–464
  unified employee portal, 459–461

Change management, 353, 359
Change management process, 410–411
Checklist, 324, 325
Clustering, 370–371
Collaboration
  benefits, 232
  challenges, 234
  requirements, 231–232
  trends, 233
Collaboration strategy, 234–235
Collaborative filtering, 245
Collaborative portal, 231
Common pitfalls, 319–320
Component view, 77
Content architecture view, 87
Content artifacts, 194
Content management, 177–197
  capabilities, 178–180
  freshness management, 185
  lifecycle management, 178, 198
  process (*see* Content management process)
  scenarios, 177
  trends, 178
  usability management, 185
Content management process, 189–190
Content migration, 185, 194–196
  artifacts for, 194
  methodologies, 194–195
  process, 195–196
Content portlet, 191–194
Content Repository API for Java, 180, 193
Content search, 190
Content services, 183
Content template, 180, 181, 196
Continuous and iterative testing, 263–264
Continuous improvement, 353, 356–357
Continuous improvement process, 356
Continuous integration, 406–407
Cookies, 133
Core integrations, 155
  BPM, 161–162
  CMS, 155–156
  ecommerce, 165–166
  knowledge management, 162–165
  reports and BI, 166–167
  search engine, 156–158
  security, 160–161
  social and collaboration, 158–160
  web frameworks, 169
  workflow, 161–162
Crawling, 203, 205–206
Cross site request forgery, 228
Cross site scripting, 228
CSRF, *see* Cross site request forgery
Cut-over strategy, 195
  big bang, 195
  iterative, 195

D

DAM, *see* Digital asset management
Data architecture, 77, 81
Denial of service, 229
Deployment view, 84–85
Design considerations, 98
Detailed design, 94
Digital asset management, 181
Digital marketing, 11
Disaster recovery, 369, 372, 373

E

Elastic scalability, 21
End-user testing, 260
Enterprise digital vision, 25
Enterprise information portal, 29
Enterprise integration trends, 430
Enterprise opportunities, 18
Enterprise search, 199–211
Enterprise service bus, 146, 157
ESB, *see* Enterprise service bus
Event consumer portlet
  JSP, 477–478
  portlet class, 477
  portlet XML, 478
Event producer portlet
  JSP, 475–476
  Portlet class, 475
  portlet XML, 476
Events, 132–133
Experience enrichment, 286
Experience impact analysis, 288
Experience improvement plan, 289
Extensions, 169

F

Facebook integration, 159, 160
Fallback testing, 256
Feature set, 55–61
Fitment analysis, 38–40
Functional capability view, 63–74
Function point estimate, 398

G

Governance, 391–398

H

Hello World portlet, 471–474
  JSP, 472
  portlet class, 472
  portlet XML, 474
Host security, 327
Hypercollaborative platform, 21

I

Identity and access management system, 216–217
Implementation, 387–391
Incident management process, 357–359
Indexing, 203–207
  seedlist based, 203–204
Information aggregation, 3, 6, 12
Information architecture, 83–84
Information discovery, 199, 208
Information gateway, 12
Infrastructure, 365–372
Infrastructure architecture view, 88
Infrastructure testing, 256–260
  availability, 257
  endurance, 257
  load, 257
  scalability, 257
Injection attack, 229
Inline editing, 180
Integration, 139–141, 144
  best practice, 174–175
  business process, 175
  design, 174
  development and testing, 174
Integration big picture, 142–143
Integration patterns, 169
  broker, 171
  data/functionality/process integration, 173
  gateway, 170
  message bus, 171
  proxy, 172
  publish/subscribe, 170
  request response, 173
  service aggregation, 172
  service orchestration, 172
  service wrapper, 172
Integrations, 139–155; *see also* Core integrations
  advantages, 139
  big picture, 142
  business scenarios, 140–141
  challenges, 140
  technical scenarios, 141–142
  techniques, 144–155
Integration techniques
  api-gateway based, 149
  clipping based, 153
  ESB based, 146
  feed based, 152
  iframe based, 145
  link-based, 144–155
  portlet based, 153–154
  screenscraping based, 153
  service based, 146
  widget based, 154–155
Interface testing, 256
Interoperability testing, 255
Inter-portlet communication, 116, 131
IPC, *see* Inter-portlet communication

J

JavaScript object notation, 429
Java specification request, 4, 26, 65, 116
  JSR, 116, 117, 119, 131, 132, 168, 286
JCR, *see* Content Repository API for Java
JSON, *see* JavaScript object notation
JSR, *see* Java Specification Request
JSR 168 portlet development, 471–474
JSR 286 portlet development, 474–478

K

Knowledge management, 13, 235–239
  Architecture, 235–238
  best practices, 238–239
  challenges, 238
Knowledge management portal, 27–29
Knowledge portal, *see* Knowledge management portal

L

Localization, 341–343
  content related, 341
  controlled value related, 341
  integration related, 342
  search related, 342
  site related, 341
  testing (*see* Localization testing)
  value formatting, 341
Localization testing, 341

M

Maintenance dashboard, 355–356
Managing user experience, 267

Mashups, 168
Metadata, 181, 183, 186, 196
Metadata management system, 181, 183
Metatags, 207
Migration testing, 259
MMS, *see* Metadata management system
Mobile app, 309, 314–316
Mobile-first, 307–312
Mobile portal, 311–313
Mockups, 187
Model view controller, 77, 427
Multi-channel support, 11
Multi-device testing, 253, 254
Multi-geo testing, 260
Multisite management, 68
Multi-tenancy model, 372
MVS, *see* Model view controller

N

Next-generation portals, 436–446
  accelerator, 439
  banking portal, 440–441
  hyperpersonalized, 438
  omni channel, 436–438
  reference architecture, 441–445
  web-oriented architecture, 436
NFR, *see* Nonfunctional requirement
Nonfunctional requirement, 376–378

O

Object caching, 416, 419
Omni-channel enablement, 307–316
Open source portal, 106–109
Operations
  administration, 348–350
  best practices, 355–357
  monitoring, 350–352
  release management, 345–348
  support and incident management, 357–359

P

Page layout, 135–136
  skins, 8, 65, 114
  template, 114
  themes, 8, 65, 114
Passionate engagement, 287
Penetration testing, 261
Performance, 413–424
  caching, 414–420
  critical success factor, 413
  metrics, 424
  modeling, 257–259
Performance testing, 421–424
  checklist, 423, 424
  load testing, 422
  stress testing, 422
  testing essentials, 420–424
Permission matrix, 218
Permission model, 8
Persona definition, 90, 305
Personalization, 239–245
  collaborative filtering, 245
  concepts, 241
  implicit, 243
  logical architecture, 241–243
  types, 243–245
Personalization types
  Anonymous, 244
  demographics-based, 243
  recommendation-based, 245
  rules-based, 243
  user attributes-based, 244
Personalized experience, 16
Personalized search, 69, 105, 390
Plugins, 169
PMO, *see* Program management office
Portal administration, 71
Portal analytics metrics, 338–339
Portal architecture, 63–109
Portal capabilities, 63–74
Portal container, 114, 118
Portal content, 177–197
  administration, 179, 182
  architecture, 180–183
  authoring, 186–190
  best practices, 196–197
  caching, 191
  design, 187
  metadata, 181, 183–186
  preview, 178, 182
  process, 188–190
  publishing, 197
  strategy, 184–186
  tagging, 186
Portal ecosystem, 115
Portal elements, 120–126
Portal estimation model, 398–400
Portal integration techniques, 144–155

Portal KPIs, 340
Portal objects, 120
Portal program, 382–391
Portal release plan, 401–404
Portal request processing, 118–119
  action request, 118
  render request, 118
  resource request, 119
Portal roadmap, 387–391
  definition, 387
  process, 388–391
Portal roles, 136
Portals, 3–14
  advantages, 6
  concept, 4
  core features, 5
  history, 3
  need, 12
  overview, 7–10
  technology, 4
  types, 6
Portals and UXP, 272–273
Portal server, 114
Portal server settings, 420
Portal standards, 116; *see also* Java specification request
Portal terminology, 113–114
Portal trends, 429
  business-related, 431
  external, 434
  integration related, 430
  intranet, 434
  operations-related, 432
  presentation technology, 429
  user experience related, 429
Portal user experience, 303–307
Portal UX, *see* Portal user experience
Portlet, 114, 115, 117–120
  API caching, 115, 120
  filters, 128
  JSP tags, 128
  modes, 121–122
  window states, 130
Portlet API, 122–128
Portlet communication, 131
Portlet deployment descriptor, 134; *see also* Portlet XML
Portlet interface, 122
  init, 122
  processAction, 122
  render, 122
Portlet JSP Tags, 128–130
  actionURL, 129
  defineObjects, 129
  namespace, 130
  param, 130
  property, 130
  renderURL, 129
  resourceURL, 129
Portlet lifecycle, 117
  JSR, 117, 168
Portlet modes, 121–122
  custom, 121
  edit, 121
  help, 121
  view, 121
Portlet packaging, 134
Portlet testing, 253
Portlet window states
  custom, 121
  maximized, 121
  minimized, 121, 131
  normal, 121
Portlet XML, 134, 135, 474
Post-production monitoring, 350–352
  application related, 352
  external systems related, 351
  internal systems related, 350
  metrics of, 352
Presentation testing, 251–254
  accessibility testing, 252
  broken link testing, 253
  compatibility testing, 253
  UI testing, 251
  usability testing, 252
Product evaluation, 47
Production readiness checklist, 346–348
Productivity improvement, 356–357
Program failure, 449–454
  business reasons, 449–451
  operations reasons, 454–455
  technology reasons, 451–454
Program goals, 27
Program management, 382–412
Program management office, 382, 388, 391, 392, 394, 395, 410–412
Program phases, 382–386
  architecture and design, 384–385
  development and testing, 385–386
  envision, 382–384
  maintenance and evolution, 386
Progressive enhancement, 310

Project management
  best practices, 404–411
  challenges, 381
  KPI (*see* Portal KPIs)
  stages, 382–391
Project management office, 392
Provisioning, 223
Public render parameters, 131; *see also* Inter-portlet communication

Q

Quality tools, 330

R

Regression testing, 255, 262, 263
Release management, 345–348
Representational state transfer, 146, 150
Requirement traceability matrix, 406
Responsive web design, 299
REST, *see* Representational state transfer
Risk management process, 409–410
Roadmap definition phase, 93–96
Road map strategy, 104–105
Root cause analysis, 357, 359
RWD, *see* Responsive web design

S

SaaS, *see* Software as service
SAML, *see* Security Assertion Markup Language
Search, 199–208
  attributes, 200
  best practices, 207
  process, 203
  process flow, 206
  requirements, 199
Search architecture, 201–202
Search engine optimization, 208–211
  advantages of, 209
  friendly URL, 210
  keyword optimization, 209
  monitoring and tracking, 211
  strategy, 209
  URL optimization, 210
Search portlet, 199, 201, 206
Search process, 203
Search services, 208
Secure integration, 226
Secure service invocation, 227
Security, 213–229
  architecture, 214
  assessment, 214
  introduction, 213
  prevention, 227–229
  vulnerability, 227–229
Security Assertion Markup Language, 67, 216, 229
Security proxy, 216
Security view, 76, 86
Seedlist, 203–205
Self-service, 82, 83, 104
Self-service portal, 105–107
SEO, *see* Search engine optimization
Service oriented architecture, 141, 146
Service testing, 254
Servlet and portlet, 115
Simple medium complex estimation, 398, 399
Single sign on, 218, 221
  federated SSO, 220
  web SSO, 220, 226
Sizing
  CPU, 367
  questionnaire, 365
  RAM, 365–367
Skin, 24, 114
SMC, *see* Simple medium complex estimation
SOA, *see* Service oriented architecture
Social marketing, 273
Software as service, 431, 432, 442
Solution capability evaluation, 40
Solution tenets, 25, 27
SOR, *see* System of record
SSO, *see* Single sign on
Strategy definition, 88, 90
Support and maintenance, 353
SWOT analysis, 54
System of record, 184, 198

T

Taxonomy, 187, 198
Technology assessment, 42, 44, 45
Technology evaluation, 47, 51
Test automation, 262
Testing, 247–264
  agile approach, 262–263
  best practices, 249, 252, 254
  challenges, 247
  governance, 249
  iterative testing, 249, 263–264
  metrics, 249, 253, 258, 262

success factors, 248, 260, 262
tools, 251–253
Testing framework, 248–256
Themes, 65, 114, 136
Tools and accelerators, 406, 412
Tools and frameworks, 406
Touch point analysis, 286, 289, 297
Transformation scenarios, 23
Trends in UI, 302, 316
Troubleshooting, 360–362

U

UGC, *see* User generated content
UI architecture, 299, 300
Use case view, 76, 81–83, 93
User engagement, 16, 17, 19
User experience, 267, 269, 271
User experience platform, 267–281
accelerator, 279
architecture, 277
business drivers, 270
capabilities, 268, 273, 280
case for, 268
motivations, 270
portals and UXP, 272
user engagement components, 279
views, 273
User experience view, 76
User generated content, 179, 180, 198
User management, 223
User persona definition, 306
User registration, 223
UXP, *see* User experience platform
UXP architecture, 277
UXP capabilities, 280, 281
UXP design, 287, 292
UXP views, 273–277
business view, 273
end user view, 276
operations view, 277

V

Value realization framework, 31–33
Virtualization, 368
Virtual portals, 372
Visual style guide, 306, 307
Vulnerability testing, 261, 264

W

WAP, *see* Web application firewall
Web analytics, 333–339
architecture, 336
challenges, 335
log-file based, 334
metrics, 338, 339
page tagging based, 334
setup, 337
Web application and UXP, 270
Web application firewall, 217
Web component testing, 422
Web oriented architecture, 277, 280, 283, 290
Web service portlet, 201
Web services for remote portlets, 116
Widgets, 283, 284
Wireframe, 306, 307, 316
WSRP, *see* Web services for remote portlets

X

XSS, *see* Cross site scripting